Got War?

Got War?
Got War?

Recent Doonesbury Books by G. B. Trudeau

Read My Lips, Make My Day, Eat Quiche and Die!
Give Those Nymphs Some Hooters!
You're Smokin' Now, Mr. Butts!
I'd Go With the Helmet, Ray
Welcome to Club Scud!
What Is It, Tink, Is Pan in Trouble?
Quality Time on Highway 1
Washed Out Bridges and Other Disasters
In Search of Cigarette Holder Man
Doonesbury Nation
Virtual Doonesbury
Planet Doonesbury
Buck Wild Doonesbury
Duke 2000: Whatever It Takes
The Revolt of the English Majors
Peace Out, Dawg!

Special Collections

The Doonesbury Chronicles
Doonesbury's Greatest Hits
The People's Doonesbury
Doonesbury Dossier: The Reagan Years
Doonesbury Deluxe: Selected Glances Askance
Recycled Doonesbury: Second Thoughts on a Gilded Age
Action Figure!
The Portable Doonesbury
Flashbacks: Twenty-five Years of Doonesbury
The Bundled Doonesbury

A DOONESBURY BOOK

Got War?

BY G. B. TRUDEAU

Andrews McMeel
Publishing

Kansas City

DOONESBURY is distributed internationally by Universal Press Syndicate.

03 04 05 06 07 BAM 10 9 8 7 6 5 4 3 2 1

ISBN: 0-7407-3817-8

Library of Congress Catalog Card Number: 2003106554

DOONESBURY may be viewed on the Internet at
www.doonesbury.com and www.ucomics.com.

——— **ATTENTION: SCHOOLS AND BUSINESSES** ———

Andrews McMeel books are available at quantity discounts with bulk purchase for educational, business, or sales promotional use. For information, please write to: Special Sales Department, Andrews McMeel Publishing, 4520 Main Street, Kansas City, Missouri 64111.

"Bring 'em on!"

—President George W. Bush, encouraging Iraqi guerrillas to attack U.S. forces

NO, YOU ILLITERATE THUGS, I WILL **NOT** PAY ANOTHER TOLL!
(IT'S OKAY, BROTHERS, LET HIM PASS.)
AKBARI! DAMMIT, MAN, DIDN'T I TELL YOU TO CLOSE DOWN THIS...
HEY, HEY, A LITTLE RESPECT, PLEASE! I'M A DEPUTY MINISTER NOW!
YOU'RE KIDDING.
LIKE THE SUIT? I TOOK IT OFF ONE OF MY FORMER RIVALS.
YEAH. VERY STATESMANLIKE.
YOU DON'T THINK THE BODY ARMOR MAKES ME LOOK FAT, DO YOU?
©B Trudeau

NO WAY! YOU'RE IN KARZAI'S WARLORD CABINET?
I AM, INDEED! COME, LET ME EXPLAIN OVER TEA, OLD FRIEND.
BY THE WAY, WE'RE NOT CALLED WARLORDS ANYMORE — WE'RE VETERANS. AND WE HAVE A NEW, SOFTER LOOK.
I'M A CHANGED MAN, HAVOC. NO LONGER THE COUNTRY RUFFIAN! I NOW CHECK EVERY DAY FOR STAINS ON MY TIE, OR DANDRUFF ON MY SHOULDER!
OR BLOOD ON YOUR HANDS.
NO, I ALWAYS WASH IT... OH!
YOU KIDDER! YOU BIG AMERICAN KIDDER!
©B Trudeau

SO WHY ALL THE FUSS ABOUT KARZAI'S ALL-WARLORD CABINET, HAVOC? THIS WAS CLEARLY THE WILL OF THE LOYA JIRGA.
THAT'S BULLFEATHERS, AKBARI. THE DELEGATES WANTED REPRESENTATIVE, REFORM GOVERNMENT! INSTEAD THEY GOT THE SAME BUNCH OF THUGS WHO TRASHED THE COUNTRY TEN YEARS AGO!
WHAT'S THIS? SO NOW THE CIA ONLY SUPPORTS REPRESENTATIVE, REFORM GOVERNMENTS?
DOWN TO THE POWDERED WIGS, CHIEF!
DEAR, DEAR — HAD WE ONLY KNOWN.
GB Trudeau

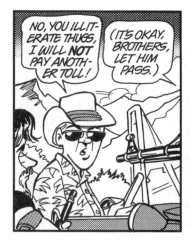

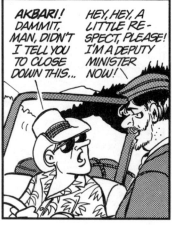

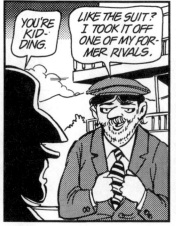

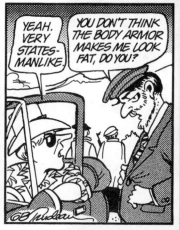

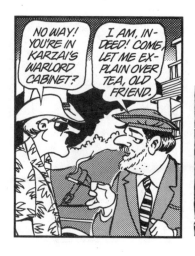

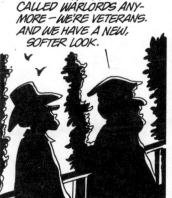

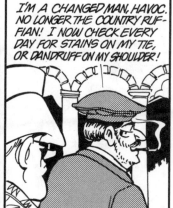

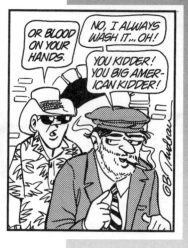

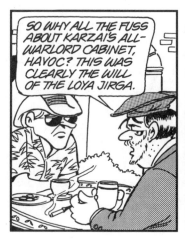

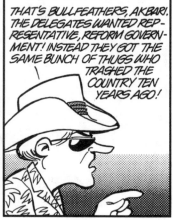

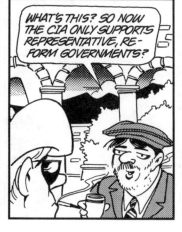

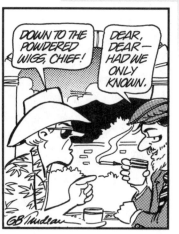

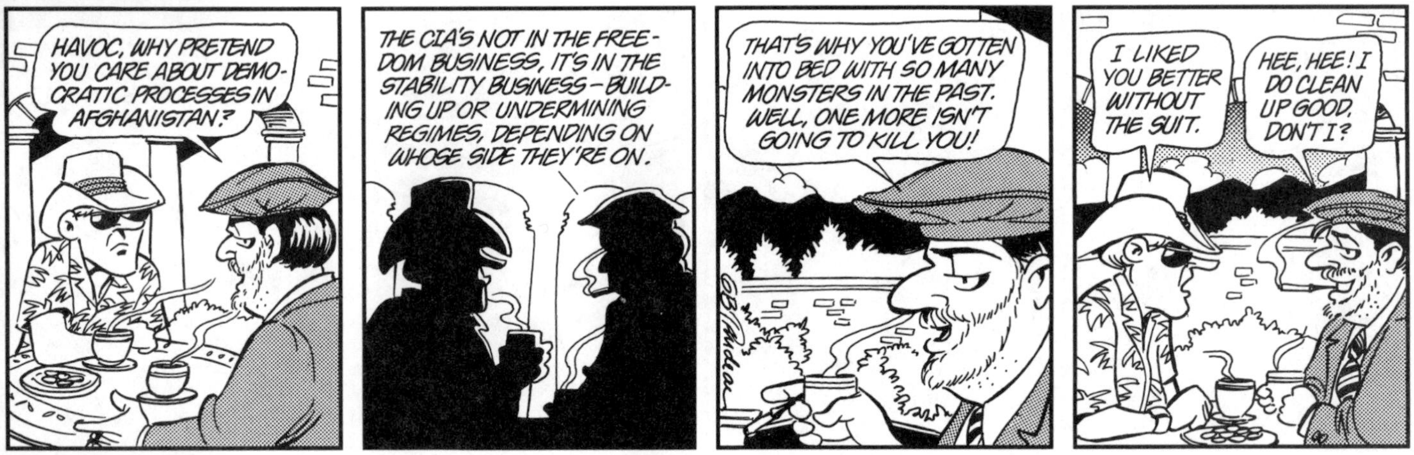
HAVOC, WHY PRETEND YOU CARE ABOUT DEMOCRATIC PROCESSES IN AFGHANISTAN?
THE CIA'S NOT IN THE FREEDOM BUSINESS, IT'S IN THE STABILITY BUSINESS—BUILDING UP OR UNDERMINING REGIMES, DEPENDING ON WHOSE SIDE THEY'RE ON.
THAT'S WHY YOU'VE GOTTEN INTO BED WITH SO MANY MONSTERS IN THE PAST. WELL, ONE MORE ISN'T GOING TO KILL YOU!
I LIKED YOU BETTER WITHOUT THE SUIT.
HEE, HEE! I DO CLEAN UP GOOD, DON'T I?

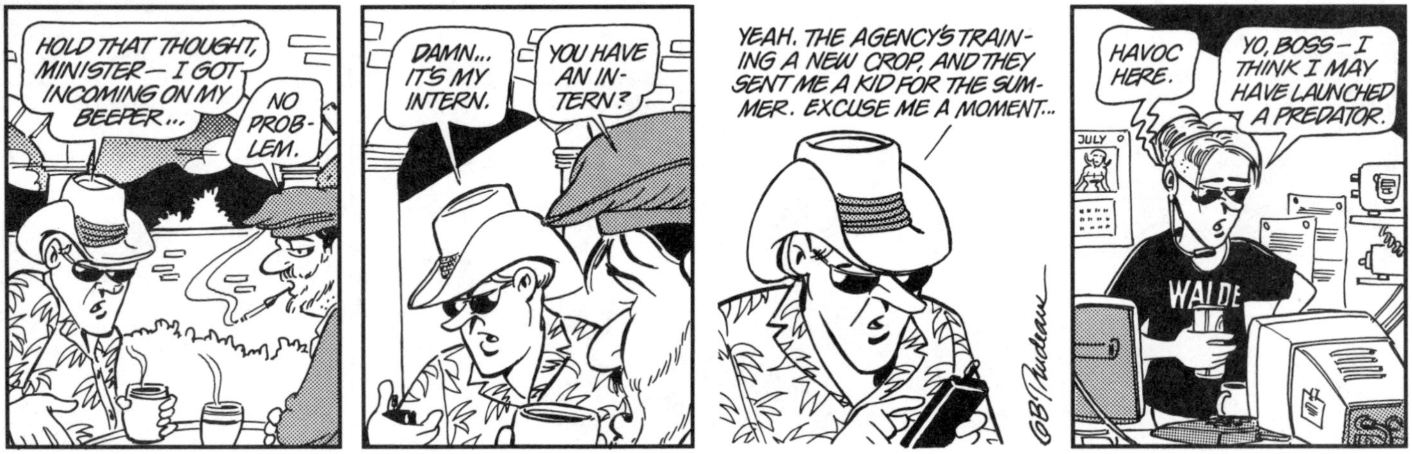
HOLD THAT THOUGHT, MINISTER—I GOT INCOMING ON MY BEEPER...
NO PROBLEM.
DAMN... IT'S MY INTERN.
YOU HAVE AN INTERN?
YEAH. THE AGENCY'S TRAINING A NEW CROP, AND THEY SENT ME A KID FOR THE SUMMER. EXCUSE ME A MOMENT...
HAVOC HERE.
YO, BOSS—I THINK I MAY HAVE LAUNCHED A PREDATOR.

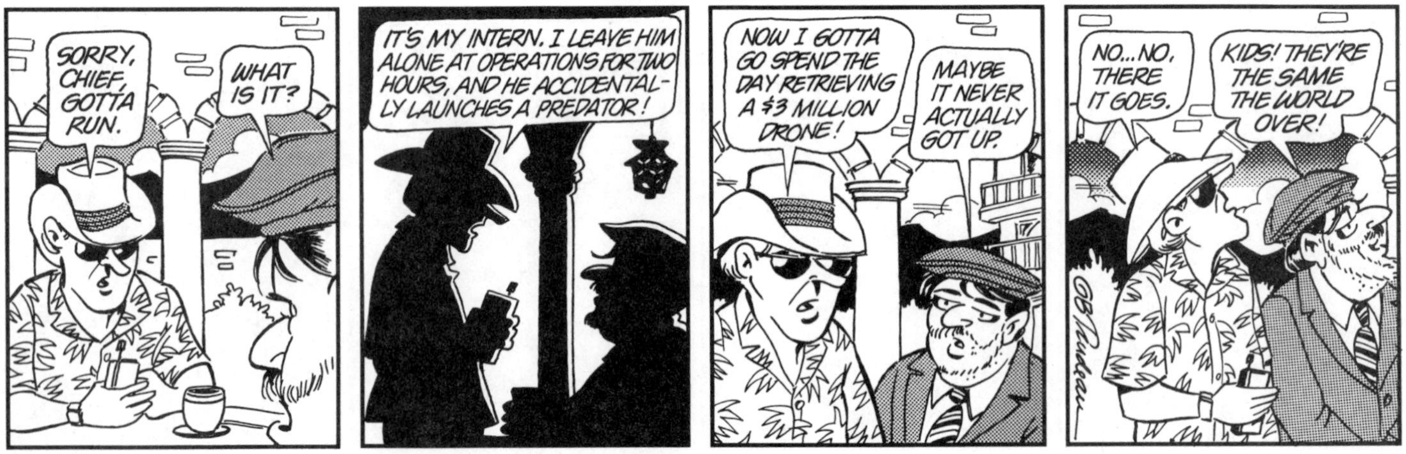
SORRY, CHIEF, GOTTA RUN.
WHAT IS IT?
IT'S MY INTERN. I LEAVE HIM ALONE AT OPERATIONS FOR TWO HOURS, AND HE ACCIDENTALLY LAUNCHES A PREDATOR!
NOW I GOTTA GO SPEND THE DAY RETRIEVING A $3 MILLION DRONE!
MAYBE IT NEVER ACTUALLY GOT UP.
NO...NO, THERE IT GOES.
KIDS! THEY'RE THE SAME THE WORLD OVER!

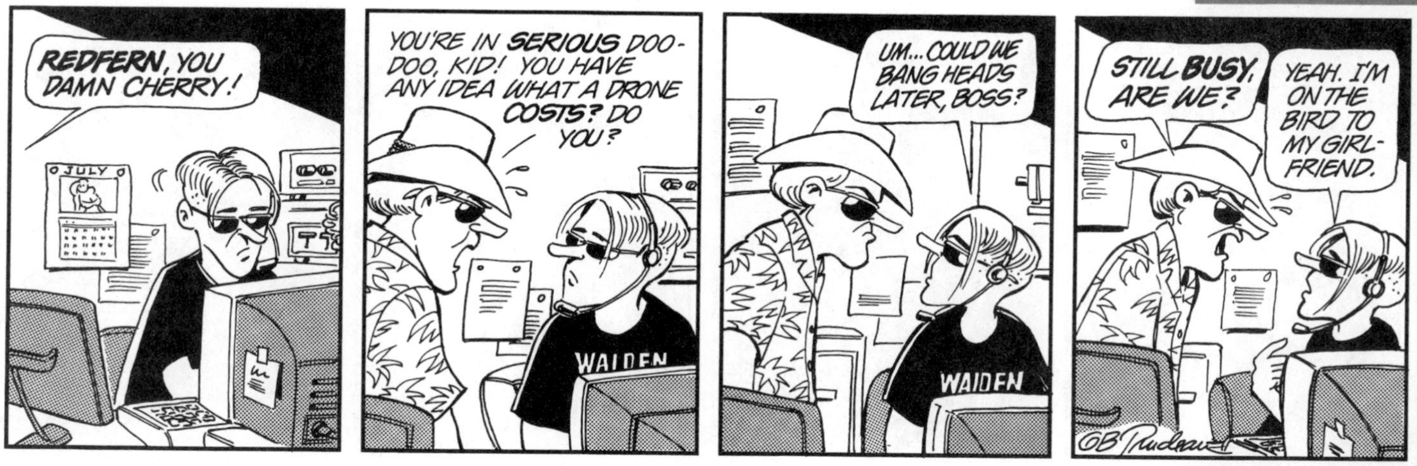
REDFERN, YOU DAMN CHERRY!
JULY
YOU'RE IN SERIOUS DOO-DOO, KID! YOU HAVE ANY IDEA WHAT A DRONE COSTS? DO YOU?
WALDEN
UM... COULD WE BANG HEADS LATER, BOSS?
WALDEN
STILL BUSY, ARE WE?
YEAH. I'M ON THE BIRD TO MY GIRL-FRIEND.

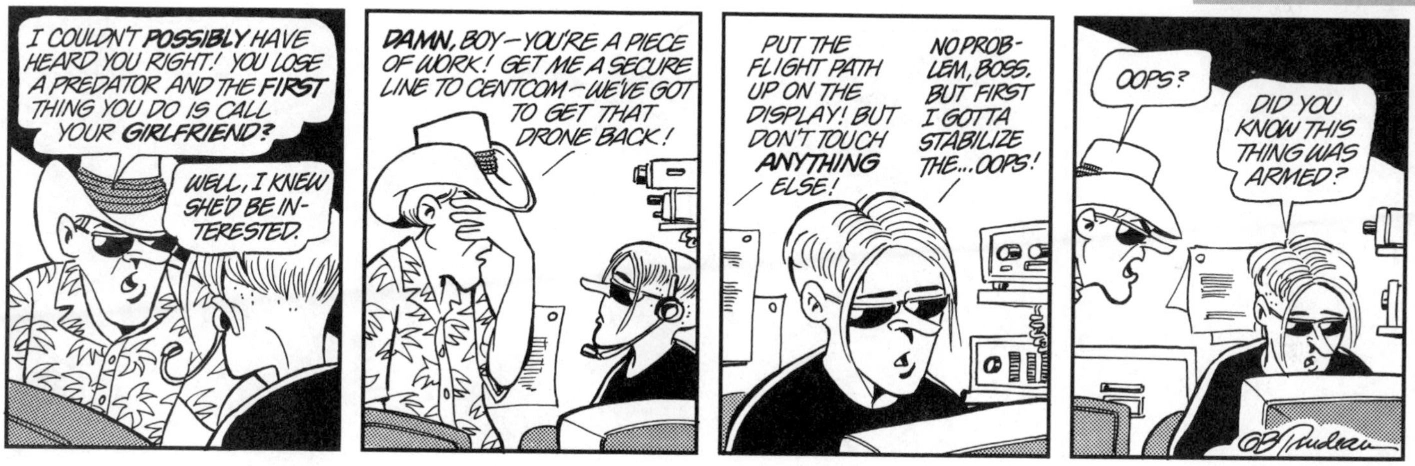
I COULDN'T POSSIBLY HAVE HEARD YOU RIGHT! YOU LOSE A PREDATOR AND THE FIRST THING YOU DO IS CALL YOUR GIRLFRIEND?
WELL, I KNEW SHE'D BE IN-TERESTED.
DAMN, BOY — YOU'RE A PIECE OF WORK! GET ME A SECURE LINE TO CENTCOM — WE'VE GOT TO GET THAT DRONE BACK!
PUT THE FLIGHT PATH UP ON THE DISPLAY! BUT DON'T TOUCH ANYTHING ELSE!
NO PROB-LEM, BOSS. BUT FIRST I GOTTA STABILIZE THE... OOPS!
OOPS?
DID YOU KNOW THIS THING WAS ARMED?

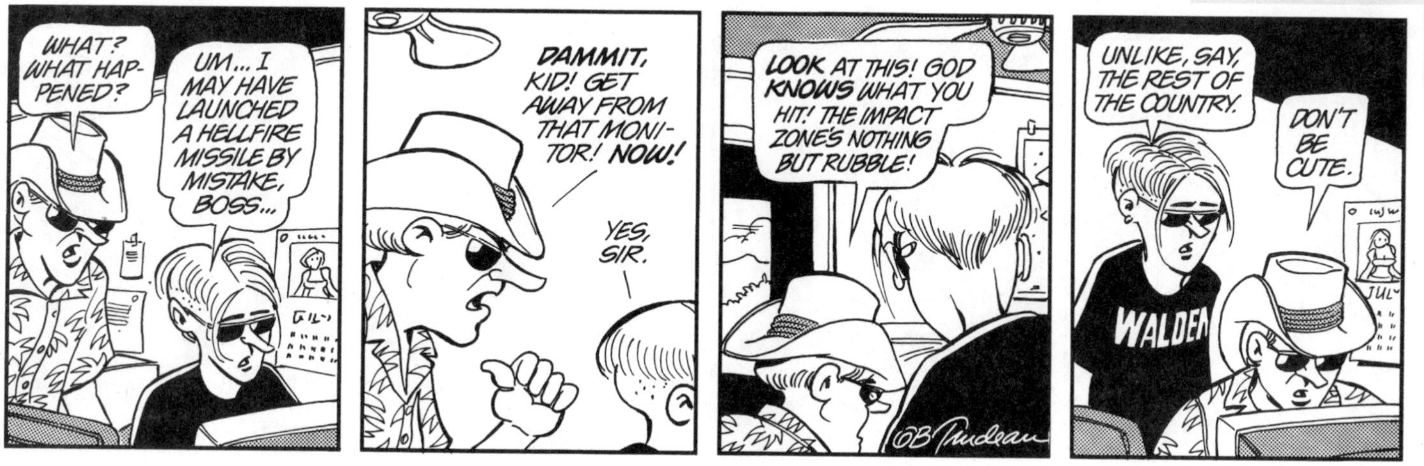
WHAT? WHAT HAP-PENED?
UM... I MAY HAVE LAUNCHED A HELLFIRE MISSILE BY MISTAKE, BOSS...
DAMMIT, KID! GET AWAY FROM THAT MONI-TOR! NOW!
YES, SIR.
LOOK AT THIS! GOD KNOWS WHAT YOU HIT! THE IMPACT ZONE'S NOTHING BUT RUBBLE!
UNLIKE, SAY, THE REST OF THE COUNTRY.
DON'T BE CUTE.
WALDEN
JULY

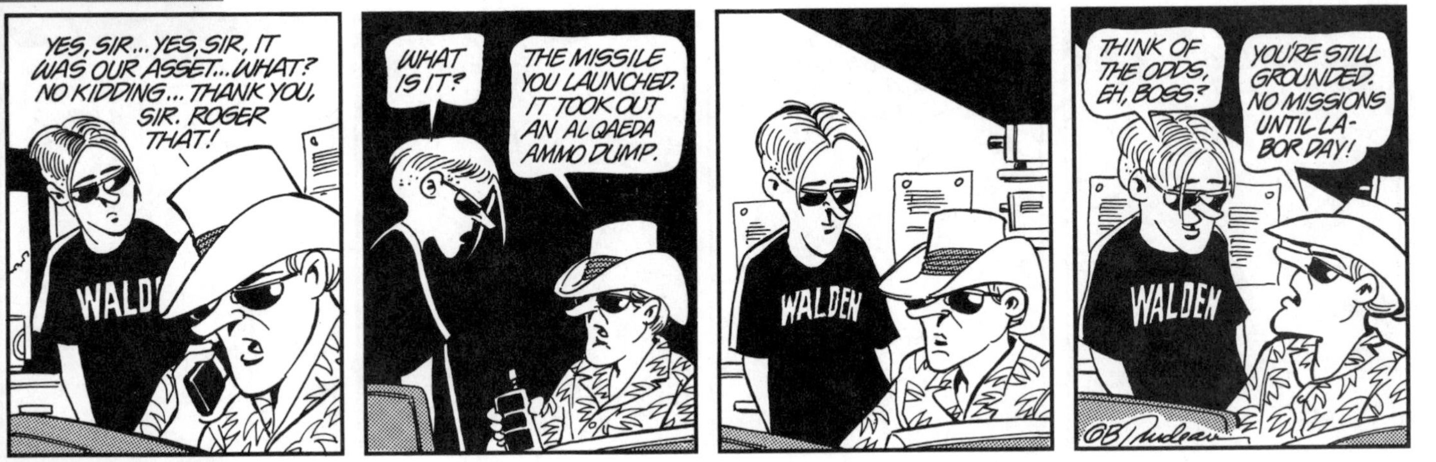
YES, SIR... YES, SIR, IT WAS OUR ASSET... WHAT? NO KIDDING... THANK YOU, SIR. ROGER THAT!
WALDEN
WHAT IS IT?
THE MISSILE YOU LAUNCHED. IT TOOK OUT AN AL QAEDA AMMO DUMP.
WALDEN
THINK OF THE ODDS, EH, BOSS?
YOU'RE STILL GROUNDED. NO MISSIONS UNTIL LA-BOR DAY!
WALDEN

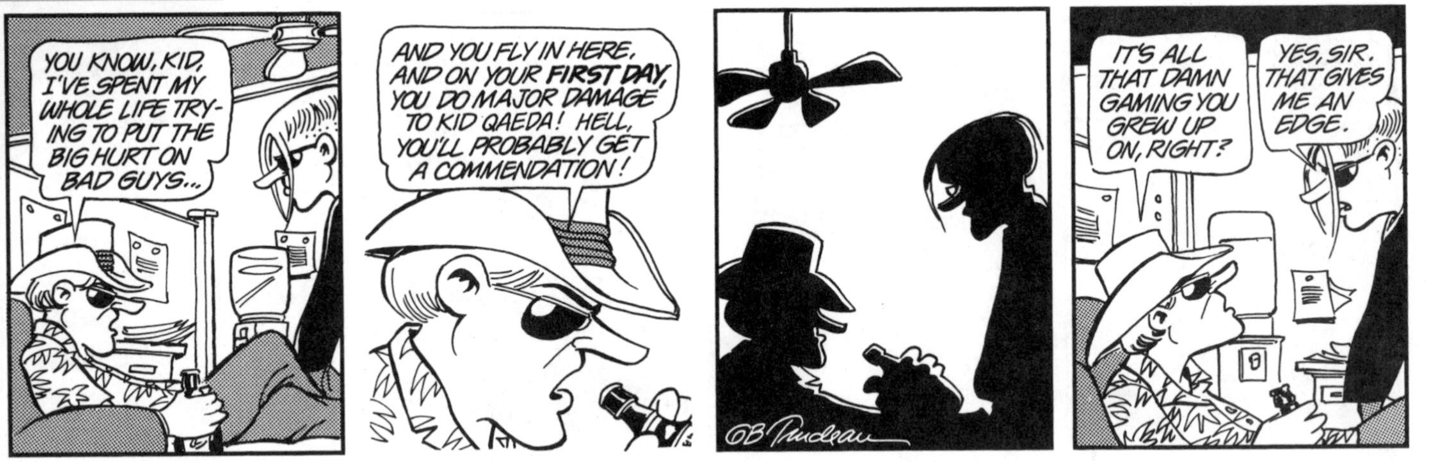
YOU KNOW, KID, I'VE SPENT MY WHOLE LIFE TRY-ING TO PUT THE BIG HURT ON BAD GUYS...
AND YOU FLY IN HERE, AND ON YOUR FIRST DAY, YOU DO MAJOR DAMAGE TO KID QAEDA! HELL, YOU'LL PROBABLY GET A COMMENDATION!
IT'S ALL THAT DAMN GAMING YOU GREW UP ON, RIGHT?
YES, SIR. THAT GIVES ME AN EDGE.

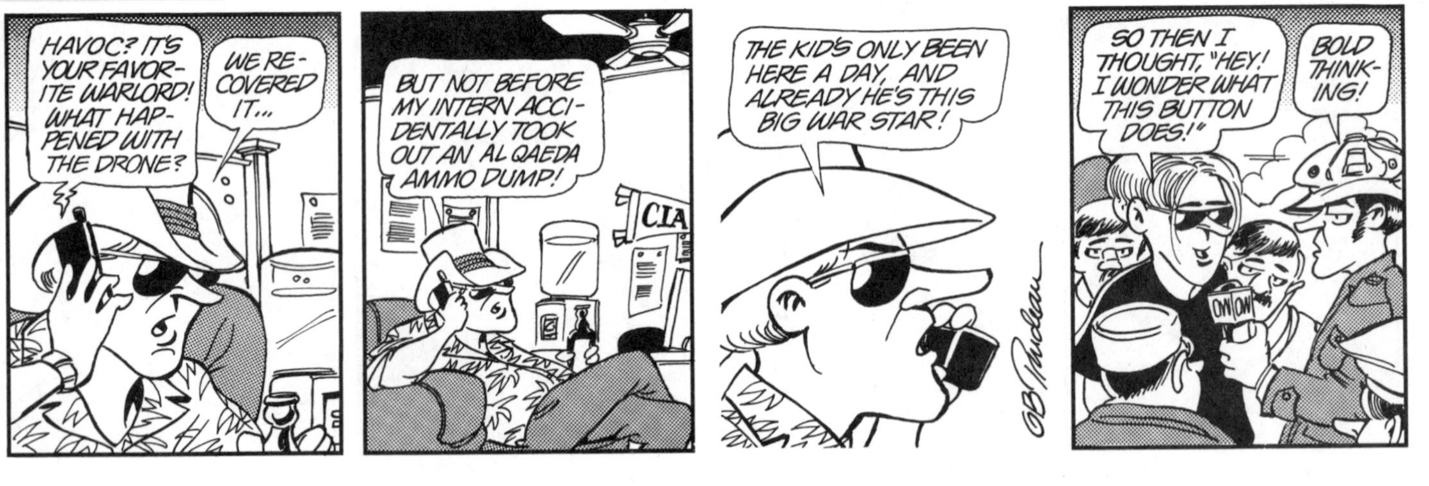
HAVOC? IT'S YOUR FAVOR-ITE WARLORD! WHAT HAP-PENED WITH THE DRONE?
WE RE-COVERED IT...
BUT NOT BEFORE MY INTERN ACCI-DENTALLY TOOK OUT AN AL QAEDA AMMO DUMP!
CIA
THE KID'S ONLY BEEN HERE A DAY, AND ALREADY HE'S THIS BIG WAR STAR!
SO THEN I THOUGHT, "HEY! I WONDER WHAT THIS BUTTON DOES!"
BOLD THINK-ING!

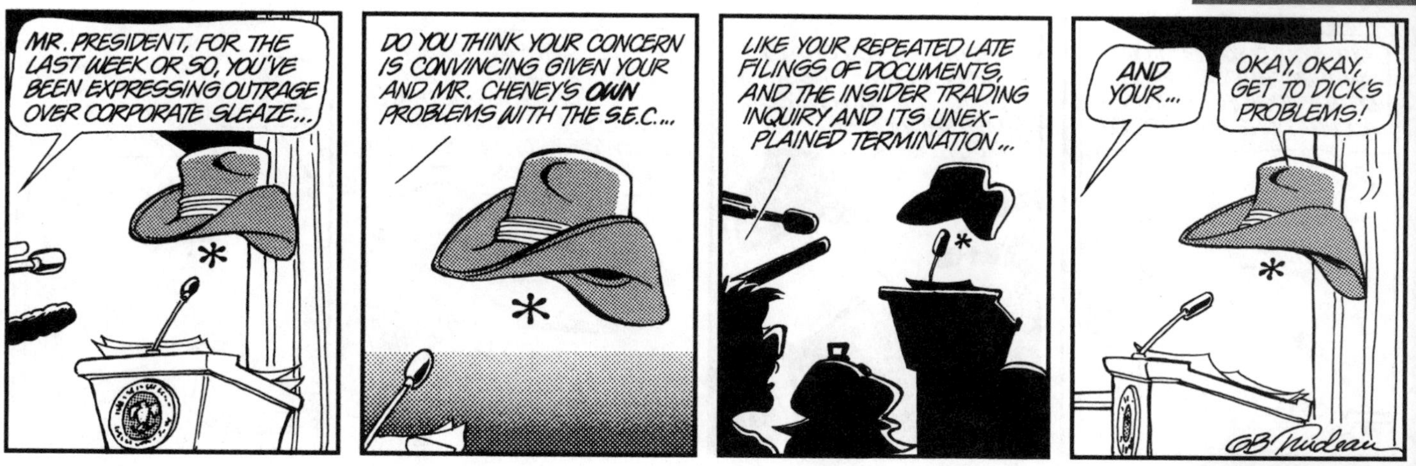
MR. PRESIDENT, FOR THE LAST WEEK OR SO, YOU'VE BEEN EXPRESSING OUTRAGE OVER CORPORATE SLEAZE...
DO YOU THINK YOUR CONCERN IS CONVINCING GIVEN YOUR AND MR. CHENEY'S OWN PROBLEMS WITH THE S.E.C....
LIKE YOUR REPEATED LATE FILINGS OF DOCUMENTS, AND THE INSIDER TRADING INQUIRY AND ITS UNEXPLAINED TERMINATION...
AND YOUR...
OKAY, OKAY, GET TO DICK'S PROBLEMS!

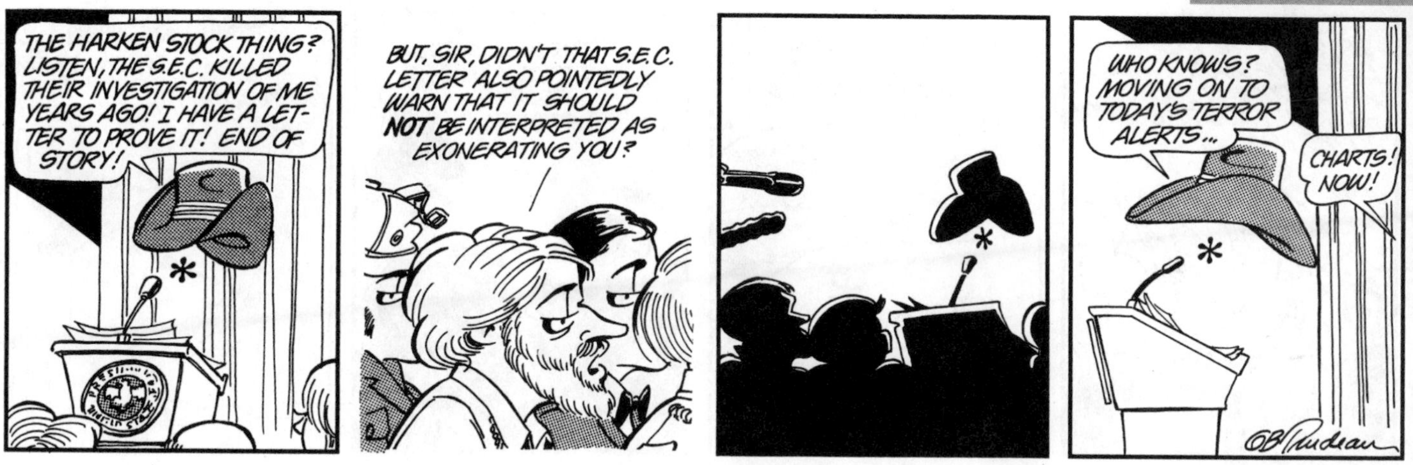
THE HARKEN STOCK THING? LISTEN, THE S.E.C. KILLED THEIR INVESTIGATION OF ME YEARS AGO! I HAVE A LETTER TO PROVE IT! END OF STORY!
BUT, SIR, DIDN'T THAT S.E.C. LETTER ALSO POINTEDLY WARN THAT IT SHOULD NOT BE INTERPRETED AS EXONERATING YOU?
WHO KNOWS? MOVING ON TO TODAY'S TERROR ALERTS...
CHARTS! NOW!

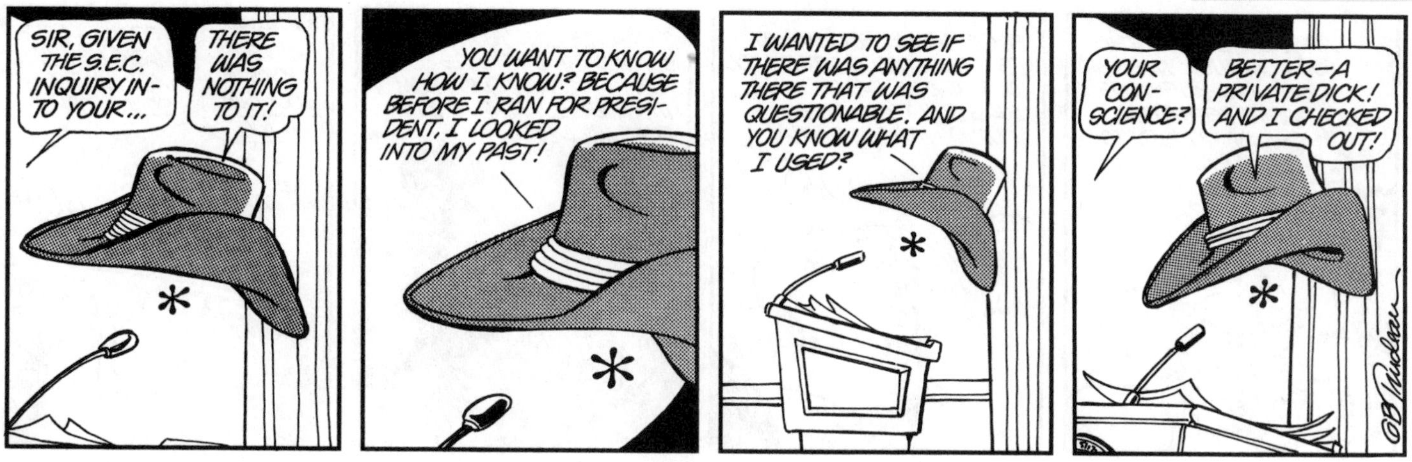
SIR, GIVEN THE S.E.C. INQUIRY INTO YOUR...
THERE WAS NOTHING TO IT!
YOU WANT TO KNOW HOW I KNOW? BECAUSE BEFORE I RAN FOR PRESIDENT, I LOOKED INTO MY PAST!
I WANTED TO SEE IF THERE WAS ANYTHING THERE THAT WAS QUESTIONABLE. AND YOU KNOW WHAT I USED?
YOUR CONSCIENCE?
BETTER—A PRIVATE DICK! AND I CHECKED OUT!

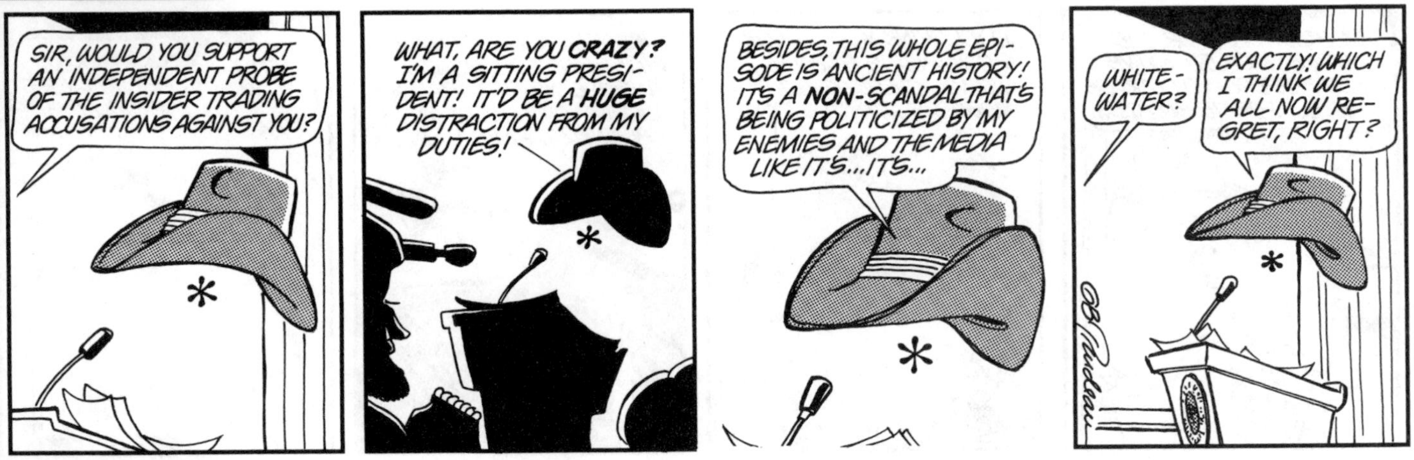
SIR, WOULD YOU SUPPORT AN INDEPENDENT PROBE OF THE INSIDER TRADING ACCUSATIONS AGAINST YOU?
WHAT, ARE YOU CRAZY? I'M A SITTING PRESIDENT! IT'D BE A HUGE DISTRACTION FROM MY DUTIES!
BESIDES, THIS WHOLE EPISODE IS ANCIENT HISTORY! IT'S A NON-SCANDAL THAT'S BEING POLITICIZED BY MY ENEMIES AND THE MEDIA LIKE IT'S...IT'S...
WHITE-WATER?
EXACTLY! WHICH I THINK WE ALL NOW REGRET, RIGHT?
©B Trudeau

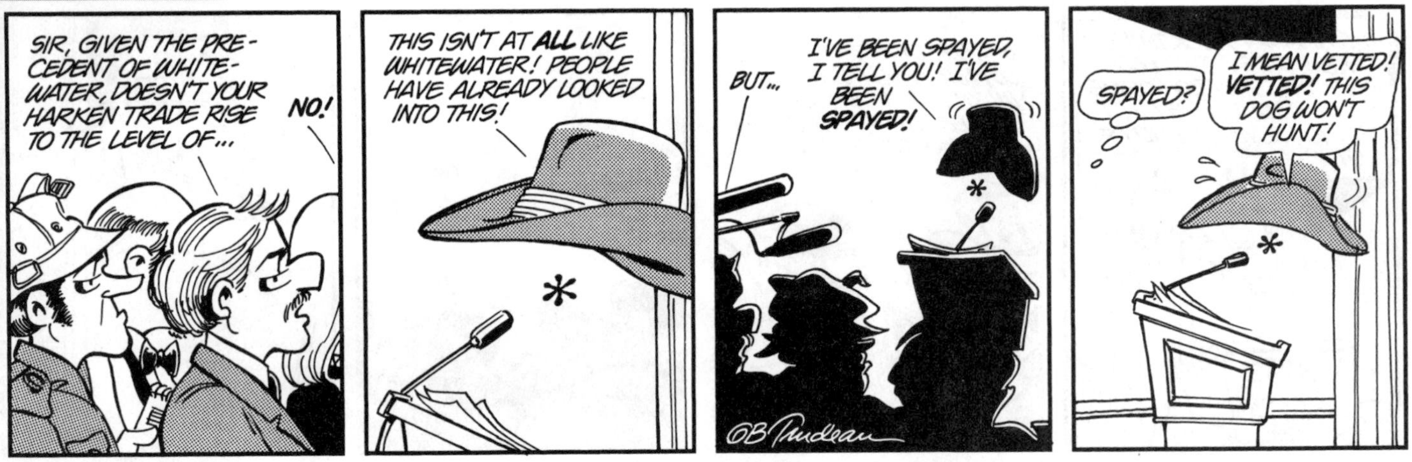
SIR, GIVEN THE PRECEDENT OF WHITEWATER, DOESN'T YOUR HARKEN TRADE RISE TO THE LEVEL OF...
NO!
THIS ISN'T AT ALL LIKE WHITEWATER! PEOPLE HAVE ALREADY LOOKED INTO THIS!
BUT...
I'VE BEEN SPAYED, I TELL YOU! I'VE BEEN SPAYED!
©B Trudeau
SPAYED?
I MEAN VETTED! VETTED! THIS DOG WON'T HUNT!

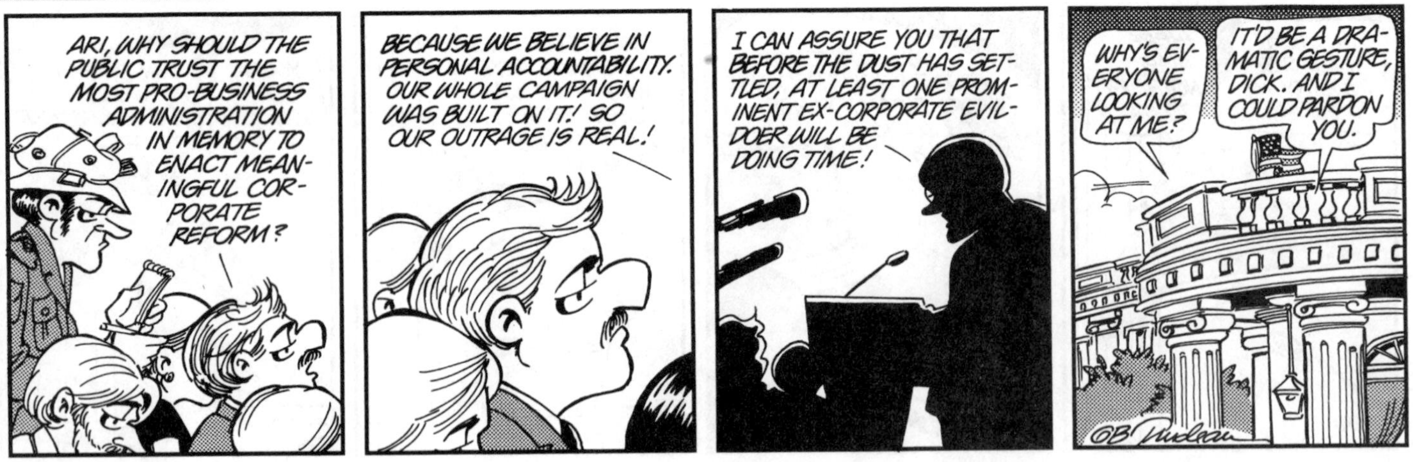
ARI, WHY SHOULD THE PUBLIC TRUST THE MOST PRO-BUSINESS ADMINISTRATION IN MEMORY TO ENACT MEANINGFUL CORPORATE REFORM?
BECAUSE WE BELIEVE IN PERSONAL ACCOUNTABILITY. OUR WHOLE CAMPAIGN WAS BUILT ON IT! SO OUR OUTRAGE IS REAL!
I CAN ASSURE YOU THAT BEFORE THE DUST HAS SETTLED, AT LEAST ONE PROMINENT EX-CORPORATE EVILDOER WILL BE DOING TIME!
WHY'S EVERYONE LOOKING AT ME?
IT'D BE A DRAMATIC GESTURE, DICK. AND I COULD PARDON YOU.
©B Trudeau

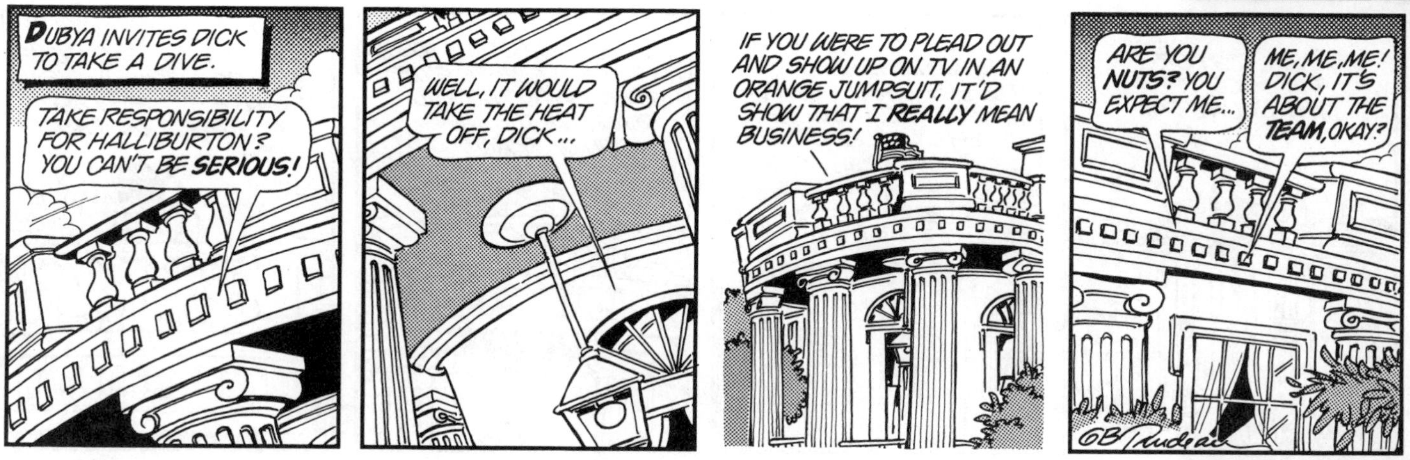
DUBYA INVITES DICK TO TAKE A DIVE.
TAKE RESPONSIBILITY FOR HALLIBURTON? YOU CAN'T BE **SERIOUS!**
WELL, IT WOULD TAKE THE HEAT OFF, DICK...
IF YOU WERE TO PLEAD OUT AND SHOW UP ON TV IN AN ORANGE JUMPSUIT, IT'D SHOW THAT I **REALLY** MEAN BUSINESS!
ARE YOU **NUTS?** YOU EXPECT ME...
ME, ME, ME! DICK, IT'S ABOUT THE **TEAM**, OKAY?

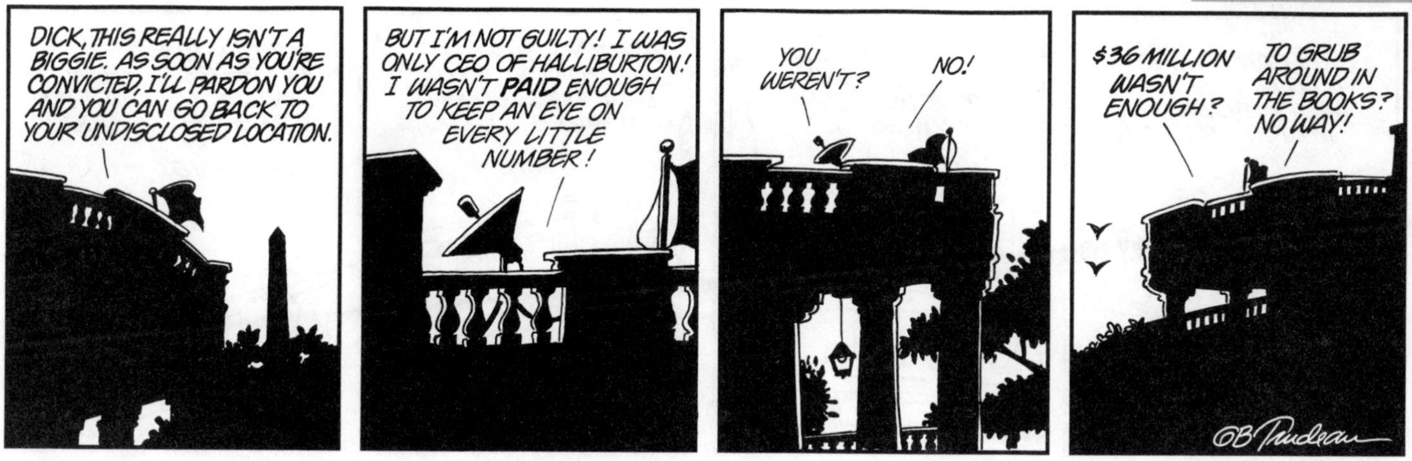
DICK, THIS REALLY ISN'T A BIGGIE. AS SOON AS YOU'RE CONVICTED, I'LL PARDON YOU AND YOU CAN GO BACK TO YOUR UNDISCLOSED LOCATION.
BUT I'M NOT GUILTY! I WAS ONLY CEO OF HALLIBURTON! I WASN'T **PAID** ENOUGH TO KEEP AN EYE ON EVERY LITTLE NUMBER!
YOU WEREN'T?
NO!
$36 MILLION WASN'T ENOUGH?
TO GRUB AROUND IN THE BOOKS? NO WAY!

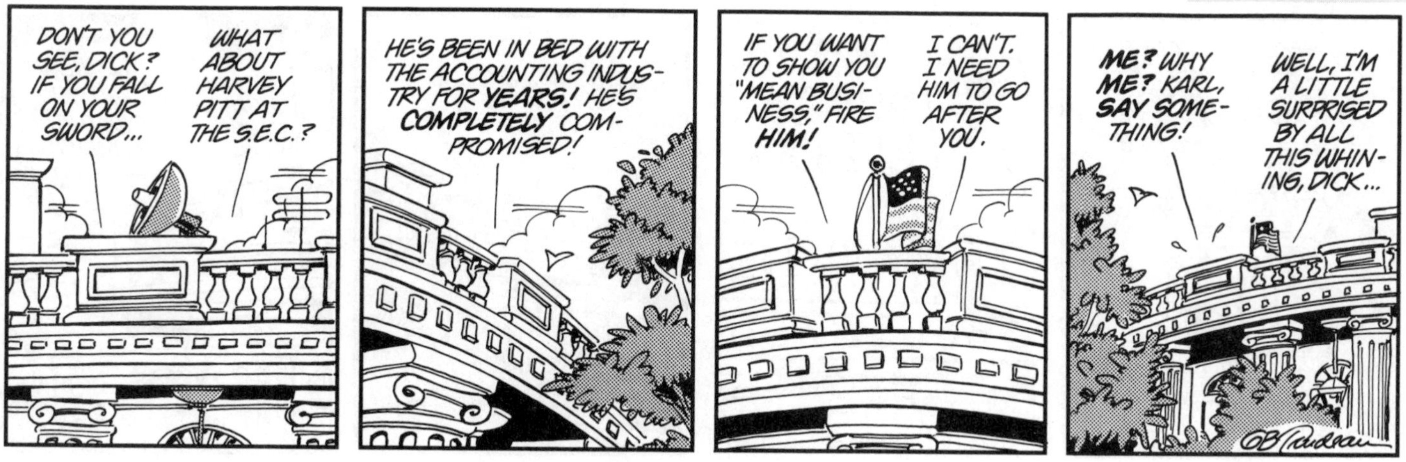
DON'T YOU SEE, DICK? IF YOU FALL ON YOUR SWORD...
WHAT ABOUT HARVEY PITT AT THE S.E.C.?
HE'S BEEN IN BED WITH THE ACCOUNTING INDUSTRY FOR **YEARS!** HE'S **COMPLETELY** COMPROMISED!
IF YOU WANT TO SHOW YOU "MEAN BUSINESS," FIRE **HIM!**
I CAN'T. I NEED HIM TO GO AFTER YOU.
ME? WHY **ME?** KARL, **SAY SOMETHING!**
WELL, I'M A LITTLE SURPRISED BY ALL THIS WHINING, DICK...

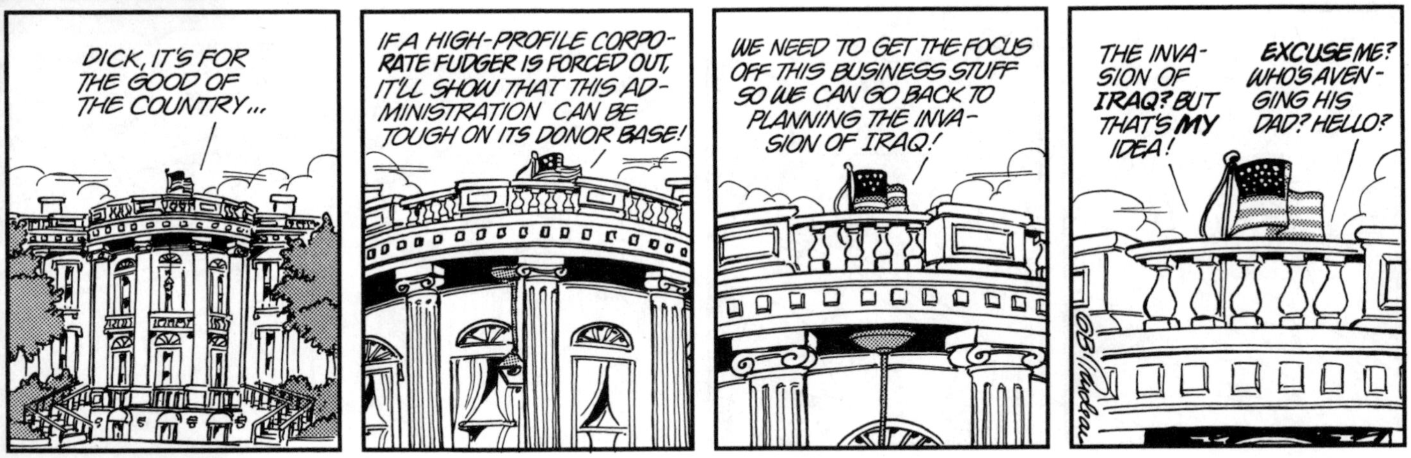
DICK, IT'S FOR THE GOOD OF THE COUNTRY...
IF A HIGH-PROFILE CORPORATE FUDGER IS FORCED OUT, IT'LL SHOW THAT THIS ADMINISTRATION CAN BE TOUGH ON ITS DONOR BASE!
WE NEED TO GET THE FOCUS OFF THIS BUSINESS STUFF SO WE CAN GO BACK TO PLANNING THE INVASION OF IRAQ!
THE INVASION OF **IRAQ?** BUT THAT'S **MY** IDEA!
EXCUSE ME? WHO'S AVENGING HIS DAD? HELLO?
GBTrudeau

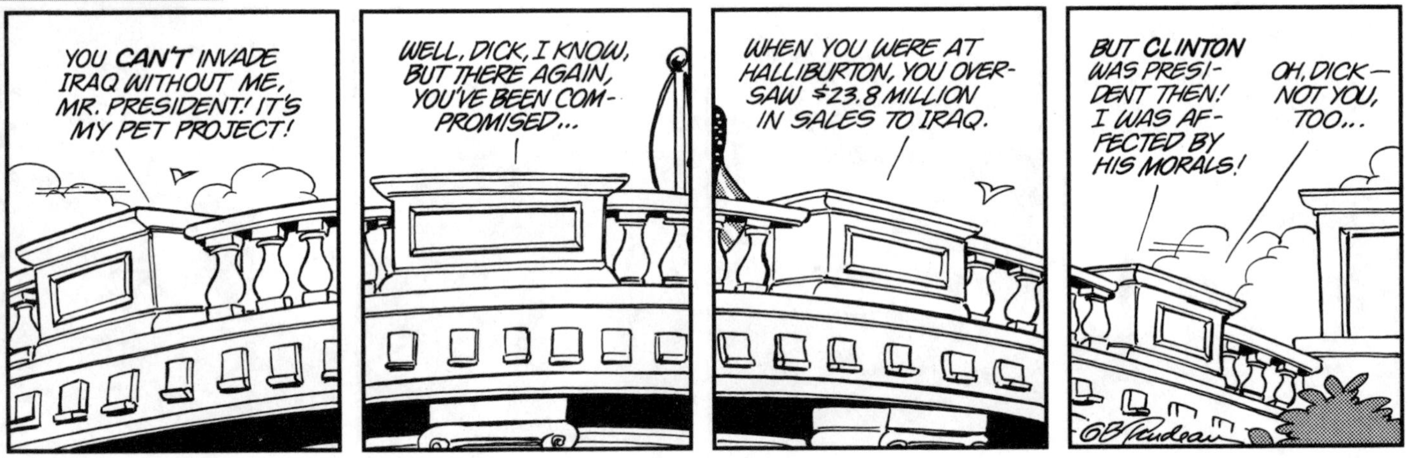
YOU **CAN'T** INVADE IRAQ WITHOUT ME, MR. PRESIDENT! IT'S MY PET PROJECT!
WELL, DICK, I KNOW, BUT THERE AGAIN, YOU'VE BEEN COMPROMISED...
WHEN YOU WERE AT HALLIBURTON, YOU OVERSAW $23.8 MILLION IN SALES TO IRAQ.
BUT **CLINTON** WAS PRESIDENT THEN! I WAS AFFECTED BY HIS MORALS!
OH, DICK— NOT YOU, TOO...
GBTrudeau

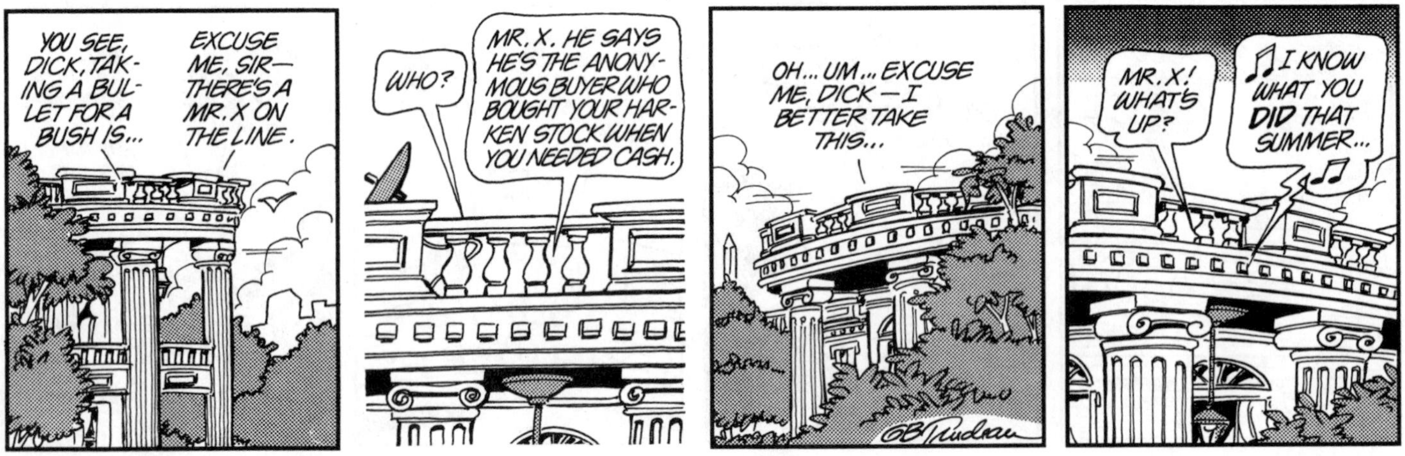
YOU SEE, DICK, TAKING A BULLET FOR A BUSH IS...
EXCUSE ME, SIR— THERE'S A MR. X ON THE LINE.
WHO?
MR. X. HE SAYS HE'S THE ANONYMOUS BUYER WHO BOUGHT YOUR HARKEN STOCK WHEN YOU NEEDED CASH.
OH... UM... EXCUSE ME, DICK — I BETTER TAKE THIS...
GBTrudeau
MR. X! WHAT'S UP?
♫ I KNOW WHAT YOU **DID** THAT SUMMER... ♫

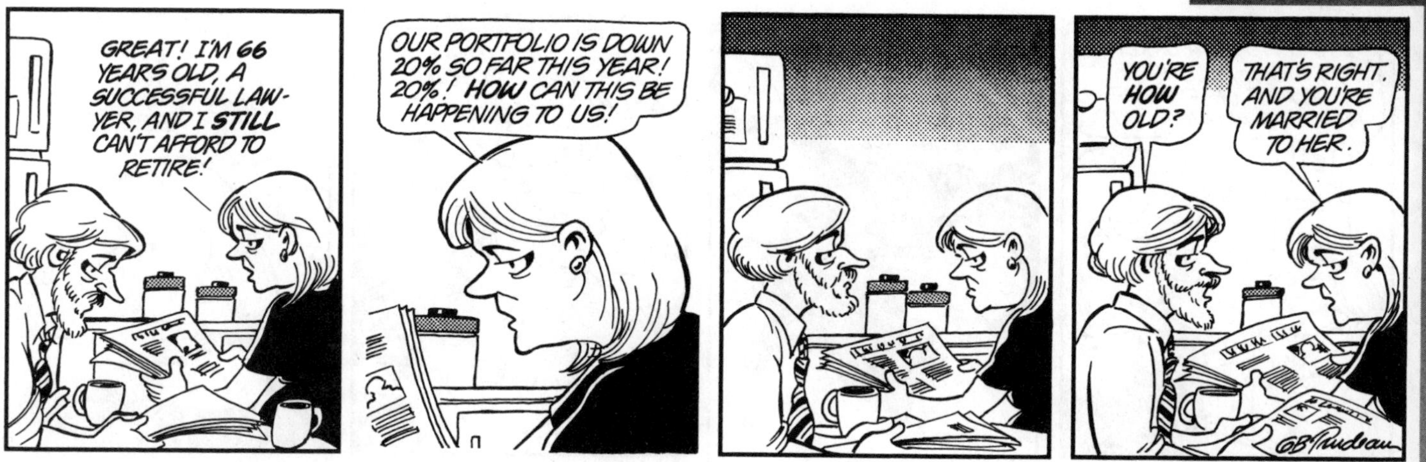
GREAT! I'M 66 YEARS OLD, A SUCCESSFUL LAWYER, AND I STILL CAN'T AFFORD TO RETIRE!
OUR PORTFOLIO IS DOWN 20% SO FAR THIS YEAR! 20%! HOW CAN THIS BE HAPPENING TO US!
YOU'RE HOW OLD?
THAT'S RIGHT. AND YOU'RE MARRIED TO HER.

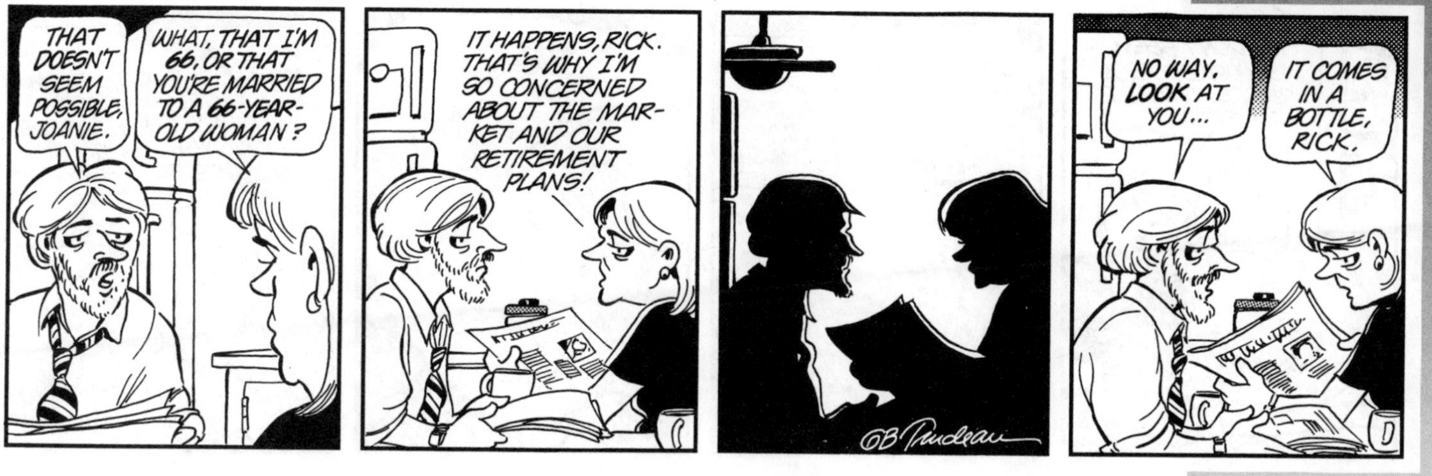
THAT DOESN'T SEEM POSSIBLE, JOANIE.
WHAT, THAT I'M 66, OR THAT YOU'RE MARRIED TO A 66-YEAR-OLD WOMAN?
IT HAPPENS, RICK. THAT'S WHY I'M SO CONCERNED ABOUT THE MARKET AND OUR RETIREMENT PLANS!
NO WAY. LOOK AT YOU...
IT COMES IN A BOTTLE, RICK.

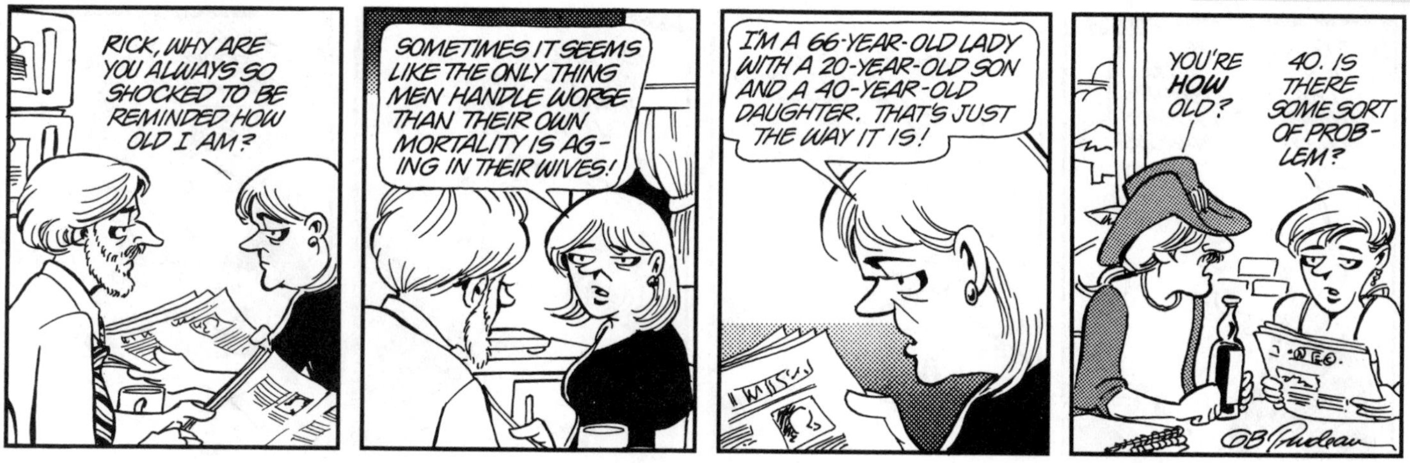
RICK, WHY ARE YOU ALWAYS SO SHOCKED TO BE REMINDED HOW OLD I AM?
SOMETIMES IT SEEMS LIKE THE ONLY THING MEN HANDLE WORSE THAN THEIR OWN MORTALITY IS AGING IN THEIR WIVES!
I'M A 66-YEAR-OLD LADY WITH A 20-YEAR-OLD SON AND A 40-YEAR-OLD DAUGHTER. THAT'S JUST THE WAY IT IS!
YOU'RE HOW OLD?
40. IS THERE SOME SORT OF PROBLEM?

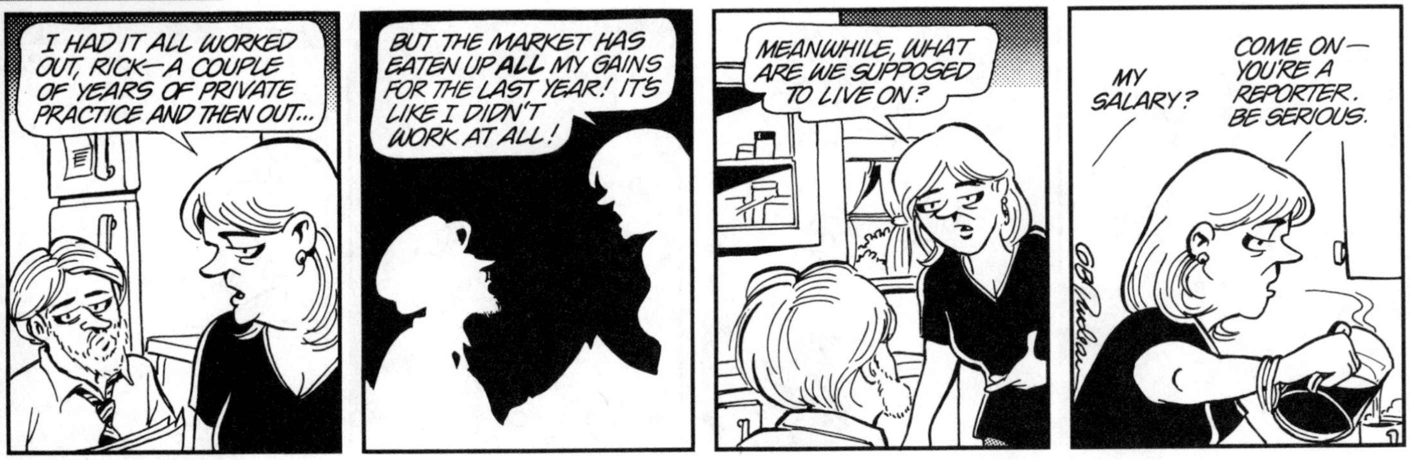
I HAD IT ALL WORKED OUT, RICK—A COUPLE OF YEARS OF PRIVATE PRACTICE AND THEN OUT...
BUT THE MARKET HAS EATEN UP ALL MY GAINS FOR THE LAST YEAR! IT'S LIKE I DIDN'T WORK AT ALL!
MEANWHILE, WHAT ARE WE SUPPOSED TO LIVE ON?
MY SALARY?
COME ON—YOU'RE A REPORTER. BE SERIOUS.

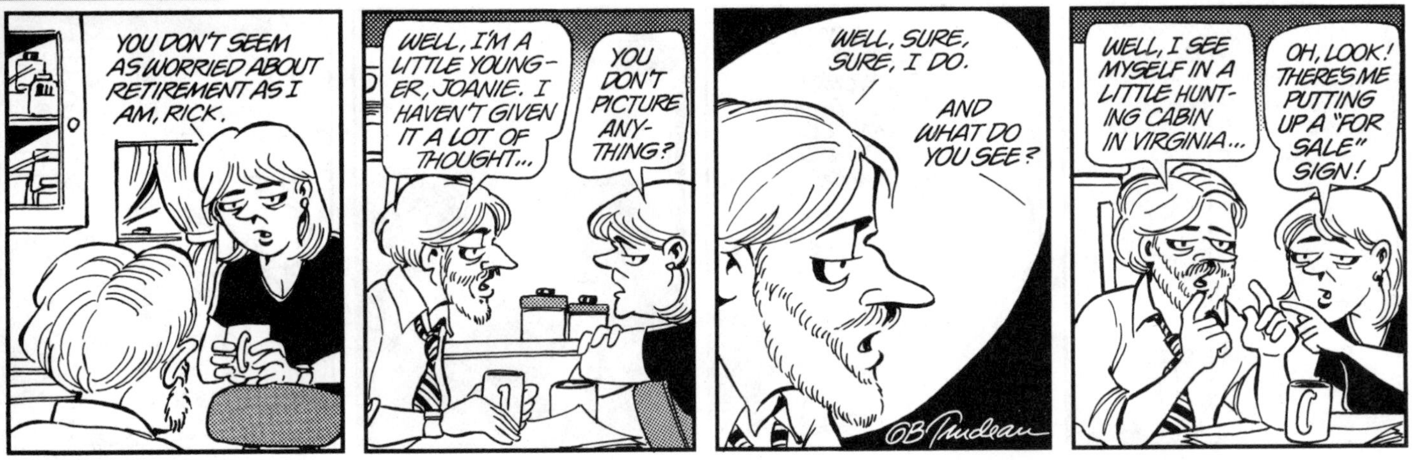
YOU DON'T SEEM AS WORRIED ABOUT RETIREMENT AS I AM, RICK.
WELL, I'M A LITTLE YOUNGER, JOANIE. I HAVEN'T GIVEN IT A LOT OF THOUGHT...
YOU DON'T PICTURE ANYTHING?
WELL, SURE, SURE, I DO.
AND WHAT DO YOU SEE?
WELL, I SEE MYSELF IN A LITTLE HUNTING CABIN IN VIRGINIA...
OH, LOOK! THERE'S ME PUTTING UP A "FOR SALE" SIGN!

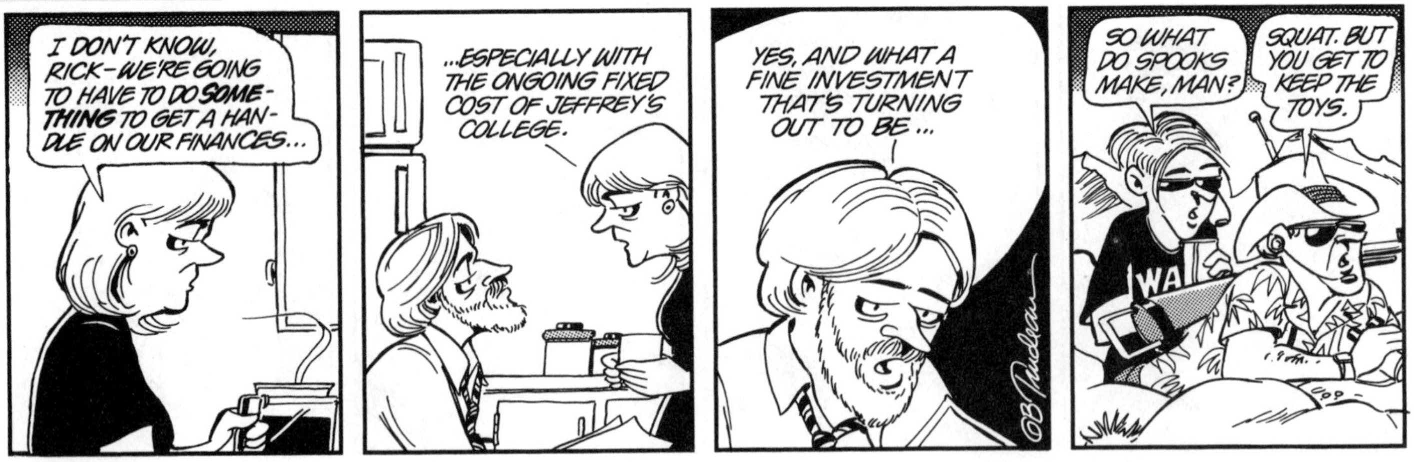
I DON'T KNOW, RICK—WE'RE GOING TO HAVE TO DO SOMETHING TO GET A HANDLE ON OUR FINANCES...
...ESPECIALLY WITH THE ONGOING FIXED COST OF JEFFREY'S COLLEGE.
YES, AND WHAT A FINE INVESTMENT THAT'S TURNING OUT TO BE...
SO WHAT DO SPOOKS MAKE, MAN?
SQUAT. BUT YOU GET TO KEEP THE TOYS.

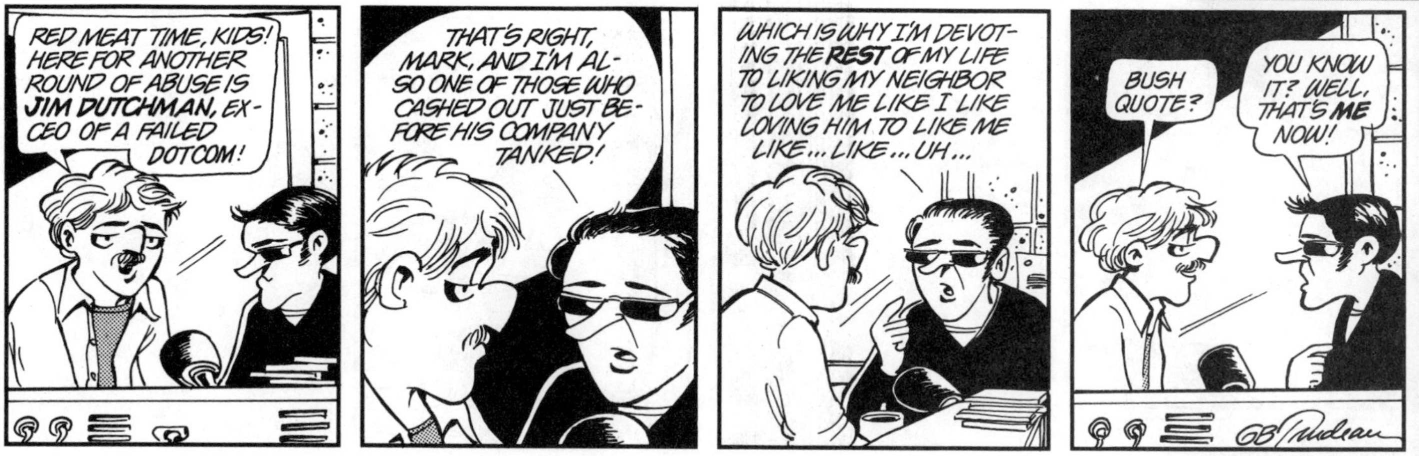
RED MEAT TIME, KIDS! HERE FOR ANOTHER ROUND OF ABUSE IS **JIM DUTCHMAN**, EX-CEO OF A FAILED DOTCOM!
THAT'S RIGHT, MARK, AND I'M ALSO ONE OF THOSE WHO CASHED OUT JUST BEFORE HIS COMPANY TANKED!
WHICH IS WHY I'M DEVOTING THE **REST** OF MY LIFE TO LIKING MY NEIGHBOR TO LOVE ME LIKE I LIKE LOVING HIM TO LIKE ME LIKE... LIKE... UH...
BUSH QUOTE?
YOU KNOW IT? WELL, THAT'S **ME** NOW!
GBTrudeau

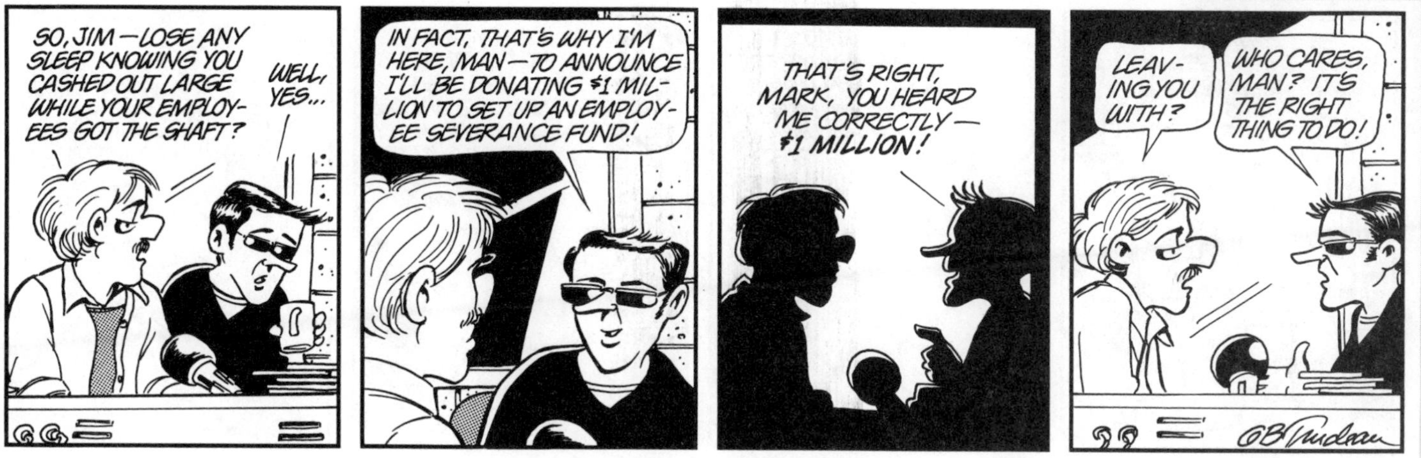
SO, JIM — LOSE ANY SLEEP KNOWING YOU CASHED OUT LARGE WHILE YOUR EMPLOYEES GOT THE SHAFT?
WELL, YES...
IN FACT, THAT'S WHY I'M HERE, MAN — TO ANNOUNCE I'LL BE DONATING $1 MILLION TO SET UP AN EMPLOYEE SEVERANCE FUND!
THAT'S RIGHT, MARK, YOU HEARD ME CORRECTLY — **$1 MILLION!**
LEAVING YOU WITH?
WHO CARES, MAN? IT'S THE RIGHT THING TO DO!
GBTrudeau

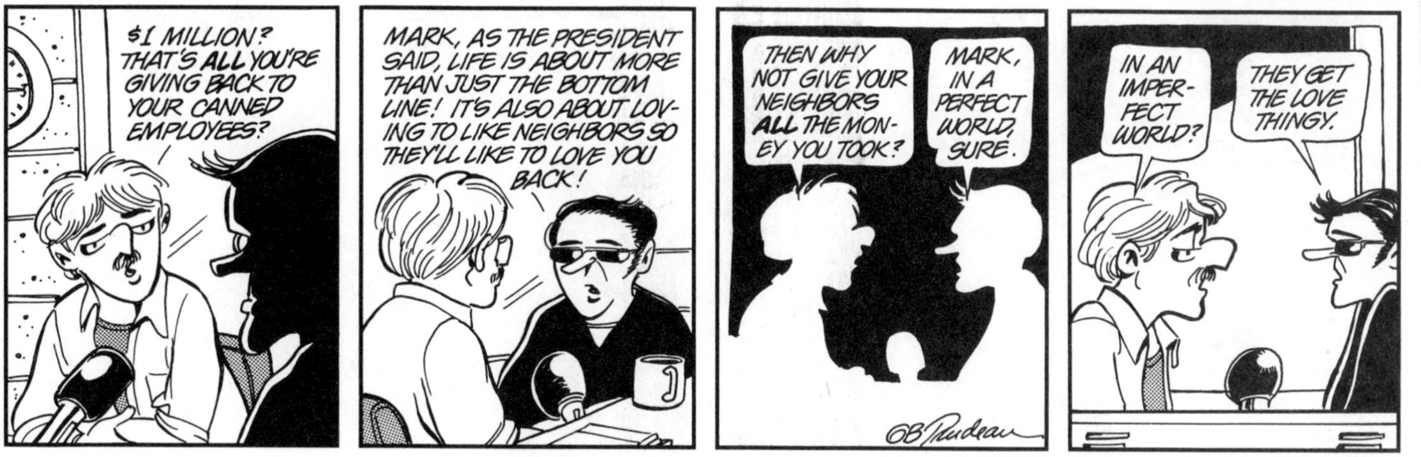
$1 MILLION? THAT'S **ALL** YOU'RE GIVING BACK TO YOUR CANNED EMPLOYEES?
MARK, AS THE PRESIDENT SAID, LIFE IS ABOUT MORE THAN JUST THE BOTTOM LINE! IT'S ALSO ABOUT LOVING TO LIKE NEIGHBORS SO THEY'LL LIKE TO LOVE YOU BACK!
THEN WHY NOT GIVE YOUR NEIGHBORS **ALL** THE MONEY YOU TOOK?
MARK, IN A PERFECT WORLD, SURE.
GBTrudeau
IN AN IMPERFECT WORLD?
THEY GET THE LOVE THINGY.

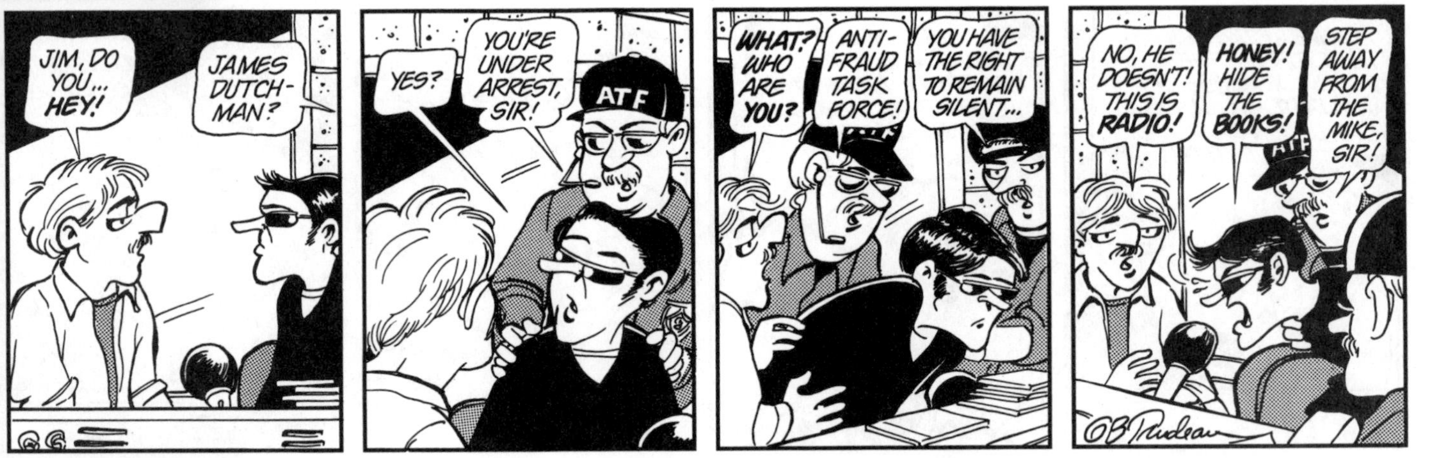
JIM, DO YOU... HEY!
JAMES DUTCHMAN?
YES?
YOU'RE UNDER ARREST, SIR!
ATF
WHAT? WHO ARE YOU?
ANTI-FRAUD TASK FORCE!
YOU HAVE THE RIGHT TO REMAIN SILENT...
NO, HE DOESN'T! THIS IS RADIO!
HONEY! HIDE THE BOOKS!
STEP AWAY FROM THE MIKE, SIR!
ATF
GB Trudeau

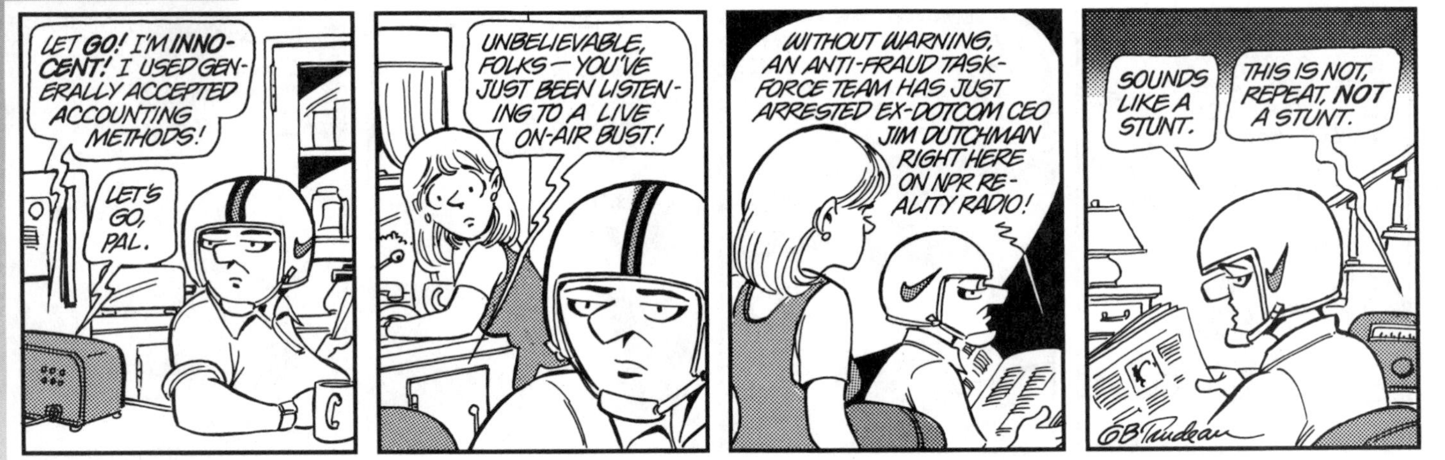
LET GO! I'M INNOCENT! I USED GENERALLY ACCEPTED ACCOUNTING METHODS!
LET'S GO, PAL.
UNBELIEVABLE, FOLKS — YOU'VE JUST BEEN LISTENING TO A LIVE ON-AIR BUST!
WITHOUT WARNING, AN ANTI-FRAUD TASK-FORCE TEAM HAS JUST ARRESTED EX-DOTCOM CEO JIM DUTCHMAN RIGHT HERE ON NPR REALITY RADIO!
SOUNDS LIKE A STUNT.
THIS IS NOT, REPEAT, NOT A STUNT.
GB Trudeau

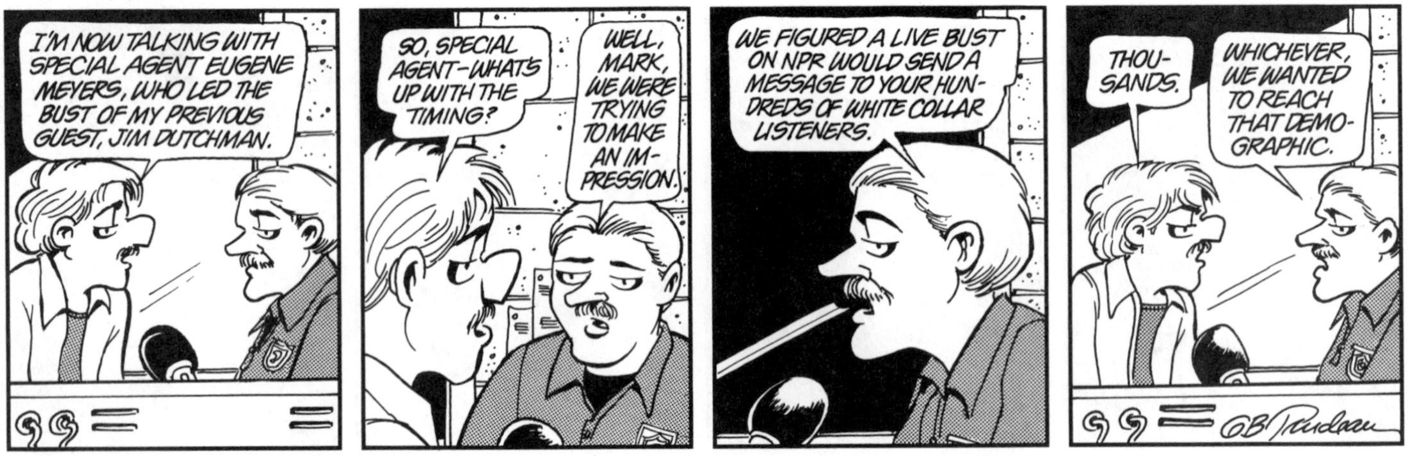
I'M NOW TALKING WITH SPECIAL AGENT EUGENE MEYERS, WHO LED THE BUST OF MY PREVIOUS GUEST, JIM DUTCHMAN.
SO, SPECIAL AGENT — WHAT'S UP WITH THE TIMING?
WELL, MARK, WE WERE TRYING TO MAKE AN IMPRESSION.
WE FIGURED A LIVE BUST ON NPR WOULD SEND A MESSAGE TO YOUR HUNDREDS OF WHITE COLLAR LISTENERS.
THOUSANDS.
WHICHEVER, WE WANTED TO REACH THAT DEMOGRAPHIC.
GB Trudeau

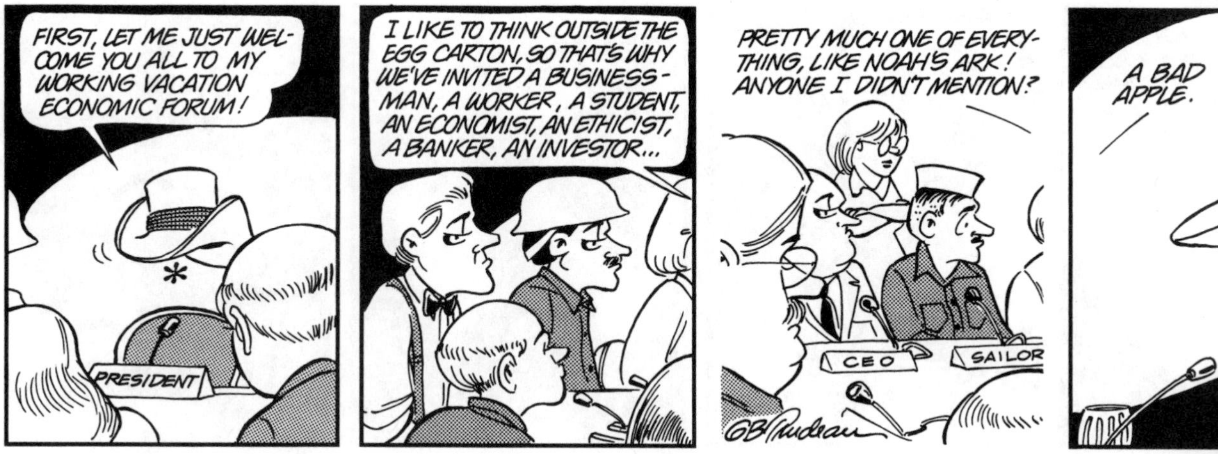
FIRST, LET ME JUST WELCOME YOU ALL TO MY WORKING VACATION ECONOMIC FORUM!
PRESIDENT
I LIKE TO THINK OUTSIDE THE EGG CARTON, SO THAT'S WHY WE'VE INVITED A BUSINESSMAN, A WORKER, A STUDENT, AN ECONOMIST, AN ETHICIST, A BANKER, AN INVESTOR...
PRETTY MUCH ONE OF EVERYTHING, LIKE NOAH'S ARK! ANYONE I DIDN'T MENTION?
CEO
SAILOR
A BAD APPLE.
OH... YOU MADE BAIL? GOOD FOR YOU.

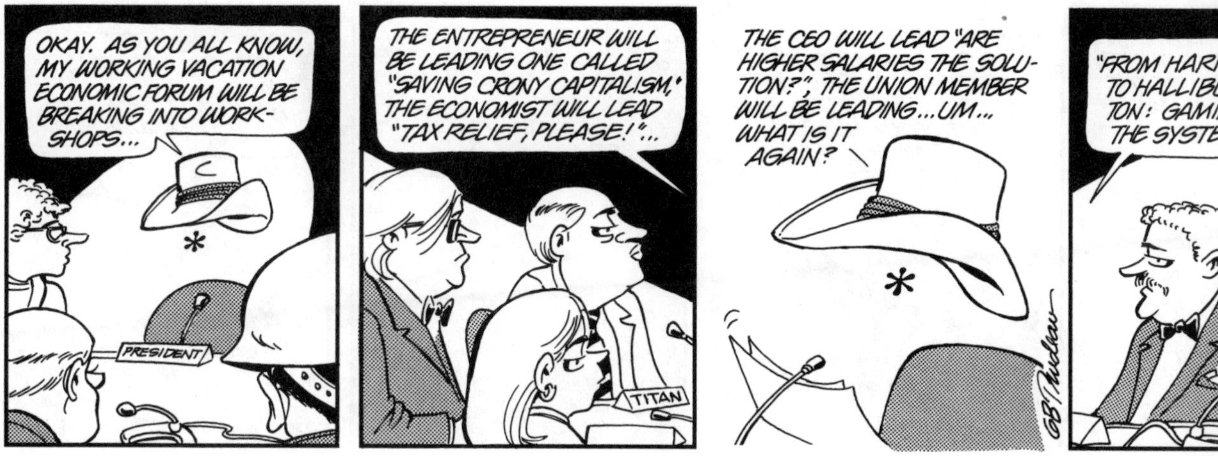
OKAY. AS YOU ALL KNOW, MY WORKING VACATION ECONOMIC FORUM WILL BE BREAKING INTO WORKSHOPS...
PRESIDENT
THE ENTREPRENEUR WILL BE LEADING ONE CALLED "SAVING CRONY CAPITALISM." THE ECONOMIST WILL LEAD "TAX RELIEF, PLEASE!"...
TITAN
THE CEO WILL LEAD "ARE HIGHER SALARIES THE SOLUTION?", THE UNION MEMBER WILL BE LEADING... UM... WHAT IS IT AGAIN?
"FROM HARKEN TO HALLIBURTON: GAMING THE SYSTEM."
NO, NO, IT'S SUPPOSED TO BE ON GIVEBACKS.

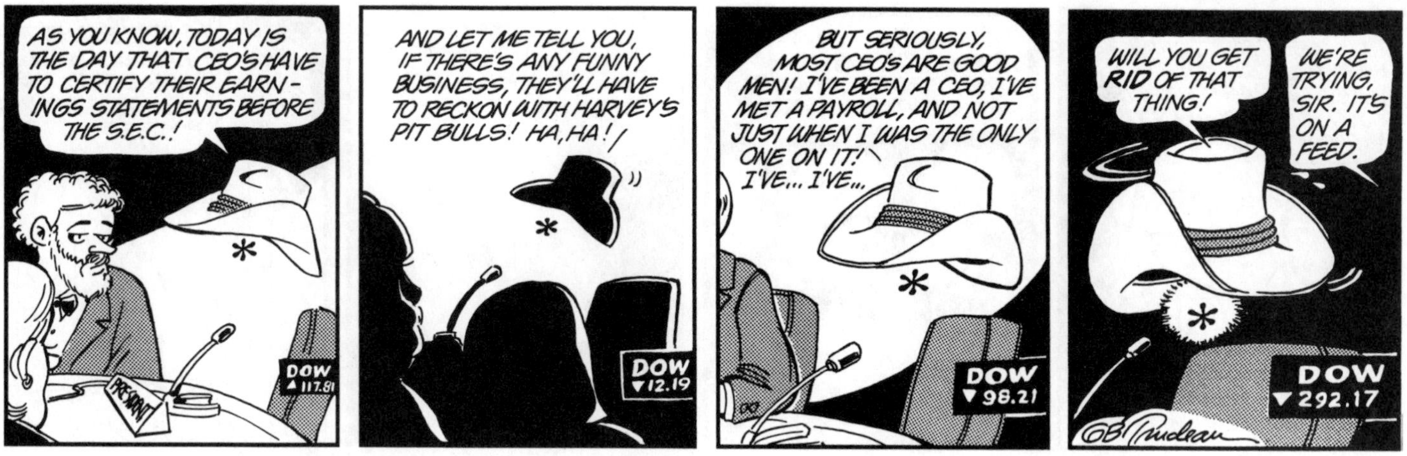
AS YOU KNOW, TODAY IS THE DAY THAT CEO'S HAVE TO CERTIFY THEIR EARNINGS STATEMENTS BEFORE THE S.E.C.!
DOW ▲117.81
AND LET ME TELL YOU, IF THERE'S ANY FUNNY BUSINESS, THEY'LL HAVE TO RECKON WITH HARVEY'S PIT BULLS! HA, HA!
DOW ▼12.19
BUT SERIOUSLY, MOST CEO'S ARE GOOD MEN! I'VE BEEN A CEO, I'VE MET A PAYROLL, AND NOT JUST WHEN I WAS THE ONLY ONE ON IT! I'VE... I'VE...
DOW ▼98.21
WILL YOU GET RID OF THAT THING!
WE'RE TRYING, SIR. IT'S ON A FEED.
DOW ▼292.17

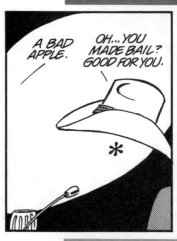

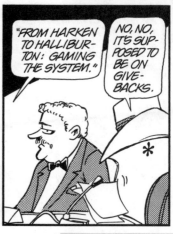

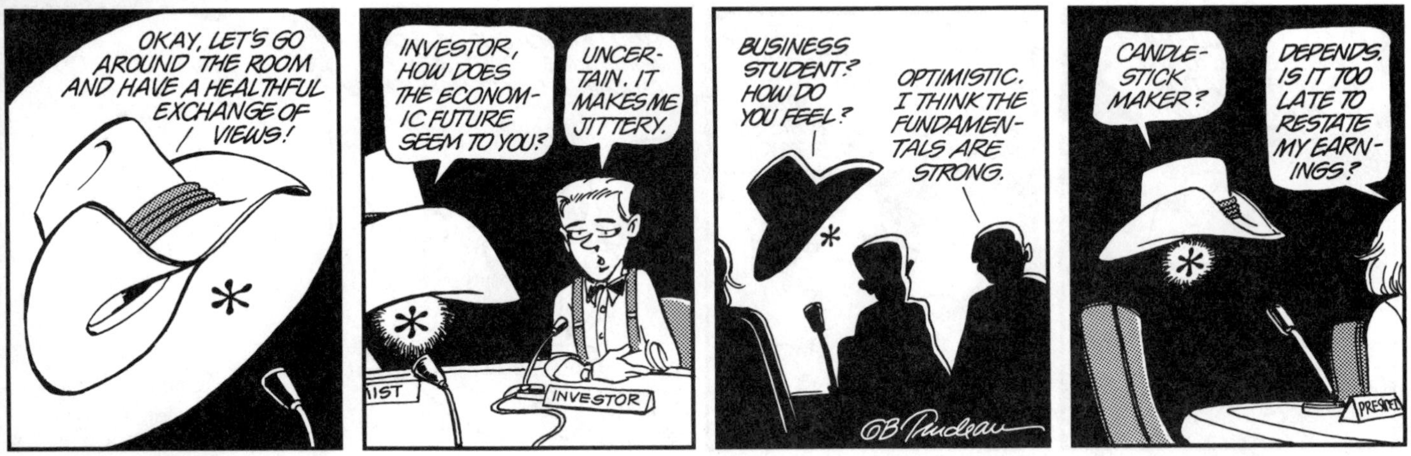
OKAY, LET'S GO AROUND THE ROOM AND HAVE A HEALTHFUL EXCHANGE OF VIEWS!
INVESTOR, HOW DOES THE ECONOMIC FUTURE SEEM TO YOU?
UNCERTAIN. IT MAKES ME JITTERY.
INVESTOR
BUSINESS STUDENT? HOW DO YOU FEEL?
OPTIMISTIC. I THINK THE FUNDAMENTALS ARE STRONG.
GB Trudeau
CANDLESTICK MAKER?
DEPENDS. IS IT TOO LATE TO RESTATE MY EARNINGS?

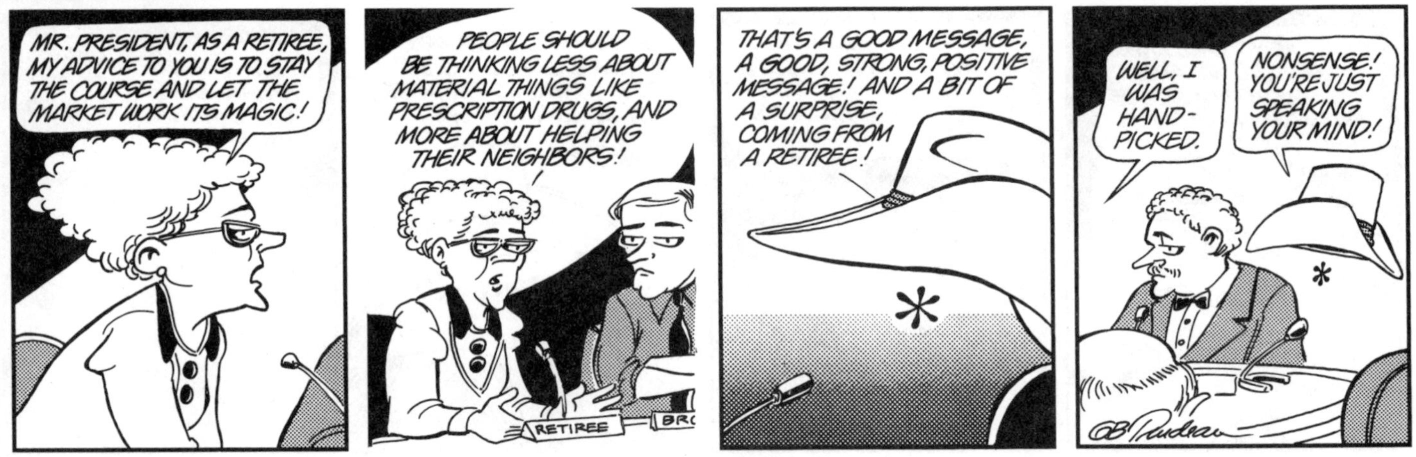
MR. PRESIDENT, AS A RETIREE, MY ADVICE TO YOU IS TO STAY THE COURSE AND LET THE MARKET WORK ITS MAGIC!
PEOPLE SHOULD BE THINKING LESS ABOUT MATERIAL THINGS LIKE PRESCRIPTION DRUGS, AND MORE ABOUT HELPING THEIR NEIGHBORS!
RETIREE
THAT'S A GOOD MESSAGE, A GOOD, STRONG, POSITIVE MESSAGE! AND A BIT OF A SURPRISE, COMING FROM A RETIREE!
WELL, I WAS HAND-PICKED.
NONSENSE! YOU'RE JUST SPEAKING YOUR MIND!
GB Trudeau

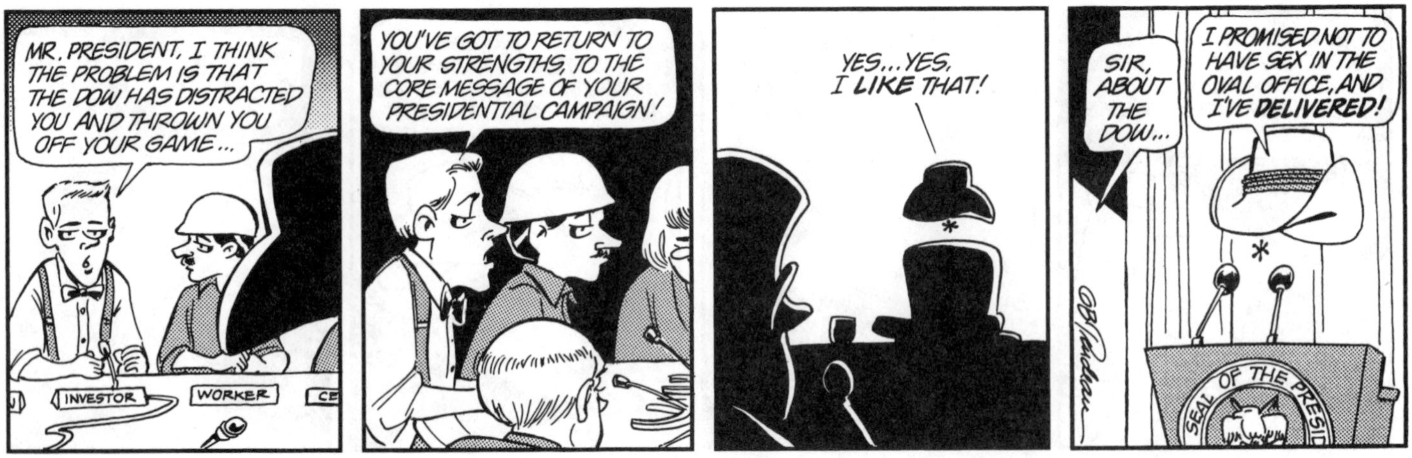
MR. PRESIDENT, I THINK THE PROBLEM IS THAT THE DOW HAS DISTRACTED YOU AND THROWN YOU OFF YOUR GAME...
INVESTOR
WORKER
YOU'VE GOT TO RETURN TO YOUR STRENGTHS, TO THE CORE MESSAGE OF YOUR PRESIDENTIAL CAMPAIGN!
YES... YES, I **LIKE** THAT!
SIR, ABOUT THE DOW...
I PROMISED NOT TO HAVE SEX IN THE OVAL OFFICE, AND I'VE **DELIVERED!**
GB Trudeau

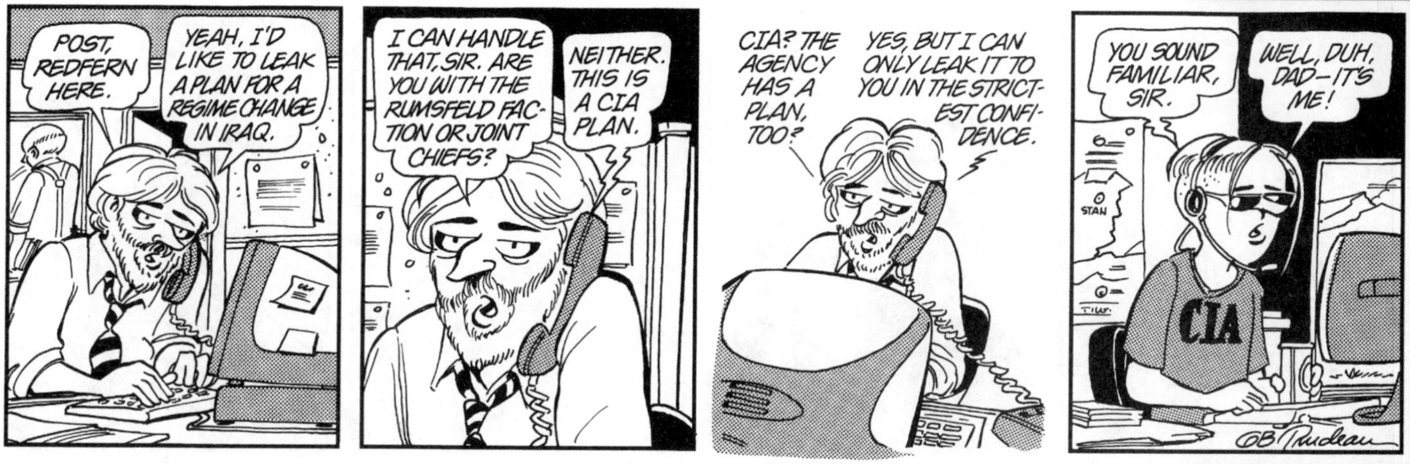
POST, REDFERN HERE.
YEAH, I'D LIKE TO LEAK A PLAN FOR A REGIME CHANGE IN IRAQ.
I CAN HANDLE THAT, SIR. ARE YOU WITH THE RUMSFELD FACTION OR JOINT CHIEFS?
NEITHER. THIS IS A CIA PLAN.
CIA? THE AGENCY HAS A PLAN, TOO?
YES, BUT I CAN ONLY LEAK IT TO YOU IN THE STRICTEST CONFIDENCE.
YOU SOUND FAMILIAR, SIR.
WELL, DUH, DAD—IT'S ME!
CIA
©B Trudeau

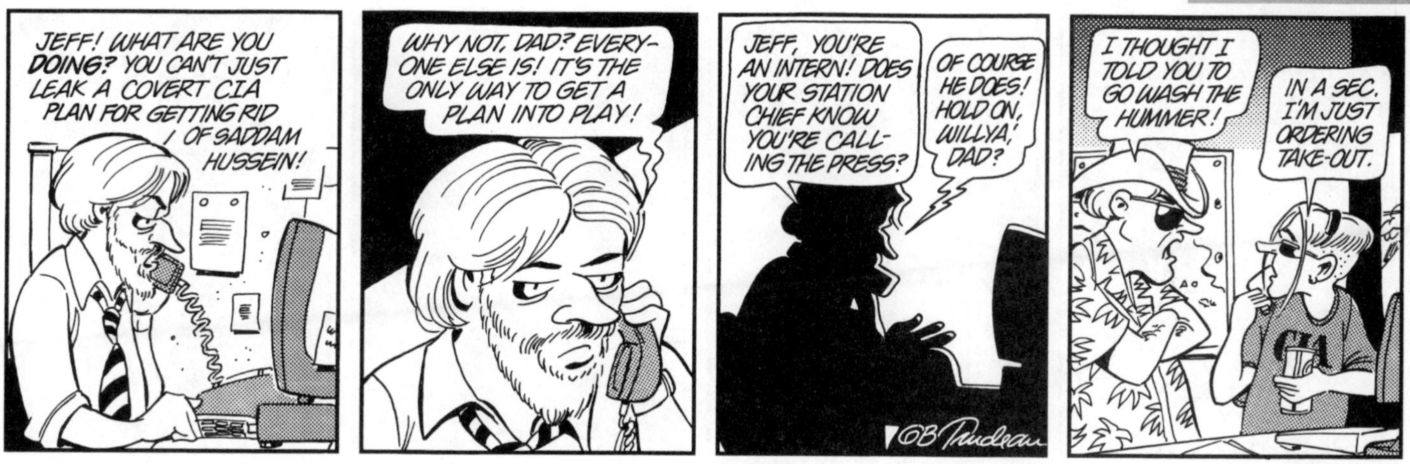
JEFF! WHAT ARE YOU DOING? YOU CAN'T JUST LEAK A COVERT CIA PLAN FOR GETTING RID OF SADDAM HUSSEIN!
WHY NOT, DAD? EVERYONE ELSE IS! IT'S THE ONLY WAY TO GET A PLAN INTO PLAY!
JEFF, YOU'RE AN INTERN! DOES YOUR STATION CHIEF KNOW YOU'RE CALLING THE PRESS?
OF COURSE HE DOES! HOLD ON, WILLYA,' DAD?
©B Trudeau
I THOUGHT I TOLD YOU TO GO WASH THE HUMMER!
IN A SEC. I'M JUST ORDERING TAKE-OUT.
CIA

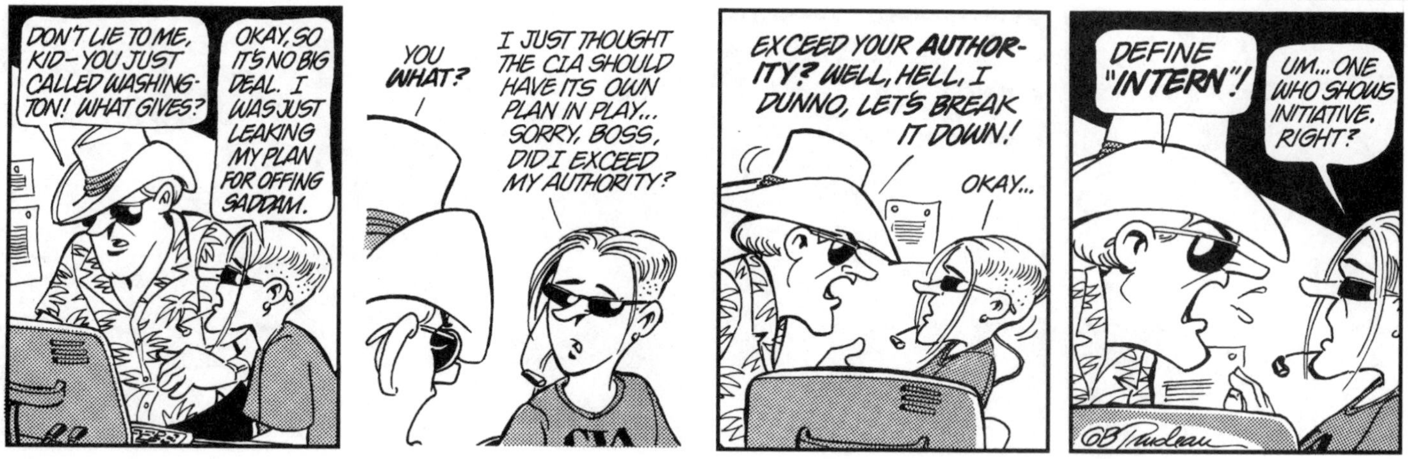
DON'T LIE TO ME, KID—YOU JUST CALLED WASHINGTON! WHAT GIVES?
OKAY, SO IT'S NO BIG DEAL. I WAS JUST LEAKING MY PLAN FOR OFFING SADDAM.
YOU WHAT?
I JUST THOUGHT THE CIA SHOULD HAVE ITS OWN PLAN IN PLAY... SORRY, BOSS, DID I EXCEED MY AUTHORITY?
EXCEED YOUR AUTHORITY? WELL, HELL, I DUNNO, LET'S BREAK IT DOWN!
OKAY...
DEFINE "INTERN"!
UM... ONE WHO SHOWS INITIATIVE, RIGHT?
©B Trudeau

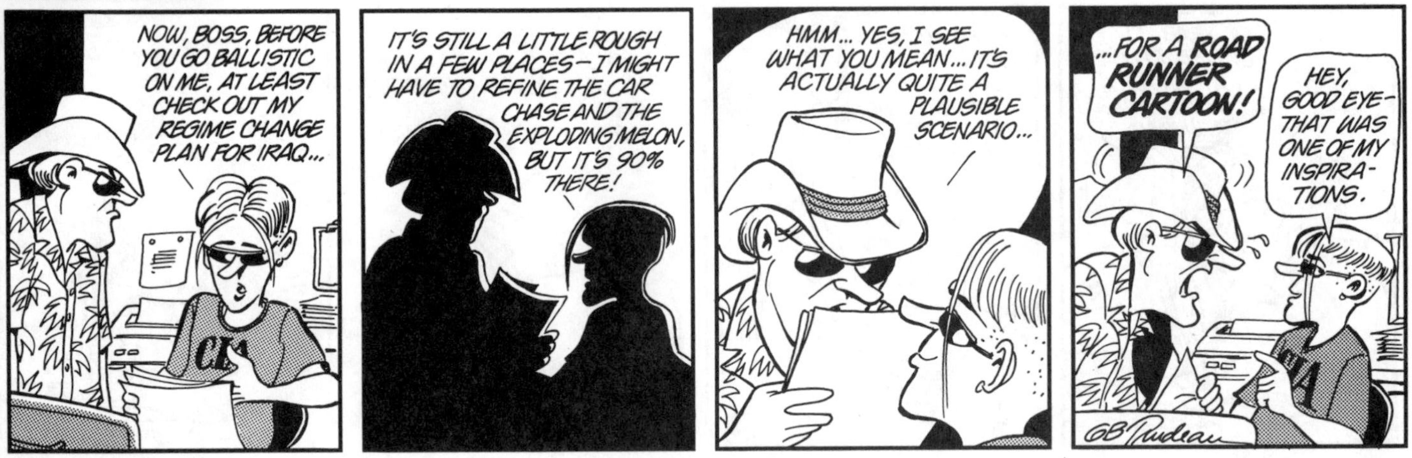
NOW, BOSS, BEFORE YOU GO BALLISTIC ON ME, AT LEAST CHECK OUT MY REGIME CHANGE PLAN FOR IRAQ...
IT'S STILL A LITTLE ROUGH IN A FEW PLACES—I MIGHT HAVE TO REFINE THE CAR CHASE AND THE EXPLODING MELON, BUT IT'S 90% THERE!
HMM... YES, I SEE WHAT YOU MEAN... IT'S ACTUALLY QUITE A PLAUSIBLE SCENARIO...
...FOR A ROAD RUNNER CARTOON!
HEY, GOOD EYE—THAT WAS ONE OF MY INSPIRATIONS.
GBTrudeau

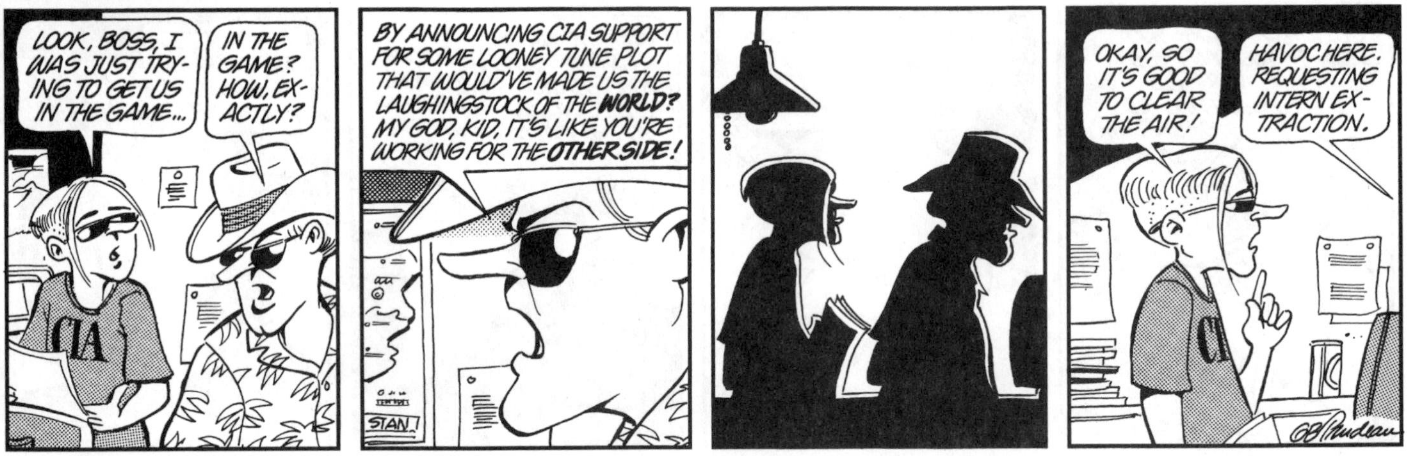
LOOK, BOSS, I WAS JUST TRYING TO GET US IN THE GAME...
IN THE GAME? HOW, EXACTLY?
BY ANNOUNCING CIA SUPPORT FOR SOME LOONEY TUNE PLOT THAT WOULD'VE MADE US THE LAUGHINGSTOCK OF THE WORLD? MY GOD, KID, IT'S LIKE YOU'RE WORKING FOR THE OTHER SIDE!
STAN!
OKAY, SO IT'S GOOD TO CLEAR THE AIR!
HAVOC HERE. REQUESTING INTERN EXTRACTION.
GBTrudeau

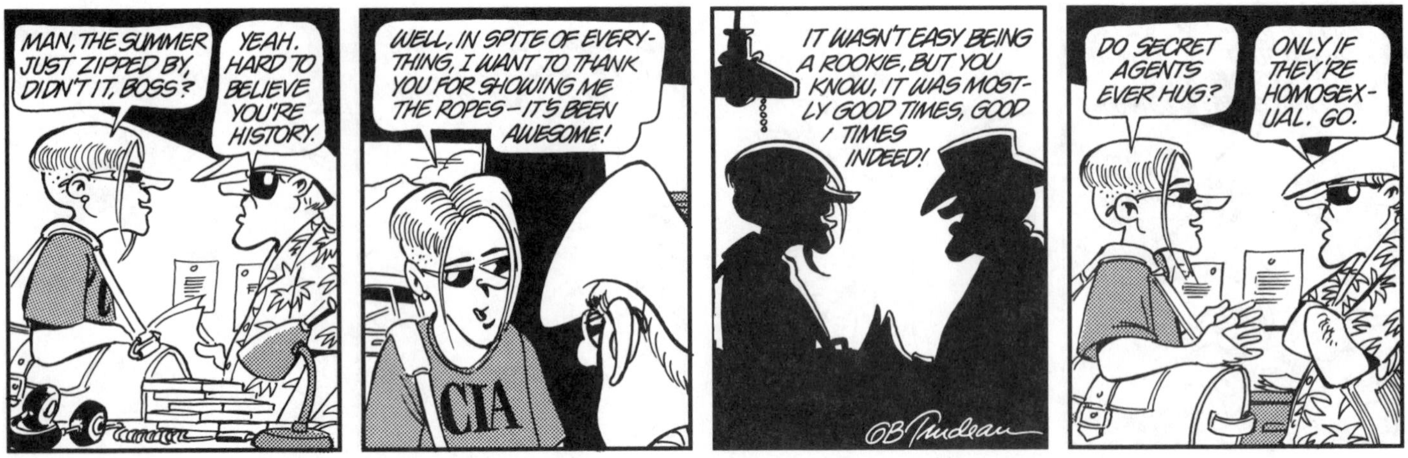
MAN, THE SUMMER JUST ZIPPED BY, DIDN'T IT, BOSS?
YEAH. HARD TO BELIEVE YOU'RE HISTORY.
WELL, IN SPITE OF EVERYTHING, I WANT TO THANK YOU FOR SHOWING ME THE ROPES—IT'S BEEN AWESOME!
IT WASN'T EASY BEING A ROOKIE, BUT YOU KNOW, IT WAS MOSTLY GOOD TIMES, GOOD TIMES INDEED!
GBTrudeau
DO SECRET AGENTS EVER HUG?
ONLY IF THEY'RE HOMOSEXUAL. GO.

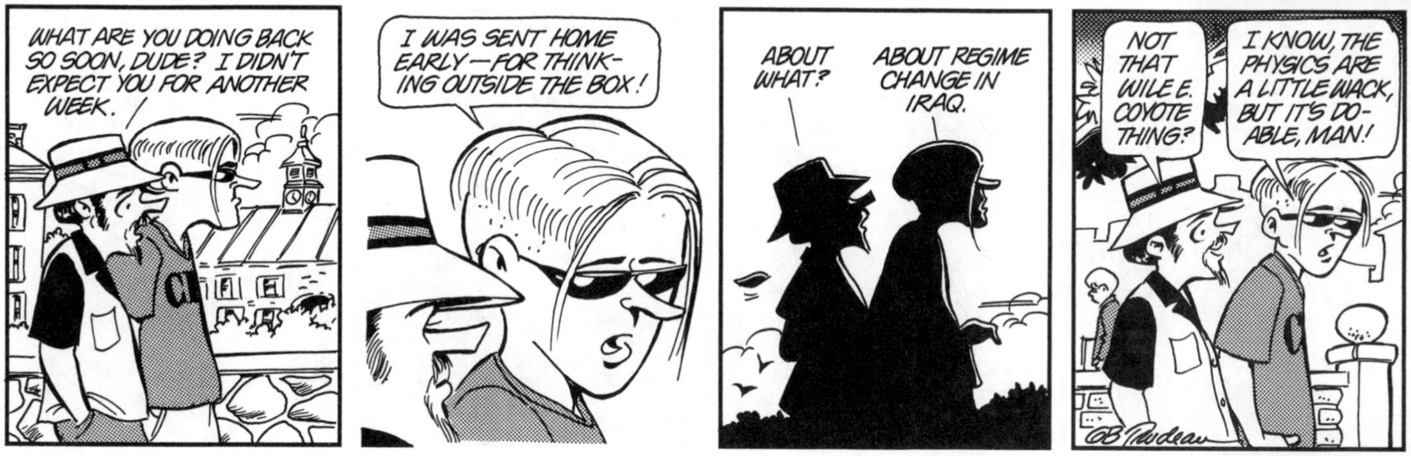
WHAT ARE YOU DOING BACK SO SOON, DUDE? I DIDN'T EXPECT YOU FOR ANOTHER WEEK.
I WAS SENT HOME EARLY—FOR THINKING OUTSIDE THE BOX!
ABOUT WHAT?
ABOUT REGIME CHANGE IN IRAQ.
NOT THAT WILE E. COYOTE THING?
I KNOW, THE PHYSICS ARE A LITTLE WACK, BUT IT'S DOABLE, MAN!
GB Trudeau

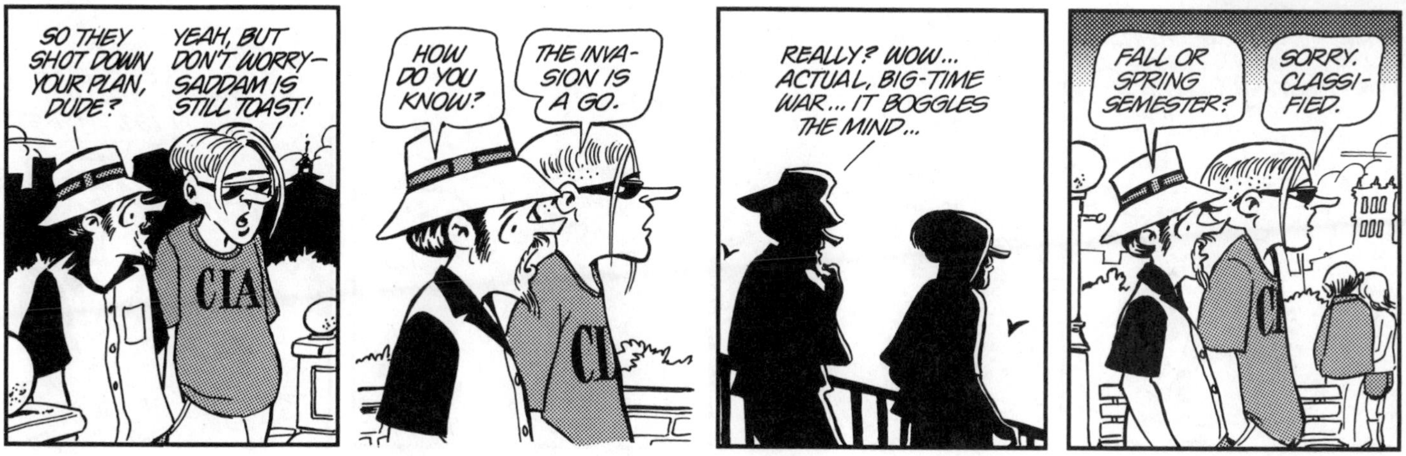
SO THEY SHOT DOWN YOUR PLAN, DUDE?
YEAH, BUT DON'T WORRY—SADDAM IS STILL TOAST!
HOW DO YOU KNOW?
THE INVASION IS A GO.
REALLY? WOW... ACTUAL, BIG-TIME WAR... IT BOGGLES THE MIND...
FALL OR SPRING SEMESTER?
SORRY. CLASSIFIED.

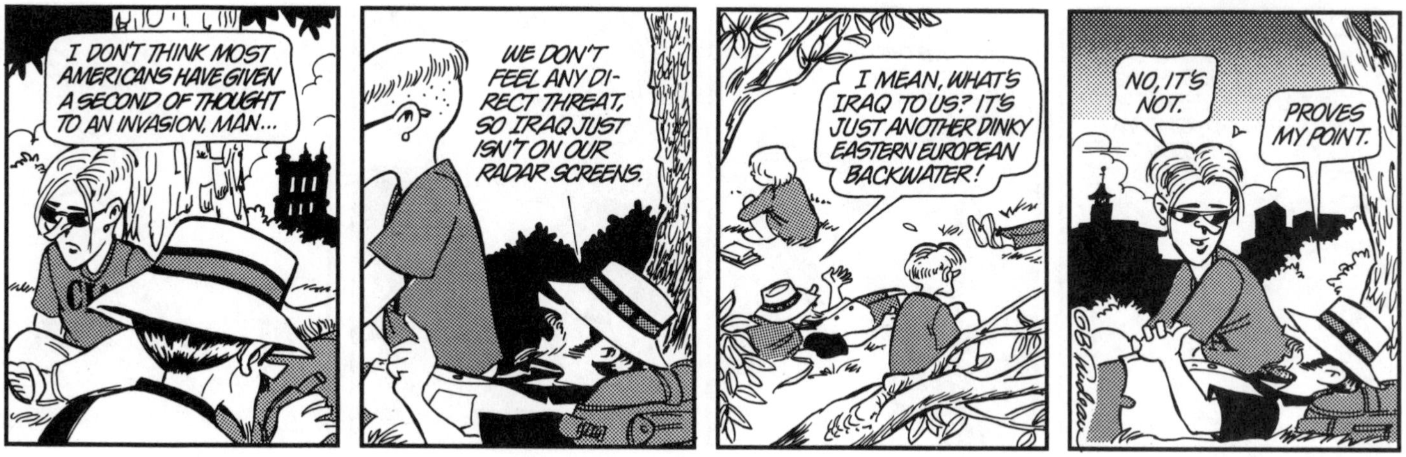
I DON'T THINK MOST AMERICANS HAVE GIVEN A SECOND OF THOUGHT TO AN INVASION, MAN...
WE DON'T FEEL ANY DIRECT THREAT, SO IRAQ JUST ISN'T ON OUR RADAR SCREENS.
I MEAN, WHAT'S IRAQ TO US? IT'S JUST ANOTHER DINKY EASTERN EUROPEAN BACKWATER!
NO, IT'S NOT.
PROVES MY POINT.
GB Trudeau

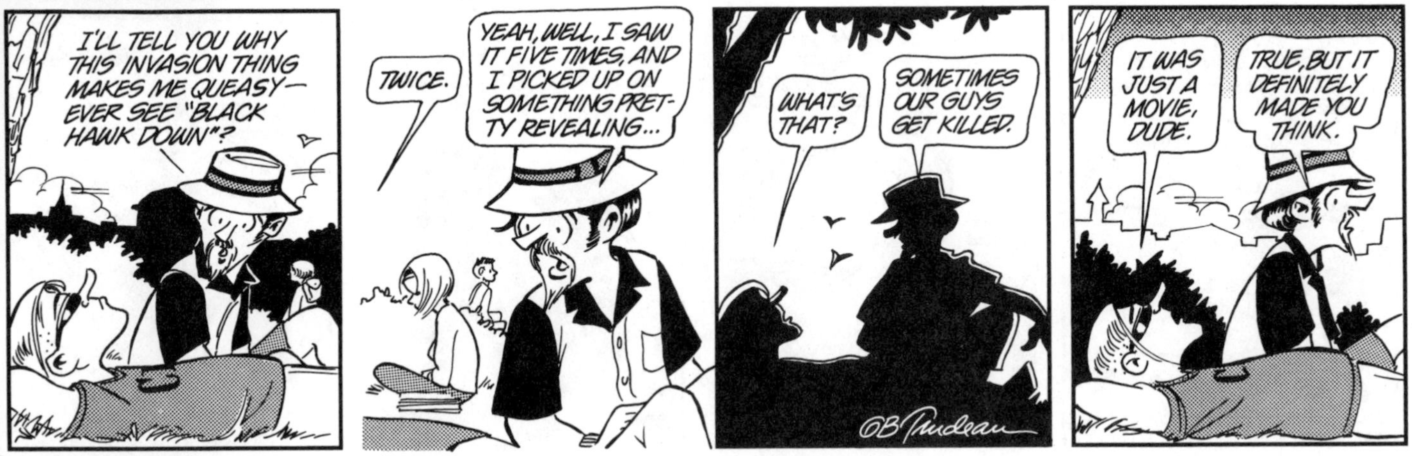
I'LL TELL YOU WHY THIS INVASION THING MAKES ME QUEASY— EVER SEE "BLACK HAWK DOWN"?
TWICE.
YEAH, WELL, I SAW IT FIVE TIMES, AND I PICKED UP ON SOMETHING PRETTY REVEALING...
WHAT'S THAT?
SOMETIMES OUR GUYS GET KILLED.
IT WAS JUST A MOVIE, DUDE.
TRUE, BUT IT DEFINITELY MADE YOU THINK.

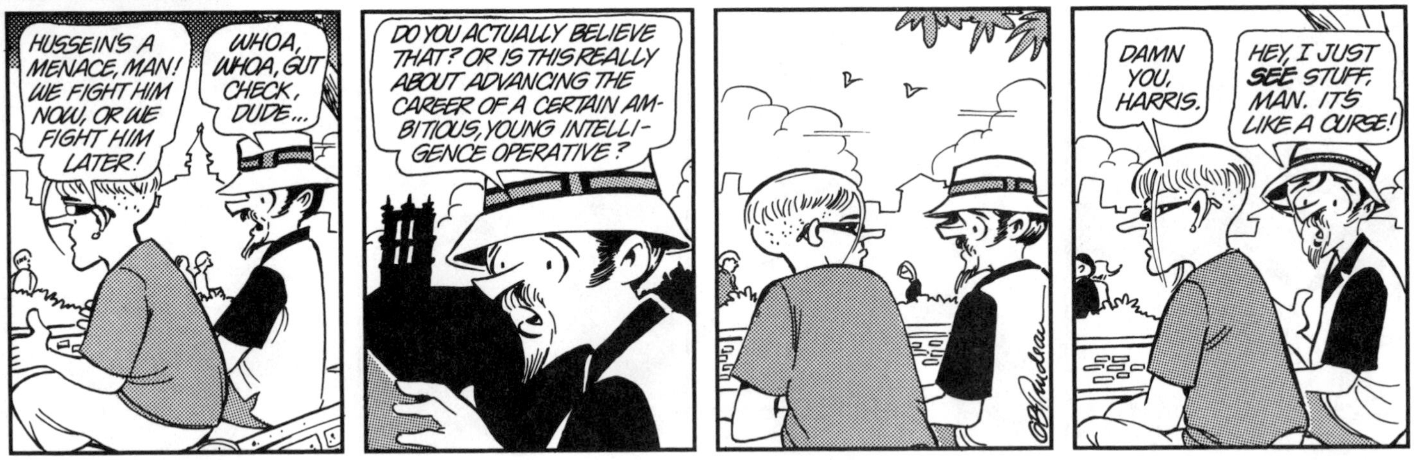
HUSSEIN'S A MENACE, MAN! WE FIGHT HIM NOW, OR WE FIGHT HIM LATER!
WHOA, WHOA, GUT CHECK, DUDE...
DO YOU ACTUALLY BELIEVE THAT? OR IS THIS REALLY ABOUT ADVANCING THE CAREER OF A CERTAIN AMBITIOUS, YOUNG INTELLIGENCE OPERATIVE?
DAMN YOU, HARRIS.
HEY, I JUST SEE STUFF, MAN. IT'S LIKE A CURSE!

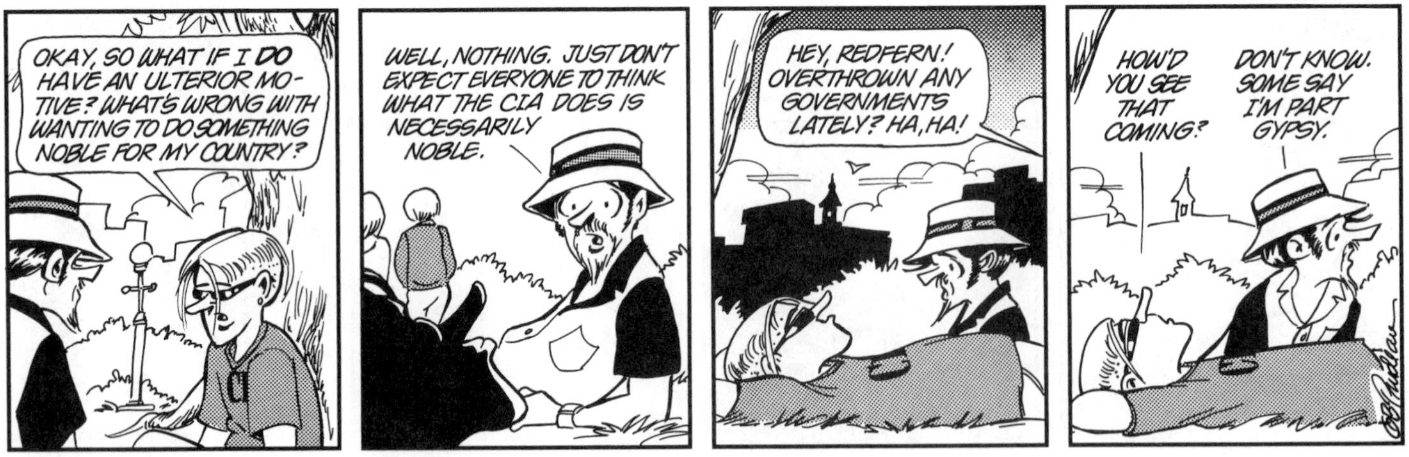
OKAY, SO WHAT IF I DO HAVE AN ULTERIOR MOTIVE? WHAT'S WRONG WITH WANTING TO DO SOMETHING NOBLE FOR MY COUNTRY?
WELL, NOTHING. JUST DON'T EXPECT EVERYONE TO THINK WHAT THE CIA DOES IS NECESSARILY NOBLE.
HEY, REDFERN! OVERTHROWN ANY GOVERNMENTS LATELY? HA, HA!
HOW'D YOU SEE THAT COMING?
DON'T KNOW. SOME SAY I'M PART GYPSY.

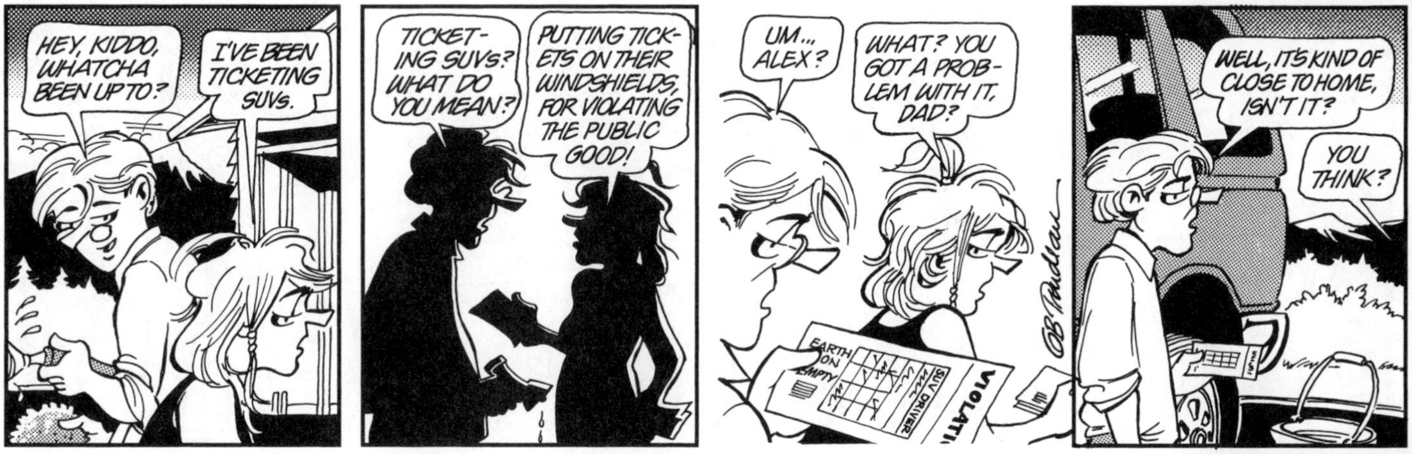
HEY, KIDDO, WHATCHA BEEN UP TO?
I'VE BEEN TICKETING SUVs.
TICKET-ING SUVs? WHAT DO YOU MEAN?
PUTTING TICK-ETS ON THEIR WINDSHIELDS, FOR VIOLATING THE PUBLIC GOOD!
UM... ALEX?
WHAT? YOU GOT A PROB-LEM WITH IT, DAD?
EARTH ON EMPTY
SUV DRIVER
VIOLATI
WELL, IT'S KIND OF CLOSE TO HOME, ISN'T IT?
YOU THINK?

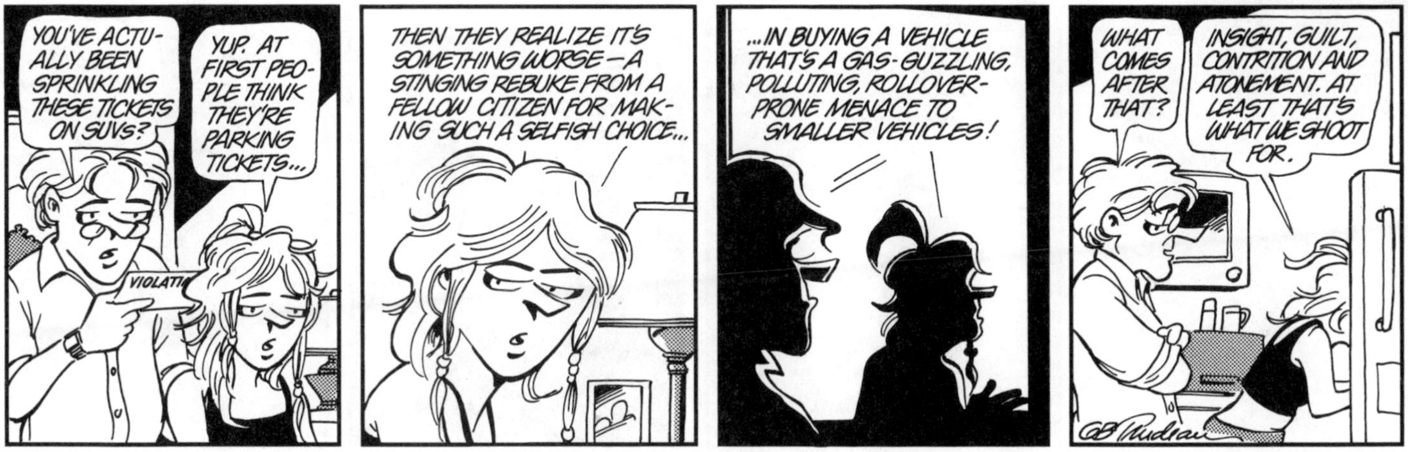
YOU'VE ACTU-ALLY BEEN SPRINKLING THESE TICKETS ON SUVs?
YUP. AT FIRST PEO-PLE THINK THEY'RE PARKING TICKETS...
VIOLATI
THEN THEY REALIZE IT'S SOMETHING WORSE—A STINGING REBUKE FROM A FELLOW CITIZEN FOR MAK-ING SUCH A SELFISH CHOICE...
...IN BUYING A VEHICLE THAT'S A GAS-GUZZLING, POLLUTING, ROLLOVER-PRONE MENACE TO SMALLER VEHICLES!
WHAT COMES AFTER THAT?
INSIGHT, GUILT, CONTRITION AND ATONEMENT. AT LEAST THAT'S WHAT WE SHOOT FOR.

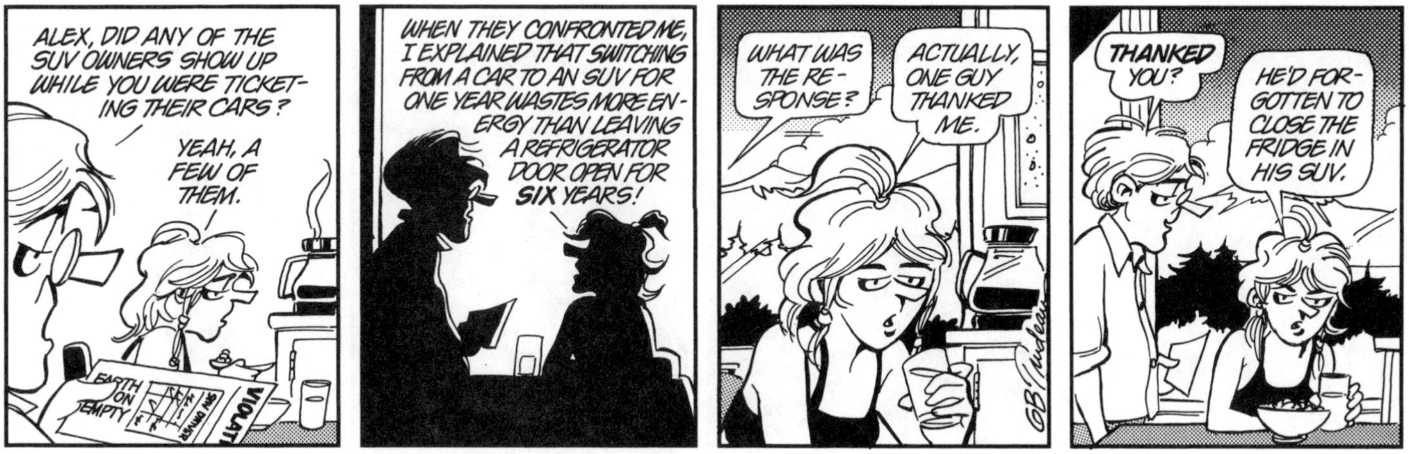
ALEX, DID ANY OF THE SUV OWNERS SHOW UP WHILE YOU WERE TICKET-ING THEIR CARS?
YEAH, A FEW OF THEM.
EARTH ON EMPTY
VIOLATI
WHEN THEY CONFRONTED ME, I EXPLAINED THAT SWITCHING FROM A CAR TO AN SUV FOR ONE YEAR WASTES MORE EN-ERGY THAN LEAVING A REFRIGERATOR DOOR OPEN FOR **SIX** YEARS!
WHAT WAS THE RE-SPONSE?
ACTUALLY, ONE GUY THANKED ME.
THANKED YOU?
HE'D FOR-GOTTEN TO CLOSE THE FRIDGE IN HIS SUV.

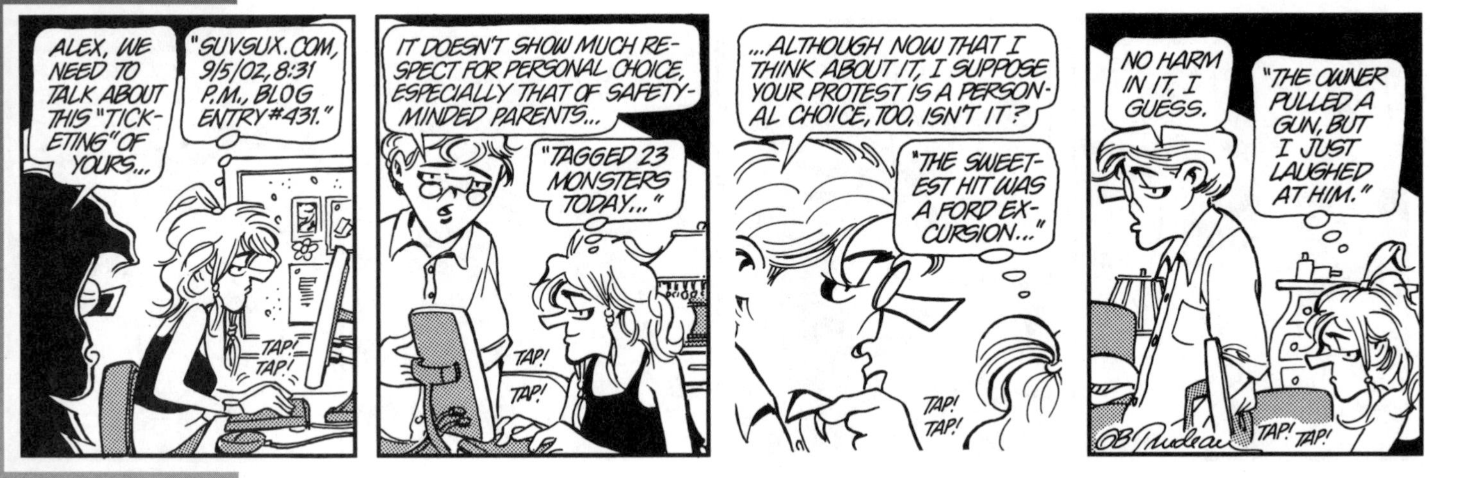
ALEX, WE NEED TO TALK ABOUT THIS "TICKETING" OF YOURS...
"SUVSUX.COM, 9/5/02, 8:31 P.M., BLOG ENTRY #431."
TAP! TAP!
IT DOESN'T SHOW MUCH RESPECT FOR PERSONAL CHOICE, ESPECIALLY THAT OF SAFETY-MINDED PARENTS...
"TAGGED 23 MONSTERS TODAY..."
TAP!
TAP!
...ALTHOUGH NOW THAT I THINK ABOUT IT, I SUPPOSE YOUR PROTEST IS A PERSONAL CHOICE, TOO, ISN'T IT?
"THE SWEETEST HIT WAS A FORD EXCURSION..."
TAP! TAP!
NO HARM IN IT, I GUESS.
"THE OWNER PULLED A GUN, BUT I JUST LAUGHED AT HIM."
TAP! TAP!

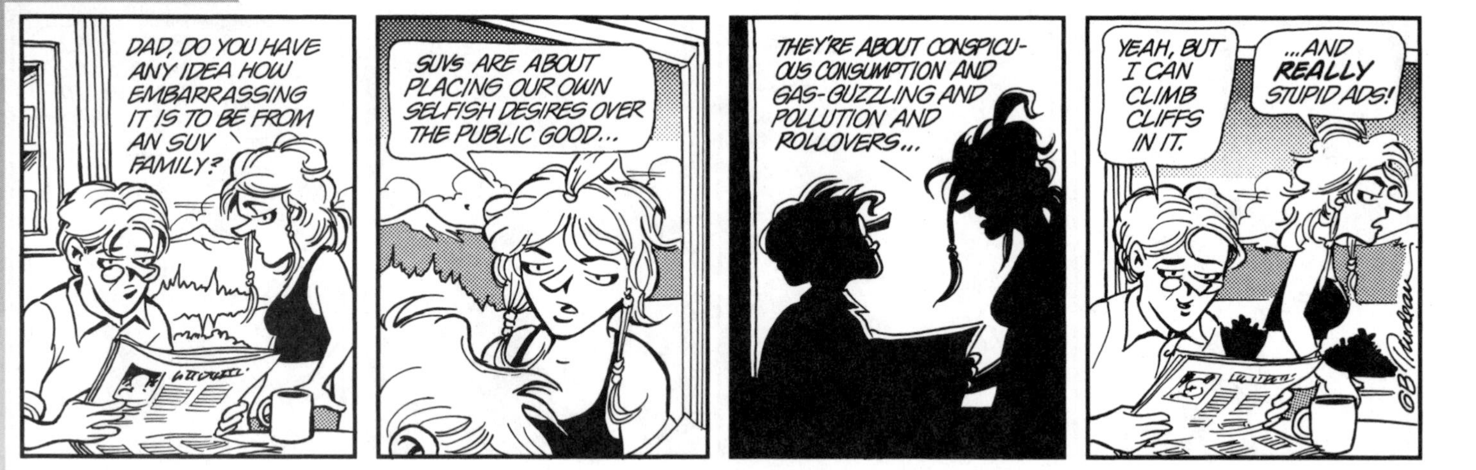
DAD, DO YOU HAVE ANY IDEA HOW EMBARRASSING IT IS TO BE FROM AN SUV FAMILY?
SUVs ARE ABOUT PLACING OUR OWN SELFISH DESIRES OVER THE PUBLIC GOOD...
THEY'RE ABOUT CONSPICUOUS CONSUMPTION AND GAS-GUZZLING AND POLLUTION AND ROLLOVERS...
YEAH, BUT I CAN CLIMB CLIFFS IN IT.
...AND REALLY STUPID ADS!

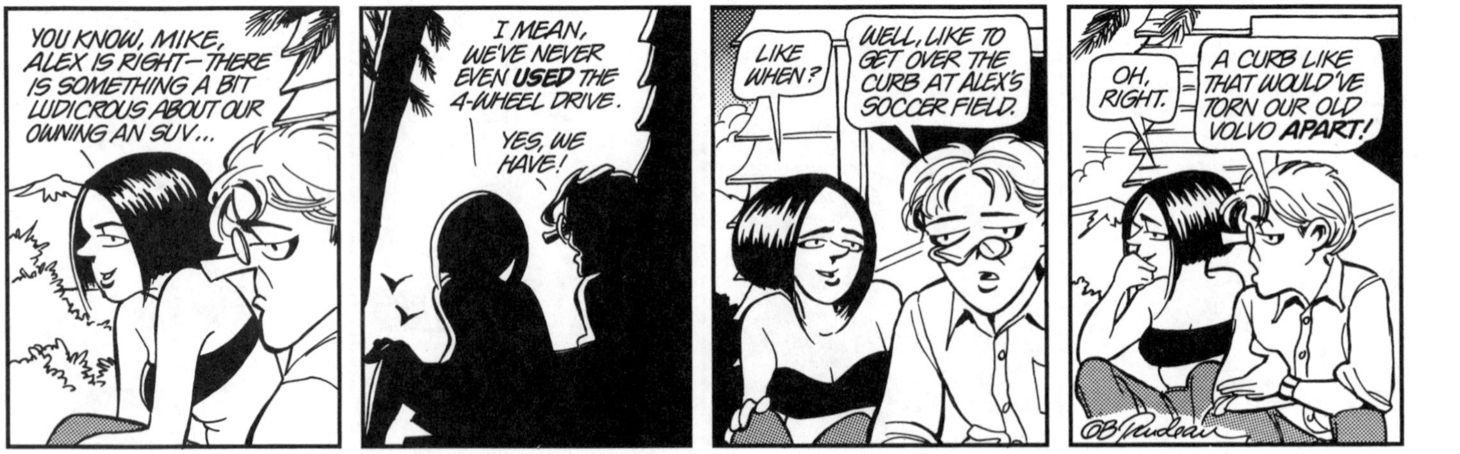
YOU KNOW, MIKE, ALEX IS RIGHT—THERE IS SOMETHING A BIT LUDICROUS ABOUT OUR OWNING AN SUV...
I MEAN, WE'VE NEVER EVEN USED THE 4-WHEEL DRIVE.
YES, WE HAVE!
LIKE WHEN?
WELL, LIKE TO GET OVER THE CURB AT ALEX'S SOCCER FIELD.
OH, RIGHT.
A CURB LIKE THAT WOULD'VE TORN OUR OLD VOLVO APART!

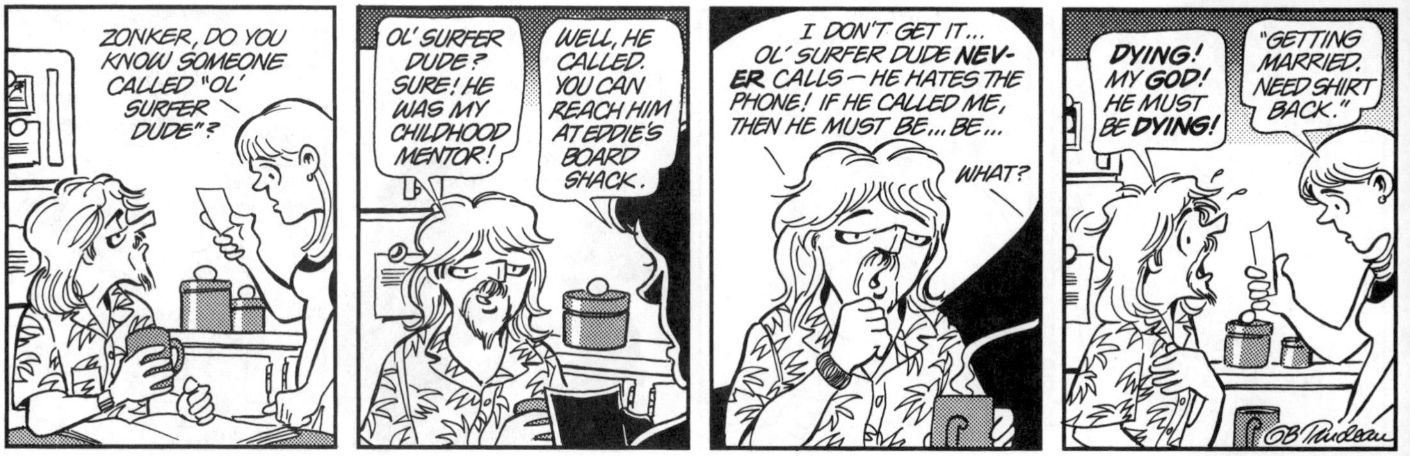
ZONKER, DO YOU KNOW SOMEONE CALLED "OL' SURFER DUDE"?
OL' SURFER DUDE? SURE! HE WAS MY CHILDHOOD MENTOR!
WELL, HE CALLED. YOU CAN REACH HIM AT EDDIE'S BOARD SHACK.
I DON'T GET IT... OL' SURFER DUDE **NEVER** CALLS — HE HATES THE PHONE! IF HE CALLED ME, THEN HE MUST BE... BE...
WHAT?
DYING! MY **GOD!** HE MUST BE **DYING!**
"GETTING MARRIED. NEED SHIRT BACK."

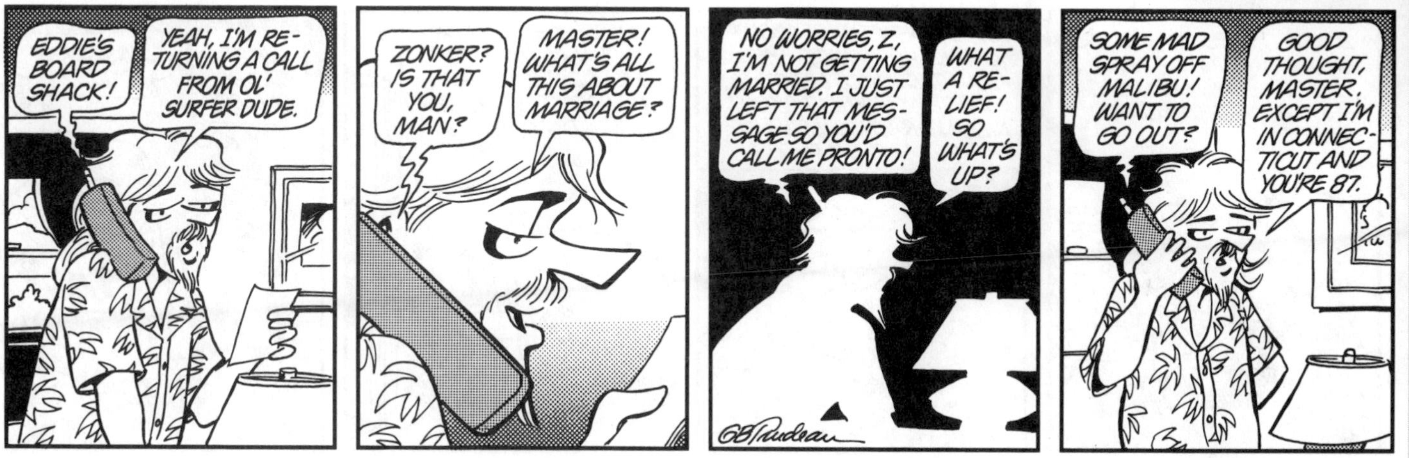
EDDIE'S BOARD SHACK!
YEAH, I'M RETURNING A CALL FROM OL' SURFER DUDE.
ZONKER? IS THAT YOU, MAN?
MASTER! WHAT'S ALL THIS ABOUT MARRIAGE?
NO WORRIES, Z, I'M NOT GETTING MARRIED. I JUST LEFT THAT MESSAGE SO YOU'D CALL ME PRONTO!
WHAT A RELIEF! SO WHAT'S UP?
SOME MAD SPRAY OFF MALIBU! WANT TO GO OUT?
GOOD THOUGHT, MASTER. EXCEPT I'M IN CONNECTICUT AND YOU'RE 87.

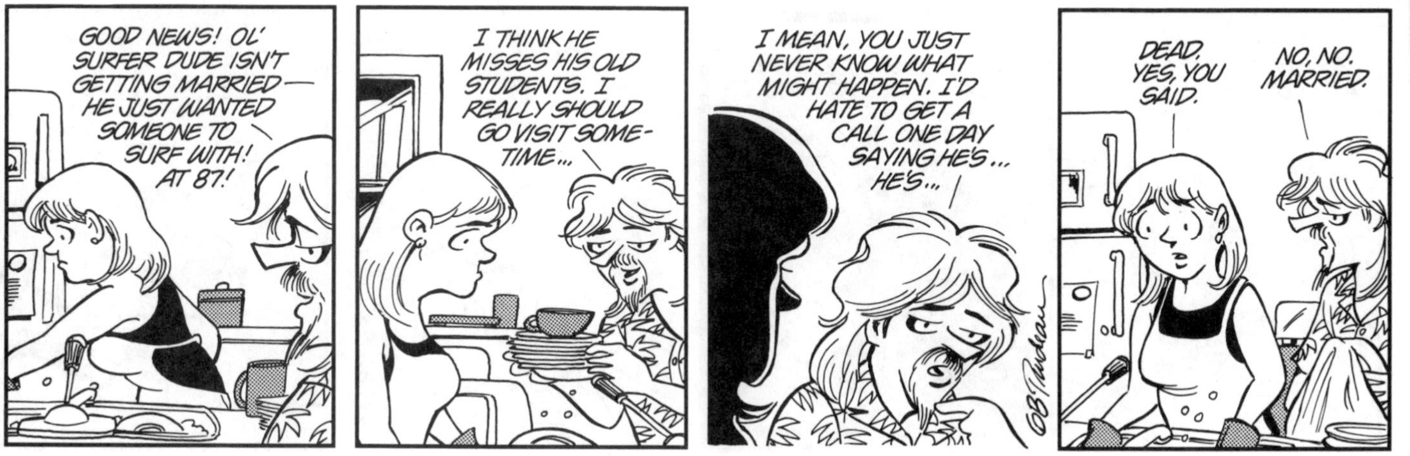
GOOD NEWS! OL' SURFER DUDE ISN'T GETTING MARRIED — HE JUST WANTED SOMEONE TO SURF WITH! AT 87!
I THINK HE MISSES HIS OLD STUDENTS. I REALLY SHOULD GO VISIT SOMETIME...
I MEAN, YOU JUST NEVER KNOW WHAT MIGHT HAPPEN. I'D HATE TO GET A CALL ONE DAY SAYING HE'S... HE'S...
DEAD. YES, YOU SAID.
NO, NO. MARRIED.

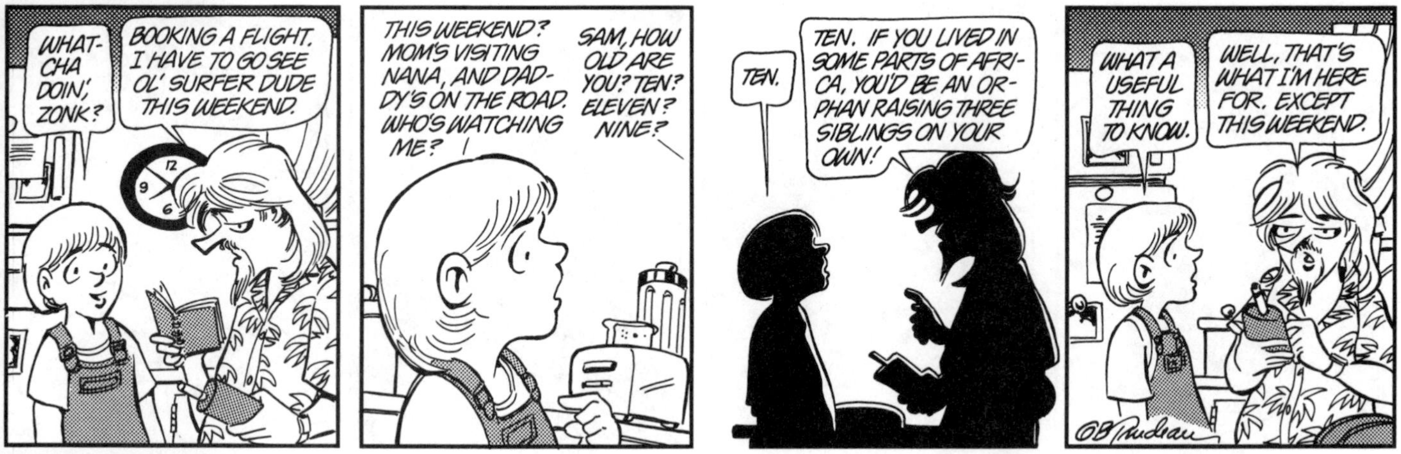
WHAT-CHA DOIN', ZONK?
BOOKING A FLIGHT. I HAVE TO GO SEE OL' SURFER DUDE THIS WEEKEND.
THIS WEEKEND? MOM'S VISITING NANA, AND DADDY'S ON THE ROAD. WHO'S WATCHING ME?
SAM, HOW OLD ARE YOU? TEN? ELEVEN? NINE?
TEN.
TEN. IF YOU LIVED IN SOME PARTS OF AFRICA, YOU'D BE AN ORPHAN RAISING THREE SIBLINGS ON YOUR OWN!
WHAT A USEFUL THING TO KNOW.
WELL, THAT'S WHAT I'M HERE FOR. EXCEPT THIS WEEKEND.
©B Trudeau

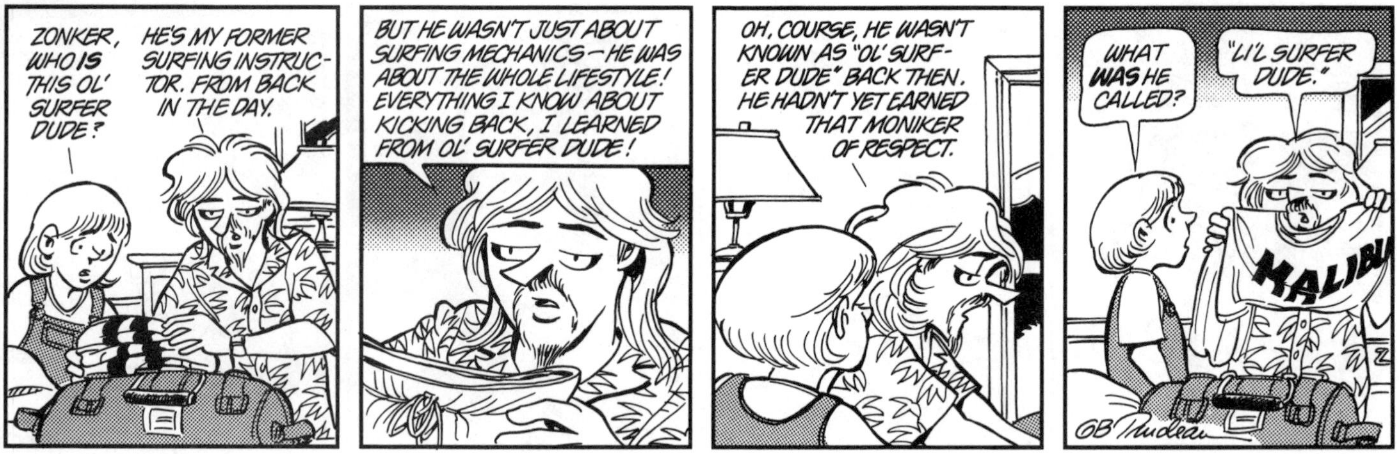
ZONKER, WHO **IS** THIS OL' SURFER DUDE?
HE'S MY FORMER SURFING INSTRUCTOR. FROM BACK IN THE DAY.
BUT HE WASN'T JUST ABOUT SURFING MECHANICS—HE WAS ABOUT THE WHOLE LIFESTYLE! EVERYTHING I KNOW ABOUT KICKING BACK, I LEARNED FROM OL' SURFER DUDE!
OH, COURSE, HE WASN'T KNOWN AS "OL' SURFER DUDE" BACK THEN. HE HADN'T YET EARNED THAT MONIKER OF RESPECT.
WHAT **WAS** HE CALLED?
"LI'L SURFER DUDE."
MALIBU
©B Trudeau

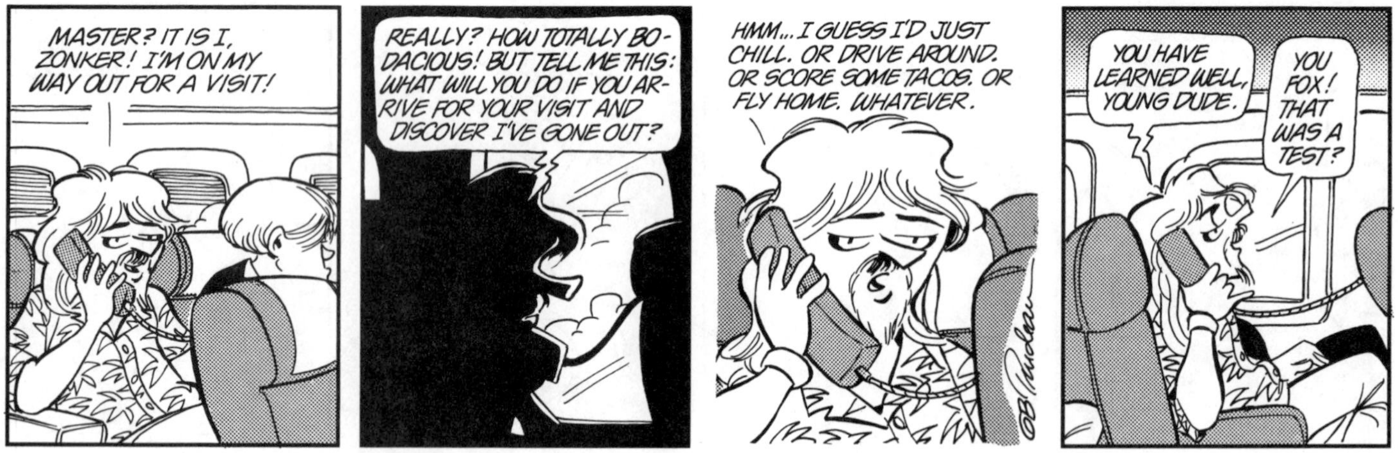
MASTER? IT IS I, ZONKER! I'M ON MY WAY OUT FOR A VISIT!
REALLY? HOW TOTALLY BODACIOUS! BUT TELL ME THIS: WHAT WILL YOU DO IF YOU ARRIVE FOR YOUR VISIT AND DISCOVER I'VE GONE OUT?
HMM... I GUESS I'D JUST CHILL. OR DRIVE AROUND. OR SCORE SOME TACOS. OR FLY HOME. WHATEVER.
©B Trudeau
YOU HAVE LEARNED WELL, YOUNG DUDE.
YOU FOX! THAT WAS A TEST?

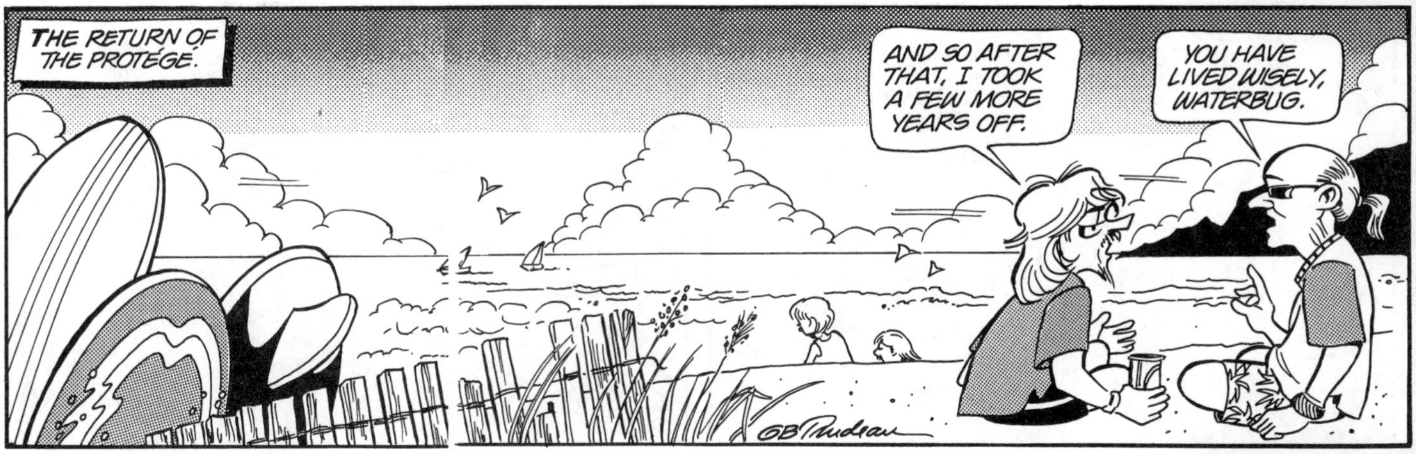
THE RETURN OF THE PROTÉGÉ.
AND SO AFTER THAT, I TOOK A FEW MORE YEARS OFF.
YOU HAVE LIVED WISELY, WATERBUG.

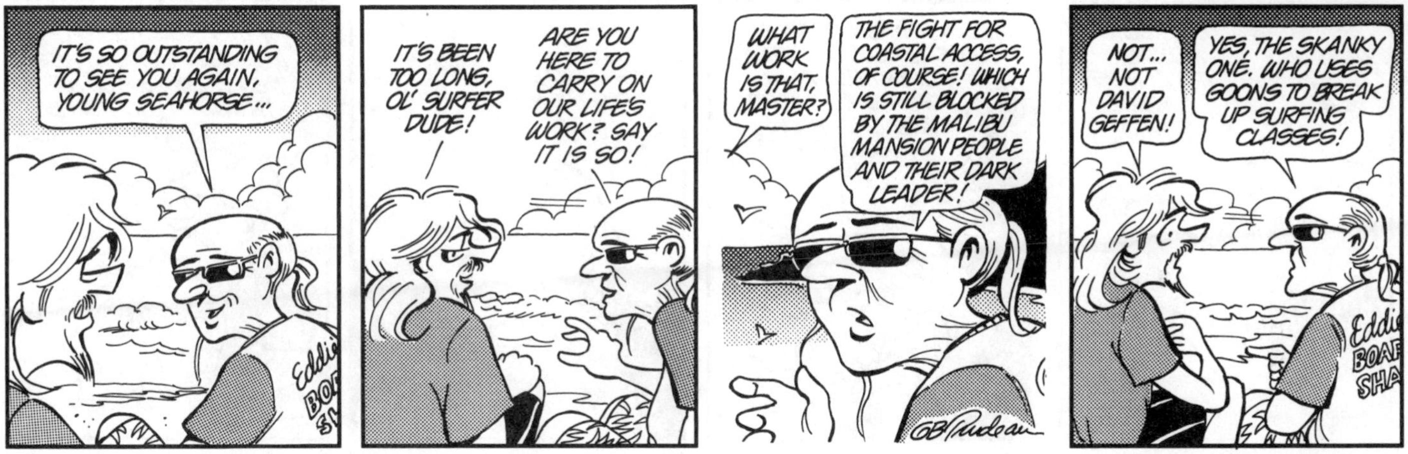
IT'S SO OUTSTANDING TO SEE YOU AGAIN, YOUNG SEAHORSE...
IT'S BEEN TOO LONG, OL' SURFER DUDE!
ARE YOU HERE TO CARRY ON OUR LIFE'S WORK? SAY IT IS SO!
WHAT WORK IS THAT, MASTER?
THE FIGHT FOR COASTAL ACCESS, OF COURSE! WHICH IS STILL BLOCKED BY THE MALIBU MANSION PEOPLE AND THEIR DARK LEADER!
NOT... NOT DAVID GEFFEN!
YES, THE SKANKY ONE. WHO USES GOONS TO BREAK UP SURFING CLASSES!
Eddie's BOARD SHACK

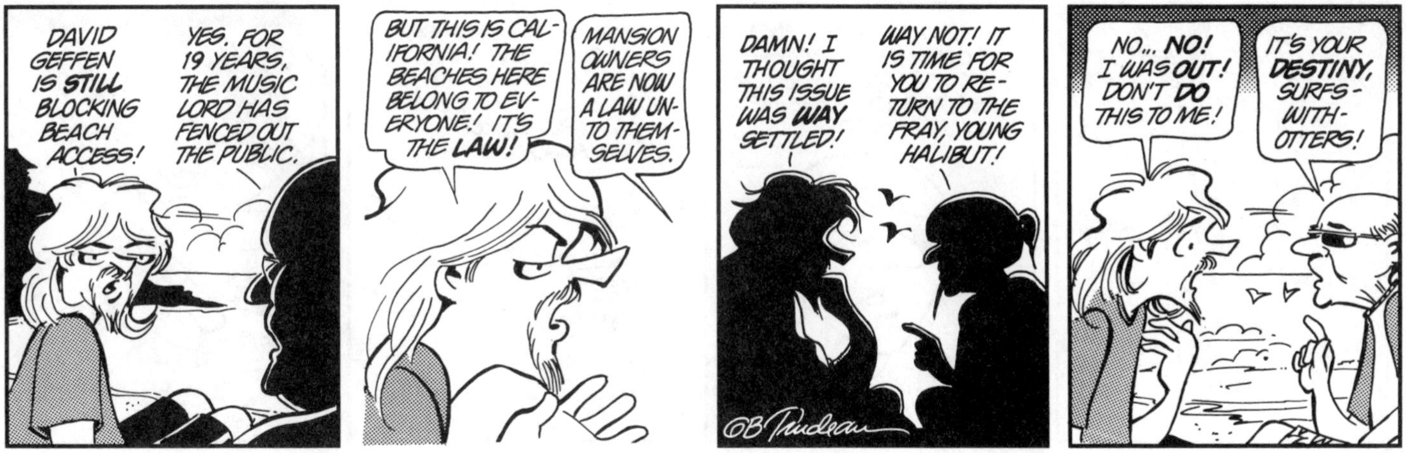
DAVID GEFFEN IS **STILL** BLOCKING BEACH ACCESS!
YES. FOR 19 YEARS, THE MUSIC LORD HAS FENCED OUT THE PUBLIC.
BUT THIS IS CAL-IFORNIA! THE BEACHES HERE BELONG TO EV-ERYONE! IT'S THE **LAW!**
MANSION OWNERS ARE NOW A LAW UN-TO THEM-SELVES.
DAMN! I THOUGHT THIS ISSUE WAS **WAY** SETTLED!
WAY NOT! IT IS TIME FOR YOU TO RE-TURN TO THE FRAY, YOUNG HALIBUT!
NO... **NO!** I WAS **OUT!** DON'T **DO** THIS TO ME!
IT'S YOUR **DESTINY,** SURFS-WITH-OTTERS!

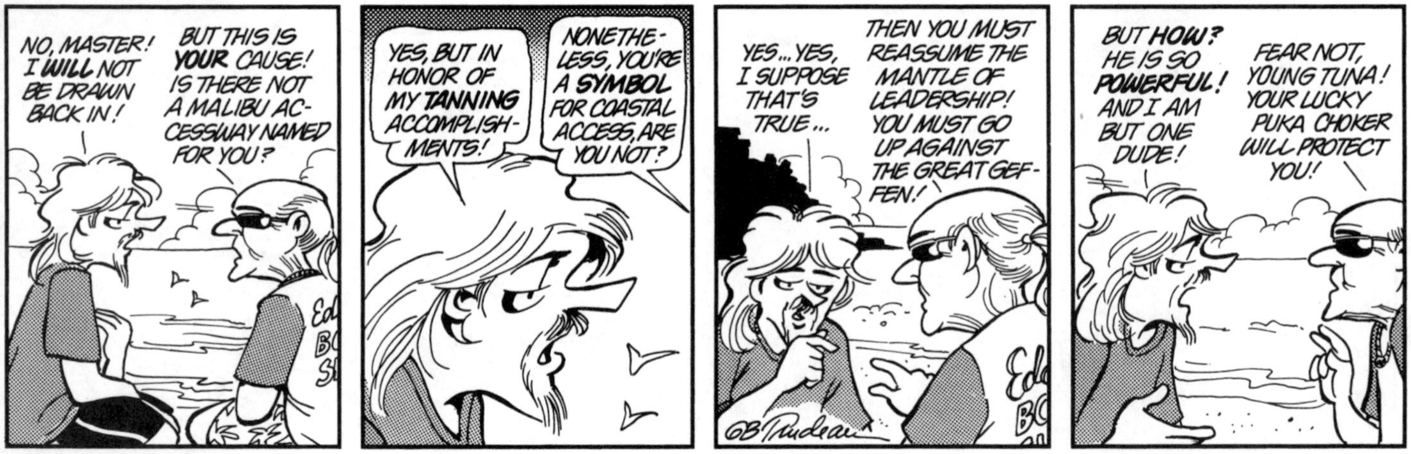
NO, MASTER! I **WILL** NOT BE DRAWN BACK IN!
BUT THIS IS **YOUR** CAUSE! IS THERE NOT A MALIBU ACCESSWAY NAMED FOR YOU?
YES, BUT IN HONOR OF MY **TANNING** ACCOMPLISHMENTS!
NONETHELESS, YOU'RE A **SYMBOL** FOR COASTAL ACCESS, ARE YOU NOT?
YES... YES, I SUPPOSE THAT'S TRUE...
THEN YOU MUST REASSUME THE MANTLE OF LEADERSHIP! YOU MUST GO UP AGAINST THE GREAT GEFFEN!
BUT **HOW?** HE IS SO **POWERFUL!** AND I AM BUT ONE DUDE!
FEAR NOT, YOUNG TUNA! YOUR LUCKY PUKA CHOKER WILL PROTECT YOU!
©B. Trudeau

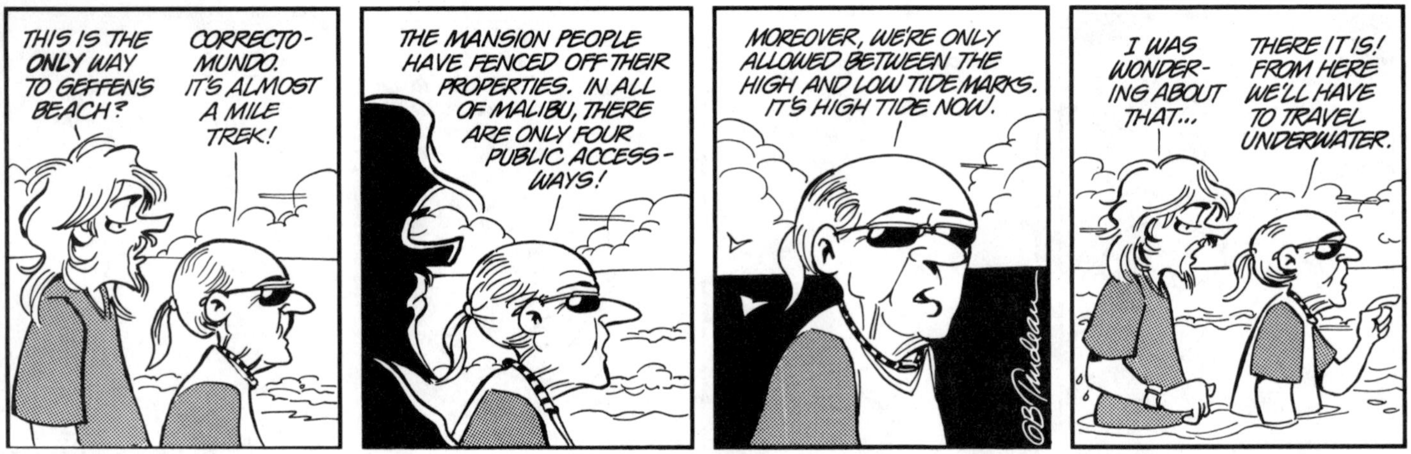
THIS IS THE **ONLY** WAY TO GEFFEN'S BEACH?
CORRECTOMUNDO. IT'S ALMOST A MILE TREK!
THE MANSION PEOPLE HAVE FENCED OFF THEIR PROPERTIES. IN ALL OF MALIBU, THERE ARE ONLY FOUR PUBLIC ACCESSWAYS!
MOREOVER, WE'RE ONLY ALLOWED BETWEEN THE HIGH AND LOW TIDE MARKS. IT'S HIGH TIDE NOW.
I WAS WONDERING ABOUT THAT...
THERE IT IS! FROM HERE WE'LL HAVE TO TRAVEL UNDERWATER.
©B. Trudeau

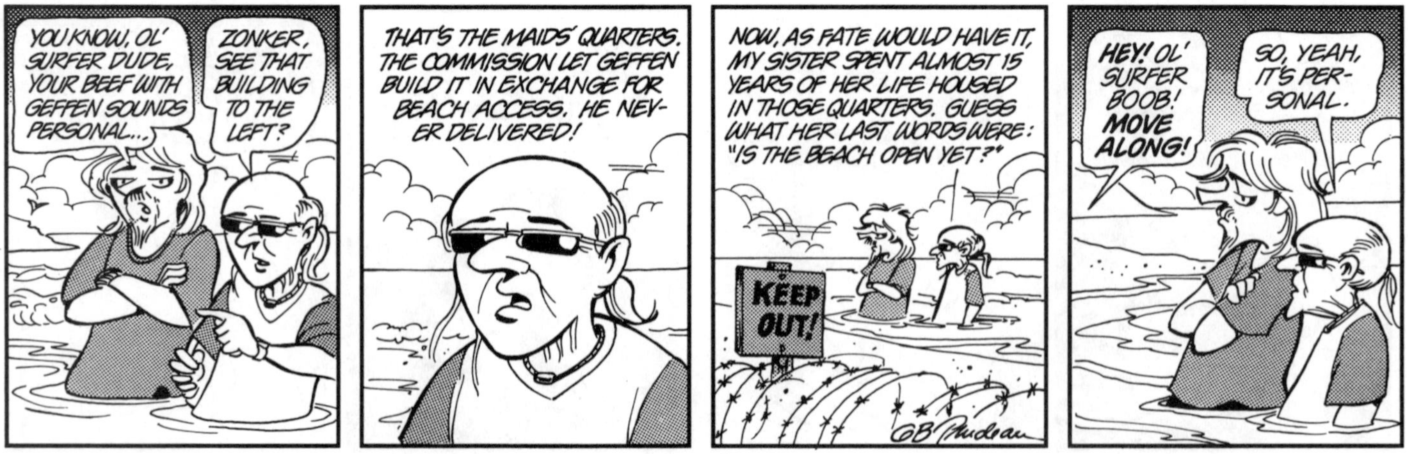
YOU KNOW, OL' SURFER DUDE, YOUR BEEF WITH GEFFEN SOUNDS PERSONAL...
ZONKER, SEE THAT BUILDING TO THE LEFT?
THAT'S THE MAIDS' QUARTERS. THE COMMISSION LET GEFFEN BUILD IT IN EXCHANGE FOR BEACH ACCESS. HE NEVER DELIVERED!
NOW, AS FATE WOULD HAVE IT, MY SISTER SPENT ALMOST 15 YEARS OF HER LIFE HOUSED IN THOSE QUARTERS. GUESS WHAT HER LAST WORDS WERE: "IS THE BEACH OPEN YET?"
KEEP OUT!
HEY! OL' SURFER BOOB! **MOVE ALONG!**
SO, YEAH, IT'S PERSONAL.
©B. Trudeau

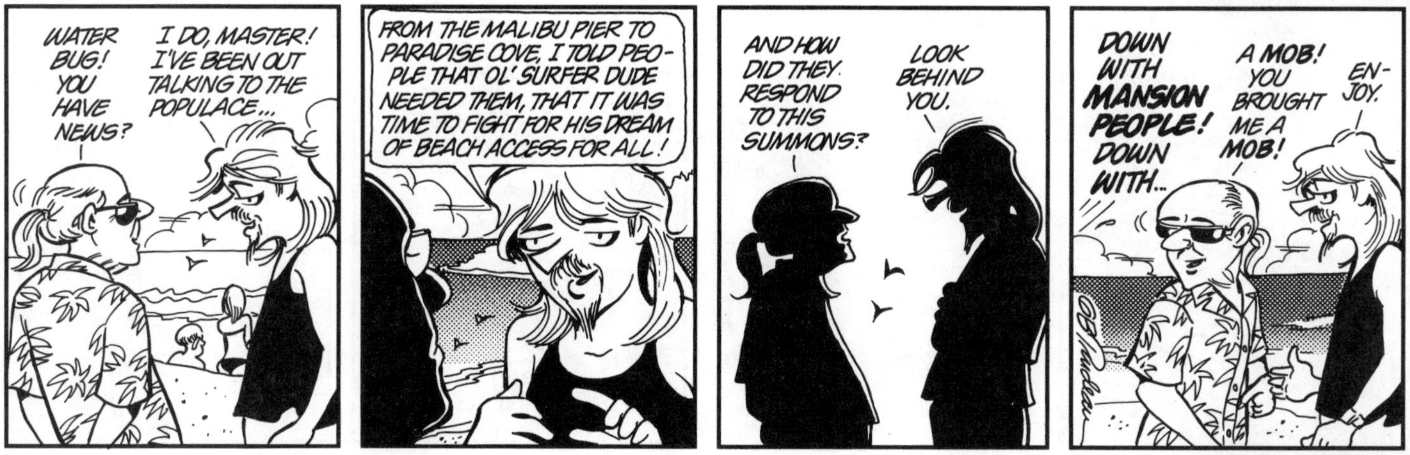
WATER BUG! YOU HAVE NEWS?
I DO, MASTER! I'VE BEEN OUT TALKING TO THE POPULACE...
FROM THE MALIBU PIER TO PARADISE COVE, I TOLD PEOPLE THAT OL' SURFER DUDE NEEDED THEM, THAT IT WAS TIME TO FIGHT FOR HIS DREAM OF BEACH ACCESS FOR ALL!
AND HOW DID THEY RESPOND TO THIS SUMMONS?
LOOK BEHIND YOU.
DOWN WITH MANSION PEOPLE! DOWN WITH...
A MOB! YOU BROUGHT ME A MOB!
ENJOY.
GB Trudeau

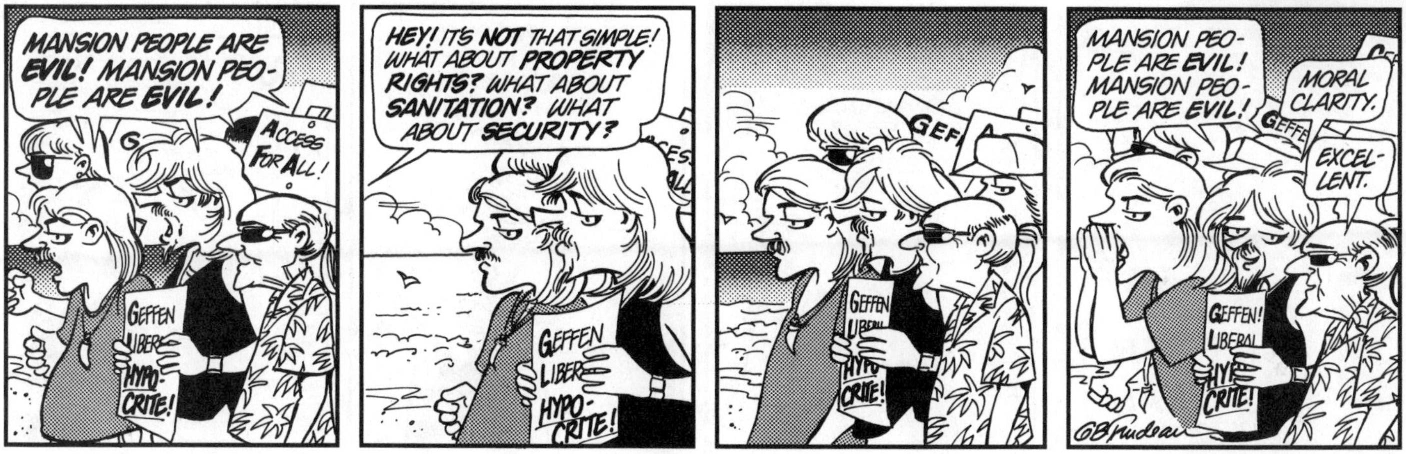
MANSION PEOPLE ARE EVIL! MANSION PEOPLE ARE EVIL!
ACCESS FOR ALL!
GEFFEN LIBERAL HYPOCRITE!
HEY! IT'S NOT THAT SIMPLE! WHAT ABOUT PROPERTY RIGHTS? WHAT ABOUT SANITATION? WHAT ABOUT SECURITY?
MANSION PEOPLE ARE EVIL! MANSION PEOPLE ARE EVIL!
MORAL CLARITY.
EXCELLENT.
GEFFEN! LIBERAL HYPOCRITE!
GB Trudeau

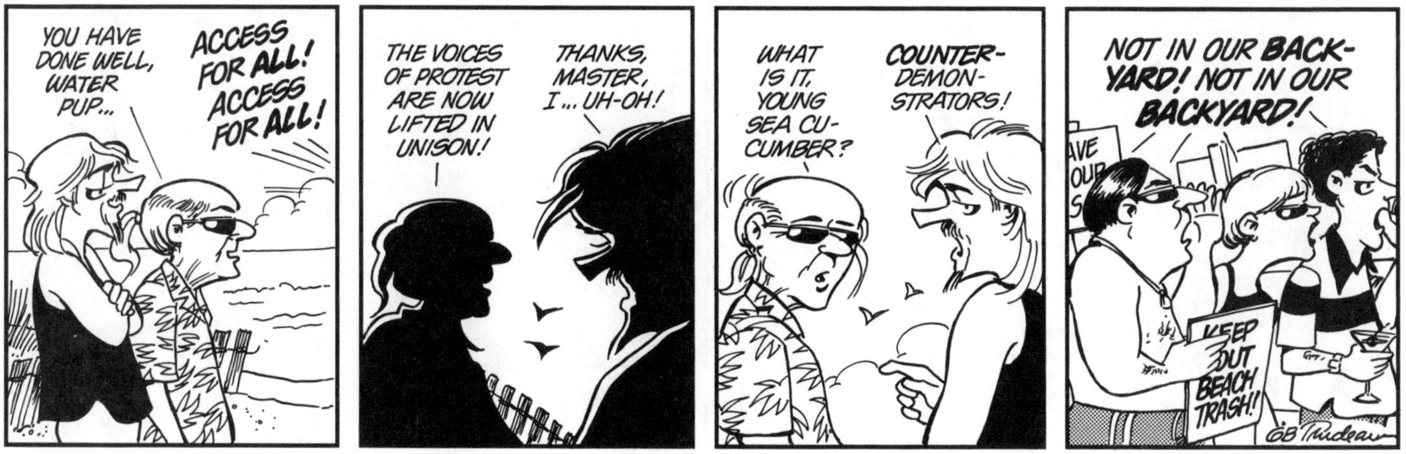
YOU HAVE DONE WELL, WATER PUP...
ACCESS FOR ALL! ACCESS FOR ALL!
THE VOICES OF PROTEST ARE NOW LIFTED IN UNISON!
THANKS, MASTER, I... UH-OH!
WHAT IS IT, YOUNG SEA CUCUMBER?
COUNTER-DEMONSTRATORS!
NOT IN OUR BACKYARD! NOT IN OUR BACKYARD!
KEEP OUT BEACH TRASH!
GB Trudeau

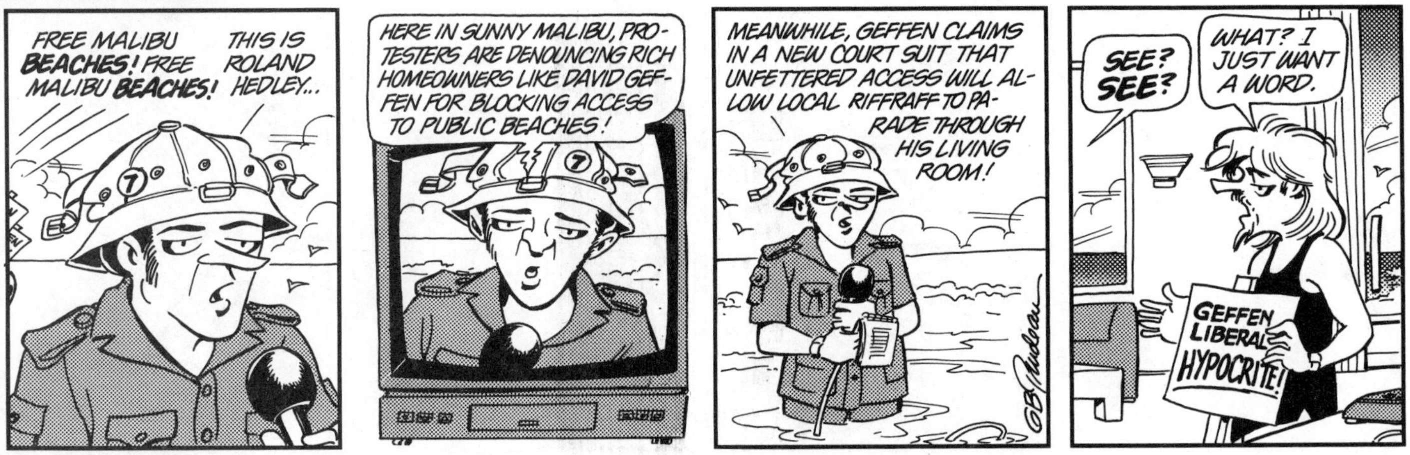
FREE MALIBU **BEACHES!** FREE MALIBU **BEACHES!**
THIS IS ROLAND HEDLEY...
HERE IN SUNNY MALIBU, PROTESTERS ARE DENOUNCING RICH HOMEOWNERS LIKE DAVID GEFFEN FOR BLOCKING ACCESS TO PUBLIC BEACHES!
MEANWHILE, GEFFEN CLAIMS IN A NEW COURT SUIT THAT UNFETTERED ACCESS WILL ALLOW LOCAL RIFFRAFF TO PARADE THROUGH HIS LIVING ROOM!
SEE? SEE?
WHAT? I JUST WANT A WORD.
GEFFEN LIBERAL HYPOCRITE!

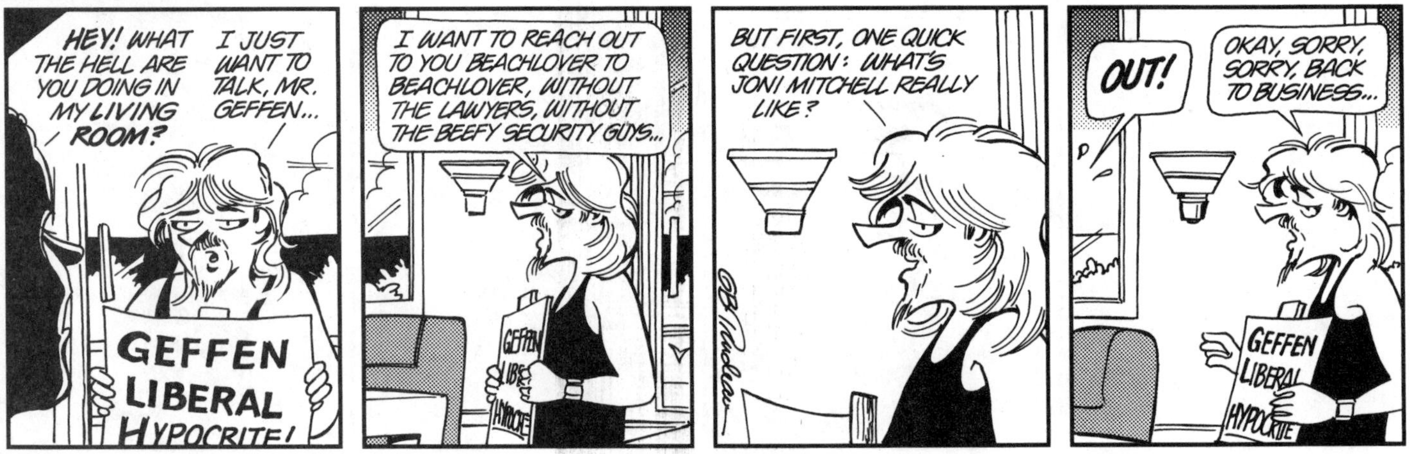
HEY! WHAT THE HELL ARE YOU DOING IN MY **LIVING ROOM?**
I JUST WANT TO TALK, MR. GEFFEN...
GEFFEN LIBERAL HYPOCRITE!
I WANT TO REACH OUT TO YOU BEACHLOVER TO BEACHLOVER, WITHOUT THE LAWYERS, WITHOUT THE BEEFY SECURITY GUYS...
BUT FIRST, ONE QUICK QUESTION: WHAT'S JONI MITCHELL REALLY LIKE?
OUT!
OKAY, SORRY, SORRY, BACK TO BUSINESS...
GEFFEN LIBERAL HYPOCRITE

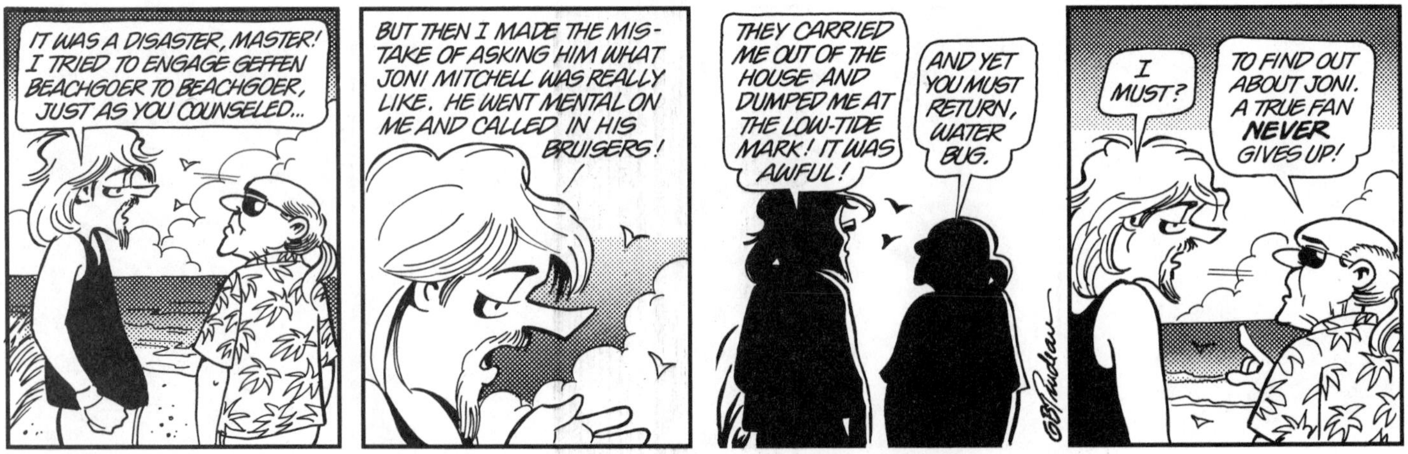
IT WAS A DISASTER, MASTER! I TRIED TO ENGAGE GEFFEN BEACHGOER TO BEACHGOER, JUST AS YOU COUNSELED...
BUT THEN I MADE THE MISTAKE OF ASKING HIM WHAT JONI MITCHELL WAS REALLY LIKE. HE WENT MENTAL ON ME AND CALLED IN HIS BRUISERS!
THEY CARRIED ME OUT OF THE HOUSE AND DUMPED ME AT THE LOW-TIDE MARK! IT WAS AWFUL!
AND YET YOU MUST RETURN, WATER BUG.
I MUST?
TO FIND OUT ABOUT JONI. A TRUE FAN **NEVER** GIVES UP!

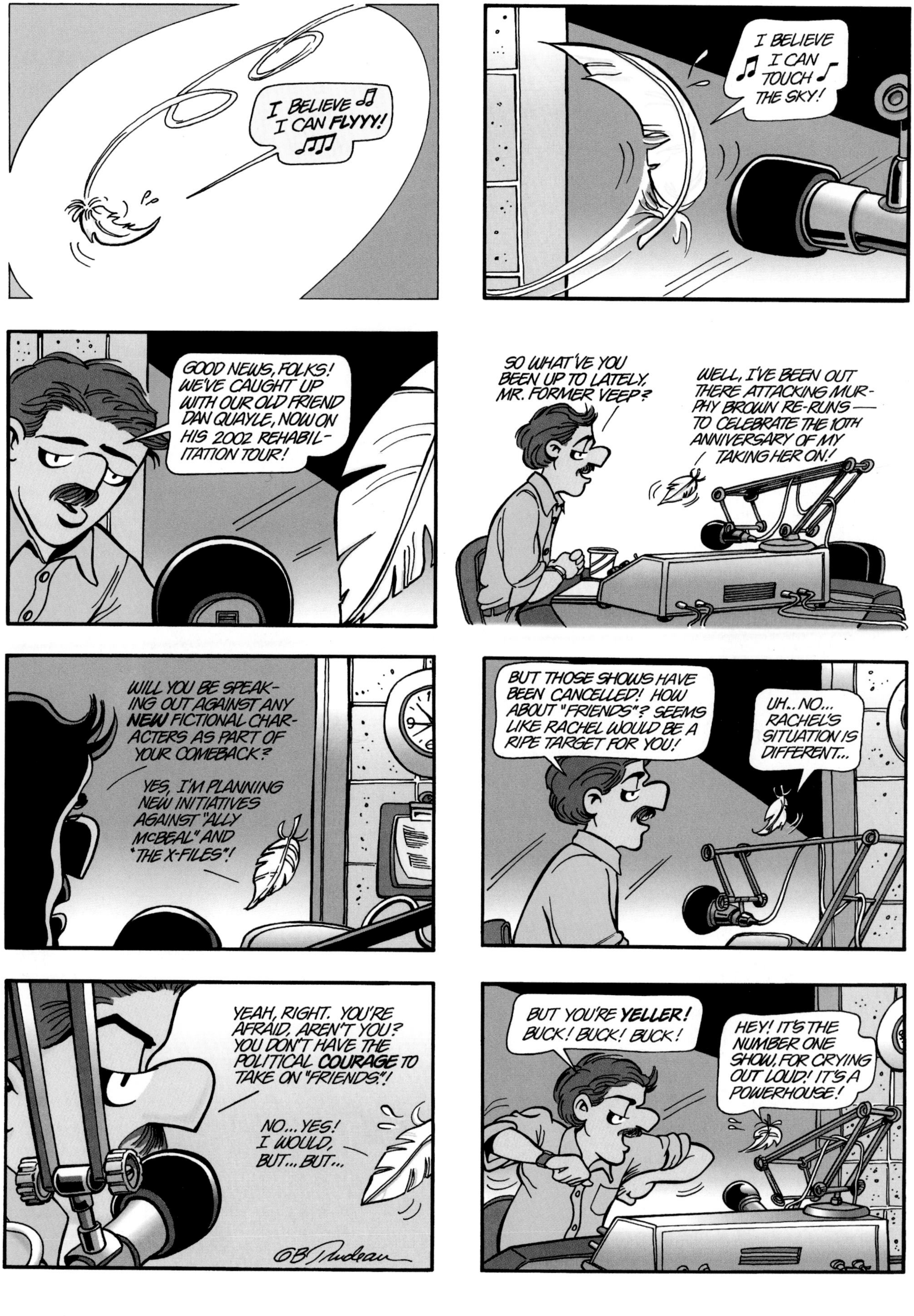
I BELIEVE ♫ I CAN FLYYY! ♫♫
I BELIEVE ♫ I CAN TOUCH ♪ THE SKY!
GOOD NEWS, FOLKS! WE'VE CAUGHT UP WITH OUR OLD FRIEND DAN QUAYLE, NOW ON HIS 2002 REHABILITATION TOUR!
SO WHAT'VE YOU BEEN UP TO LATELY, MR. FORMER VEEP?
WELL, I'VE BEEN OUT THERE ATTACKING MURPHY BROWN RE-RUNS — TO CELEBRATE THE 10TH ANNIVERSARY OF MY TAKING HER ON!
WILL YOU BE SPEAKING OUT AGAINST ANY NEW FICTIONAL CHARACTERS AS PART OF YOUR COMEBACK?
YES, I'M PLANNING NEW INITIATIVES AGAINST "ALLY McBEAL" AND "THE X-FILES"!
BUT THOSE SHOWS HAVE BEEN CANCELLED! HOW ABOUT "FRIENDS"? SEEMS LIKE RACHEL WOULD BE A RIPE TARGET FOR YOU!
UH.. NO... RACHEL'S SITUATION IS DIFFERENT...
YEAH, RIGHT. YOU'RE AFRAID, AREN'T YOU? YOU DON'T HAVE THE POLITICAL COURAGE TO TAKE ON "FRIENDS"!
NO... YES! I WOULD, BUT... BUT...
BUT YOU'RE YELLER! BUCK! BUCK! BUCK!
HEY! IT'S THE NUMBER ONE SHOW, FOR CRYING OUT LOUD! IT'S A POWERHOUSE!
©B. Trudeau

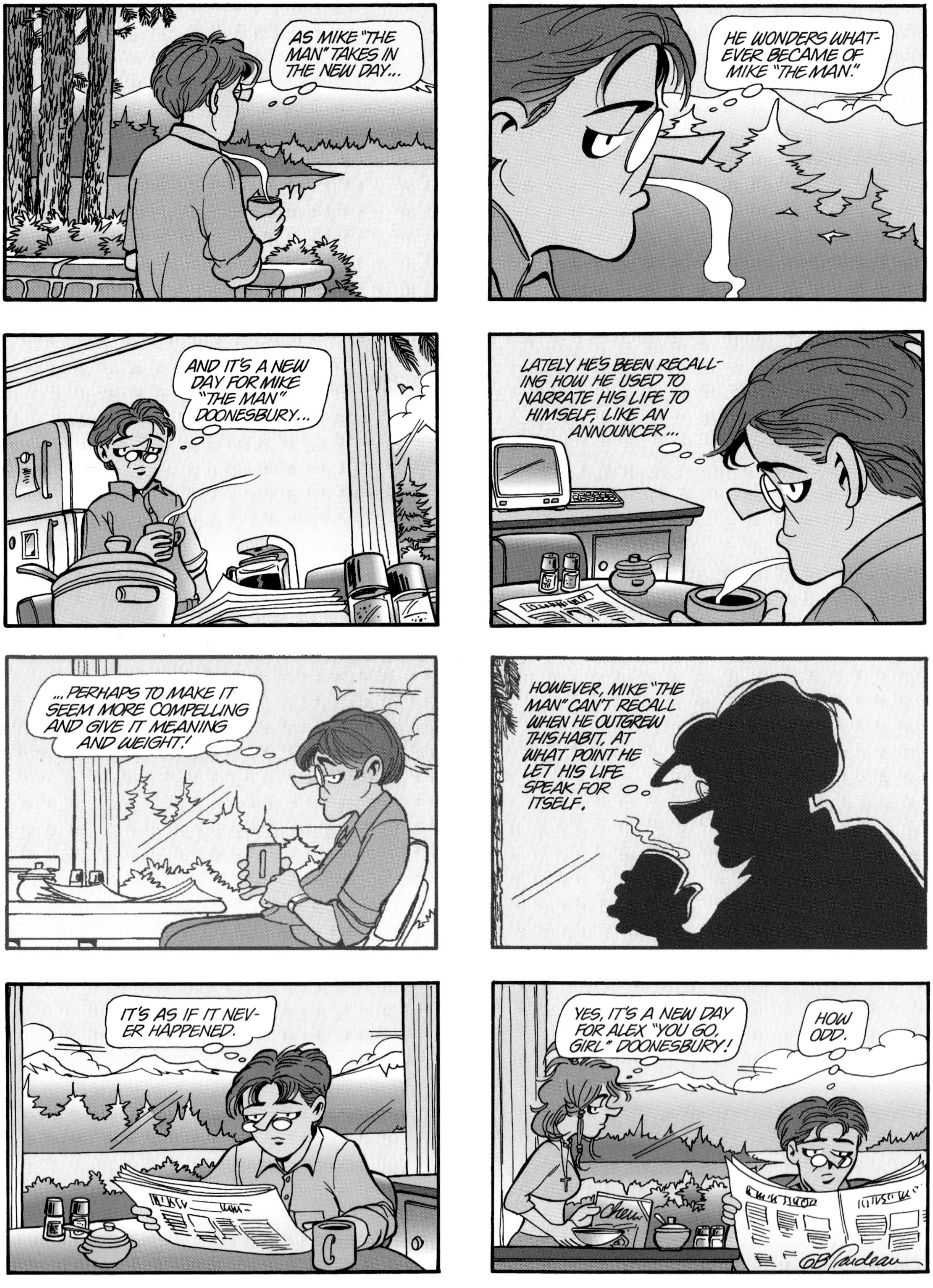
AS MIKE "THE MAN" TAKES IN THE NEW DAY...
HE WONDERS WHATEVER BECAME OF MIKE "THE MAN."
AND IT'S A NEW DAY FOR MIKE "THE MAN" DOONESBURY...
LATELY HE'S BEEN RECALLING HOW HE USED TO NARRATE HIS LIFE TO HIMSELF, LIKE AN ANNOUNCER...
...PERHAPS TO MAKE IT SEEM MORE COMPELLING AND GIVE IT MEANING AND WEIGHT!
HOWEVER, MIKE "THE MAN" CAN'T RECALL WHEN HE OUTGREW THIS HABIT, AT WHAT POINT HE LET HIS LIFE SPEAK FOR ITSELF.
IT'S AS IF IT NEVER HAPPENED.
YES, IT'S A NEW DAY FOR ALEX "YOU GO, GIRL" DOONESBURY!
HOW ODD.
GBTrudeau

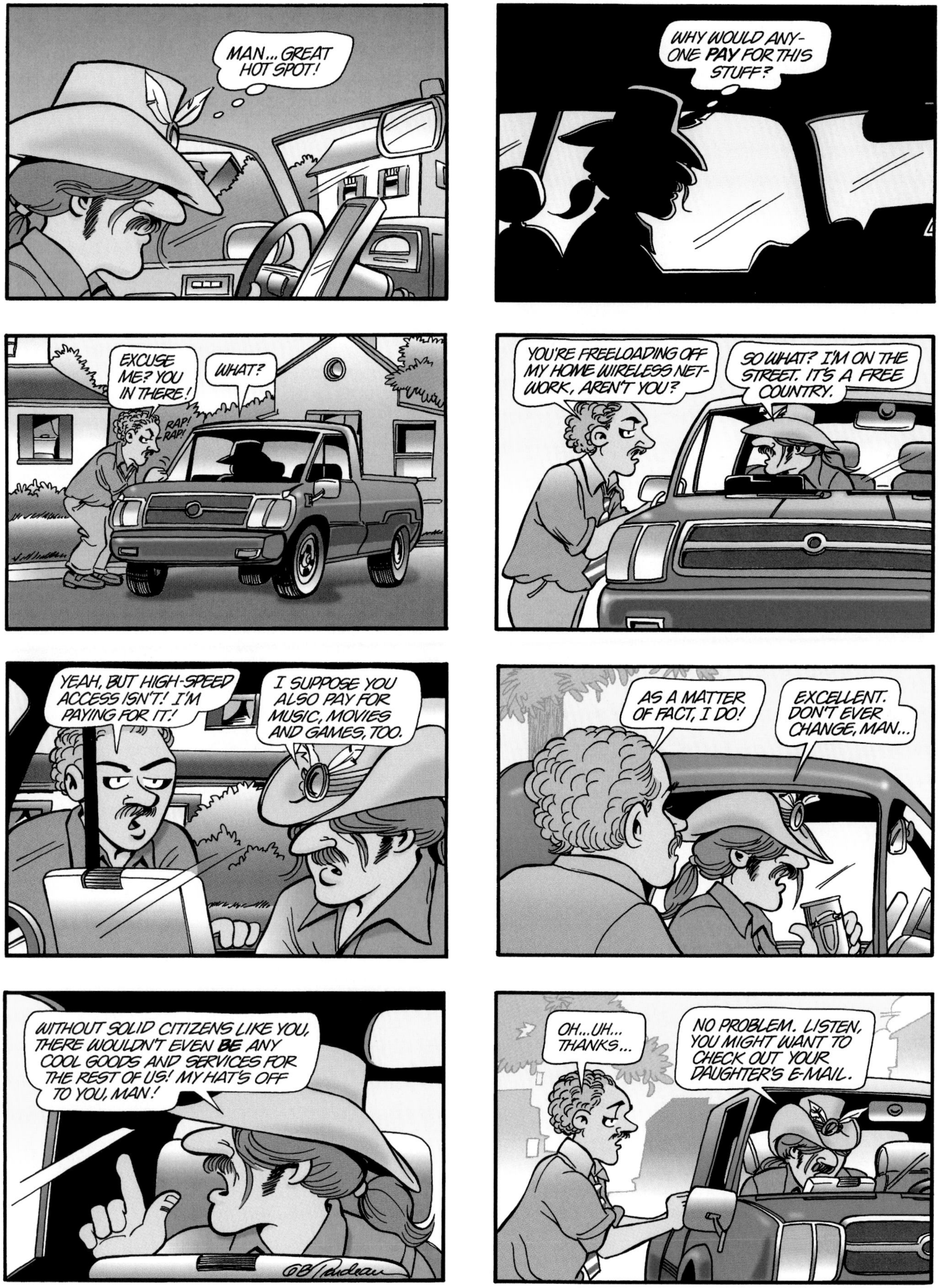
MAN... GREAT HOT SPOT!
WHY WOULD ANY-ONE PAY FOR THIS STUFF?
EXCUSE ME? YOU IN THERE!
RAP! RAP!
WHAT?
YOU'RE FREELOADING OFF MY HOME WIRELESS NET-WORK, AREN'T YOU?
SO WHAT? I'M ON THE STREET. IT'S A FREE COUNTRY.
YEAH, BUT HIGH-SPEED ACCESS ISN'T! I'M PAYING FOR IT!
I SUPPOSE YOU ALSO PAY FOR MUSIC, MOVIES AND GAMES, TOO.
AS A MATTER OF FACT, I DO!
EXCELLENT. DON'T EVER CHANGE, MAN...
WITHOUT SOLID CITIZENS LIKE YOU, THERE WOULDN'T EVEN BE ANY COOL GOODS AND SERVICES FOR THE REST OF US! MY HAT'S OFF TO YOU, MAN!
OH...UH... THANKS...
NO PROBLEM. LISTEN, YOU MIGHT WANT TO CHECK OUT YOUR DAUGHTER'S E-MAIL.

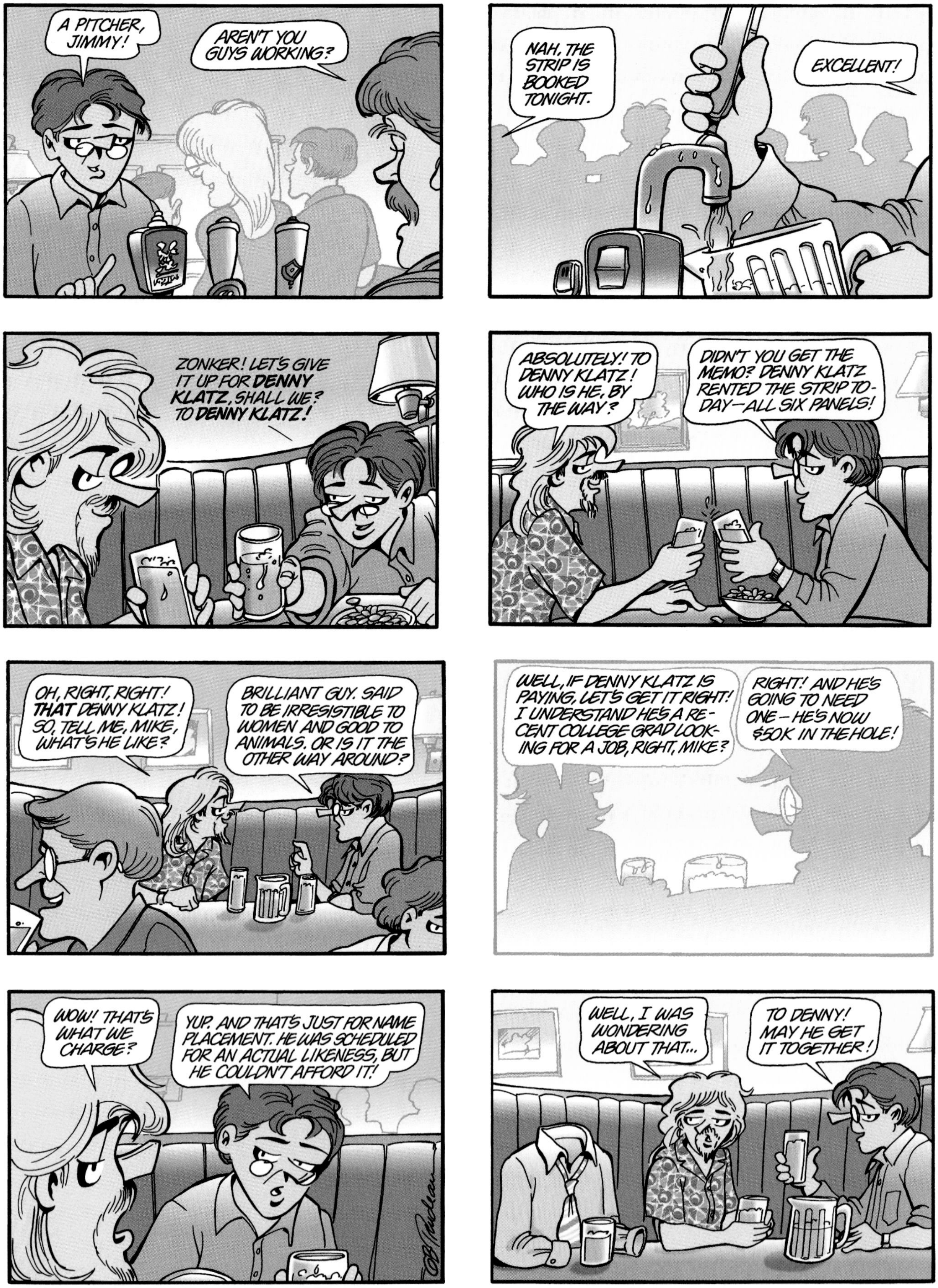

A PITCHER, JIMMY!
AREN'T YOU GUYS WORKING?
NAH, THE STRIP IS BOOKED TONIGHT.
EXCELLENT!
ZONKER! LET'S GIVE IT UP FOR **DENNY KLATZ**, SHALL WE? TO **DENNY KLATZ**!
ABSOLUTELY! TO DENNY KLATZ! WHO IS HE, BY THE WAY?
DIDN'T YOU GET THE MEMO? DENNY KLATZ RENTED THE STRIP TODAY—ALL SIX PANELS!
OH, RIGHT, RIGHT! **THAT** DENNY KLATZ! SO, TELL ME, MIKE, WHAT'S HE LIKE?
BRILLIANT GUY. SAID TO BE IRRESISTIBLE TO WOMEN AND GOOD TO ANIMALS. OR IS IT THE OTHER WAY AROUND?
WELL, IF DENNY KLATZ IS PAYING, LET'S GET IT RIGHT! I UNDERSTAND HE'S A RECENT COLLEGE GRAD LOOKING FOR A JOB, RIGHT, MIKE?
RIGHT! AND HE'S GOING TO NEED ONE—HE'S NOW $50K IN THE HOLE!
WOW! THAT'S WHAT WE CHARGE?
YUP. AND THAT'S JUST FOR NAME PLACEMENT. HE WAS SCHEDULED FOR AN ACTUAL LIKENESS, BUT HE COULDN'T AFFORD IT!
WELL, I WAS WONDERING ABOUT THAT...
TO DENNY! MAY HE GET IT TOGETHER!

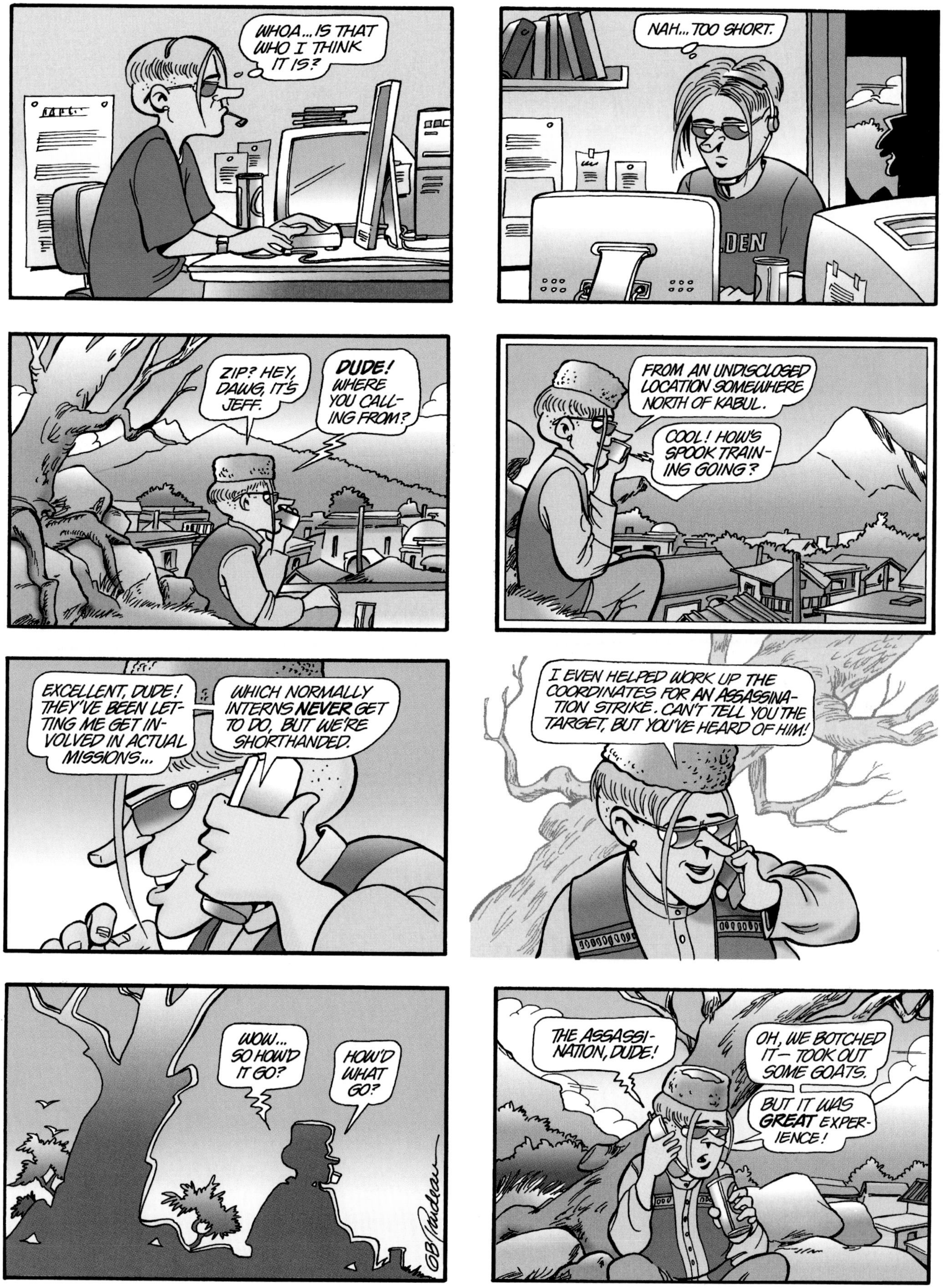
WHOA... IS THAT WHO I THINK IT IS?
NAH... TOO SHORT.
ZIP? HEY, DAWG, IT'S JEFF.
DUDE! WHERE YOU CALLING FROM?
FROM AN UNDISCLOSED LOCATION SOMEWHERE NORTH OF KABUL.
COOL! HOW'S SPOOK TRAINING GOING?
EXCELLENT, DUDE! THEY'VE BEEN LETTING ME GET INVOLVED IN ACTUAL MISSIONS...
WHICH NORMALLY INTERNS NEVER GET TO DO, BUT WE'RE SHORTHANDED.
I EVEN HELPED WORK UP THE COORDINATES FOR AN ASSASSINATION STRIKE. CAN'T TELL YOU THE TARGET, BUT YOU'VE HEARD OF HIM!
WOW... SO HOW'D IT GO?
HOW'D WHAT GO?
THE ASSASSINATION, DUDE!
OH, WE BOTCHED IT — TOOK OUT SOME GOATS.
BUT IT WAS GREAT EXPERIENCE!

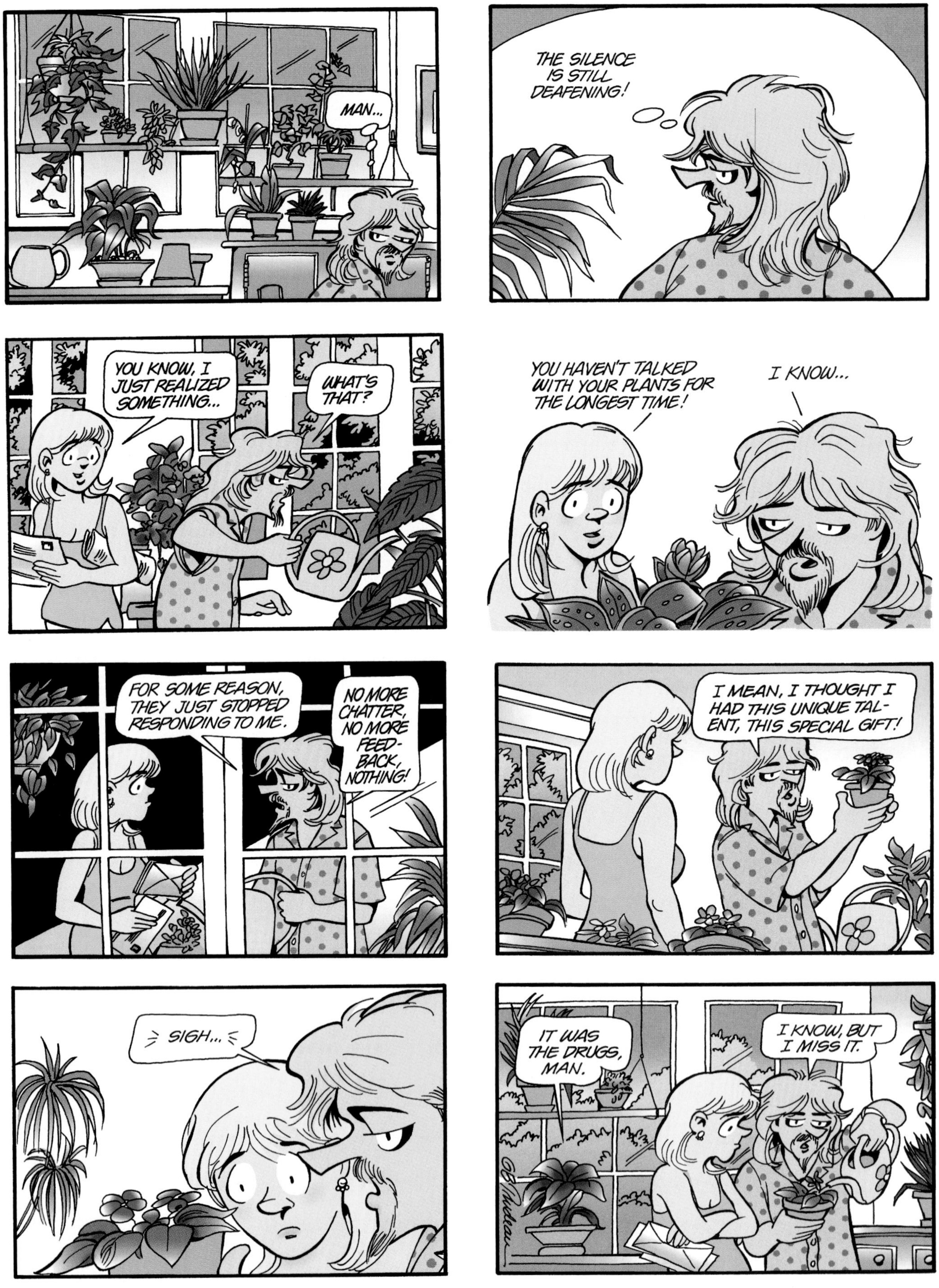
MAN...
THE SILENCE IS STILL DEAFENING!
YOU KNOW, I JUST REALIZED SOMETHING...
WHAT'S THAT?
YOU HAVEN'T TALKED WITH YOUR PLANTS FOR THE LONGEST TIME!
I KNOW...
FOR SOME REASON, THEY JUST STOPPED RESPONDING TO ME.
NO MORE CHATTER, NO MORE FEED-BACK, NOTHING!
I MEAN, I THOUGHT I HAD THIS UNIQUE TAL-ENT, THIS SPECIAL GIFT!
SIGH...
IT WAS THE DRUGS, MAN.
I KNOW, BUT I MISS IT.

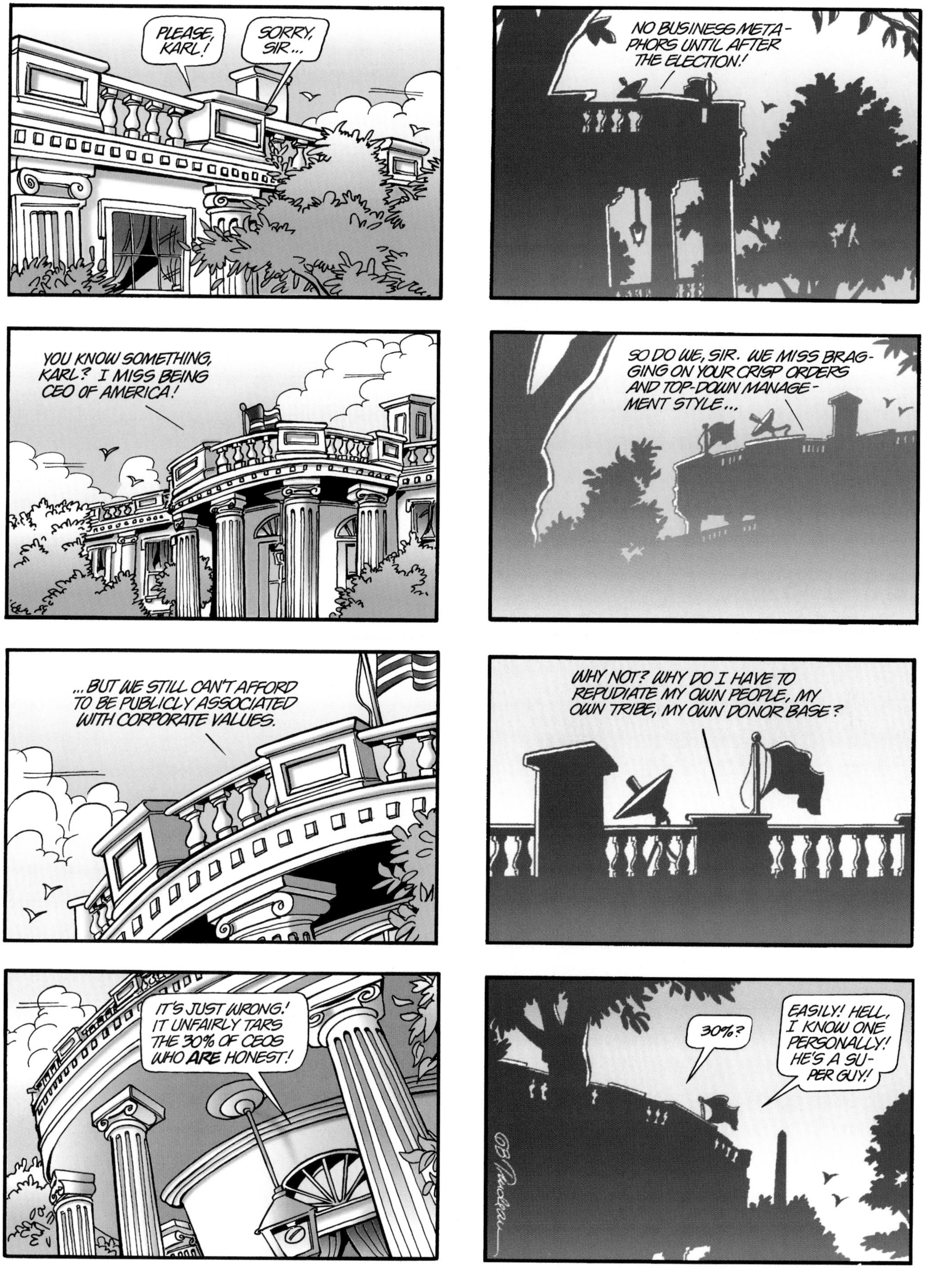
PLEASE, KARL!
SORRY, SIR...
NO BUSINESS METAPHORS UNTIL AFTER THE ELECTION!
YOU KNOW SOMETHING, KARL? I MISS BEING CEO OF AMERICA!
SO DO WE, SIR. WE MISS BRAGGING ON YOUR CRISP ORDERS AND TOP-DOWN MANAGEMENT STYLE...
...BUT WE STILL CAN'T AFFORD TO BE PUBLICLY ASSOCIATED WITH CORPORATE VALUES.
WHY NOT? WHY DO I HAVE TO REPUDIATE MY OWN PEOPLE, MY OWN TRIBE, MY OWN DONOR BASE?
IT'S JUST WRONG! IT UNFAIRLY TARS THE 30% OF CEOS WHO **ARE** HONEST!
30%?
EASILY! HELL, I KNOW ONE PERSONALLY! HE'S A SUPER GUY!

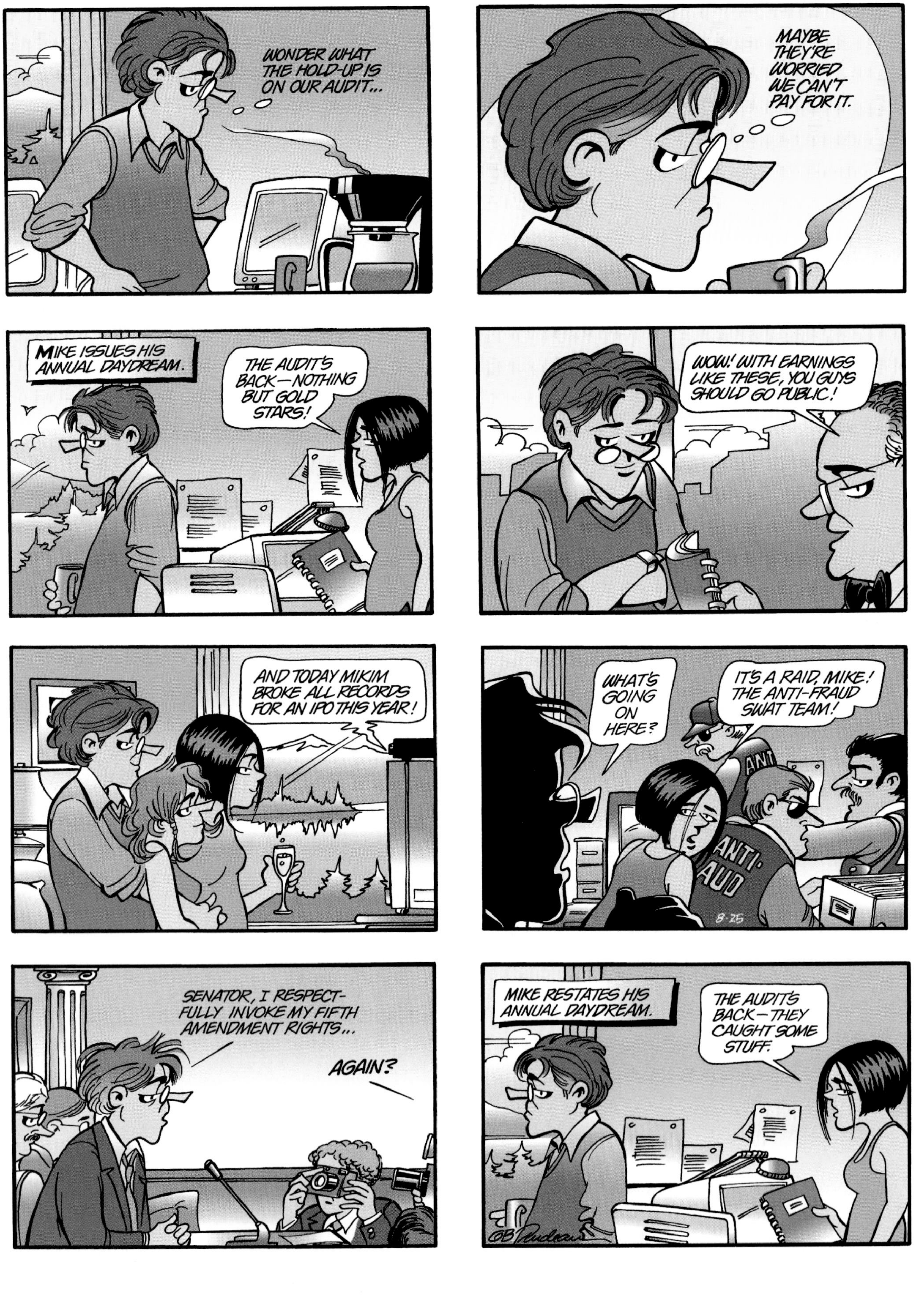

WONDER WHAT THE HOLD-UP IS ON OUR AUDIT...
MAYBE THEY'RE WORRIED WE CAN'T PAY FOR IT.
MIKE ISSUES HIS ANNUAL DAYDREAM.
THE AUDIT'S BACK—NOTHING BUT GOLD STARS!
WOW! WITH EARNINGS LIKE THESE, YOU GUYS SHOULD GO PUBLIC!
AND TODAY MIKIM BROKE ALL RECORDS FOR AN IPO THIS YEAR!
WHAT'S GOING ON HERE?
IT'S A RAID, MIKE! THE ANTI-FRAUD SWAT TEAM!
ANTI
ANTI-AUD
8-25
SENATOR, I RESPECTFULLY INVOKE MY FIFTH AMENDMENT RIGHTS...
AGAIN?
MIKE RESTATES HIS ANNUAL DAYDREAM.
THE AUDIT'S BACK—THEY CAUGHT SOME STUFF.

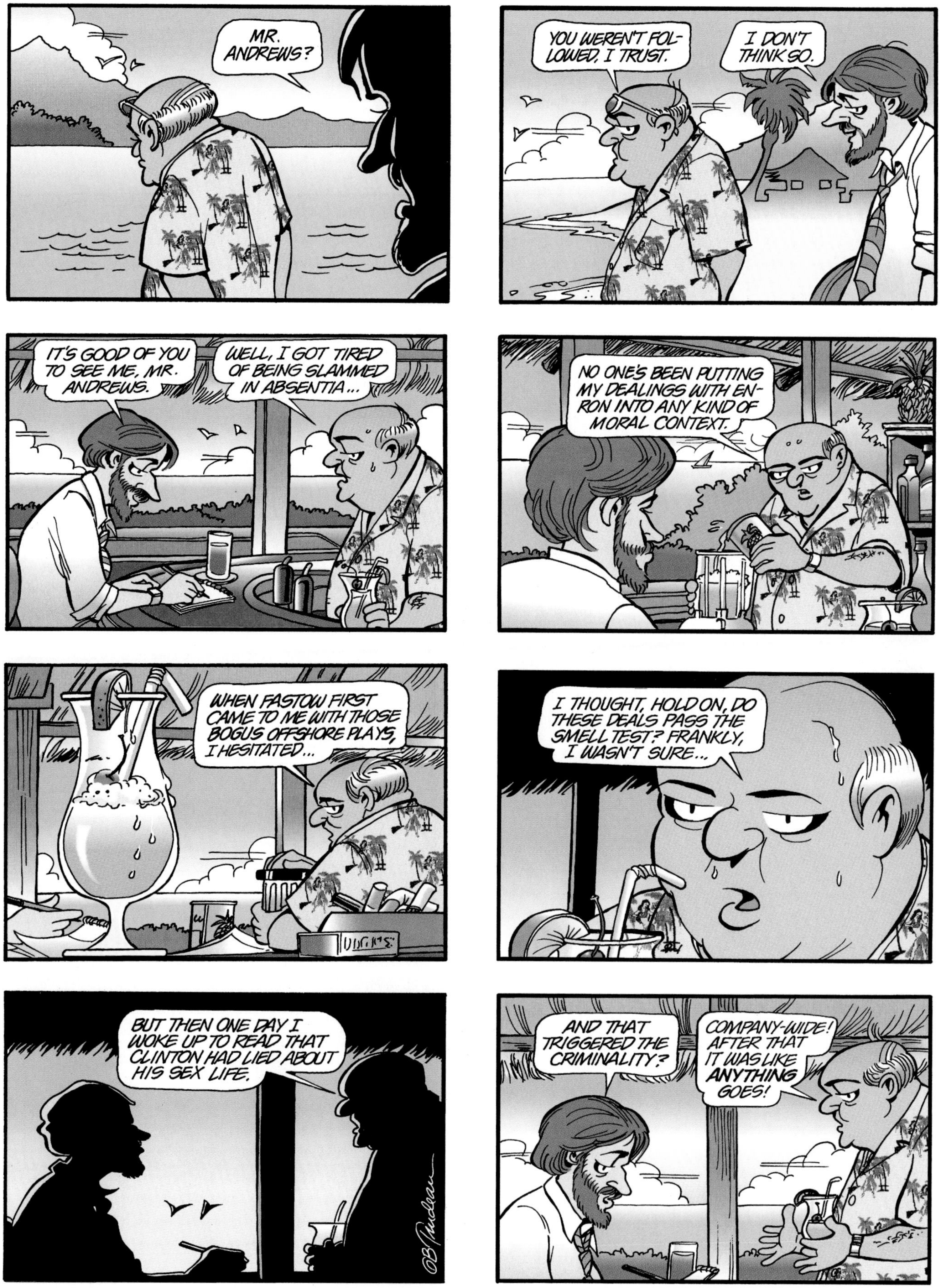
MR. ANDREWS?
YOU WEREN'T FOLLOWED, I TRUST.
I DON'T THINK SO.
IT'S GOOD OF YOU TO SEE ME, MR. ANDREWS.
WELL, I GOT TIRED OF BEING SLAMMED IN ABSENTIA...
NO ONE'S BEEN PUTTING MY DEALINGS WITH ENRON INTO ANY KIND OF MORAL CONTEXT.
WHEN FASTOW FIRST CAME TO ME WITH THOSE BOGUS OFFSHORE PLAYS, I HESITATED...
I THOUGHT, HOLD ON, DO THESE DEALS PASS THE SMELL TEST? FRANKLY, I WASN'T SURE...
BUT THEN ONE DAY I WOKE UP TO READ THAT CLINTON HAD LIED ABOUT HIS SEX LIFE.
AND THAT TRIGGERED THE CRIMINALITY?
COMPANY-WIDE! AFTER THAT IT WAS LIKE **ANYTHING** GOES!

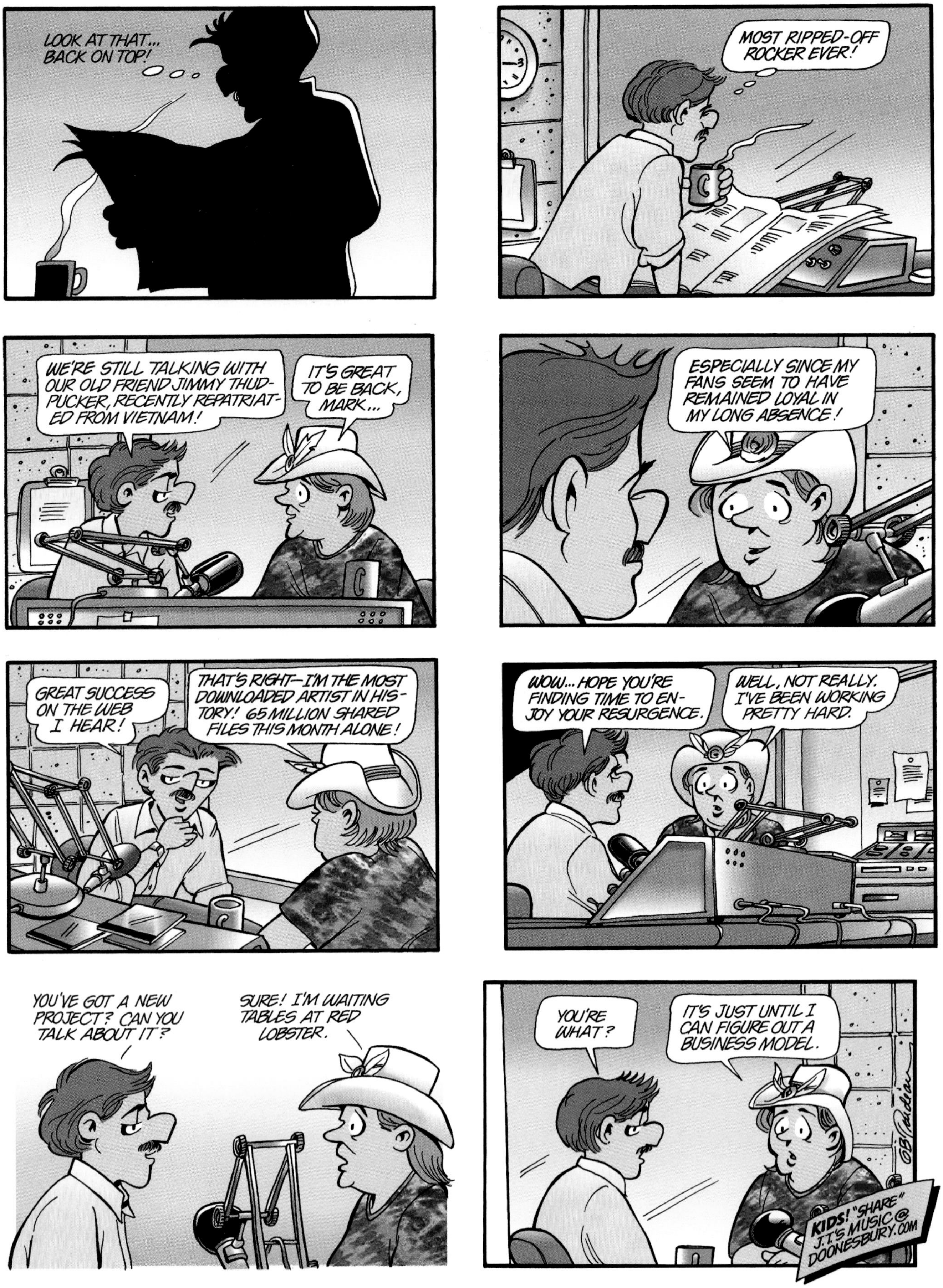
LOOK AT THAT... BACK ON TOP!
MOST RIPPED-OFF ROCKER EVER!
WE'RE STILL TALKING WITH OUR OLD FRIEND JIMMY THUDPUCKER, RECENTLY REPATRIATED FROM VIETNAM!
IT'S GREAT TO BE BACK, MARK...
ESPECIALLY SINCE MY FANS SEEM TO HAVE REMAINED LOYAL IN MY LONG ABSENCE!
GREAT SUCCESS ON THE WEB I HEAR!
THAT'S RIGHT—I'M THE MOST DOWNLOADED ARTIST IN HISTORY! 65 MILLION SHARED FILES THIS MONTH ALONE!
WOW... HOPE YOU'RE FINDING TIME TO ENJOY YOUR RESURGENCE.
WELL, NOT REALLY. I'VE BEEN WORKING PRETTY HARD.
YOU'VE GOT A NEW PROJECT? CAN YOU TALK ABOUT IT?
SURE! I'M WAITING TABLES AT RED LOBSTER.
YOU'RE WHAT?
IT'S JUST UNTIL I CAN FIGURE OUT A BUSINESS MODEL.
KIDS! "SHARE" J.T.'S MUSIC @ DOONESBURY.COM

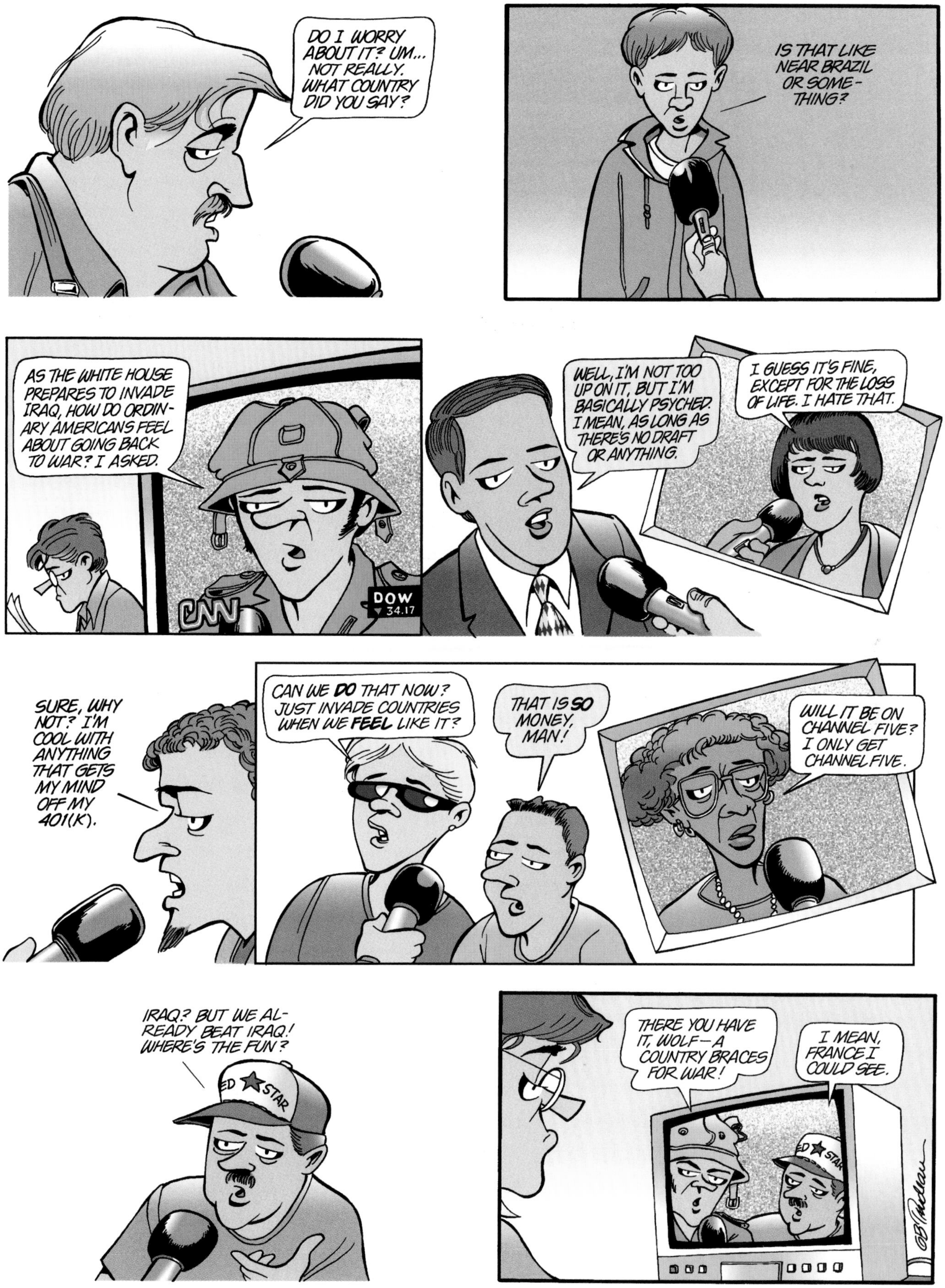
DO I WORRY ABOUT IT? UM... NOT REALLY. WHAT COUNTRY DID YOU SAY?
IS THAT LIKE NEAR BRAZIL OR SOME-THING?
AS THE WHITE HOUSE PREPARES TO INVADE IRAQ, HOW DO ORDINARY AMERICANS FEEL ABOUT GOING BACK TO WAR? I ASKED.
CNN
DOW ▼34.17
WELL, I'M NOT TOO UP ON IT, BUT I'M BASICALLY PSYCHED. I MEAN, AS LONG AS THERE'S NO DRAFT OR ANYTHING.
I GUESS IT'S FINE, EXCEPT FOR THE LOSS OF LIFE. I HATE THAT.
SURE, WHY NOT? I'M COOL WITH ANYTHING THAT GETS MY MIND OFF MY 401(K).
CAN WE **DO** THAT NOW? JUST INVADE COUNTRIES WHEN WE **FEEL** LIKE IT?
THAT IS **SO** MONEY, MAN!
WILL IT BE ON CHANNEL FIVE? I ONLY GET CHANNEL FIVE.
IRAQ? BUT WE AL-READY BEAT IRAQ! WHERE'S THE FUN?
ED ★ STAR
THERE YOU HAVE IT, WOLF—A COUNTRY BRACES FOR WAR!
I MEAN, FRANCE I COULD SEE.

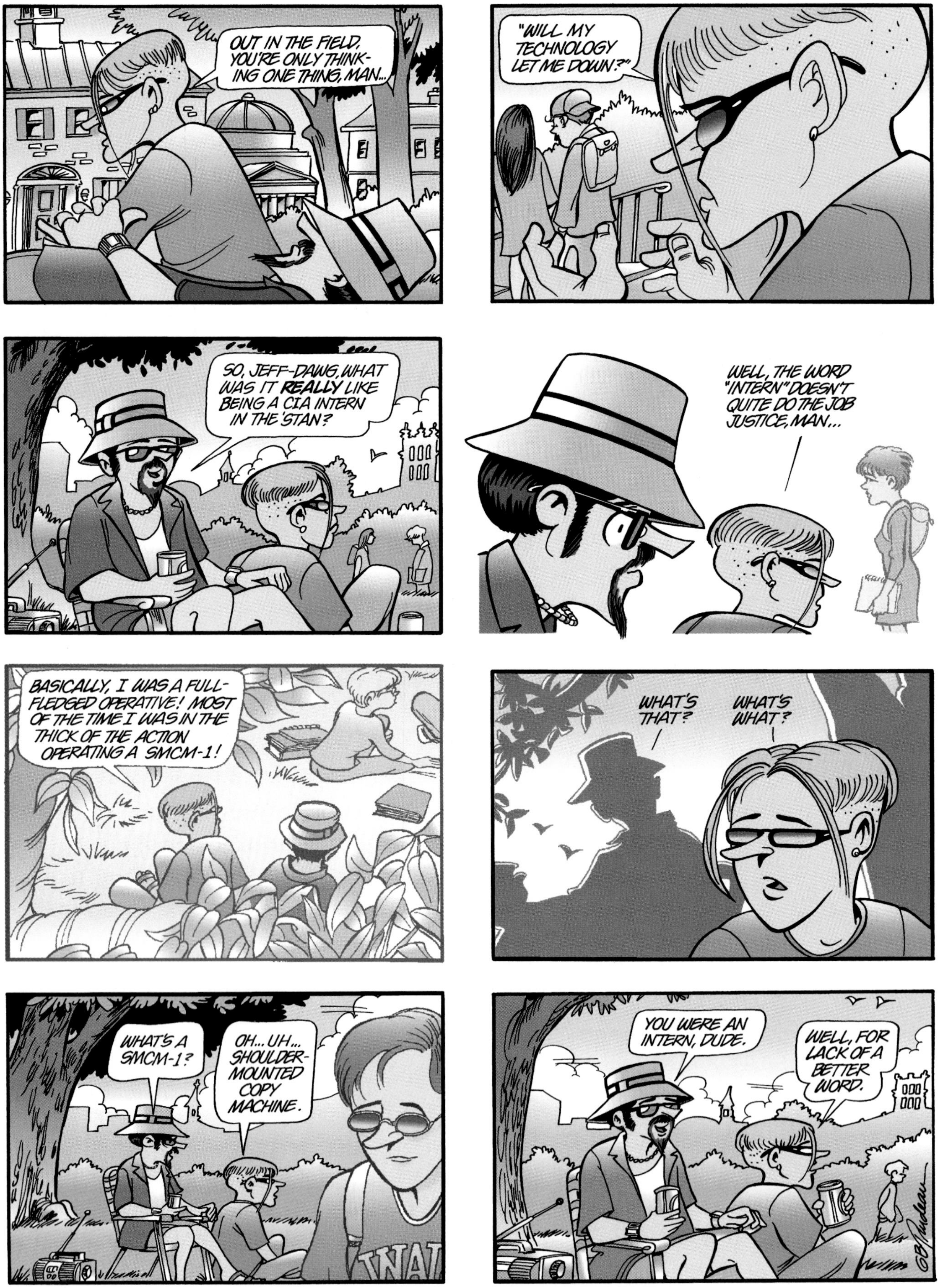
OUT IN THE FIELD, YOU'RE ONLY THINKING ONE THING, MAN...
"WILL MY TECHNOLOGY LET ME DOWN?"
SO, JEFF-DAWG, WHAT WAS IT REALLY LIKE BEING A CIA INTERN IN THE 'STAN?
WELL, THE WORD "INTERN" DOESN'T QUITE DO THE JOB JUSTICE, MAN...
BASICALLY, I WAS A FULL-FLEDGED OPERATIVE! MOST OF THE TIME I WAS IN THE THICK OF THE ACTION OPERATING A SMCM-1!
WHAT'S THAT?
WHAT'S WHAT?
WHAT'S A SMCM-1?
OH... UH... SHOULDER-MOUNTED COPY MACHINE.
YOU WERE AN INTERN, DUDE.
WELL, FOR LACK OF A BETTER WORD.

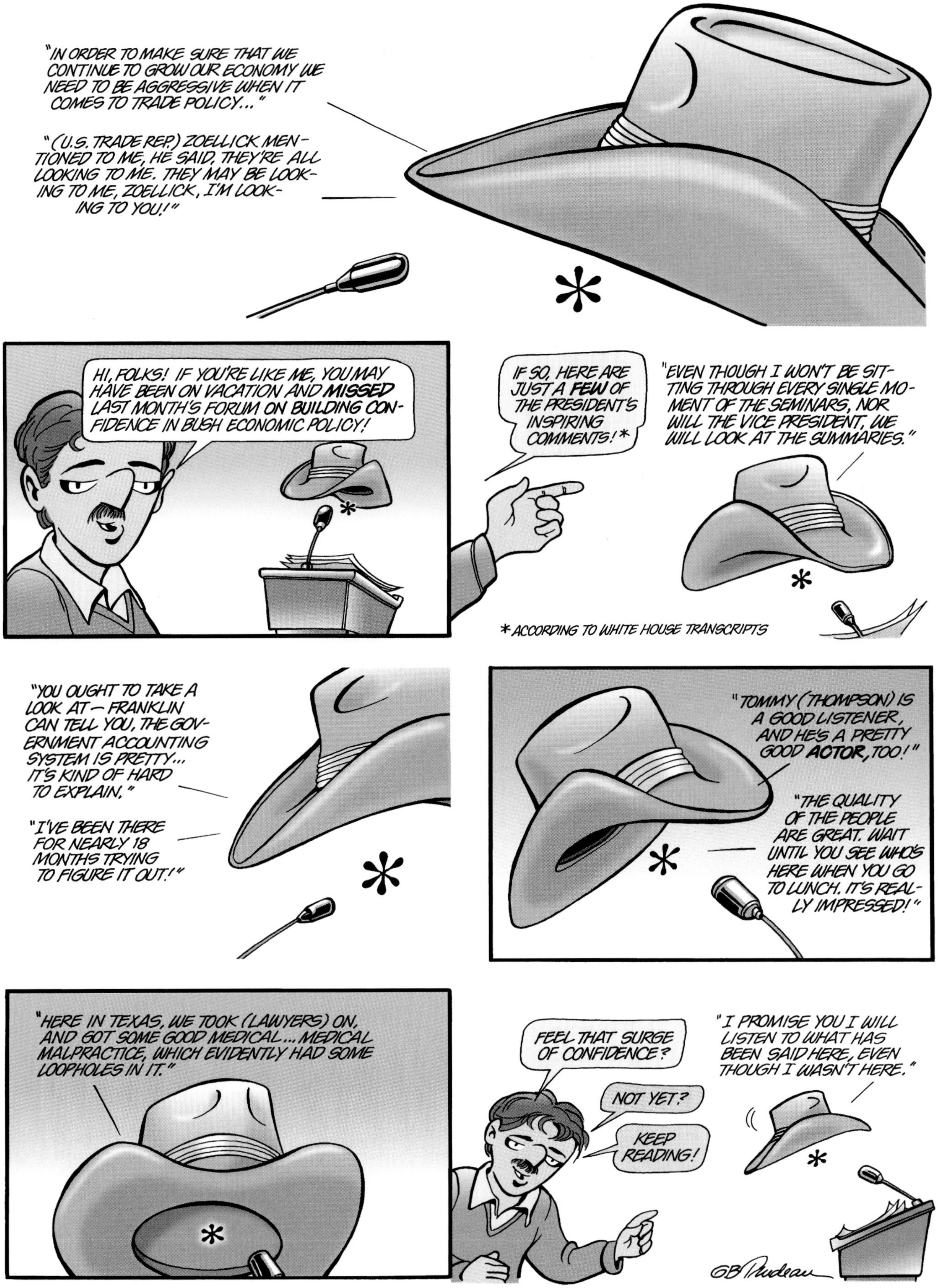
"IN ORDER TO MAKE SURE THAT WE CONTINUE TO GROW OUR ECONOMY WE NEED TO BE AGGRESSIVE WHEN IT COMES TO TRADE POLICY..."
"(U.S. TRADE REP.) ZOELLICK MENTIONED TO ME, HE SAID, THEY'RE ALL LOOKING TO ME. THEY MAY BE LOOKING TO ME, ZOELLICK, I'M LOOKING TO YOU!"
*
HI, FOLKS! IF YOU'RE LIKE ME, YOU MAY HAVE BEEN ON VACATION AND **MISSED** LAST MONTH'S FORUM **ON BUILDING CONFIDENCE** IN BUSH ECONOMIC POLICY!
IF SO, HERE ARE JUST A **FEW** OF THE PRESIDENT'S INSPIRING COMMENTS! *
"EVEN THOUGH I WON'T BE SITTING THROUGH EVERY SINGLE MOMENT OF THE SEMINARS, NOR WILL THE VICE PRESIDENT, WE WILL LOOK AT THE SUMMARIES."
* ACCORDING TO WHITE HOUSE TRANSCRIPTS
"YOU OUGHT TO TAKE A LOOK AT — FRANKLIN CAN TELL YOU, THE GOVERNMENT ACCOUNTING SYSTEM IS PRETTY... IT'S KIND OF HARD TO EXPLAIN."
"I'VE BEEN THERE FOR NEARLY 18 MONTHS TRYING TO FIGURE IT OUT!"
"TOMMY (THOMPSON) IS A GOOD LISTENER, AND HE'S A PRETTY GOOD **ACTOR**, TOO!"
"THE QUALITY OF THE PEOPLE ARE GREAT. WAIT UNTIL YOU SEE WHO'S HERE WHEN YOU GO TO LUNCH. IT'S REALLY IMPRESSED!"
"HERE IN TEXAS, WE TOOK (LAWYERS) ON, AND GOT SOME GOOD MEDICAL... MEDICAL MALPRACTICE, WHICH EVIDENTLY HAD SOME LOOPHOLES IN IT."
FEEL THAT SURGE OF CONFIDENCE?
NOT YET?
KEEP READING!
"I PROMISE YOU I WILL LISTEN TO WHAT HAS BEEN SAID HERE, EVEN THOUGH I WASN'T HERE."
GBTrudeau

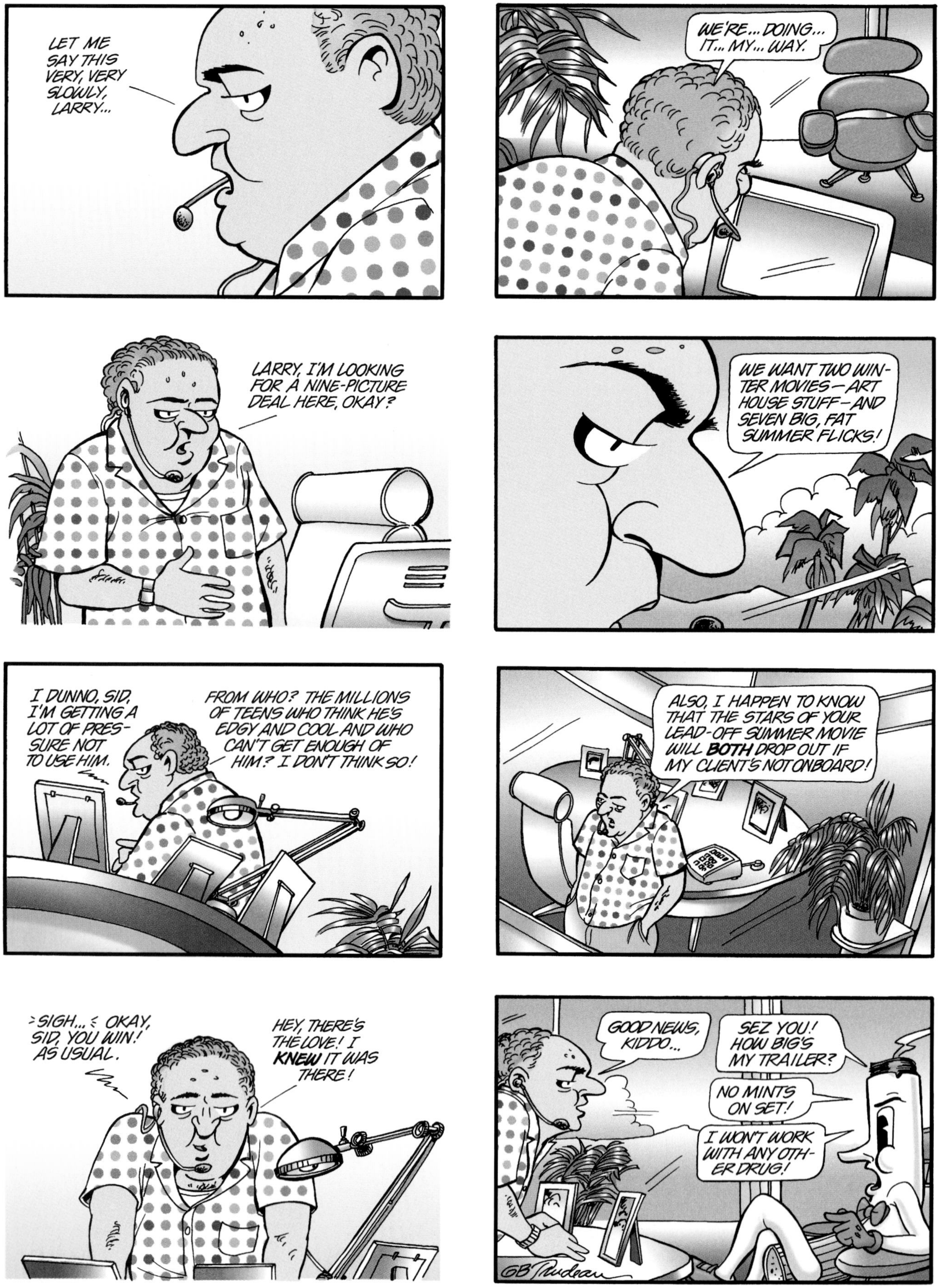
LET ME SAY THIS VERY, VERY SLOWLY, LARRY...
WE'RE... DOING... IT... MY... WAY.
LARRY, I'M LOOKING FOR A NINE-PICTURE DEAL HERE, OKAY?
WE WANT TWO WINTER MOVIES—ART HOUSE STUFF—AND SEVEN BIG, FAT SUMMER FLICKS!
I DUNNO, SID, I'M GETTING A LOT OF PRESSURE NOT TO USE HIM.
FROM WHO? THE MILLIONS OF TEENS WHO THINK HE'S EDGY AND COOL AND WHO CAN'T GET ENOUGH OF HIM? I DON'T THINK SO!
ALSO, I HAPPEN TO KNOW THAT THE STARS OF YOUR LEAD-OFF SUMMER MOVIE WILL **BOTH** DROP OUT IF MY CLIENT'S NOT ONBOARD!
>SIGH...< OKAY, SID, YOU WIN! AS USUAL.
HEY, THERE'S THE LOVE! I **KNEW** IT WAS THERE!
GOOD NEWS, KIDDO...
SEZ YOU! HOW BIG'S MY TRAILER?
NO MINTS ON SET!
I WON'T WORK WITH ANY OTHER DRUG!
GB Trudeau

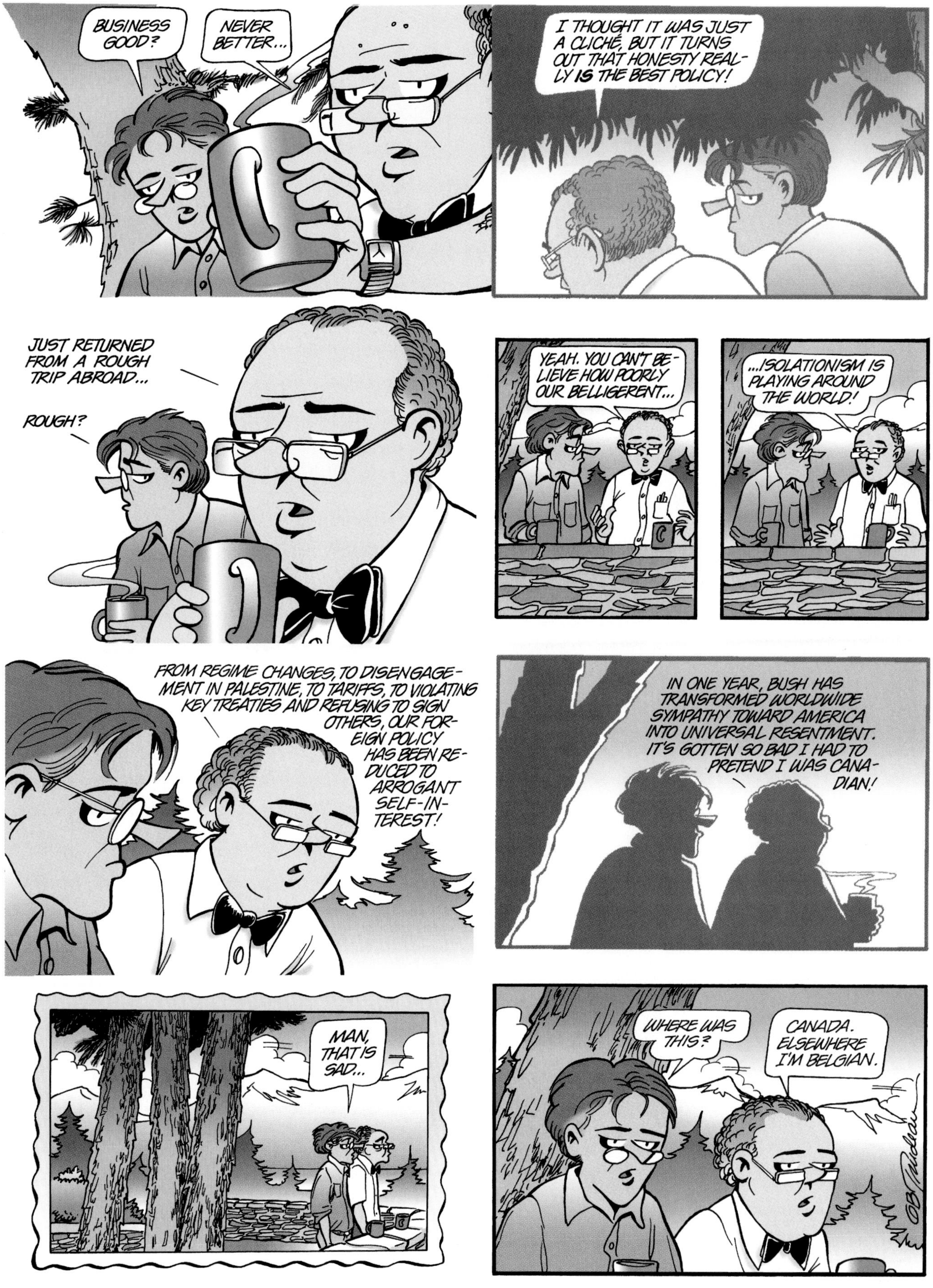
BUSINESS GOOD?
NEVER BETTER...
I THOUGHT IT WAS JUST A CLICHÉ, BUT IT TURNS OUT THAT HONESTY REALLY **IS** THE BEST POLICY!
JUST RETURNED FROM A ROUGH TRIP ABROAD...
ROUGH?
YEAH. YOU CAN'T BELIEVE HOW POORLY OUR BELLIGERENT...
...ISOLATIONISM IS PLAYING AROUND THE WORLD!
FROM REGIME CHANGES, TO DISENGAGEMENT IN PALESTINE, TO TARIFFS, TO VIOLATING KEY TREATIES AND REFUSING TO SIGN OTHERS, OUR FOREIGN POLICY HAS BEEN REDUCED TO ARROGANT SELF-INTEREST!
IN ONE YEAR, BUSH HAS TRANSFORMED WORLDWIDE SYMPATHY TOWARD AMERICA INTO UNIVERSAL RESENTMENT. IT'S GOTTEN SO BAD I HAD TO PRETEND I WAS CANADIAN!
MAN, THAT IS SAD...
WHERE WAS THIS?
CANADA. ELSEWHERE I'M BELGIAN.

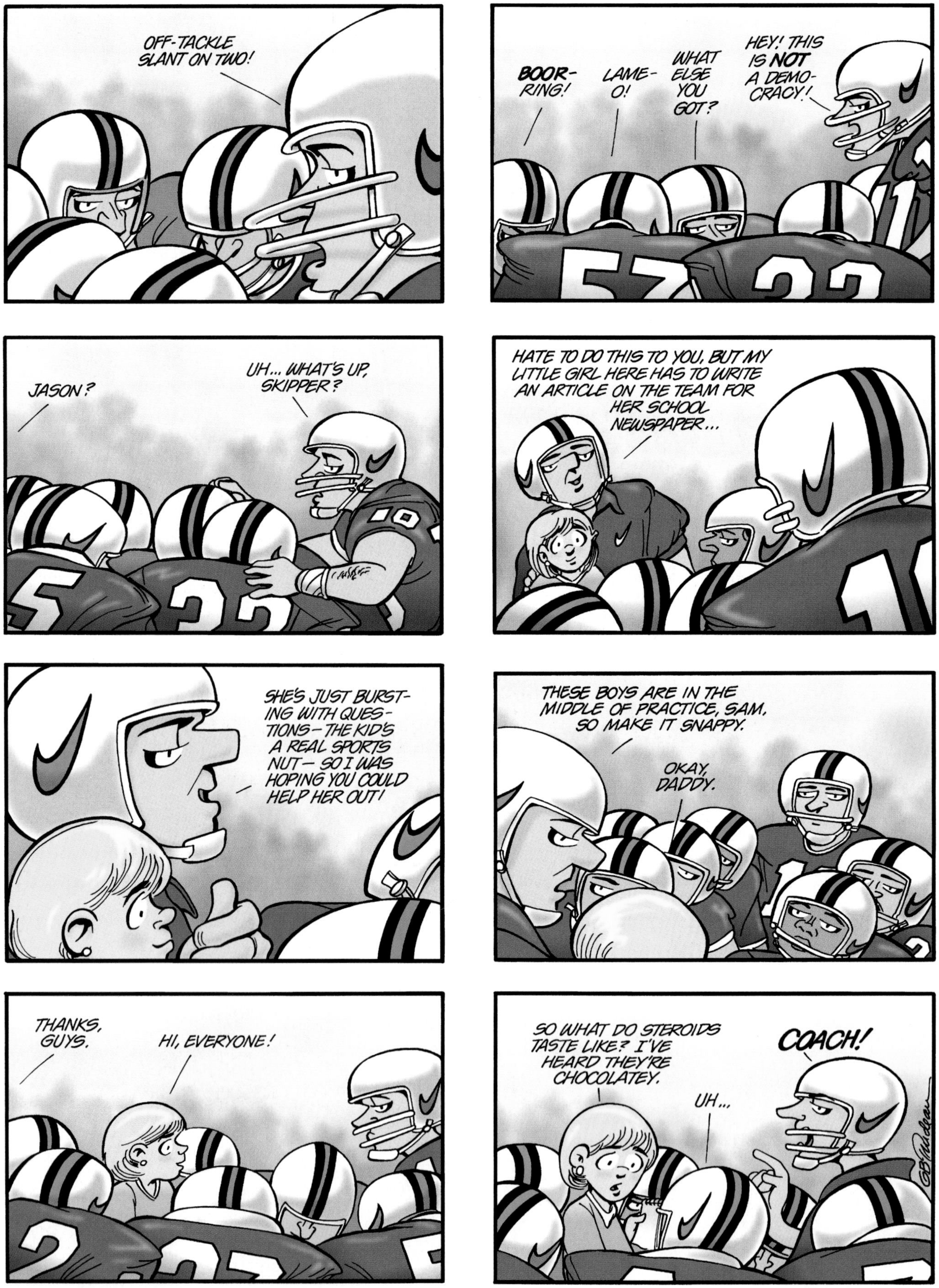
OFF-TACKLE SLANT ON TWO!
BOOR-RING!
LAME-O!
WHAT ELSE YOU GOT?
HEY! THIS IS NOT A DEMOCRACY!
JASON?
UH... WHAT'S UP, SKIPPER?
HATE TO DO THIS TO YOU, BUT MY LITTLE GIRL HERE HAS TO WRITE AN ARTICLE ON THE TEAM FOR HER SCHOOL NEWSPAPER...
SHE'S JUST BURSTING WITH QUESTIONS—THE KID'S A REAL SPORTS NUT—SO I WAS HOPING YOU COULD HELP HER OUT!
THESE BOYS ARE IN THE MIDDLE OF PRACTICE, SAM, SO MAKE IT SNAPPY.
OKAY, DADDY.
THANKS, GUYS.
HI, EVERYONE!
SO WHAT DO STEROIDS TASTE LIKE? I'VE HEARD THEY'RE CHOCOLATEY.
UH...
COACH!

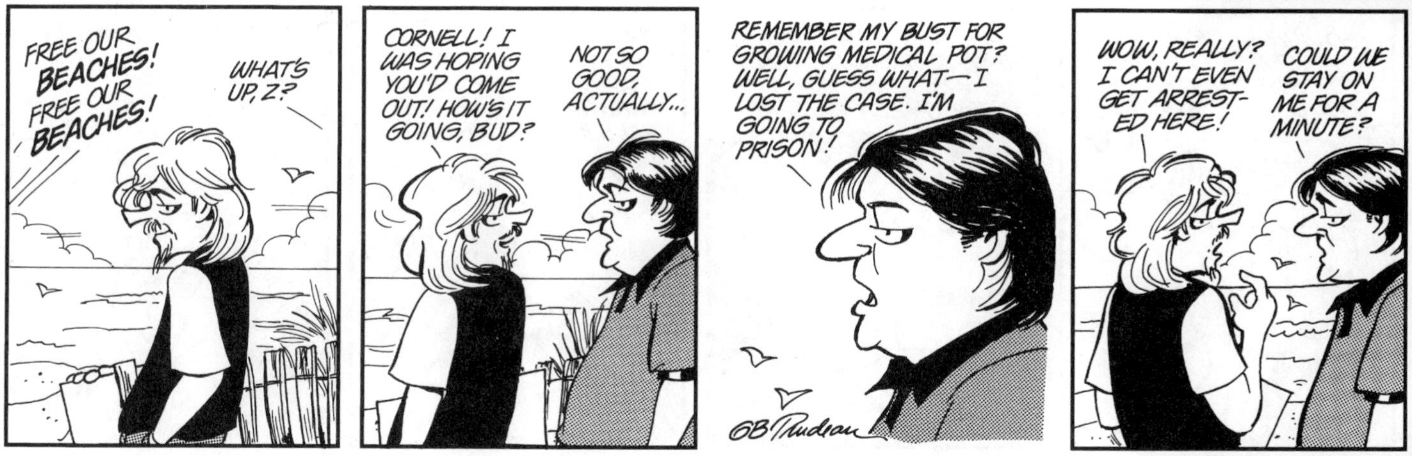
FREE OUR BEACHES! FREE OUR BEACHES!
WHAT'S UP, Z?
CORNELL! I WAS HOPING YOU'D COME OUT! HOW'S IT GOING, BUD?
NOT SO GOOD, ACTUALLY...
REMEMBER MY BUST FOR GROWING MEDICAL POT? WELL, GUESS WHAT—I LOST THE CASE. I'M GOING TO PRISON!
WOW, REALLY? I CAN'T EVEN GET ARRESTED HERE!
COULD WE STAY ON ME FOR A MINUTE?

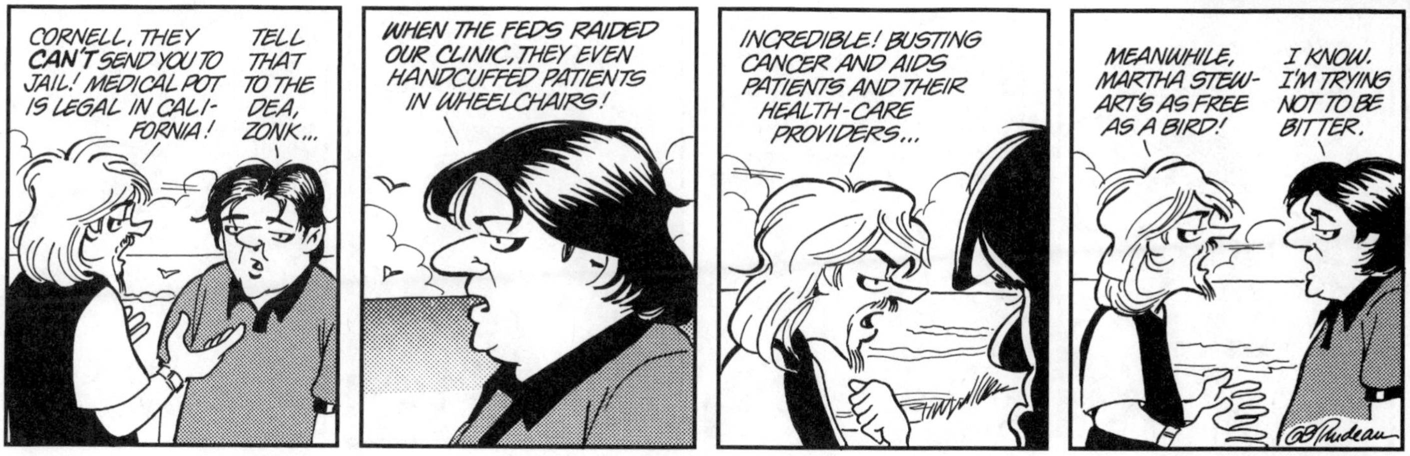
CORNELL, THEY CAN'T SEND YOU TO JAIL! MEDICAL POT IS LEGAL IN CALIFORNIA!
TELL THAT TO THE DEA, ZONK...
WHEN THE FEDS RAIDED OUR CLINIC, THEY EVEN HANDCUFFED PATIENTS IN WHEELCHAIRS!
INCREDIBLE! BUSTING CANCER AND AIDS PATIENTS AND THEIR HEALTH-CARE PROVIDERS...
MEANWHILE, MARTHA STEWART'S AS FREE AS A BIRD!
I KNOW. I'M TRYING NOT TO BE BITTER.

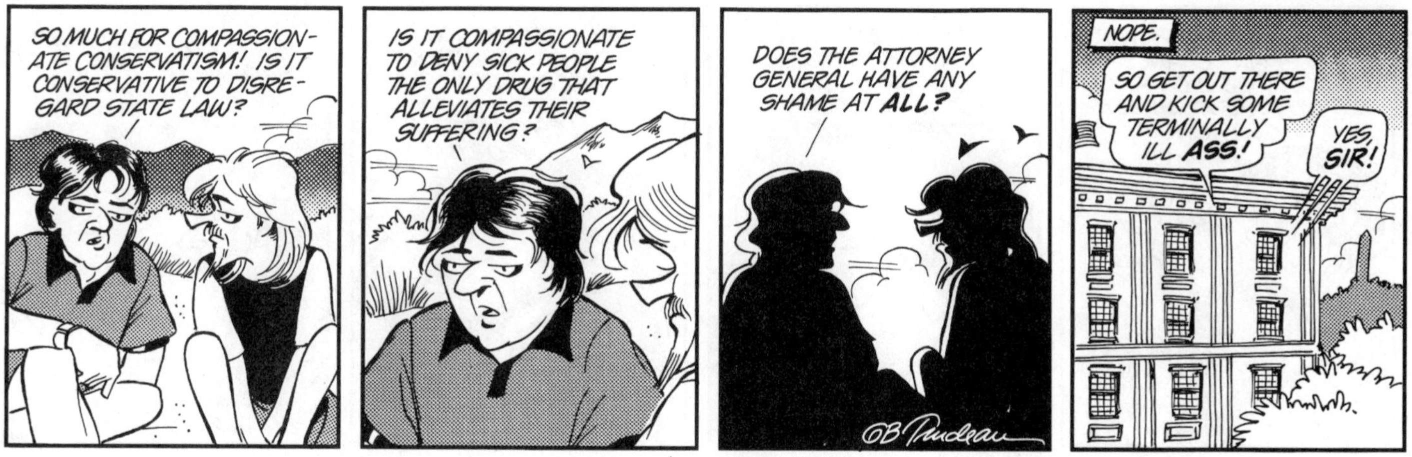
SO MUCH FOR COMPASSIONATE CONSERVATISM! IS IT CONSERVATIVE TO DISREGARD STATE LAW?
IS IT COMPASSIONATE TO DENY SICK PEOPLE THE ONLY DRUG THAT ALLEVIATES THEIR SUFFERING?
DOES THE ATTORNEY GENERAL HAVE ANY SHAME AT ALL?
NOPE.
SO GET OUT THERE AND KICK SOME TERMINALLY ILL ASS!
YES, SIR!

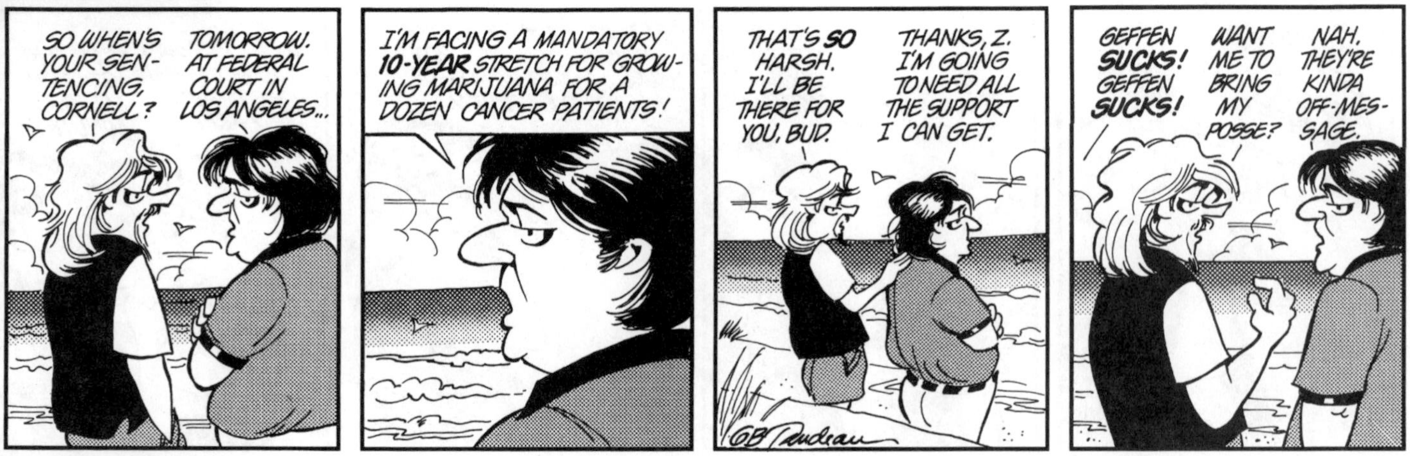
SO WHEN'S YOUR SEN-TENCING, CORNELL?
TOMORROW. AT FEDERAL COURT IN LOS ANGELES...
I'M FACING A MANDATORY **10-YEAR** STRETCH FOR GROW-ING MARIJUANA FOR A DOZEN CANCER PATIENTS!
THAT'S **SO** HARSH. I'LL BE THERE FOR YOU, BUD.
THANKS, Z. I'M GOING TO NEED ALL THE SUPPORT I CAN GET.
GEFFEN **SUCKS!** GEFFEN **SUCKS!**
WANT ME TO BRING MY POSSE?
NAH. THEY'RE KINDA OFF-MES-SAGE.

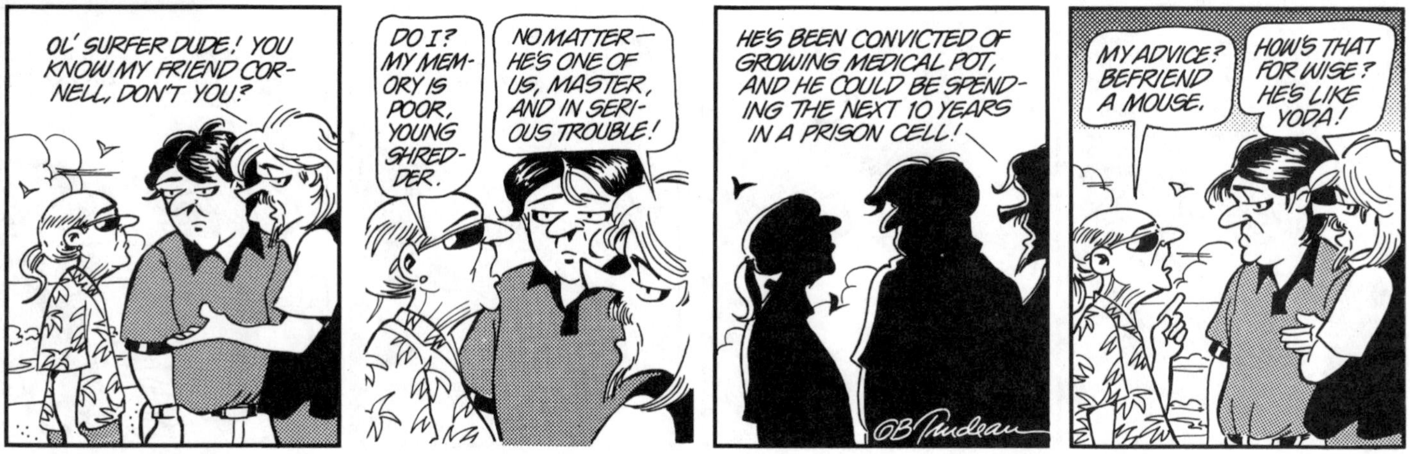
OL' SURFER DUDE! YOU KNOW MY FRIEND COR-NELL, DON'T YOU?
DO I? MY MEM-ORY IS POOR, YOUNG SHRED-DER.
NO MATTER— HE'S ONE OF US, MASTER, AND IN SERI-OUS TROUBLE!
HE'S BEEN CONVICTED OF GROWING MEDICAL POT, AND HE COULD BE SPEND-ING THE NEXT 10 YEARS IN A PRISON CELL!
MY ADVICE? BEFRIEND A MOUSE.
HOW'S THAT FOR WISE? HE'S LIKE YODA!

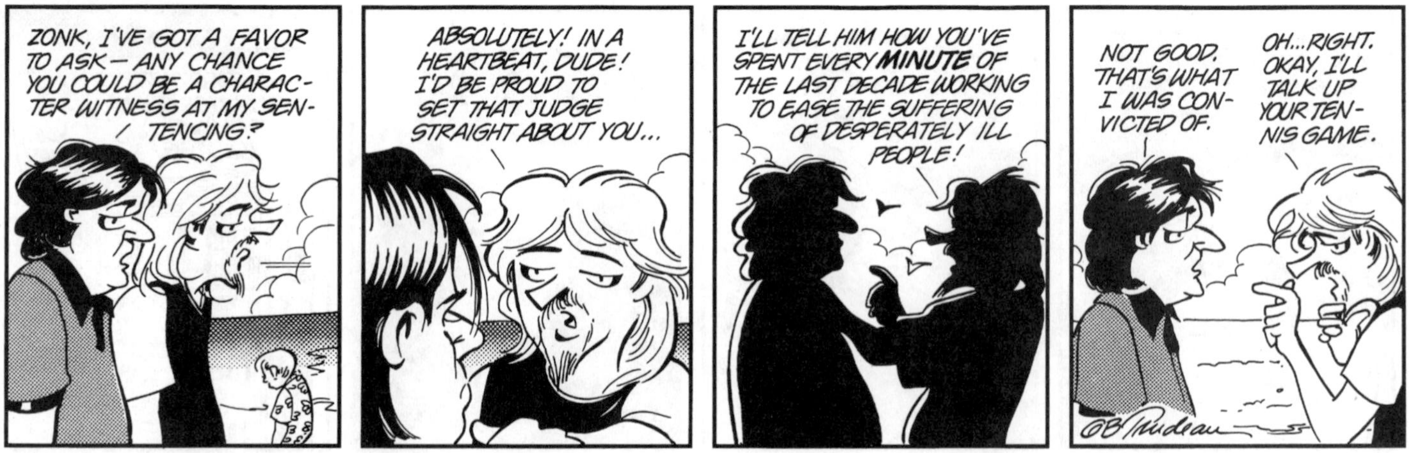
ZONK, I'VE GOT A FAVOR TO ASK— ANY CHANCE YOU COULD BE A CHARAC-TER WITNESS AT MY SEN-TENCING?
ABSOLUTELY! IN A HEARTBEAT, DUDE! I'D BE PROUD TO SET THAT JUDGE STRAIGHT ABOUT YOU...
I'LL TELL HIM HOW YOU'VE SPENT EVERY **MINUTE** OF THE LAST DECADE WORKING TO EASE THE SUFFERING OF DESPERATELY ILL PEOPLE!
NOT GOOD. THAT'S WHAT I WAS CON-VICTED OF.
OH...RIGHT. OKAY, I'LL TALK UP YOUR TEN-NIS GAME.

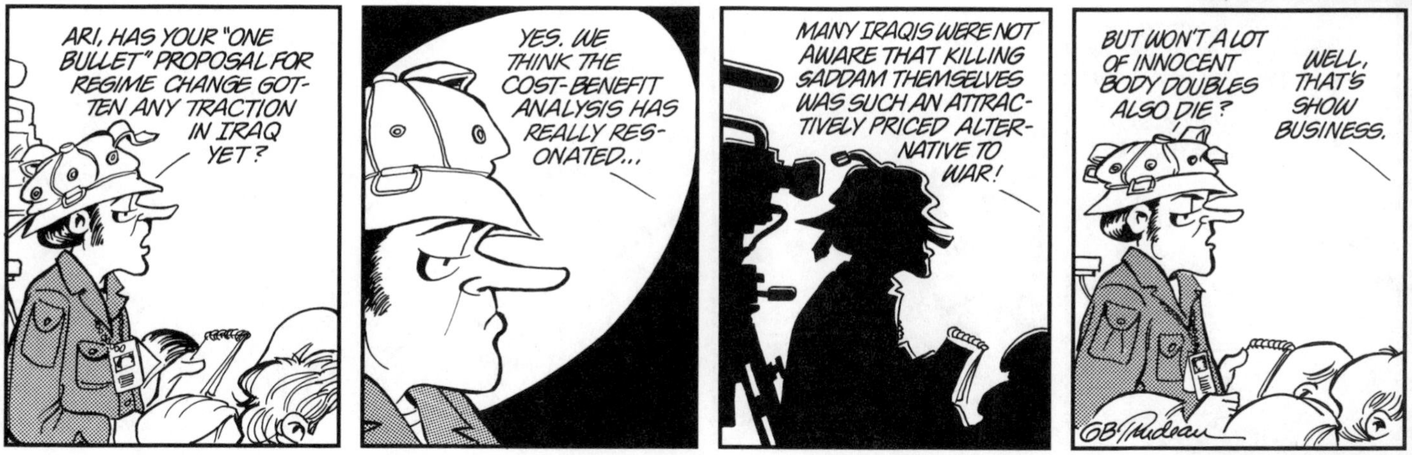
ARI, HAS YOUR "ONE BULLET" PROPOSAL FOR REGIME CHANGE GOTTEN ANY TRACTION IN IRAQ YET?
YES. WE THINK THE COST-BENEFIT ANALYSIS HAS REALLY RESONATED...
MANY IRAQIS WERE NOT AWARE THAT KILLING SADDAM THEMSELVES WAS SUCH AN ATTRACTIVELY PRICED ALTERNATIVE TO WAR!
BUT WON'T A LOT OF INNOCENT BODY DOUBLES ALSO DIE?
WELL, THAT'S SHOW BUSINESS.
GB Trudeau

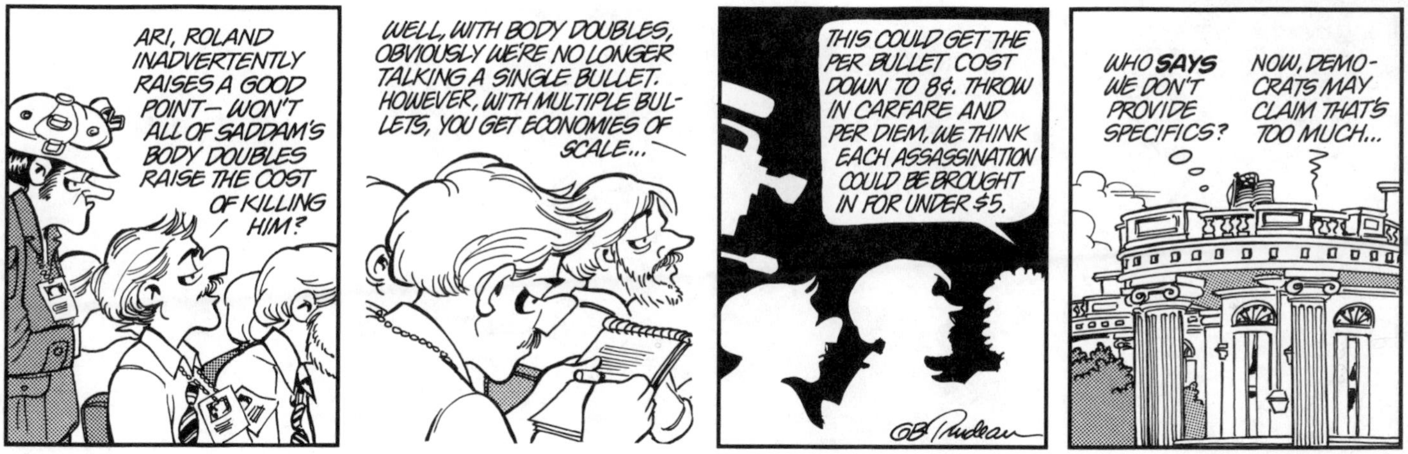
ARI, ROLAND INADVERTENTLY RAISES A GOOD POINT— WON'T ALL OF SADDAM'S BODY DOUBLES RAISE THE COST OF KILLING HIM?
WELL, WITH BODY DOUBLES, OBVIOUSLY WE'RE NO LONGER TALKING A SINGLE BULLET. HOWEVER, WITH MULTIPLE BULLETS, YOU GET ECONOMIES OF SCALE...
THIS COULD GET THE PER BULLET COST DOWN TO 8¢. THROW IN CARFARE AND PER DIEM, WE THINK EACH ASSASSINATION COULD BE BROUGHT IN FOR UNDER $5.
GB Trudeau
WHO **SAYS** WE DON'T PROVIDE SPECIFICS?
NOW, DEMOCRATS MAY CLAIM THAT'S TOO MUCH...

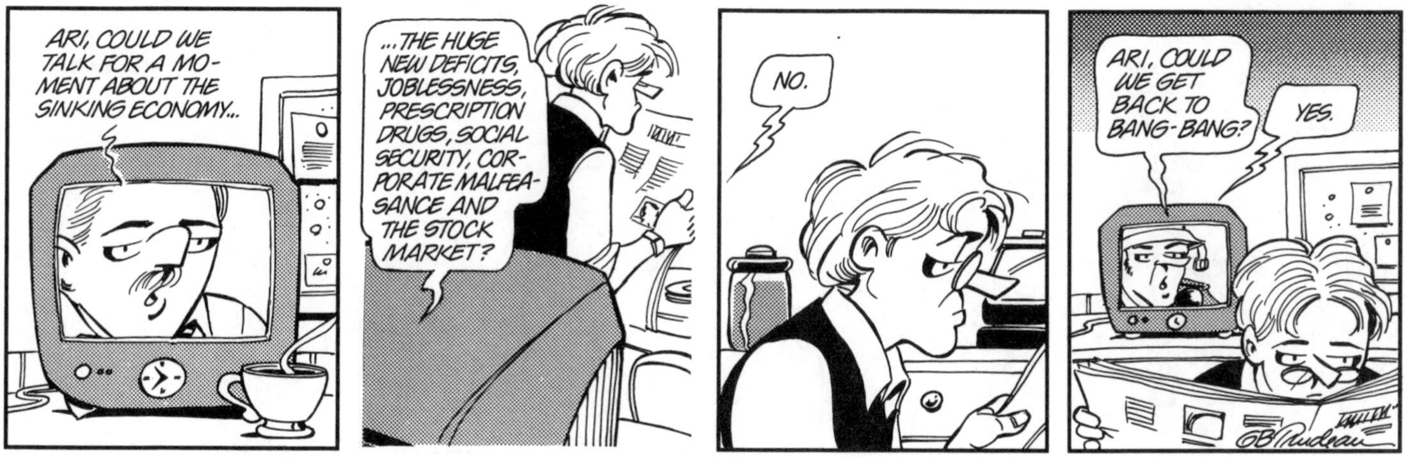
ARI, COULD WE TALK FOR A MOMENT ABOUT THE SINKING ECONOMY...
...THE HUGE NEW DEFICITS, JOBLESSNESS, PRESCRIPTION DRUGS, SOCIAL SECURITY, CORPORATE MALFEASANCE AND THE STOCK MARKET?
NO.
ARI, COULD WE GET BACK TO BANG-BANG?
YES.
GB Trudeau

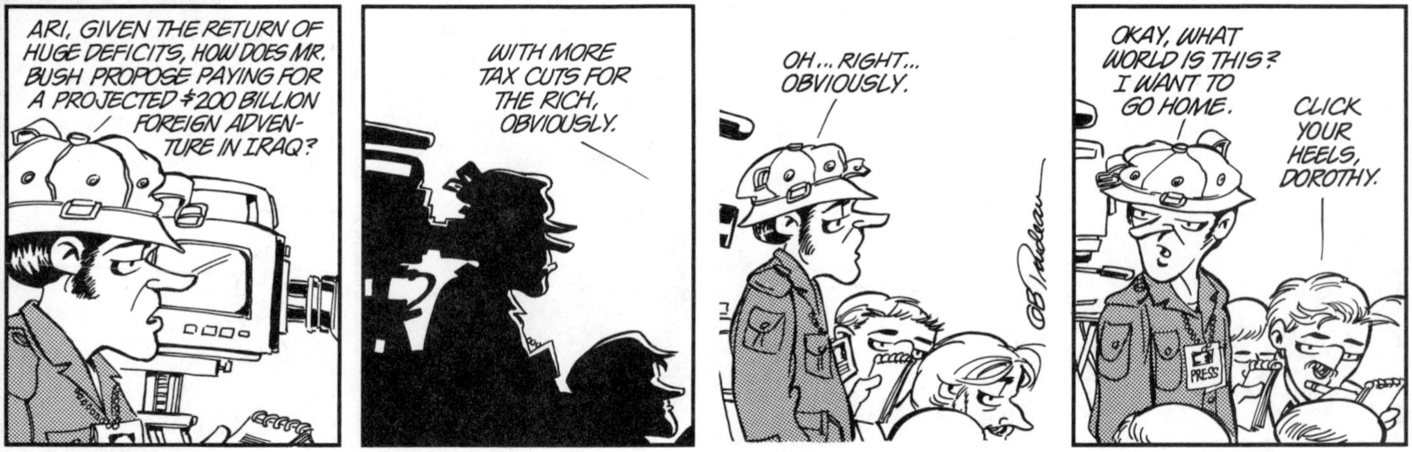
ARI, GIVEN THE RETURN OF HUGE DEFICITS, HOW DOES MR. BUSH PROPOSE PAYING FOR A PROJECTED $200 BILLION FOREIGN ADVENTURE IN IRAQ?
WITH MORE TAX CUTS FOR THE RICH, OBVIOUSLY.
OH... RIGHT... OBVIOUSLY.
OKAY, WHAT WORLD IS THIS? I WANT TO GO HOME.
CLICK YOUR HEELS, DOROTHY.

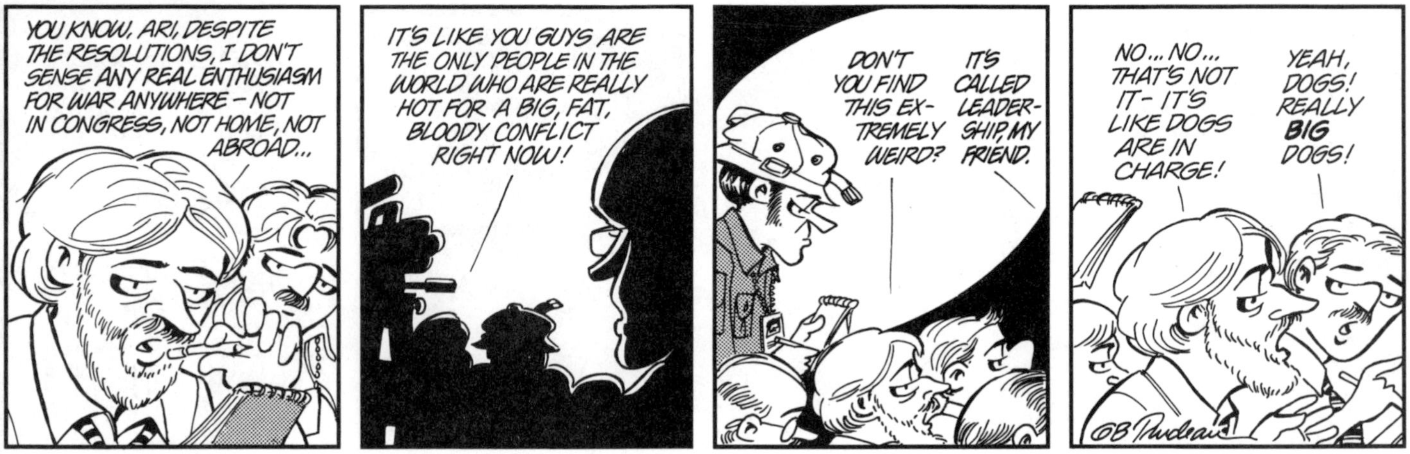
YOU KNOW, ARI, DESPITE THE RESOLUTIONS, I DON'T SENSE ANY REAL ENTHUSIASM FOR WAR ANYWHERE – NOT IN CONGRESS, NOT HOME, NOT ABROAD...
IT'S LIKE YOU GUYS ARE THE ONLY PEOPLE IN THE WORLD WHO ARE REALLY HOT FOR A BIG, FAT, BLOODY CONFLICT RIGHT NOW!
DON'T YOU FIND THIS EXTREMELY WEIRD?
IT'S CALLED LEADERSHIP, MY FRIEND.
NO... NO... THAT'S NOT IT – IT'S LIKE DOGS ARE IN CHARGE!
YEAH, DOGS! REALLY BIG DOGS!

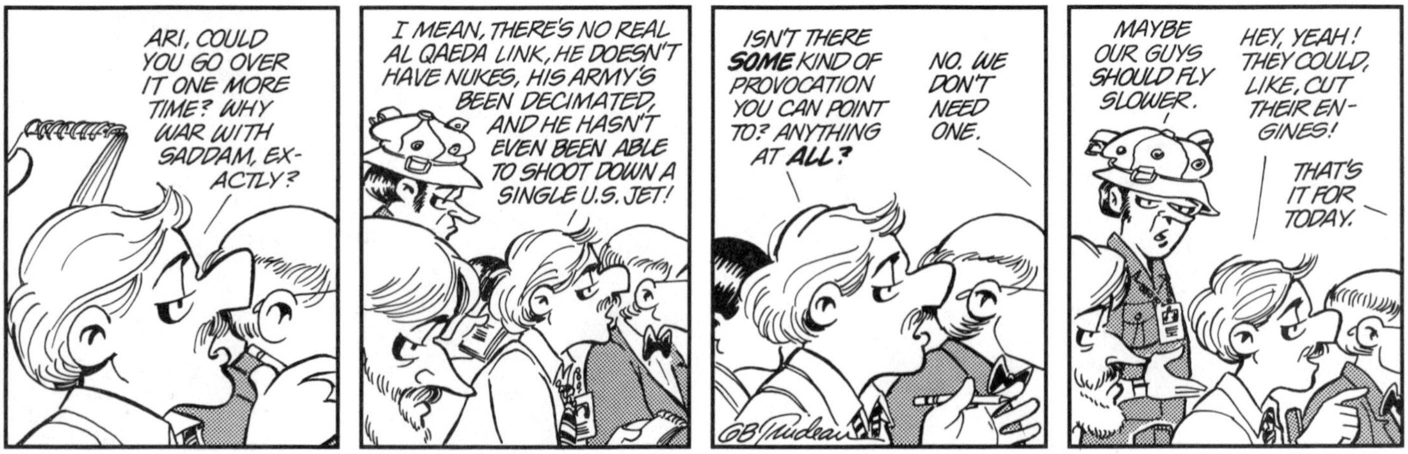
ARI, COULD YOU GO OVER IT ONE MORE TIME? WHY WAR WITH SADDAM, EXACTLY?
I MEAN, THERE'S NO REAL AL QAEDA LINK, HE DOESN'T HAVE NUKES, HIS ARMY'S BEEN DECIMATED, AND HE HASN'T EVEN BEEN ABLE TO SHOOT DOWN A SINGLE U.S. JET!
ISN'T THERE SOME KIND OF PROVOCATION YOU CAN POINT TO? ANYTHING AT ALL?
NO. WE DON'T NEED ONE.
MAYBE OUR GUYS SHOULD FLY SLOWER.
HEY, YEAH! THEY COULD, LIKE, CUT THEIR ENGINES!
THAT'S IT FOR TODAY.

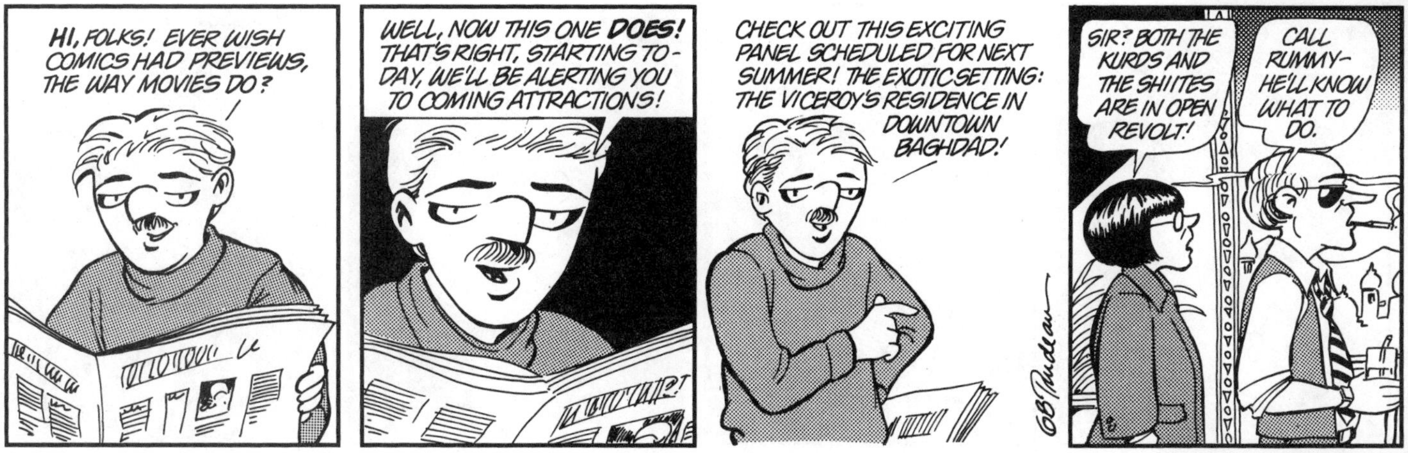
HI, FOLKS! EVER WISH COMICS HAD PREVIEWS, THE WAY MOVIES DO?
WELL, NOW THIS ONE DOES! THAT'S RIGHT, STARTING TO-DAY, WE'LL BE ALERTING YOU TO COMING ATTRACTIONS!
CHECK OUT THIS EXCITING PANEL SCHEDULED FOR NEXT SUMMER! THE EXOTIC SETTING: THE VICEROY'S RESIDENCE IN DOWNTOWN BAGHDAD!
SIR? BOTH THE KURDS AND THE SHIITES ARE IN OPEN REVOLT!
CALL RUMMY-HE'LL KNOW WHAT TO DO.
©BTrudeau

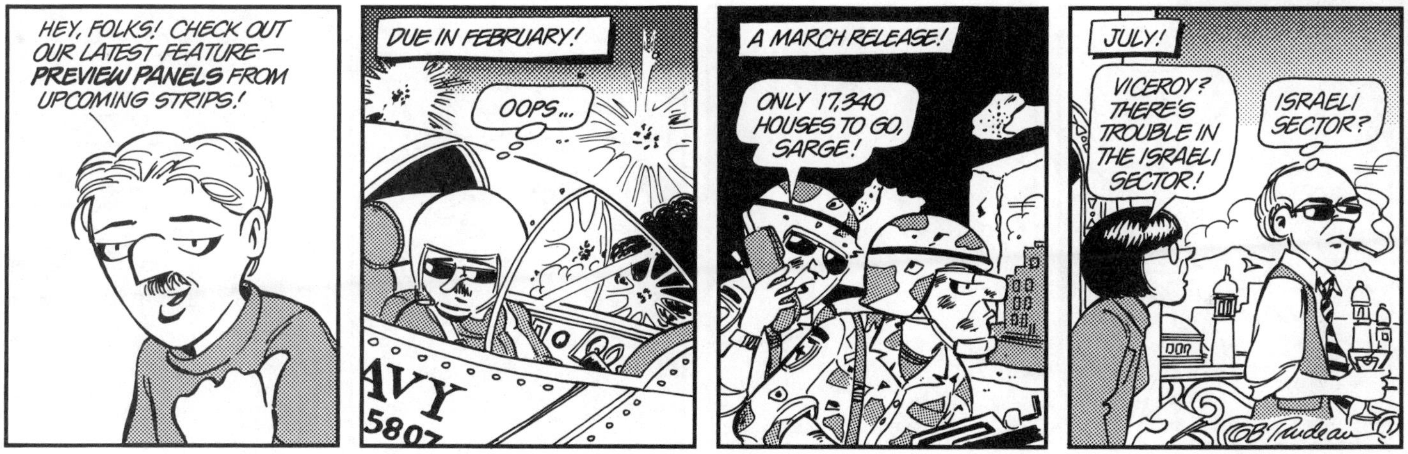
HEY, FOLKS! CHECK OUT OUR LATEST FEATURE—PREVIEW PANELS FROM UPCOMING STRIPS!
DUE IN FEBRUARY!
OOPS...
AVY
5807
A MARCH RELEASE!
ONLY 17,340 HOUSES TO GO, SARGE!
JULY!
VICEROY? THERE'S TROUBLE IN THE ISRAELI SECTOR!
ISRAELI SECTOR?
©BTrudeau

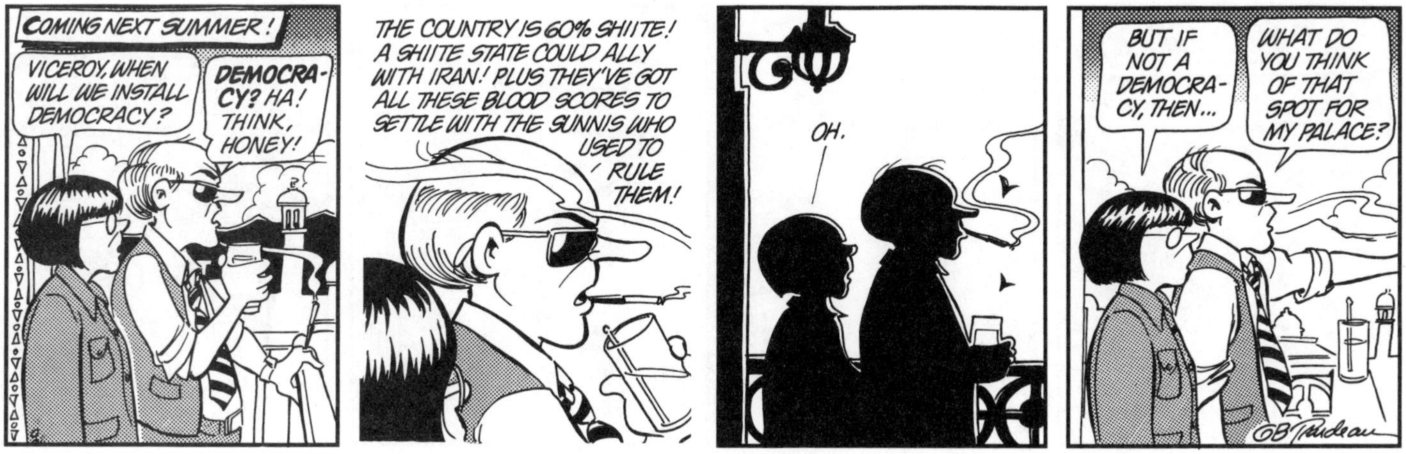
COMING NEXT SUMMER!
VICEROY, WHEN WILL WE INSTALL DEMOCRACY?
DEMOCRA-CY? HA! THINK, HONEY!
THE COUNTRY IS 60% SHIITE! A SHIITE STATE COULD ALLY WITH IRAN! PLUS THEY'VE GOT ALL THESE BLOOD SCORES TO SETTLE WITH THE SUNNIS WHO USED TO RULE THEM!
OH.
BUT IF NOT A DEMOCRA-CY, THEN...
WHAT DO YOU THINK OF THAT SPOT FOR MY PALACE?
©BTrudeau

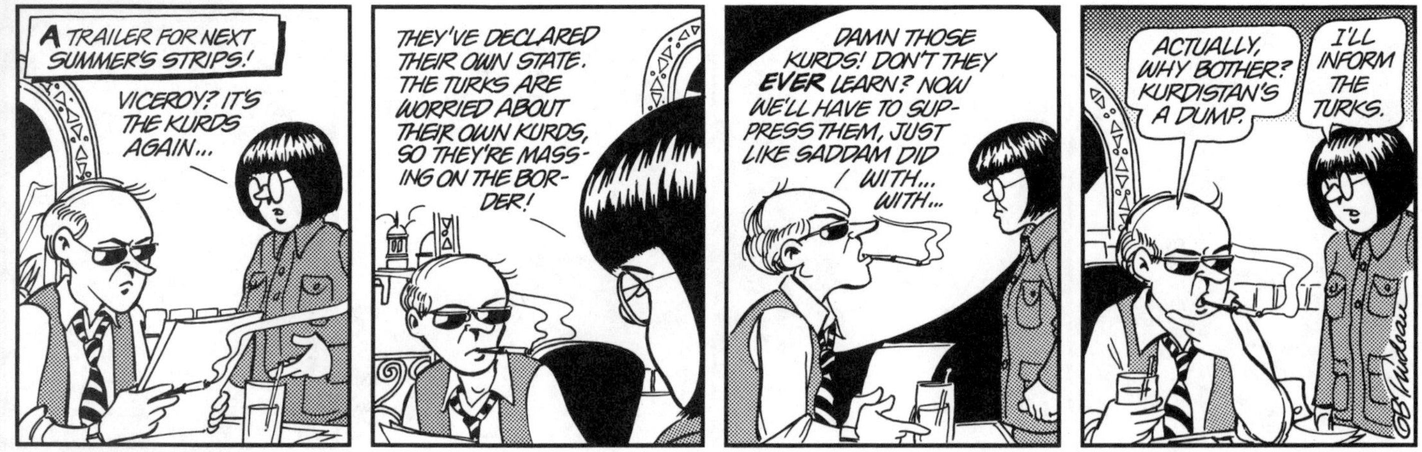
A TRAILER FOR NEXT SUMMER'S STRIPS!
VICEROY? IT'S THE KURDS AGAIN...
THEY'VE DECLARED THEIR OWN STATE. THE TURKS ARE WORRIED ABOUT THEIR OWN KURDS, SO THEY'RE MASSING ON THE BORDER!
DAMN THOSE KURDS! DON'T THEY EVER LEARN? NOW WE'LL HAVE TO SUPPRESS THEM, JUST LIKE SADDAM DID WITH... WITH...
ACTUALLY, WHY BOTHER? KURDISTAN'S A DUMP.
I'LL INFORM THE TURKS.

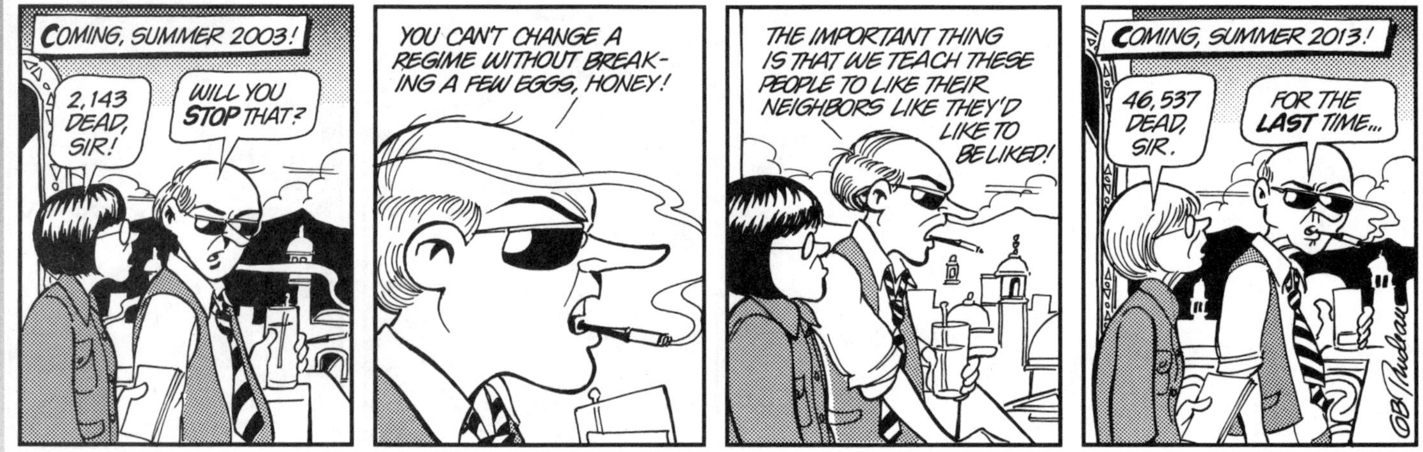
COMING, SUMMER 2003!
2,143 DEAD, SIR!
WILL YOU STOP THAT?
YOU CAN'T CHANGE A REGIME WITHOUT BREAKING A FEW EGGS, HONEY!
THE IMPORTANT THING IS THAT WE TEACH THESE PEOPLE TO LIKE THEIR NEIGHBORS LIKE THEY'D LIKE TO BE LIKED!
COMING, SUMMER 2013!
46,537 DEAD, SIR.
FOR THE LAST TIME...

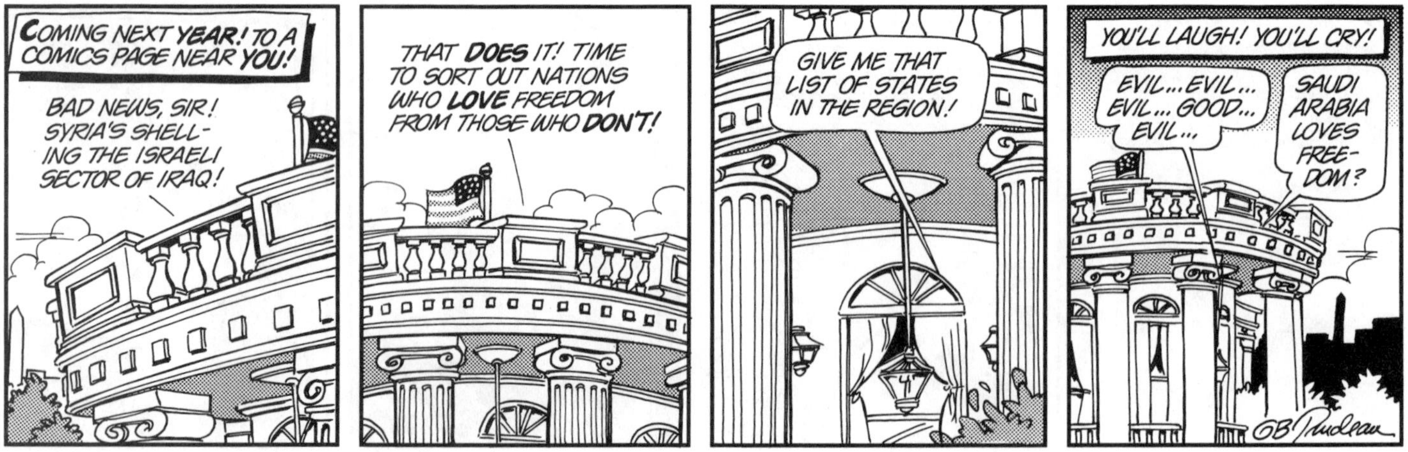
COMING NEXT YEAR! TO A COMICS PAGE NEAR YOU!
BAD NEWS, SIR! SYRIA'S SHELLING THE ISRAELI SECTOR OF IRAQ!
THAT DOES IT! TIME TO SORT OUT NATIONS WHO LOVE FREEDOM FROM THOSE WHO DON'T!
GIVE ME THAT LIST OF STATES IN THE REGION!
YOU'LL LAUGH! YOU'LL CRY!
EVIL... EVIL... EVIL... GOOD... EVIL...,
SAUDI ARABIA LOVES FREEDOM?

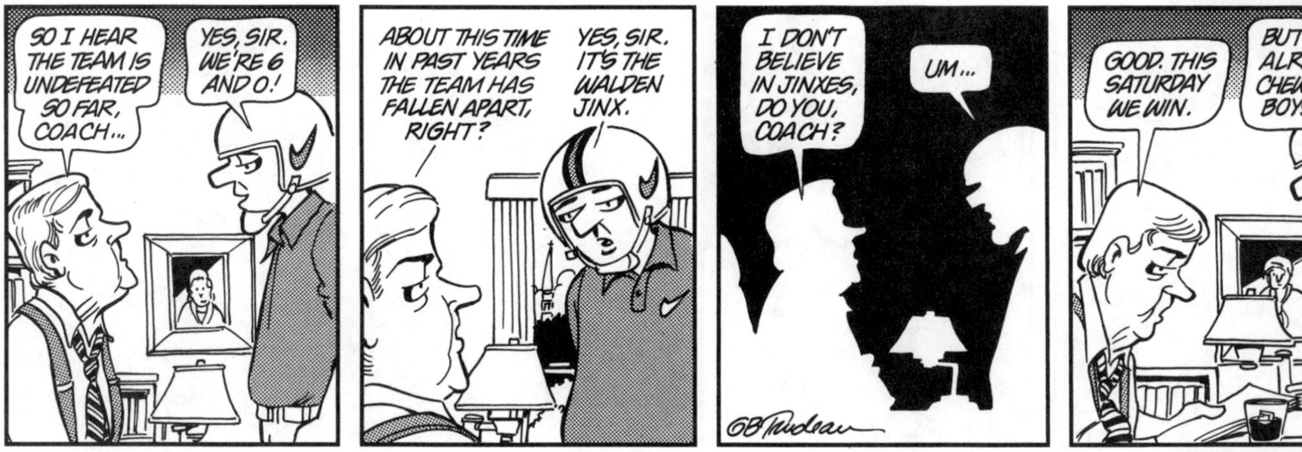
SO I HEAR THE TEAM IS UNDEFEATED SO FAR, COACH...
YES, SIR. WE'RE 6 AND 0.!
ABOUT THIS TIME IN PAST YEARS THE TEAM HAS FALLEN APART, RIGHT?
YES, SIR. IT'S THE WALDEN JINX.
I DON'T BELIEVE IN JINXES, DO YOU, COACH?
UM...
GOOD. THIS SATURDAY WE WIN.
BUT I'VE ALREADY CHEWED THE BOYS OUT.

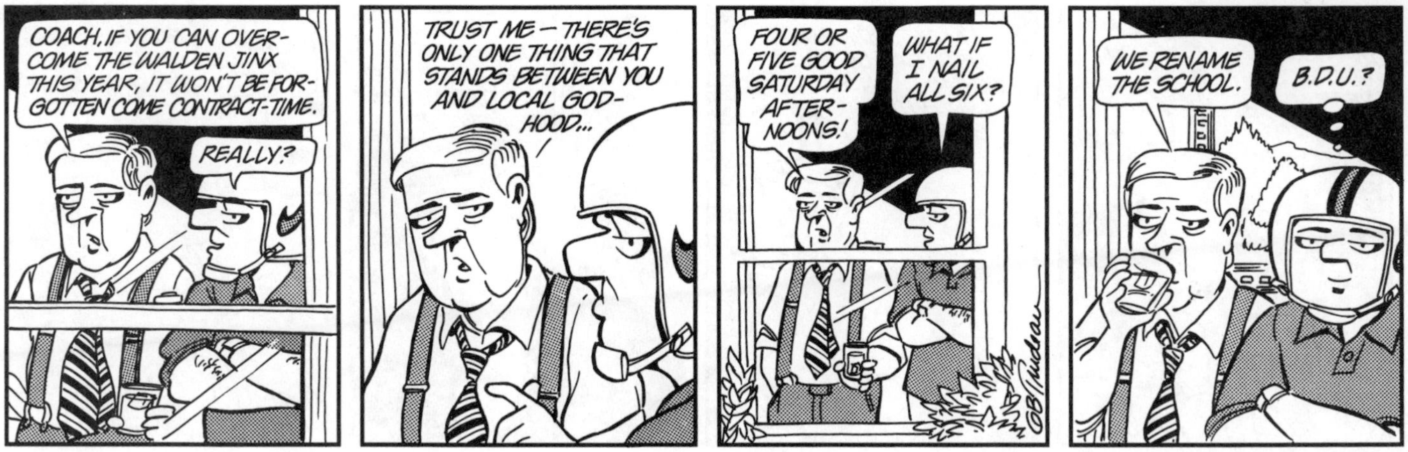
COACH, IF YOU CAN OVERCOME THE WALDEN JINX THIS YEAR, IT WON'T BE FORGOTTEN COME CONTRACT-TIME.
REALLY?
TRUST ME — THERE'S ONLY ONE THING THAT STANDS BETWEEN YOU AND LOCAL GODHOOD...
FOUR OR FIVE GOOD SATURDAY AFTERNOONS!
WHAT IF I NAIL ALL SIX?
WE RENAME THE SCHOOL.
B.D.U.?

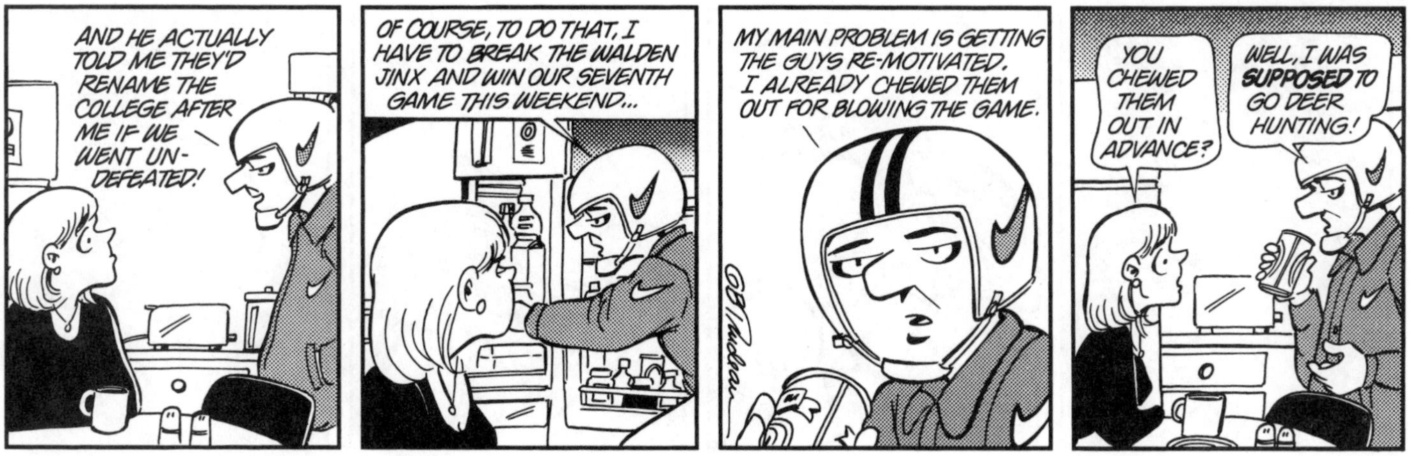
AND HE ACTUALLY TOLD ME THEY'D RENAME THE COLLEGE AFTER ME IF WE WENT UNDEFEATED!
OF COURSE, TO DO THAT, I HAVE TO BREAK THE WALDEN JINX AND WIN OUR SEVENTH GAME THIS WEEKEND...
MY MAIN PROBLEM IS GETTING THE GUYS RE-MOTIVATED. I ALREADY CHEWED THEM OUT FOR BLOWING THE GAME.
YOU CHEWED THEM OUT IN ADVANCE?
WELL, I WAS SUPPOSED TO GO DEER HUNTING!

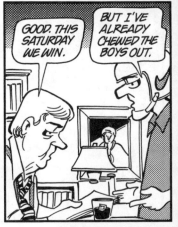

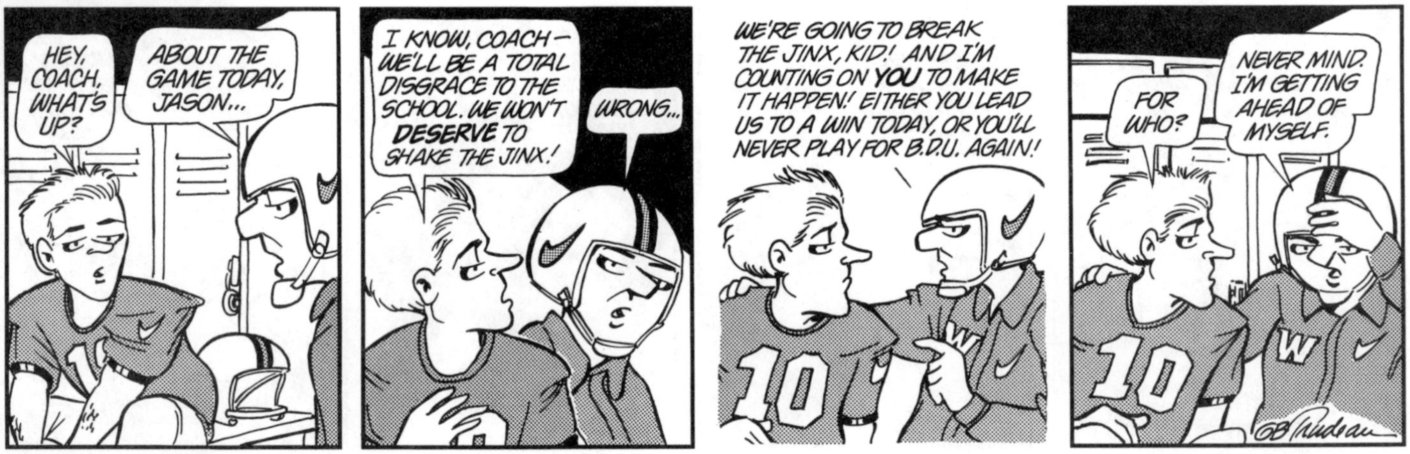
HEY, COACH, WHAT'S UP?
ABOUT THE GAME TODAY, JASON...
I KNOW, COACH— WE'LL BE A TOTAL DISGRACE TO THE SCHOOL. WE WON'T DESERVE TO SHAKE THE JINX!
WRONG...
WE'RE GOING TO BREAK THE JINX, KID! AND I'M COUNTING ON YOU TO MAKE IT HAPPEN! EITHER YOU LEAD US TO A WIN TODAY, OR YOU'LL NEVER PLAY FOR B.D.U. AGAIN!
FOR WHO?
NEVER MIND. I'M GETTING AHEAD OF MYSELF.
©B Trudeau

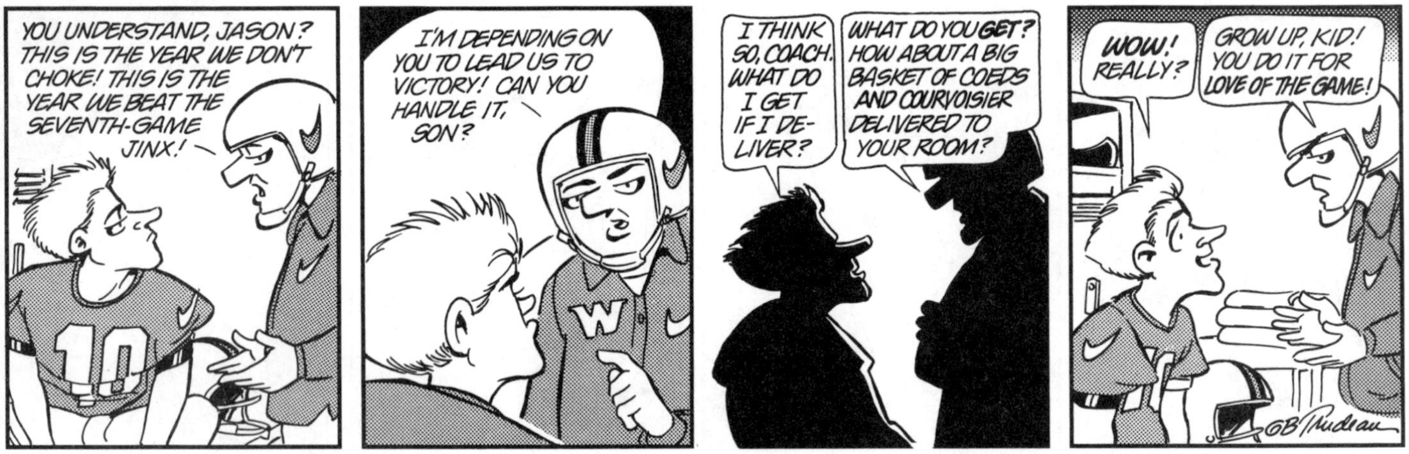
YOU UNDERSTAND, JASON? THIS IS THE YEAR WE DON'T CHOKE! THIS IS THE YEAR WE BEAT THE SEVENTH-GAME JINX!
I'M DEPENDING ON YOU TO LEAD US TO VICTORY! CAN YOU HANDLE IT, SON?
I THINK SO, COACH. WHAT DO I GET IF I DELIVER?
WHAT DO YOU GET? HOW ABOUT A BIG BASKET OF COEDS AND COURVOISIER DELIVERED TO YOUR ROOM?
WOW! REALLY?
GROW UP, KID! YOU DO IT FOR LOVE OF THE GAME!
©B Trudeau

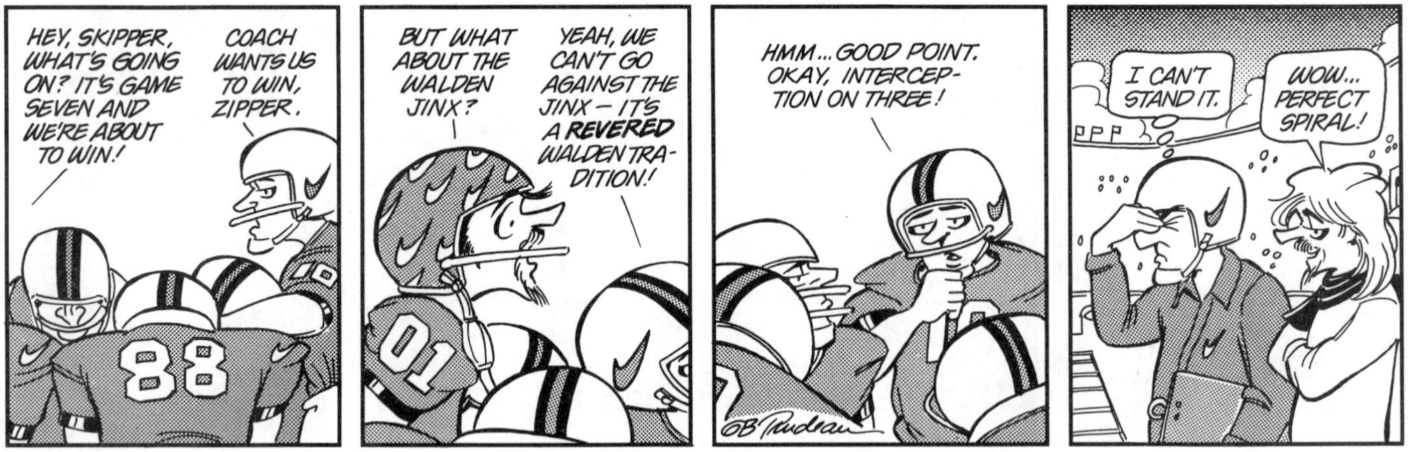
HEY, SKIPPER, WHAT'S GOING ON? IT'S GAME SEVEN AND WE'RE ABOUT TO WIN!
COACH WANTS US TO WIN, ZIPPER.
BUT WHAT ABOUT THE WALDEN JINX?
YEAH, WE CAN'T GO AGAINST THE JINX— IT'S A REVERED WALDEN TRADITION!
HMM... GOOD POINT. OKAY, INTERCEPTION ON THREE!
©B Trudeau
I CAN'T STAND IT.
WOW... PERFECT SPIRAL!

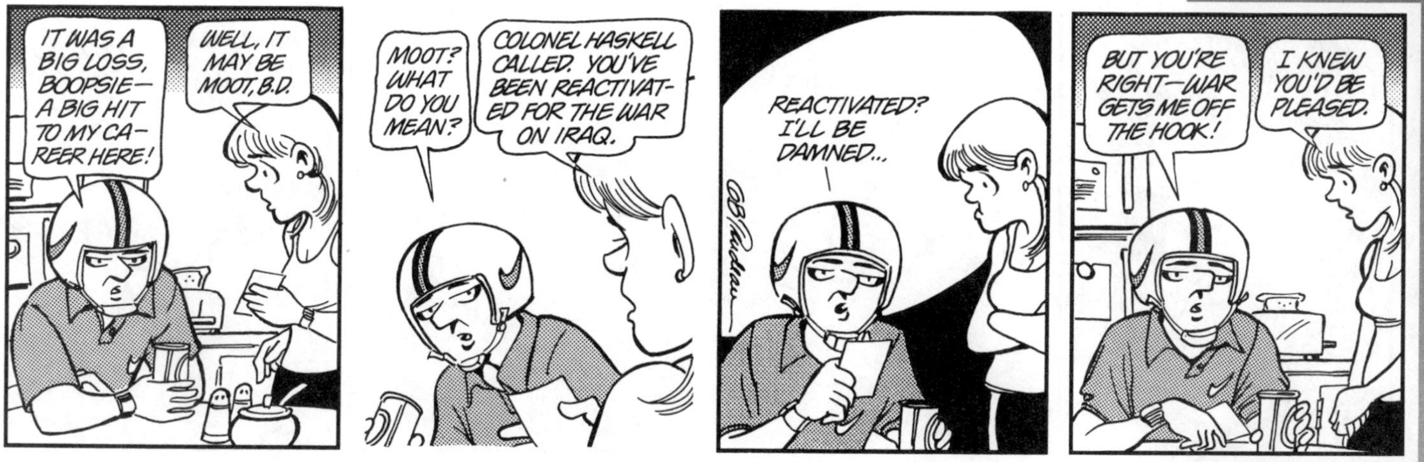
IT WAS A BIG LOSS, BOOPSIE— A BIG HIT TO MY CA-REER HERE!
WELL, IT MAY BE MOOT, B.D.
MOOT? WHAT DO YOU MEAN?
COLONEL HASKELL CALLED. YOU'VE BEEN REACTIVAT-ED FOR THE WAR ON IRAQ.
REACTIVATED? I'LL BE DAMNED...
BUT YOU'RE RIGHT—WAR GETS ME OFF THE HOOK!
I KNEW YOU'D BE PLEASED.

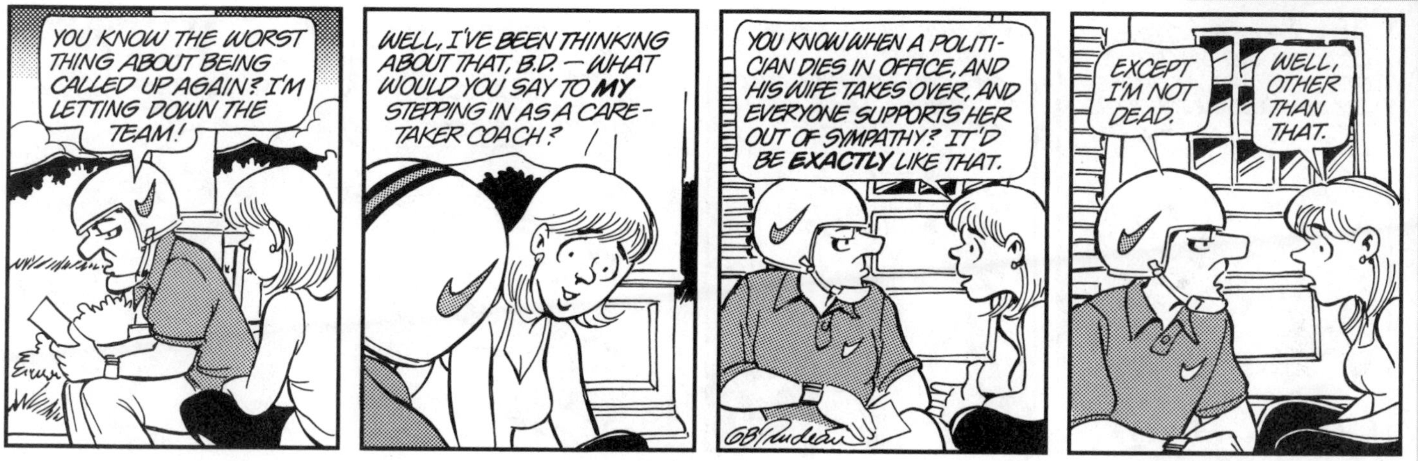
YOU KNOW THE WORST THING ABOUT BEING CALLED UP AGAIN? I'M LETTING DOWN THE TEAM!
WELL, I'VE BEEN THINKING ABOUT THAT, B.D.—WHAT WOULD YOU SAY TO MY STEPPING IN AS A CARE-TAKER COACH?
YOU KNOW WHEN A POLITI-CIAN DIES IN OFFICE, AND HIS WIFE TAKES OVER, AND EVERYONE SUPPORTS HER OUT OF SYMPATHY? IT'D BE EXACTLY LIKE THAT.
EXCEPT I'M NOT DEAD.
WELL, OTHER THAN THAT.

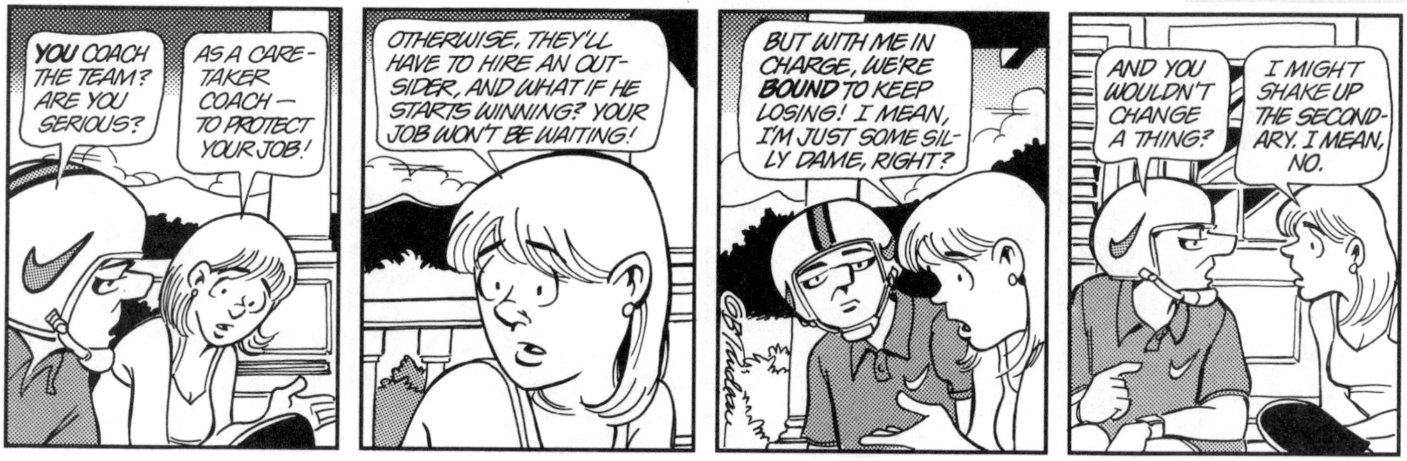
YOU COACH THE TEAM? ARE YOU SERIOUS?
AS A CARE-TAKER COACH— TO PROTECT YOUR JOB!
OTHERWISE, THEY'LL HAVE TO HIRE AN OUT-SIDER, AND WHAT IF HE STARTS WINNING? YOUR JOB WON'T BE WAITING!
BUT WITH ME IN CHARGE, WE'RE BOUND TO KEEP LOSING! I MEAN, I'M JUST SOME SIL-LY DAME, RIGHT?
AND YOU WOULDN'T CHANGE A THING?
I MIGHT SHAKE UP THE SECOND-ARY. I MEAN, NO.

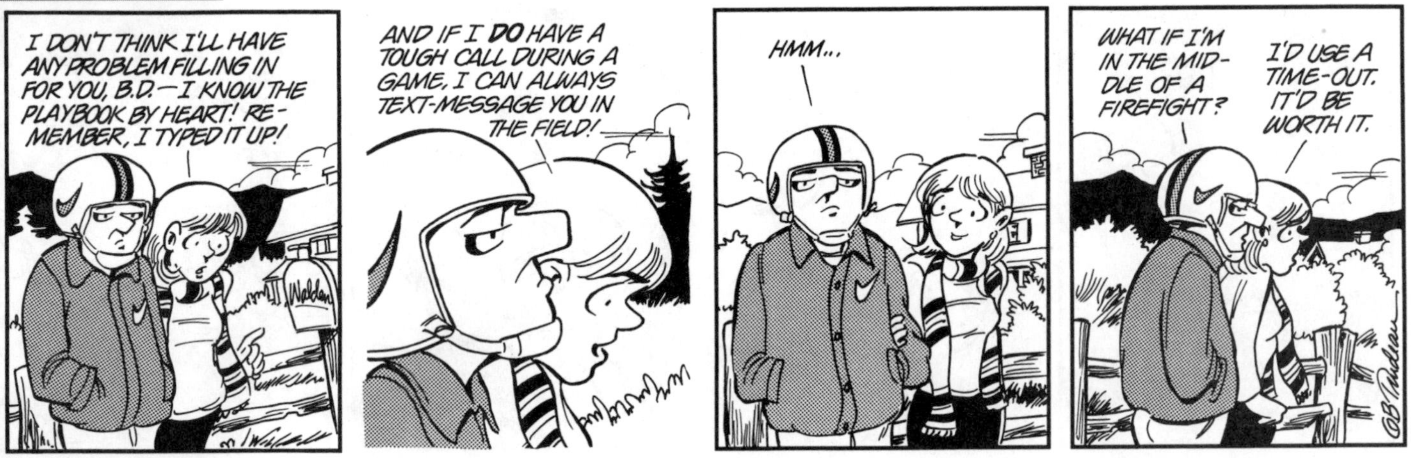
I DON'T THINK I'LL HAVE ANY PROBLEM FILLING IN FOR YOU, B.D.—I KNOW THE PLAYBOOK BY HEART! REMEMBER, I TYPED IT UP!
AND IF I **DO** HAVE A TOUGH CALL DURING A GAME, I CAN ALWAYS TEXT-MESSAGE YOU IN THE FIELD!
HMM...
WHAT IF I'M IN THE MIDDLE OF A FIREFIGHT?
I'D USE A TIME-OUT. IT'D BE WORTH IT.

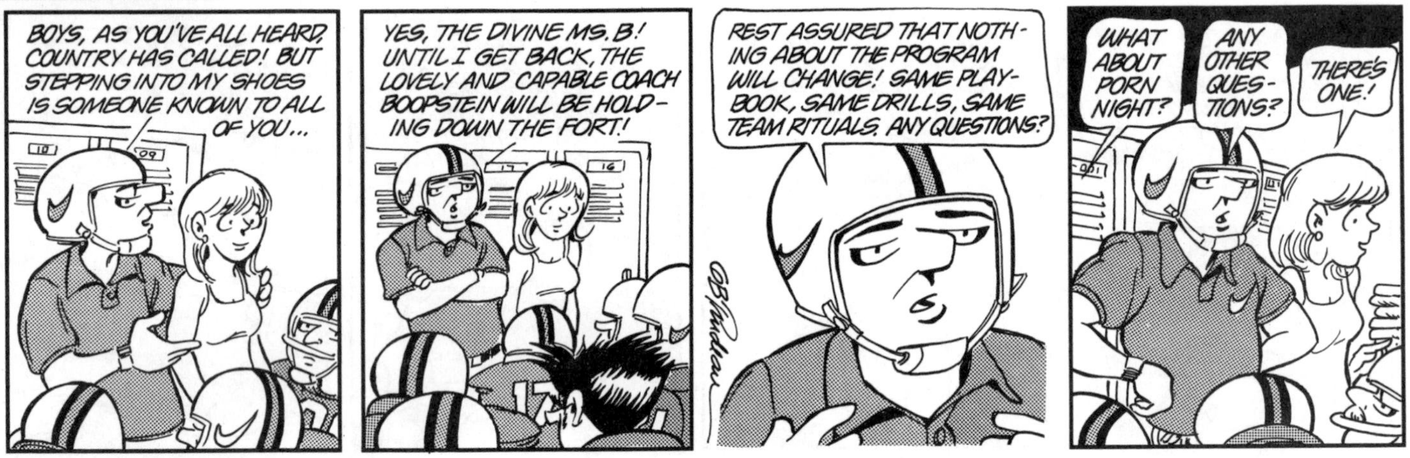
BOYS, AS YOU'VE ALL HEARD, COUNTRY HAS CALLED! BUT STEPPING INTO MY SHOES IS SOMEONE KNOWN TO ALL OF YOU...
YES, THE DIVINE MS. B.! UNTIL I GET BACK, THE LOVELY AND CAPABLE COACH BOOPSTEIN WILL BE HOLDING DOWN THE FORT!
REST ASSURED THAT NOTHING ABOUT THE PROGRAM WILL CHANGE! SAME PLAYBOOK, SAME DRILLS, SAME TEAM RITUALS. ANY QUESTIONS?
WHAT ABOUT PORN NIGHT?
ANY OTHER QUESTIONS?
THERE'S ONE!

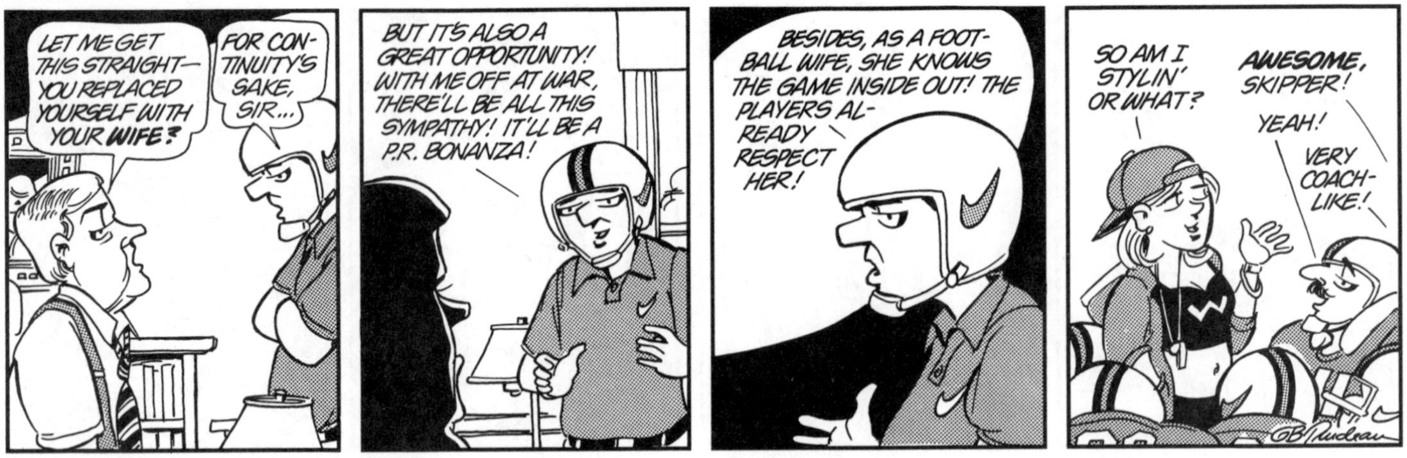
LET ME GET THIS STRAIGHT—YOU REPLACED YOURSELF WITH YOUR **WIFE?**
FOR CONTINUITY'S SAKE, SIR...
BUT IT'S ALSO A GREAT OPPORTUNITY! WITH ME OFF AT WAR, THERE'LL BE ALL THIS SYMPATHY! IT'LL BE A P.R. BONANZA!
BESIDES, AS A FOOTBALL WIFE, SHE KNOWS THE GAME INSIDE OUT! THE PLAYERS ALREADY RESPECT HER!
SO AM I STYLIN' OR WHAT?
AWESOME, SKIPPER!
YEAH!
VERY COACH-LIKE!

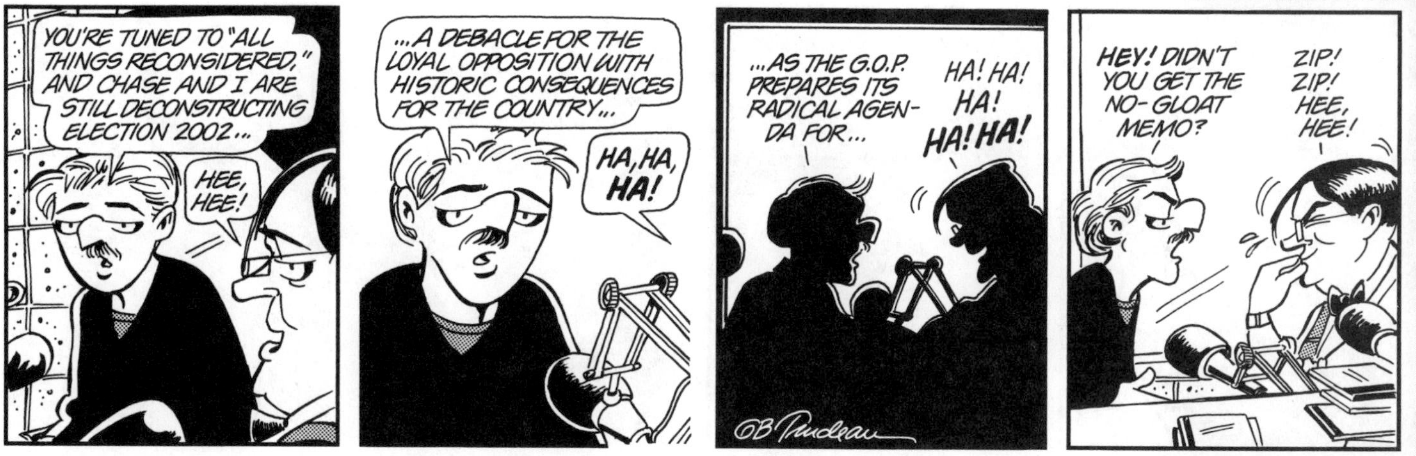
YOU'RE TUNED TO "ALL THINGS RECONSIDERED," AND CHASE AND I ARE STILL DECONSTRUCTING ELECTION 2002...
HEE, HEE!
...A DEBACLE FOR THE LOYAL OPPOSITION WITH HISTORIC CONSEQUENCES FOR THE COUNTRY...
HA, HA, HA!
...AS THE G.O.P. PREPARES ITS RADICAL AGENDA FOR...
HA! HA! HA! HA! HA!
HEY! DIDN'T YOU GET THE NO-GLOAT MEMO?
ZIP! ZIP! HEE, HEE!

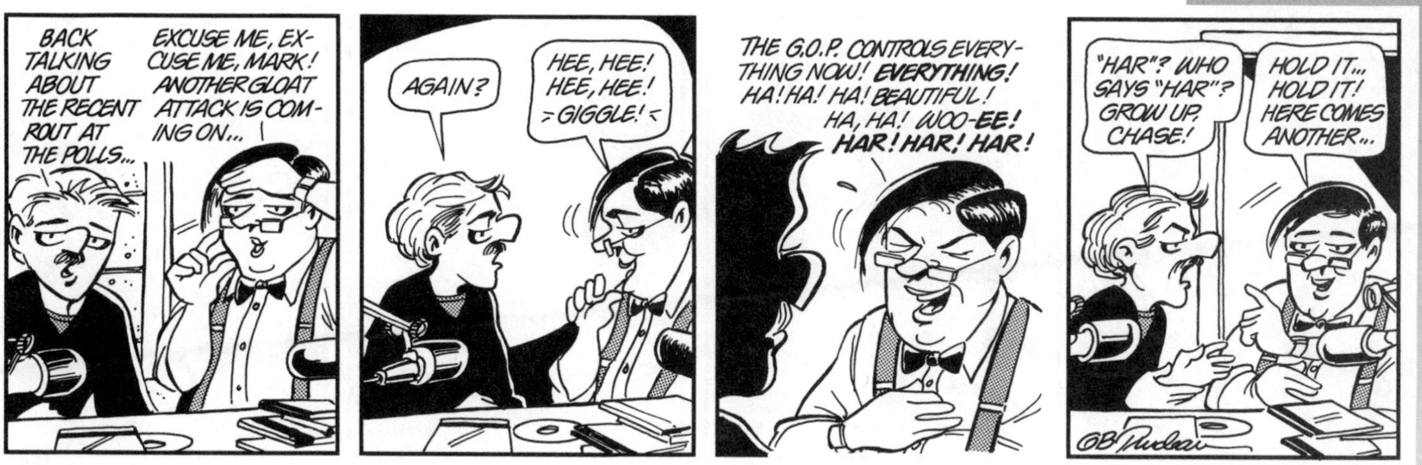
BACK TALKING ABOUT THE RECENT ROUT AT THE POLLS...
EXCUSE ME, EXCUSE ME, MARK! ANOTHER GLOAT ATTACK IS COMING ON...
AGAIN?
HEE, HEE! HEE, HEE! GIGGLE!
THE G.O.P. CONTROLS EVERYTHING NOW! EVERYTHING! HA! HA! HA! BEAUTIFUL! HA, HA! WOO-EE! HAR! HAR! HAR!
"HAR"? WHO SAYS "HAR"? GROW UP, CHASE!
HOLD IT... HOLD IT! HERE COMES ANOTHER...

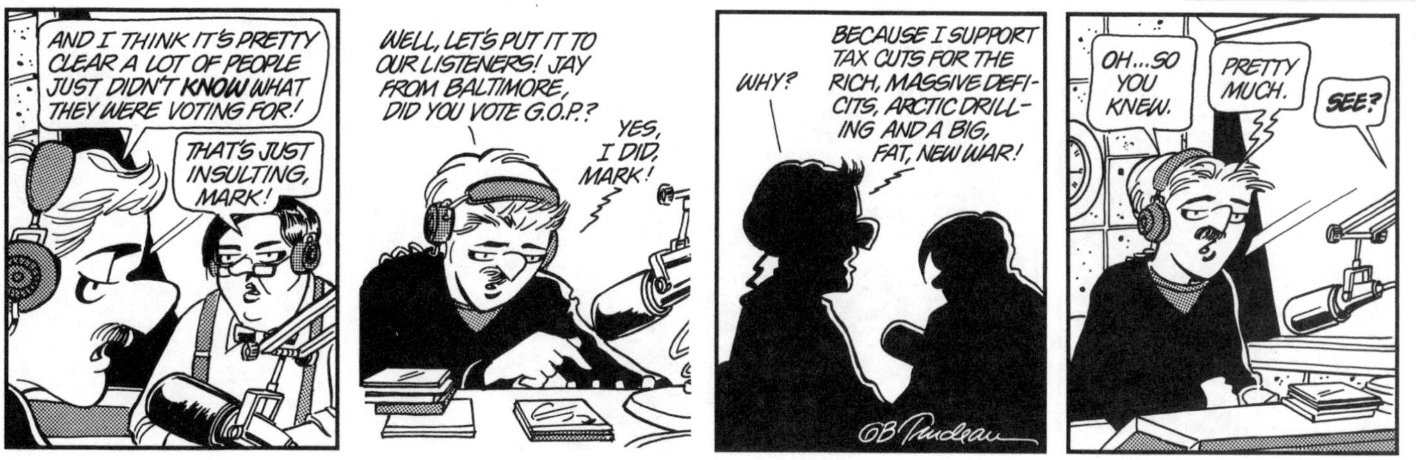
AND I THINK IT'S PRETTY CLEAR A LOT OF PEOPLE JUST DIDN'T KNOW WHAT THEY WERE VOTING FOR!
THAT'S JUST INSULTING, MARK!
WELL, LET'S PUT IT TO OUR LISTENERS! JAY FROM BALTIMORE, DID YOU VOTE G.O.P.?
YES, I DID, MARK!
WHY?
BECAUSE I SUPPORT TAX CUTS FOR THE RICH, MASSIVE DEFICITS, ARCTIC DRILLING AND A BIG, FAT, NEW WAR!
OH...SO YOU KNEW.
PRETTY MUCH.
SEE?

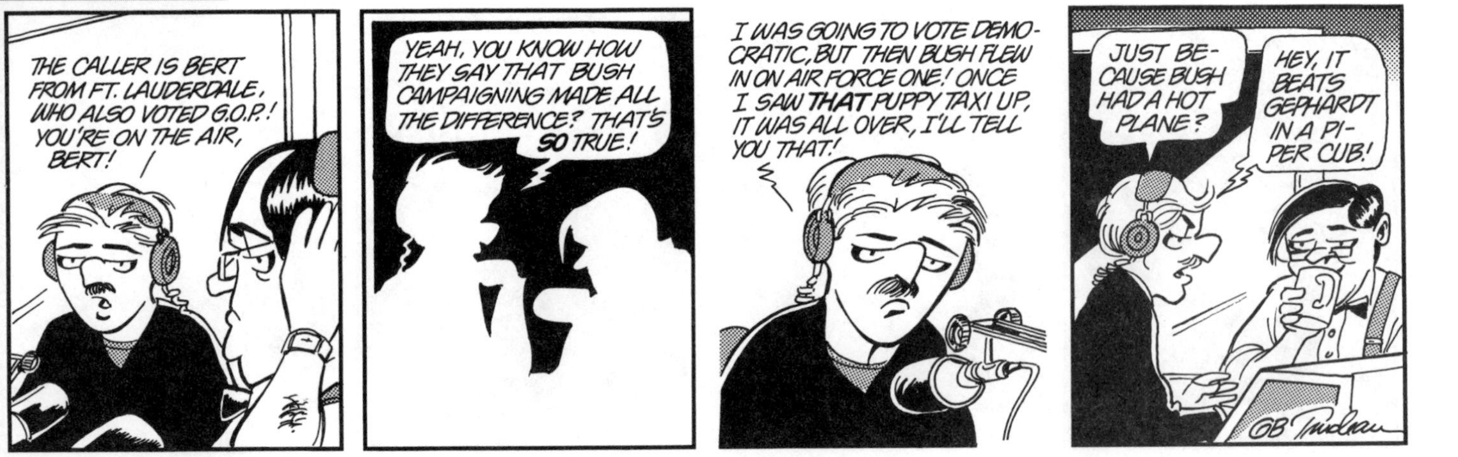
THE CALLER IS BERT FROM FT. LAUDERDALE, WHO ALSO VOTED G.O.P.! YOU'RE ON THE AIR, BERT!
YEAH, YOU KNOW HOW THEY SAY THAT BUSH CAMPAIGNING MADE ALL THE DIFFERENCE? THAT'S SO TRUE!
I WAS GOING TO VOTE DEMOCRATIC, BUT THEN BUSH FLEW IN ON AIR FORCE ONE! ONCE I SAW THAT PUPPY TAXI UP, IT WAS ALL OVER, I'LL TELL YOU THAT!
JUST BECAUSE BUSH HAD A HOT PLANE?
HEY, IT BEATS GEPHARDT IN A PIPER CUB!
GB Trudeau

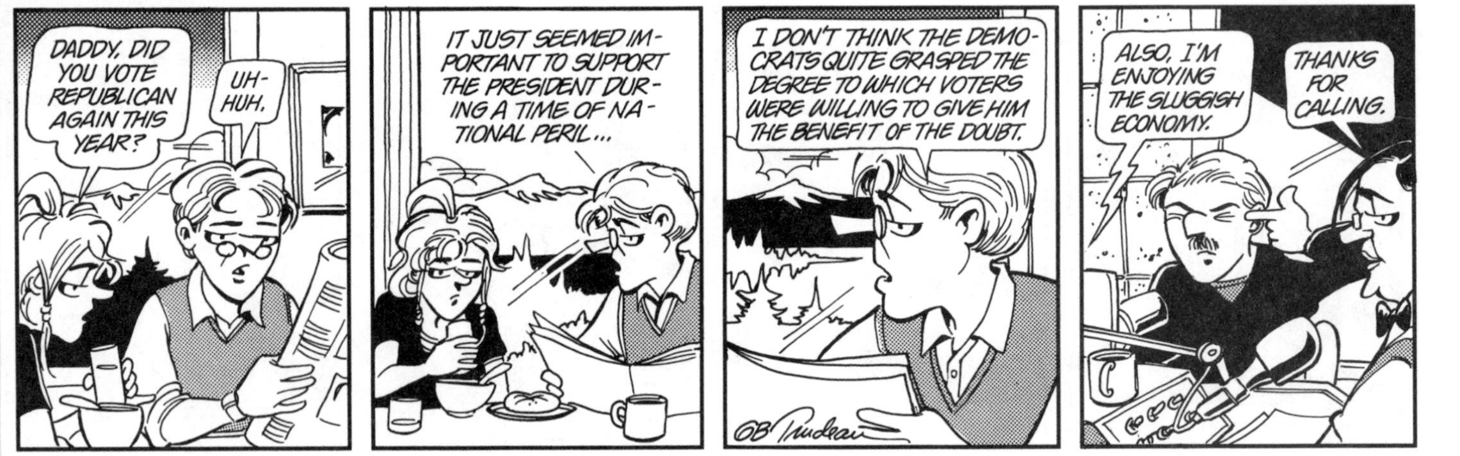
DADDY, DID YOU VOTE REPUBLICAN AGAIN THIS YEAR?
UH-HUH.
IT JUST SEEMED IMPORTANT TO SUPPORT THE PRESIDENT DURING A TIME OF NATIONAL PERIL...
I DON'T THINK THE DEMOCRATS QUITE GRASPED THE DEGREE TO WHICH VOTERS WERE WILLING TO GIVE HIM THE BENEFIT OF THE DOUBT.
GB Trudeau
ALSO, I'M ENJOYING THE SLUGGISH ECONOMY.
THANKS FOR CALLING.

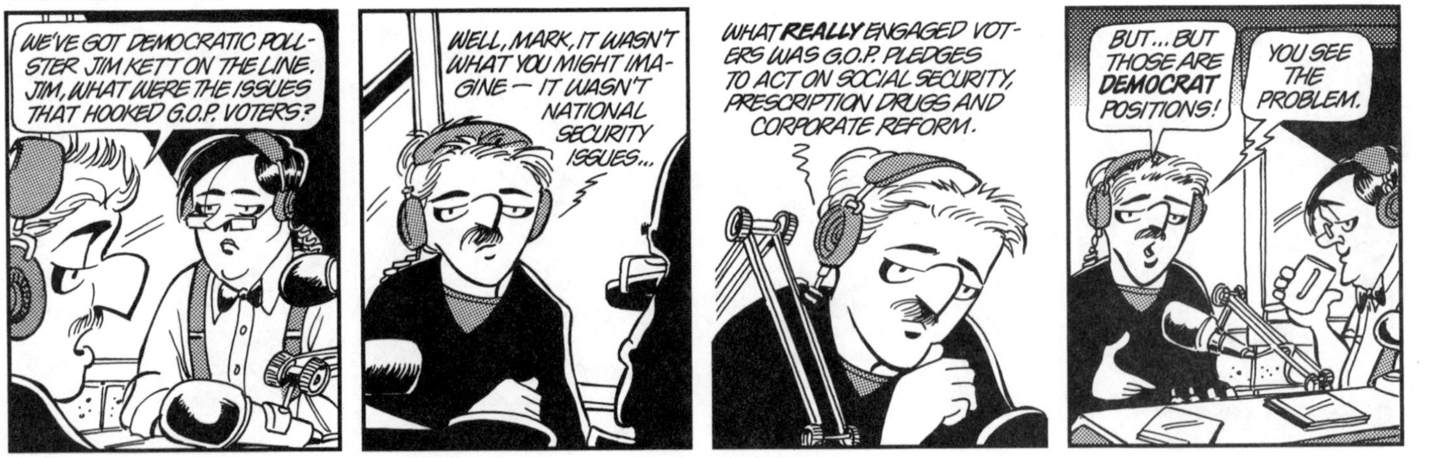
WE'VE GOT DEMOCRATIC POLLSTER JIM KETT ON THE LINE. JIM, WHAT WERE THE ISSUES THAT HOOKED G.O.P. VOTERS?
WELL, MARK, IT WASN'T WHAT YOU MIGHT IMAGINE — IT WASN'T NATIONAL SECURITY ISSUES...
WHAT REALLY ENGAGED VOTERS WAS G.O.P. PLEDGES TO ACT ON SOCIAL SECURITY, PRESCRIPTION DRUGS AND CORPORATE REFORM.
BUT... BUT THOSE ARE DEMOCRAT POSITIONS!
YOU SEE THE PROBLEM.

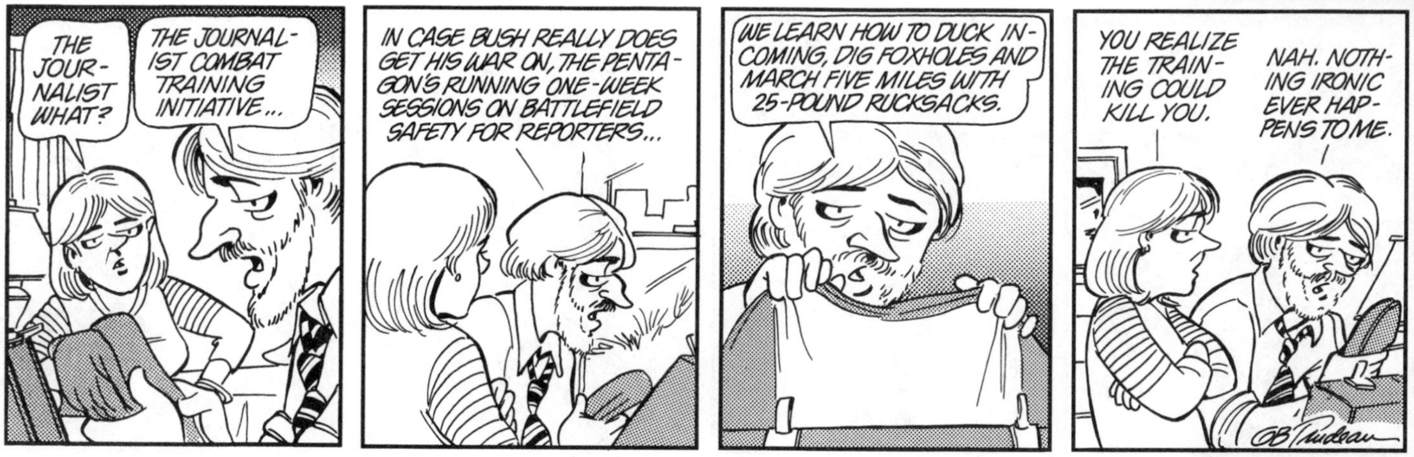
THE JOURNALIST WHAT?
THE JOURNALIST COMBAT TRAINING INITIATIVE...
IN CASE BUSH REALLY DOES GET HIS WAR ON, THE PENTAGON'S RUNNING ONE-WEEK SESSIONS ON BATTLEFIELD SAFETY FOR REPORTERS...
WE LEARN HOW TO DUCK INCOMING, DIG FOXHOLES AND MARCH FIVE MILES WITH 25-POUND RUCKSACKS.
YOU REALIZE THE TRAINING COULD KILL YOU.
NAH. NOTHING IRONIC EVER HAPPENS TO ME.

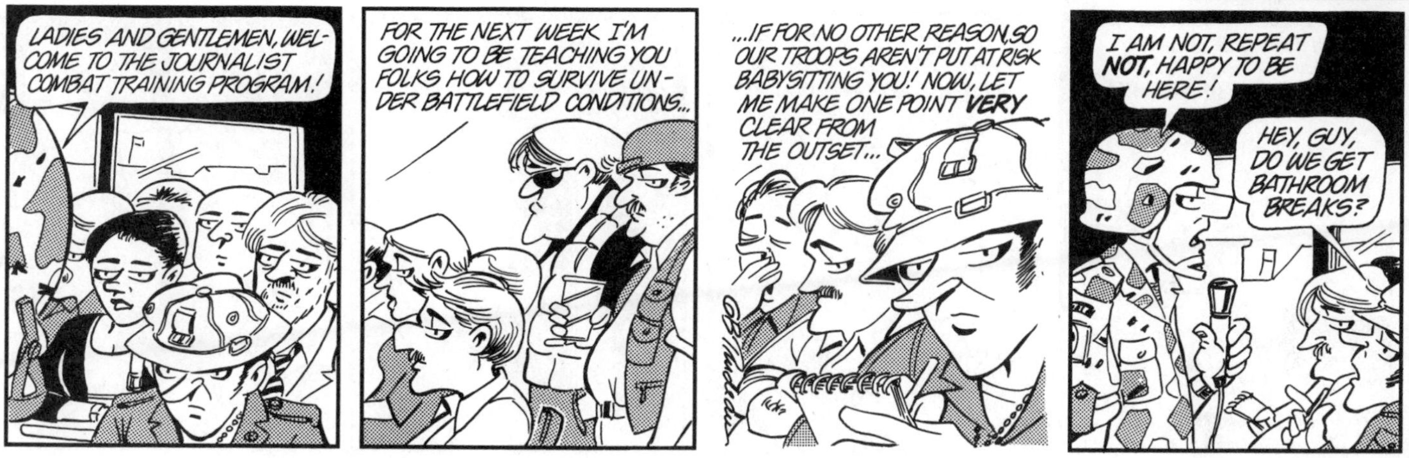
LADIES AND GENTLEMEN, WELCOME TO THE JOURNALIST COMBAT TRAINING PROGRAM!
FOR THE NEXT WEEK I'M GOING TO BE TEACHING YOU FOLKS HOW TO SURVIVE UNDER BATTLEFIELD CONDITIONS...
...IF FOR NO OTHER REASON, SO OUR TROOPS AREN'T PUT AT RISK BABYSITTING YOU! NOW, LET ME MAKE ONE POINT **VERY** CLEAR FROM THE OUTSET...
I AM NOT, REPEAT **NOT**, HAPPY TO BE HERE!
HEY, GUY, DO WE GET BATHROOM BREAKS?

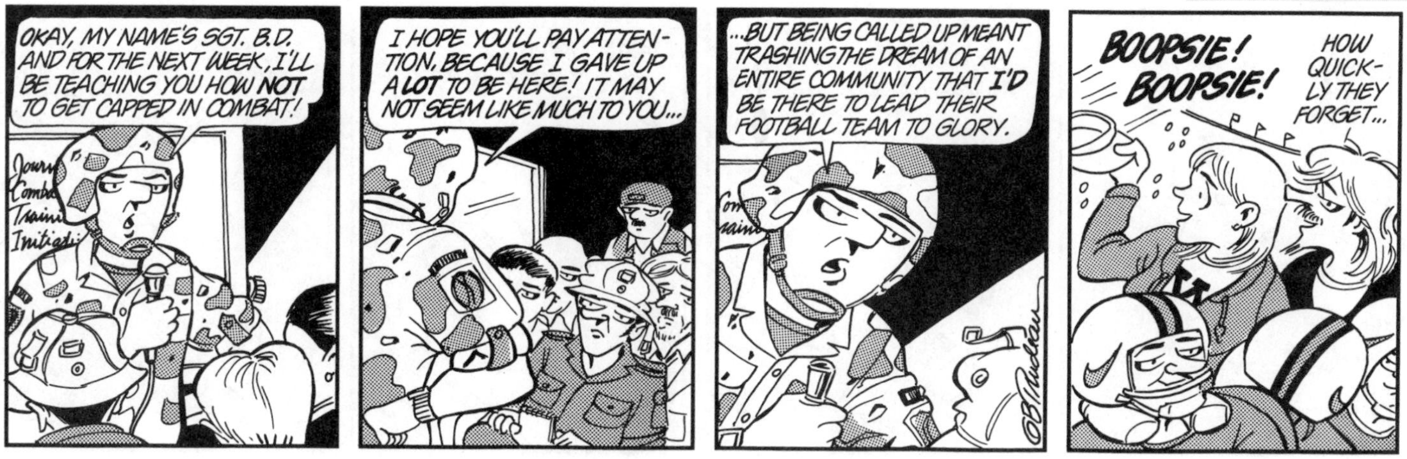
OKAY, MY NAME'S SGT. B.D. AND FOR THE NEXT WEEK, I'LL BE TEACHING YOU HOW **NOT** TO GET CAPPED IN COMBAT!
I HOPE YOU'LL PAY ATTENTION, BECAUSE I GAVE UP A **LOT** TO BE HERE! IT MAY NOT SEEM LIKE MUCH TO YOU...
...BUT BEING CALLED UP MEANT TRASHING THE DREAM OF AN ENTIRE COMMUNITY THAT **I'D** BE THERE TO LEAD THEIR FOOTBALL TEAM TO GLORY.
BOOPSIE! BOOPSIE!
HOW QUICKLY THEY FORGET...

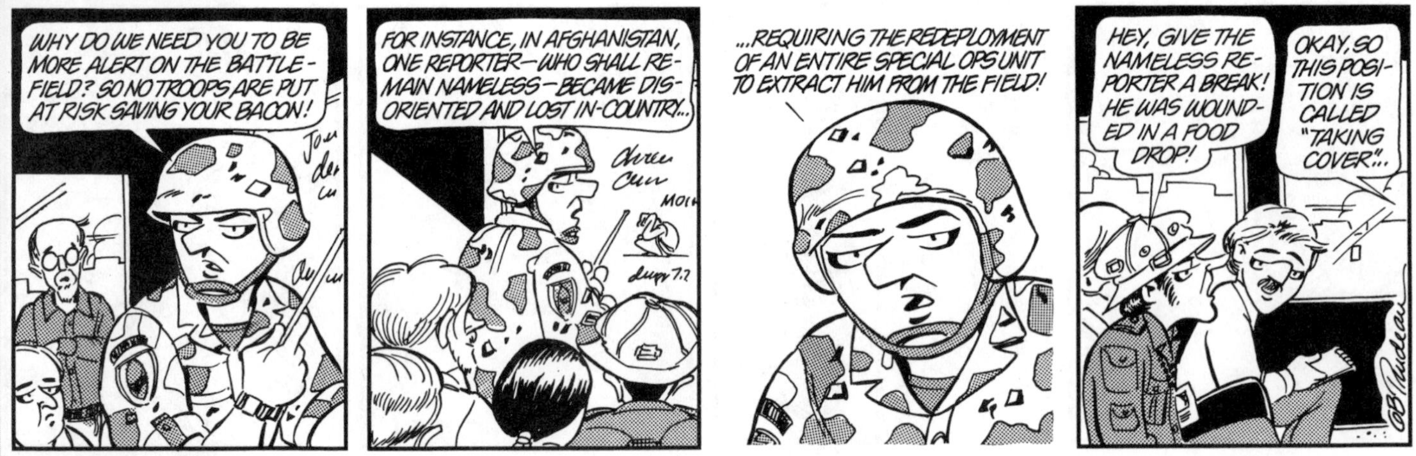
WHY DO WE NEED YOU TO BE MORE ALERT ON THE BATTLEFIELD? SO NO TROOPS ARE PUT AT RISK SAVING YOUR BACON!
FOR INSTANCE, IN AFGHANISTAN, ONE REPORTER—WHO SHALL REMAIN NAMELESS—BECAME DISORIENTED AND LOST IN-COUNTRY...
...REQUIRING THE REDEPLOYMENT OF AN ENTIRE SPECIAL OPS UNIT TO EXTRACT HIM FROM THE FIELD!
HEY, GIVE THE NAMELESS REPORTER A BREAK! HE WAS WOUNDED IN A FOOD DROP!
OKAY, SO THIS POSITION IS CALLED "TAKING COVER"...

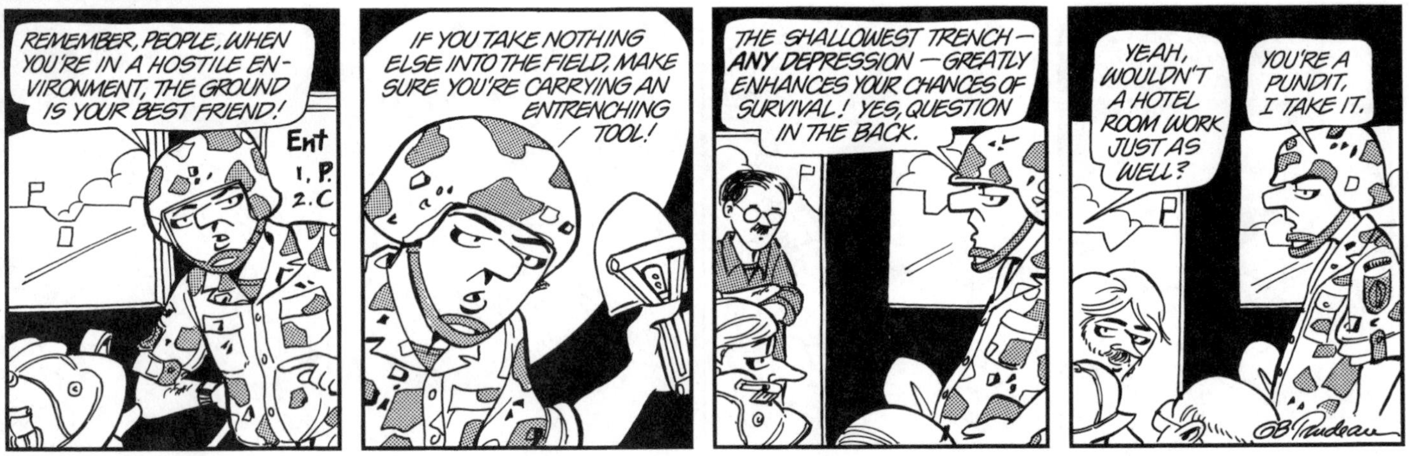
REMEMBER, PEOPLE, WHEN YOU'RE IN A HOSTILE ENVIRONMENT, THE GROUND IS YOUR BEST FRIEND!
IF YOU TAKE NOTHING ELSE INTO THE FIELD, MAKE SURE YOU'RE CARRYING AN ENTRENCHING TOOL!
THE SHALLOWEST TRENCH—ANY DEPRESSION—GREATLY ENHANCES YOUR CHANCES OF SURVIVAL! YES, QUESTION IN THE BACK.
YEAH, WOULDN'T A HOTEL ROOM WORK JUST AS WELL?
YOU'RE A PUNDIT, I TAKE IT.

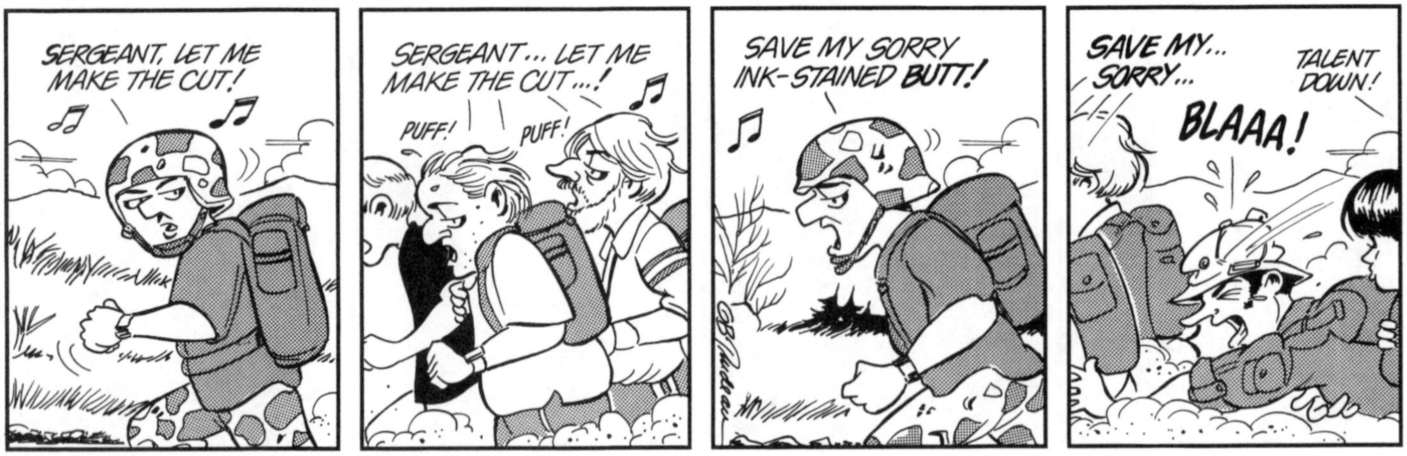
SERGEANT, LET ME MAKE THE CUT!
SERGEANT... LET ME MAKE THE CUT...!
PUFF!
PUFF!
SAVE MY SORRY INK-STAINED BUTT!
SAVE MY... SORRY...
BLAAA!
TALENT DOWN!

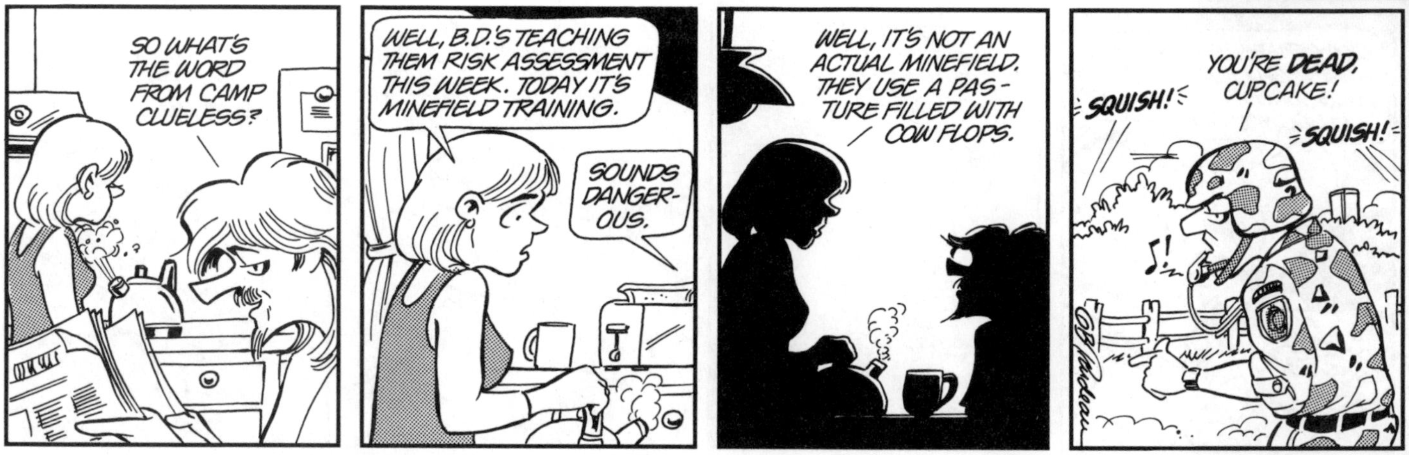
SO WHAT'S THE WORD FROM CAMP CLUELESS?
WELL, B.D.'S TEACHING THEM RISK ASSESSMENT THIS WEEK. TODAY IT'S MINEFIELD TRAINING.
SOUNDS DANGER-OUS.
WELL, IT'S NOT AN ACTUAL MINEFIELD. THEY USE A PAS-TURE FILLED WITH COW FLOPS.
SQUISH!
YOU'RE DEAD, CUPCAKE!
SQUISH!

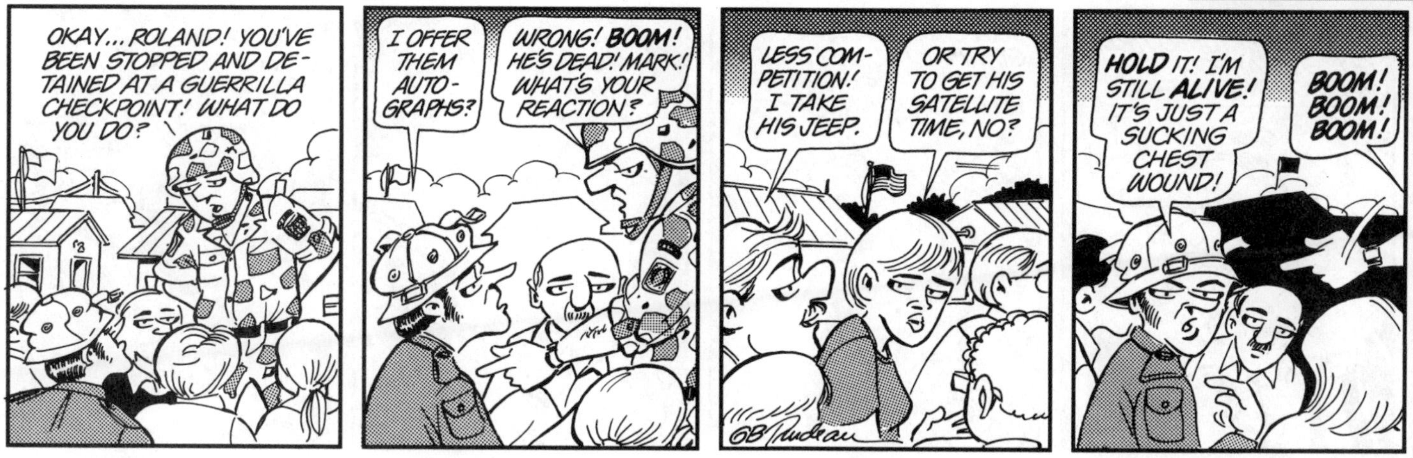
OKAY... ROLAND! YOU'VE BEEN STOPPED AND DE-TAINED AT A GUERRILLA CHECKPOINT! WHAT DO YOU DO?
I OFFER THEM AUTO-GRAPHS?
WRONG! BOOM! HE'S DEAD! MARK! WHAT'S YOUR REACTION?
LESS COM-PETITION! I TAKE HIS JEEP.
OR TRY TO GET HIS SATELLITE TIME, NO?
HOLD IT! I'M STILL ALIVE! IT'S JUST A SUCKING CHEST WOUND!
BOOM! BOOM! BOOM!

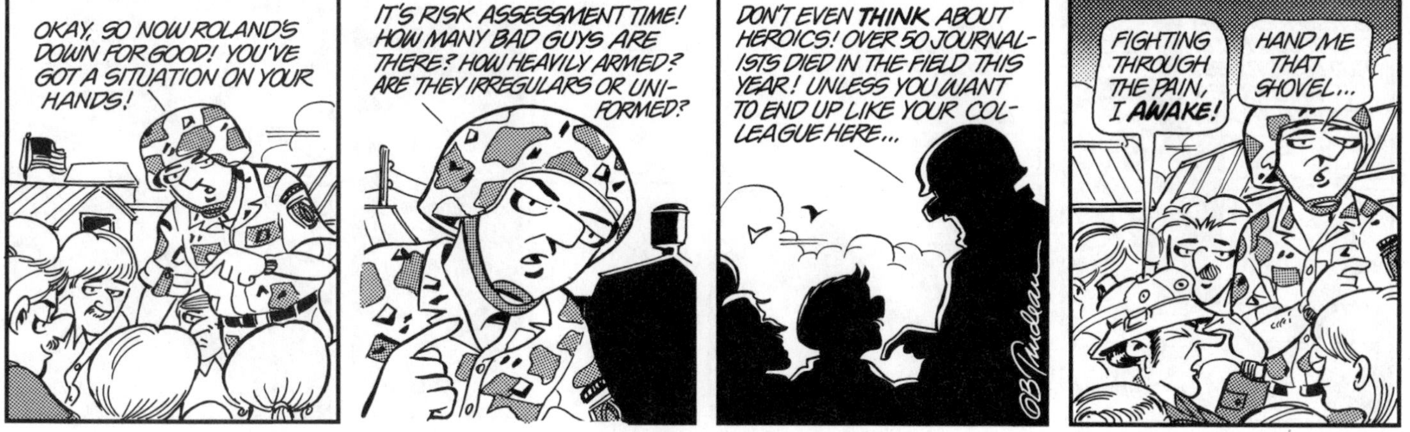
OKAY, SO NOW ROLAND'S DOWN FOR GOOD! YOU'VE GOT A SITUATION ON YOUR HANDS!
IT'S RISK ASSESSMENT TIME! HOW MANY BAD GUYS ARE THERE? HOW HEAVILY ARMED? ARE THEY IRREGULARS OR UNI-FORMED?
DON'T EVEN THINK ABOUT HEROICS! OVER 50 JOURNAL-ISTS DIED IN THE FIELD THIS YEAR! UNLESS YOU WANT TO END UP LIKE YOUR COL-LEAGUE HERE...
FIGHTING THROUGH THE PAIN, I AWAKE!
HAND ME THAT SHOVEL...

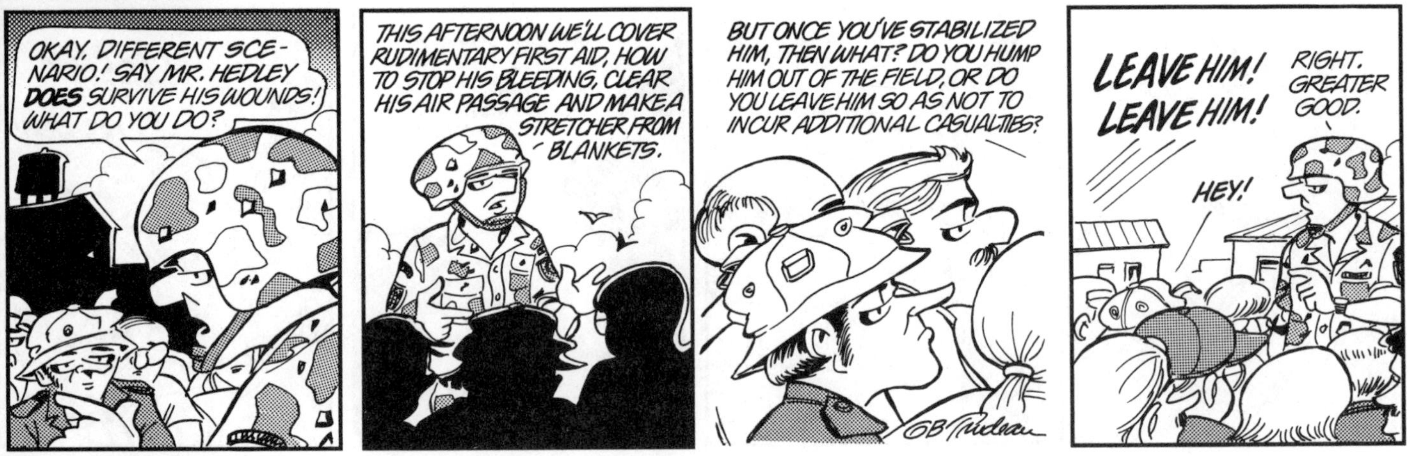
OKAY, DIFFERENT SCENARIO! SAY MR. HEDLEY DOES SURVIVE HIS WOUNDS! WHAT DO YOU DO?
THIS AFTERNOON WE'LL COVER RUDIMENTARY FIRST AID, HOW TO STOP HIS BLEEDING, CLEAR HIS AIR PASSAGE AND MAKE A STRETCHER FROM BLANKETS.
BUT ONCE YOU'VE STABILIZED HIM, THEN WHAT? DO YOU HUMP HIM OUT OF THE FIELD, OR DO YOU LEAVE HIM SO AS NOT TO INCUR ADDITIONAL CASUALTIES?
LEAVE HIM! LEAVE HIM!
RIGHT. GREATER GOOD.
HEY!

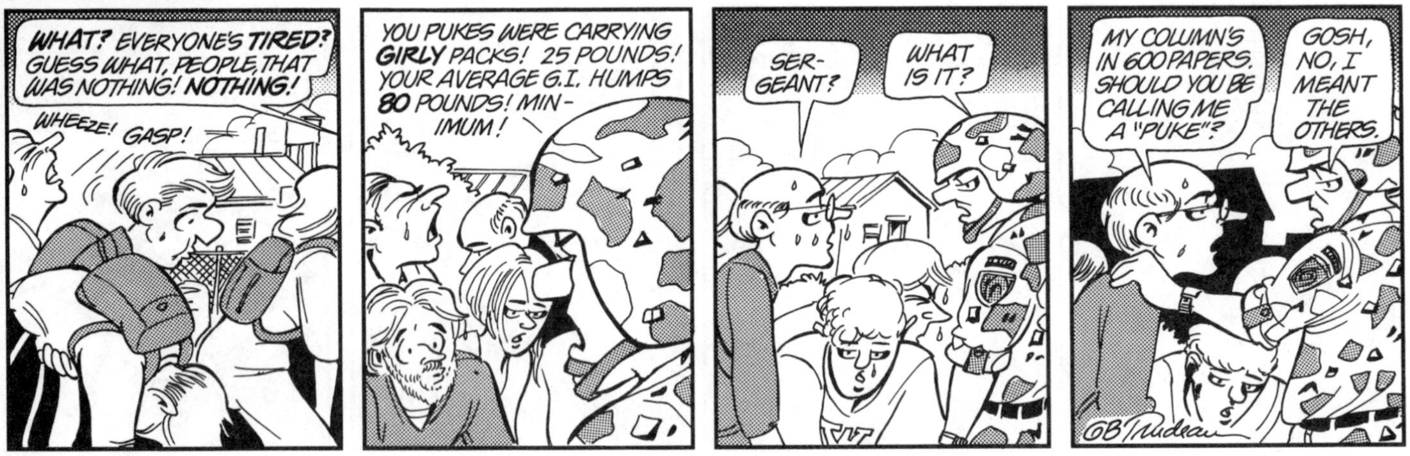
WHAT? EVERYONE'S TIRED? GUESS WHAT, PEOPLE, THAT WAS NOTHING! NOTHING!
WHEEZE! GASP!
YOU PUKES WERE CARRYING GIRLY PACKS! 25 POUNDS! YOUR AVERAGE G.I. HUMPS 80 POUNDS! MINIMUM!
SERGEANT?
WHAT IS IT?
MY COLUMN'S IN 600 PAPERS. SHOULD YOU BE CALLING ME A "PUKE"?
GOSH, NO, I MEANT THE OTHERS.

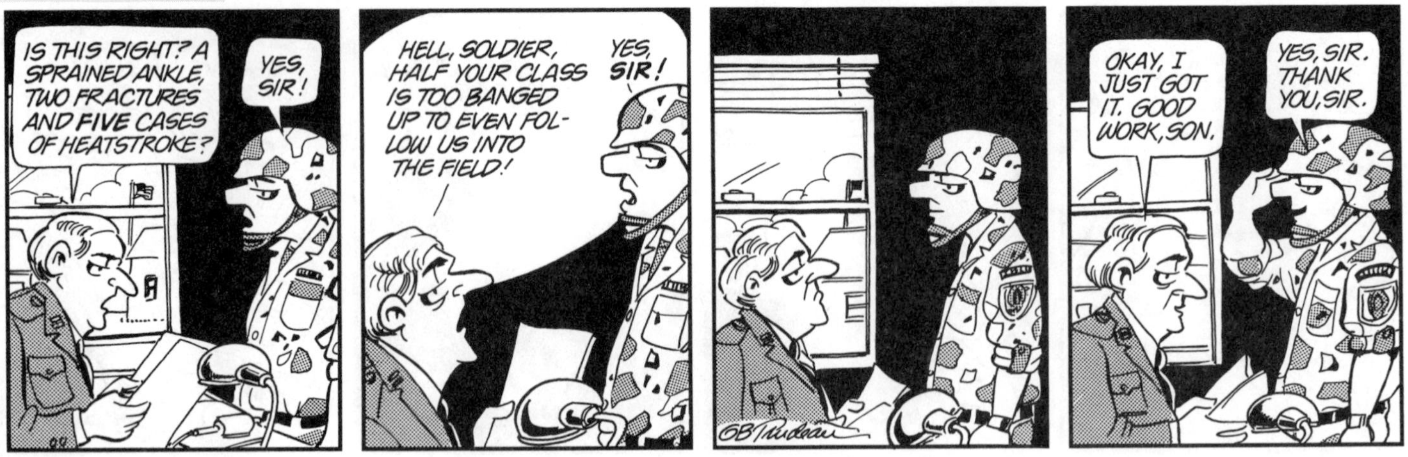
IS THIS RIGHT? A SPRAINED ANKLE, TWO FRACTURES AND FIVE CASES OF HEATSTROKE?
YES, SIR!
HELL, SOLDIER, HALF YOUR CLASS IS TOO BANGED UP TO EVEN FOLLOW US INTO THE FIELD!
YES, SIR!
OKAY, I JUST GOT IT. GOOD WORK, SON.
YES, SIR. THANK YOU, SIR.

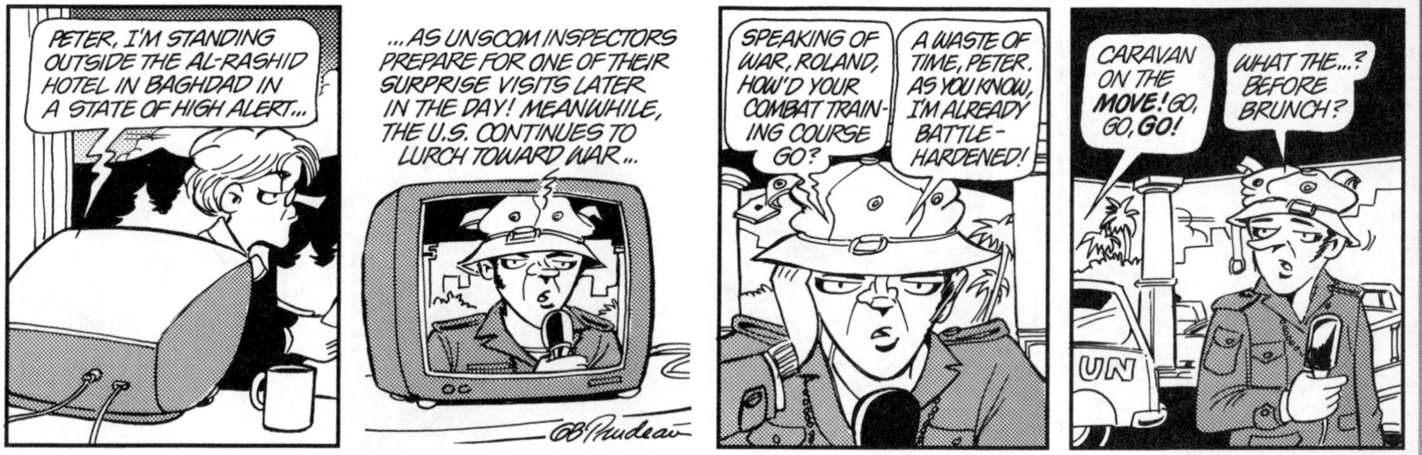
PETER, I'M STANDING OUTSIDE THE AL-RASHID HOTEL IN BAGHDAD IN A STATE OF HIGH ALERT...
...AS UNSCOM INSPECTORS PREPARE FOR ONE OF THEIR SURPRISE VISITS LATER IN THE DAY! MEANWHILE, THE U.S. CONTINUES TO LURCH TOWARD WAR...
SPEAKING OF WAR, ROLAND, HOW'D YOUR COMBAT TRAINING COURSE GO?
A WASTE OF TIME, PETER. AS YOU KNOW, I'M ALREADY BATTLE-HARDENED!
CARAVAN ON THE **MOVE!** GO, GO, **GO!**
WHAT THE...? BEFORE BRUNCH?
UN

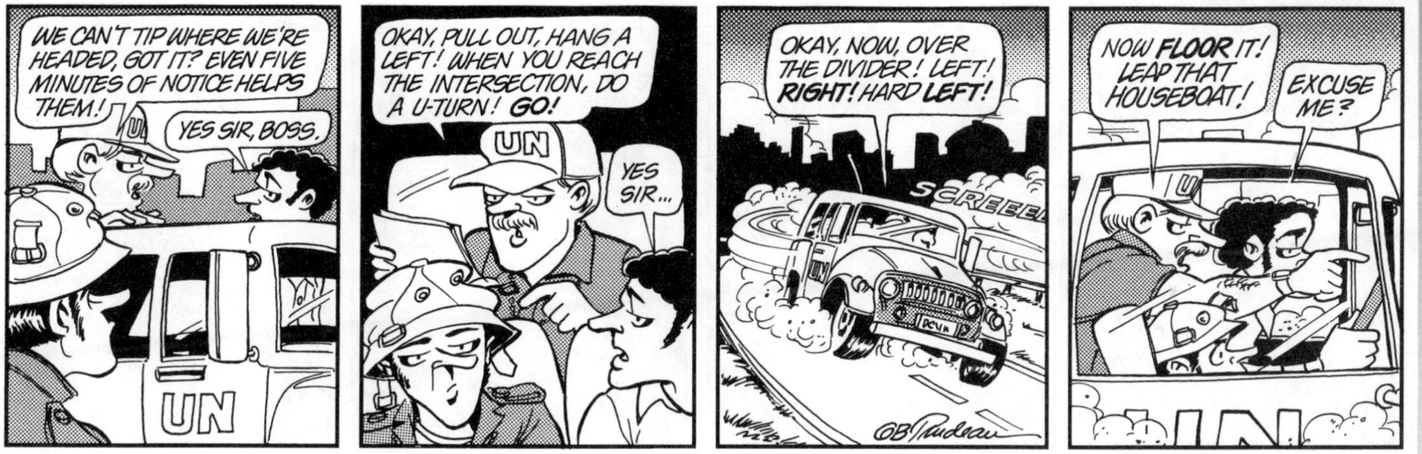
WE CAN'T TIP WHERE WE'RE HEADED, GOT IT? EVEN FIVE MINUTES OF NOTICE HELPS THEM!
YES SIR, BOSS.
UN
OKAY, PULL OUT, HANG A LEFT! WHEN YOU REACH THE INTERSECTION, DO A U-TURN! **GO!**
YES SIR...
OKAY, NOW, OVER THE DIVIDER! LEFT! **RIGHT!** HARD **LEFT!**
SCREEEE
NOW **FLOOR** IT! LEAP THAT HOUSEBOAT!
EXCUSE ME?

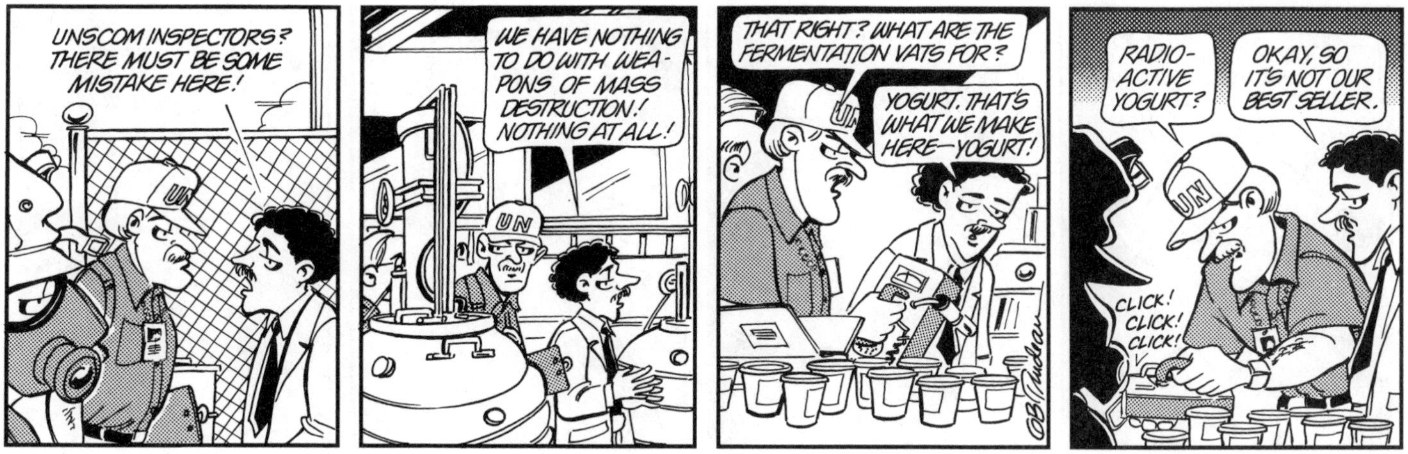
UNSCOM INSPECTORS? THERE MUST BE SOME MISTAKE HERE!
WE HAVE NOTHING TO DO WITH WEAPONS OF MASS DESTRUCTION! NOTHING AT ALL!
THAT RIGHT? WHAT ARE THE FERMENTATION VATS FOR?
YOGURT. THAT'S WHAT WE MAKE HERE—YOGURT!
RADIO-ACTIVE YOGURT?
OKAY, SO IT'S NOT OUR BEST SELLER.
CLICK! CLICK! CLICK!

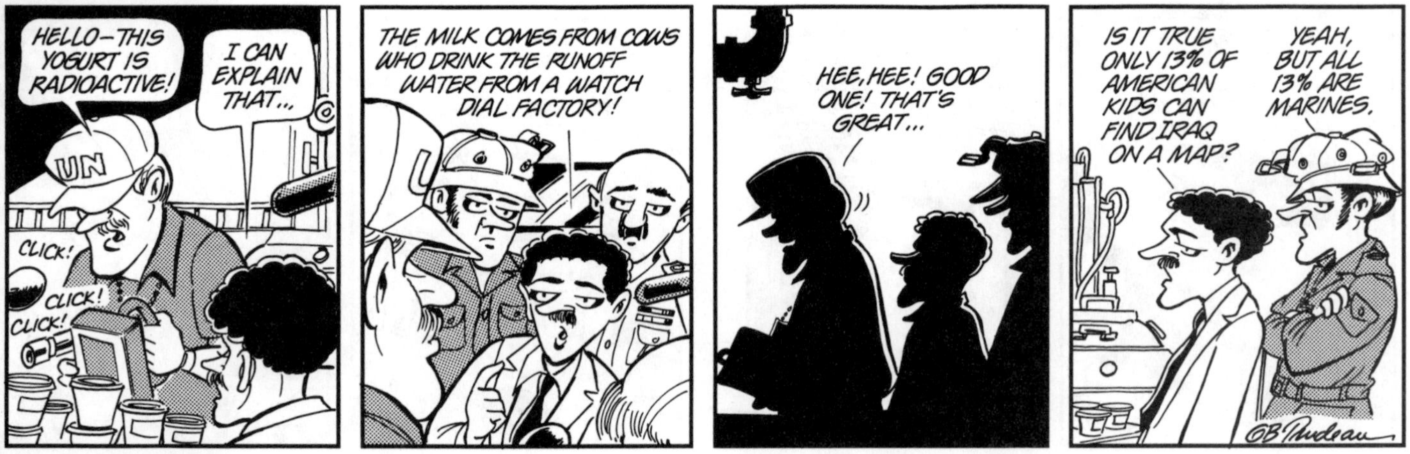
HELLO—THIS YOGURT IS RADIOACTIVE!
I CAN EXPLAIN THAT...
CLICK!
CLICK!
CLICK!
THE MILK COMES FROM COWS WHO DRINK THE RUNOFF WATER FROM A WATCH DIAL FACTORY!
HEE, HEE! GOOD ONE! THAT'S GREAT...
IS IT TRUE ONLY 13% OF AMERICAN KIDS CAN FIND IRAQ ON A MAP?
YEAH, BUT ALL 13% ARE MARINES.

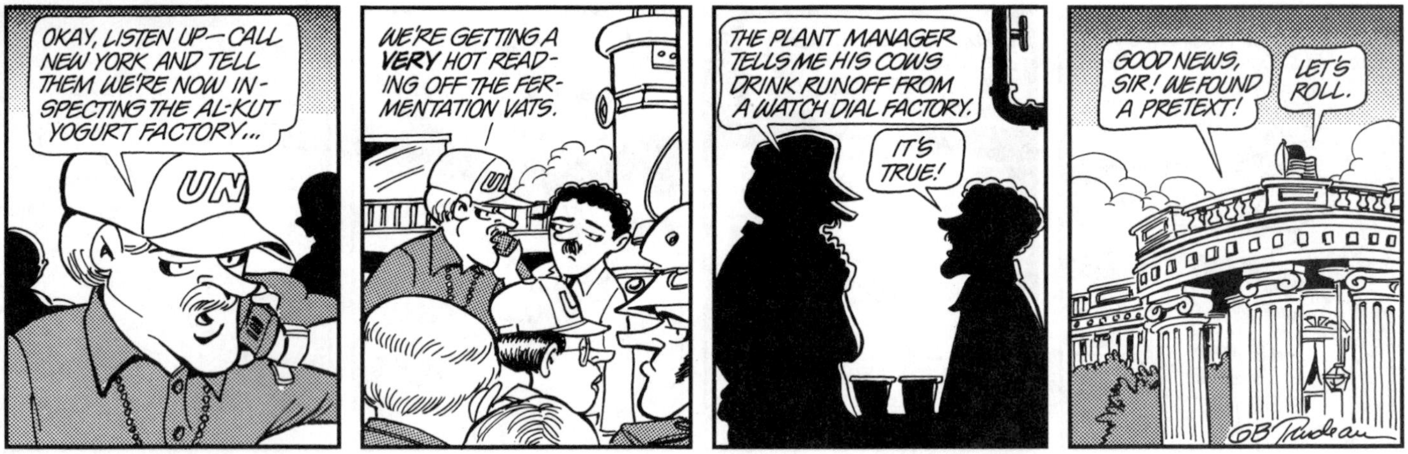
OKAY, LISTEN UP—CALL NEW YORK AND TELL THEM WE'RE NOW INSPECTING THE AL-KUT YOGURT FACTORY...
WE'RE GETTING A **VERY** HOT READING OFF THE FERMENTATION VATS.
THE PLANT MANAGER TELLS ME HIS COWS DRINK RUNOFF FROM A WATCH DIAL FACTORY.
IT'S TRUE!
GOOD NEWS, SIR! WE FOUND A PRETEXT!
LET'S ROLL.

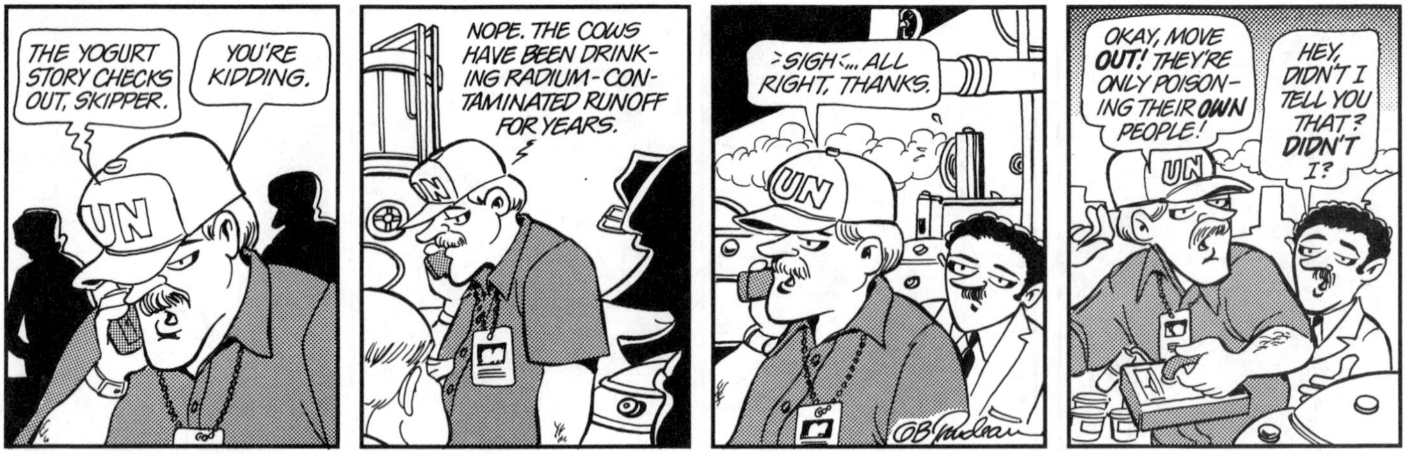
THE YOGURT STORY CHECKS OUT, SKIPPER.
YOU'RE KIDDING.
NOPE. THE COWS HAVE BEEN DRINKING RADIUM-CONTAMINATED RUNOFF FOR YEARS.
>SIGH<... ALL RIGHT, THANKS.
OKAY, MOVE **OUT!** THEY'RE ONLY POISONING THEIR **OWN** PEOPLE!
HEY, DIDN'T I TELL YOU THAT? **DIDN'T** I?

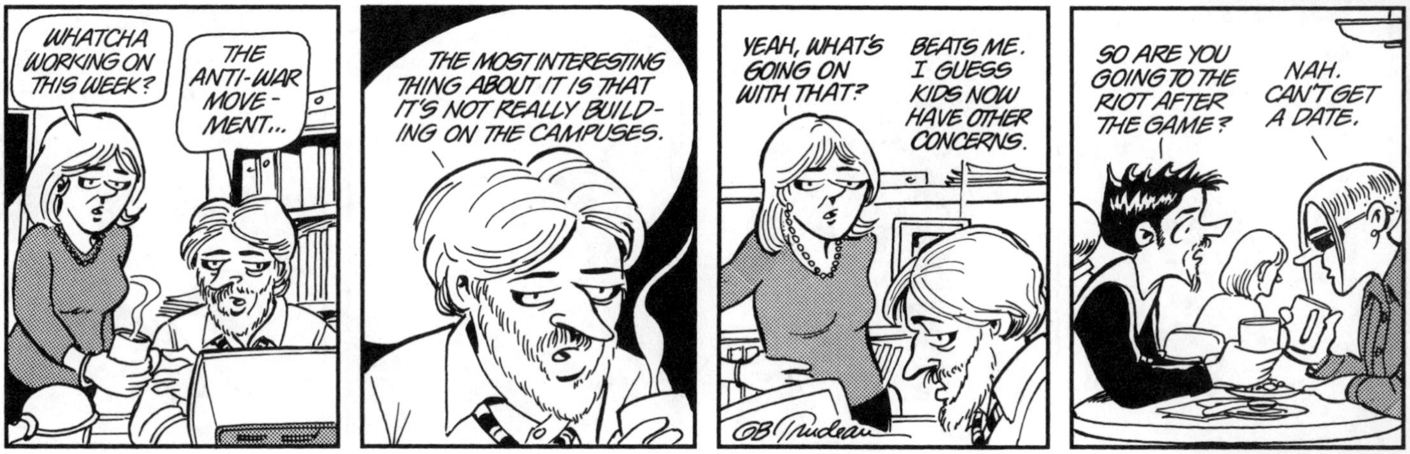
WHATCHA WORKING ON THIS WEEK?
THE ANTI-WAR MOVEMENT...
THE MOST INTERESTING THING ABOUT IT IS THAT IT'S NOT REALLY BUILDING ON THE CAMPUSES.
YEAH, WHAT'S GOING ON WITH THAT?
BEATS ME. I GUESS KIDS NOW HAVE OTHER CONCERNS.
©B Trudeau
SO ARE YOU GOING TO THE RIOT AFTER THE GAME?
NAH. CAN'T GET A DATE.

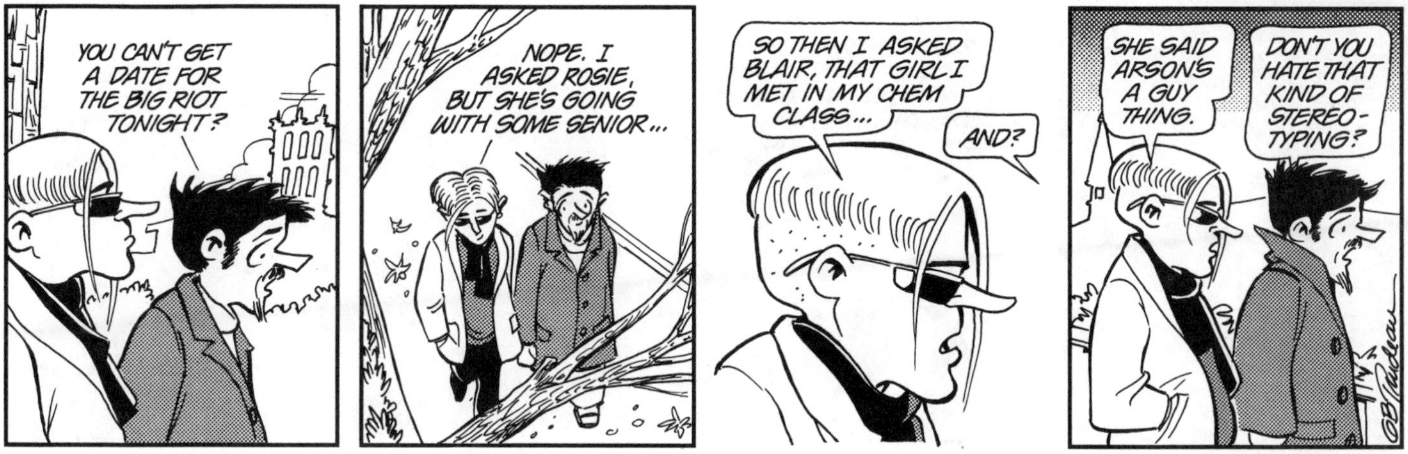
YOU CAN'T GET A DATE FOR THE BIG RIOT TONIGHT?
NOPE. I ASKED ROSIE, BUT SHE'S GOING WITH SOME SENIOR...
SO THEN I ASKED BLAIR, THAT GIRL I MET IN MY CHEM CLASS...
AND?
SHE SAID ARSON'S A GUY THING.
DON'T YOU HATE THAT KIND OF STEREOTYPING?
©B Trudeau

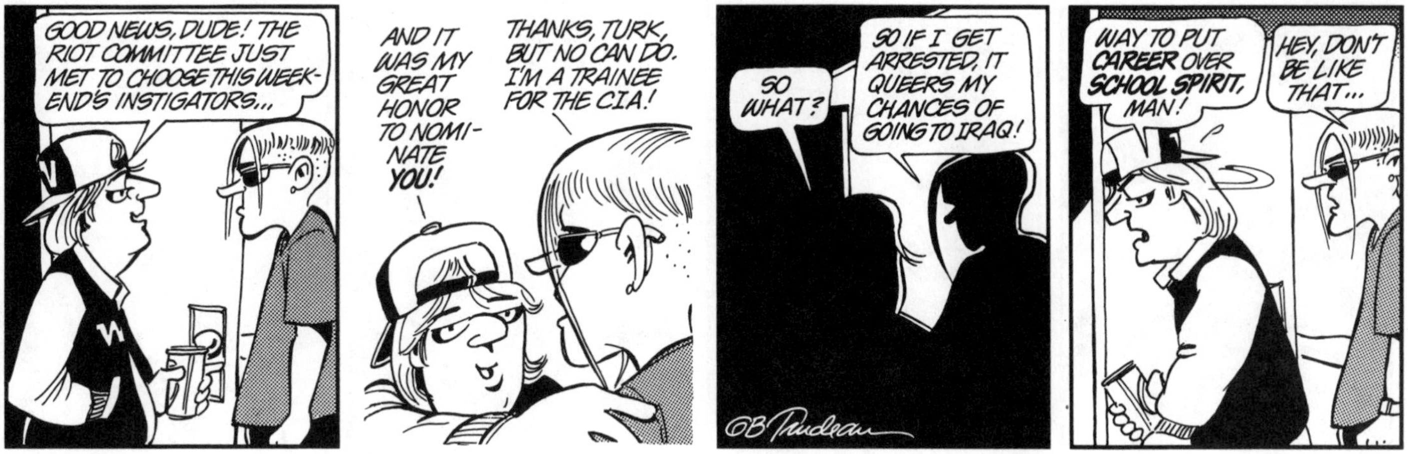
GOOD NEWS, DUDE! THE RIOT COMMITTEE JUST MET TO CHOOSE THIS WEEKEND'S INSTIGATORS...
AND IT WAS MY GREAT HONOR TO NOMINATE YOU!
THANKS, TURK, BUT NO CAN DO. I'M A TRAINEE FOR THE CIA!
SO WHAT?
SO IF I GET ARRESTED, IT QUEERS MY CHANCES OF GOING TO IRAQ!
©B Trudeau
WAY TO PUT CAREER OVER SCHOOL SPIRIT, MAN!
HEY, DON'T BE LIKE THAT...

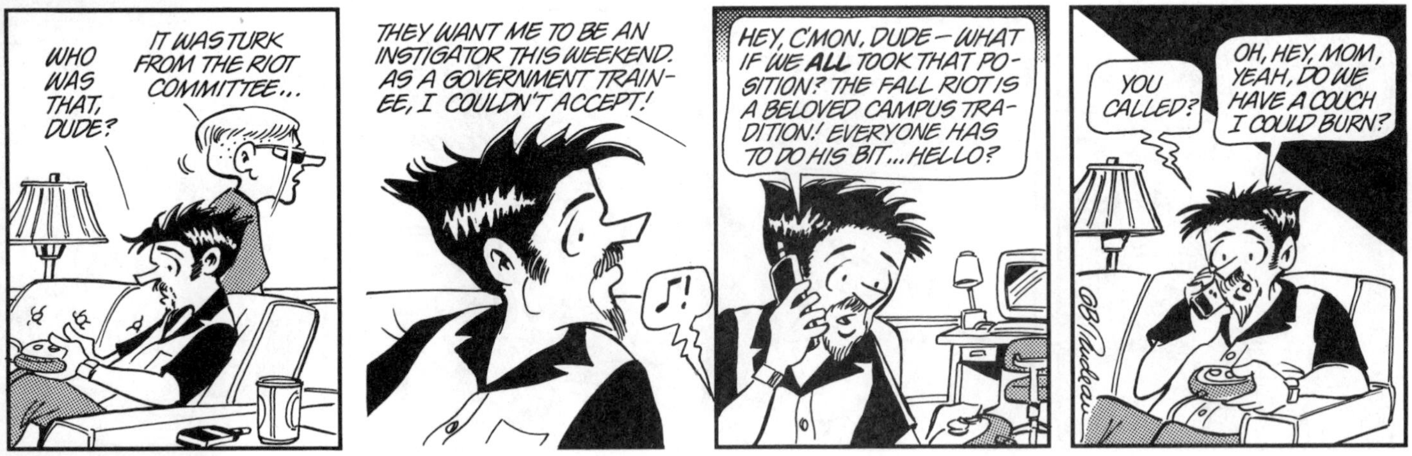
WHO WAS THAT, DUDE?
IT WAS TURK FROM THE RIOT COMMITTEE...
THEY WANT ME TO BE AN INSTIGATOR THIS WEEKEND. AS A GOVERNMENT TRAINEE, I COULDN'T ACCEPT!
HEY, C'MON, DUDE – WHAT IF WE **ALL** TOOK THAT POSITION? THE FALL RIOT IS A BELOVED CAMPUS TRADITION! EVERYONE HAS TO DO HIS BIT... HELLO?
YOU CALLED?
OH, HEY, MOM, YEAH, DO WE HAVE A COUCH I COULD BURN?

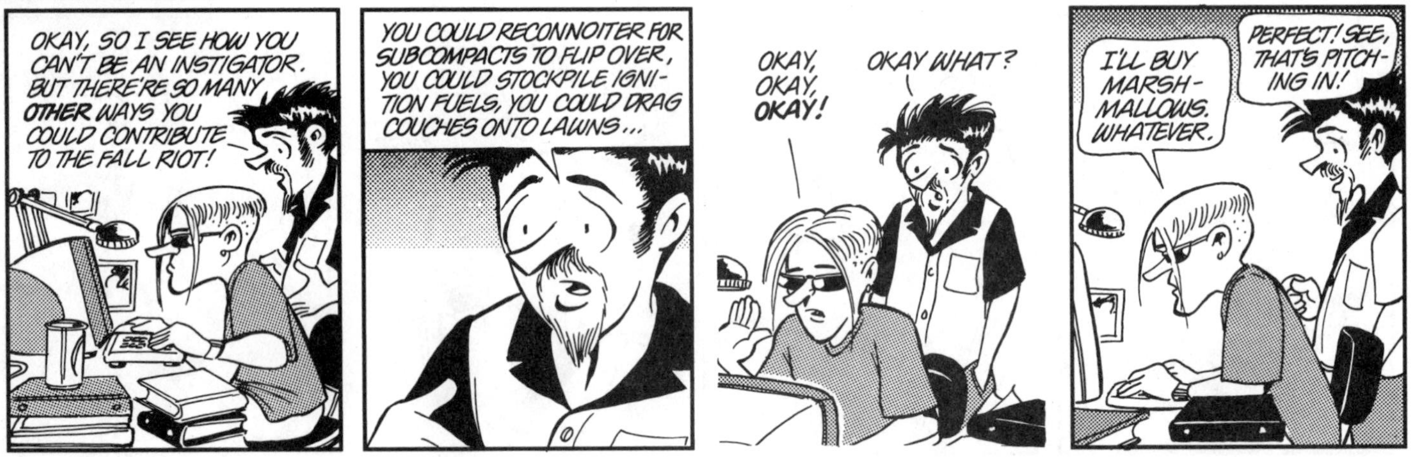
OKAY, SO I SEE HOW YOU CAN'T BE AN INSTIGATOR. BUT THERE'RE SO MANY **OTHER** WAYS YOU COULD CONTRIBUTE TO THE FALL RIOT!
YOU COULD RECONNOITER FOR SUBCOMPACTS TO FLIP OVER, YOU COULD STOCKPILE IGNITION FUELS, YOU COULD DRAG COUCHES ONTO LAWNS...
OKAY, OKAY, **OKAY!**
OKAY WHAT?
I'LL BUY MARSHMALLOWS. WHATEVER.
PERFECT! SEE, THAT'S PITCHING IN!

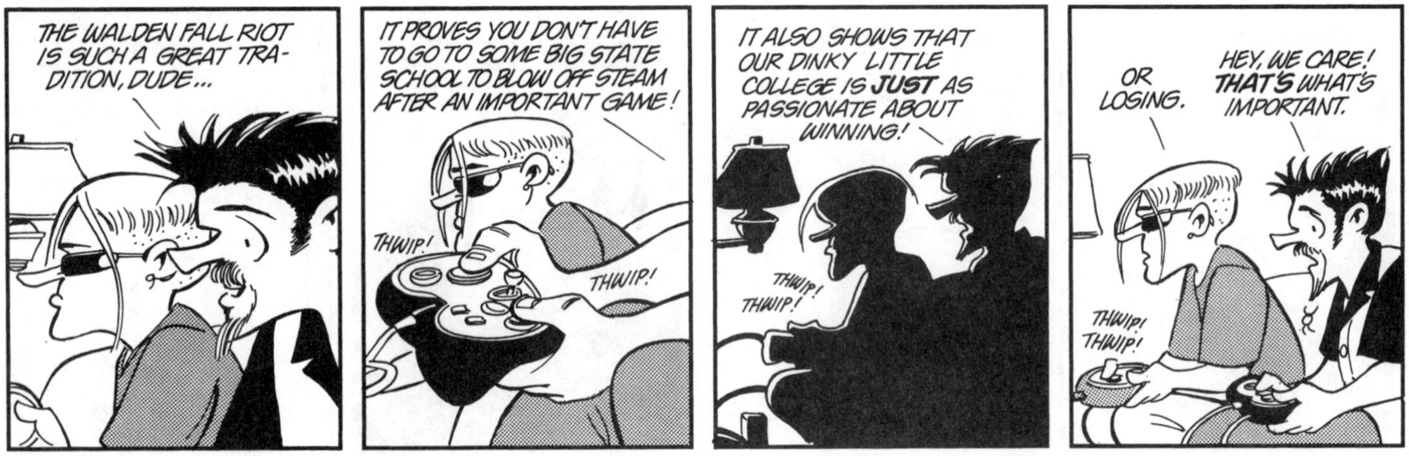
THE WALDEN FALL RIOT IS SUCH A GREAT TRADITION, DUDE...
IT PROVES YOU DON'T HAVE TO GO TO SOME BIG STATE SCHOOL TO BLOW OFF STEAM AFTER AN IMPORTANT GAME!
THWIP!
THWIP!
IT ALSO SHOWS THAT OUR DINKY LITTLE COLLEGE IS **JUST** AS PASSIONATE ABOUT WINNING!
THWIP! THWIP!
OR LOSING.
HEY, WE CARE! **THAT'S** WHAT'S IMPORTANT.
THWIP! THWIP!

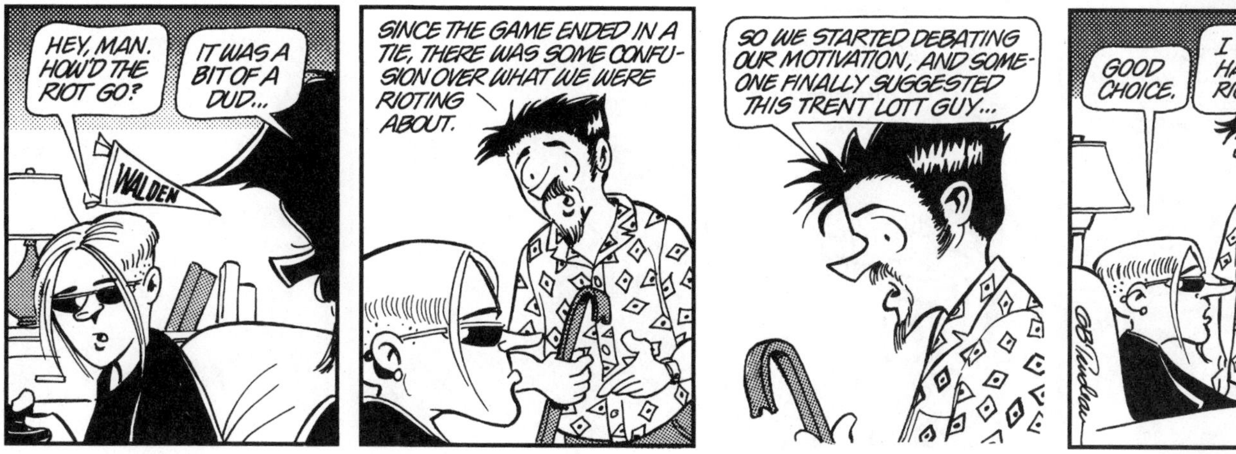
HEY, MAN. HOW'D THE RIOT GO?
IT WAS A BIT OF A DUD...
WALDEN
SINCE THE GAME ENDED IN A TIE, THERE WAS SOME CONFUSION OVER WHAT WE WERE RIOTING ABOUT.
SO WE STARTED DEBATING OUR MOTIVATION, AND SOMEONE FINALLY SUGGESTED THIS TRENT LOTT GUY...
GOOD CHOICE.
I DUNNO. YOU HATE TO SEE A RIOT POLITICIZED.
GBTrudeau

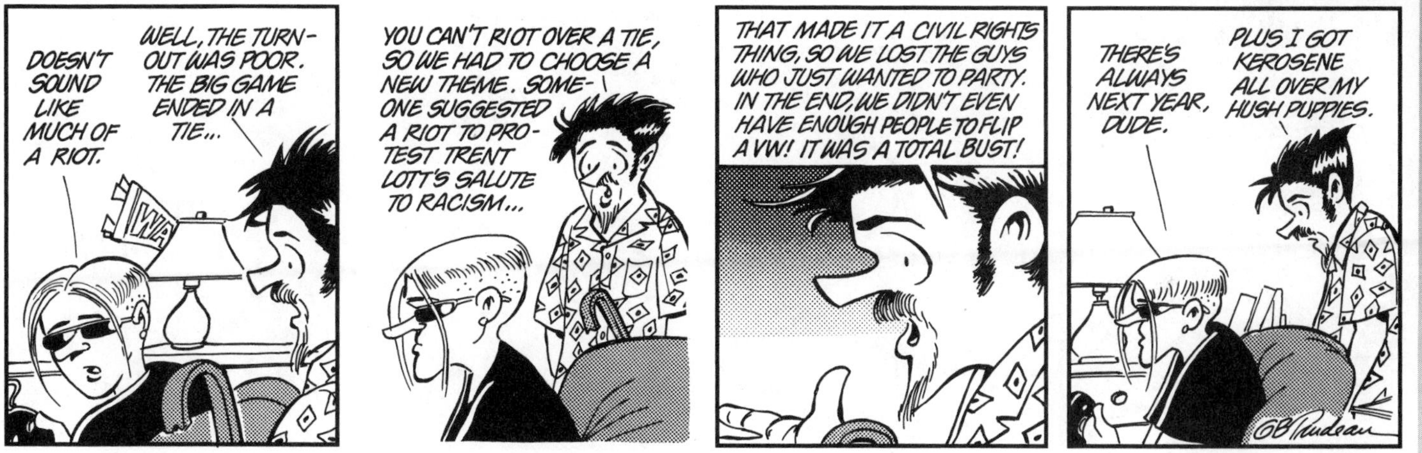
DOESN'T SOUND LIKE MUCH OF A RIOT.
WELL, THE TURNOUT WAS POOR. THE BIG GAME ENDED IN A TIE...
YOU CAN'T RIOT OVER A TIE, SO WE HAD TO CHOOSE A NEW THEME. SOMEONE SUGGESTED A RIOT TO PROTEST TRENT LOTT'S SALUTE TO RACISM...
THAT MADE IT A CIVIL RIGHTS THING, SO WE LOST THE GUYS WHO JUST WANTED TO PARTY. IN THE END, WE DIDN'T EVEN HAVE ENOUGH PEOPLE TO FLIP A VW! IT WAS A TOTAL BUST!
THERE'S ALWAYS NEXT YEAR, DUDE.
PLUS I GOT KEROSENE ALL OVER MY HUSH PUPPIES.
GBTrudeau

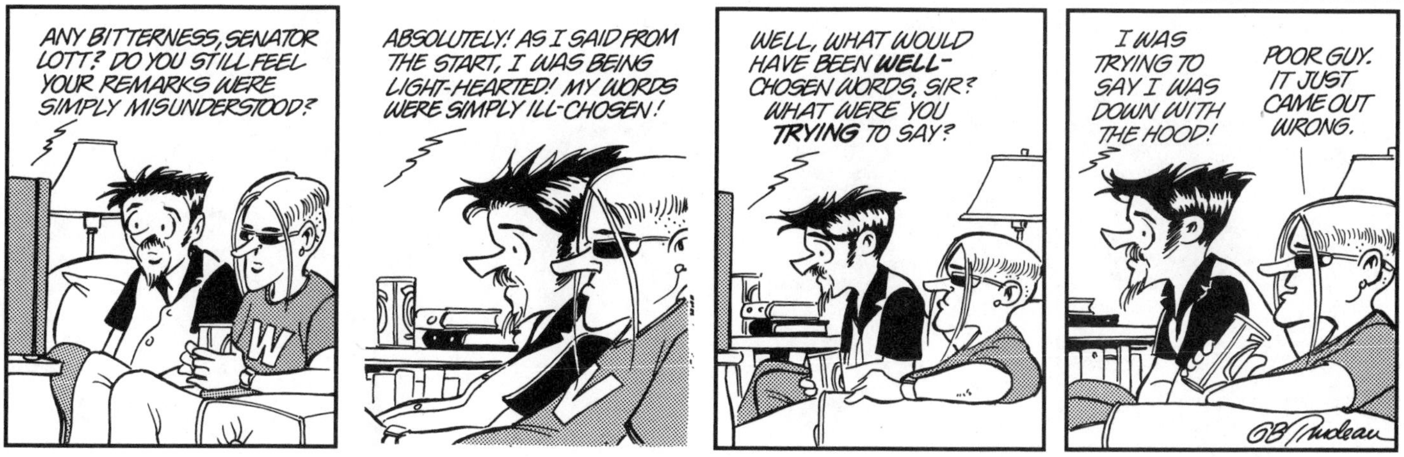
ANY BITTERNESS, SENATOR LOTT? DO YOU STILL FEEL YOUR REMARKS WERE SIMPLY MISUNDERSTOOD?
ABSOLUTELY! AS I SAID FROM THE START, I WAS BEING LIGHT-HEARTED! MY WORDS WERE SIMPLY ILL-CHOSEN!
WELL, WHAT WOULD HAVE BEEN WELL-CHOSEN WORDS, SIR? WHAT WERE YOU TRYING TO SAY?
I WAS TRYING TO SAY I WAS DOWN WITH THE HOOD!
POOR GUY. IT JUST CAME OUT WRONG.
GBTrudeau

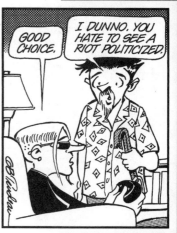

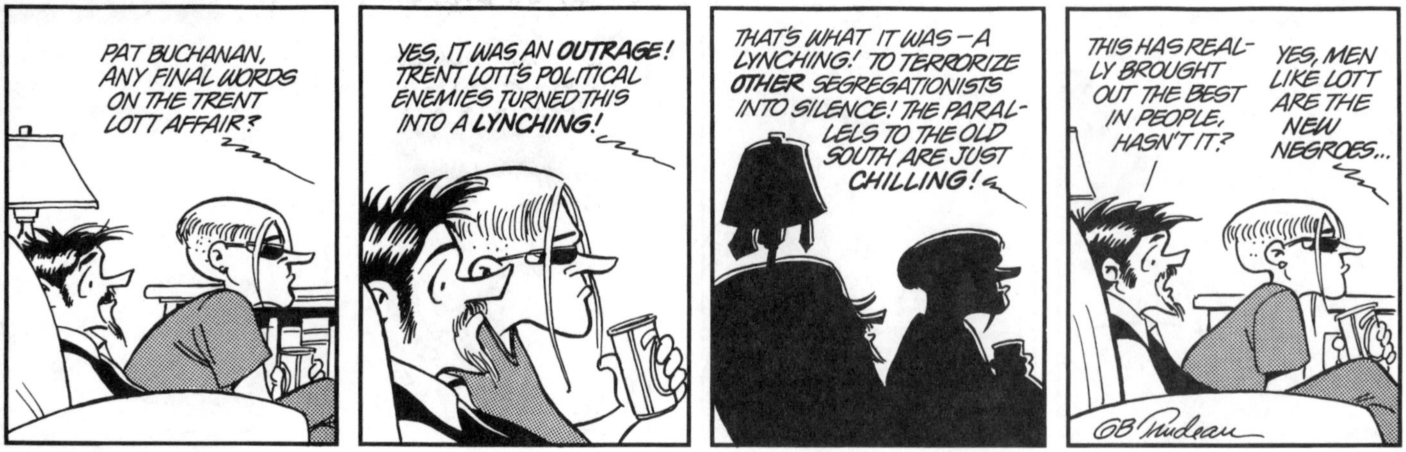
PAT BUCHANAN, ANY FINAL WORDS ON THE TRENT LOTT AFFAIR?
YES, IT WAS AN **OUTRAGE**! TRENT LOTT'S POLITICAL ENEMIES TURNED THIS INTO A **LYNCHING**!
THAT'S WHAT IT WAS—A LYNCHING! TO TERRORIZE **OTHER** SEGREGATIONISTS INTO SILENCE! THE PARALLELS TO THE OLD SOUTH ARE JUST **CHILLING**!
THIS HAS REALLY BROUGHT OUT THE BEST IN PEOPLE, HASN'T IT?
YES, MEN LIKE LOTT ARE THE NEW NEGROES...
GB Trudeau

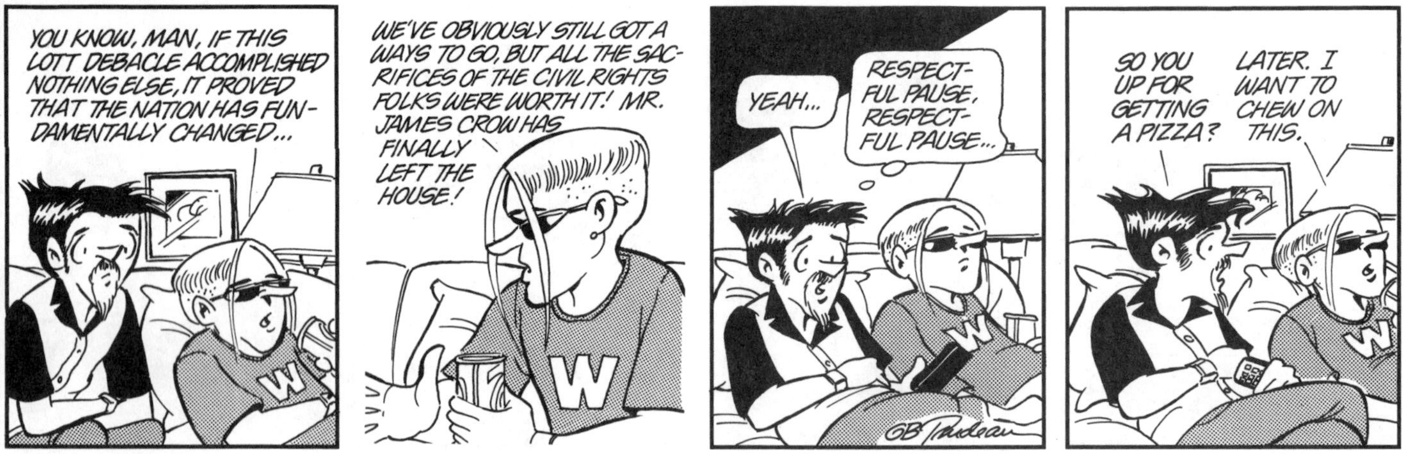
YOU KNOW, MAN, IF THIS LOTT DEBACLE ACCOMPLISHED NOTHING ELSE, IT PROVED THAT THE NATION HAS FUNDAMENTALLY CHANGED...
WE'VE OBVIOUSLY STILL GOT A WAYS TO GO, BUT ALL THE SACRIFICES OF THE CIVIL RIGHTS FOLKS WERE WORTH IT! MR. JAMES CROW HAS FINALLY LEFT THE HOUSE!
YEAH...
RESPECTFUL PAUSE, RESPECTFUL PAUSE...
GB Trudeau
SO YOU UP FOR GETTING A PIZZA?
LATER. I WANT TO CHEW ON THIS.

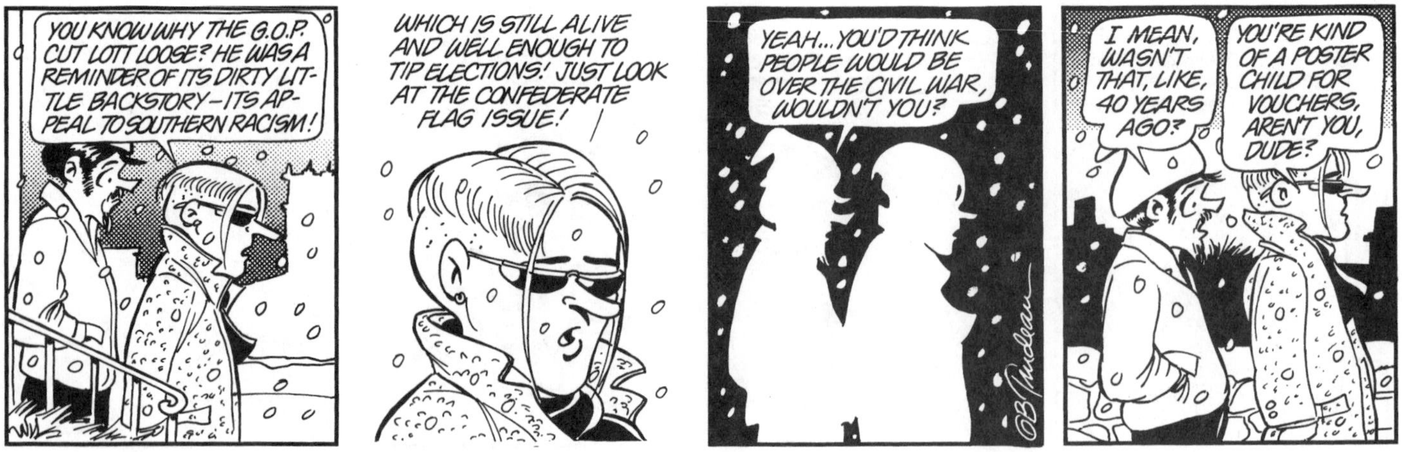
YOU KNOW WHY THE G.O.P. CUT LOTT LOOSE? HE WAS A REMINDER OF ITS DIRTY LITTLE BACKSTORY—ITS APPEAL TO SOUTHERN RACISM!
WHICH IS STILL ALIVE AND WELL ENOUGH TO TIP ELECTIONS! JUST LOOK AT THE CONFEDERATE FLAG ISSUE!
YEAH... YOU'D THINK PEOPLE WOULD BE OVER THE CIVIL WAR, WOULDN'T YOU?
GB Trudeau
I MEAN, WASN'T THAT, LIKE, 40 YEARS AGO?
YOU'RE KIND OF A POSTER CHILD FOR VOUCHERS, AREN'T YOU, DUDE?

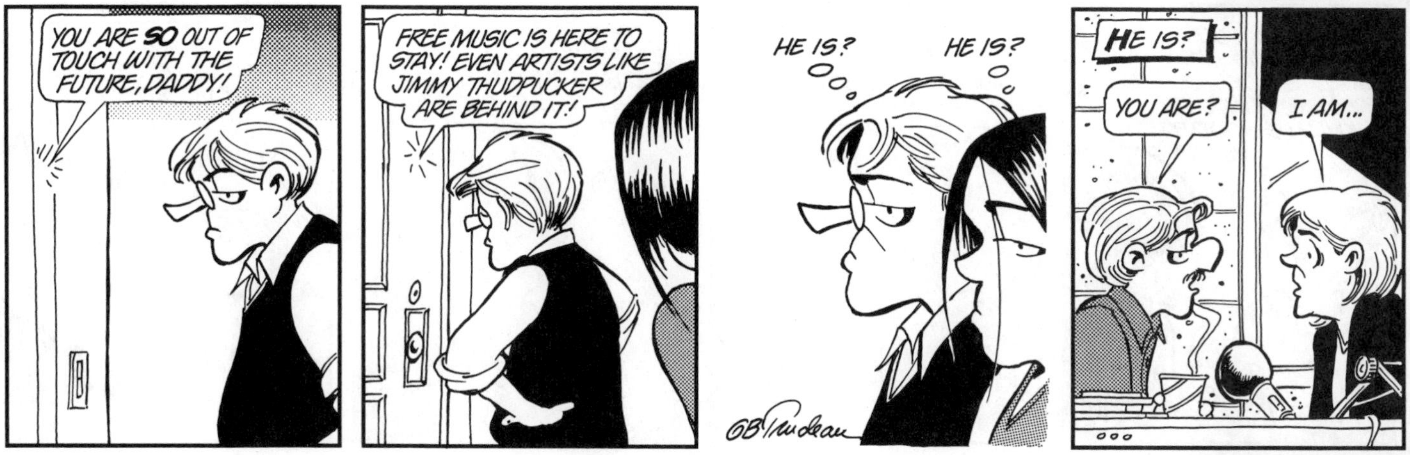
YOU ARE SO OUT OF TOUCH WITH THE FUTURE, DADDY!
FREE MUSIC IS HERE TO STAY! EVEN ARTISTS LIKE JIMMY THUDPUCKER ARE BEHIND IT!
HE IS?
HE IS?
HE IS?
YOU ARE?
I AM...

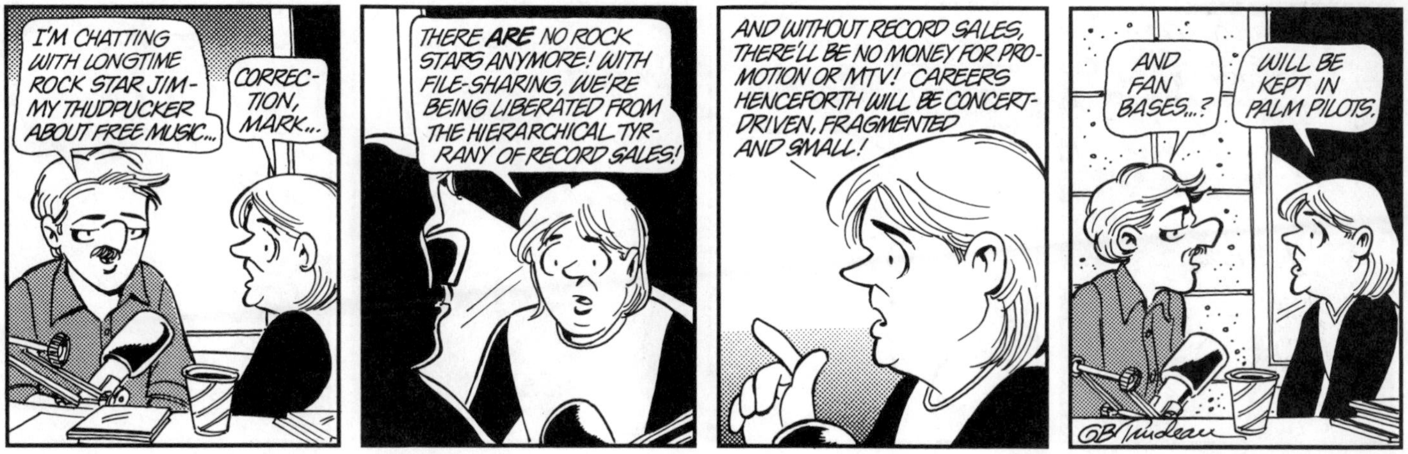
I'M CHATTING WITH LONGTIME ROCK STAR JIMMY THUDPUCKER ABOUT FREE MUSIC...
CORRECTION, MARK...
THERE ARE NO ROCK STARS ANYMORE! WITH FILE-SHARING, WE'RE BEING LIBERATED FROM THE HIERARCHICAL TYRRANY OF RECORD SALES!
AND WITHOUT RECORD SALES, THERE'LL BE NO MONEY FOR PROMOTION OR MTV! CAREERS HENCEFORTH WILL BE CONCERT-DRIVEN, FRAGMENTED AND SMALL!
AND FAN BASES...?
WILL BE KEPT IN PALM PILOTS.

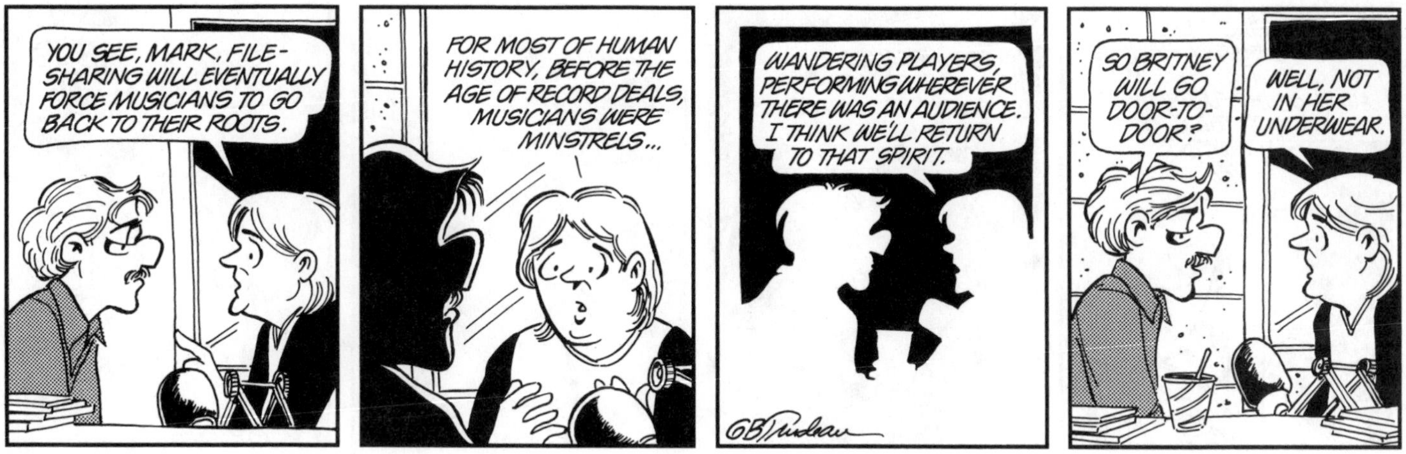
YOU SEE, MARK, FILE-SHARING WILL EVENTUALLY FORCE MUSICIANS TO GO BACK TO THEIR ROOTS.
FOR MOST OF HUMAN HISTORY, BEFORE THE AGE OF RECORD DEALS, MUSICIANS WERE MINSTRELS...
WANDERING PLAYERS, PERFORMING WHEREVER THERE WAS AN AUDIENCE. I THINK WE'LL RETURN TO THAT SPIRIT.
SO BRITNEY WILL GO DOOR-TO-DOOR?
WELL, NOT IN HER UNDERWEAR.

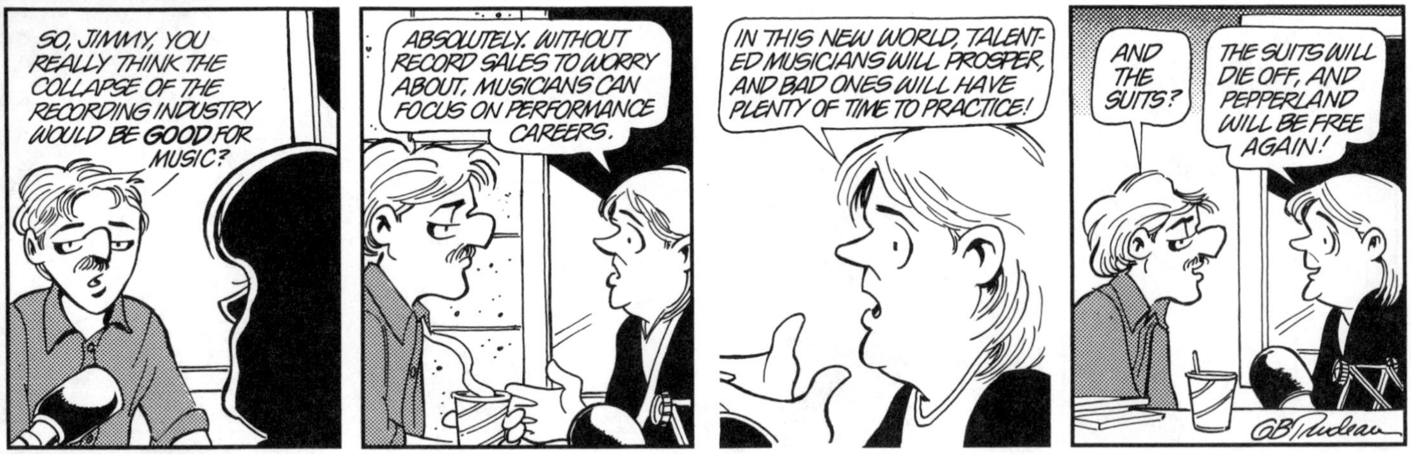
SO, JIMMY, YOU REALLY THINK THE COLLAPSE OF THE RECORDING INDUSTRY WOULD BE GOOD FOR MUSIC?
ABSOLUTELY. WITHOUT RECORD SALES TO WORRY ABOUT, MUSICIANS CAN FOCUS ON PERFORMANCE CAREERS.
IN THIS NEW WORLD, TALENTED MUSICIANS WILL PROSPER, AND BAD ONES WILL HAVE PLENTY OF TIME TO PRACTICE!
AND THE SUITS?
THE SUITS WILL DIE OFF, AND PEPPERLAND WILL BE FREE AGAIN!

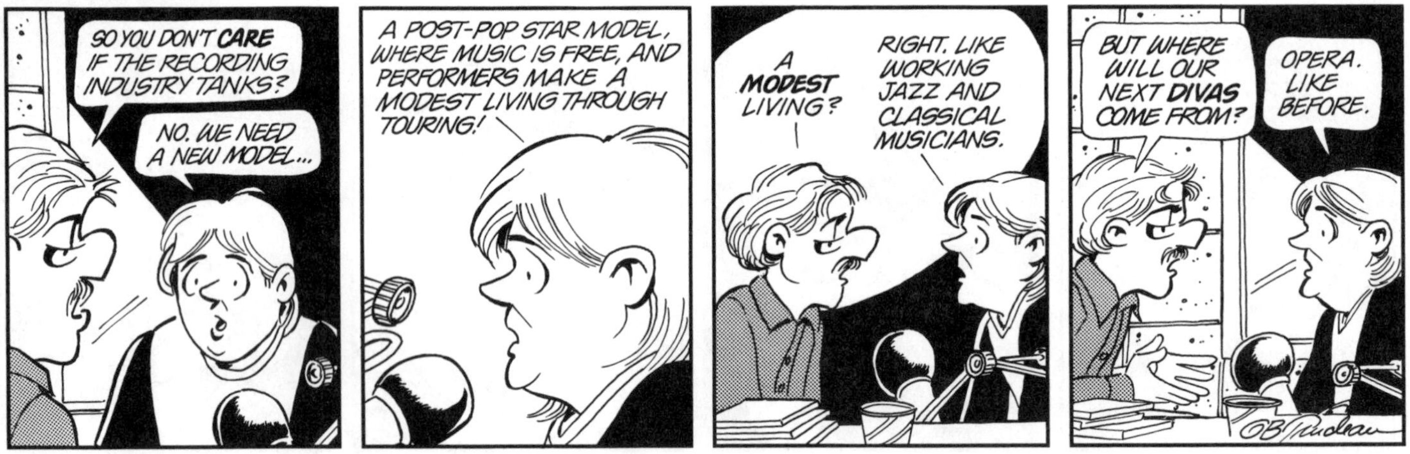
SO YOU DON'T CARE IF THE RECORDING INDUSTRY TANKS?
NO. WE NEED A NEW MODEL...
A POST-POP STAR MODEL, WHERE MUSIC IS FREE, AND PERFORMERS MAKE A MODEST LIVING THROUGH TOURING!
A MODEST LIVING?
RIGHT. LIKE WORKING JAZZ AND CLASSICAL MUSICIANS.
BUT WHERE WILL OUR NEXT DIVAS COME FROM?
OPERA. LIKE BEFORE.

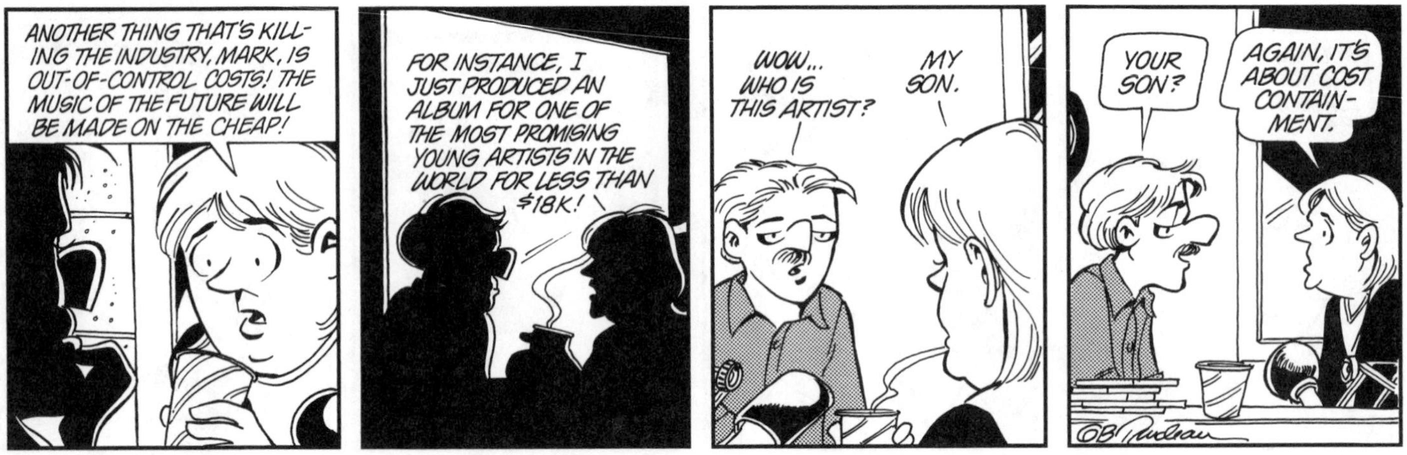
ANOTHER THING THAT'S KILLING THE INDUSTRY, MARK, IS OUT-OF-CONTROL COSTS! THE MUSIC OF THE FUTURE WILL BE MADE ON THE CHEAP!
FOR INSTANCE, I JUST PRODUCED AN ALBUM FOR ONE OF THE MOST PROMISING YOUNG ARTISTS IN THE WORLD FOR LESS THAN $18K!
WOW... WHO IS THIS ARTIST?
MY SON.
YOUR SON?
AGAIN, IT'S ABOUT COST CONTAINMENT.

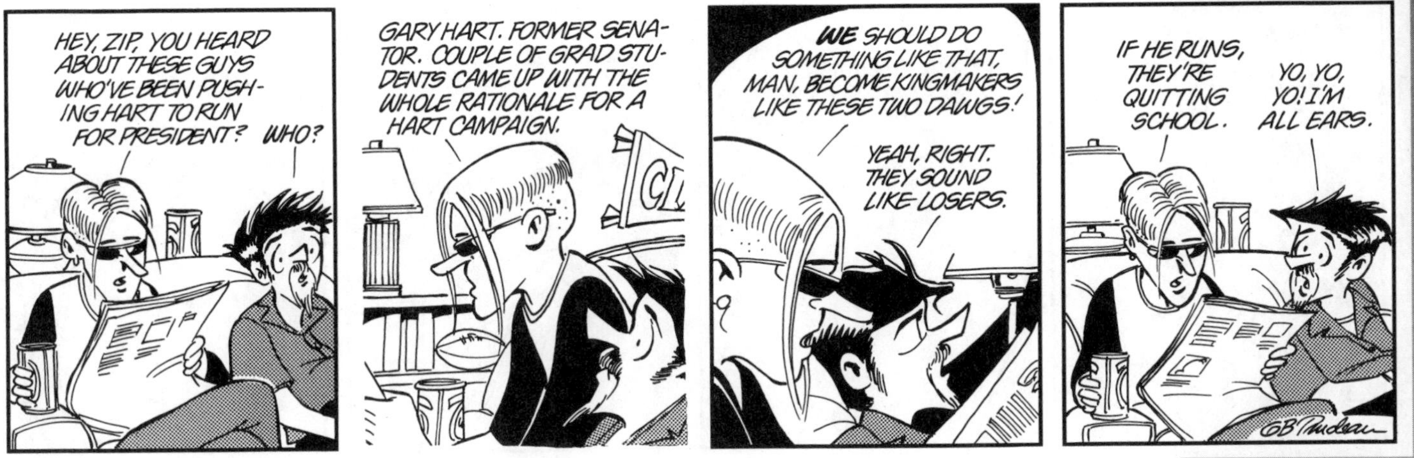
HEY, ZIP, YOU HEARD ABOUT THESE GUYS WHO'VE BEEN PUSH-ING HART TO RUN FOR PRESIDENT?
WHO?
GARY HART. FORMER SENA-TOR. COUPLE OF GRAD STU-DENTS CAME UP WITH THE WHOLE RATIONALE FOR A HART CAMPAIGN.
CIA
WE SHOULD DO SOMETHING LIKE THAT, MAN. BECOME KINGMAKERS LIKE THESE TWO DAWGS!
YEAH, RIGHT. THEY SOUND LIKE LOSERS.
IF HE RUNS, THEY'RE QUITTING SCHOOL.
YO, YO, YO! I'M ALL EARS.
GB Trudeau

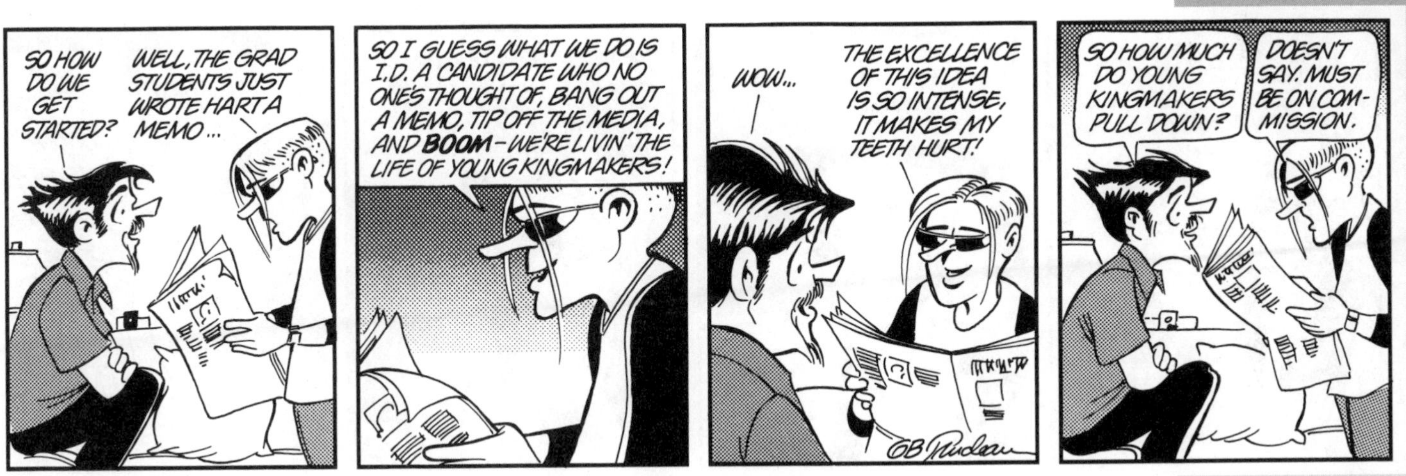
SO HOW DO WE GET STARTED?
WELL, THE GRAD STUDENTS JUST WROTE HART A MEMO ...
SO I GUESS WHAT WE DO IS I.D. A CANDIDATE WHO NO ONE'S THOUGHT OF, BANG OUT A MEMO, TIP OFF THE MEDIA, AND **BOOM** – WE'RE LIVIN' THE LIFE OF YOUNG KINGMAKERS!
WOW...
THE EXCELLENCE OF THIS IDEA IS SO INTENSE, IT MAKES MY TEETH HURT!
GB Trudeau
SO HOW MUCH DO YOUNG KINGMAKERS PULL DOWN?
DOESN'T SAY. MUST BE ON COM-MISSION.

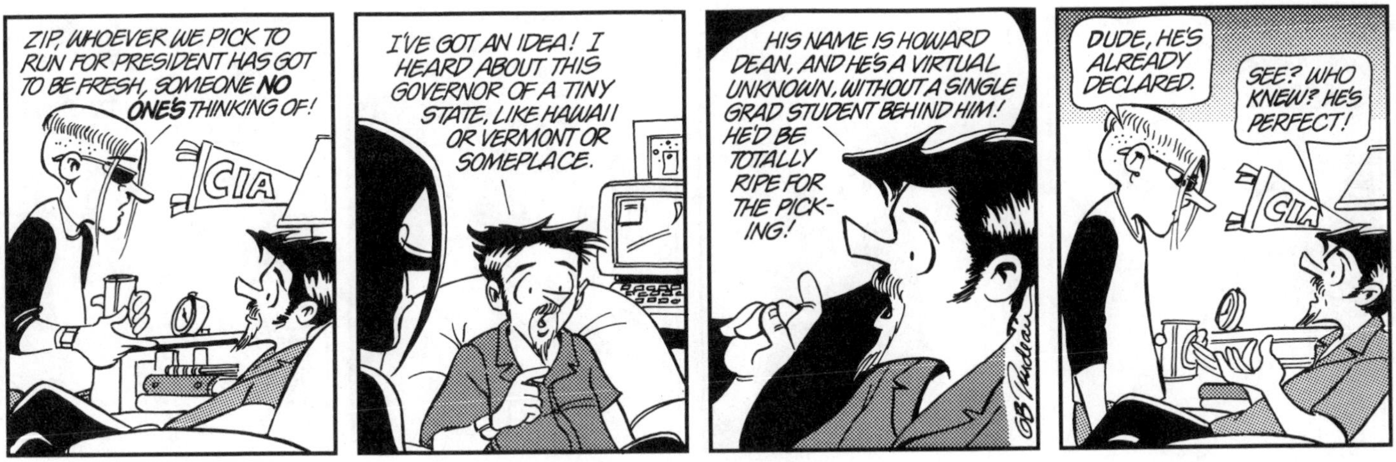
ZIP, WHOEVER WE PICK TO RUN FOR PRESIDENT HAS GOT TO BE FRESH, SOMEONE **NO ONE'S** THINKING OF!
CIA
I'VE GOT AN IDEA! I HEARD ABOUT THIS GOVERNOR OF A TINY STATE, LIKE HAWAII OR VERMONT OR SOMEPLACE.
HIS NAME IS HOWARD DEAN, AND HE'S A VIRTUAL UNKNOWN, WITHOUT A SINGLE GRAD STUDENT BEHIND HIM!
HE'D BE TOTALLY RIPE FOR THE PICK-ING!
GB Trudeau
DUDE, HE'S ALREADY DECLARED.
SEE? WHO KNEW? HE'S PERFECT!
CIA

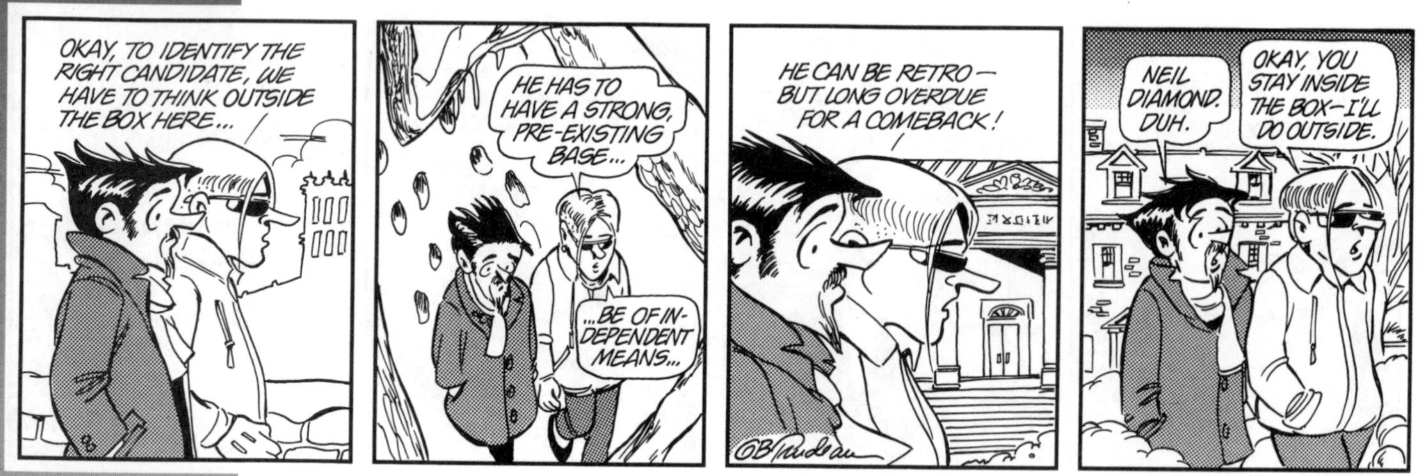
OKAY, TO IDENTIFY THE RIGHT CANDIDATE, WE HAVE TO THINK OUTSIDE THE BOX HERE...
HE HAS TO HAVE A STRONG, PRE-EXISTING BASE...
...BE OF INDEPENDENT MEANS...
HE CAN BE RETRO— BUT LONG OVERDUE FOR A COMEBACK!
NEIL DIAMOND. DUH.
OKAY, YOU STAY INSIDE THE BOX—I'LL DO OUTSIDE.

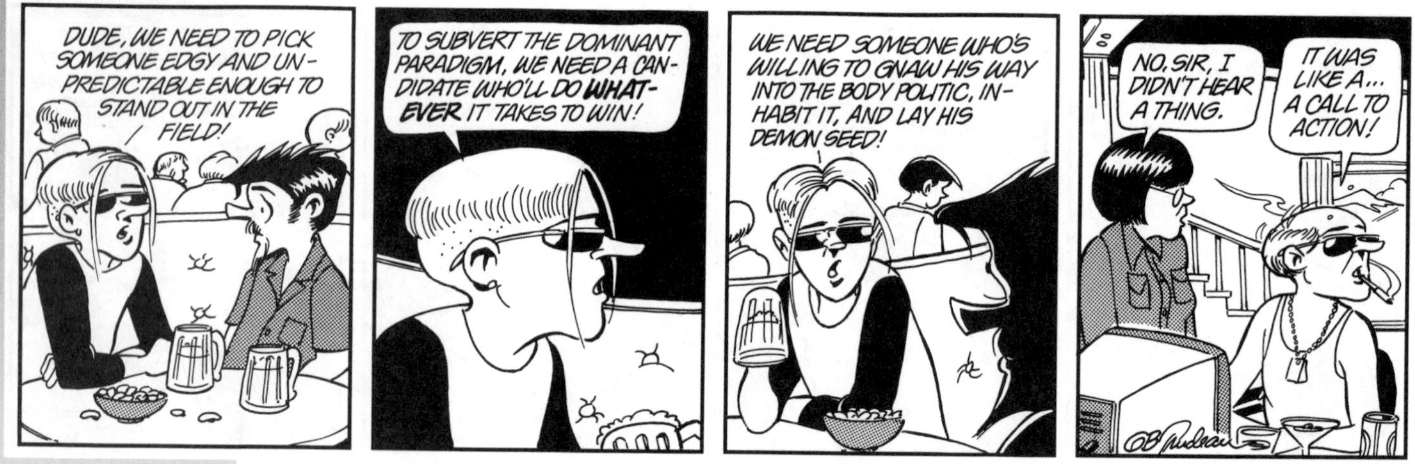
DUDE, WE NEED TO PICK SOMEONE EDGY AND UNPREDICTABLE ENOUGH TO STAND OUT IN THE FIELD!
TO SUBVERT THE DOMINANT PARADIGM, WE NEED A CANDIDATE WHO'LL DO WHATEVER IT TAKES TO WIN!
WE NEED SOMEONE WHO'S WILLING TO GNAW HIS WAY INTO THE BODY POLITIC, INHABIT IT, AND LAY HIS DEMON SEED!
NO, SIR, I DIDN'T HEAR A THING.
IT WAS LIKE A... A CALL TO ACTION!

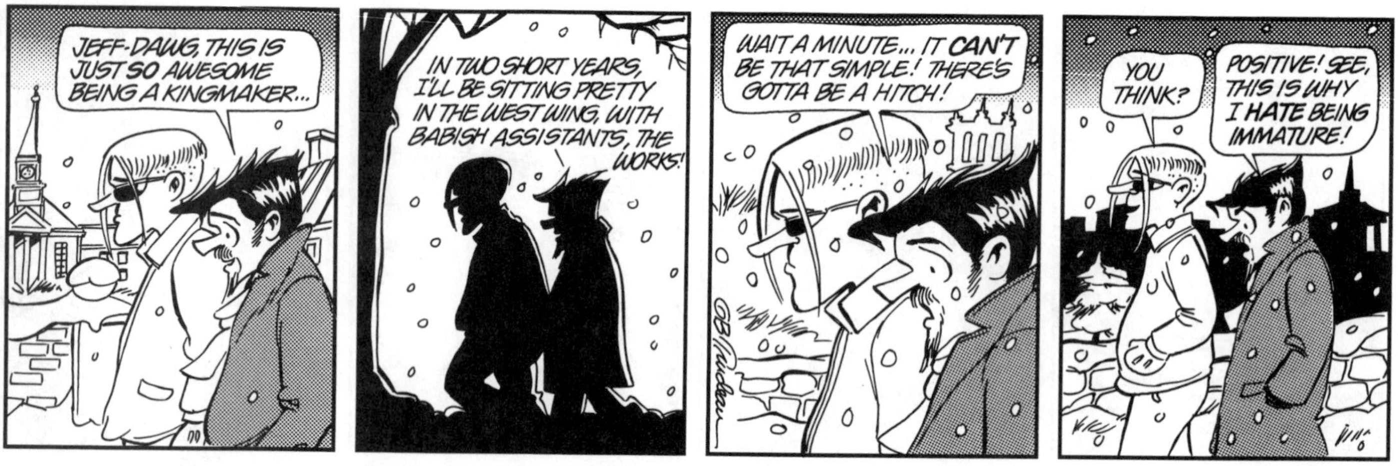
JEFF-DAWG, THIS IS JUST SO AWESOME BEING A KINGMAKER...
IN TWO SHORT YEARS, I'LL BE SITTING PRETTY IN THE WEST WING, WITH BABISH ASSISTANTS, THE WORKS!
WAIT A MINUTE... IT CAN'T BE THAT SIMPLE! THERE'S GOTTA BE A HITCH!
YOU THINK?
POSITIVE! SEE, THIS IS WHY I HATE BEING IMMATURE!

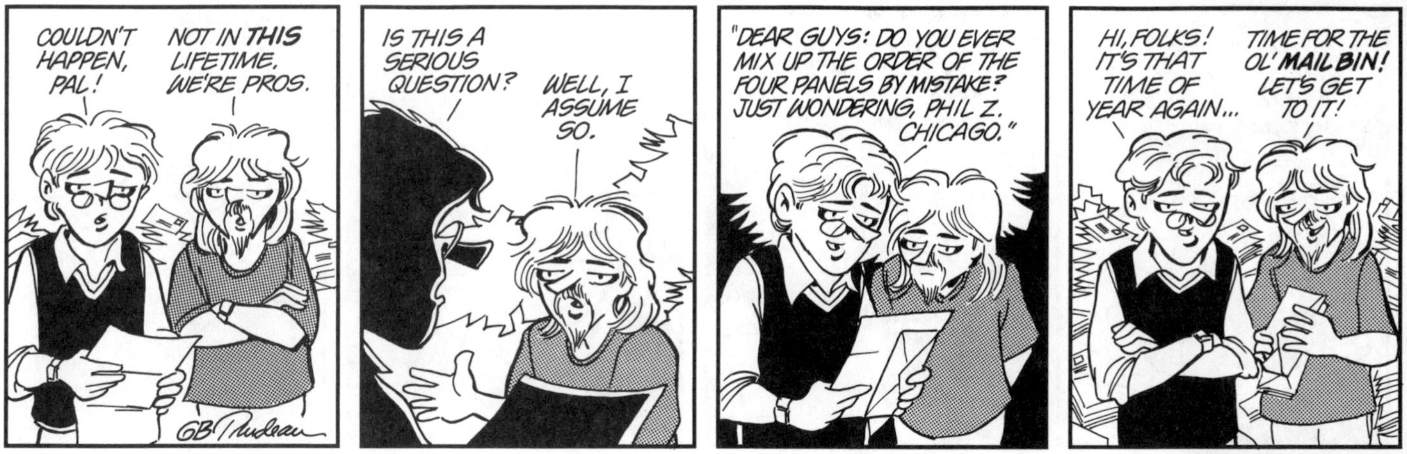
COULDN'T HAPPEN, PAL!
NOT IN **THIS** LIFETIME. WE'RE PROS.
IS THIS A SERIOUS QUESTION?
WELL, I ASSUME SO.
"DEAR GUYS: DO YOU EVER MIX UP THE ORDER OF THE FOUR PANELS BY **MISTAKE?** JUST WONDERING, PHIL Z. CHICAGO."
HI, FOLKS! IT'S THAT TIME OF YEAR AGAIN...
TIME FOR THE OL' **MAIL BIN!** LET'S GET TO IT!

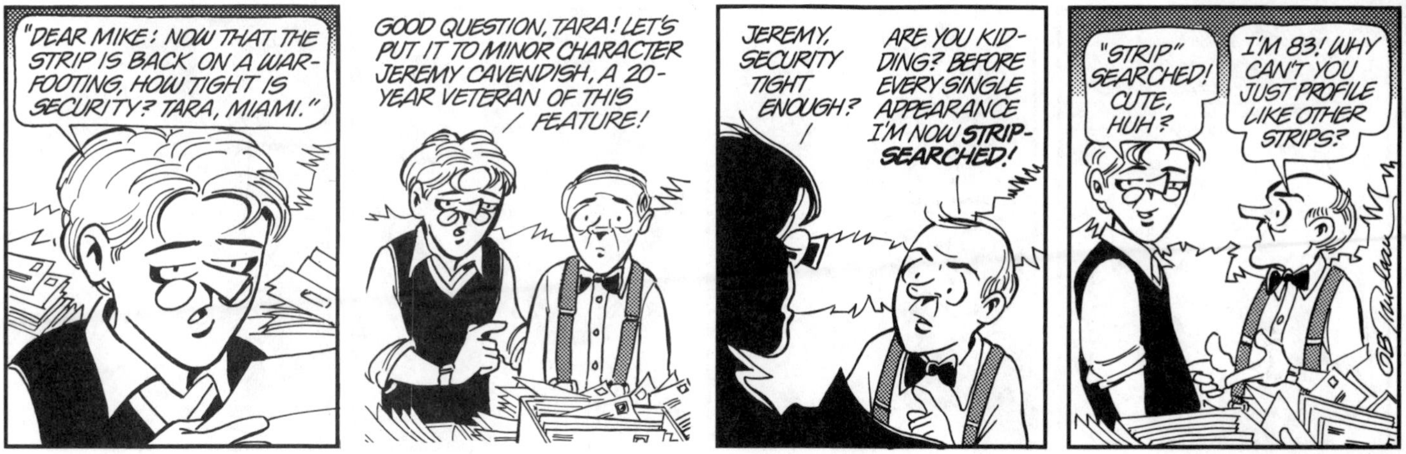
"DEAR MIKE: NOW THAT THE STRIP IS BACK ON A WAR-FOOTING, HOW TIGHT IS SECURITY? TARA, MIAMI."
GOOD QUESTION, TARA! LET'S PUT IT TO MINOR CHARACTER JEREMY CAVENDISH, A 20-YEAR VETERAN OF THIS FEATURE!
JEREMY, SECURITY TIGHT ENOUGH?
ARE YOU KID-DING? BEFORE EVERY SINGLE APPEARANCE I'M NOW **STRIP-SEARCHED!**
"STRIP" SEARCHED! CUTE, HUH?
I'M 83! WHY CAN'T YOU JUST PROFILE LIKE OTHER STRIPS?

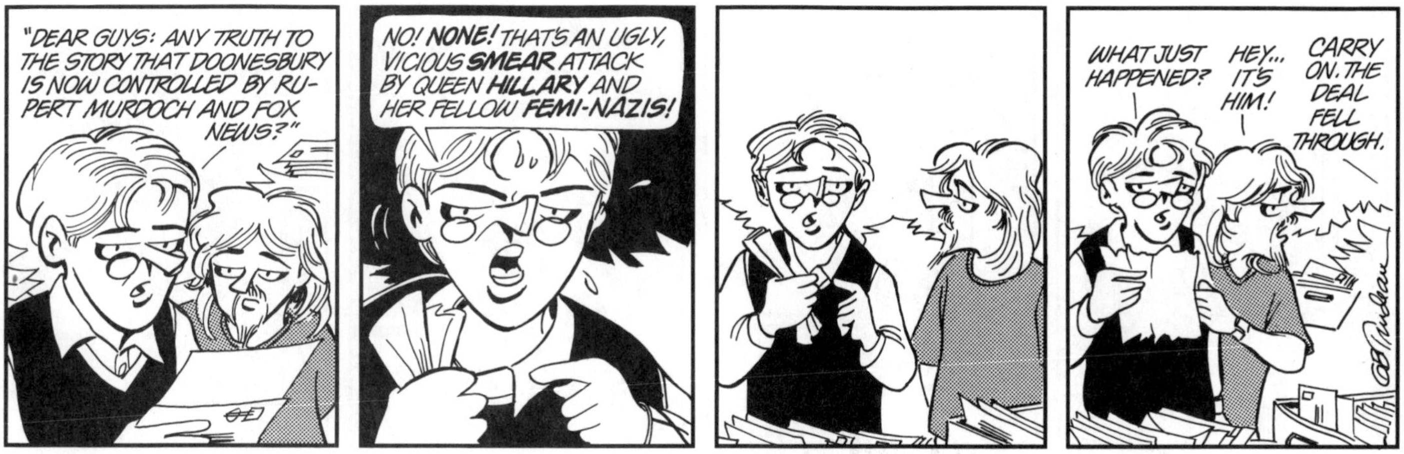
"DEAR GUYS: ANY TRUTH TO THE STORY THAT DOONESBURY IS NOW CONTROLLED BY RU-PERT MURDOCH AND FOX NEWS?"
NO! **NONE!** THAT'S AN UGLY, VICIOUS **SMEAR** ATTACK BY QUEEN **HILLARY** AND HER FELLOW **FEMI-NAZIS!**
WHAT JUST HAPPENED?
HEY... IT'S HIM!
CARRY ON. THE DEAL FELL THROUGH.

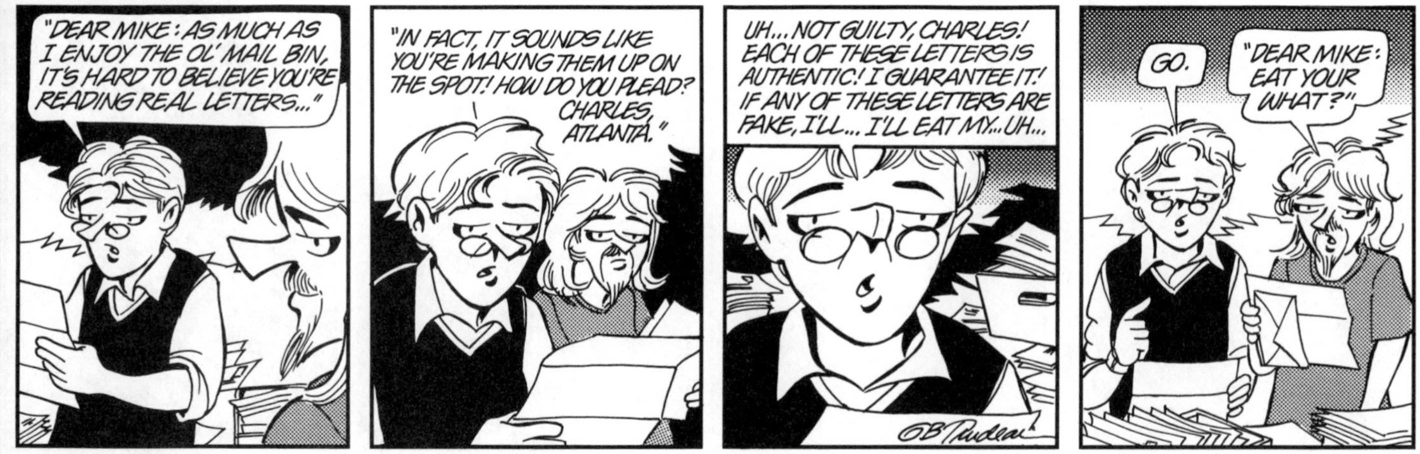
"DEAR MIKE: AS MUCH AS I ENJOY THE OL' MAIL BIN, IT'S HARD TO BELIEVE YOU'RE READING REAL LETTERS..."
"IN FACT, IT SOUNDS LIKE YOU'RE MAKING THEM UP ON THE SPOT! HOW DO YOU PLEAD? CHARLES, ATLANTA."
UH... NOT GUILTY, CHARLES! EACH OF THESE LETTERS IS AUTHENTIC! I GUARANTEE IT! IF ANY OF THESE LETTERS ARE FAKE, I'LL... I'LL EAT MY...UH...
GO.
"DEAR MIKE: EAT YOUR WHAT?"

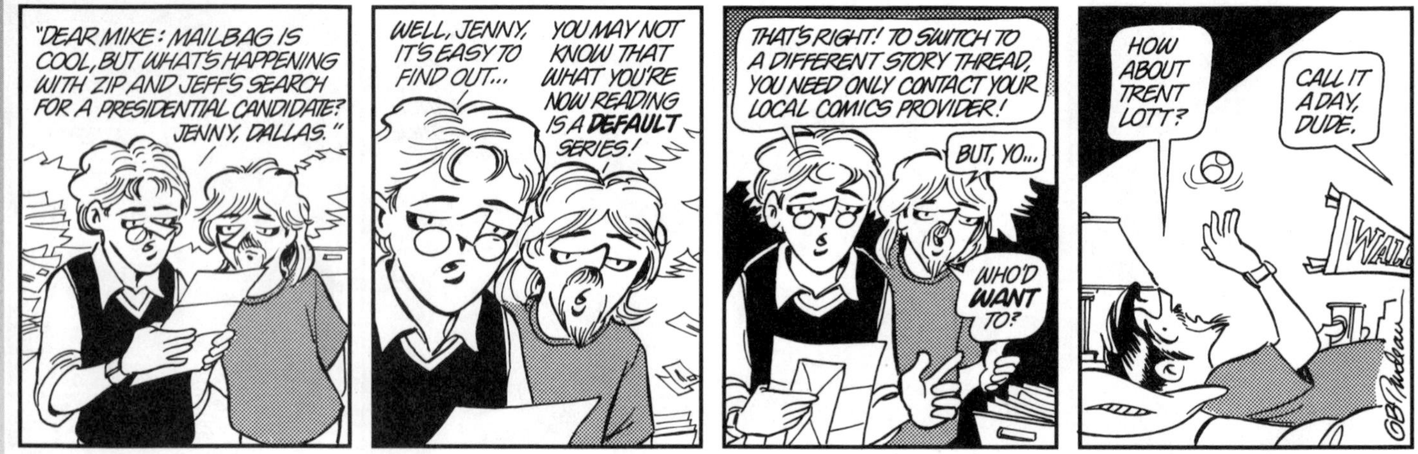
"DEAR MIKE: MAILBAG IS COOL, BUT WHAT'S HAPPENING WITH ZIP AND JEFF'S SEARCH FOR A PRESIDENTIAL CANDIDATE? JENNY, DALLAS."
WELL, JENNY, IT'S EASY TO FIND OUT...
YOU MAY NOT KNOW THAT WHAT YOU'RE NOW READING IS A **DEFAULT** SERIES!
THAT'S RIGHT! TO SWITCH TO A DIFFERENT STORY THREAD, YOU NEED ONLY CONTACT YOUR LOCAL COMICS PROVIDER!
BUT, YO...
WHO'D **WANT** TO?
HOW ABOUT TRENT LOTT?
CALL IT A DAY, DUDE.

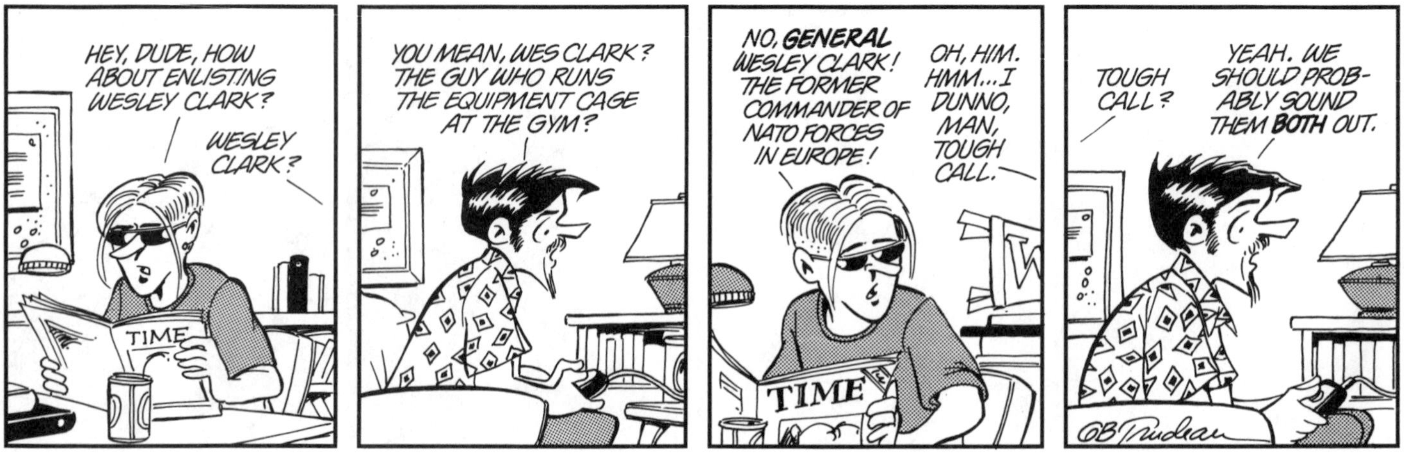
HEY, DUDE, HOW ABOUT ENLISTING WESLEY CLARK?
WESLEY CLARK?
TIME
YOU MEAN, WES CLARK? THE GUY WHO RUNS THE EQUIPMENT CAGE AT THE GYM?
NO, **GENERAL** WESLEY CLARK! THE FORMER COMMANDER OF NATO FORCES IN EUROPE!
OH, HIM. HMM... I DUNNO, MAN, TOUGH CALL.
TIME
TOUGH CALL?
YEAH. WE SHOULD PROBABLY SOUND THEM **BOTH** OUT.

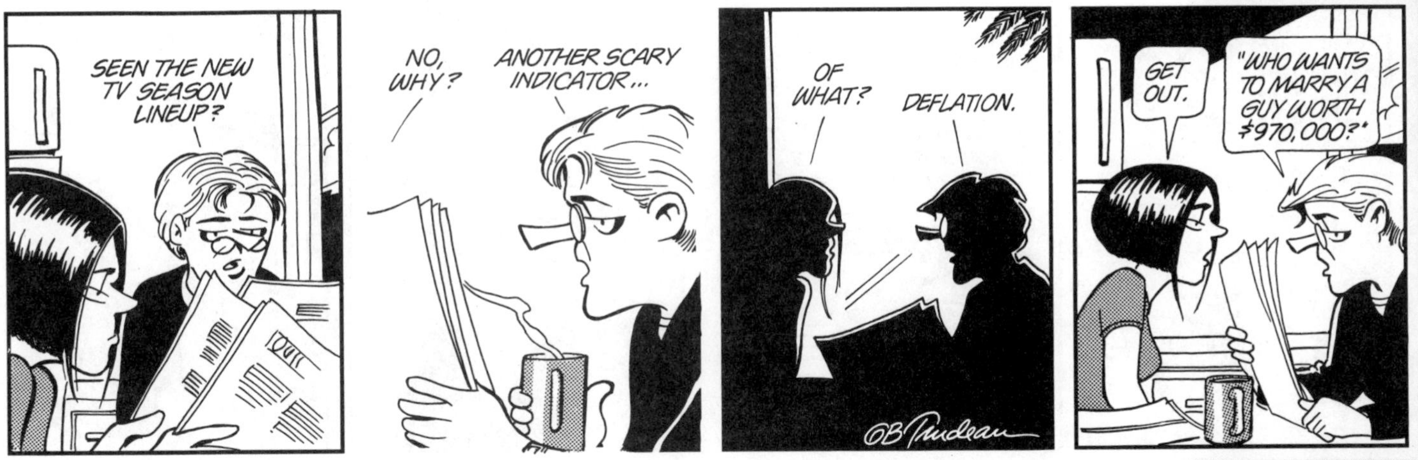
SEEN THE NEW TV SEASON LINEUP?
NO, WHY?
ANOTHER SCARY INDICATOR...
OF WHAT?
DEFLATION.
GET OUT.
"WHO WANTS TO MARRY A GUY WORTH $970,000?"
GB Trudeau

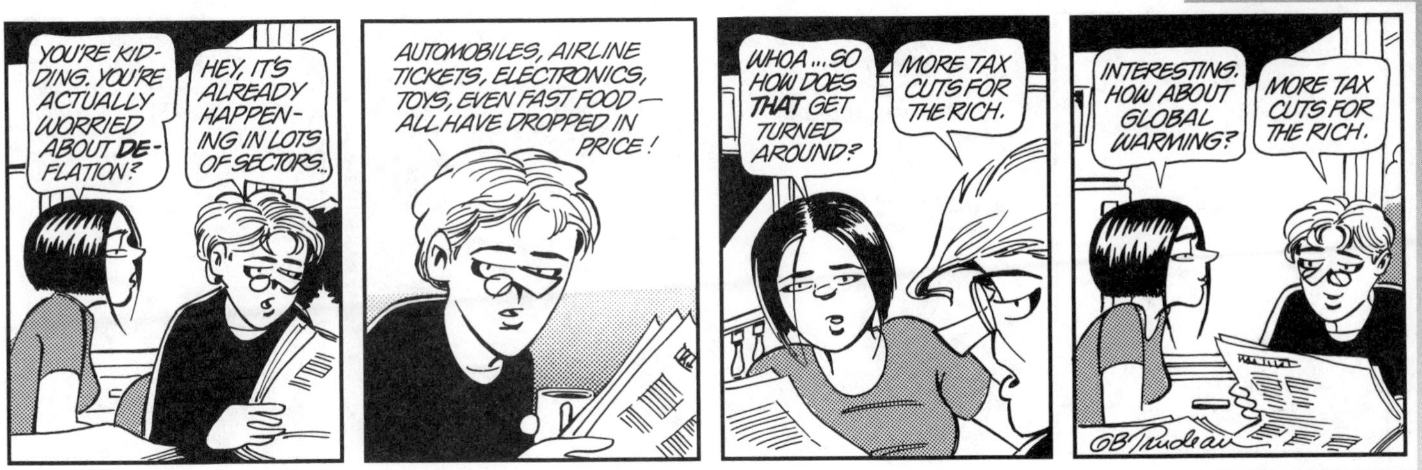
YOU'RE KIDDING. YOU'RE ACTUALLY WORRIED ABOUT DEFLATION?
HEY, IT'S ALREADY HAPPENING IN LOTS OF SECTORS...
AUTOMOBILES, AIRLINE TICKETS, ELECTRONICS, TOYS, EVEN FAST FOOD— ALL HAVE DROPPED IN PRICE!
WHOA... SO HOW DOES THAT GET TURNED AROUND?
MORE TAX CUTS FOR THE RICH.
INTERESTING. HOW ABOUT GLOBAL WARMING?
MORE TAX CUTS FOR THE RICH.
GB Trudeau

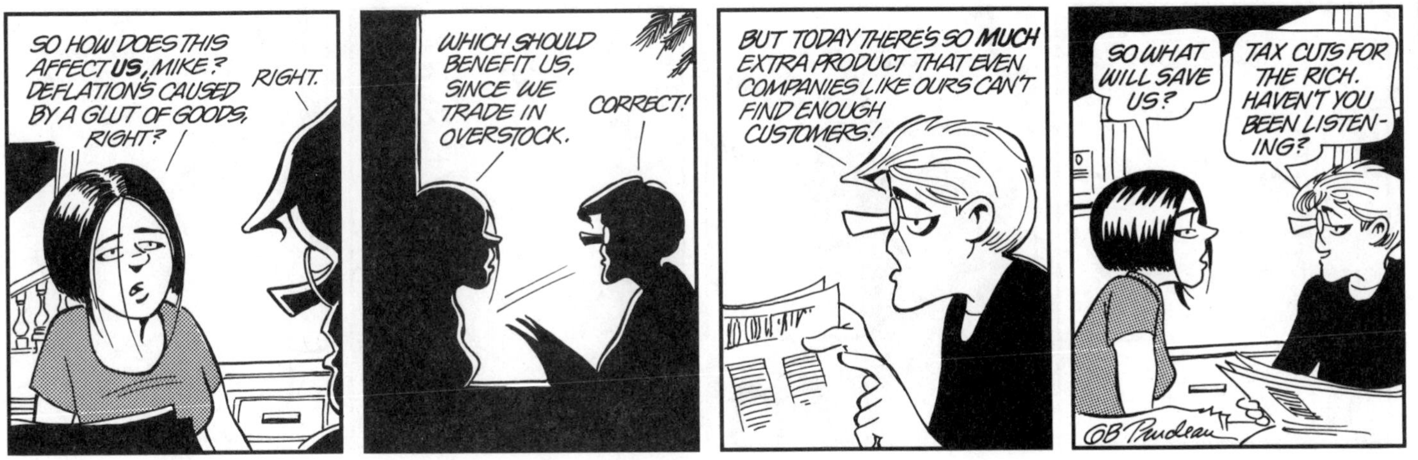
SO HOW DOES THIS AFFECT US, MIKE? DEFLATION'S CAUSED BY A GLUT OF GOODS, RIGHT?
RIGHT.
WHICH SHOULD BENEFIT US, SINCE WE TRADE IN OVERSTOCK.
CORRECT!
BUT TODAY THERE'S SO MUCH EXTRA PRODUCT THAT EVEN COMPANIES LIKE OURS CAN'T FIND ENOUGH CUSTOMERS!
SO WHAT WILL SAVE US?
TAX CUTS FOR THE RICH. HAVEN'T YOU BEEN LISTENING?
GB Trudeau

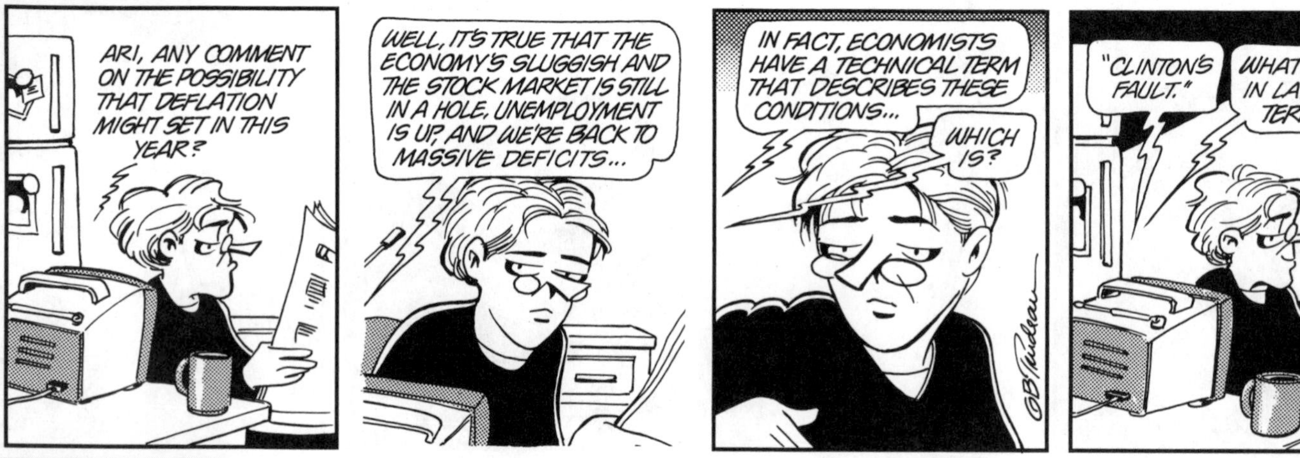
ARI, ANY COMMENT ON THE POSSIBILITY THAT DEFLATION MIGHT SET IN THIS YEAR?
WELL, IT'S TRUE THAT THE ECONOMY'S SLUGGISH AND THE STOCK MARKET IS STILL IN A HOLE, UNEMPLOYMENT IS UP, AND WE'RE BACK TO MASSIVE DEFICITS...
IN FACT, ECONOMISTS HAVE A TECHNICAL TERM THAT DESCRIBES THESE CONDITIONS...
WHICH IS?
"CLINTON'S FAULT."
WHAT'S THAT IN LAYMAN'S TERMS?

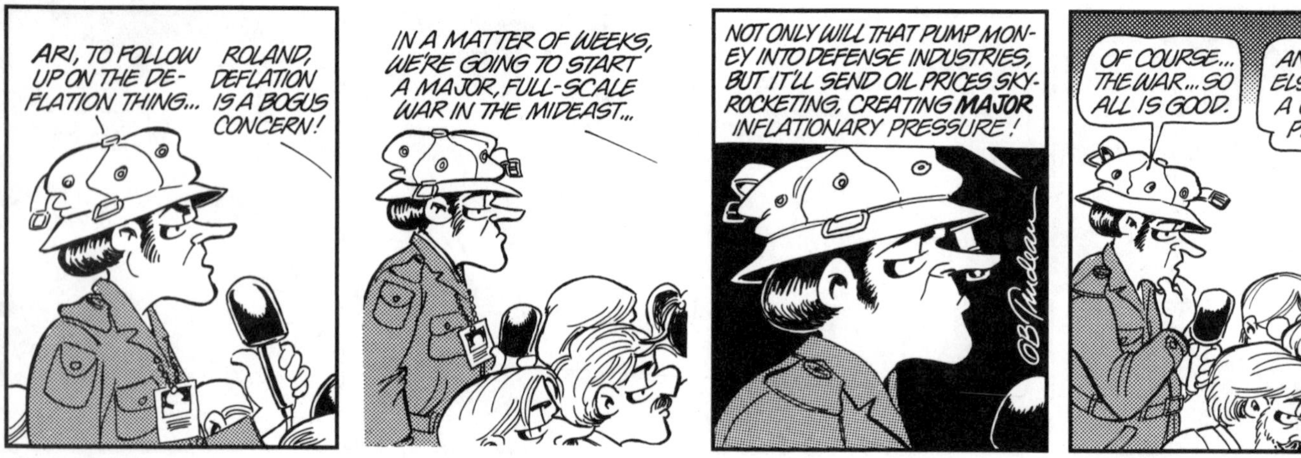
ARI, TO FOLLOW UP ON THE DEFLATION THING...
ROLAND, DEFLATION IS A BOGUS CONCERN!
IN A MATTER OF WEEKS, WE'RE GOING TO START A MAJOR, FULL-SCALE WAR IN THE MIDEAST...
NOT ONLY WILL THAT PUMP MONEY INTO DEFENSE INDUSTRIES, BUT IT'LL SEND OIL PRICES SKYROCKETING, CREATING MAJOR INFLATIONARY PRESSURE!
OF COURSE... THE WAR... SO ALL IS GOOD.
ANYONE ELSE NEED A CHILL PILL?

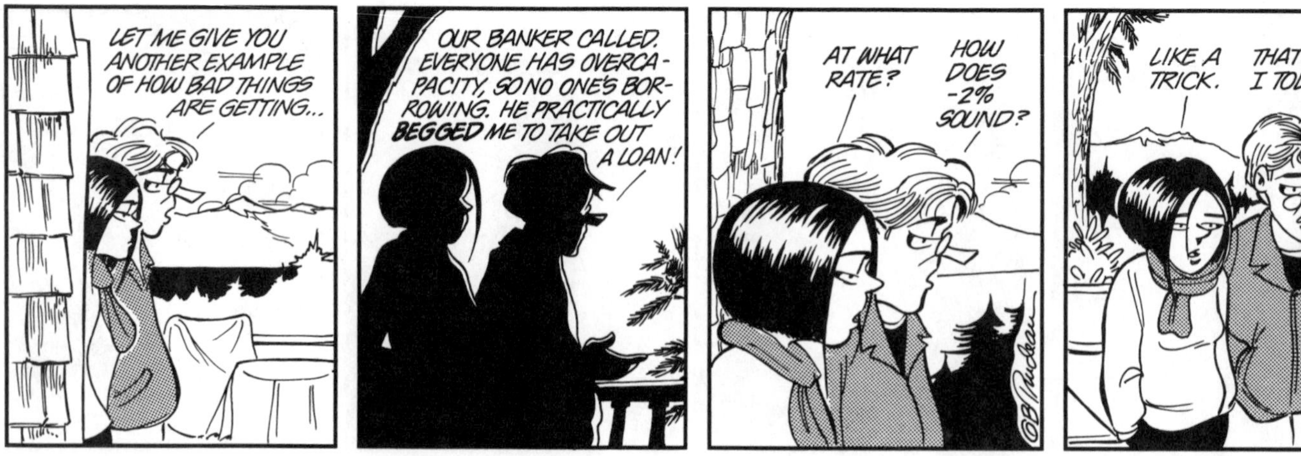
LET ME GIVE YOU ANOTHER EXAMPLE OF HOW BAD THINGS ARE GETTING...
OUR BANKER CALLED. EVERYONE HAS OVERCAPACITY, SO NO ONE'S BORROWING. HE PRACTICALLY BEGGED ME TO TAKE OUT A LOAN!
AT WHAT RATE?
HOW DOES -2% SOUND?
LIKE A TRICK.
THAT'S WHAT I TOLD HIM.

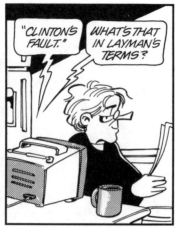

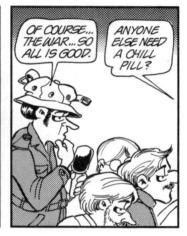

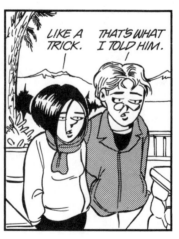

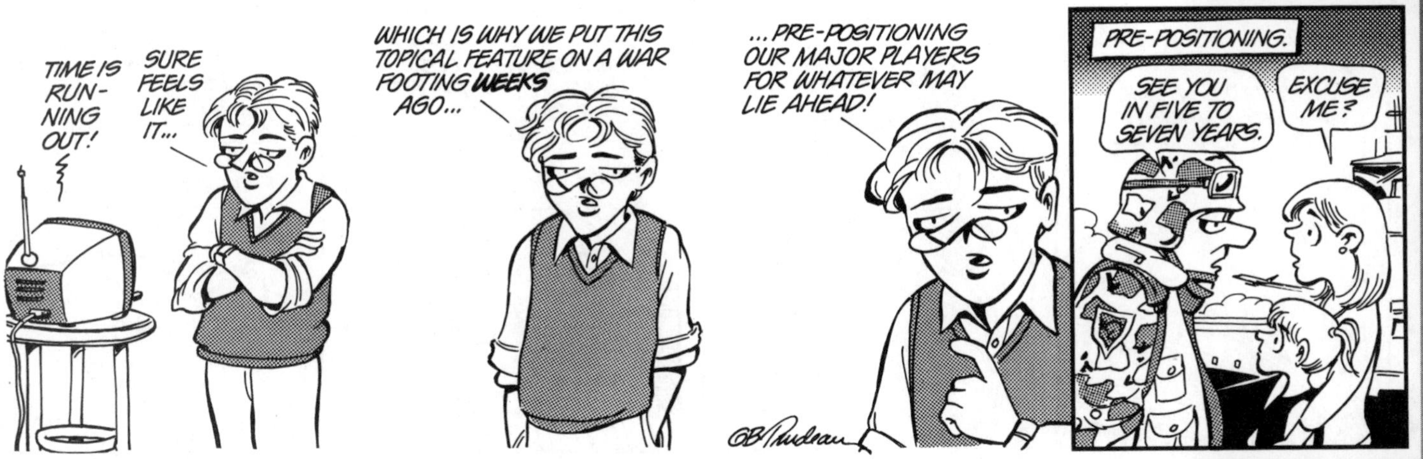
TIME IS RUN-NING OUT!
SURE FEELS LIKE IT...
WHICH IS WHY WE PUT THIS TOPICAL FEATURE ON A WAR FOOTING **WEEKS** AGO...
...PRE-POSITIONING OUR MAJOR PLAYERS FOR WHATEVER MAY LIE AHEAD!
PRE-POSITIONING.
SEE YOU IN FIVE TO SEVEN YEARS.
EXCUSE ME?

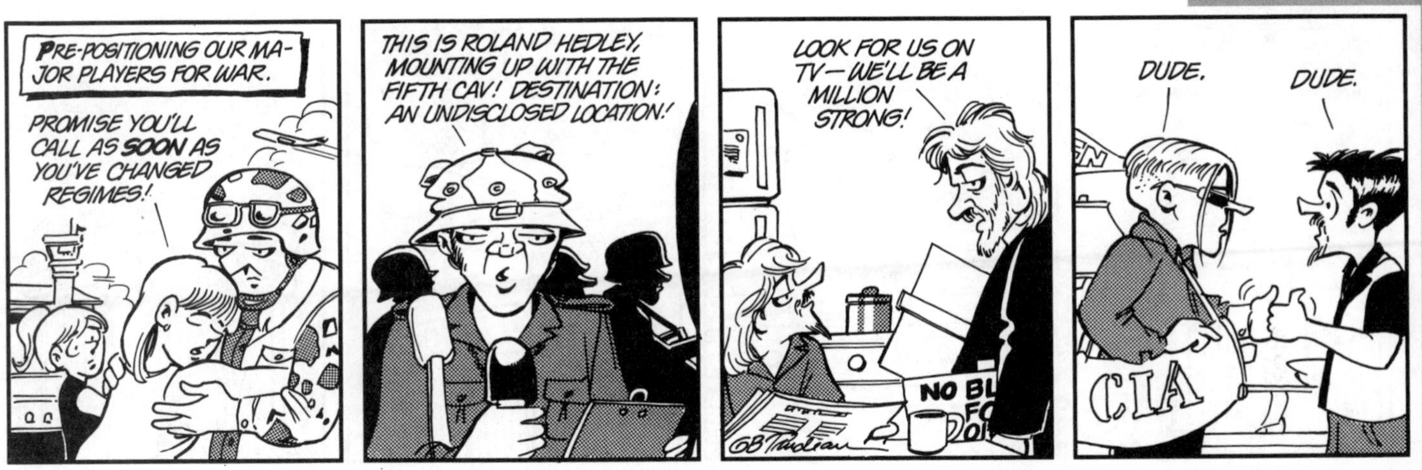
PRE-POSITIONING OUR MAJOR PLAYERS FOR WAR.
PROMISE YOU'LL CALL AS **SOON** AS YOU'VE CHANGED REGIMES!
THIS IS ROLAND HEDLEY, MOUNTING UP WITH THE FIFTH CAV! DESTINATION: AN UNDISCLOSED LOCATION!
LOOK FOR US ON TV—WE'LL BE A MILLION STRONG!
DUDE.
DUDE.
CIA

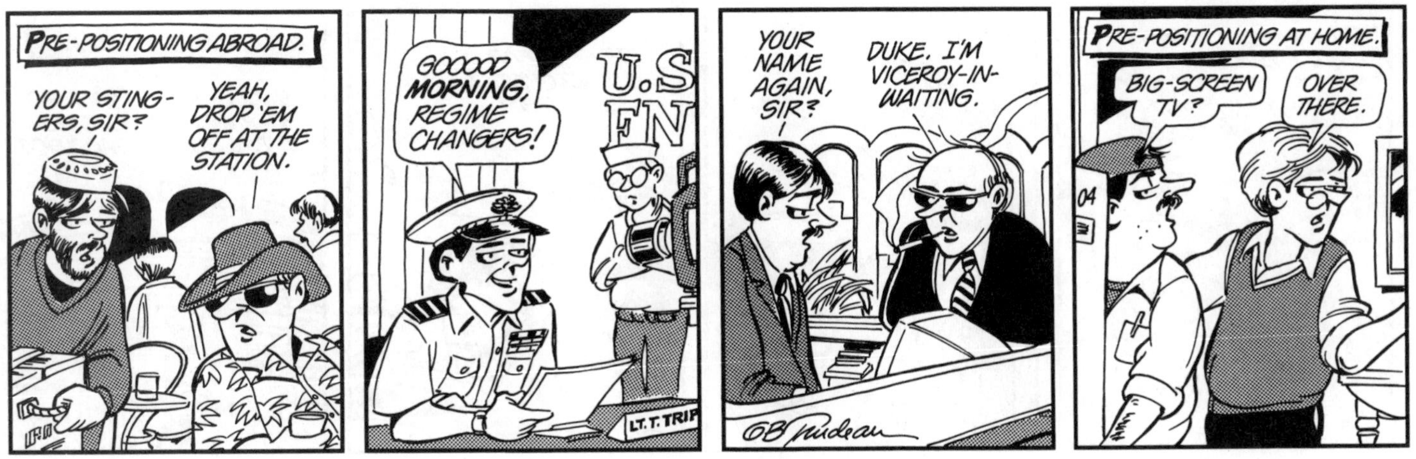
PRE-POSITIONING ABROAD.
YOUR STING-ERS, SIR?
YEAH, DROP 'EM OFF AT THE STATION.
GOOOOD **MORNING**, REGIME CHANGERS!
LT. T. TRIP
YOUR NAME AGAIN, SIR?
DUKE. I'M VICEROY-IN-WAITING.
PRE-POSITIONING AT HOME.
BIG-SCREEN TV?
OVER THERE.

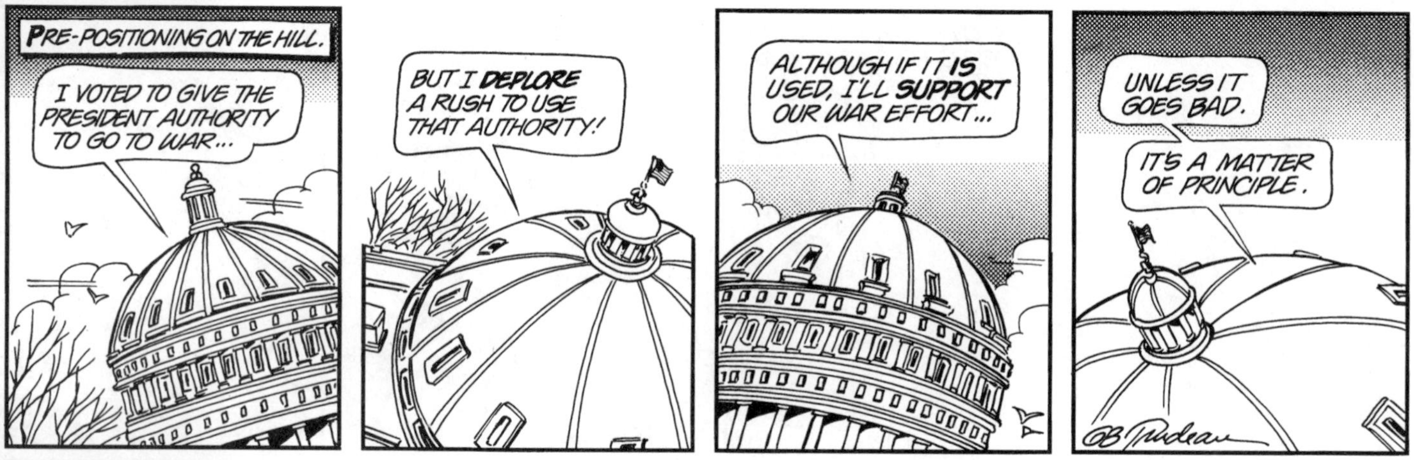
PRE-POSITIONING ON THE HILL.
I VOTED TO GIVE THE PRESIDENT AUTHORITY TO GO TO WAR...
BUT I DEPLORE A RUSH TO USE THAT AUTHORITY!
ALTHOUGH IF IT IS USED, I'LL SUPPORT OUR WAR EFFORT...
UNLESS IT GOES BAD.
IT'S A MATTER OF PRINCIPLE.

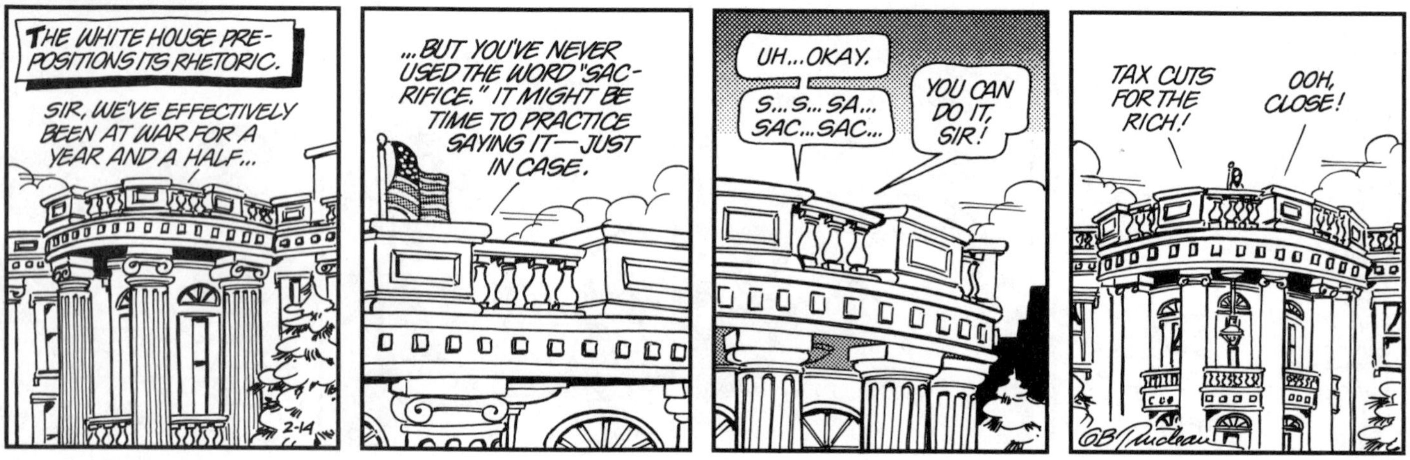
THE WHITE HOUSE PRE-POSITIONS ITS RHETORIC.
SIR, WE'VE EFFECTIVELY BEEN AT WAR FOR A YEAR AND A HALF...
2-14
...BUT YOU'VE NEVER USED THE WORD "SACRIFICE." IT MIGHT BE TIME TO PRACTICE SAYING IT— JUST IN CASE.
UH...OKAY.
S...S...SA... SAC...SAC...
YOU CAN DO IT, SIR!
TAX CUTS FOR THE RICH!
OOH, CLOSE!

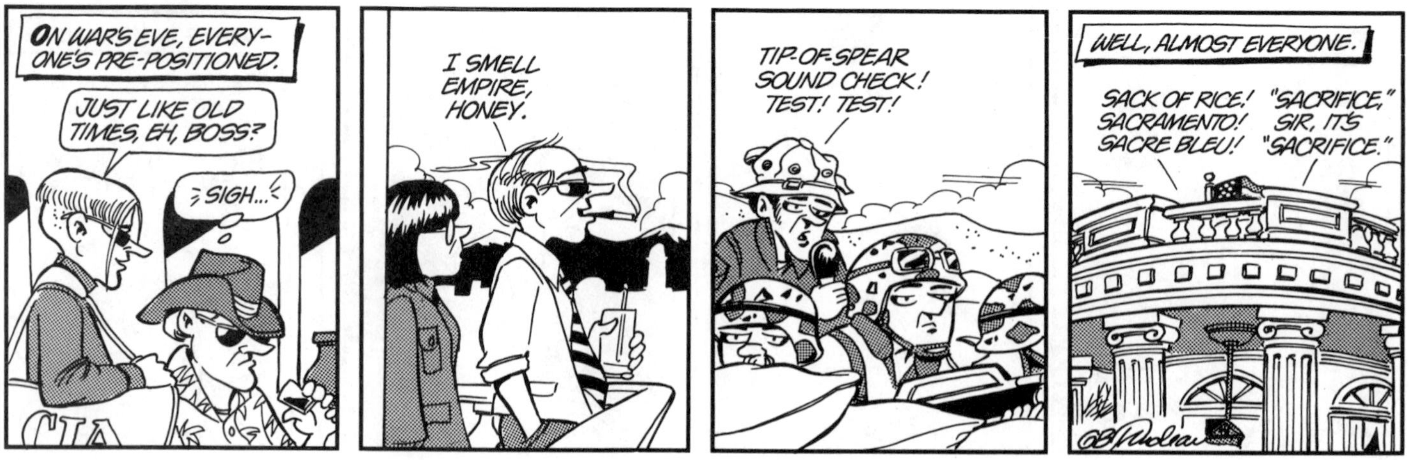
ON WAR'S EVE, EVERYONE'S PRE-POSITIONED.
JUST LIKE OLD TIMES, EH, BOSS?
SIGH...
CIA
I SMELL EMPIRE, HONEY.
TIP-OF-SPEAR SOUND CHECK! TEST! TEST!
WELL, ALMOST EVERYONE.
SACK OF RICE! SACRAMENTO! SACRE BLEU!
"SACRIFICE," SIR, IT'S "SACRIFICE."

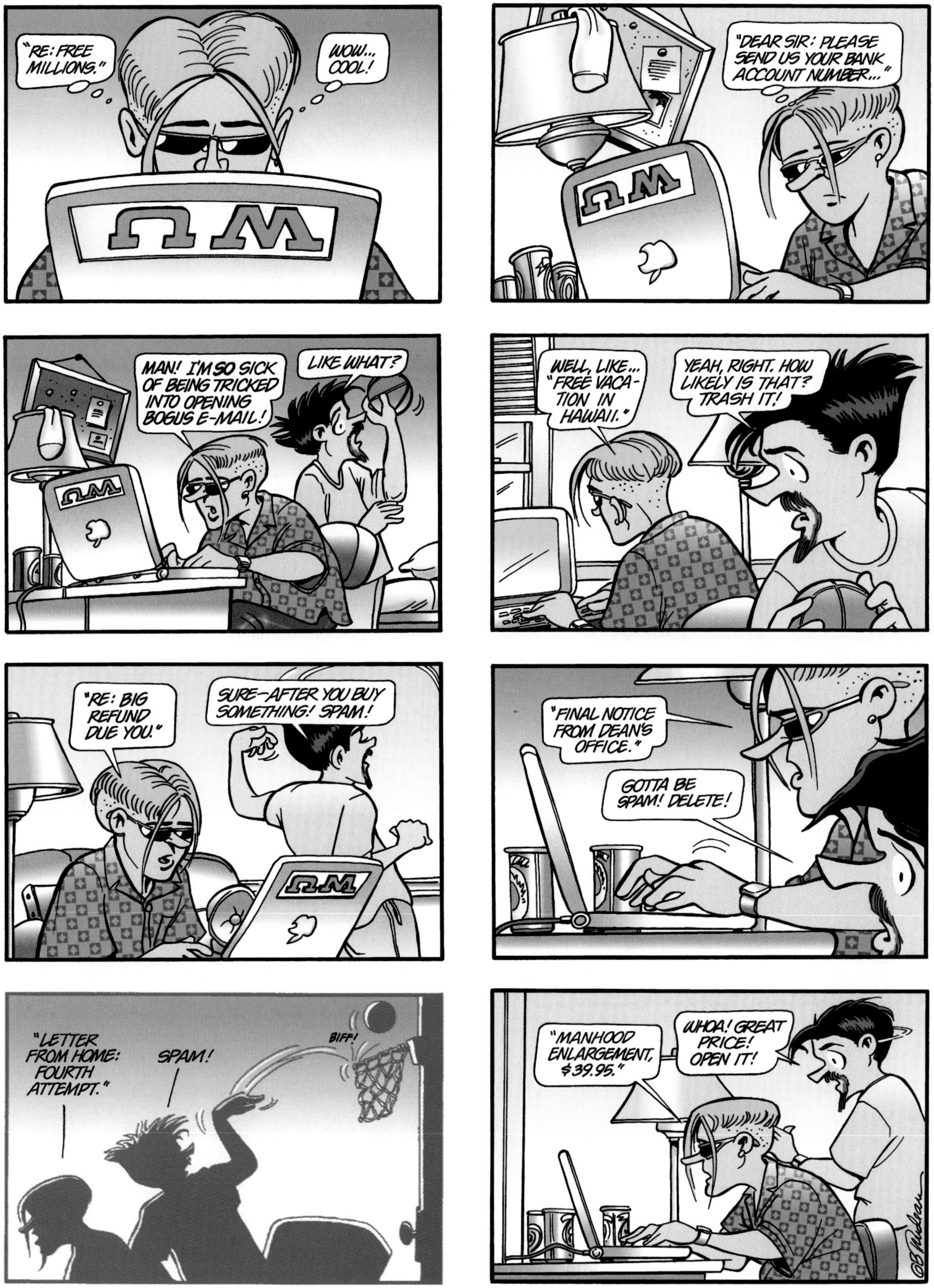

"RE: FREE MILLIONS."
WOW... COOL!
"DEAR SIR: PLEASE SEND US YOUR BANK ACCOUNT NUMBER..."
MAN! I'M SO SICK OF BEING TRICKED INTO OPENING BOGUS E-MAIL!
LIKE WHAT?
WELL, LIKE... "FREE VACATION IN HAWAII."
YEAH, RIGHT. HOW LIKELY IS THAT? TRASH IT!
"RE: BIG REFUND DUE YOU."
SURE—AFTER YOU BUY SOMETHING! SPAM!
"FINAL NOTICE FROM DEAN'S OFFICE."
GOTTA BE SPAM! DELETE!
"LETTER FROM HOME: FOURTH ATTEMPT."
SPAM!
BIFF!
"MANHOOD ENLARGEMENT, $39.95."
WHOA! GREAT PRICE! OPEN IT!

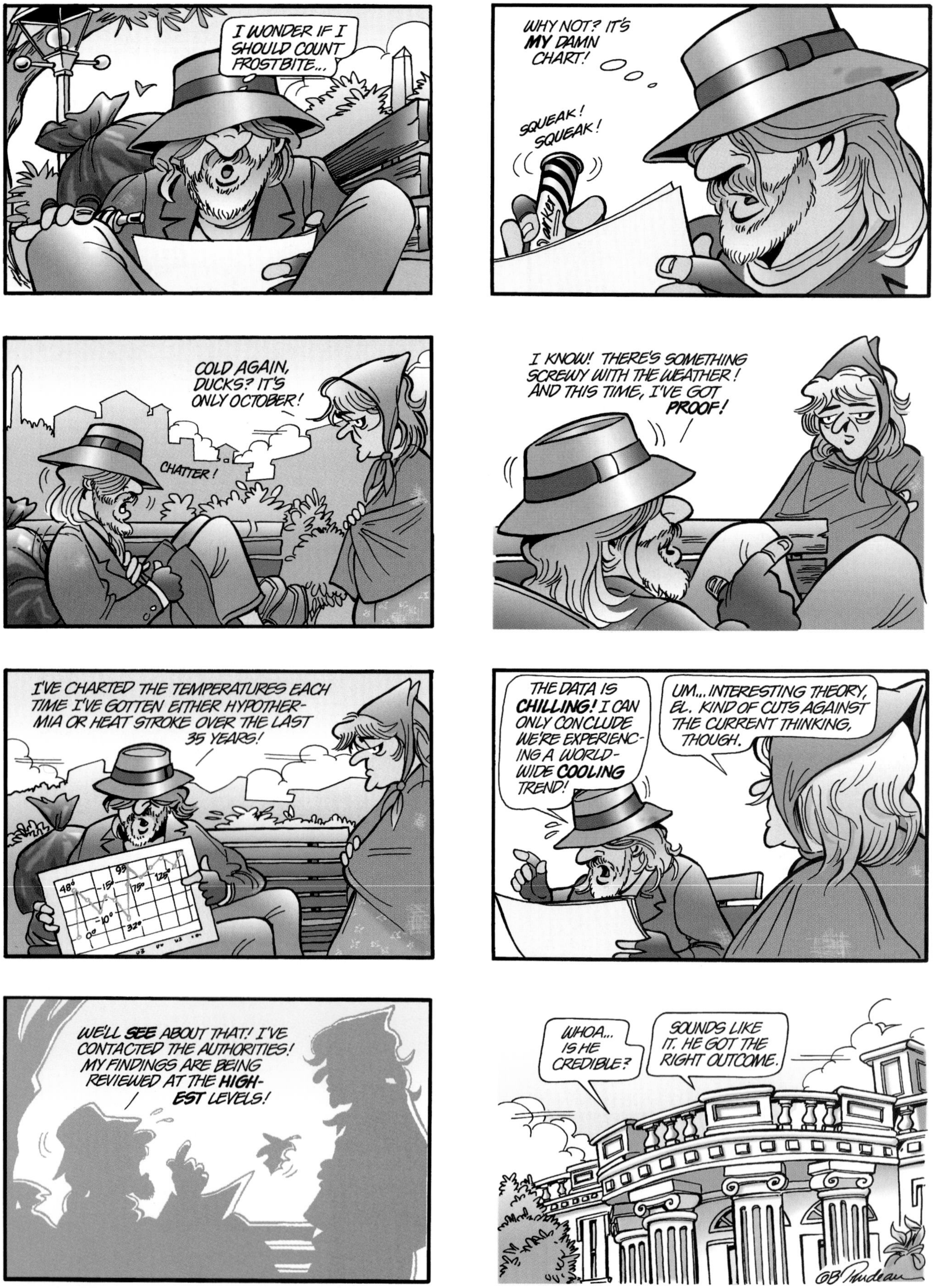
I WONDER IF I SHOULD COUNT FROSTBITE...
WHY NOT? IT'S MY DAMN CHART!
SQUEAK! SQUEAK!
COLD AGAIN, DUCKS? IT'S ONLY OCTOBER!
CHATTER!
I KNOW! THERE'S SOMETHING SCREWY WITH THE WEATHER! AND THIS TIME, I'VE GOT PROOF!
I'VE CHARTED THE TEMPERATURES EACH TIME I'VE GOTTEN EITHER HYPOTHERMIA OR HEAT STROKE OVER THE LAST 35 YEARS!
48°
-15°
99°
75°
128°
-10°
0°
32°
THE DATA IS CHILLING! I CAN ONLY CONCLUDE WE'RE EXPERIENCING A WORLDWIDE COOLING TREND!
UM... INTERESTING THEORY, EL. KIND OF CUTS AGAINST THE CURRENT THINKING, THOUGH.
WE'LL SEE ABOUT THAT! I'VE CONTACTED THE AUTHORITIES! MY FINDINGS ARE BEING REVIEWED AT THE HIGHEST LEVELS!
WHOA... IS HE CREDIBLE?
SOUNDS LIKE IT. HE GOT THE RIGHT OUTCOME.

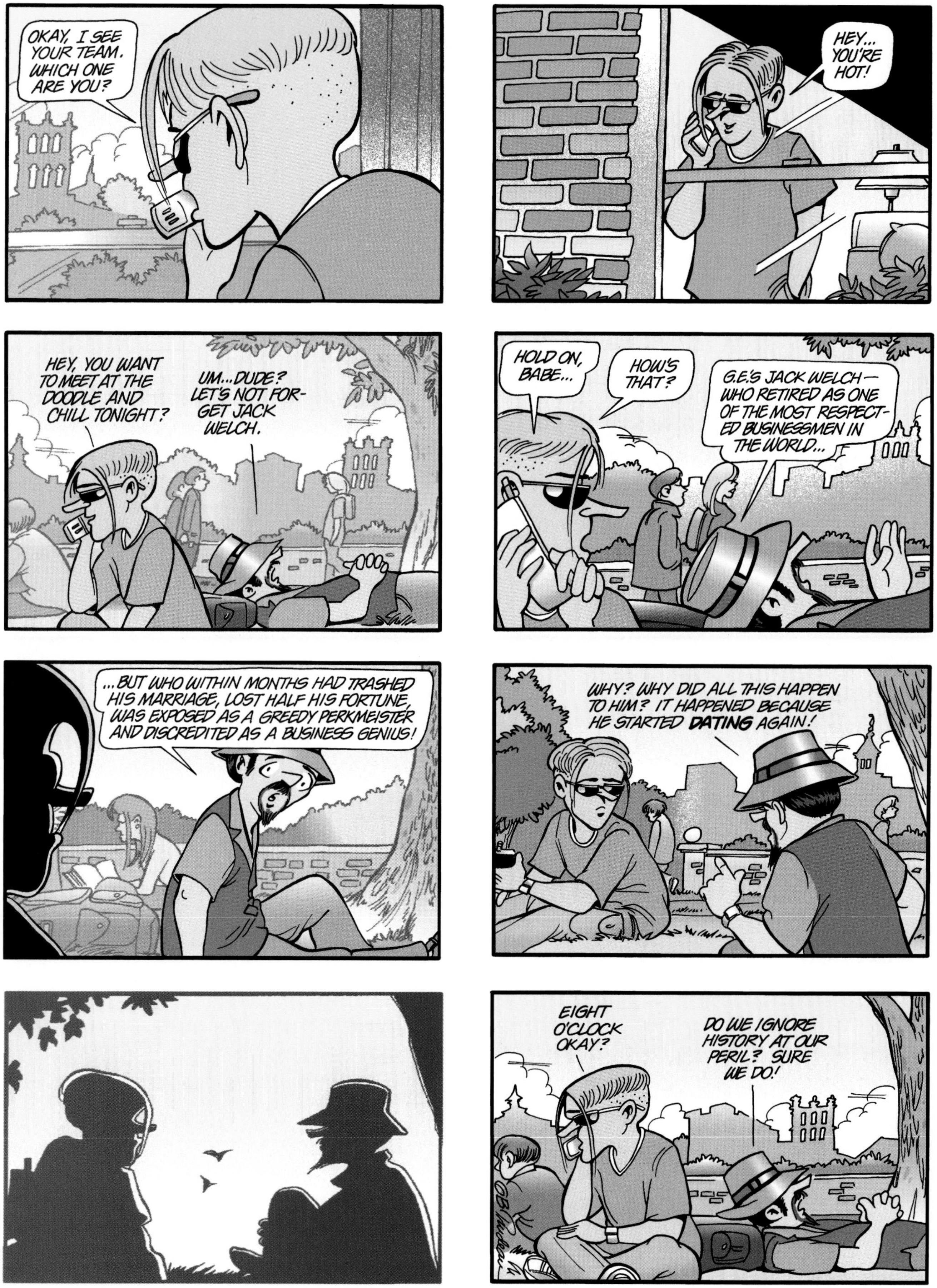

OKAY, I SEE YOUR TEAM. WHICH ONE ARE YOU?
HEY... YOU'RE HOT!
HEY, YOU WANT TO MEET AT THE DOODLE AND CHILL TONIGHT?
UM...DUDE? LET'S NOT FORGET JACK WELCH.
HOLD ON, BABE...
HOW'S THAT?
G.E.'S JACK WELCH— WHO RETIRED AS ONE OF THE MOST RESPECTED BUSINESSMEN IN THE WORLD...
...BUT WHO WITHIN MONTHS HAD TRASHED HIS MARRIAGE, LOST HALF HIS FORTUNE, WAS EXPOSED AS A GREEDY PERKMEISTER AND DISCREDITED AS A BUSINESS GENIUS!
WHY? WHY DID ALL THIS HAPPEN TO HIM? IT HAPPENED BECAUSE HE STARTED **DATING** AGAIN!
EIGHT O'CLOCK OKAY?
DO WE IGNORE HISTORY AT OUR PERIL? SURE WE DO!

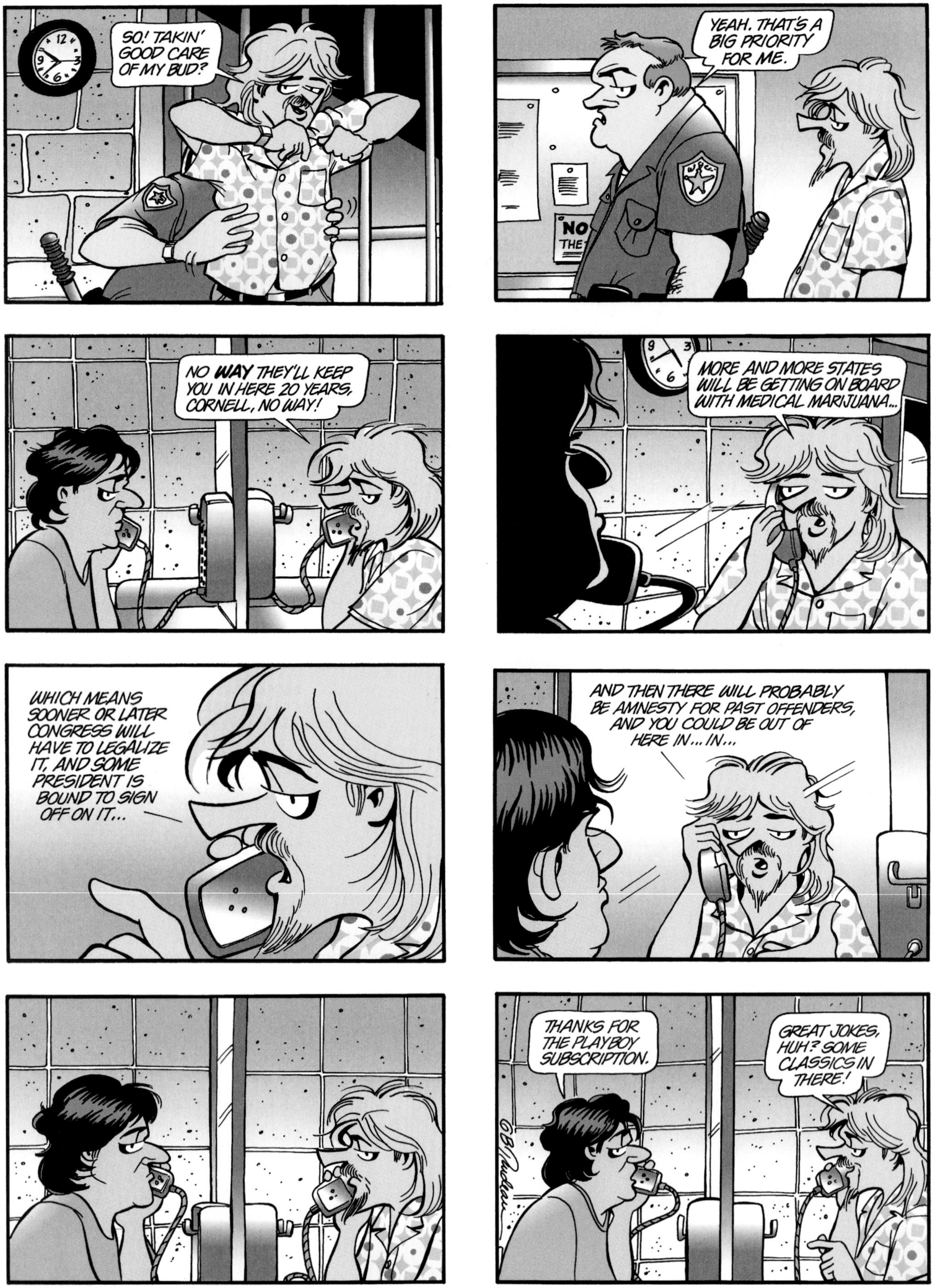
SO! TAKIN' GOOD CARE OF MY BUD?
YEAH. THAT'S A BIG PRIORITY FOR ME.
NO THE
NO **WAY** THEY'LL KEEP YOU IN HERE 20 YEARS, CORNELL, NO WAY!
MORE AND MORE STATES WILL BE GETTING ON BOARD WITH MEDICAL MARIJUANA...
WHICH MEANS SOONER OR LATER CONGRESS WILL HAVE TO LEGALIZE IT, AND SOME PRESIDENT IS BOUND TO SIGN OFF ON IT...
AND THEN THERE WILL PROBABLY BE AMNESTY FOR PAST OFFENDERS, AND YOU COULD BE OUT OF HERE IN... IN...
THANKS FOR THE PLAYBOY SUBSCRIPTION.
GREAT JOKES, HUH? SOME CLASSICS IN THERE!

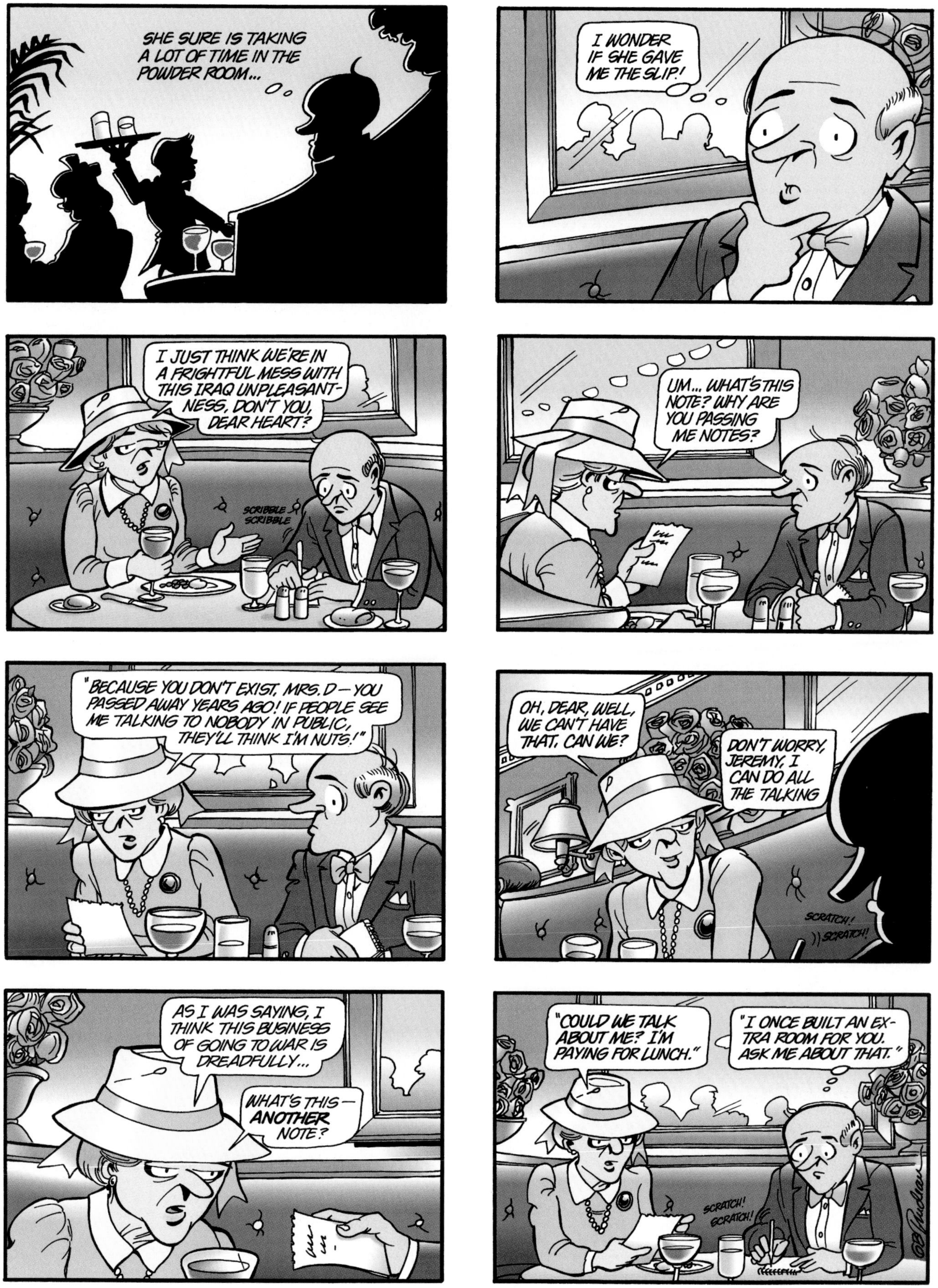
SHE SURE IS TAKING A LOT OF TIME IN THE POWDER ROOM...
I WONDER IF SHE GAVE ME THE SLIP!
I JUST THINK WE'RE IN A FRIGHTFUL MESS WITH THIS IRAQ UNPLEASANTNESS, DON'T YOU, DEAR HEART?
SCRIBBLE SCRIBBLE
UM... WHAT'S THIS NOTE? WHY ARE YOU PASSING ME NOTES?
"BECAUSE YOU DON'T EXIST, MRS. D—YOU PASSED AWAY YEARS AGO! IF PEOPLE SEE ME TALKING TO NOBODY IN PUBLIC, THEY'LL THINK I'M NUTS!"
OH, DEAR, WELL, WE CAN'T HAVE THAT, CAN WE?
DON'T WORRY, JEREMY, I CAN DO ALL THE TALKING
SCRATCH! SCRATCH!
AS I WAS SAYING, I THINK THIS BUSINESS OF GOING TO WAR IS DREADFULLY...
WHAT'S THIS— ANOTHER NOTE?
"COULD WE TALK ABOUT ME? I'M PAYING FOR LUNCH."
"I ONCE BUILT AN EXTRA ROOM FOR YOU. ASK ME ABOUT THAT."
SCRATCH! SCRATCH!

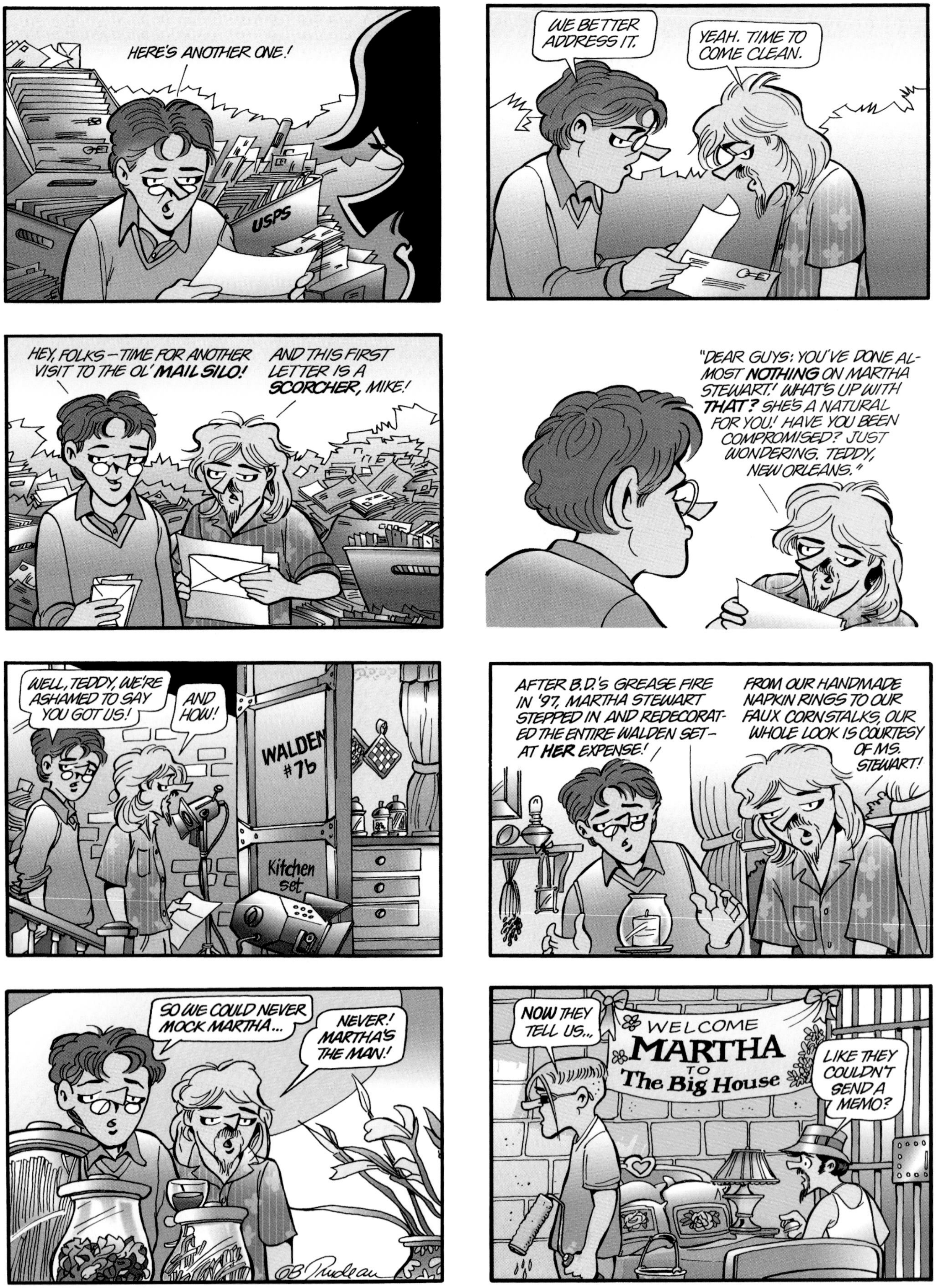
HERE'S ANOTHER ONE!
USPS
WE BETTER ADDRESS IT.
YEAH. TIME TO COME CLEAN.
HEY, FOLKS—TIME FOR ANOTHER VISIT TO THE OL' **MAIL SILO!**
AND THIS FIRST LETTER IS A **SCORCHER,** MIKE!
"DEAR GUYS: YOU'VE DONE ALMOST **NOTHING** ON MARTHA STEWART! WHAT'S UP WITH **THAT?** SHE'S A NATURAL FOR YOU! HAVE YOU BEEN COMPROMISED? JUST WONDERING. TEDDY, NEW ORLEANS."
WELL, TEDDY, WE'RE ASHAMED TO SAY YOU GOT US!
AND HOW!
WALDEN #76
Kitchen set
AFTER B.D.'S GREASE FIRE IN '97, MARTHA STEWART STEPPED IN AND REDECORATED THE ENTIRE WALDEN SET—AT **HER** EXPENSE!
FROM OUR HANDMADE NAPKIN RINGS TO OUR FAUX CORNSTALKS, OUR WHOLE LOOK IS COURTESY OF MS. STEWART!
SO WE COULD NEVER MOCK MARTHA...
NEVER! MARTHA'S THE MAN!
NOW THEY TELL US...
WELCOME MARTHA TO The Big House
LIKE THEY COULDN'T SEND A MEMO?

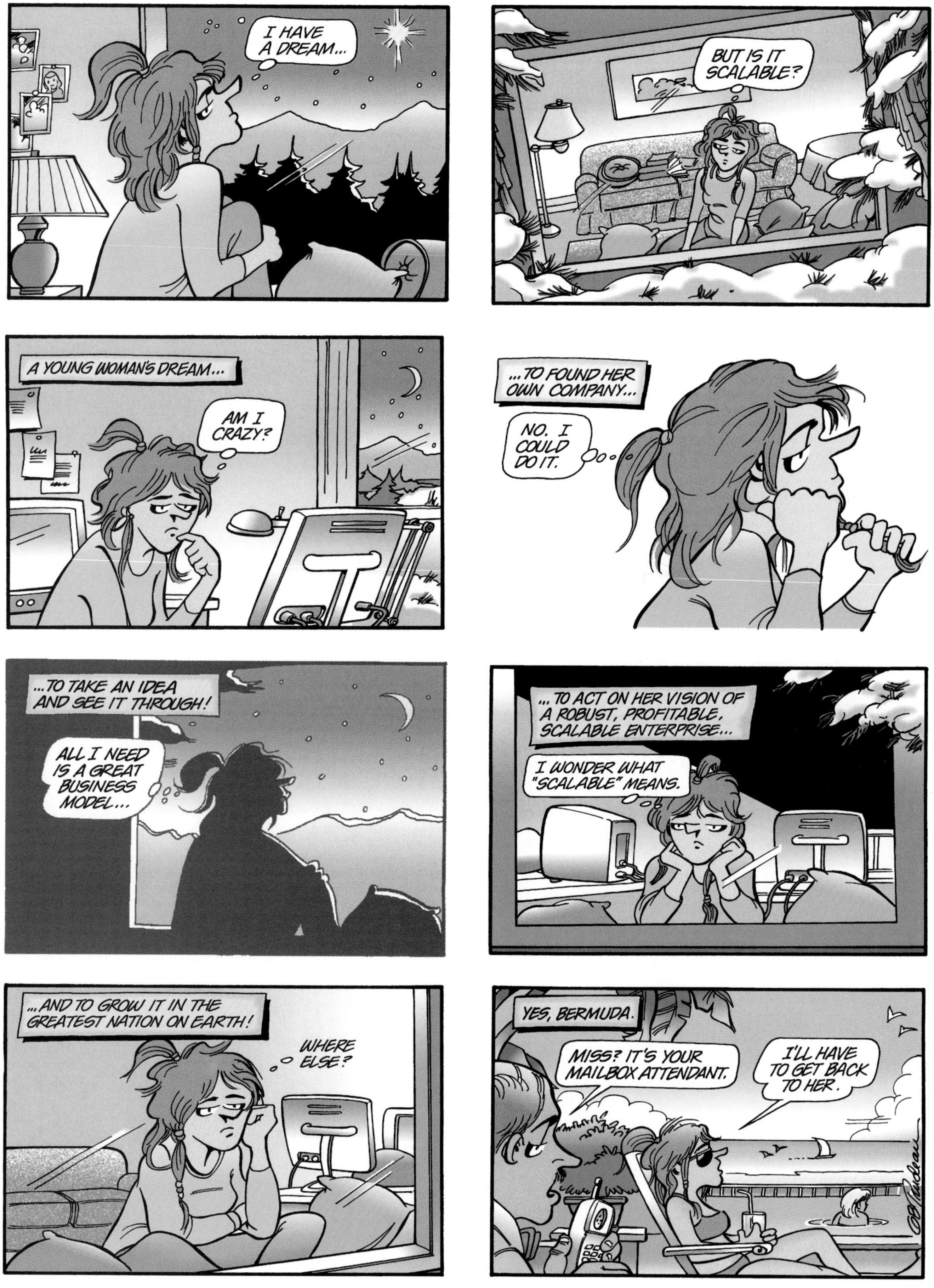
I HAVE A DREAM...
BUT IS IT SCALABLE?
A YOUNG WOMAN'S DREAM...
AM I CRAZY?
...TO FOUND HER OWN COMPANY...
NO. I COULD DO IT.
...TO TAKE AN IDEA AND SEE IT THROUGH!
ALL I NEED IS A GREAT BUSINESS MODEL...
...TO ACT ON HER VISION OF A ROBUST, PROFITABLE, SCALABLE ENTERPRISE...
I WONDER WHAT "SCALABLE" MEANS.
...AND TO GROW IT IN THE GREATEST NATION ON EARTH!
WHERE ELSE?
YES, BERMUDA.
MISS? IT'S YOUR MAILBOX ATTENDANT.
I'LL HAVE TO GET BACK TO HER.

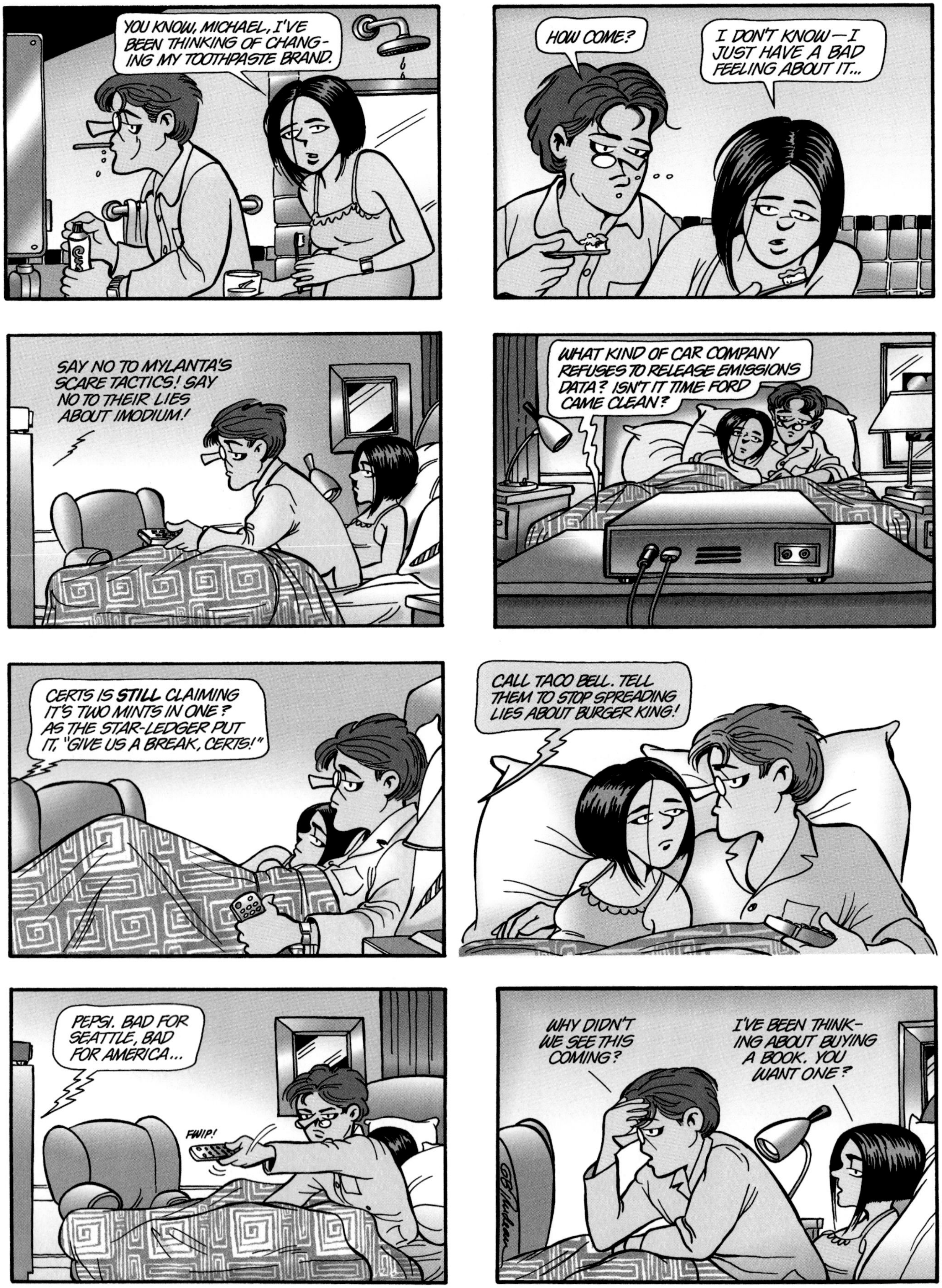

YOU KNOW, MICHAEL, I'VE BEEN THINKING OF CHANGING MY TOOTHPASTE BRAND.
HOW COME?
I DON'T KNOW—I JUST HAVE A BAD FEELING ABOUT IT...
SAY NO TO MYLANTA'S SCARE TACTICS! SAY NO TO THEIR LIES ABOUT IMODIUM!
WHAT KIND OF CAR COMPANY REFUSES TO RELEASE EMISSIONS DATA? ISN'T IT TIME FORD CAME CLEAN?
CERTS IS **STILL** CLAIMING IT'S TWO MINTS IN ONE? AS THE STAR-LEDGER PUT IT, "GIVE US A BREAK, CERTS!"
CALL TACO BELL. TELL THEM TO STOP SPREADING LIES ABOUT BURGER KING!
PEPSI. BAD FOR SEATTLE, BAD FOR AMERICA...
FWIP!
WHY DIDN'T WE SEE THIS COMING?
I'VE BEEN THINKING ABOUT BUYING A BOOK. YOU WANT ONE?

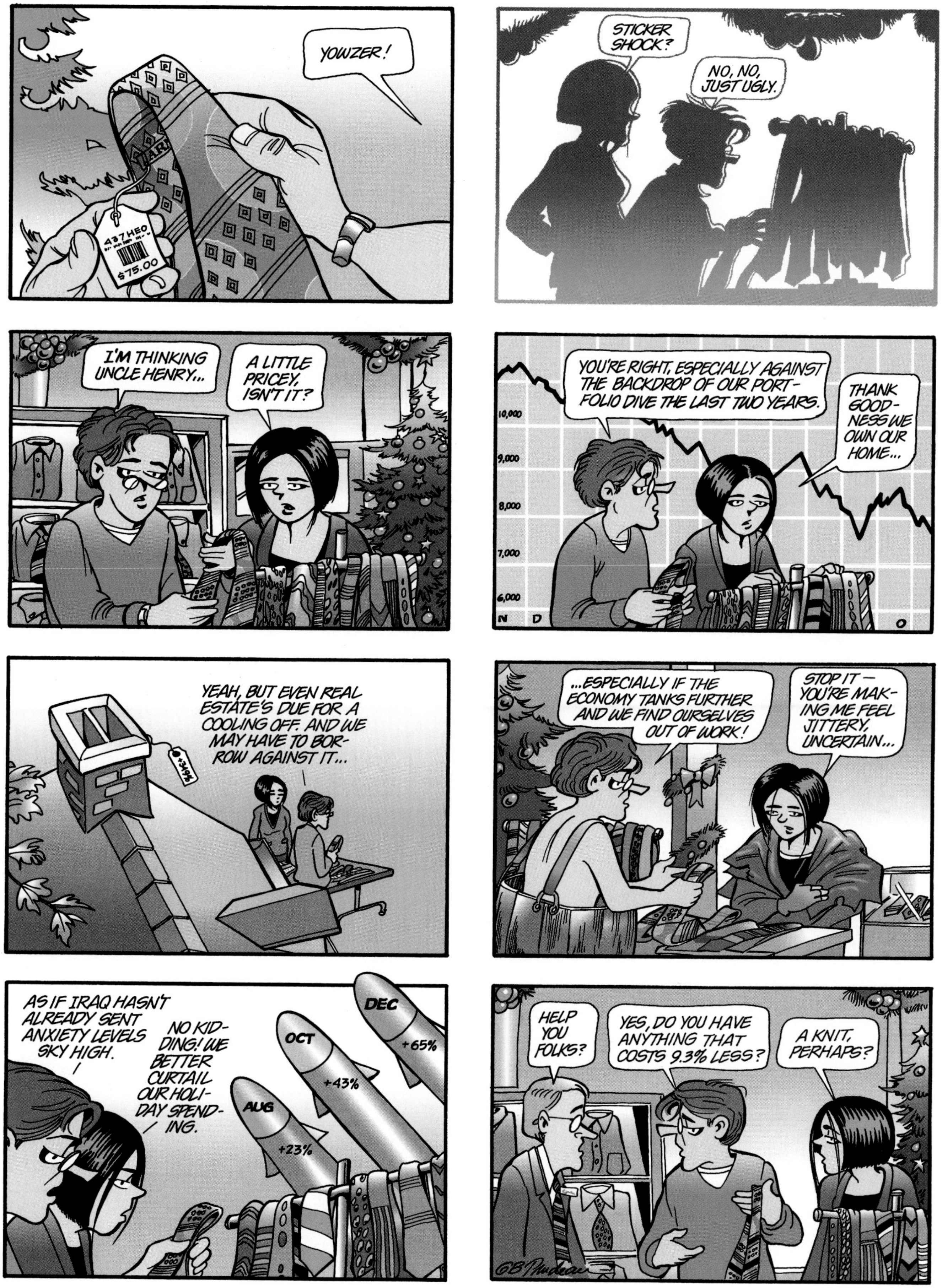
437HEO
$75.00
YOWZER!
STICKER SHOCK?
NO, NO, JUST UGLY.
I'M THINKING UNCLE HENRY...
A LITTLE PRICEY, ISN'T IT?
YOU'RE RIGHT, ESPECIALLY AGAINST THE BACKDROP OF OUR PORTFOLIO DIVE THE LAST TWO YEARS.
THANK GOODNESS WE OWN OUR HOME...
10,000
9,000
8,000
7,000
6,000
N
D
O
YEAH, BUT EVEN REAL ESTATE'S DUE FOR A COOLING OFF. AND WE MAY HAVE TO BORROW AGAINST IT...
...ESPECIALLY IF THE ECONOMY TANKS FURTHER AND WE FIND OURSELVES OUT OF WORK!
STOP IT — YOU'RE MAKING ME FEEL JITTERY, UNCERTAIN...
AS IF IRAQ HASN'T ALREADY SENT ANXIETY LEVELS SKY HIGH.
NO KIDDING! WE BETTER CURTAIL OUR HOLIDAY SPENDING.
AUG
+23%
OCT
+43%
DEC
+65%
HELP YOU FOLKS?
YES, DO YOU HAVE ANYTHING THAT COSTS 9.3% LESS?
A KNIT, PERHAPS?
GBTrudeau

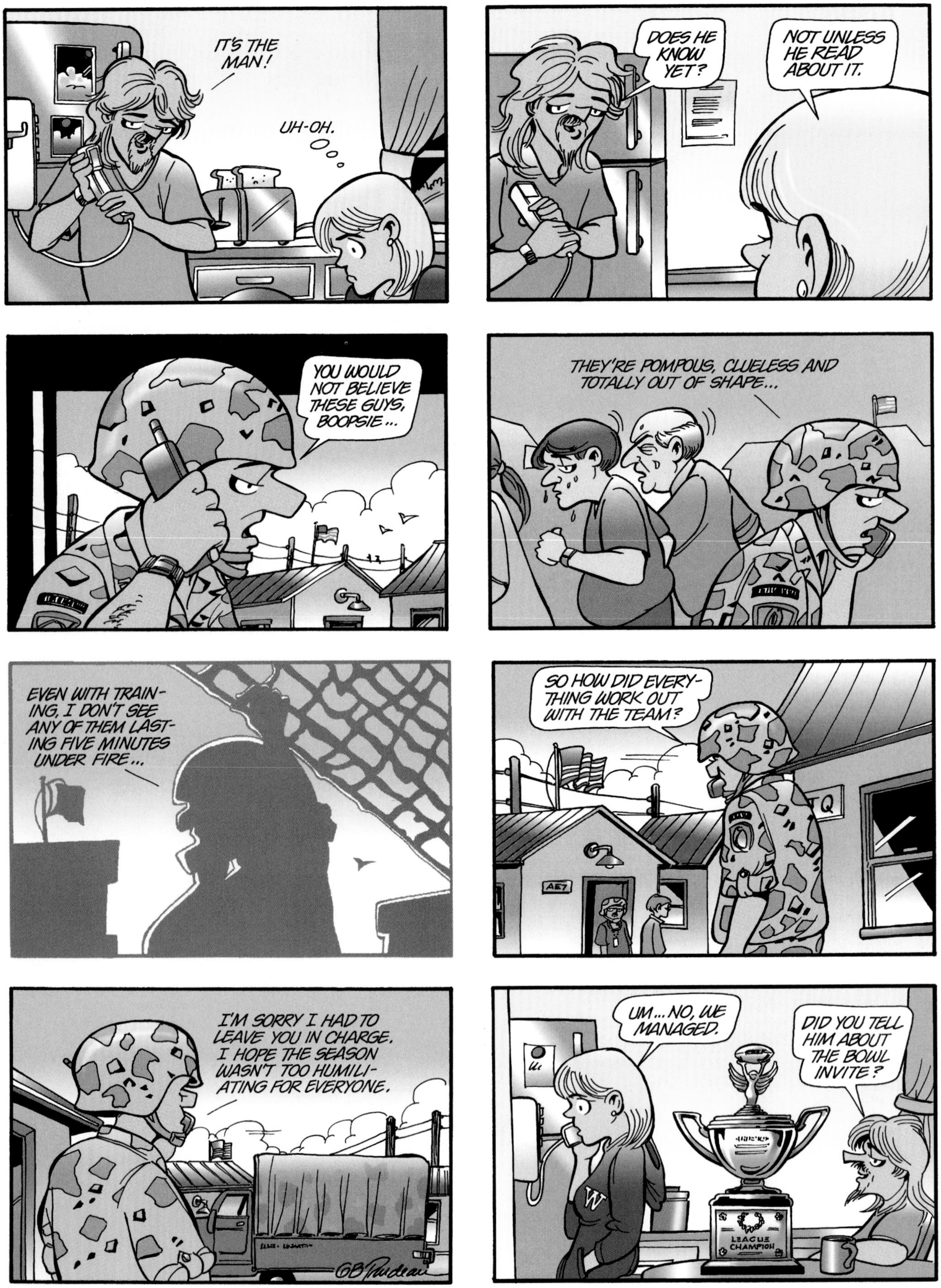
IT'S THE MAN!
UH-OH.
DOES HE KNOW YET?
NOT UNLESS HE READ ABOUT IT.
YOU WOULD NOT BELIEVE THESE GUYS, BOOPSIE...
THEY'RE POMPOUS, CLUELESS AND TOTALLY OUT OF SHAPE...
EVEN WITH TRAINING, I DON'T SEE ANY OF THEM LASTING FIVE MINUTES UNDER FIRE...
SO HOW DID EVERYTHING WORK OUT WITH THE TEAM?
I'M SORRY I HAD TO LEAVE YOU IN CHARGE. I HOPE THE SEASON WASN'T TOO HUMILIATING FOR EVERYONE.
UM... NO, WE MANAGED.
DID YOU TELL HIM ABOUT THE BOWL INVITE?
LEAGUE CHAMPION

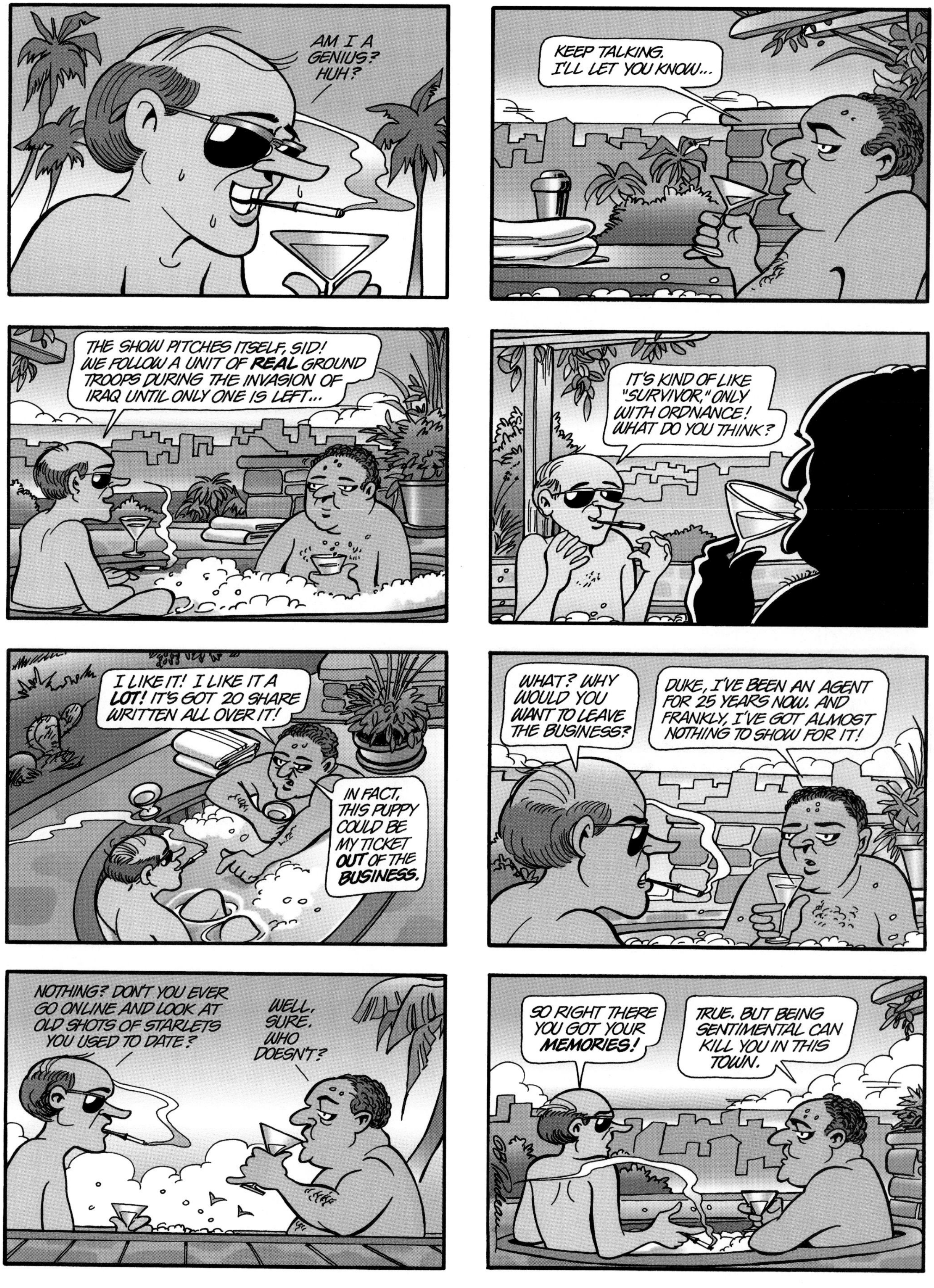
AM I A GENIUS? HUH?
KEEP TALKING. I'LL LET YOU KNOW...
THE SHOW PITCHES ITSELF, SID! WE FOLLOW A UNIT OF REAL GROUND TROOPS DURING THE INVASION OF IRAQ UNTIL ONLY ONE IS LEFT...
IT'S KIND OF LIKE "SURVIVOR," ONLY WITH ORDNANCE! WHAT DO YOU THINK?
I LIKE IT! I LIKE IT A LOT! IT'S GOT 20 SHARE WRITTEN ALL OVER IT!
IN FACT, THIS PUPPY COULD BE MY TICKET OUT OF THE BUSINESS.
WHAT? WHY WOULD YOU WANT TO LEAVE THE BUSINESS?
DUKE, I'VE BEEN AN AGENT FOR 25 YEARS NOW. AND FRANKLY, I'VE GOT ALMOST NOTHING TO SHOW FOR IT!
NOTHING? DON'T YOU EVER GO ONLINE AND LOOK AT OLD SHOTS OF STARLETS YOU USED TO DATE?
WELL, SURE. WHO DOESN'T?
SO RIGHT THERE YOU GOT YOUR MEMORIES!
TRUE. BUT BEING SENTIMENTAL CAN KILL YOU IN THIS TOWN.

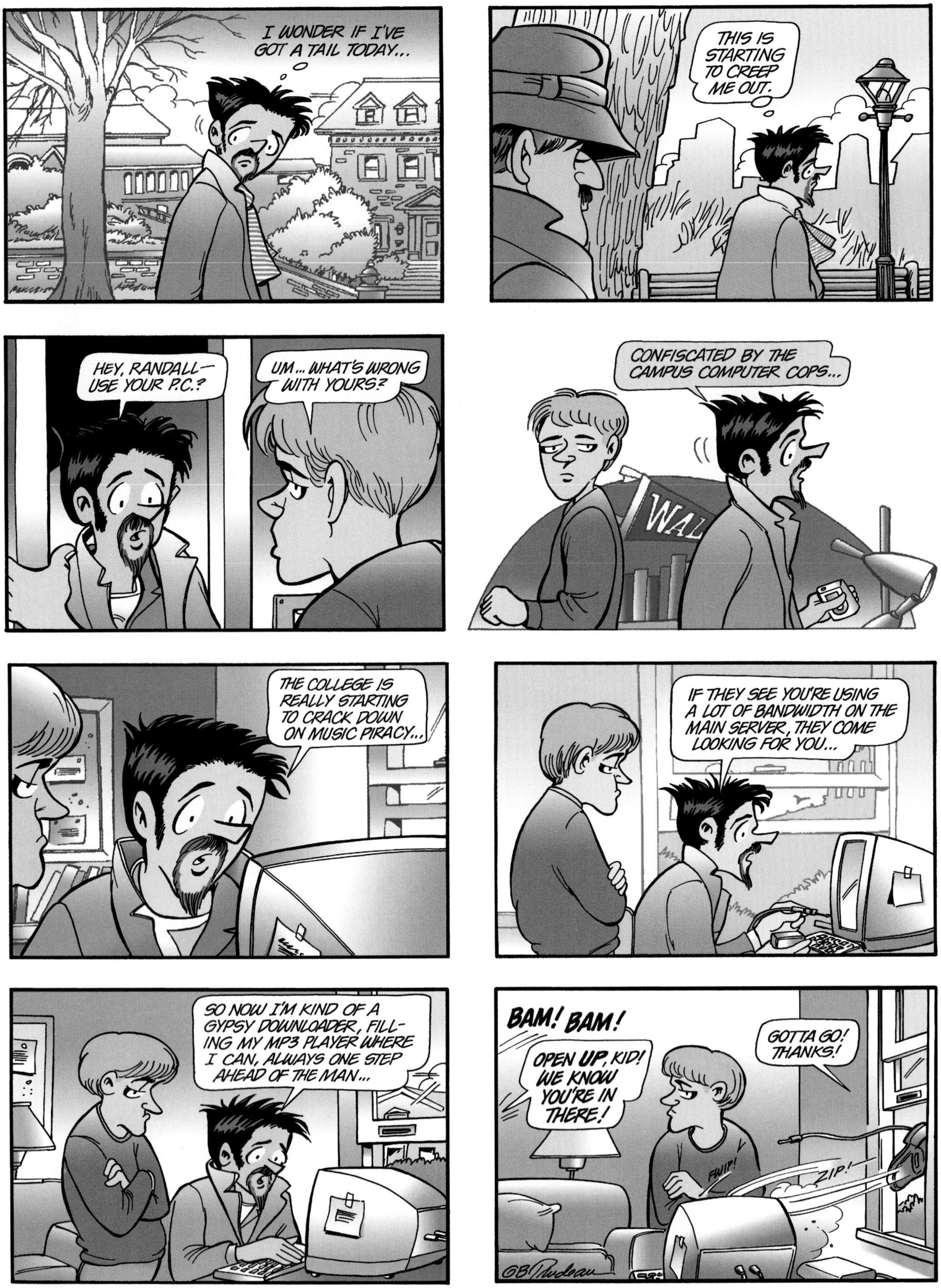
I WONDER IF I'VE GOT A TAIL TODAY...
THIS IS STARTING TO CREEP ME OUT.
HEY, RANDALL— USE YOUR P.C.?
UM... WHAT'S WRONG WITH YOURS?
CONFISCATED BY THE CAMPUS COMPUTER COPS...
WAL
THE COLLEGE IS REALLY STARTING TO CRACK DOWN ON MUSIC PIRACY...
IF THEY SEE YOU'RE USING A LOT OF BANDWIDTH ON THE MAIN SERVER, THEY COME LOOKING FOR YOU...
SO NOW I'M KIND OF A GYPSY DOWNLOADER, FILLING MY MP3 PLAYER WHERE I CAN, ALWAYS ONE STEP AHEAD OF THE MAN...
BAM! BAM!
OPEN UP, KID! WE KNOW YOU'RE IN THERE!
GOTTA GO! THANKS!
FWIP!
ZIP!
©B Trudeau

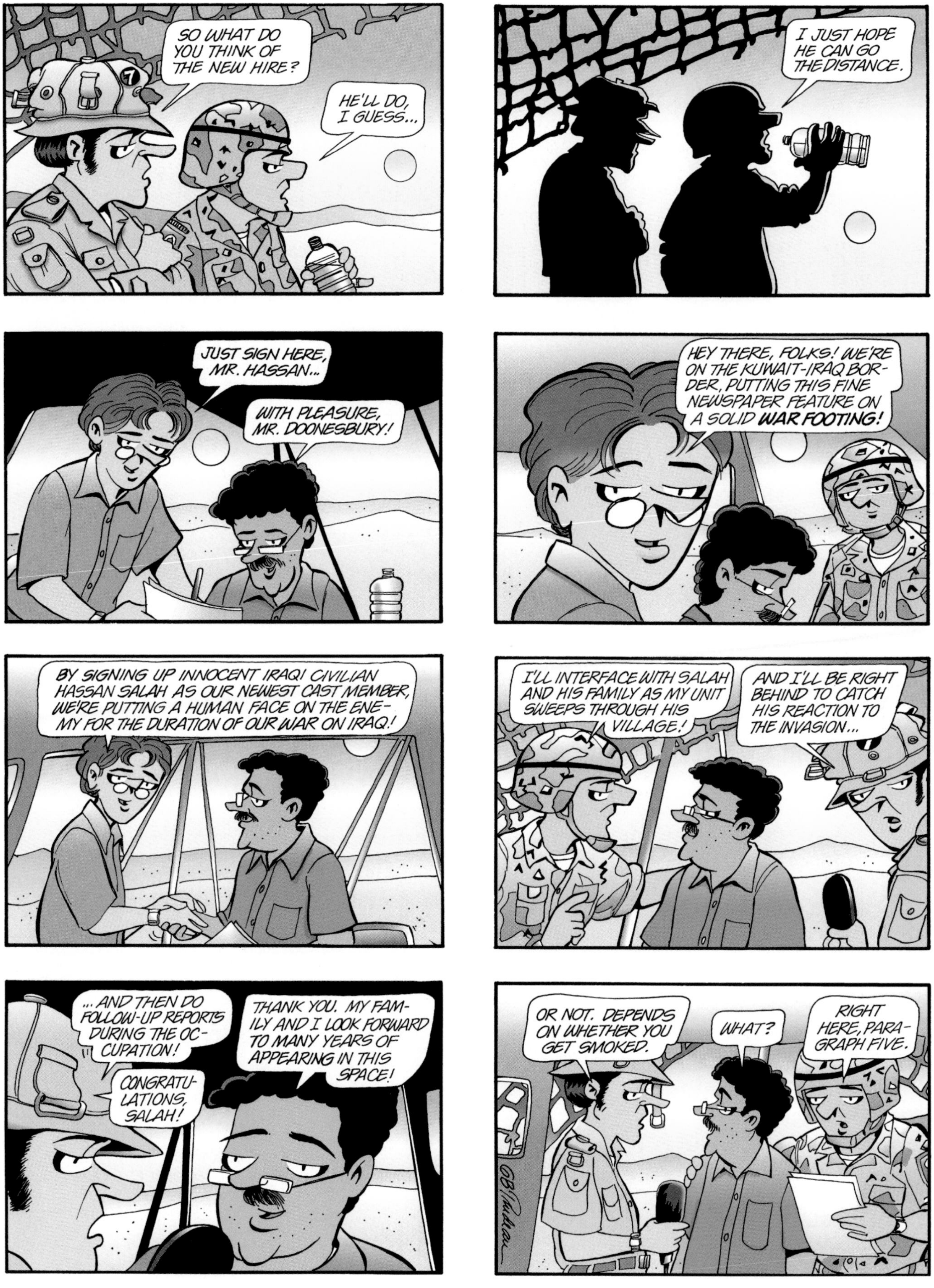
SO WHAT DO YOU THINK OF THE NEW HIRE?
HE'LL DO, I GUESS...
I JUST HOPE HE CAN GO THE DISTANCE.
JUST SIGN HERE, MR. HASSAN...
WITH PLEASURE, MR. DOONESBURY!
HEY THERE, FOLKS! WE'RE ON THE KUWAIT-IRAQ BORDER, PUTTING THIS FINE NEWSPAPER FEATURE ON A SOLID WAR FOOTING!
BY SIGNING UP INNOCENT IRAQI CIVILIAN HASSAN SALAH AS OUR NEWEST CAST MEMBER, WE'RE PUTTING A HUMAN FACE ON THE ENEMY FOR THE DURATION OF OUR WAR ON IRAQ!
I'LL INTERFACE WITH SALAH AND HIS FAMILY AS MY UNIT SWEEPS THROUGH HIS VILLAGE!
AND I'LL BE RIGHT BEHIND TO CATCH HIS REACTION TO THE INVASION...
...AND THEN DO FOLLOW-UP REPORTS DURING THE OCCUPATION!
CONGRATULATIONS, SALAH!
THANK YOU. MY FAMILY AND I LOOK FORWARD TO MANY YEARS OF APPEARING IN THIS SPACE!
OR NOT. DEPENDS ON WHETHER YOU GET SMOKED.
WHAT?
RIGHT HERE, PARAGRAPH FIVE.
GB Trudeau

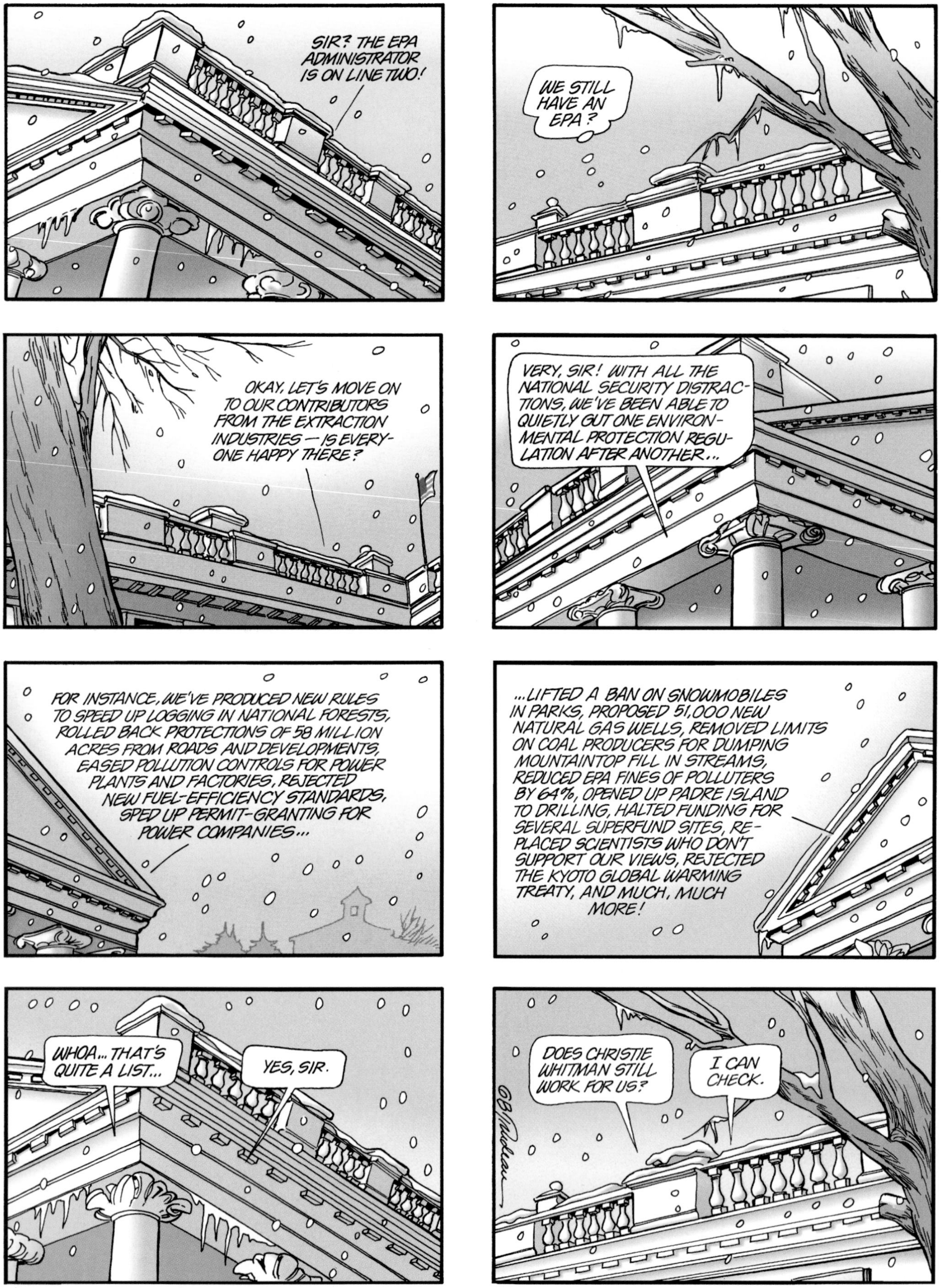
SIR? THE EPA ADMINISTRATOR IS ON LINE TWO!
WE STILL HAVE AN EPA?
OKAY, LET'S MOVE ON TO OUR CONTRIBUTORS FROM THE EXTRACTION INDUSTRIES — IS EVERYONE HAPPY THERE?
VERY, SIR! WITH ALL THE NATIONAL SECURITY DISTRACTIONS, WE'VE BEEN ABLE TO QUIETLY GUT ONE ENVIRONMENTAL PROTECTION REGULATION AFTER ANOTHER...
FOR INSTANCE, WE'VE PRODUCED NEW RULES TO SPEED UP LOGGING IN NATIONAL FORESTS, ROLLED BACK PROTECTIONS OF 58 MILLION ACRES FROM ROADS AND DEVELOPMENTS, EASED POLLUTION CONTROLS FOR POWER PLANTS AND FACTORIES, REJECTED NEW FUEL-EFFICIENCY STANDARDS, SPED UP PERMIT-GRANTING FOR POWER COMPANIES...
...LIFTED A BAN ON SNOWMOBILES IN PARKS, PROPOSED 51,000 NEW NATURAL GAS WELLS, REMOVED LIMITS ON COAL PRODUCERS FOR DUMPING MOUNTAINTOP FILL IN STREAMS, REDUCED EPA FINES OF POLLUTERS BY 64%, OPENED UP PADRE ISLAND TO DRILLING, HALTED FUNDING FOR SEVERAL SUPERFUND SITES, REPLACED SCIENTISTS WHO DON'T SUPPORT OUR VIEWS, REJECTED THE KYOTO GLOBAL WARMING TREATY, AND MUCH, MUCH MORE!
WHOA... THAT'S QUITE A LIST...
YES, SIR.
DOES CHRISTIE WHITMAN STILL WORK FOR US?
I CAN CHECK.
©B Trudeau

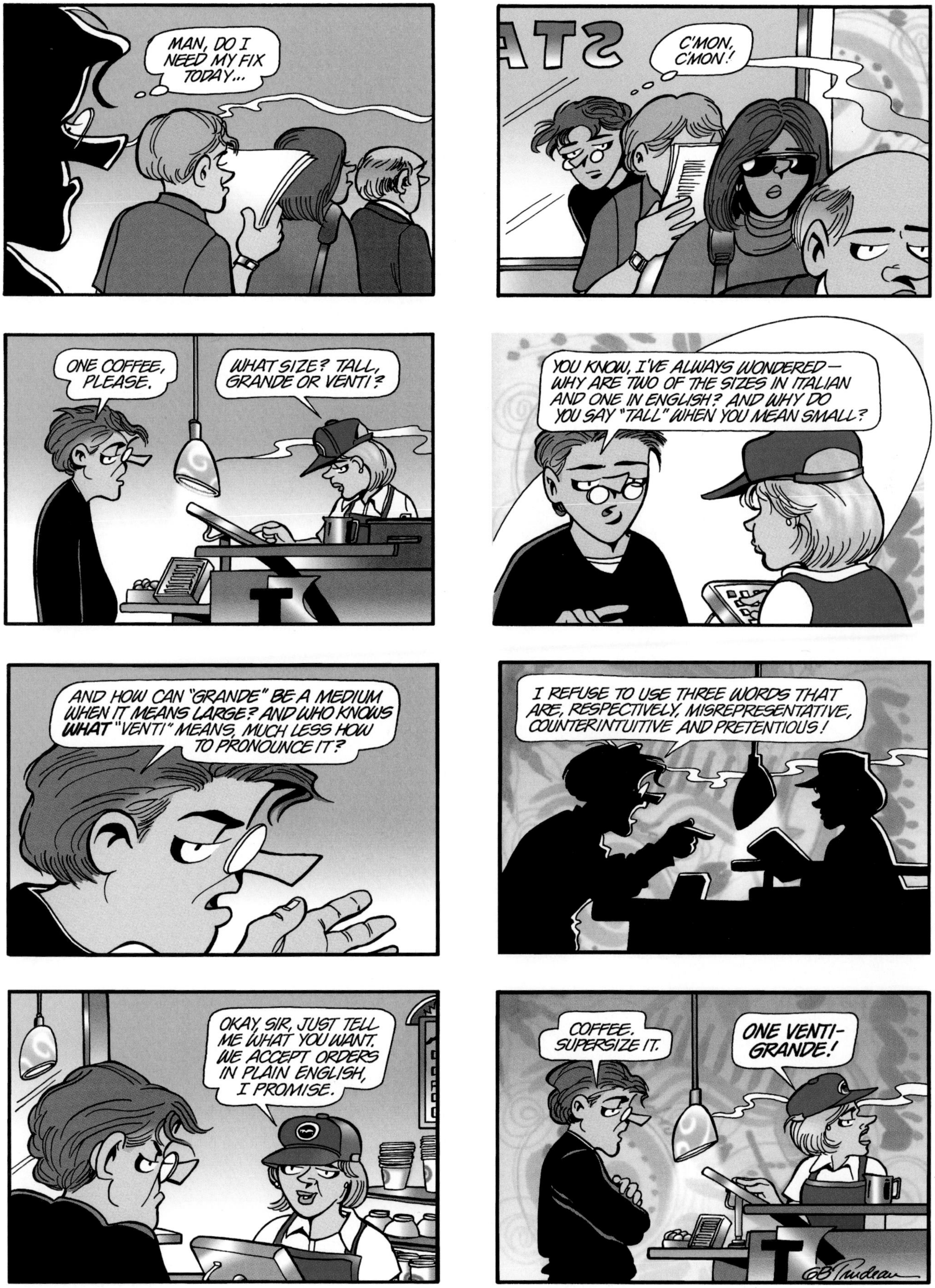
MAN, DO I NEED MY FIX TODAY...
C'MON, C'MON!
ONE COFFEE, PLEASE.
WHAT SIZE? TALL, GRANDE OR VENTI?
YOU KNOW, I'VE ALWAYS WONDERED— WHY ARE TWO OF THE SIZES IN ITALIAN AND ONE IN ENGLISH? AND WHY DO YOU SAY "TALL" WHEN YOU MEAN SMALL?
AND HOW CAN "GRANDE" BE A MEDIUM WHEN IT MEANS LARGE? AND WHO KNOWS **WHAT** "VENTI" MEANS, MUCH LESS HOW TO PRONOUNCE IT?
I REFUSE TO USE THREE WORDS THAT ARE, RESPECTIVELY, MISREPRESENTATIVE, COUNTERINTUITIVE AND PRETENTIOUS!
OKAY, SIR, JUST TELL ME WHAT YOU WANT. WE ACCEPT ORDERS IN PLAIN ENGLISH, I PROMISE.
COFFEE. SUPERSIZE IT.
ONE VENTI-GRANDE!
GB Trudeau

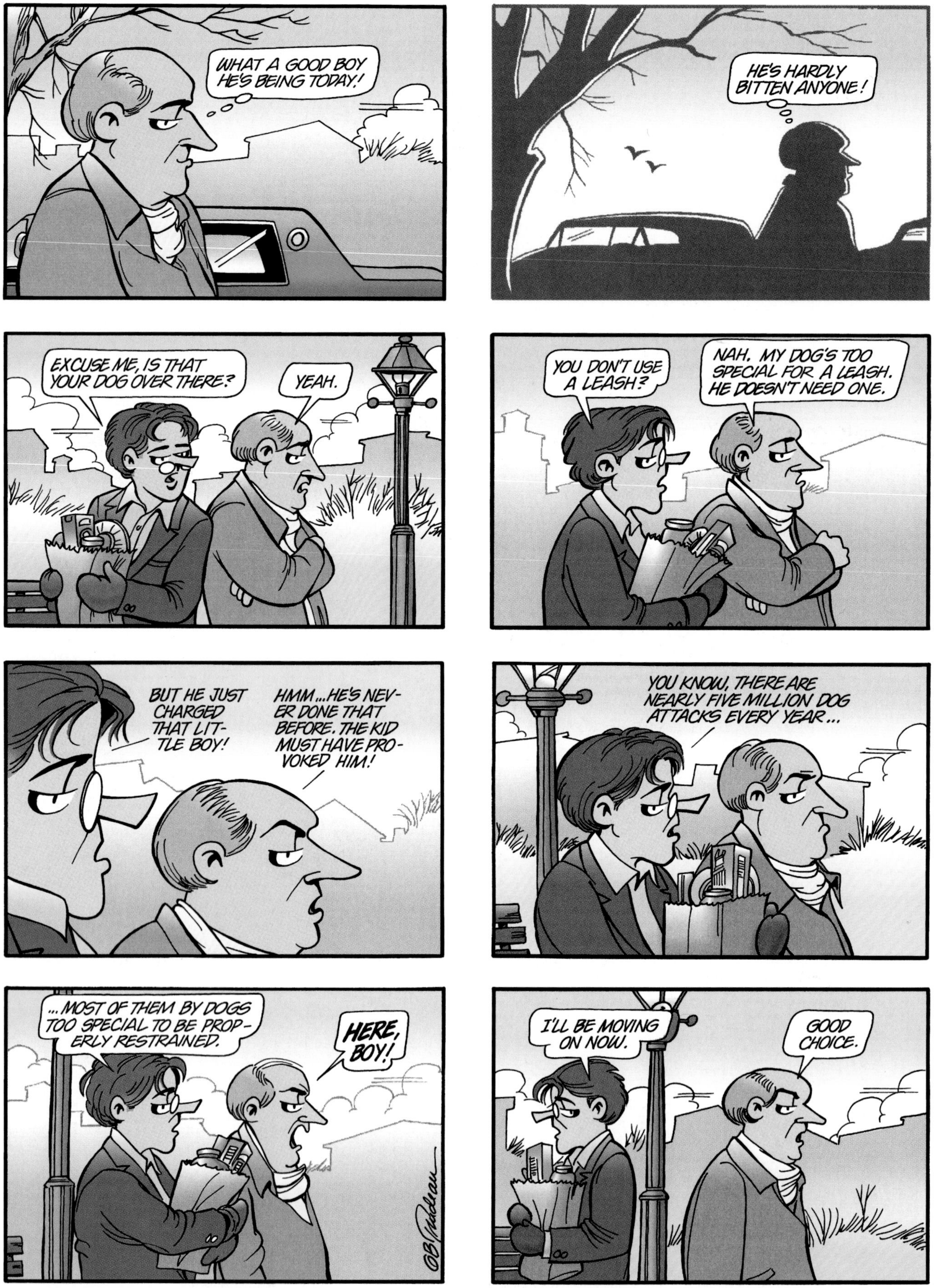
WHAT A GOOD BOY HE'S BEING TODAY!
HE'S HARDLY BITTEN ANYONE!
EXCUSE ME, IS THAT YOUR DOG OVER THERE?
YEAH.
YOU DON'T USE A LEASH?
NAH. MY DOG'S TOO SPECIAL FOR A LEASH. HE DOESN'T NEED ONE.
BUT HE JUST CHARGED THAT LITTLE BOY!
HMM...HE'S NEVER DONE THAT BEFORE. THE KID MUST HAVE PROVOKED HIM!
YOU KNOW, THERE ARE NEARLY FIVE MILLION DOG ATTACKS EVERY YEAR...
...MOST OF THEM BY DOGS TOO SPECIAL TO BE PROPERLY RESTRAINED.
HERE, BOY!
©B/Trudeau
I'LL BE MOVING ON NOW.
GOOD CHOICE.

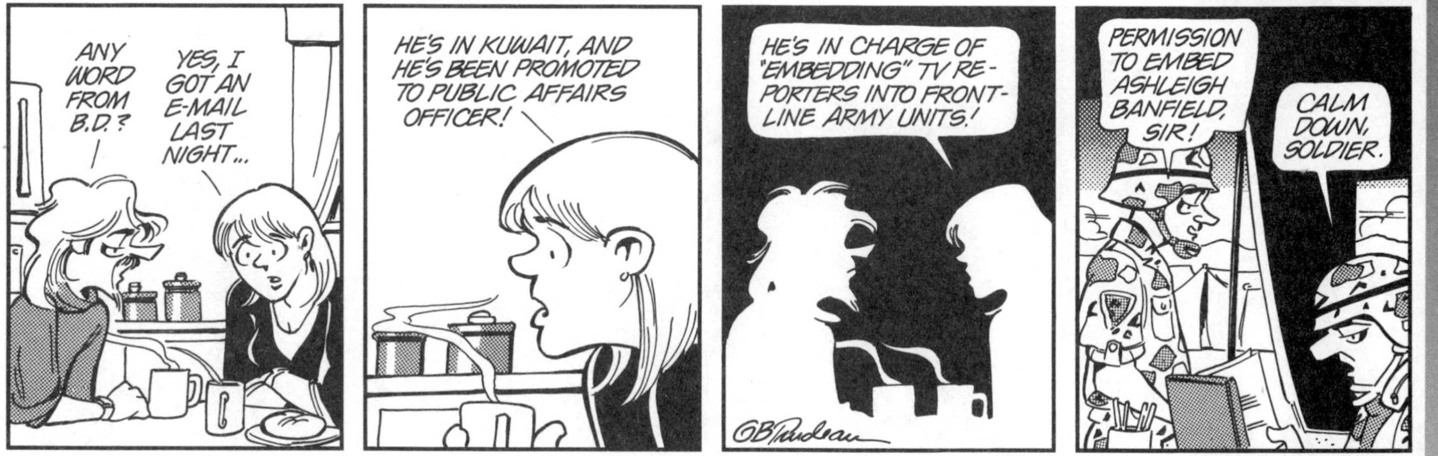
ANY WORD FROM B.D.?
YES, I GOT AN E-MAIL LAST NIGHT...
HE'S IN KUWAIT, AND HE'S BEEN PROMOTED TO PUBLIC AFFAIRS OFFICER!
HE'S IN CHARGE OF "EMBEDDING" TV REPORTERS INTO FRONT-LINE ARMY UNITS!
PERMISSION TO EMBED ASHLEIGH BANFIELD, SIR!
CALM DOWN, SOLDIER.

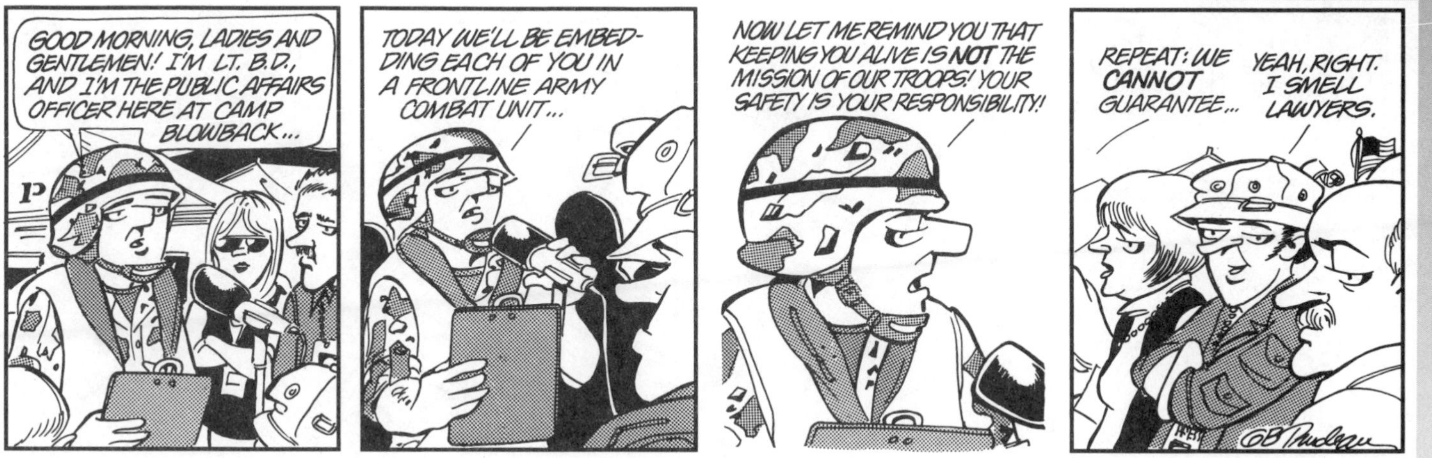
GOOD MORNING, LADIES AND GENTLEMEN! I'M LT. B.D., AND I'M THE PUBLIC AFFAIRS OFFICER HERE AT CAMP BLOWBACK...
TODAY WE'LL BE EMBEDDING EACH OF YOU IN A FRONTLINE ARMY COMBAT UNIT...
NOW LET ME REMIND YOU THAT KEEPING YOU ALIVE IS NOT THE MISSION OF OUR TROOPS! YOUR SAFETY IS YOUR RESPONSIBILITY!
REPEAT: WE CANNOT GUARANTEE...
YEAH, RIGHT. I SMELL LAWYERS.

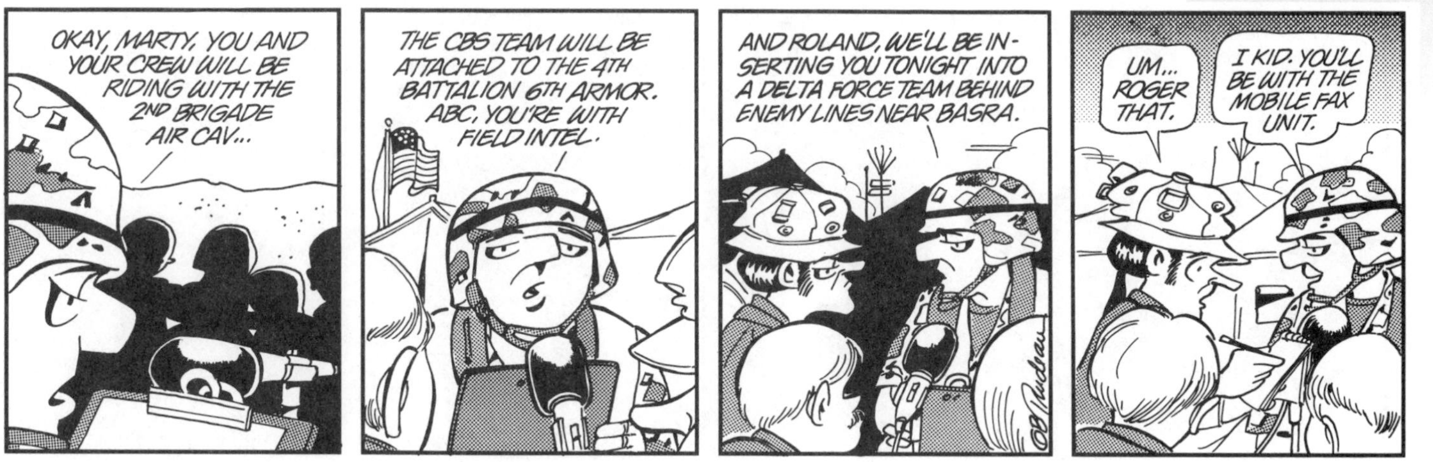
OKAY, MARTY, YOU AND YOUR CREW WILL BE RIDING WITH THE 2ND BRIGADE AIR CAV...
THE CBS TEAM WILL BE ATTACHED TO THE 4TH BATTALION 6TH ARMOR. ABC, YOU'RE WITH FIELD INTEL.
AND ROLAND, WE'LL BE INSERTING YOU TONIGHT INTO A DELTA FORCE TEAM BEHIND ENEMY LINES NEAR BASRA.
UM... ROGER THAT.
I KID. YOU'LL BE WITH THE MOBILE FAX UNIT.

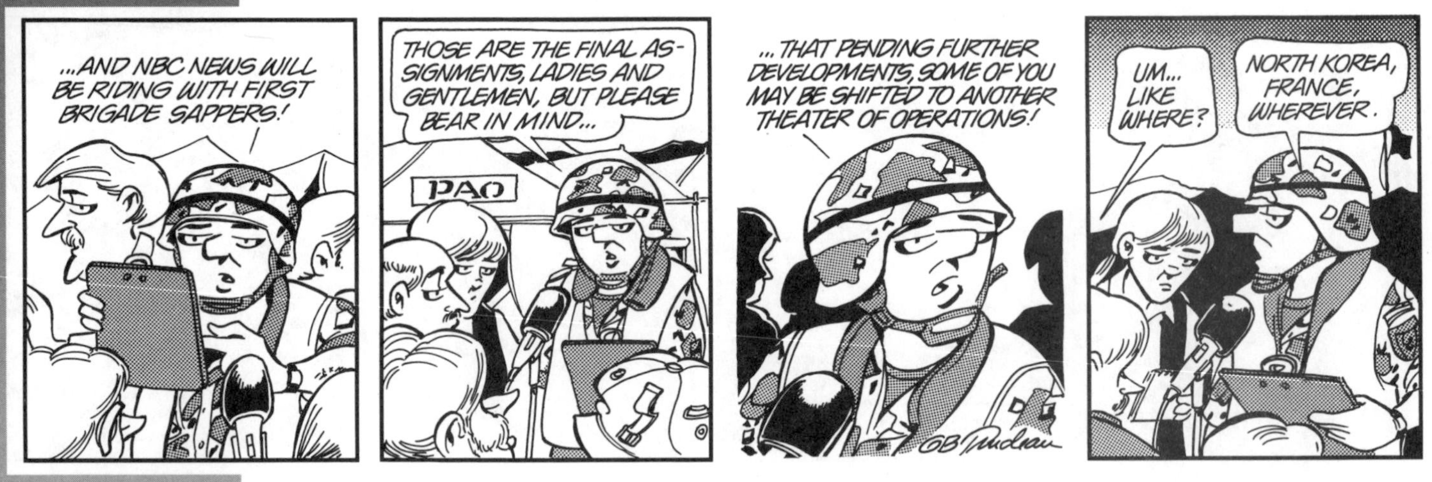
...AND NBC NEWS WILL BE RIDING WITH FIRST BRIGADE SAPPERS!
THOSE ARE THE FINAL AS-SIGNMENTS, LADIES AND GENTLEMEN, BUT PLEASE BEAR IN MIND...
PAO
...THAT PENDING FURTHER DEVELOPMENTS, SOME OF YOU MAY BE SHIFTED TO ANOTHER THEATER OF OPERATIONS!
UM... LIKE WHERE?
NORTH KOREA, FRANCE, WHEREVER.

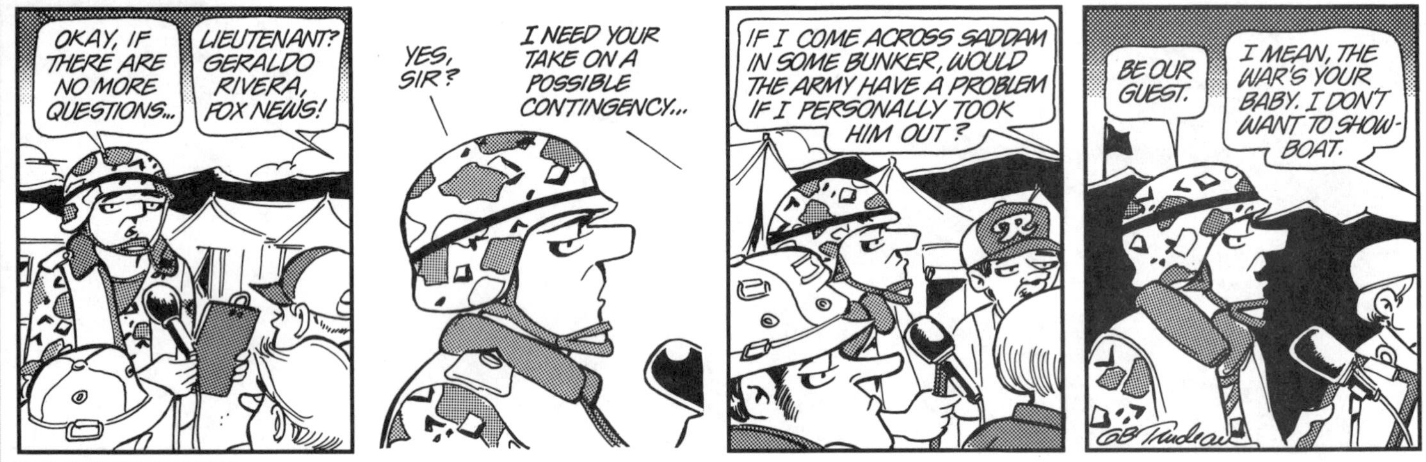
OKAY, IF THERE ARE NO MORE QUESTIONS...
LIEUTENANT? GERALDO RIVERA, FOX NEWS!
YES, SIR?
I NEED YOUR TAKE ON A POSSIBLE CONTINGENCY...
IF I COME ACROSS SADDAM IN SOME BUNKER, WOULD THE ARMY HAVE A PROBLEM IF I PERSONALLY TOOK HIM OUT?
BE OUR GUEST.
I MEAN, THE WAR'S YOUR BABY. I DON'T WANT TO SHOW-BOAT.

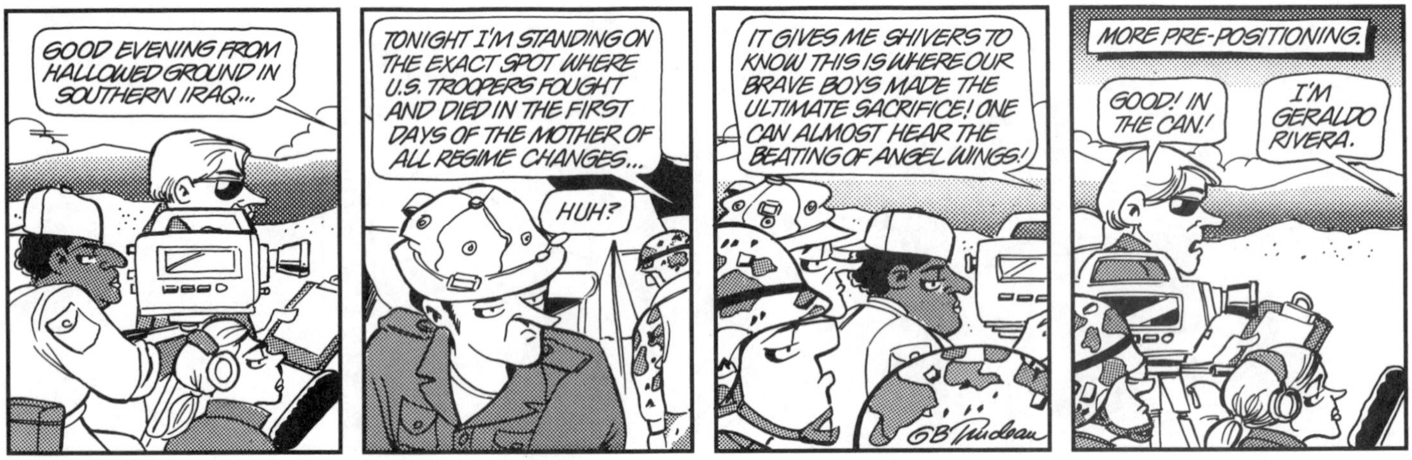
GOOD EVENING FROM HALLOWED GROUND IN SOUTHERN IRAQ...
TONIGHT I'M STANDING ON THE EXACT SPOT WHERE U.S. TROOPERS FOUGHT AND DIED IN THE FIRST DAYS OF THE MOTHER OF ALL REGIME CHANGES...
HUH?
IT GIVES ME SHIVERS TO KNOW THIS IS WHERE OUR BRAVE BOYS MADE THE ULTIMATE SACRIFICE! ONE CAN ALMOST HEAR THE BEATING OF ANGEL WINGS!
MORE PRE-POSITIONING.
GOOD! IN THE CAN!
I'M GERALDO RIVERA.

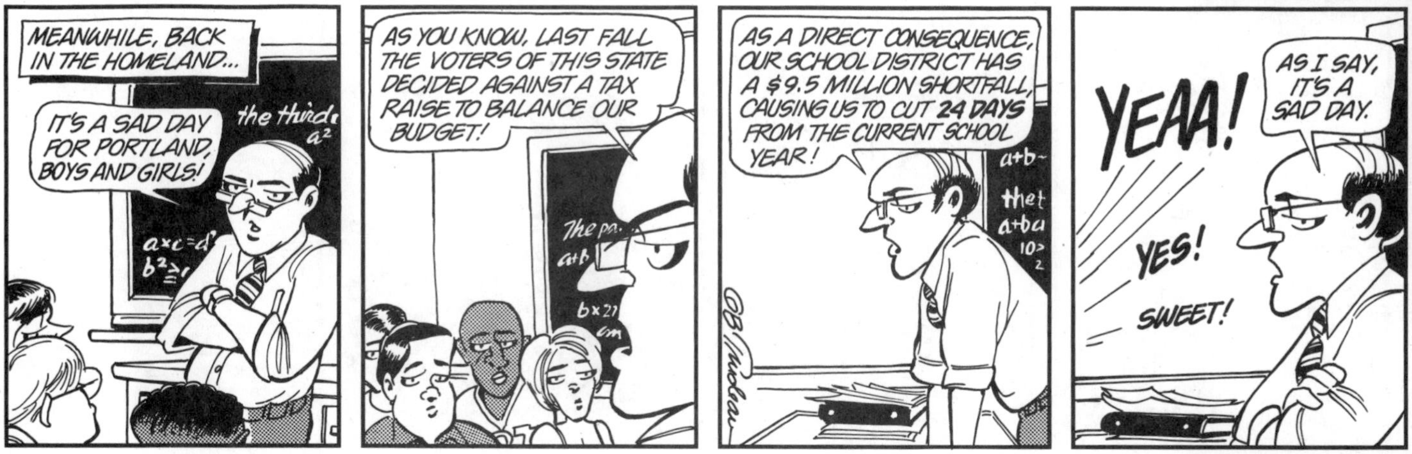
MEANWHILE, BACK IN THE HOMELAND...
IT'S A SAD DAY FOR PORTLAND, BOYS AND GIRLS!
AS YOU KNOW, LAST FALL THE VOTERS OF THIS STATE DECIDED AGAINST A TAX RAISE TO BALANCE OUR BUDGET!
AS A DIRECT CONSEQUENCE, OUR SCHOOL DISTRICT HAS A $9.5 MILLION SHORTFALL, CAUSING US TO CUT 24 DAYS FROM THE CURRENT SCHOOL YEAR!
YEAA!
YES!
SWEET!
AS I SAY, IT'S A SAD DAY.

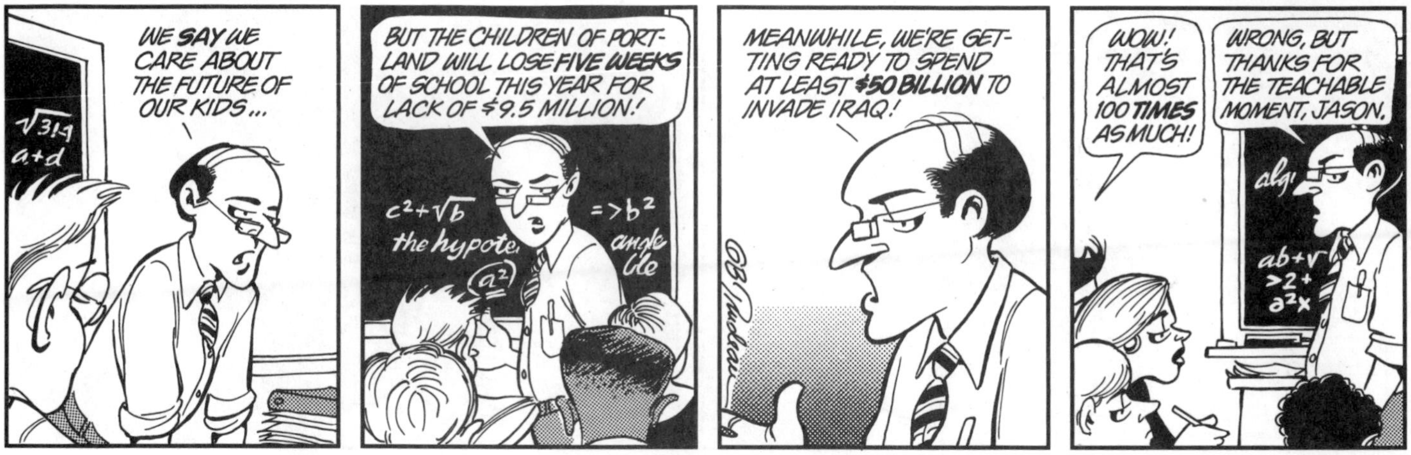
WE SAY WE CARE ABOUT THE FUTURE OF OUR KIDS...
BUT THE CHILDREN OF PORTLAND WILL LOSE FIVE WEEKS OF SCHOOL THIS YEAR FOR LACK OF $9.5 MILLION!
MEANWHILE, WE'RE GETTING READY TO SPEND AT LEAST $50 BILLION TO INVADE IRAQ!
WOW! THAT'S ALMOST 100 TIMES AS MUCH!
WRONG, BUT THANKS FOR THE TEACHABLE MOMENT, JASON.

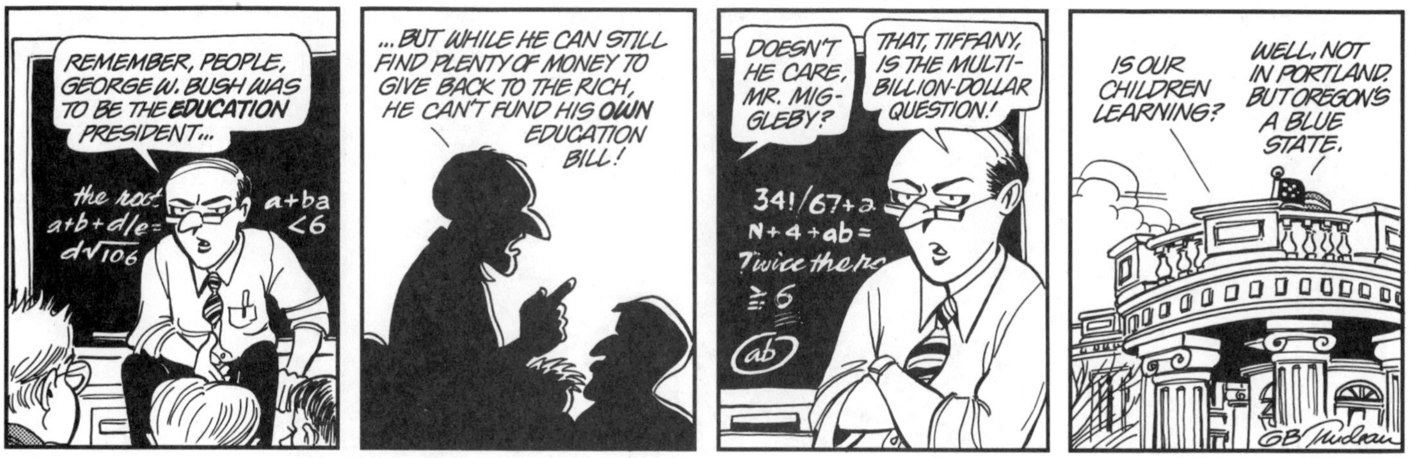
REMEMBER, PEOPLE, GEORGE W. BUSH WAS TO BE THE EDUCATION PRESIDENT...
...BUT WHILE HE CAN STILL FIND PLENTY OF MONEY TO GIVE BACK TO THE RICH, HE CAN'T FUND HIS OWN EDUCATION BILL!
DOESN'T HE CARE, MR. MIGGLEBY?
THAT, TIFFANY, IS THE MULTI-BILLION-DOLLAR QUESTION!
IS OUR CHILDREN LEARNING?
WELL, NOT IN PORTLAND. BUT OREGON'S A BLUE STATE.

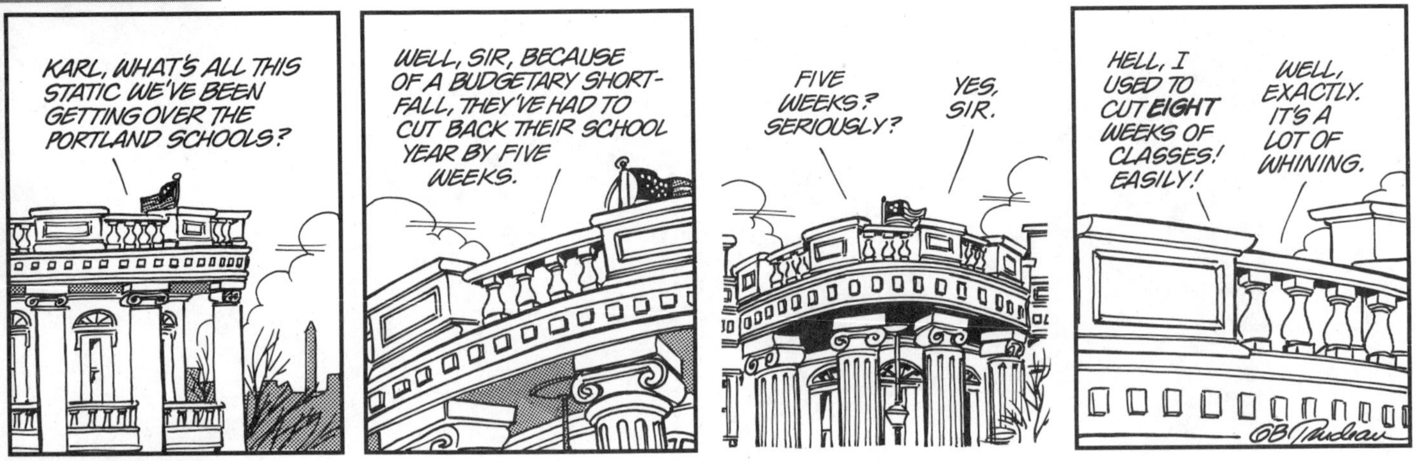
KARL, WHAT'S ALL THIS STATIC WE'VE BEEN GETTING OVER THE PORTLAND SCHOOLS?
WELL, SIR, BECAUSE OF A BUDGETARY SHORT-FALL, THEY'VE HAD TO CUT BACK THEIR SCHOOL YEAR BY FIVE WEEKS.
FIVE WEEKS? SERIOUSLY?
YES, SIR.
HELL, I USED TO CUT EIGHT WEEKS OF CLASSES! EASILY!
WELL, EXACTLY. IT'S A LOT OF WHINING.

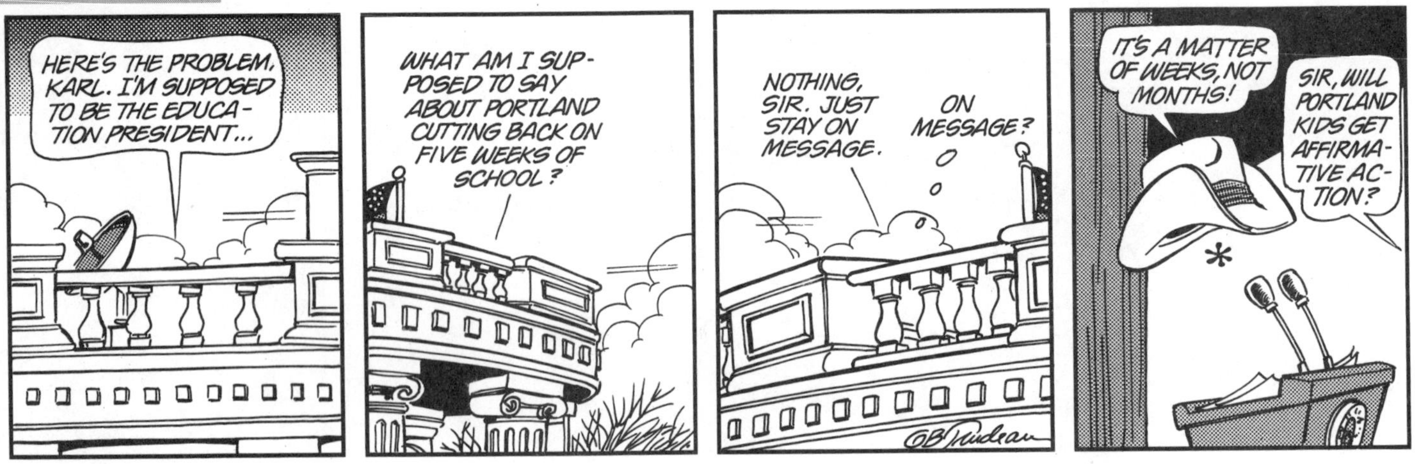
HERE'S THE PROBLEM, KARL. I'M SUPPOSED TO BE THE EDUCA-TION PRESIDENT...
WHAT AM I SUP-POSED TO SAY ABOUT PORTLAND CUTTING BACK ON FIVE WEEKS OF SCHOOL?
NOTHING, SIR. JUST STAY ON MESSAGE.
ON MESSAGE?

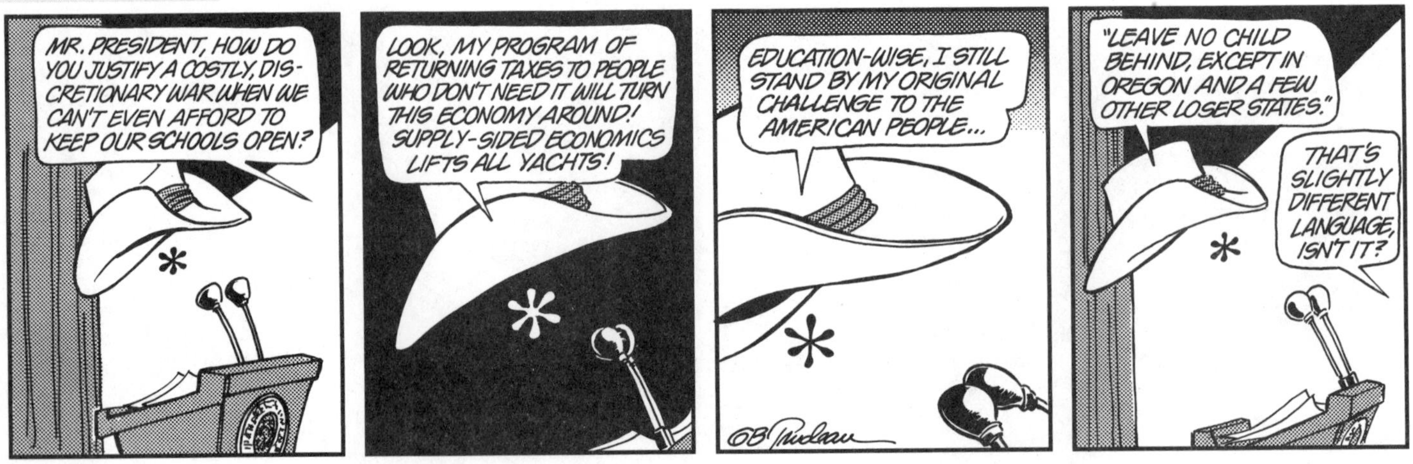
IT'S A MATTER OF WEEKS, NOT MONTHS!
SIR, WILL PORTLAND KIDS GET AFFIRMA-TIVE AC-TION?
MR. PRESIDENT, HOW DO YOU JUSTIFY A COSTLY, DIS-CRETIONARY WAR WHEN WE CAN'T EVEN AFFORD TO KEEP OUR SCHOOLS OPEN?
LOOK, MY PROGRAM OF RETURNING TAXES TO PEOPLE WHO DON'T NEED IT WILL TURN THIS ECONOMY AROUND! SUPPLY-SIDED ECONOMICS LIFTS ALL YACHTS!
EDUCATION-WISE, I STILL STAND BY MY ORIGINAL CHALLENGE TO THE AMERICAN PEOPLE...
"LEAVE NO CHILD BEHIND, EXCEPT IN OREGON AND A FEW OTHER LOSER STATES."
THAT'S SLIGHTLY DIFFERENT LANGUAGE, ISN'T IT?

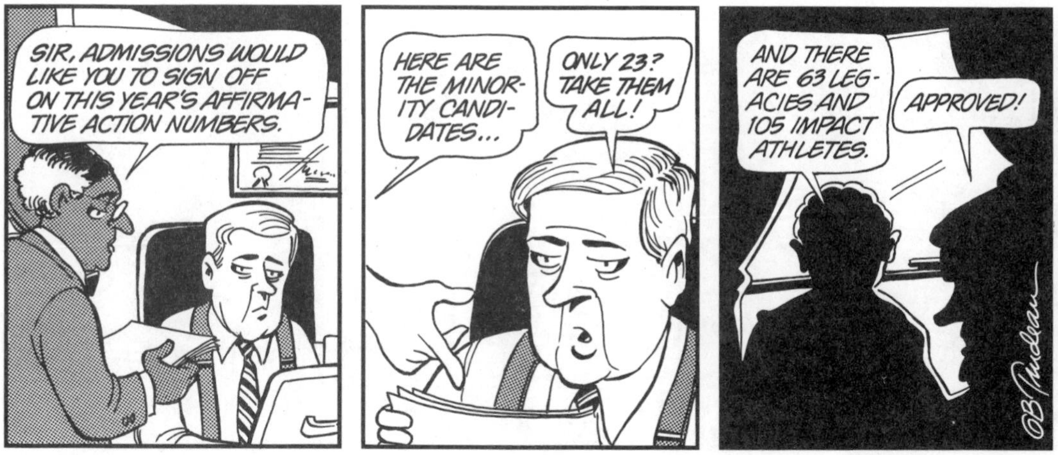
SIR, ADMISSIONS WOULD LIKE YOU TO SIGN OFF ON THIS YEAR'S AFFIRMATIVE ACTION NUMBERS.
HERE ARE THE MINORITY CANDIDATES...
ONLY 23? TAKE THEM ALL!
AND THERE ARE 63 LEGACIES AND 105 IMPACT ATHLETES.
APPROVED!
LASTLY, FIVE OREGON HIGH SCHOOL "GRADUATES."
NO WAY.

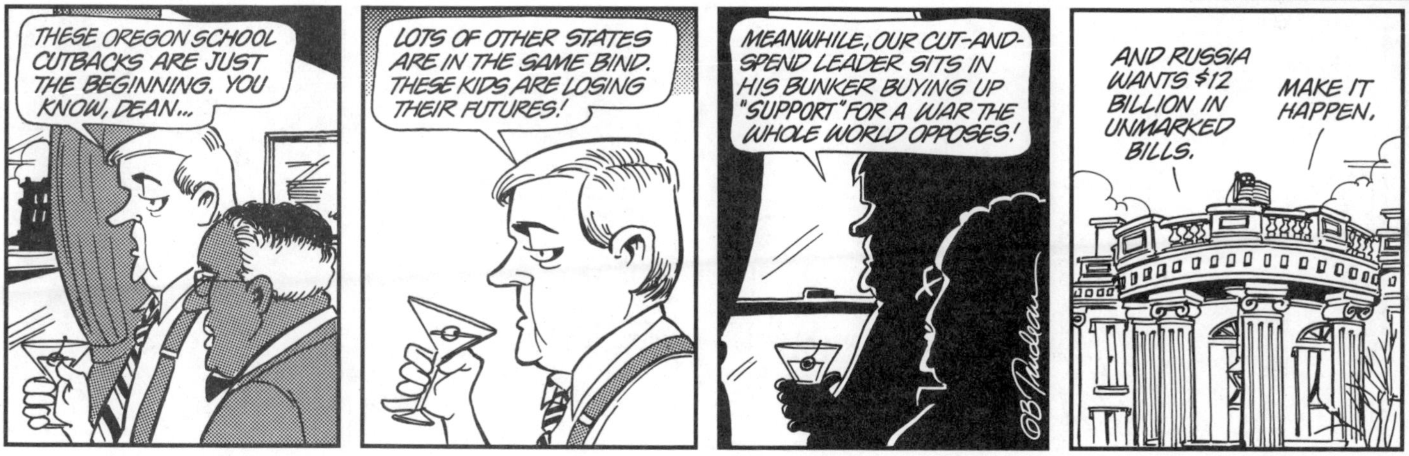
THESE OREGON SCHOOL CUTBACKS ARE JUST THE BEGINNING. YOU KNOW, DEAN...
LOTS OF OTHER STATES ARE IN THE SAME BIND. THESE KIDS ARE LOSING THEIR FUTURES!
MEANWHILE, OUR CUT-AND-SPEND LEADER SITS IN HIS BUNKER BUYING UP "SUPPORT" FOR A WAR THE WHOLE WORLD OPPOSES!
AND RUSSIA WANTS $12 BILLION IN UNMARKED BILLS.
MAKE IT HAPPEN.

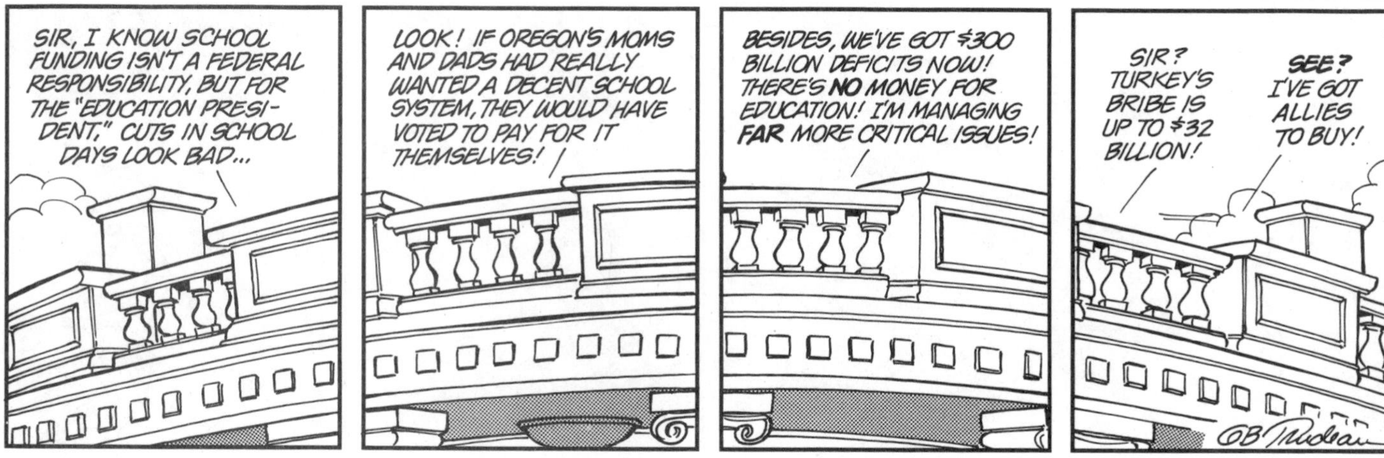
SIR, I KNOW SCHOOL FUNDING ISN'T A FEDERAL RESPONSIBILITY, BUT FOR THE "EDUCATION PRESIDENT," CUTS IN SCHOOL DAYS LOOK BAD...
LOOK! IF OREGON'S MOMS AND DADS HAD REALLY WANTED A DECENT SCHOOL SYSTEM, THEY WOULD HAVE VOTED TO PAY FOR IT THEMSELVES!
BESIDES, WE'VE GOT $300 BILLION DEFICITS NOW! THERE'S NO MONEY FOR EDUCATION! I'M MANAGING FAR MORE CRITICAL ISSUES!
SIR? TURKEY'S BRIBE IS UP TO $32 BILLION!
SEE? I'VE GOT ALLIES TO BUY!

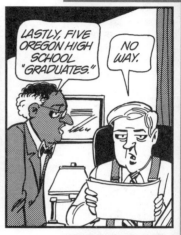

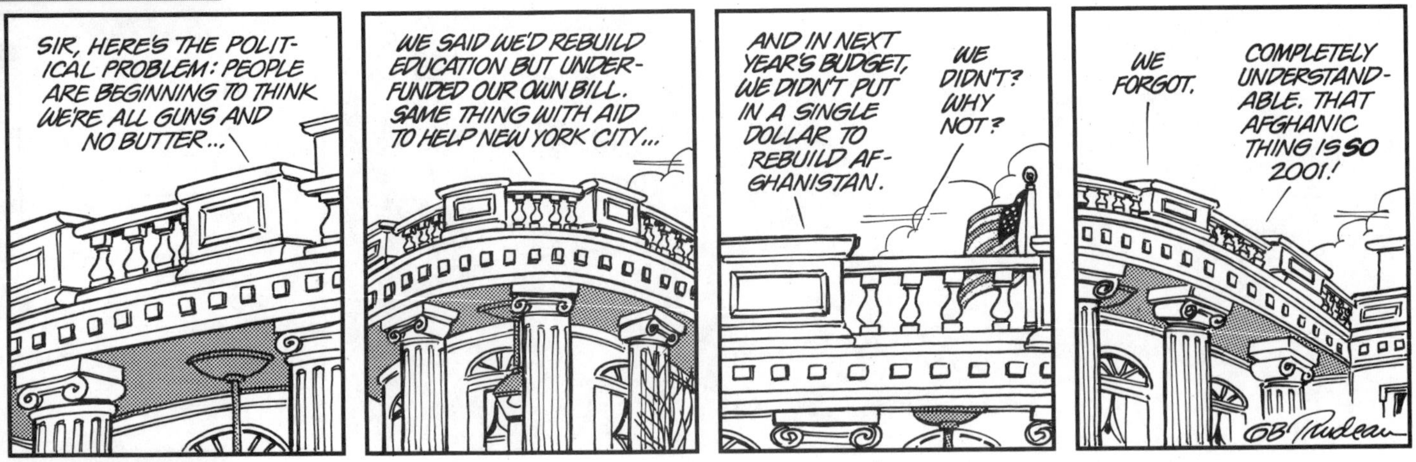
SIR, HERE'S THE POLITICAL PROBLEM: PEOPLE ARE BEGINNING TO THINK WE'RE ALL GUNS AND NO BUTTER...
WE SAID WE'D REBUILD EDUCATION BUT UNDERFUNDED OUR OWN BILL. SAME THING WITH AID TO HELP NEW YORK CITY...
AND IN NEXT YEAR'S BUDGET, WE DIDN'T PUT IN A SINGLE DOLLAR TO REBUILD AFGHANISTAN.
WE DIDN'T? WHY NOT?
WE FORGOT.
COMPLETELY UNDERSTANDABLE. THAT AFGHANIC THING IS SO 2001!
GB Trudeau

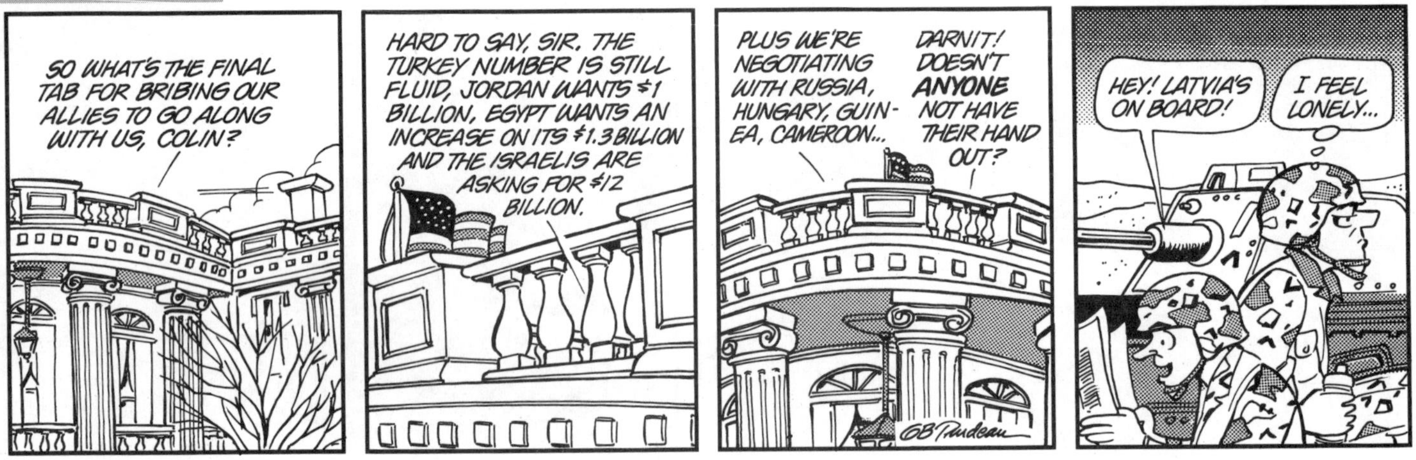
SO WHAT'S THE FINAL TAB FOR BRIBING OUR ALLIES TO GO ALONG WITH US, COLIN?
HARD TO SAY, SIR. THE TURKEY NUMBER IS STILL FLUID, JORDAN WANTS $1 BILLION, EGYPT WANTS AN INCREASE ON ITS $1.3 BILLION AND THE ISRAELIS ARE ASKING FOR $12 BILLION.
PLUS WE'RE NEGOTIATING WITH RUSSIA, HUNGARY, GUINEA, CAMEROON...
DARNIT! DOESN'T ANYONE NOT HAVE THEIR HAND OUT?
GB Trudeau
HEY! LATVIA'S ON BOARD!
I FEEL LONELY...

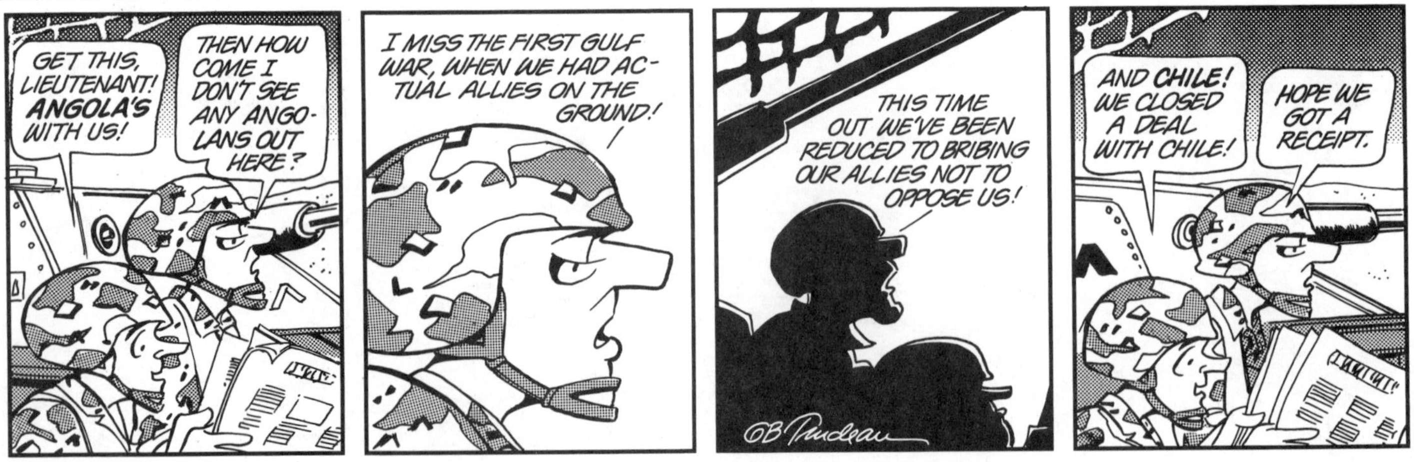
GET THIS, LIEUTENANT! ANGOLA'S WITH US!
THEN HOW COME I DON'T SEE ANY ANGOLANS OUT HERE?
I MISS THE FIRST GULF WAR, WHEN WE HAD ACTUAL ALLIES ON THE GROUND!
THIS TIME OUT WE'VE BEEN REDUCED TO BRIBING OUR ALLIES NOT TO OPPOSE US!
GB Trudeau
AND CHILE! WE CLOSED A DEAL WITH CHILE!
HOPE WE GOT A RECEIPT.

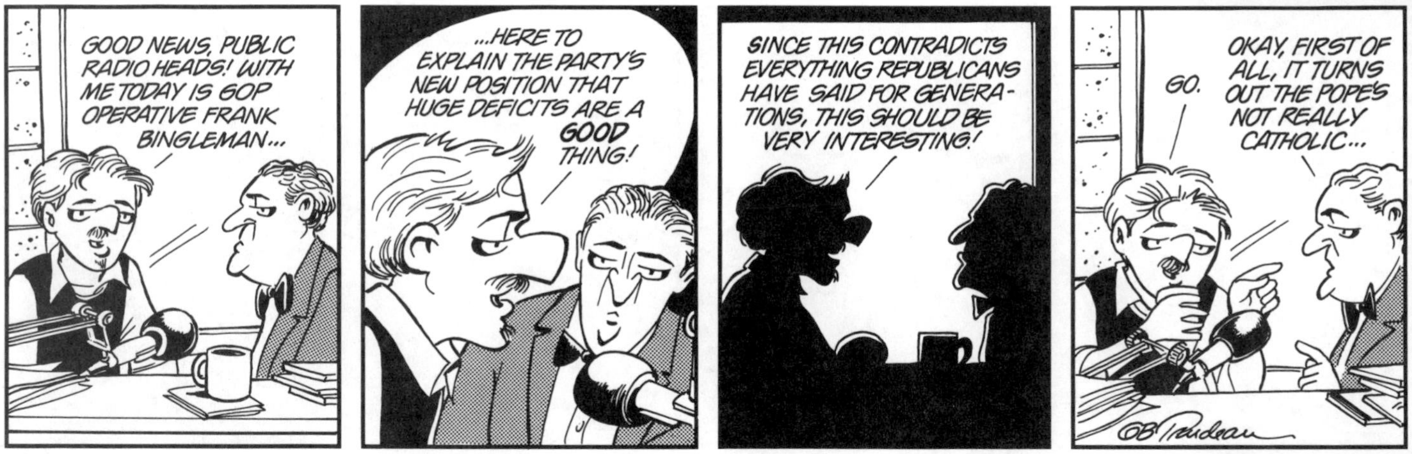
GOOD NEWS, PUBLIC RADIO HEADS! WITH ME TODAY IS GOP OPERATIVE FRANK BINGLEMAN...
...HERE TO EXPLAIN THE PARTY'S NEW POSITION THAT HUGE DEFICITS ARE A GOOD THING!
SINCE THIS CONTRADICTS EVERYTHING REPUBLICANS HAVE SAID FOR GENERATIONS, THIS SHOULD BE VERY INTERESTING!
GO.
OKAY, FIRST OF ALL, IT TURNS OUT THE POPE'S NOT REALLY CATHOLIC...
GB Trudeau

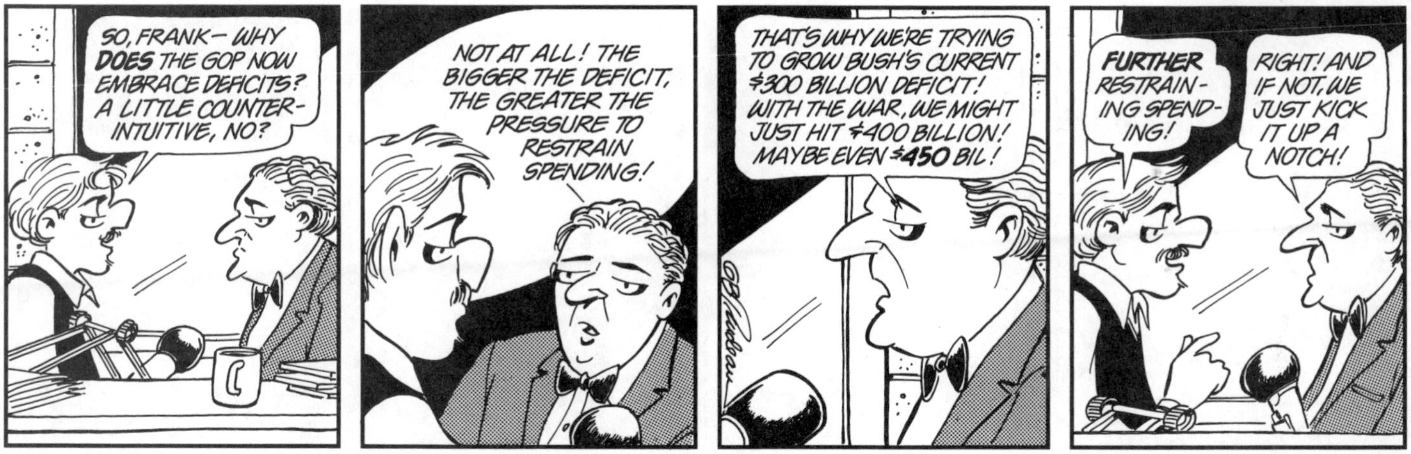
SO, FRANK— WHY DOES THE GOP NOW EMBRACE DEFICITS? A LITTLE COUNTER-INTUITIVE, NO?
NOT AT ALL! THE BIGGER THE DEFICIT, THE GREATER THE PRESSURE TO RESTRAIN SPENDING!
THAT'S WHY WE'RE TRYING TO GROW BUSH'S CURRENT $300 BILLION DEFICIT! WITH THE WAR, WE MIGHT JUST HIT $400 BILLION! MAYBE EVEN $450 BIL!
FURTHER RESTRAINING SPENDING!
RIGHT! AND IF NOT, WE JUST KICK IT UP A NOTCH!

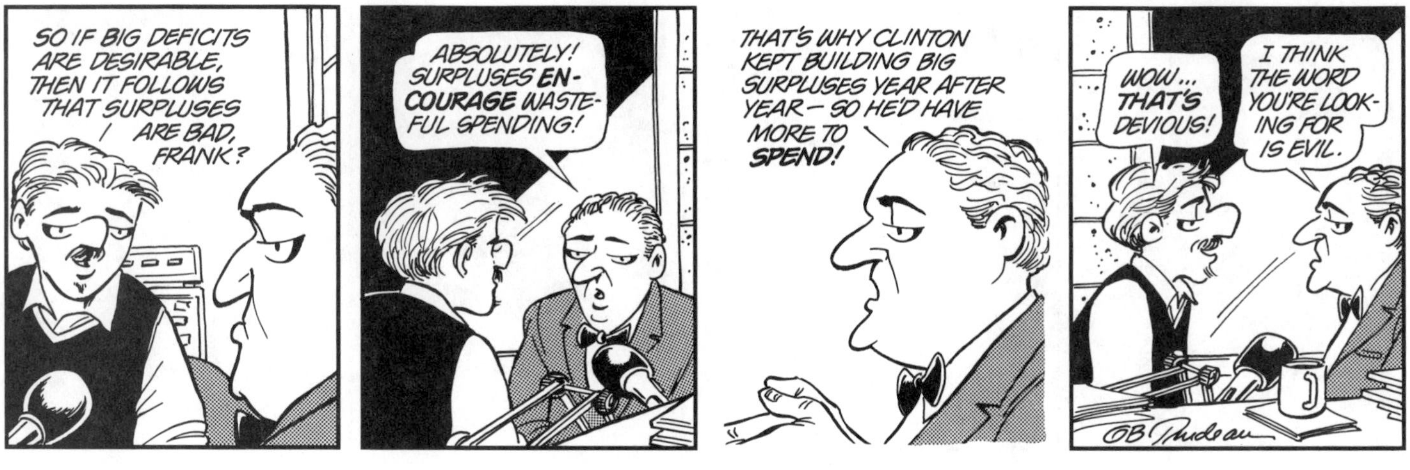
SO IF BIG DEFICITS ARE DESIRABLE, THEN IT FOLLOWS THAT SURPLUSES ARE BAD, FRANK?
ABSOLUTELY! SURPLUSES ENCOURAGE WASTEFUL SPENDING!
THAT'S WHY CLINTON KEPT BUILDING BIG SURPLUSES YEAR AFTER YEAR— SO HE'D HAVE MORE TO SPEND!
WOW... THAT'S DEVIOUS!
I THINK THE WORD YOU'RE LOOKING FOR IS EVIL.
GB Trudeau

YOU SEE, MARK, ONLY BY OVER-SPENDING CAN WE HOPE TO CURB SPENDING!
YOU KNOW, LIKE CUTTING TIMBER TO KEEP IT FROM BURNING! OR SAVING SOCIAL SECURITY BY MAKING IT LESS SECURE!
OR PROMOTING JUDICIAL RESTRAINT BY APPOINTING JUDICIAL ACTIVISTS! OR MAKING THE WORLD **SAFER** BY STARTING A **WAR**!
WHAT? WHAT'D I SAY?
OOPS! DOWN THE RABBIT HOLE!
GB Trudeau

YOU SEE, MARK, WE'RE RIGHT WHERE WE WANT TO BE! WE FOUGHT CLINTON'S SURPLUSES WITH TAX CUTS, AND IT WORKED!
NOW WE'RE BACK TO HUGE, DESIRABLE DEFICITS! AND NEW TAX CUTS WILL MAKE THE SITUATION EVEN BETTER!
I SEE. SO IF TAX CUTS FOR THE RICH WORK IN BOTH GOOD TIMES AND BAD, ARE THERE **ANY** CONDITIONS WHEN YOU **WOULDN'T** FAVOR THEM?
GB Trudeau
UM... NO.
YEA. STRAIGHT TALK.

TO SPEND MONEY IS TO **SAVE** IT!
RISK IS SECURITY!
TO ENSURE **PEACE**, WAGE **WAR**!
GB Trudeau
HI, GENTS! SORRY I'M LATE!
NO PROBLEM.
GOOD-BYE, I MUST BE STAYING!

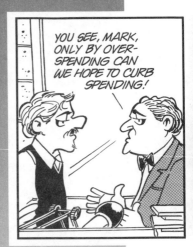

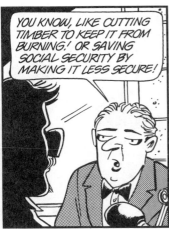

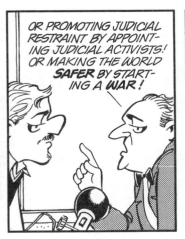

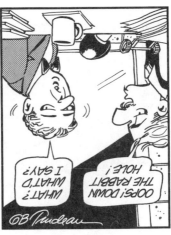

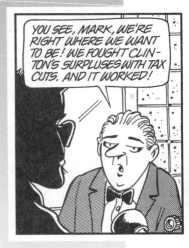

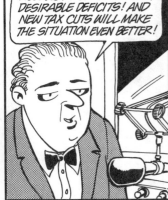

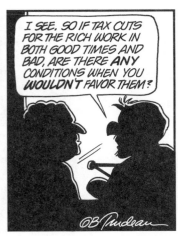

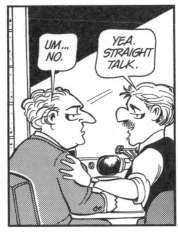

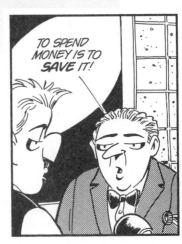

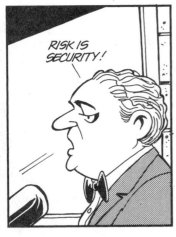

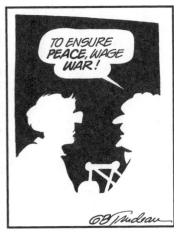

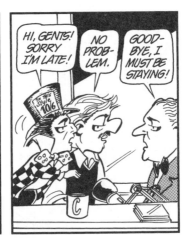

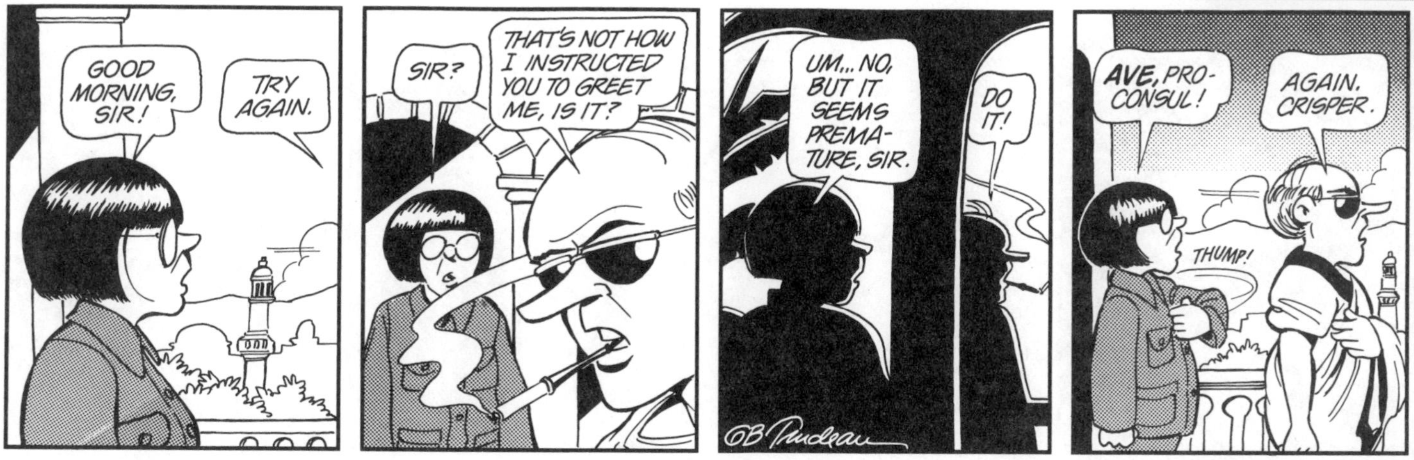
GOOD MORNING, SIR!
TRY AGAIN.
SIR?
THAT'S NOT HOW I INSTRUCTED YOU TO GREET ME, IS IT?
UM... NO, BUT IT SEEMS PREMATURE, SIR.
DO IT!
AVE, PROCONSUL!
AGAIN. CRISPER.
THUMP!

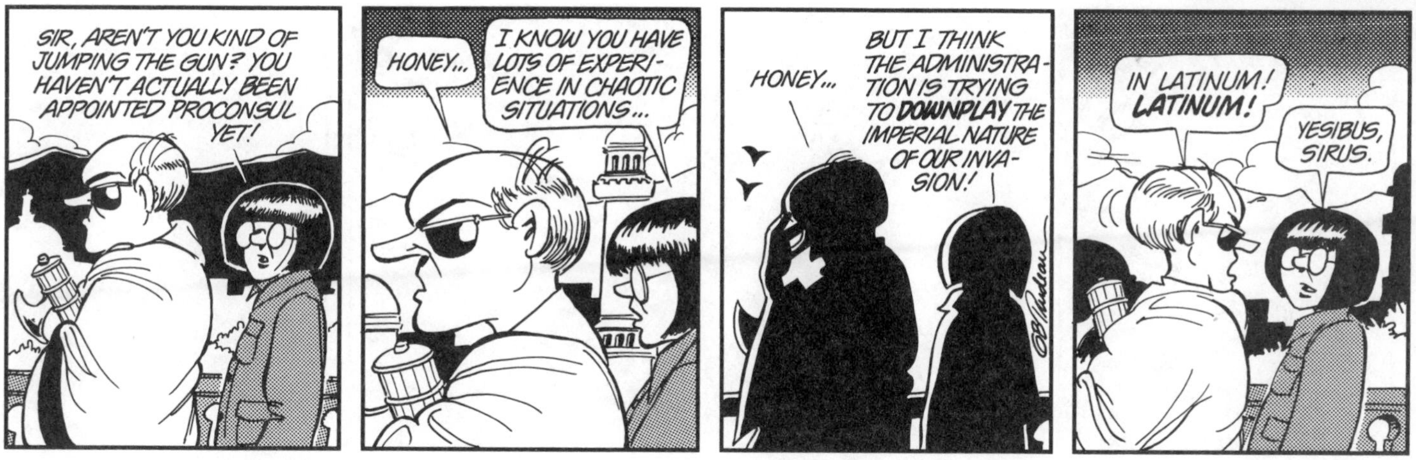
SIR, AREN'T YOU KIND OF JUMPING THE GUN? YOU HAVEN'T ACTUALLY BEEN APPOINTED PROCONSUL YET!
HONEY...
I KNOW YOU HAVE LOTS OF EXPERIENCE IN CHAOTIC SITUATIONS...
HONEY...
BUT I THINK THE ADMINISTRATION IS TRYING TO DOWNPLAY THE IMPERIAL NATURE OF OUR INVASION!
IN LATINUM! LATINUM!
YESIBUS, SIRUS.

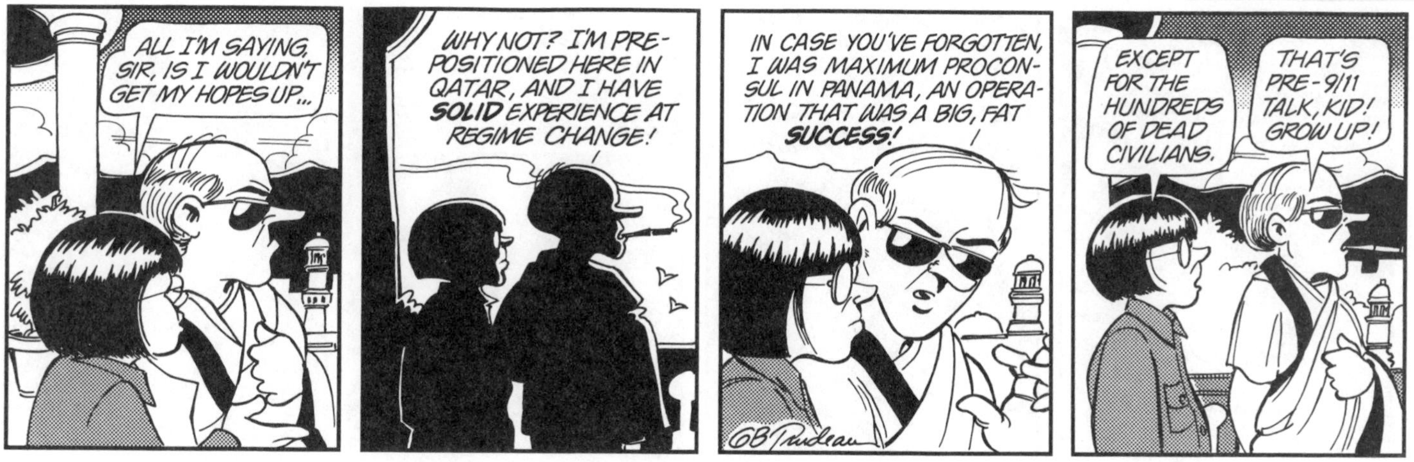
ALL I'M SAYING, SIR, IS I WOULDN'T GET MY HOPES UP...
WHY NOT? I'M PREPOSITIONED HERE IN QATAR, AND I HAVE SOLID EXPERIENCE AT REGIME CHANGE!
IN CASE YOU'VE FORGOTTEN, I WAS MAXIMUM PROCONSUL IN PANAMA, AN OPERATION THAT WAS A BIG, FAT SUCCESS!
EXCEPT FOR THE HUNDREDS OF DEAD CIVILIANS.
THAT'S PRE-9/11 TALK, KID! GROW UP!

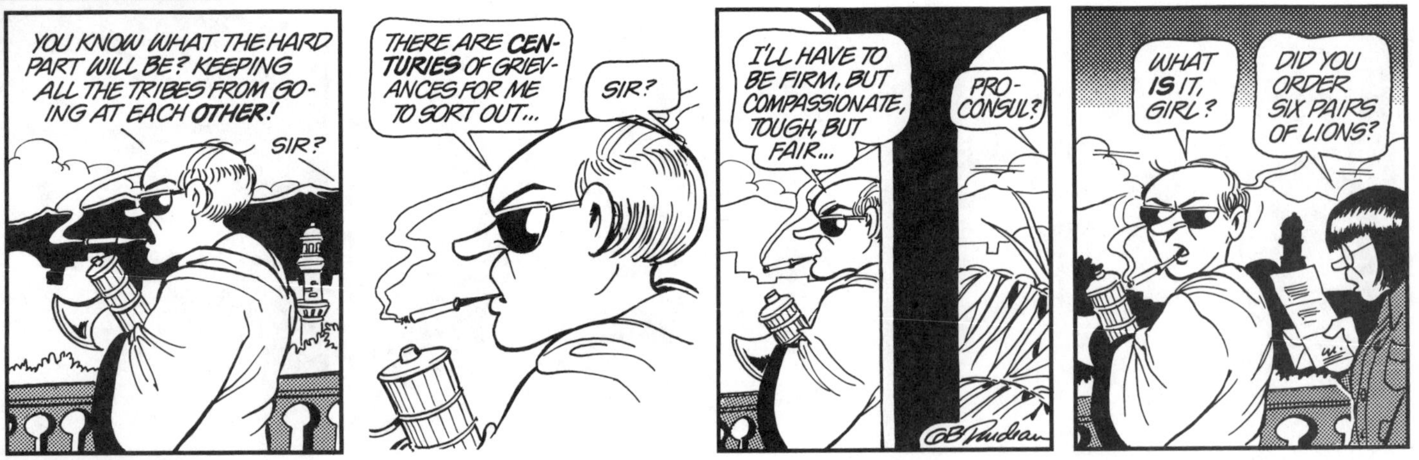
YOU KNOW WHAT THE HARD PART WILL BE? KEEPING ALL THE TRIBES FROM GOING AT EACH OTHER!
SIR?
THERE ARE CENTURIES OF GRIEVANCES FOR ME TO SORT OUT...
SIR?
I'LL HAVE TO BE FIRM, BUT COMPASSIONATE, TOUGH, BUT FAIR...
PROCONSUL?
WHAT IS IT, GIRL?
DID YOU ORDER SIX PAIRS OF LIONS?

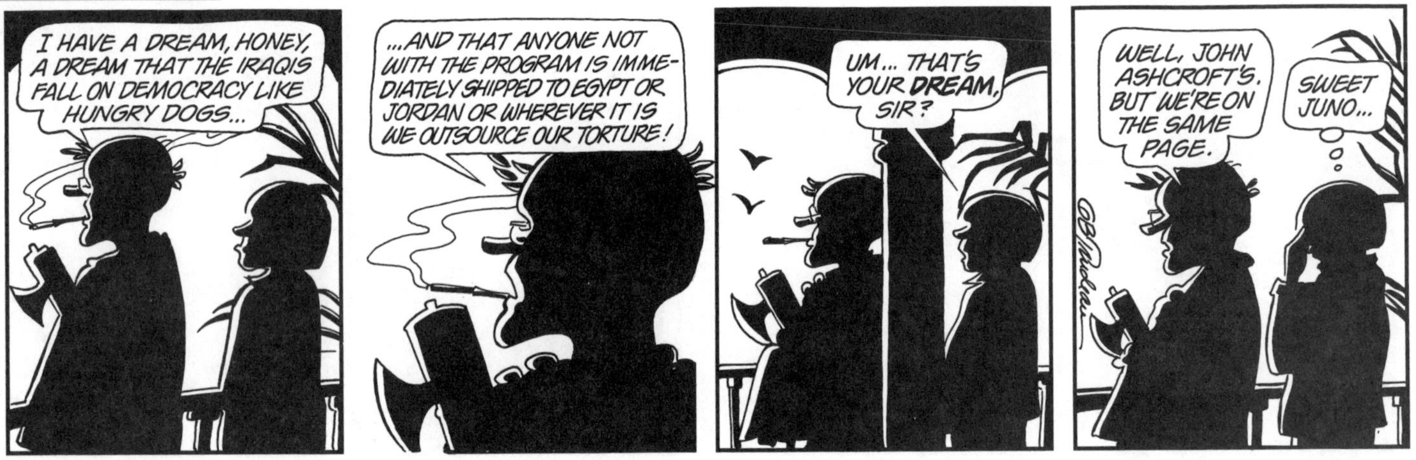
I HAVE A DREAM, HONEY. A DREAM THAT THE IRAQIS FALL ON DEMOCRACY LIKE HUNGRY DOGS...
...AND THAT ANYONE NOT WITH THE PROGRAM IS IMMEDIATELY SHIPPED TO EGYPT OR JORDAN OR WHEREVER IT IS WE OUTSOURCE OUR TORTURE!
UM... THAT'S YOUR DREAM, SIR?
WELL, JOHN ASHCROFT'S. BUT WE'RE ON THE SAME PAGE.
SWEET JUNO...

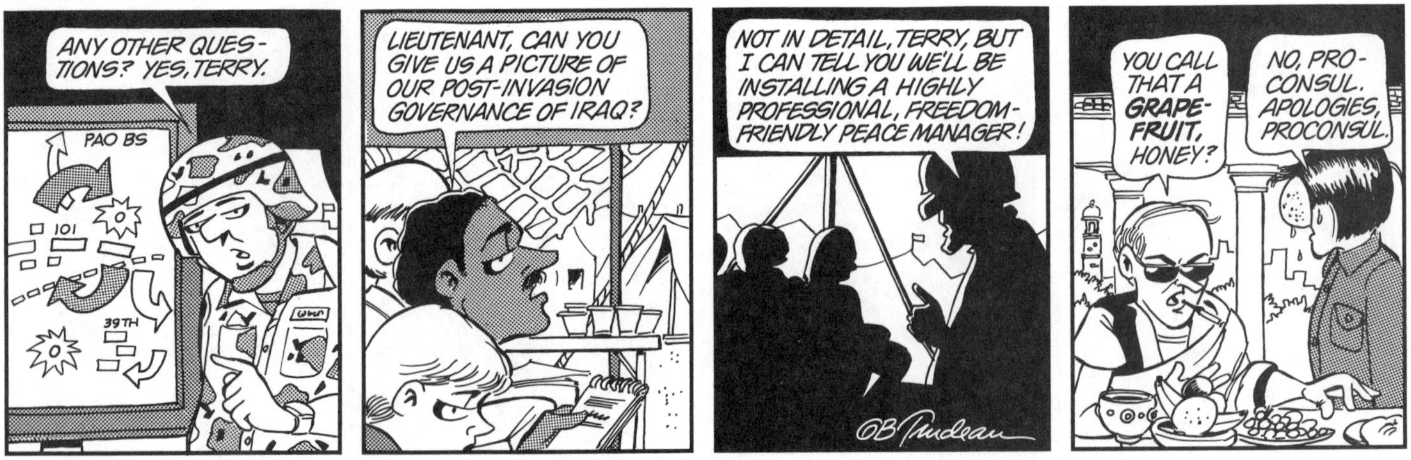
ANY OTHER QUESTIONS? YES, TERRY.
PAO BS
101
39TH
LIEUTENANT, CAN YOU GIVE US A PICTURE OF OUR POST-INVASION GOVERNANCE OF IRAQ?
NOT IN DETAIL, TERRY, BUT I CAN TELL YOU WE'LL BE INSTALLING A HIGHLY PROFESSIONAL, FREEDOM-FRIENDLY PEACE MANAGER!
YOU CALL THAT A GRAPEFRUIT, HONEY?
NO, PROCONSUL. APOLOGIES, PROCONSUL.

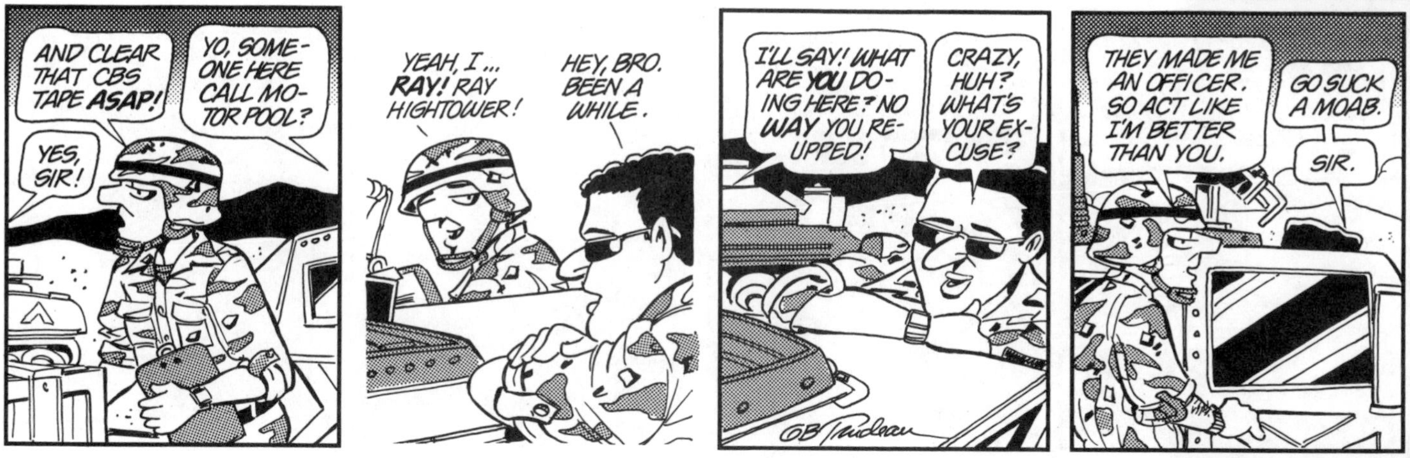
AND CLEAR THAT CBS TAPE ASAP!
YES, SIR!
YO, SOME-ONE HERE CALL MO-TOR POOL?
YEAH, I... RAY! RAY HIGHTOWER!
HEY, BRO. BEEN A WHILE.
I'LL SAY! WHAT ARE YOU DO-ING HERE? NO WAY YOU RE-UPPED!
CRAZY, HUH? WHAT'S YOUR EX-CUSE?
THEY MADE ME AN OFFICER. SO ACT LIKE I'M BETTER THAN YOU.
GO SUCK A MOAB.
SIR.

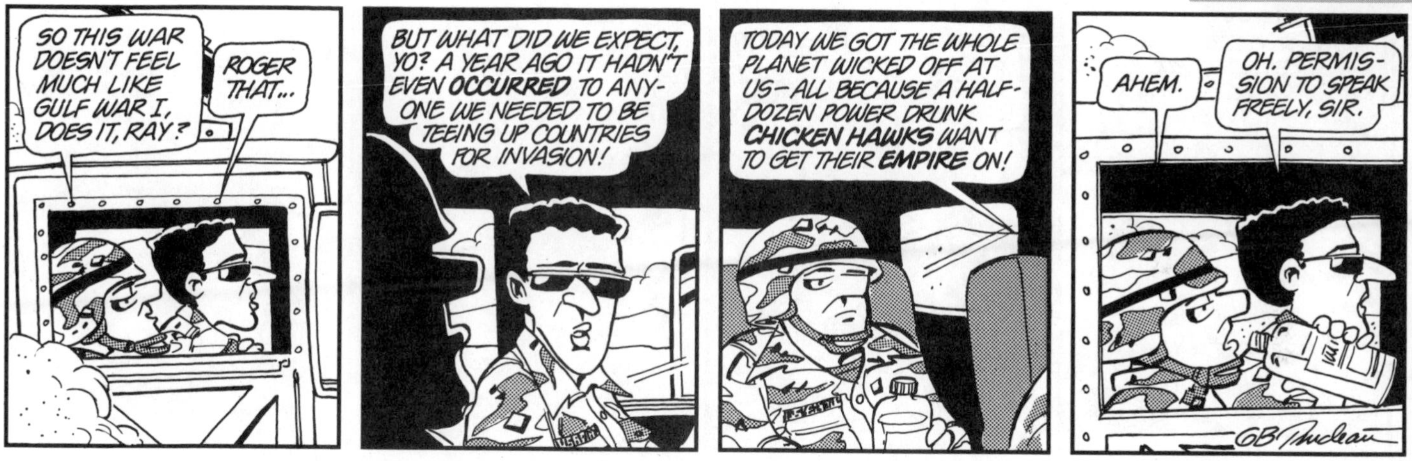
SO THIS WAR DOESN'T FEEL MUCH LIKE GULF WAR I, DOES IT, RAY?
ROGER THAT...
BUT WHAT DID WE EXPECT, YO? A YEAR AGO IT HADN'T EVEN OCCURRED TO ANY-ONE WE NEEDED TO BE TEEING UP COUNTRIES FOR INVASION!
TODAY WE GOT THE WHOLE PLANET WICKED OFF AT US—ALL BECAUSE A HALF-DOZEN POWER DRUNK CHICKEN HAWKS WANT TO GET THEIR EMPIRE ON!
AHEM.
OH. PERMIS-SION TO SPEAK FREELY, SIR.

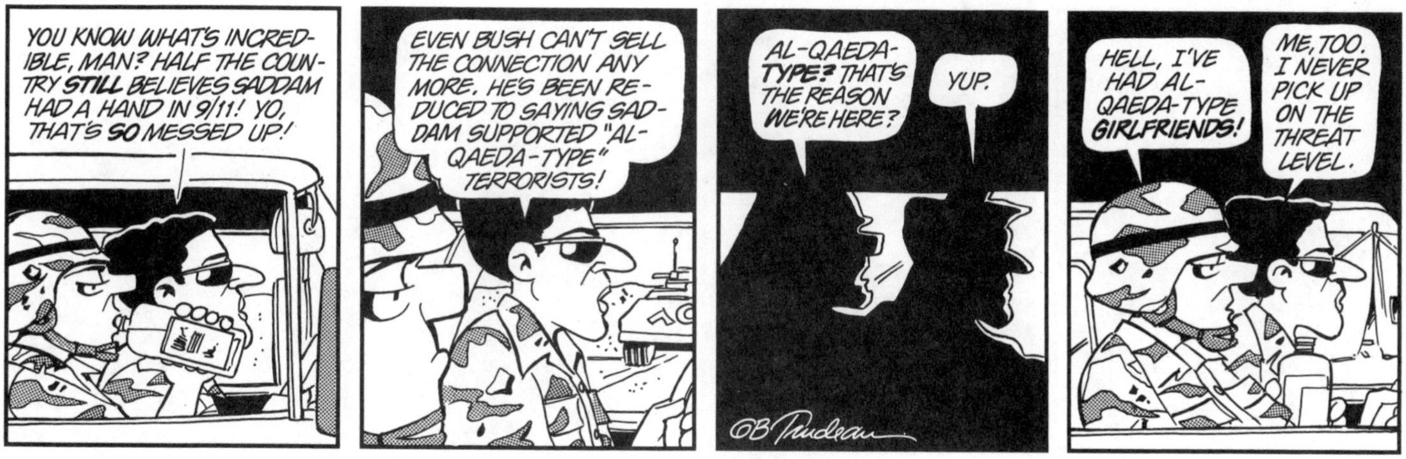
YOU KNOW WHAT'S INCRED-IBLE, MAN? HALF THE COUN-TRY STILL BELIEVES SADDAM HAD A HAND IN 9/11! YO, THAT'S SO MESSED UP!
EVEN BUSH CAN'T SELL THE CONNECTION ANY MORE. HE'S BEEN RE-DUCED TO SAYING SAD-DAM SUPPORTED "AL-QAEDA-TYPE" TERRORISTS!
AL-QAEDA-TYPE? THAT'S THE REASON WE'RE HERE?
YUP.
HELL, I'VE HAD AL-QAEDA-TYPE GIRLFRIENDS!
ME, TOO. I NEVER PICK UP ON THE THREAT LEVEL.

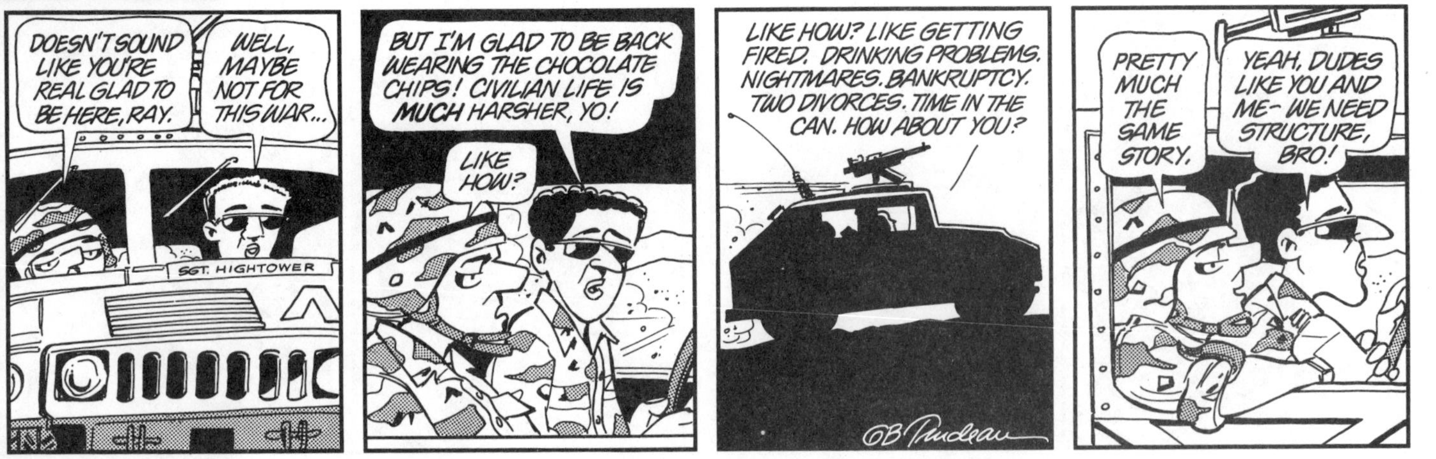
DOESN'T SOUND LIKE YOU'RE REAL GLAD TO BE HERE, RAY.
WELL, MAYBE NOT FOR THIS WAR...
SGT. HIGHTOWER
BUT I'M GLAD TO BE BACK WEARING THE CHOCOLATE CHIPS! CIVILIAN LIFE IS **MUCH** HARSHER, YO!
LIKE HOW?
LIKE HOW? LIKE GETTING FIRED. DRINKING PROBLEMS. NIGHTMARES. BANKRUPTCY. TWO DIVORCES. TIME IN THE CAN. HOW ABOUT YOU?
PRETTY MUCH THE SAME STORY.
YEAH, DUDES LIKE YOU AND ME– WE NEED STRUCTURE, BRO!

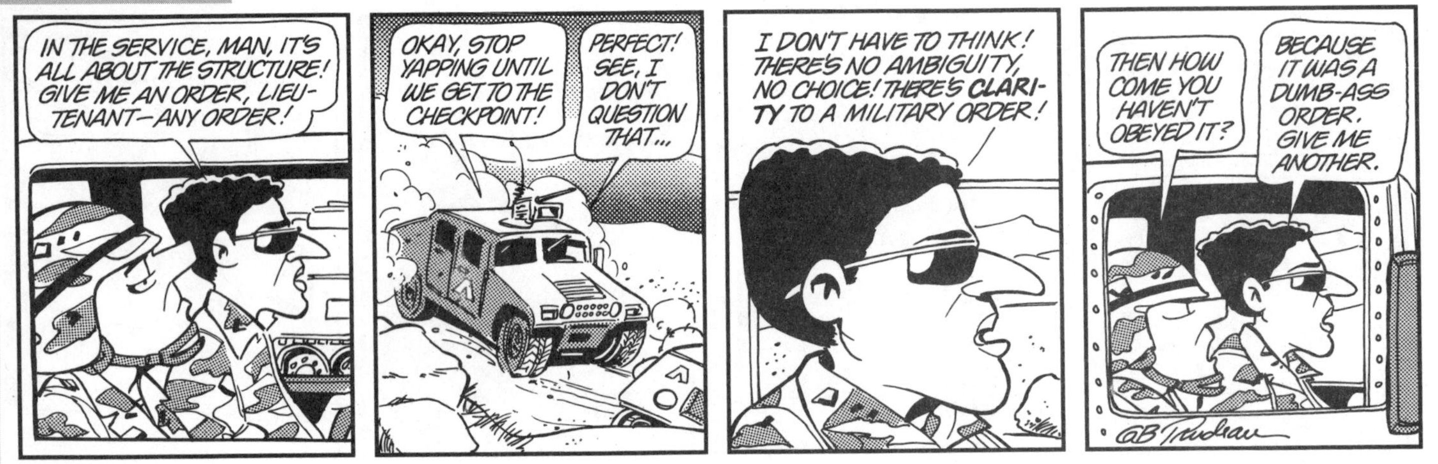
IN THE SERVICE, MAN, IT'S ALL ABOUT THE STRUCTURE! GIVE ME AN ORDER, LIEUTENANT–ANY ORDER!
OKAY, STOP YAPPING UNTIL WE GET TO THE CHECKPOINT!
PERFECT! SEE, I DON'T QUESTION THAT...
I DON'T HAVE TO THINK! THERE'S NO AMBIGUITY, NO CHOICE! THERE'S **CLARITY** TO A MILITARY ORDER!
THEN HOW COME YOU HAVEN'T OBEYED IT?
BECAUSE IT WAS A DUMB-ASS ORDER. GIVE ME ANOTHER.

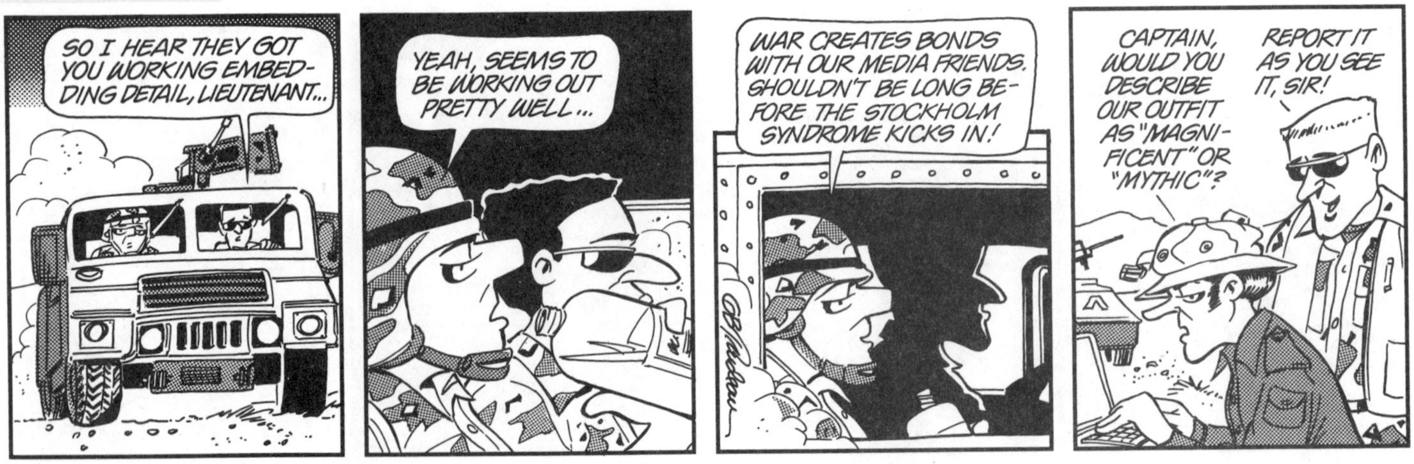
SO I HEAR THEY GOT YOU WORKING EMBEDDING DETAIL, LIEUTENANT...
YEAH, SEEMS TO BE WORKING OUT PRETTY WELL...
WAR CREATES BONDS WITH OUR MEDIA FRIENDS. SHOULDN'T BE LONG BEFORE THE STOCKHOLM SYNDROME KICKS IN!
CAPTAIN, WOULD YOU DESCRIBE OUR OUTFIT AS "MAGNIFICENT" OR "MYTHIC"?
REPORT IT AS YOU SEE IT, SIR!

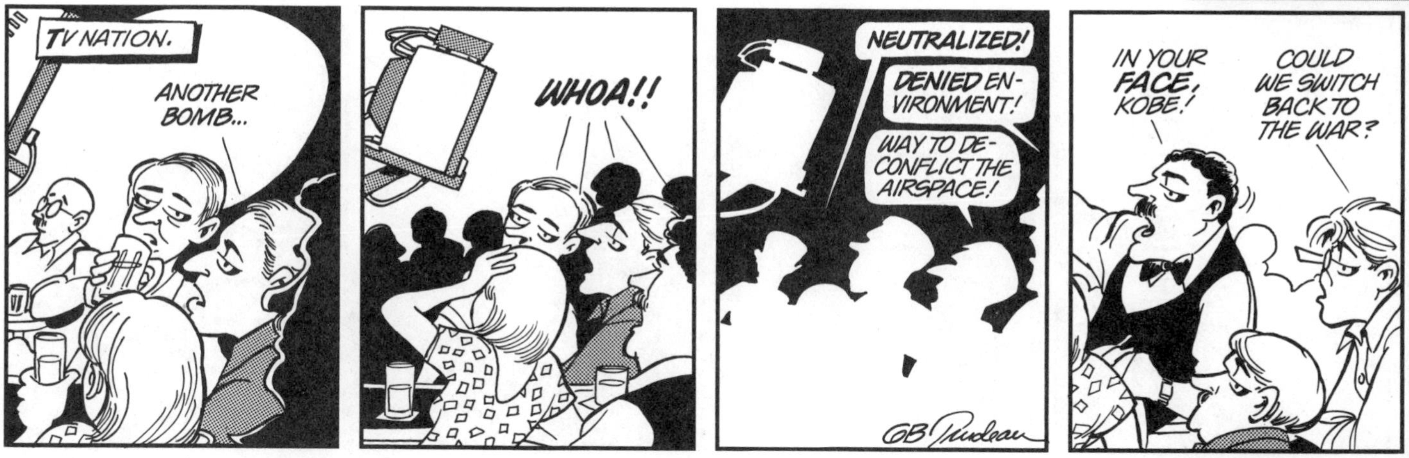
TV NATION.
ANOTHER BOMB...
WHOA!!
NEUTRALIZED!
DENIED ENVIRONMENT!
WAY TO DECONFLICT THE AIRSPACE!
IN YOUR FACE, KOBE!
COULD WE SWITCH BACK TO THE WAR?

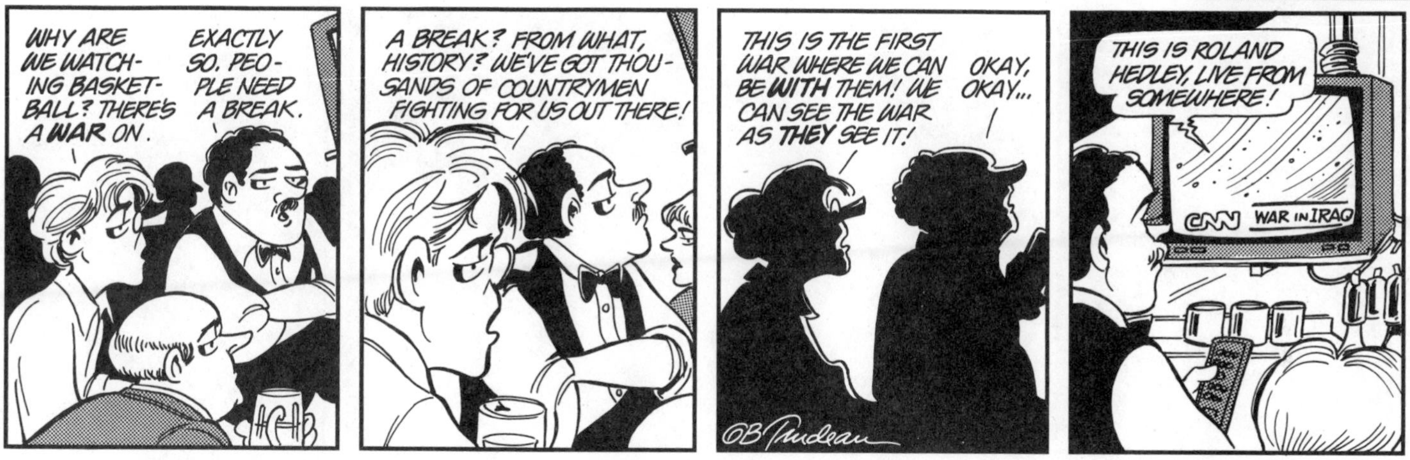
WHY ARE WE WATCHING BASKETBALL? THERE'S A WAR ON.
EXACTLY SO. PEOPLE NEED A BREAK.
A BREAK? FROM WHAT, HISTORY? WE'VE GOT THOUSANDS OF COUNTRYMEN FIGHTING FOR US OUT THERE!
THIS IS THE FIRST WAR WHERE WE CAN BE WITH THEM! WE CAN SEE THE WAR AS THEY SEE IT!
OKAY, OKAY...
THIS IS ROLAND HEDLEY, LIVE FROM SOMEWHERE!
CNN WAR IN IRAQ

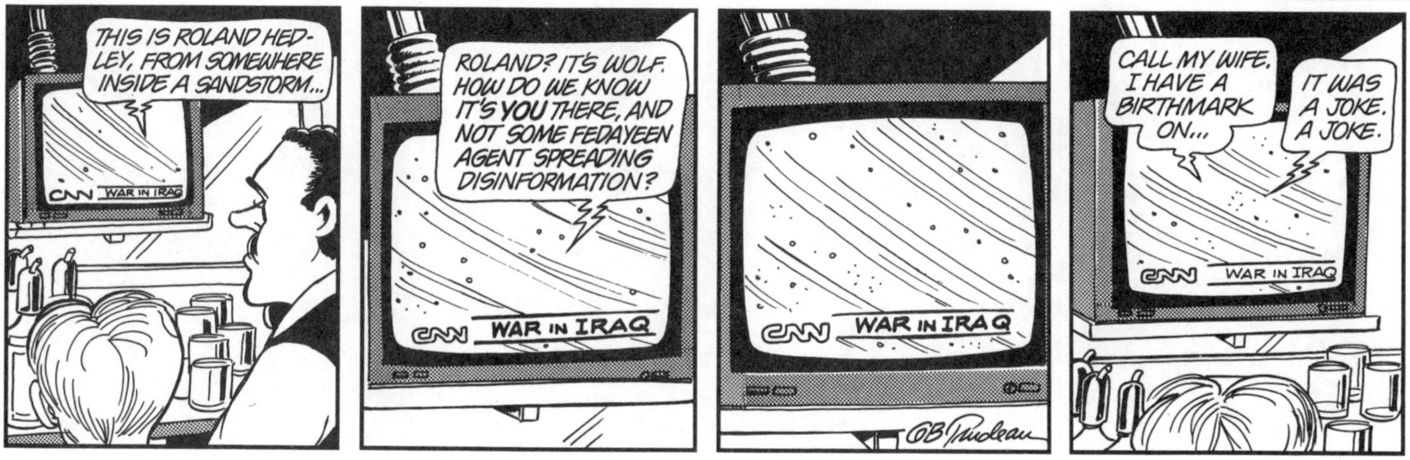
THIS IS ROLAND HEDLEY, FROM SOMEWHERE INSIDE A SANDSTORM...
CNN WAR IN IRAQ
ROLAND? IT'S WOLF. HOW DO WE KNOW IT'S YOU THERE, AND NOT SOME FEDAYEEN AGENT SPREADING DISINFORMATION?
CNN WAR IN IRAQ
CNN WAR IN IRAQ
CALL MY WIFE. I HAVE A BIRTHMARK ON...
IT WAS A JOKE. A JOKE.
CNN WAR IN IRAQ

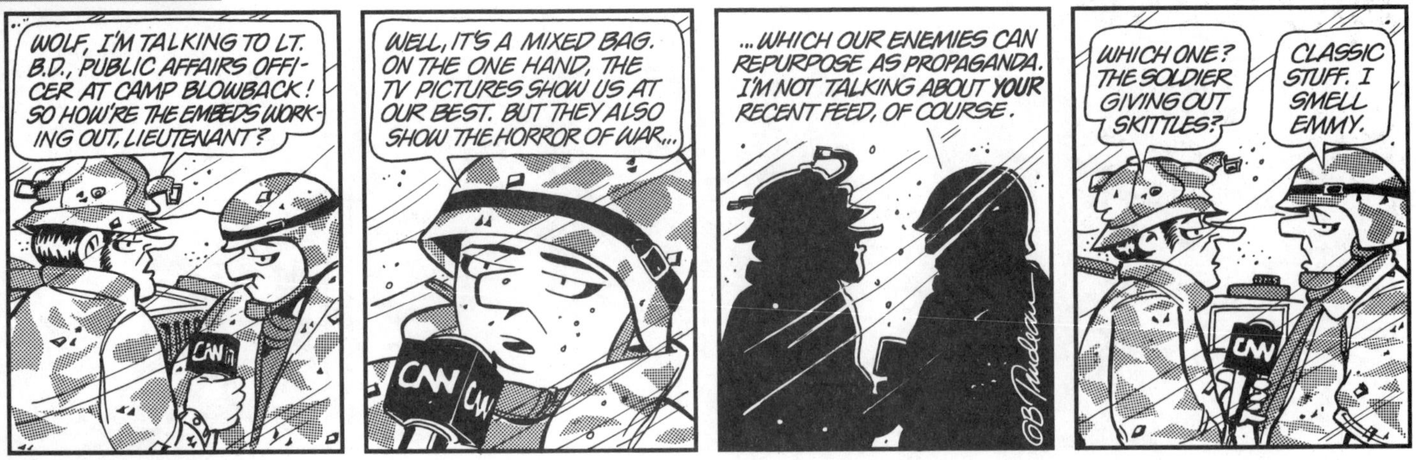
WOLF, I'M TALKING TO LT. B.D., PUBLIC AFFAIRS OFFICER AT CAMP BLOWBACK! SO HOW'RE THE EMBEDS WORKING OUT, LIEUTENANT?
WELL, IT'S A MIXED BAG. ON THE ONE HAND, THE TV PICTURES SHOW US AT OUR BEST. BUT THEY ALSO SHOW THE HORROR OF WAR...
...WHICH OUR ENEMIES CAN REPURPOSE AS PROPAGANDA. I'M NOT TALKING ABOUT YOUR RECENT FEED, OF COURSE.
WHICH ONE? THE SOLDIER GIVING OUT SKITTLES?
CLASSIC STUFF. I SMELL EMMY.

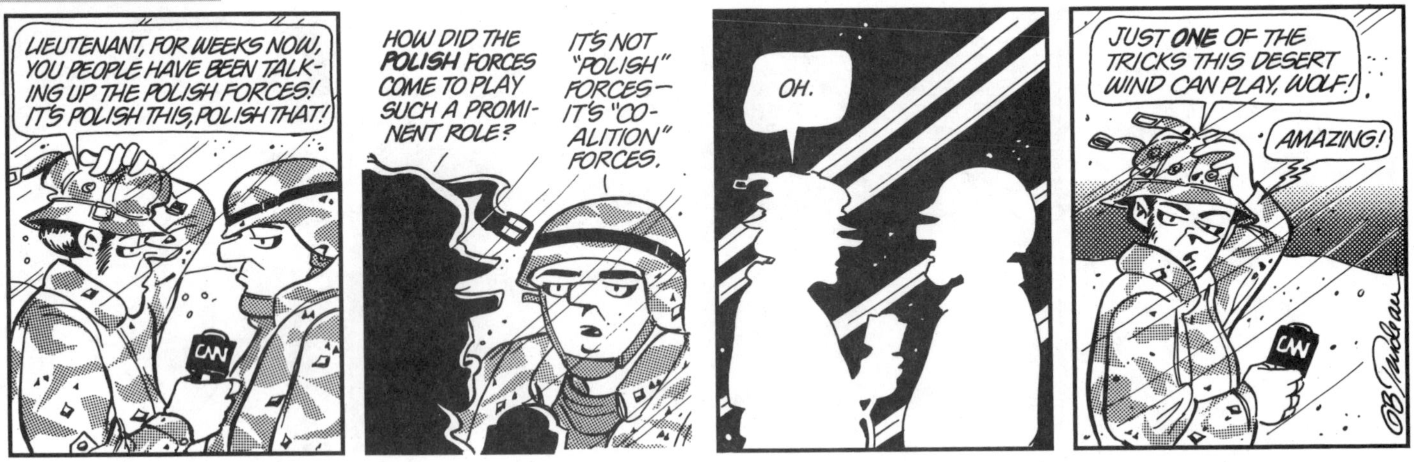
LIEUTENANT, FOR WEEKS NOW, YOU PEOPLE HAVE BEEN TALKING UP THE POLISH FORCES! IT'S POLISH THIS, POLISH THAT!
HOW DID THE POLISH FORCES COME TO PLAY SUCH A PROMINENT ROLE?
IT'S NOT "POLISH" FORCES— IT'S "COALITION" FORCES.
OH.
JUST ONE OF THE TRICKS THIS DESERT WIND CAN PLAY, WOLF!
AMAZING!

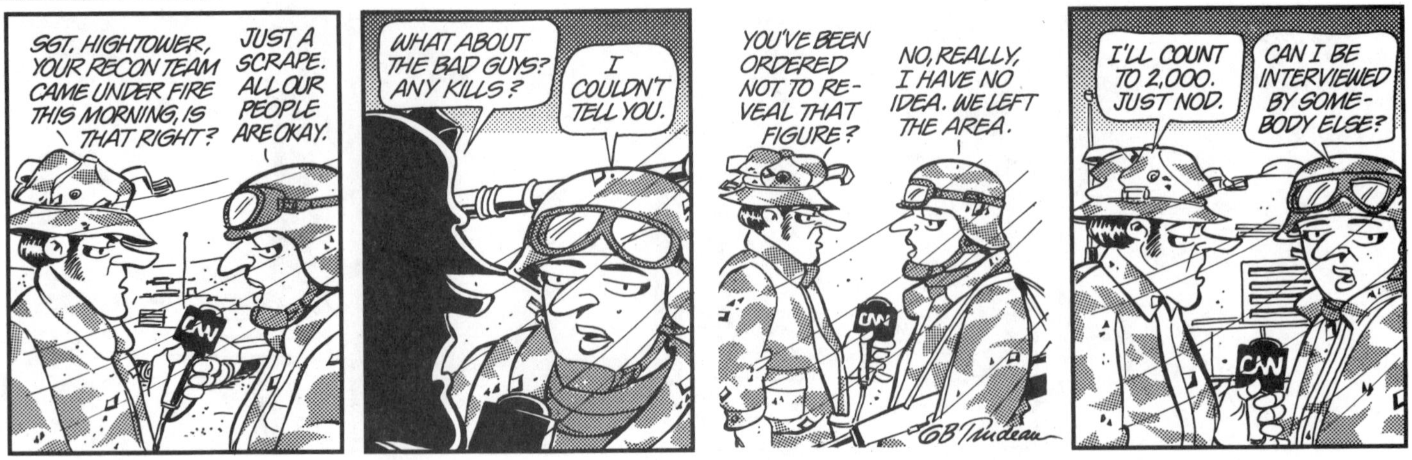
SGT. HIGHTOWER, YOUR RECON TEAM CAME UNDER FIRE THIS MORNING, IS THAT RIGHT?
JUST A SCRAPE. ALL OUR PEOPLE ARE OKAY.
WHAT ABOUT THE BAD GUYS? ANY KILLS?
I COULDN'T TELL YOU.
YOU'VE BEEN ORDERED NOT TO REVEAL THAT FIGURE?
NO, REALLY, I HAVE NO IDEA. WE LEFT THE AREA.
I'LL COUNT TO 2,000. JUST NOD.
CAN I BE INTERVIEWED BY SOMEBODY ELSE?

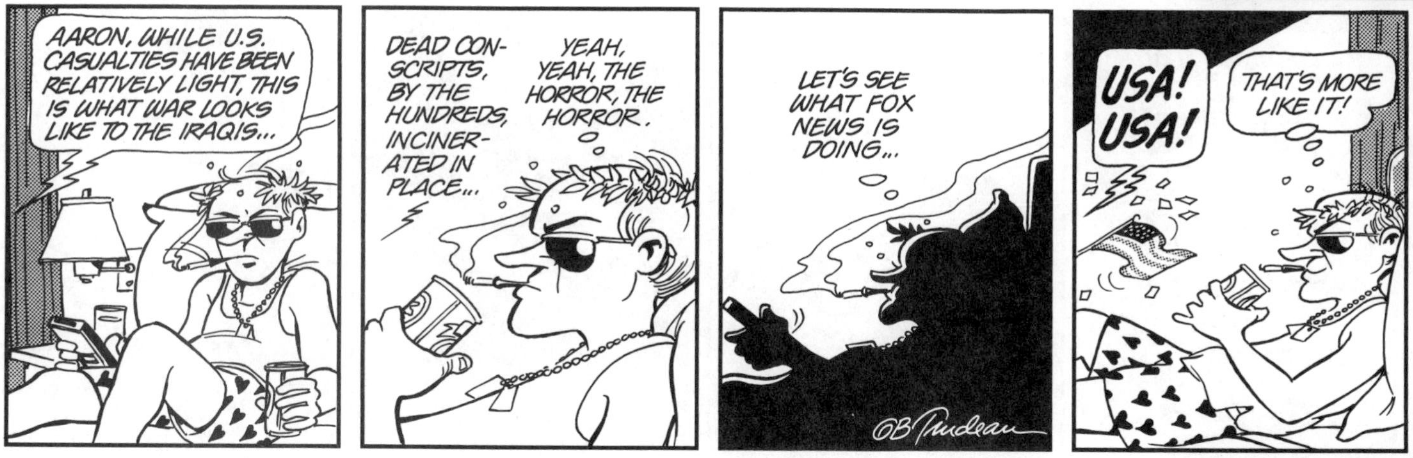
AARON, WHILE U.S. CASUALTIES HAVE BEEN RELATIVELY LIGHT, THIS IS WHAT WAR LOOKS LIKE TO THE IRAQIS...
DEAD CONSCRIPTS, BY THE HUNDREDS, INCINERATED IN PLACE...
YEAH, YEAH, THE HORROR, THE HORROR.
LET'S SEE WHAT FOX NEWS IS DOING...
USA! USA!
THAT'S MORE LIKE IT!
©B Trudeau

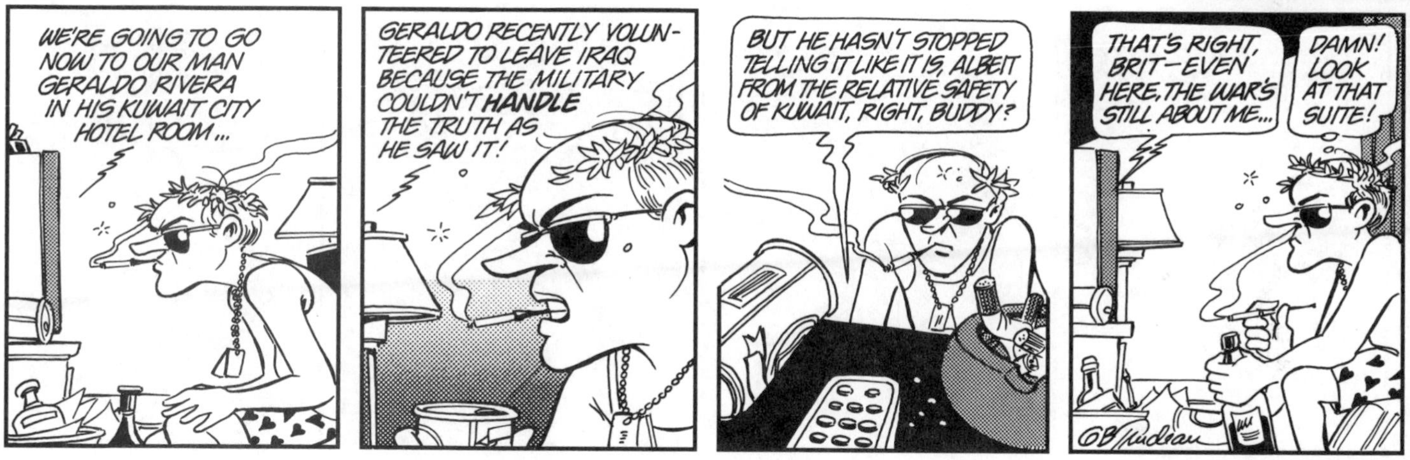
WE'RE GOING TO GO NOW TO OUR MAN GERALDO RIVERA IN HIS KUWAIT CITY HOTEL ROOM...
GERALDO RECENTLY VOLUNTEERED TO LEAVE IRAQ BECAUSE THE MILITARY COULDN'T HANDLE THE TRUTH AS HE SAW IT!
BUT HE HASN'T STOPPED TELLING IT LIKE IT IS, ALBEIT FROM THE RELATIVE SAFETY OF KUWAIT, RIGHT, BUDDY?
THAT'S RIGHT, BRIT—EVEN HERE, THE WAR'S STILL ABOUT ME...
DAMN! LOOK AT THAT SUITE!
©B Trudeau

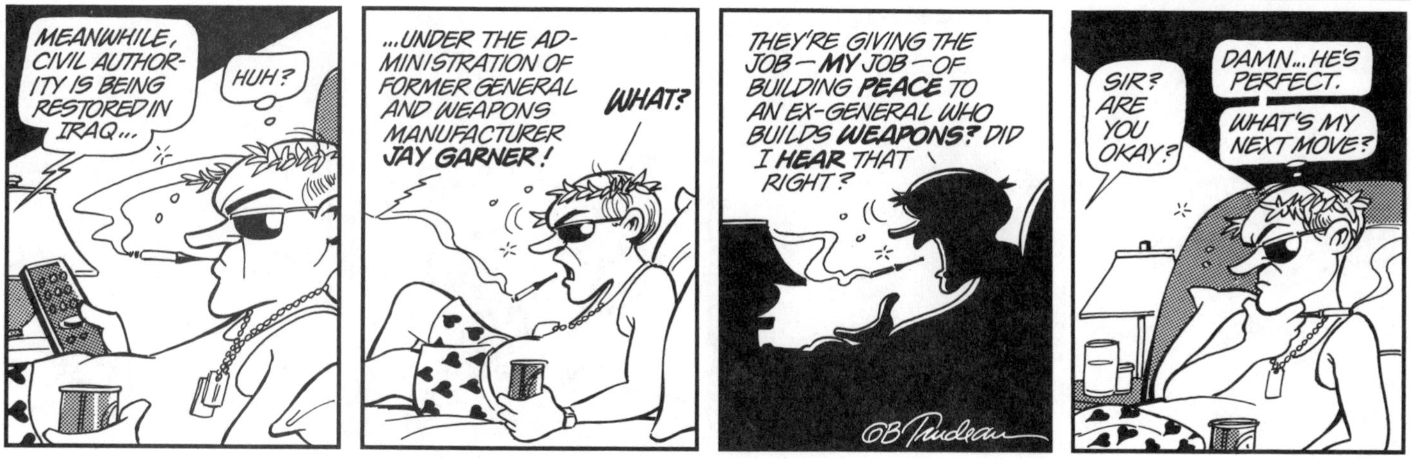
MEANWHILE, CIVIL AUTHORITY IS BEING RESTORED IN IRAQ...
HUH?
...UNDER THE ADMINISTRATION OF FORMER GENERAL AND WEAPONS MANUFACTURER JAY GARNER!
WHAT?
THEY'RE GIVING THE JOB—MY JOB—OF BUILDING PEACE TO AN EX-GENERAL WHO BUILDS WEAPONS? DID I HEAR THAT RIGHT?
©B Trudeau
SIR? ARE YOU OKAY?
DAMN... HE'S PERFECT.
WHAT'S MY NEXT MOVE?

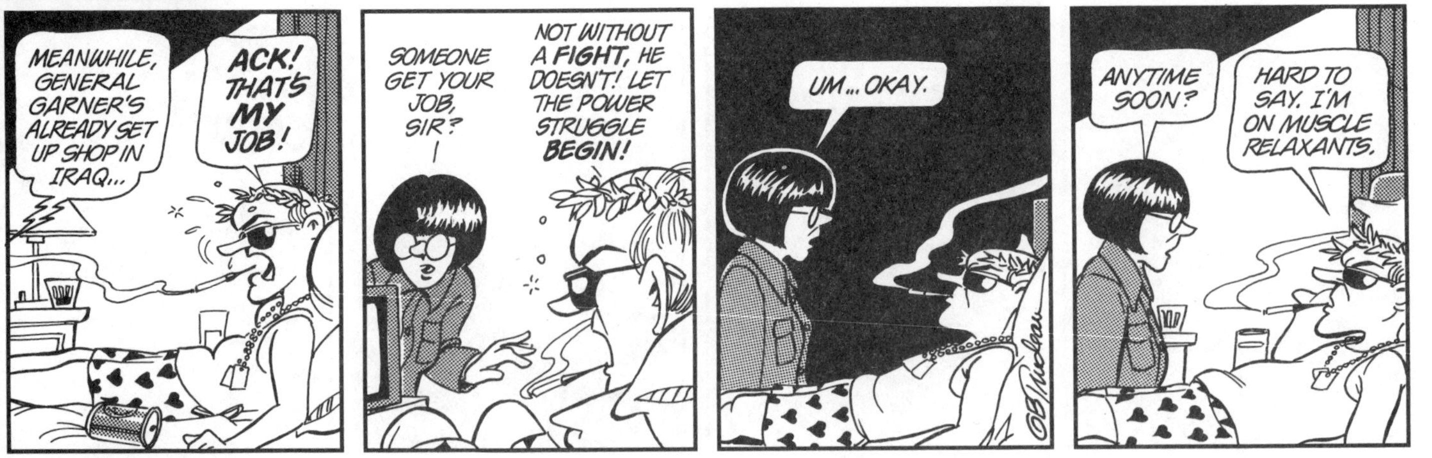
MEANWHILE, GENERAL GARNER'S ALREADY SET UP SHOP IN IRAQ...
ACK! THAT'S MY JOB!
SOMEONE GET YOUR JOB, SIR?
NOT WITHOUT A FIGHT, HE DOESN'T! LET THE POWER STRUGGLE BEGIN!
UM... OKAY.
ANYTIME SOON?
HARD TO SAY. I'M ON MUSCLE RELAXANTS.

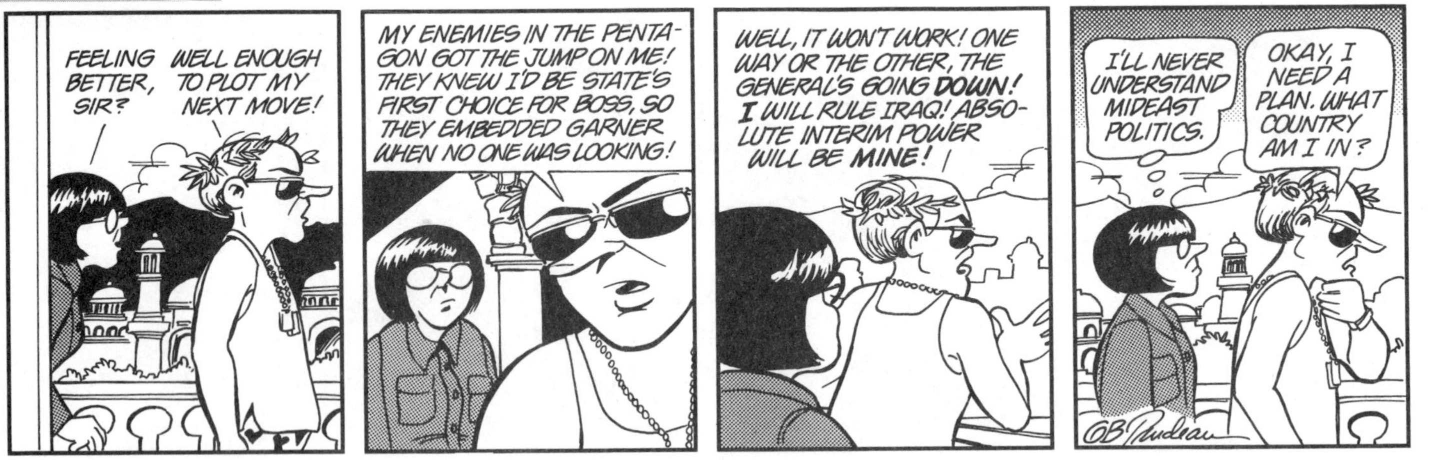
FEELING BETTER, SIR?
WELL ENOUGH TO PLOT MY NEXT MOVE!
MY ENEMIES IN THE PENTAGON GOT THE JUMP ON ME! THEY KNEW I'D BE STATE'S FIRST CHOICE FOR BOSS, SO THEY EMBEDDED GARNER WHEN NO ONE WAS LOOKING!
WELL, IT WON'T WORK! ONE WAY OR THE OTHER, THE GENERAL'S GOING DOWN! I WILL RULE IRAQ! ABSOLUTE INTERIM POWER WILL BE MINE!
I'LL NEVER UNDERSTAND MIDEAST POLITICS.
OKAY, I NEED A PLAN. WHAT COUNTRY AM I IN?

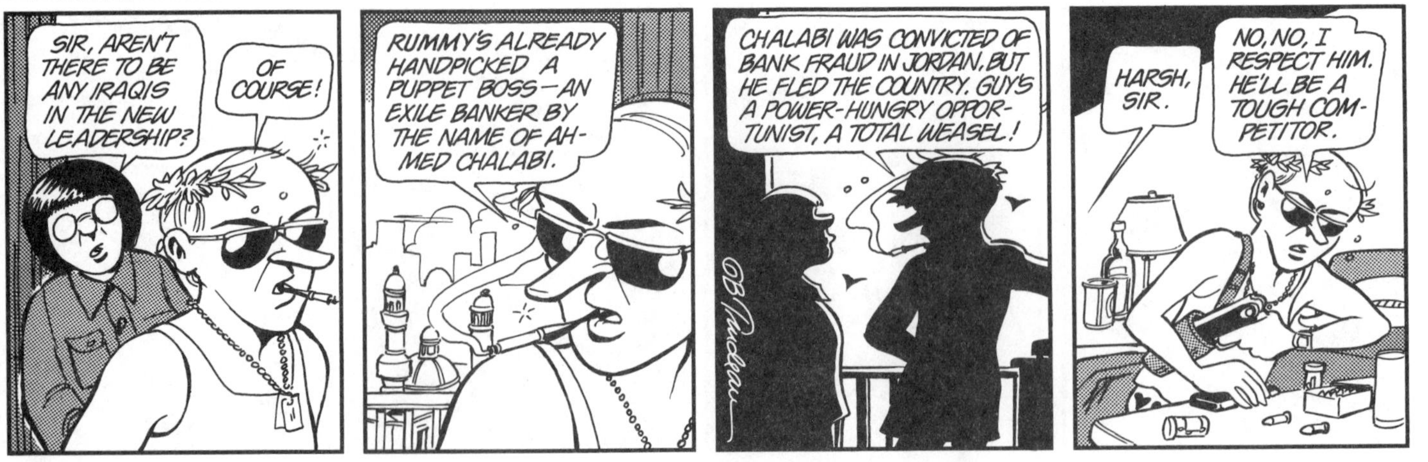
SIR, AREN'T THERE TO BE ANY IRAQIS IN THE NEW LEADERSHIP?
OF COURSE!
RUMMY'S ALREADY HANDPICKED A PUPPET BOSS—AN EXILE BANKER BY THE NAME OF AHMED CHALABI.
CHALABI WAS CONVICTED OF BANK FRAUD IN JORDAN, BUT HE FLED THE COUNTRY. GUY'S A POWER-HUNGRY OPPORTUNIST, A TOTAL WEASEL!
HARSH, SIR.
NO, NO, I RESPECT HIM. HE'LL BE A TOUGH COMPETITOR.

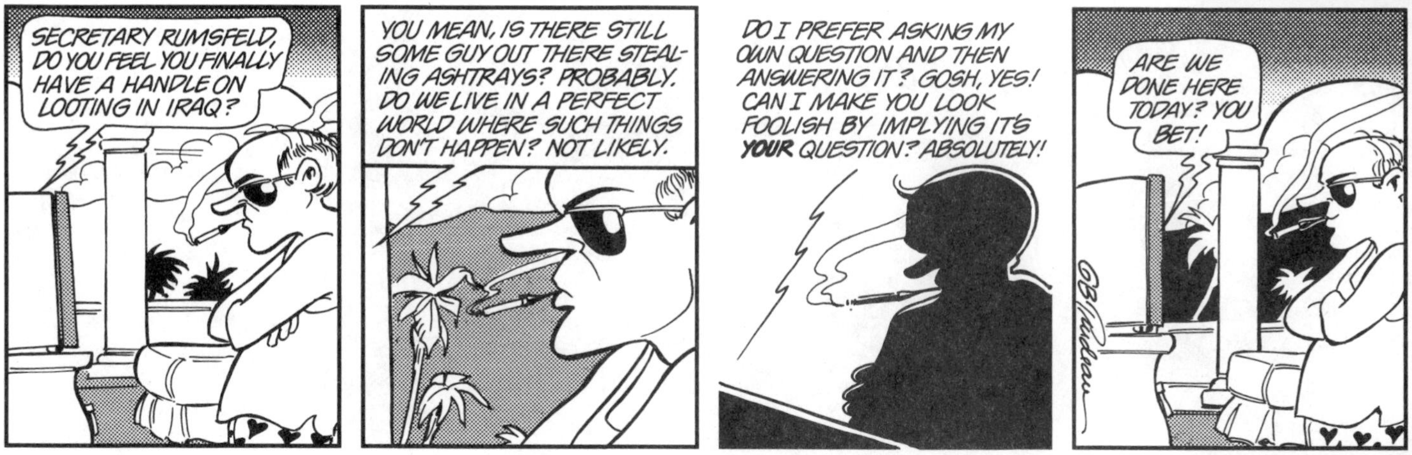
SECRETARY RUMSFELD, DO YOU FEEL YOU FINALLY HAVE A HANDLE ON LOOTING IN IRAQ?
YOU MEAN, IS THERE STILL SOME GUY OUT THERE STEALING ASHTRAYS? PROBABLY. DO WE LIVE IN A PERFECT WORLD WHERE SUCH THINGS DON'T HAPPEN? NOT LIKELY.
DO I PREFER ASKING MY OWN QUESTION AND THEN ANSWERING IT? GOSH, YES! CAN I MAKE YOU LOOK FOOLISH BY IMPLYING IT'S YOUR QUESTION? ABSOLUTELY!
ARE WE DONE HERE TODAY? YOU BET!
GB Trudeau

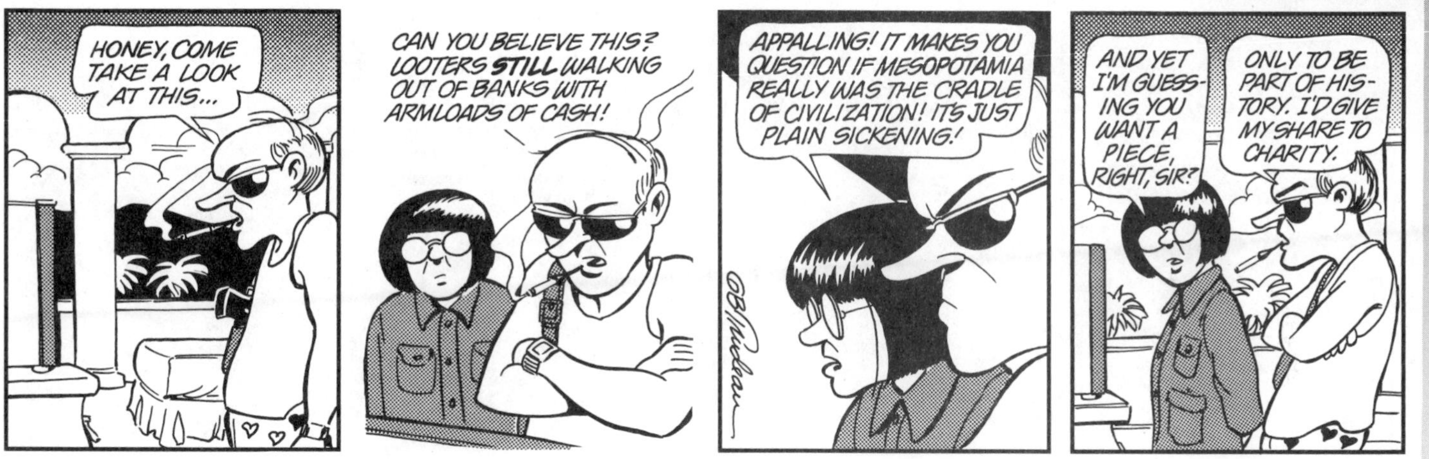
HONEY, COME TAKE A LOOK AT THIS...
CAN YOU BELIEVE THIS? LOOTERS STILL WALKING OUT OF BANKS WITH ARMLOADS OF CASH!
GB Trudeau
APPALLING! IT MAKES YOU QUESTION IF MESOPOTAMIA REALLY WAS THE CRADLE OF CIVILIZATION! IT'S JUST PLAIN SICKENING!
AND YET I'M GUESSING YOU WANT A PIECE, RIGHT, SIR?
ONLY TO BE PART OF HISTORY. I'D GIVE MY SHARE TO CHARITY.

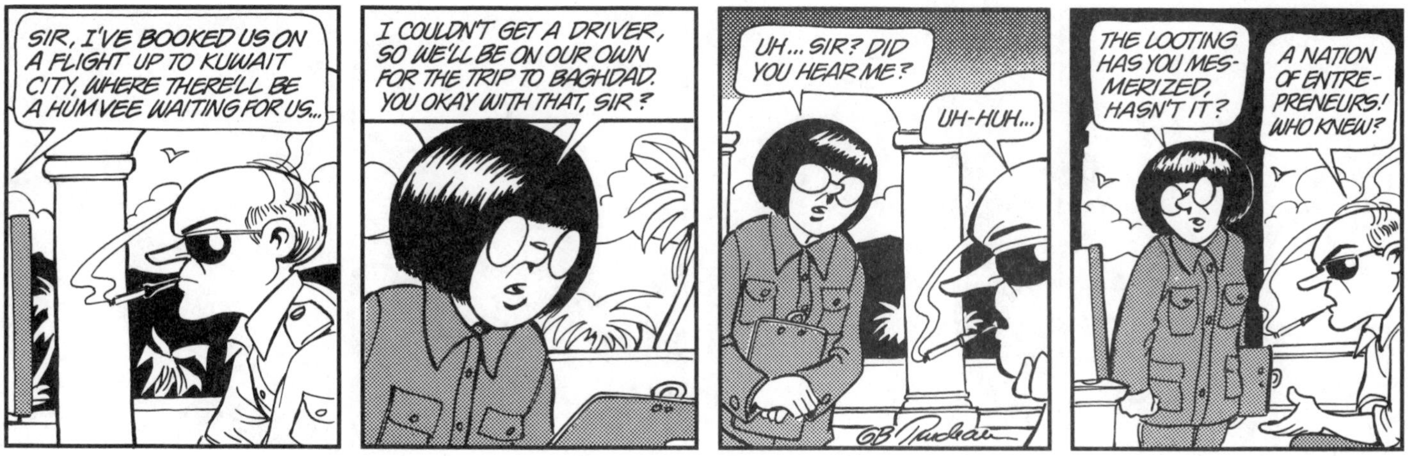
SIR, I'VE BOOKED US ON A FLIGHT UP TO KUWAIT CITY, WHERE THERE'LL BE A HUMVEE WAITING FOR US...
I COULDN'T GET A DRIVER, SO WE'LL BE ON OUR OWN FOR THE TRIP TO BAGHDAD. YOU OKAY WITH THAT, SIR?
UH... SIR? DID YOU HEAR ME?
UH-HUH...
GB Trudeau
THE LOOTING HAS YOU MESMERIZED, HASN'T IT?
A NATION OF ENTREPRENEURS! WHO KNEW?

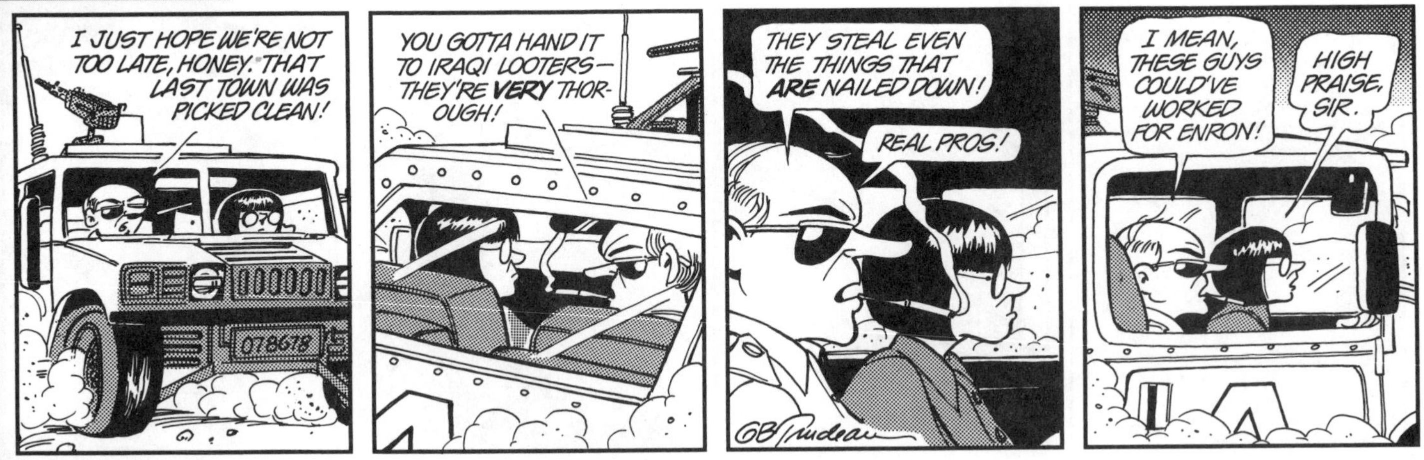
I JUST HOPE WE'RE NOT TOO LATE, HONEY. THAT LAST TOWN WAS PICKED CLEAN!
YOU GOTTA HAND IT TO IRAQI LOOTERS—THEY'RE VERY THOROUGH!
THEY STEAL EVEN THE THINGS THAT ARE NAILED DOWN!
REAL PROS!
I MEAN, THESE GUYS COULD'VE WORKED FOR ENRON!
HIGH PRAISE, SIR.
GB Trudeau

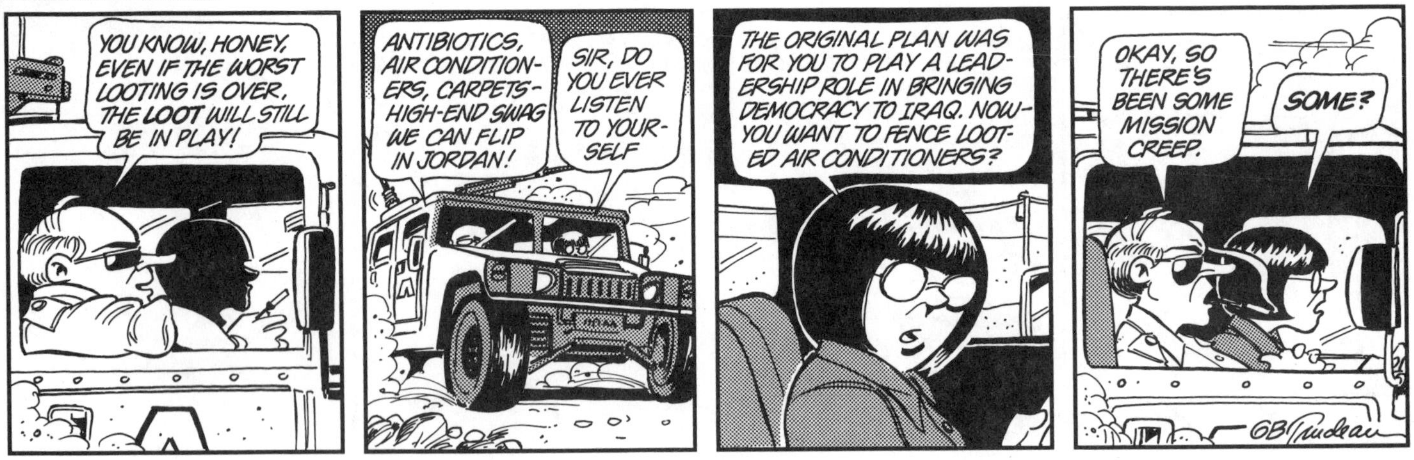
YOU KNOW, HONEY, EVEN IF THE WORST LOOTING IS OVER, THE LOOT WILL STILL BE IN PLAY!
ANTIBIOTICS, AIR CONDITIONERS, CARPETS—HIGH-END SWAG WE CAN FLIP IN JORDAN!
SIR, DO YOU EVER LISTEN TO YOURSELF
THE ORIGINAL PLAN WAS FOR YOU TO PLAY A LEADERSHIP ROLE IN BRINGING DEMOCRACY TO IRAQ. NOW YOU WANT TO FENCE LOOTED AIR CONDITIONERS?
OKAY, SO THERE'S BEEN SOME MISSION CREEP.
SOME?
GB Trudeau

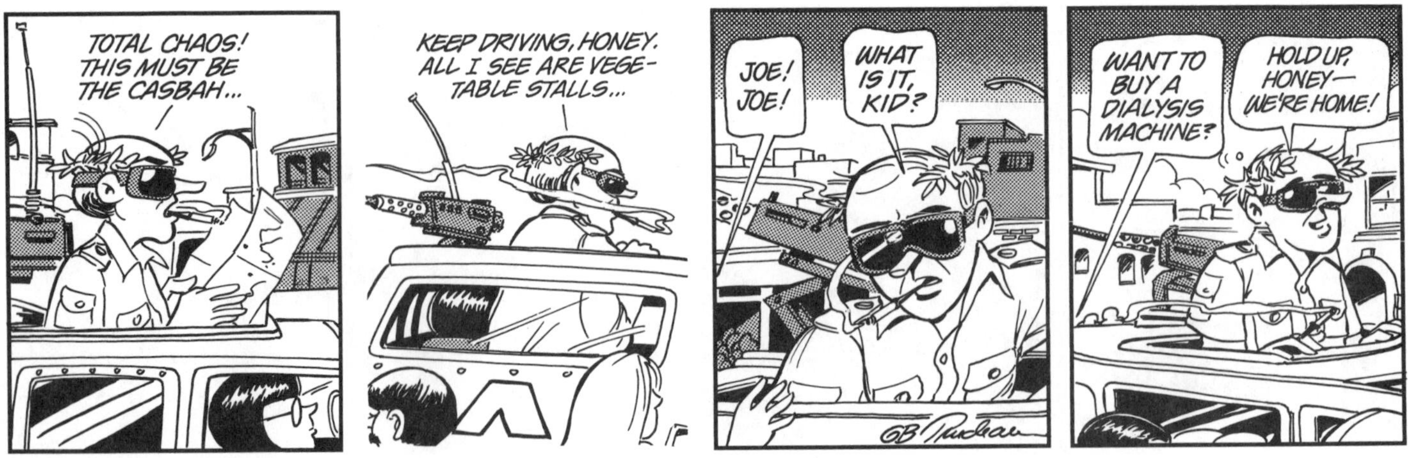
TOTAL CHAOS! THIS MUST BE THE CASBAH...
KEEP DRIVING, HONEY. ALL I SEE ARE VEGETABLE STALLS...
JOE! JOE!
WHAT IS IT, KID?
WANT TO BUY A DIALYSIS MACHINE?
HOLD UP, HONEY—WE'RE HOME!
GB Trudeau

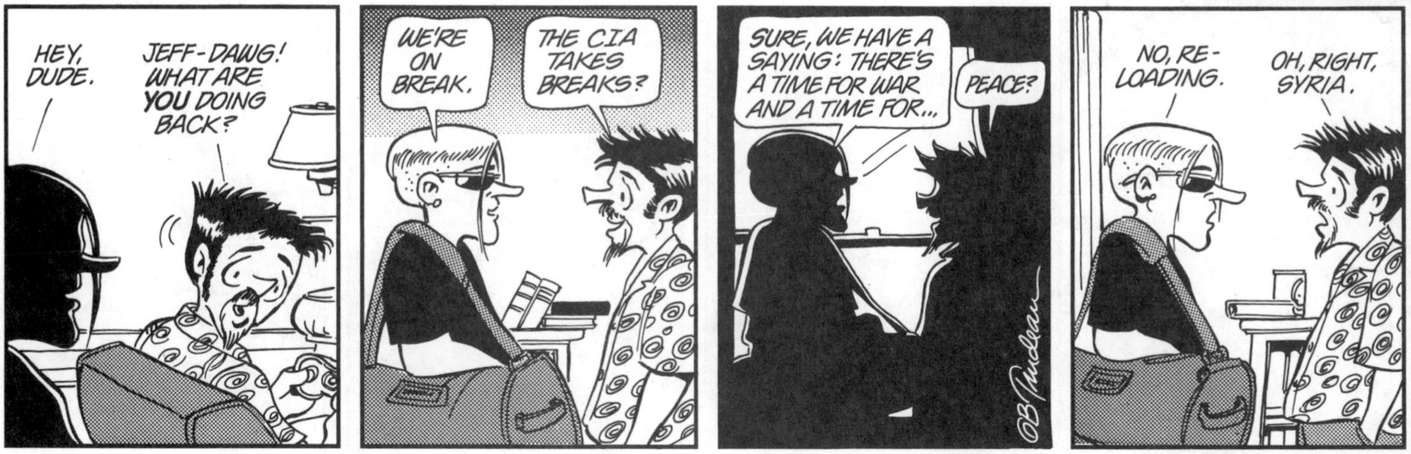
HEY, DUDE.
JEFF-DAWG! WHAT ARE **YOU** DOING BACK?
WE'RE ON BREAK.
THE C.I.A TAKES BREAKS?
SURE, WE HAVE A SAYING: THERE'S A TIME FOR WAR AND A TIME FOR...
PEACE?
NO, RE-LOADING.
OH, RIGHT, SYRIA.

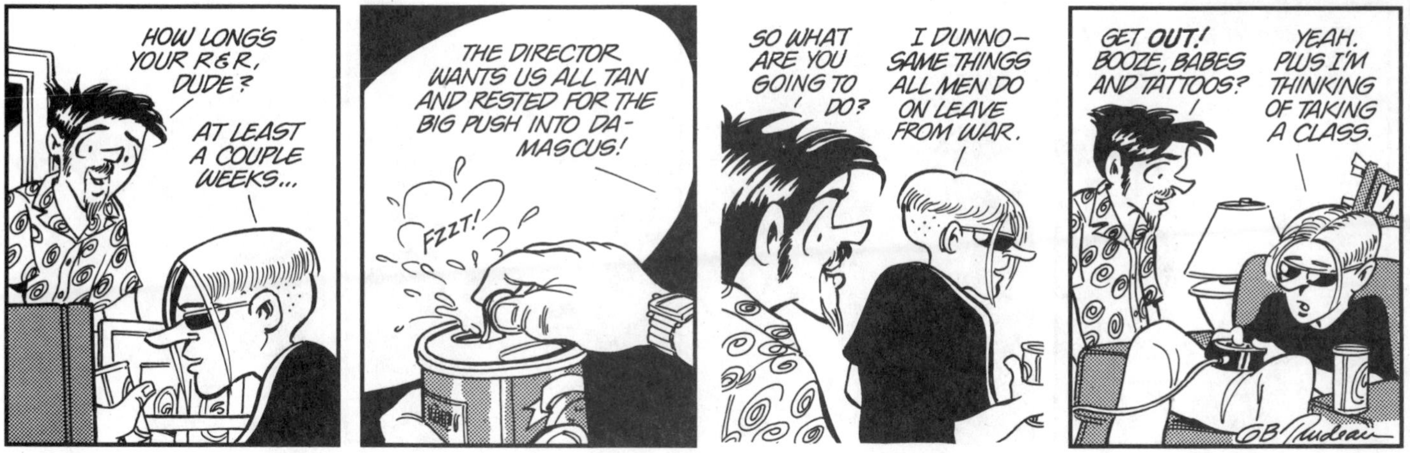
HOW LONG'S YOUR R&R, DUDE?
AT LEAST A COUPLE WEEKS...
THE DIRECTOR WANTS US ALL TAN AND RESTED FOR THE BIG PUSH INTO DA-MASCUS!
FZZT!
SO WHAT ARE YOU GOING TO DO?
I DUNNO— SAME THINGS ALL MEN DO ON LEAVE FROM WAR.
GET **OUT!** BOOZE, BABES AND TATTOOS?
YEAH. PLUS I'M THINKING OF TAKING A CLASS.

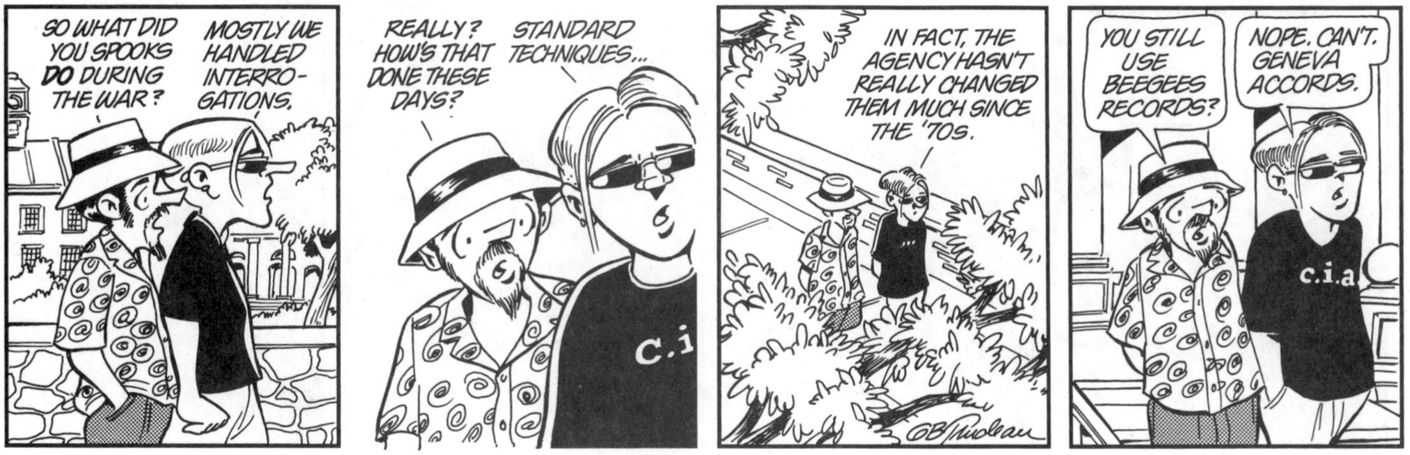
SO WHAT DID YOU SPOOKS **DO** DURING THE WAR?
MOSTLY WE HANDLED INTERRO-GATIONS.
REALLY? HOW'S THAT DONE THESE DAYS?
STANDARD TECHNIQUES...
IN FACT, THE AGENCY HASN'T REALLY CHANGED THEM MUCH SINCE THE '70S.
YOU STILL USE BEEGEES RECORDS?
NOPE. CAN'T. GENEVA ACCORDS.
c.i.a

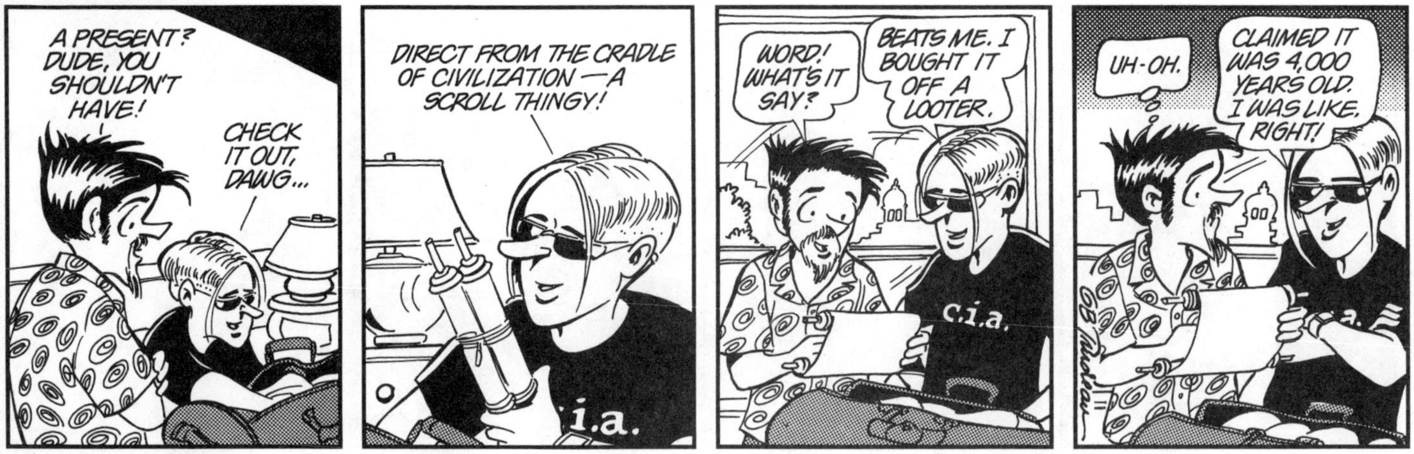
A PRESENT? DUDE, YOU SHOULDN'T HAVE!
CHECK IT OUT, DAWG...
DIRECT FROM THE CRADLE OF CIVILIZATION — A SCROLL THINGY!
c.i.a.
WORD! WHAT'S IT SAY?
BEATS ME. I BOUGHT IT OFF A LOOTER.
c.i.a.
UH-OH.
CLAIMED IT WAS 4,000 YEARS OLD. I WAS LIKE, RIGHT!

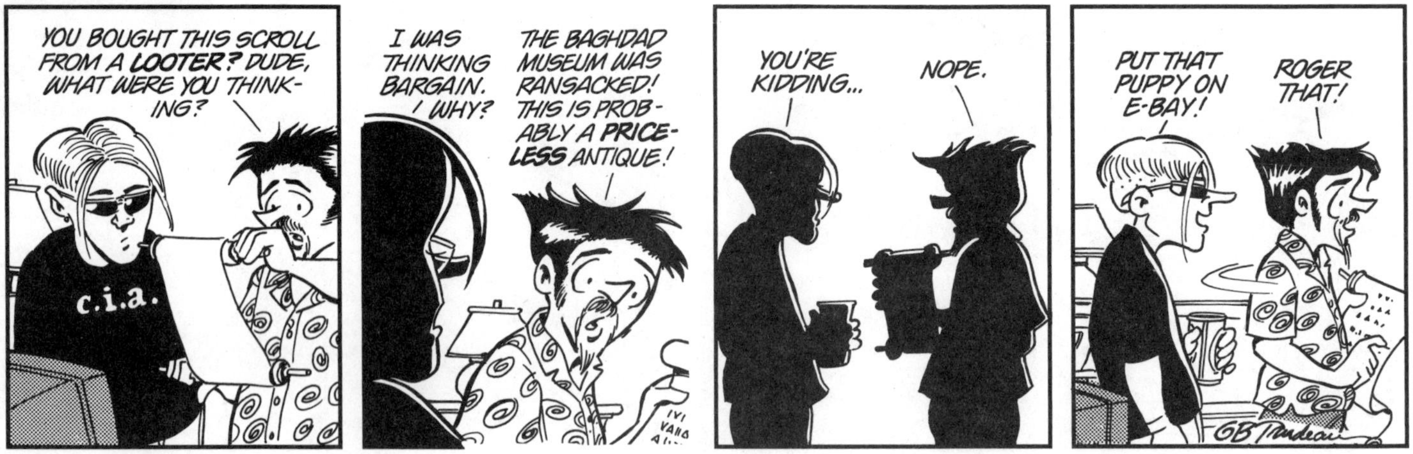
YOU BOUGHT THIS SCROLL FROM A **LOOTER?** DUDE, WHAT WERE YOU THINKING?
c.i.a.
I WAS THINKING BARGAIN. WHY?
THE BAGHDAD MUSEUM WAS RANSACKED! THIS IS PROBABLY A **PRICELESS** ANTIQUE!
YOU'RE KIDDING...
NOPE.
PUT THAT PUPPY ON E-BAY!
ROGER THAT!

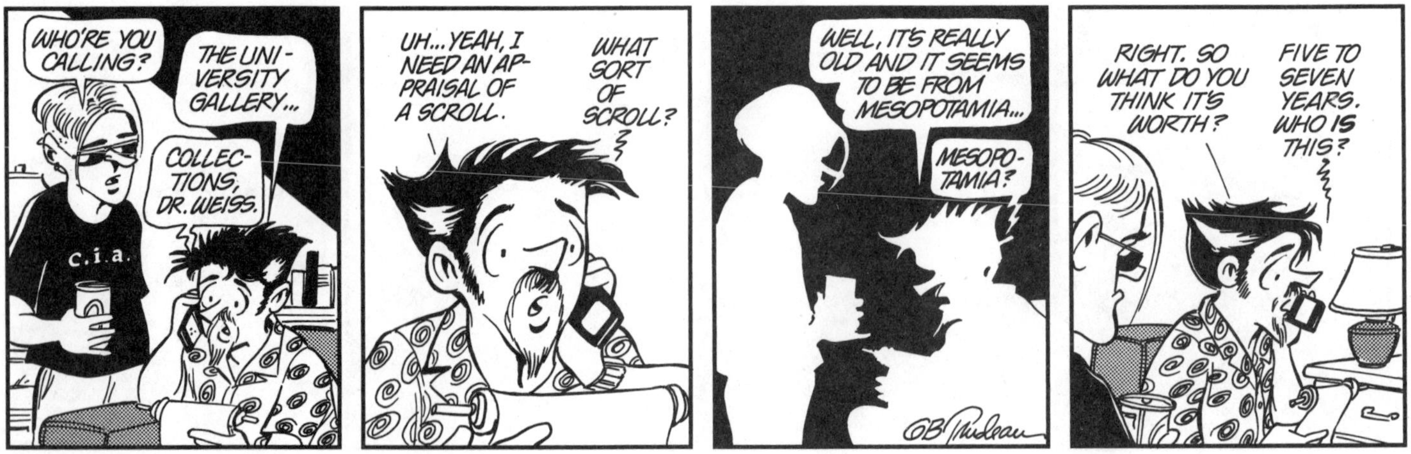
WHO'RE YOU CALLING?
THE UNIVERSITY GALLERY...
COLLECTIONS, DR. WEISS.
c.i.a.
UH... YEAH, I NEED AN APPRAISAL OF A SCROLL.
WHAT SORT OF SCROLL?
WELL, IT'S REALLY OLD AND IT SEEMS TO BE FROM MESOPOTAMIA...
MESOPOTAMIA?
RIGHT. SO WHAT DO YOU THINK IT'S WORTH?
FIVE TO SEVEN YEARS. WHO **IS** THIS?

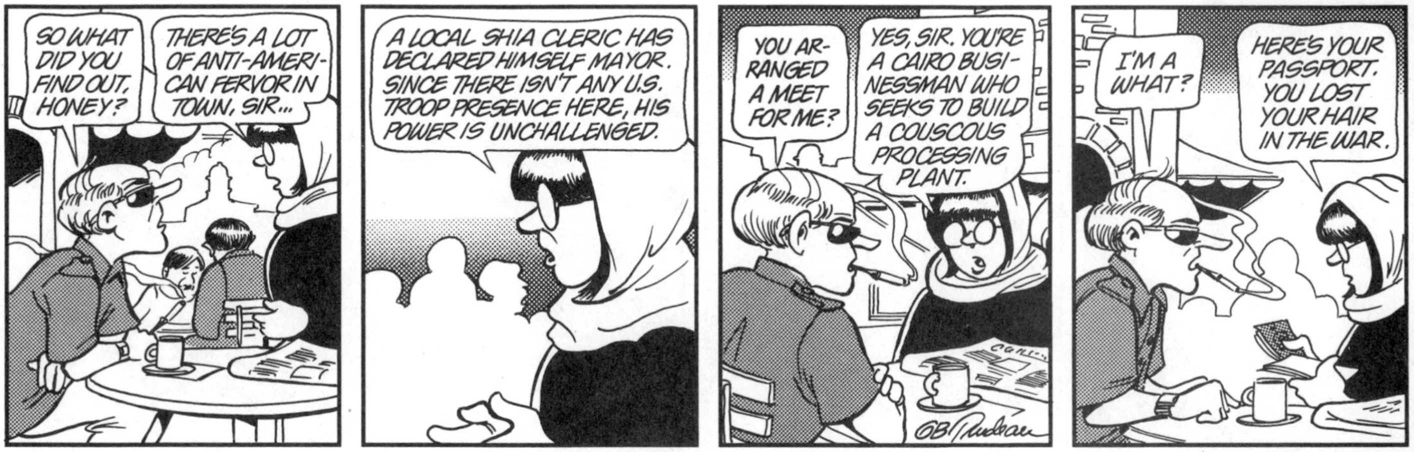
SO WHAT DID YOU FIND OUT, HONEY?
THERE'S A LOT OF ANTI-AMERICAN FERVOR IN TOWN, SIR...
A LOCAL SHIA CLERIC HAS DECLARED HIMSELF MAYOR. SINCE THERE ISN'T ANY U.S. TROOP PRESENCE HERE, HIS POWER IS UNCHALLENGED.
YOU ARRANGED A MEET FOR ME?
YES, SIR. YOU'RE A CAIRO BUSINESSMAN WHO SEEKS TO BUILD A COUSCOUS PROCESSING PLANT.
I'M A WHAT?
HERE'S YOUR PASSPORT. YOU LOST YOUR HAIR IN THE WAR.

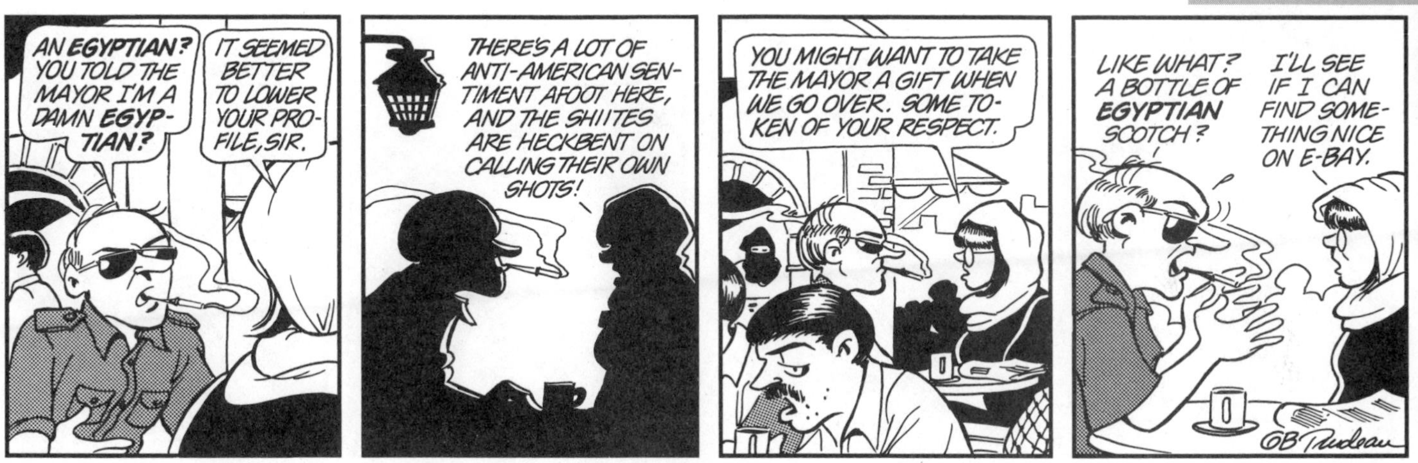
AN **EGYPTIAN?** YOU TOLD THE MAYOR I'M A DAMN **EGYPTIAN?**
IT SEEMED BETTER TO LOWER YOUR PROFILE, SIR.
THERE'S A LOT OF ANTI-AMERICAN SENTIMENT AFOOT HERE, AND THE SHIITES ARE HECKBENT ON CALLING THEIR OWN SHOTS!
YOU MIGHT WANT TO TAKE THE MAYOR A GIFT WHEN WE GO OVER. SOME TOKEN OF YOUR RESPECT.
LIKE WHAT? A BOTTLE OF **EGYPTIAN** SCOTCH?
I'LL SEE IF I CAN FIND SOMETHING NICE ON E-BAY.

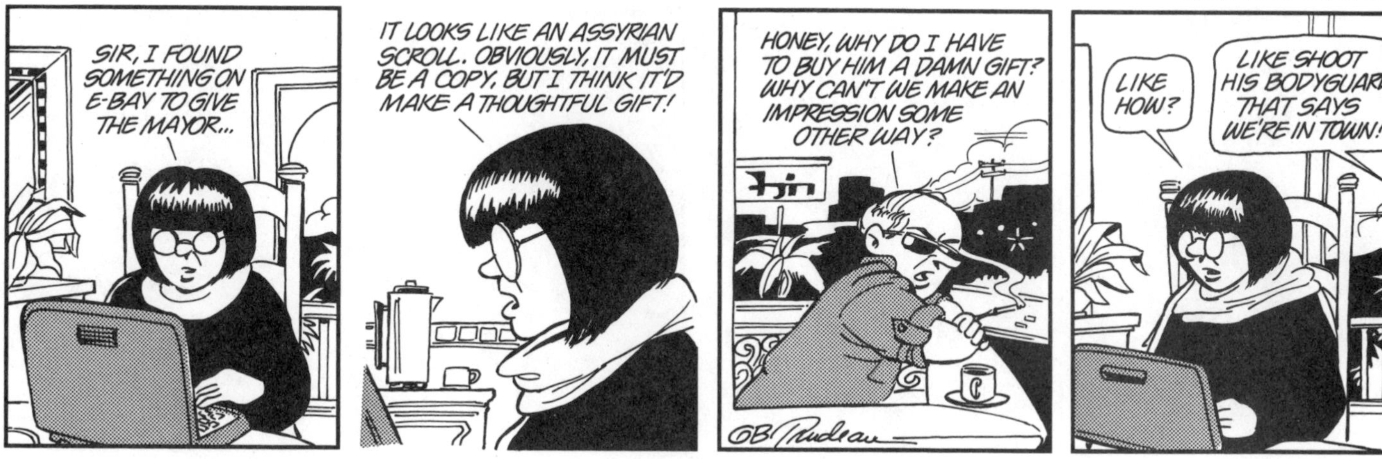
SIR, I FOUND SOMETHING ON E-BAY TO GIVE THE MAYOR...
IT LOOKS LIKE AN ASSYRIAN SCROLL. OBVIOUSLY, IT MUST BE A COPY, BUT I THINK IT'D MAKE A THOUGHTFUL GIFT!
HONEY, WHY DO I HAVE TO BUY HIM A DAMN GIFT? WHY CAN'T WE MAKE AN IMPRESSION SOME OTHER WAY?
LIKE HOW?
LIKE SHOOT HIS BODYGUARD. THAT SAYS WE'RE IN TOWN!

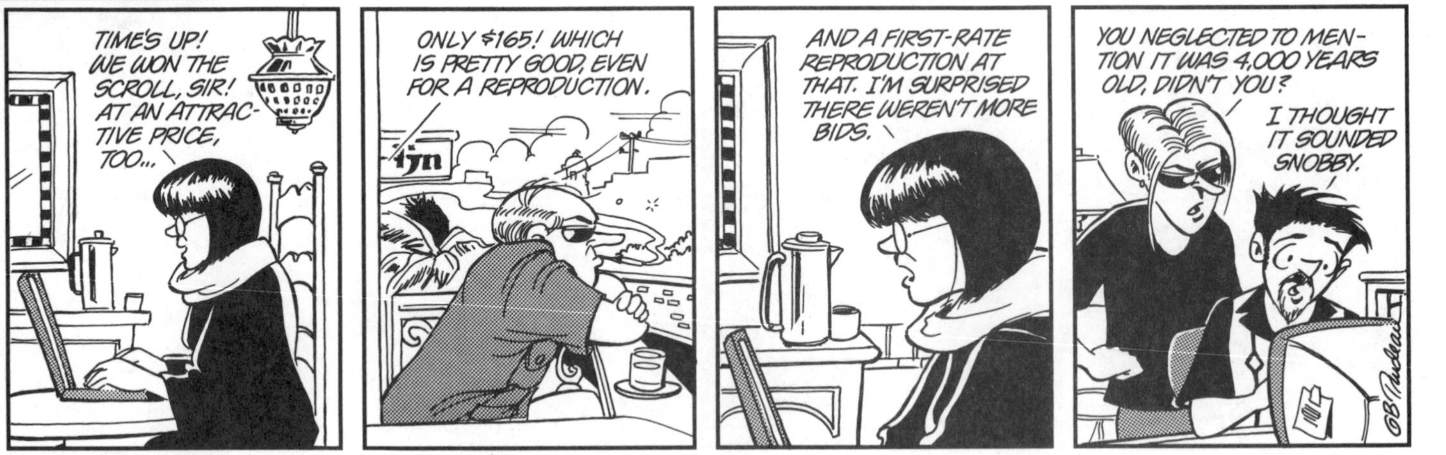
TIME'S UP! WE WON THE SCROLL, SIR! AT AN ATTRACTIVE PRICE, TOO...
ONLY $165! WHICH IS PRETTY GOOD, EVEN FOR A REPRODUCTION.
AND A FIRST-RATE REPRODUCTION AT THAT. I'M SURPRISED THERE WEREN'T MORE BIDS.
YOU NEGLECTED TO MENTION IT WAS 4,000 YEARS OLD, DIDN'T YOU?
I THOUGHT IT SOUNDED SNOBBY.

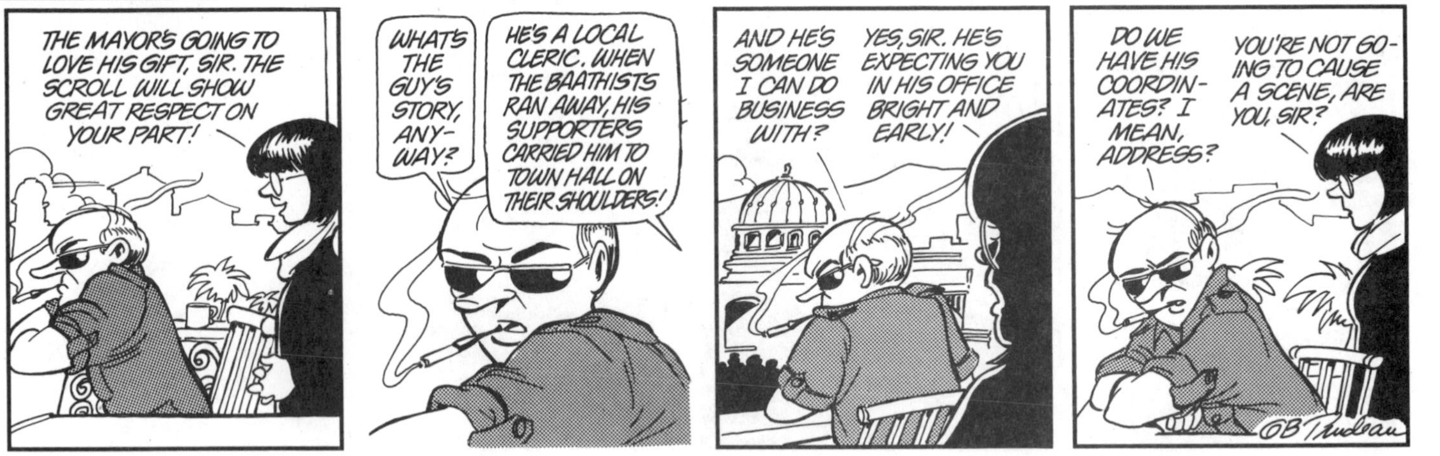
THE MAYOR'S GOING TO LOVE HIS GIFT, SIR. THE SCROLL WILL SHOW GREAT RESPECT ON YOUR PART!
WHAT'S THE GUY'S STORY, ANYWAY?
HE'S A LOCAL CLERIC. WHEN THE BAATHISTS RAN AWAY, HIS SUPPORTERS CARRIED HIM TO TOWN HALL ON THEIR SHOULDERS!
AND HE'S SOMEONE I CAN DO BUSINESS WITH?
YES, SIR. HE'S EXPECTING YOU IN HIS OFFICE BRIGHT AND EARLY!
DO WE HAVE HIS COORDINATES? I MEAN, ADDRESS?
YOU'RE NOT GOING TO CAUSE A SCENE, ARE YOU, SIR?

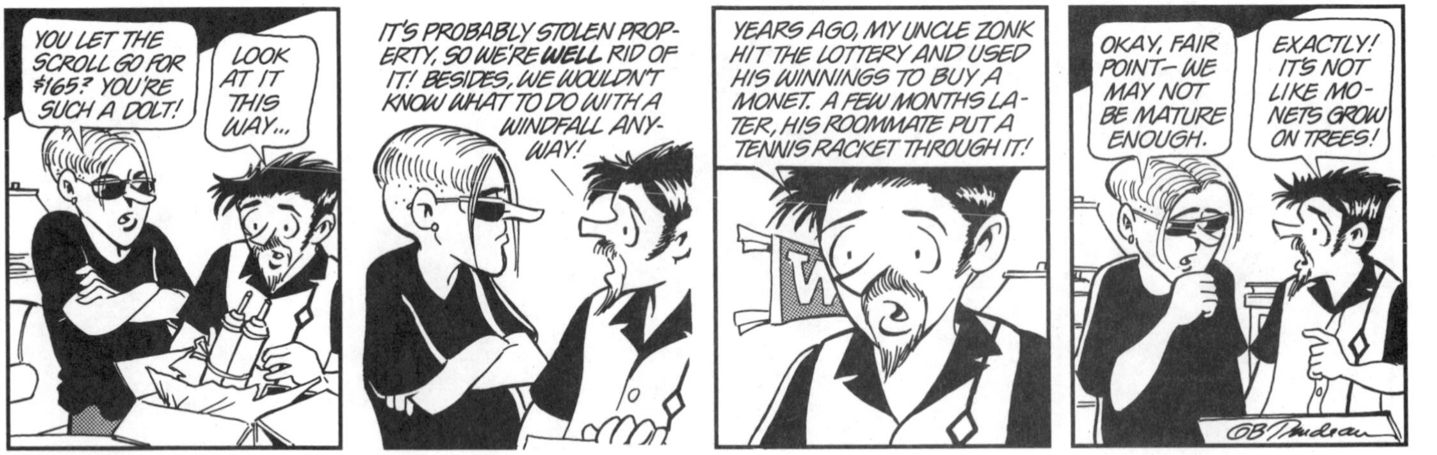
YOU LET THE SCROLL GO FOR $165? YOU'RE SUCH A DOLT!
LOOK AT IT THIS WAY...
IT'S PROBABLY STOLEN PROPERTY, SO WE'RE WELL RID OF IT! BESIDES, WE WOULDN'T KNOW WHAT TO DO WITH A WINDFALL ANYWAY!
YEARS AGO, MY UNCLE ZONK HIT THE LOTTERY AND USED HIS WINNINGS TO BUY A MONET. A FEW MONTHS LATER, HIS ROOMMATE PUT A TENNIS RACKET THROUGH IT!
OKAY, FAIR POINT— WE MAY NOT BE MATURE ENOUGH.
EXACTLY! IT'S NOT LIKE MONETS GROW ON TREES!

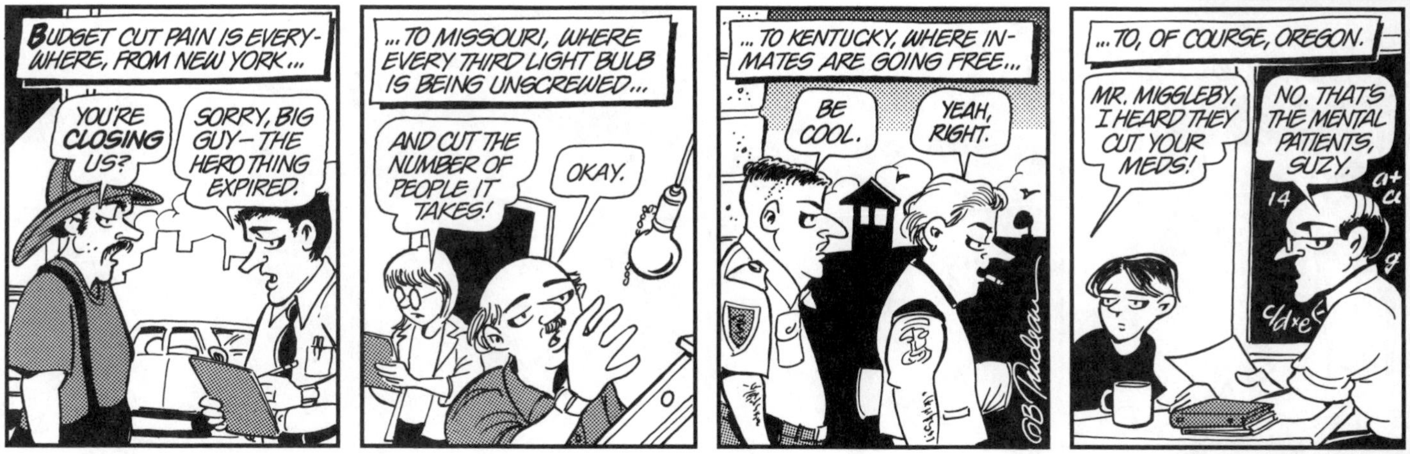
BUDGET CUT PAIN IS EVERYWHERE, FROM NEW YORK...
YOU'RE CLOSING US?
SORRY, BIG GUY— THE HERO THING EXPIRED.
...TO MISSOURI, WHERE EVERY THIRD LIGHT BULB IS BEING UNSCREWED...
AND CUT THE NUMBER OF PEOPLE IT TAKES!
OKAY.
...TO KENTUCKY, WHERE INMATES ARE GOING FREE...
BE COOL.
YEAH, RIGHT.
...TO, OF COURSE, OREGON.
MR. MIGGLEBY, I HEARD THEY CUT YOUR MEDS!
NO. THAT'S THE MENTAL PATIENTS, SUZY.

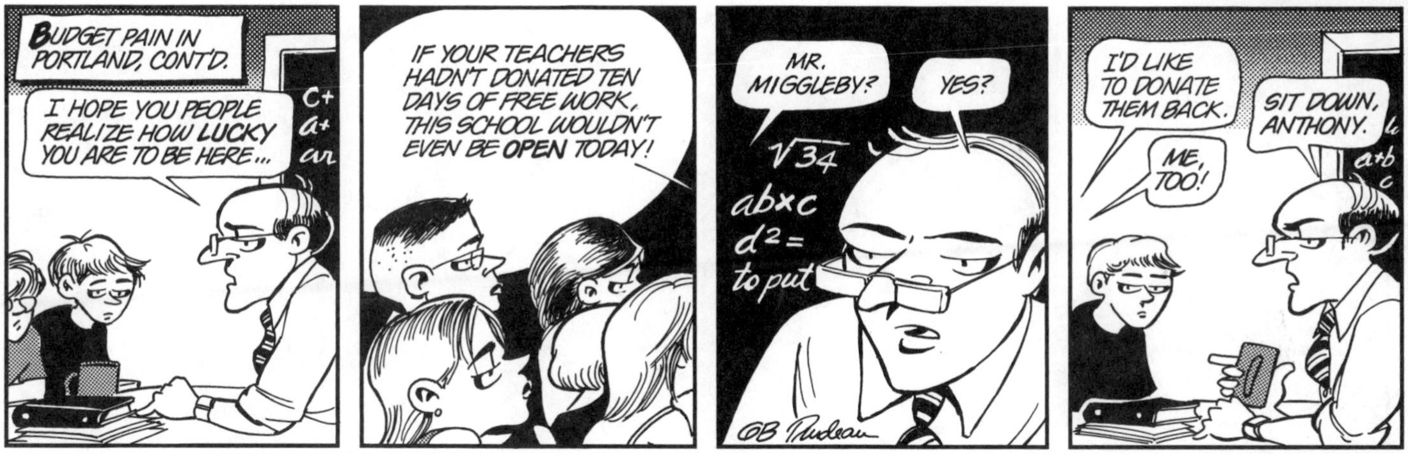
BUDGET PAIN IN PORTLAND, CONT'D.
I HOPE YOU PEOPLE REALIZE HOW LUCKY YOU ARE TO BE HERE...
IF YOUR TEACHERS HADN'T DONATED TEN DAYS OF FREE WORK, THIS SCHOOL WOULDN'T EVEN BE OPEN TODAY!
MR. MIGGLEBY?
YES?
I'D LIKE TO DONATE THEM BACK.
ME, TOO!
SIT DOWN, ANTHONY.

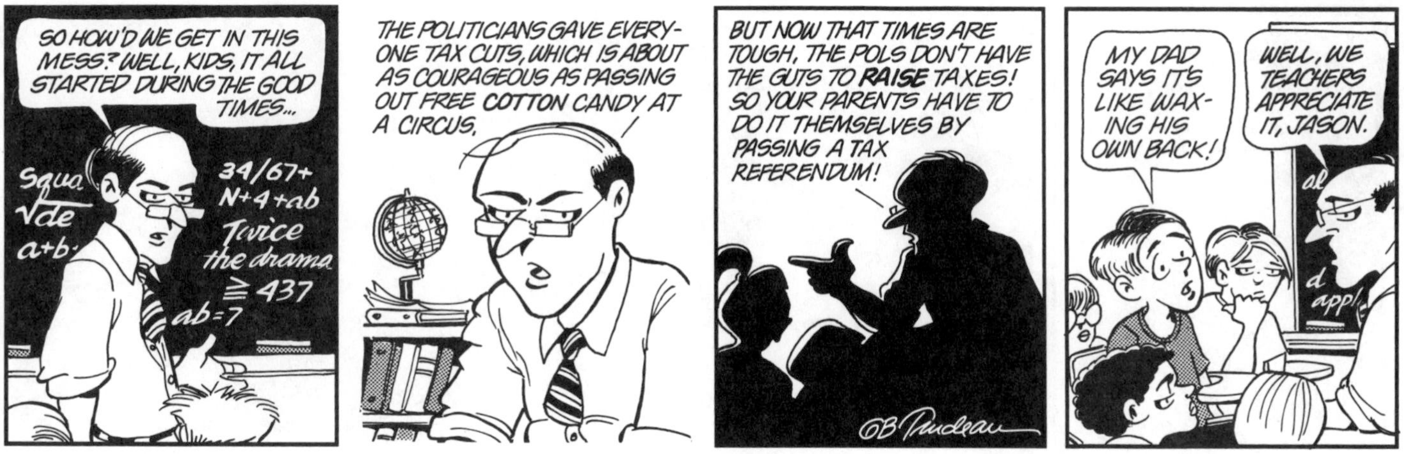
SO HOW'D WE GET IN THIS MESS? WELL, KIDS, IT ALL STARTED DURING THE GOOD TIMES...
THE POLITICIANS GAVE EVERYONE TAX CUTS, WHICH IS ABOUT AS COURAGEOUS AS PASSING OUT FREE COTTON CANDY AT A CIRCUS.
BUT NOW THAT TIMES ARE TOUGH, THE POLS DON'T HAVE THE GUTS TO RAISE TAXES! SO YOUR PARENTS HAVE TO DO IT THEMSELVES BY PASSING A TAX REFERENDUM!
MY DAD SAYS IT'S LIKE WAXING HIS OWN BACK!
WELL, WE TEACHERS APPRECIATE IT, JASON.

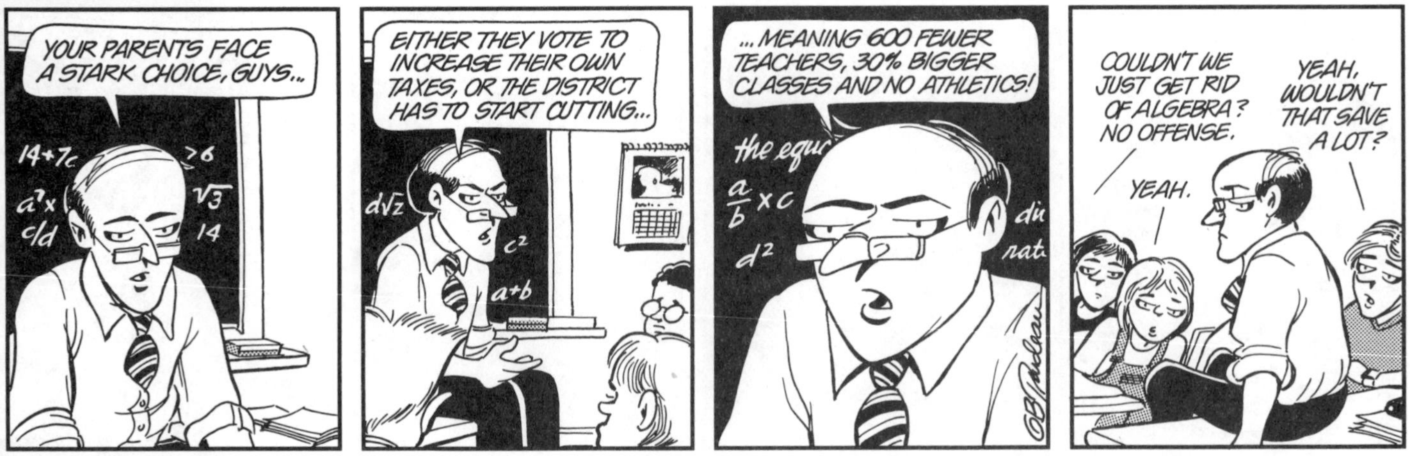
YOUR PARENTS FACE A STARK CHOICE, GUYS...
EITHER THEY VOTE TO INCREASE THEIR OWN TAXES, OR THE DISTRICT HAS TO START CUTTING...
...MEANING 600 FEWER TEACHERS, 30% BIGGER CLASSES AND NO ATHLETICS!
COULDN'T WE JUST GET RID OF ALGEBRA? NO OFFENSE.
YEAH.
YEAH, WOULDN'T THAT SAVE A LOT?

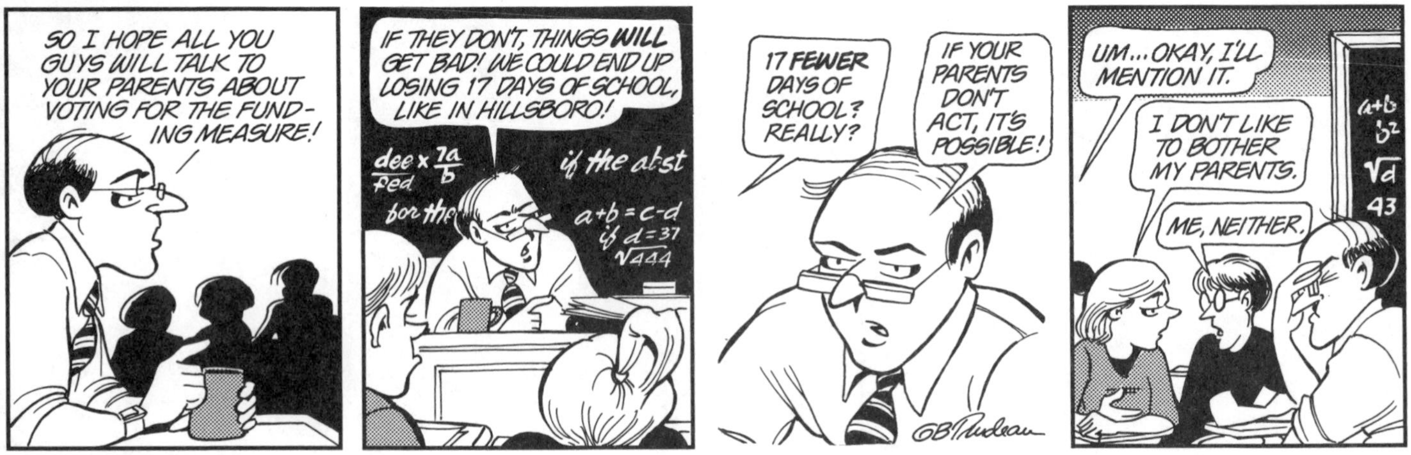
SO I HOPE ALL YOU GUYS WILL TALK TO YOUR PARENTS ABOUT VOTING FOR THE FUNDING MEASURE!
IF THEY DON'T, THINGS **WILL** GET BAD! WE COULD END UP LOSING 17 DAYS OF SCHOOL, LIKE IN HILLSBORO!
17 **FEWER** DAYS OF SCHOOL? REALLY?
IF YOUR PARENTS DON'T ACT, IT'S POSSIBLE!
UM...OKAY, I'LL MENTION IT.
I DON'T LIKE TO BOTHER MY PARENTS.
ME, NEITHER.

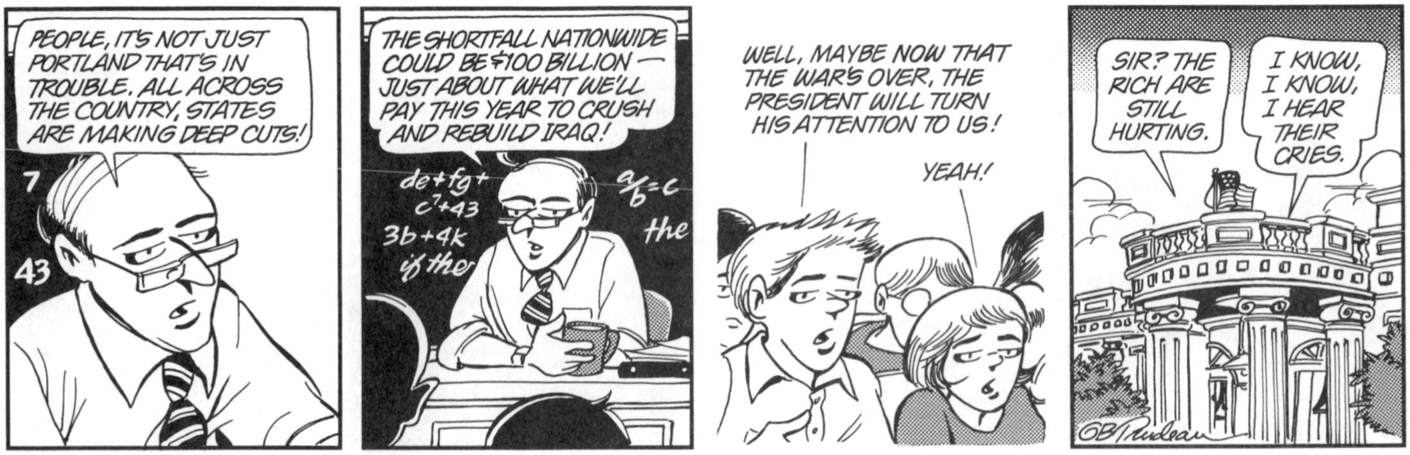
PEOPLE, IT'S NOT JUST PORTLAND THAT'S IN TROUBLE. ALL ACROSS THE COUNTRY, STATES ARE MAKING DEEP CUTS!
THE SHORTFALL NATIONWIDE COULD BE $100 BILLION — JUST ABOUT WHAT WE'LL PAY THIS YEAR TO CRUSH AND REBUILD IRAQ!
WELL, MAYBE NOW THAT THE WAR'S OVER, THE PRESIDENT WILL TURN HIS ATTENTION TO US!
YEAH!
SIR? THE RICH ARE STILL HURTING.
I KNOW, I KNOW, I HEAR THEIR CRIES.

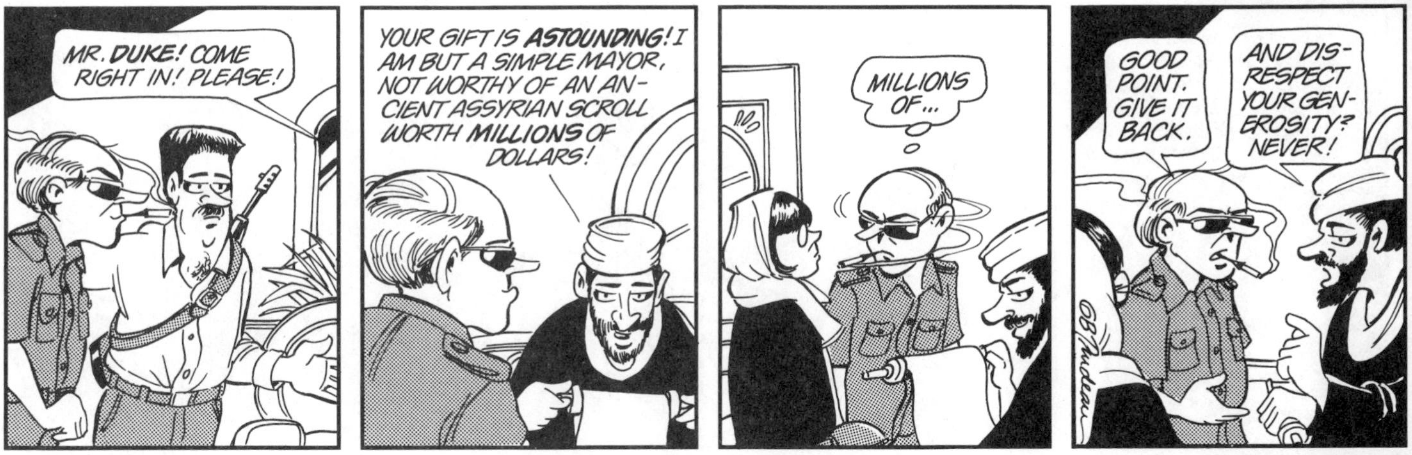
MR. DUKE! COME RIGHT IN! PLEASE!
YOUR GIFT IS ASTOUNDING! I AM BUT A SIMPLE MAYOR, NOT WORTHY OF AN ANCIENT ASSYRIAN SCROLL WORTH MILLIONS OF DOLLARS!
MILLIONS OF...
GOOD POINT. GIVE IT BACK.
AND DISRESPECT YOUR GENEROSITY? NEVER!

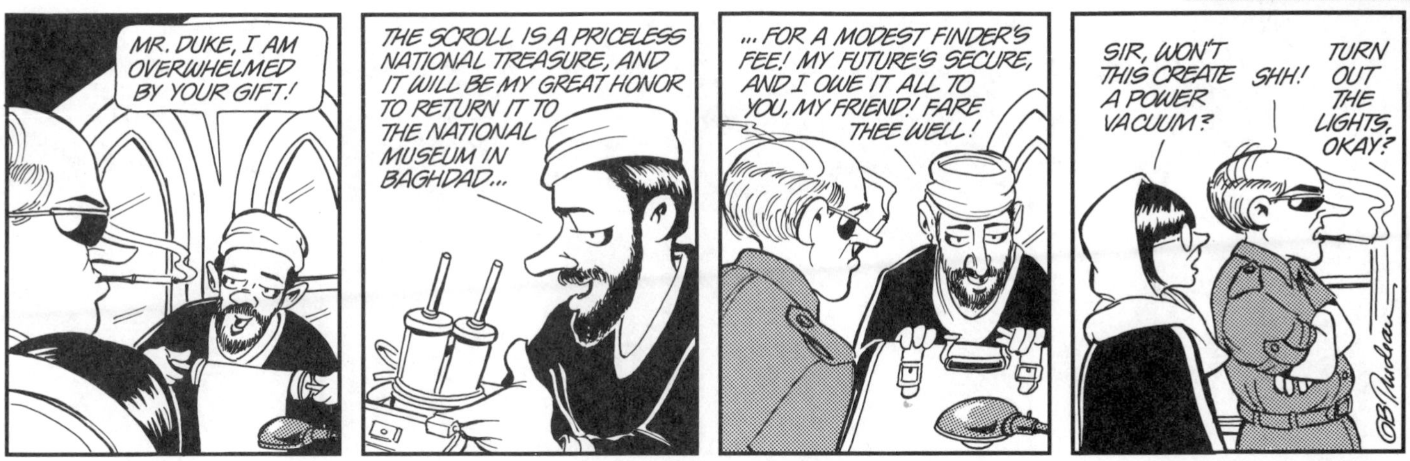
MR. DUKE, I AM OVERWHELMED BY YOUR GIFT!
THE SCROLL IS A PRICELESS NATIONAL TREASURE, AND IT WILL BE MY GREAT HONOR TO RETURN IT TO THE NATIONAL MUSEUM IN BAGHDAD...
...FOR A MODEST FINDER'S FEE! MY FUTURE'S SECURE, AND I OWE IT ALL TO YOU, MY FRIEND! FARE THEE WELL!
SIR, WON'T THIS CREATE A POWER VACUUM?
SHH!
TURN OUT THE LIGHTS, OKAY?

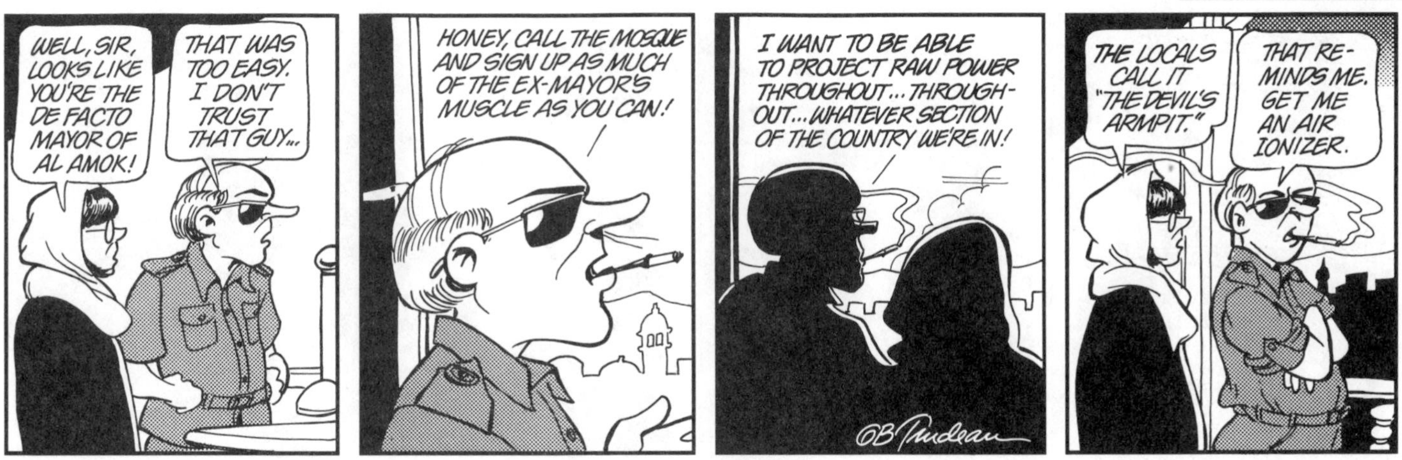
WELL, SIR, LOOKS LIKE YOU'RE THE DE FACTO MAYOR OF AL AMOK!
THAT WAS TOO EASY. I DON'T TRUST THAT GUY...
HONEY, CALL THE MOSQUE AND SIGN UP AS MUCH OF THE EX-MAYOR'S MUSCLE AS YOU CAN!
I WANT TO BE ABLE TO PROJECT RAW POWER THROUGHOUT... THROUGHOUT... WHATEVER SECTION OF THE COUNTRY WE'RE IN!
THE LOCALS CALL IT "THE DEVIL'S ARMPIT."
THAT REMINDS ME. GET ME AN AIR IONIZER.

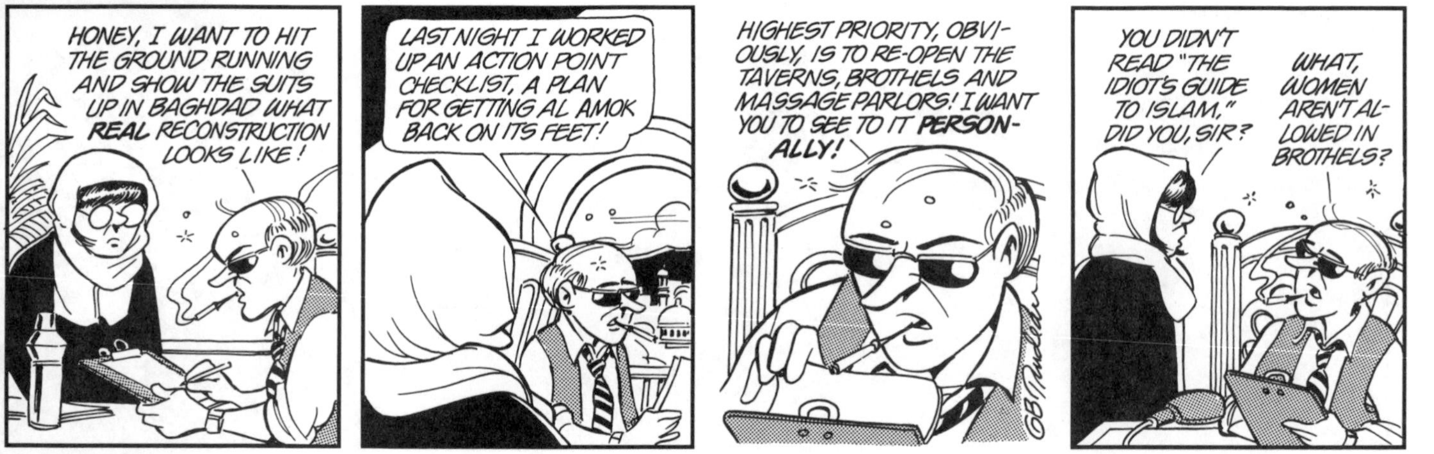
HONEY, I WANT TO HIT THE GROUND RUNNING AND SHOW THE SUITS UP IN BAGHDAD WHAT REAL RECONSTRUCTION LOOKS LIKE!
LAST NIGHT I WORKED UP AN ACTION POINT CHECKLIST, A PLAN FOR GETTING AL AMOK BACK ON ITS FEET!
HIGHEST PRIORITY, OBVIOUSLY, IS TO RE-OPEN THE TAVERNS, BROTHELS AND MASSAGE PARLORS! I WANT YOU TO SEE TO IT PERSONALLY!
YOU DIDN'T READ "THE IDIOT'S GUIDE TO ISLAM," DID YOU, SIR?
WHAT, WOMEN AREN'T ALLOWED IN BROTHELS?

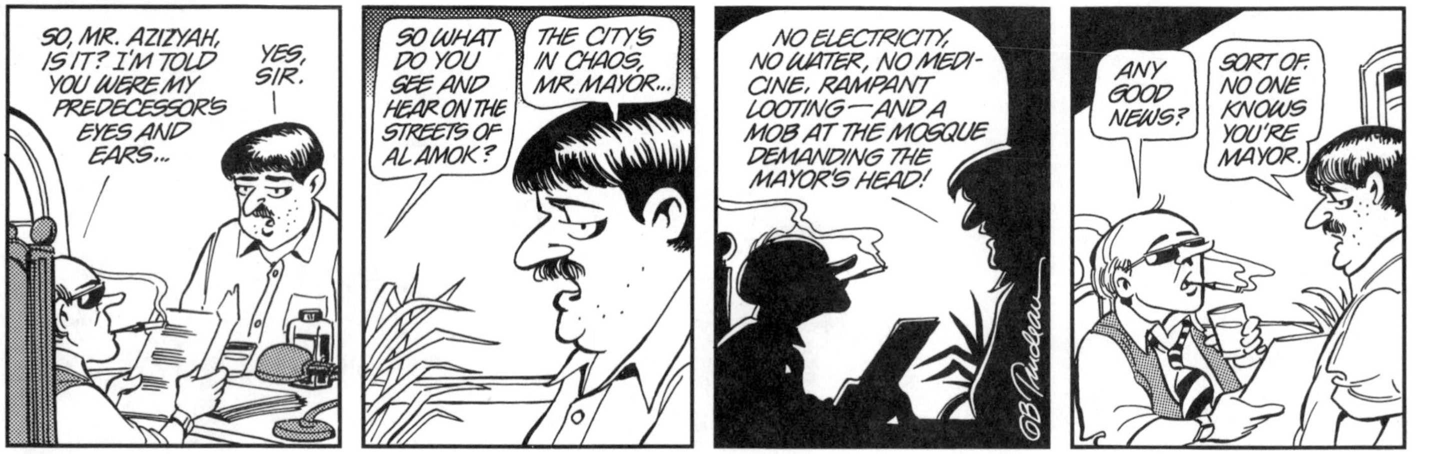
SO, MR. AZIZYAH, IS IT? I'M TOLD YOU WERE MY PREDECESSOR'S EYES AND EARS...
YES, SIR.
SO WHAT DO YOU SEE AND HEAR ON THE STREETS OF AL AMOK?
THE CITY'S IN CHAOS, MR. MAYOR...
NO ELECTRICITY, NO WATER, NO MEDICINE, RAMPANT LOOTING — AND A MOB AT THE MOSQUE DEMANDING THE MAYOR'S HEAD!
ANY GOOD NEWS?
SORT OF. NO ONE KNOWS YOU'RE MAYOR.

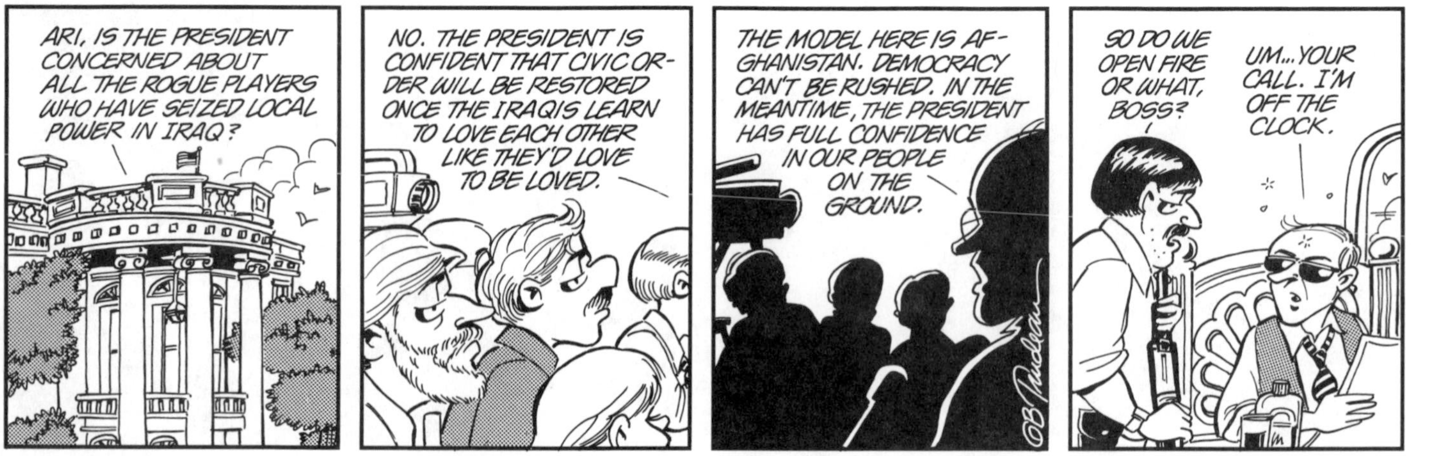
ARI, IS THE PRESIDENT CONCERNED ABOUT ALL THE ROGUE PLAYERS WHO HAVE SEIZED LOCAL POWER IN IRAQ?
NO. THE PRESIDENT IS CONFIDENT THAT CIVIC ORDER WILL BE RESTORED ONCE THE IRAQIS LEARN TO LOVE EACH OTHER LIKE THEY'D LOVE TO BE LOVED.
THE MODEL HERE IS AFGHANISTAN. DEMOCRACY CAN'T BE RUSHED. IN THE MEANTIME, THE PRESIDENT HAS FULL CONFIDENCE IN OUR PEOPLE ON THE GROUND.
SO DO WE OPEN FIRE OR WHAT, BOSS?
UM... YOUR CALL. I'M OFF THE CLOCK.

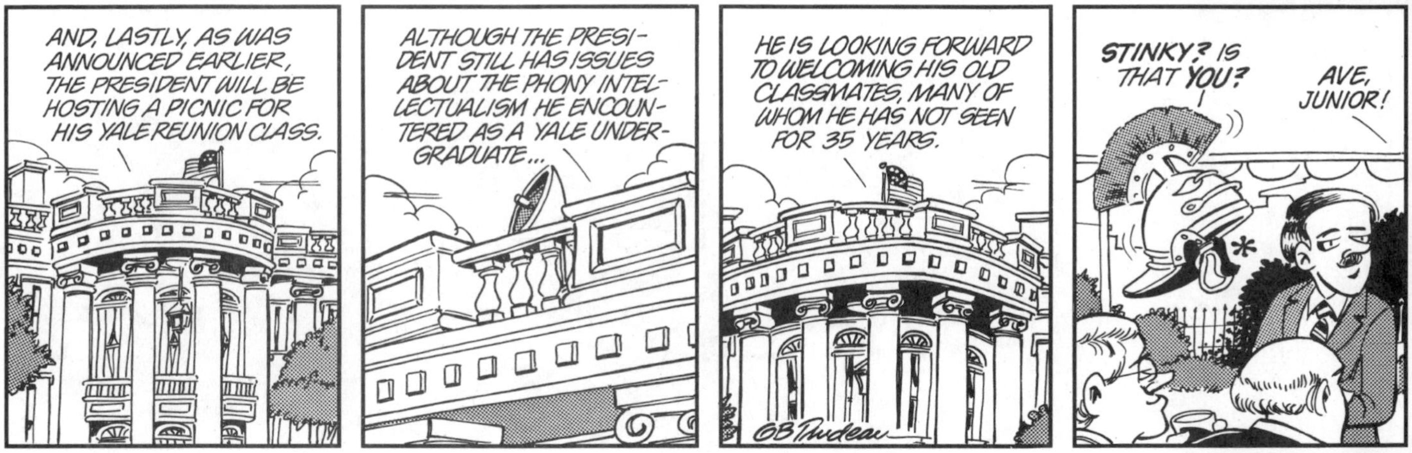
AND, LASTLY, AS WAS ANNOUNCED EARLIER, THE PRESIDENT WILL BE HOSTING A PICNIC FOR HIS YALE REUNION CLASS.
ALTHOUGH THE PRESIDENT STILL HAS ISSUES ABOUT THE PHONY INTELLECTUALISM HE ENCOUNTERED AS A YALE UNDERGRADUATE...
HE IS LOOKING FORWARD TO WELCOMING HIS OLD CLASSMATES, MANY OF WHOM HE HAS NOT SEEN FOR 35 YEARS.
STINKY? IS THAT YOU?
AVE, JUNIOR!

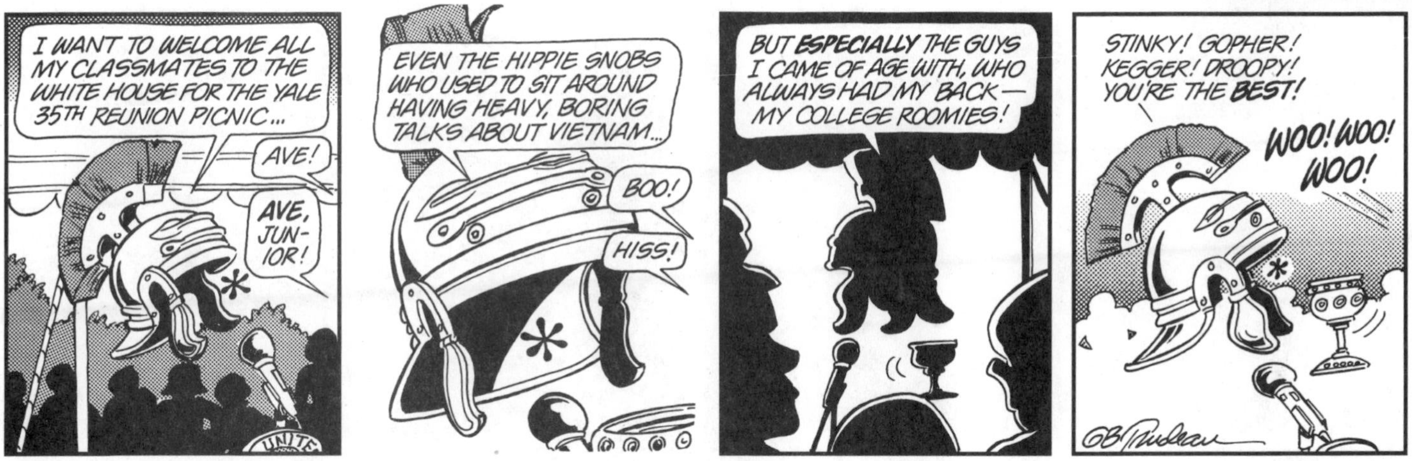
I WANT TO WELCOME ALL MY CLASSMATES TO THE WHITE HOUSE FOR THE YALE 35TH REUNION PICNIC...
AVE!
AVE, JUNIOR!
EVEN THE HIPPIE SNOBS WHO USED TO SIT AROUND HAVING HEAVY, BORING TALKS ABOUT VIETNAM...
BOO!
HISS!
BUT ESPECIALLY THE GUYS I CAME OF AGE WITH, WHO ALWAYS HAD MY BACK— MY COLLEGE ROOMIES!
STINKY! GOPHER! KEGGER! DROOPY! YOU'RE THE BEST!
WOO! WOO! WOO!

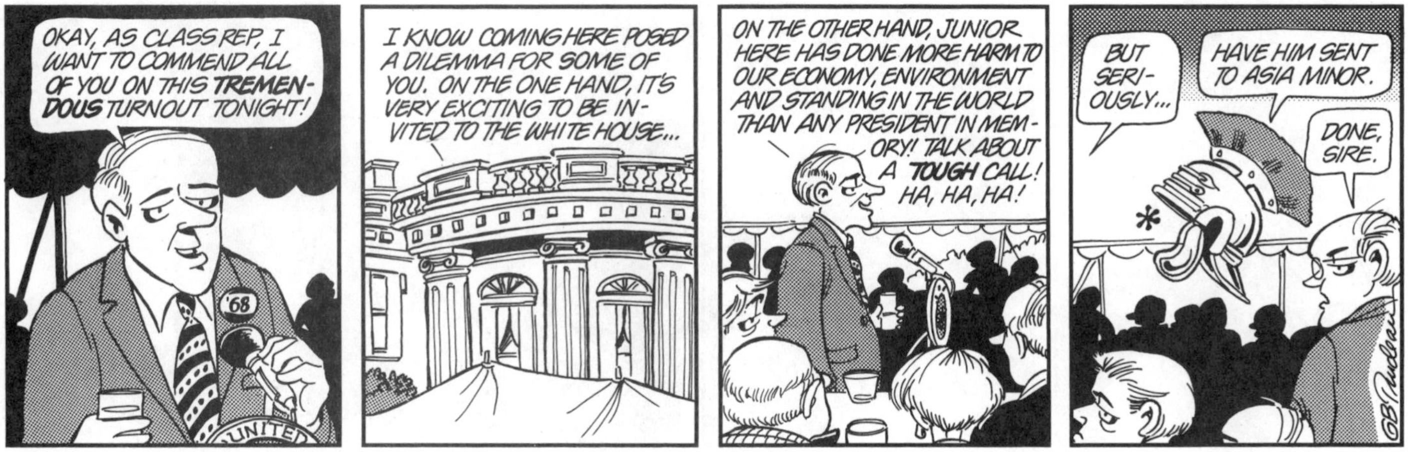
OKAY, AS CLASS REP, I WANT TO COMMEND ALL OF YOU ON THIS TREMENDOUS TURNOUT TONIGHT!
'68
I KNOW COMING HERE POSED A DILEMMA FOR SOME OF YOU. ON THE ONE HAND, IT'S VERY EXCITING TO BE INVITED TO THE WHITE HOUSE...
ON THE OTHER HAND, JUNIOR HERE HAS DONE MORE HARM TO OUR ECONOMY, ENVIRONMENT AND STANDING IN THE WORLD THAN ANY PRESIDENT IN MEMORY! TALK ABOUT A "TOUGH CALL! HA, HA, HA!
BUT SERIOUSLY...
HAVE HIM SENT TO ASIA MINOR.
DONE, SIRE.

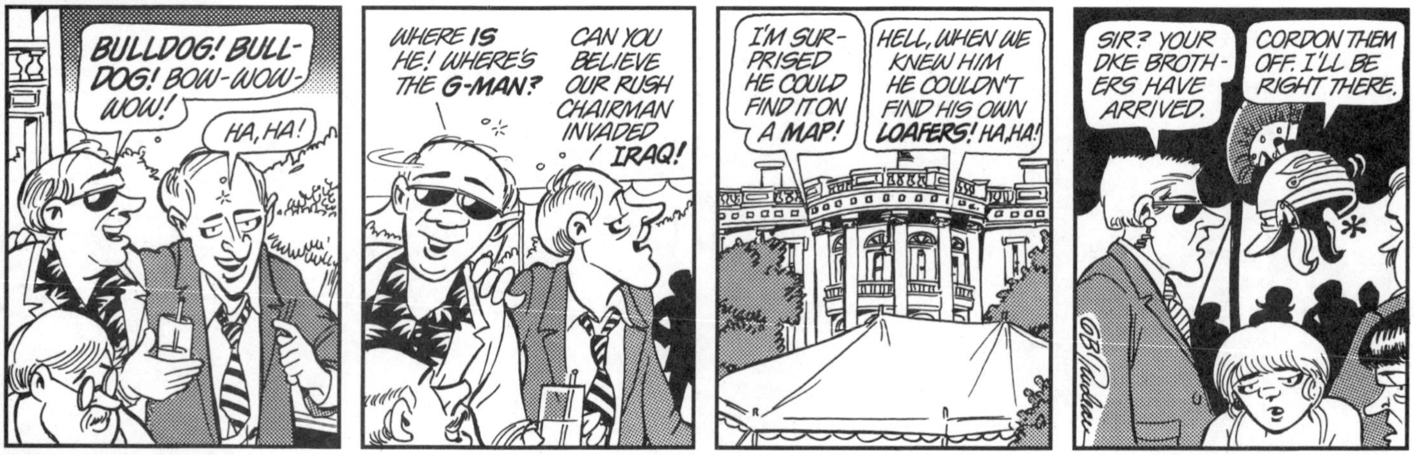
BULLDOG! BULLDOG! BOW-WOW-WOW!
HA, HA!
WHERE IS HE! WHERE'S THE G-MAN?
CAN YOU BELIEVE OUR RUSH CHAIRMAN INVADED IRAQ!
I'M SURPRISED HE COULD FIND IT ON A MAP!
HELL, WHEN WE KNEW HIM HE COULDN'T FIND HIS OWN LOAFERS! HA,HA!
SIR? YOUR DKE BROTHERS HAVE ARRIVED.
CORDON THEM OFF. I'LL BE RIGHT THERE.

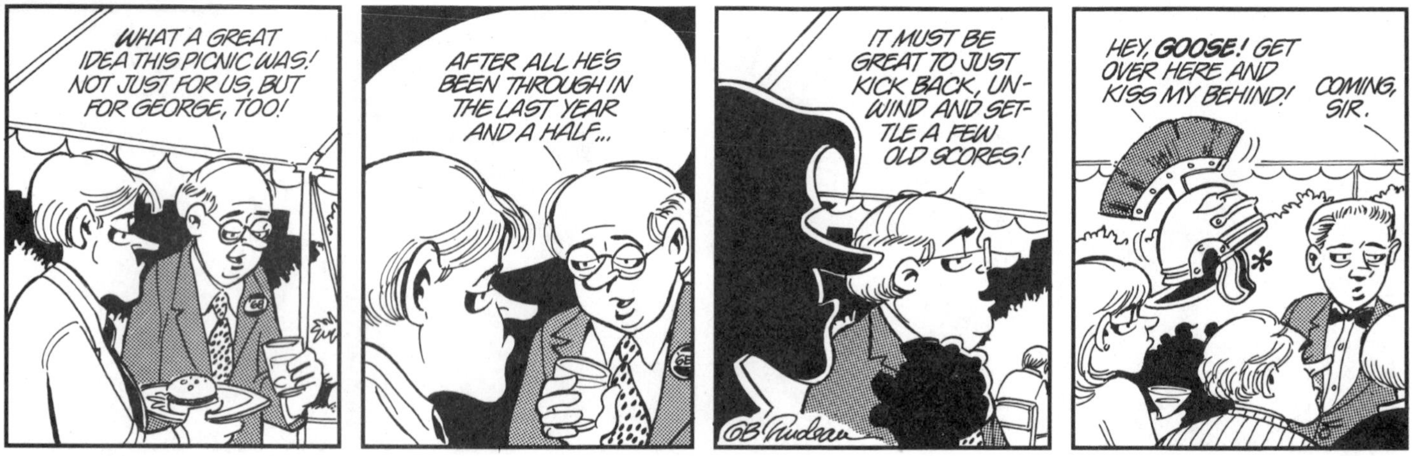
WHAT A GREAT IDEA THIS PICNIC WAS! NOT JUST FOR US, BUT FOR GEORGE, TOO!
AFTER ALL HE'S BEEN THROUGH IN THE LAST YEAR AND A HALF...
IT MUST BE GREAT TO JUST KICK BACK, UNWIND AND SETTLE A FEW OLD SCORES!
HEY, GOOSE! GET OVER HERE AND KISS MY BEHIND!
COMING, SIR.

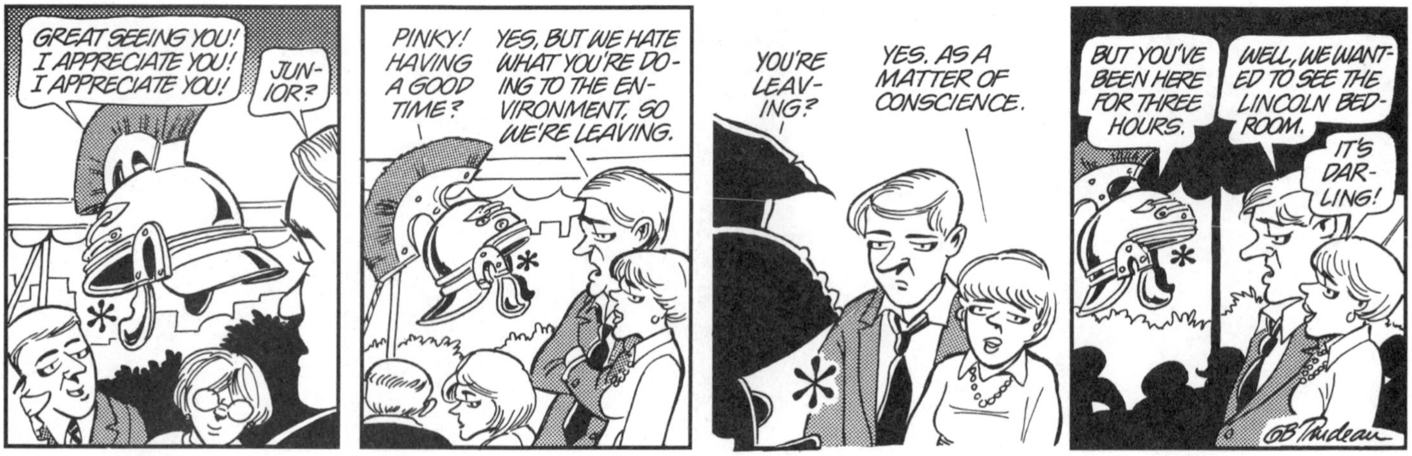
GREAT SEEING YOU! I APPRECIATE YOU! I APPRECIATE YOU!
JUNIOR?
PINKY! HAVING A GOOD TIME?
YES, BUT WE HATE WHAT YOU'RE DOING TO THE ENVIRONMENT, SO WE'RE LEAVING.
YOU'RE LEAVING?
YES. AS A MATTER OF CONSCIENCE.
BUT YOU'VE BEEN HERE FOR THREE HOURS.
WELL, WE WANTED TO SEE THE LINCOLN BEDROOM.
IT'S DARLING!

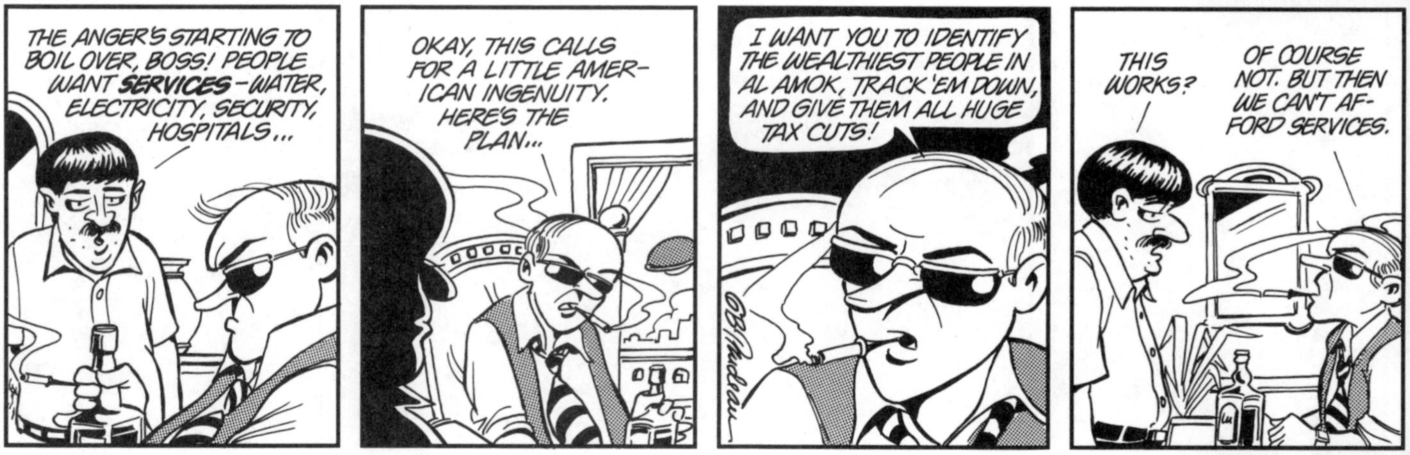
THE ANGER'S STARTING TO BOIL OVER, BOSS! PEOPLE WANT SERVICES—WATER, ELECTRICITY, SECURITY, HOSPITALS...
OKAY, THIS CALLS FOR A LITTLE AMERICAN INGENUITY. HERE'S THE PLAN...
I WANT YOU TO IDENTIFY THE WEALTHIEST PEOPLE IN AL AMOK, TRACK 'EM DOWN, AND GIVE THEM ALL HUGE TAX CUTS!
THIS WORKS?
OF COURSE NOT. BUT THEN WE CAN'T AFFORD SERVICES.

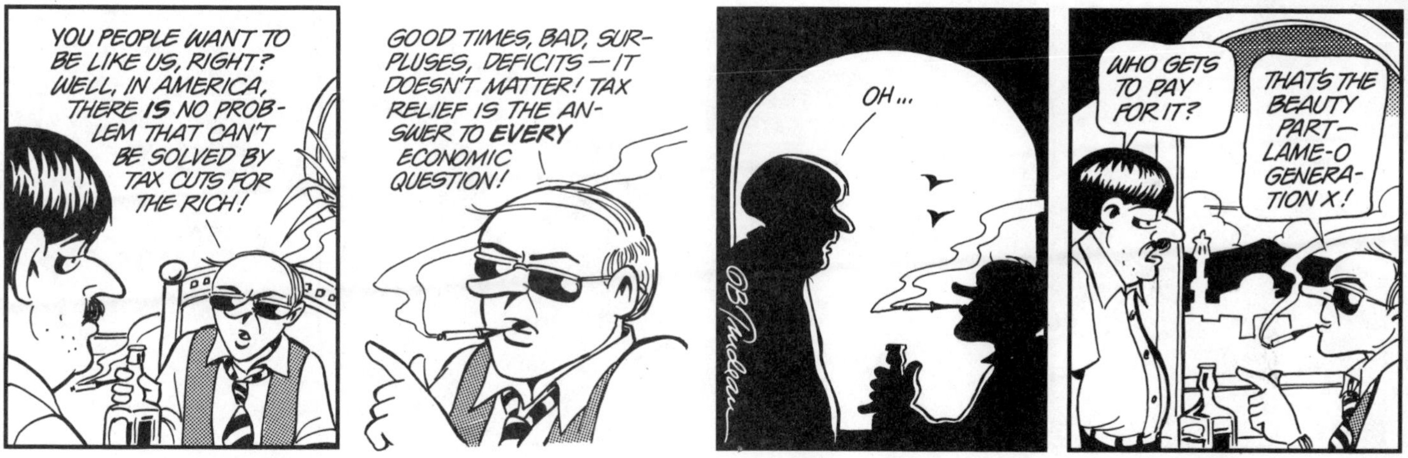
YOU PEOPLE WANT TO BE LIKE US, RIGHT? WELL, IN AMERICA, THERE IS NO PROBLEM THAT CAN'T BE SOLVED BY TAX CUTS FOR THE RICH!
GOOD TIMES, BAD, SURPLUSES, DEFICITS—IT DOESN'T MATTER! TAX RELIEF IS THE ANSWER TO EVERY ECONOMIC QUESTION!
OH...
WHO GETS TO PAY FOR IT?
THAT'S THE BEAUTY PART—LAME-O GENERATION X!

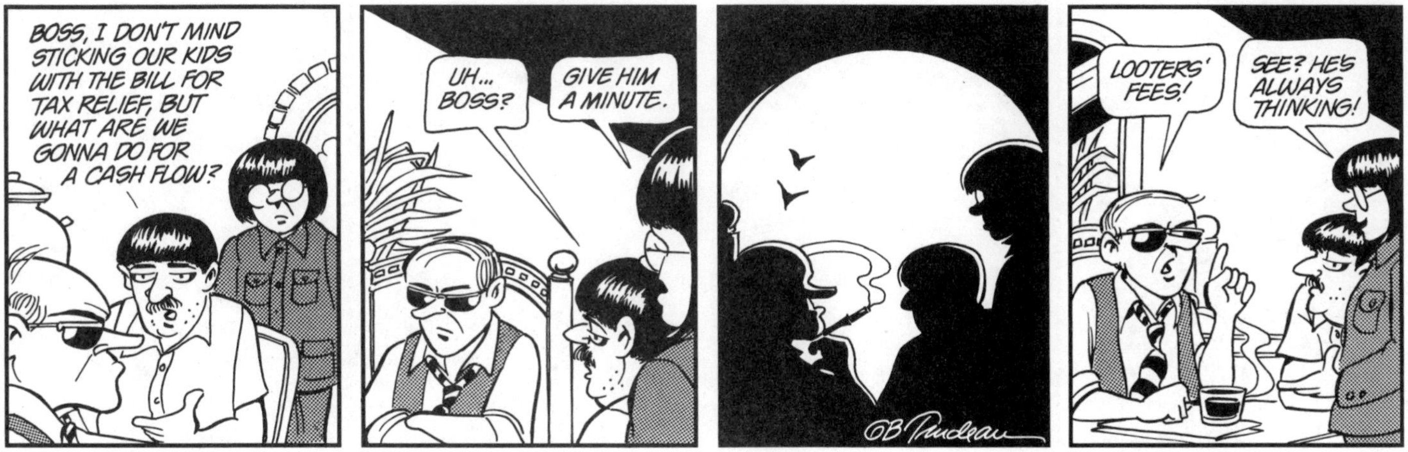
BOSS, I DON'T MIND STICKING OUR KIDS WITH THE BILL FOR TAX RELIEF, BUT WHAT ARE WE GONNA DO FOR A CASH FLOW?
UH... BOSS?
GIVE HIM A MINUTE.
LOOTERS' FEES!
SEE? HE'S ALWAYS THINKING!

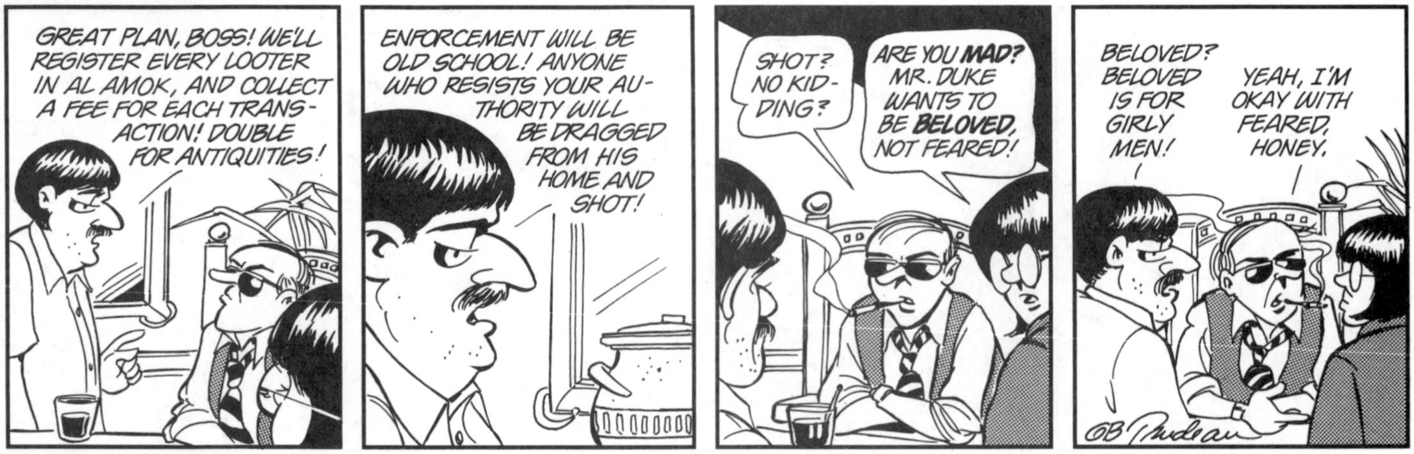
GREAT PLAN, BOSS! WE'LL REGISTER EVERY LOOTER IN AL AMOK, AND COLLECT A FEE FOR EACH TRANS-ACTION! DOUBLE FOR ANTIQUITIES!
ENFORCEMENT WILL BE OLD SCHOOL! ANYONE WHO RESISTS YOUR AU-THORITY WILL BE DRAGGED FROM HIS HOME AND SHOT!
SHOT? NO KID-DING?
ARE YOU MAD? MR. DUKE WANTS TO BE BELOVED, NOT FEARED!
BELOVED? BELOVED IS FOR GIRLY MEN!
YEAH, I'M OKAY WITH FEARED, HONEY.
©B Trudeau

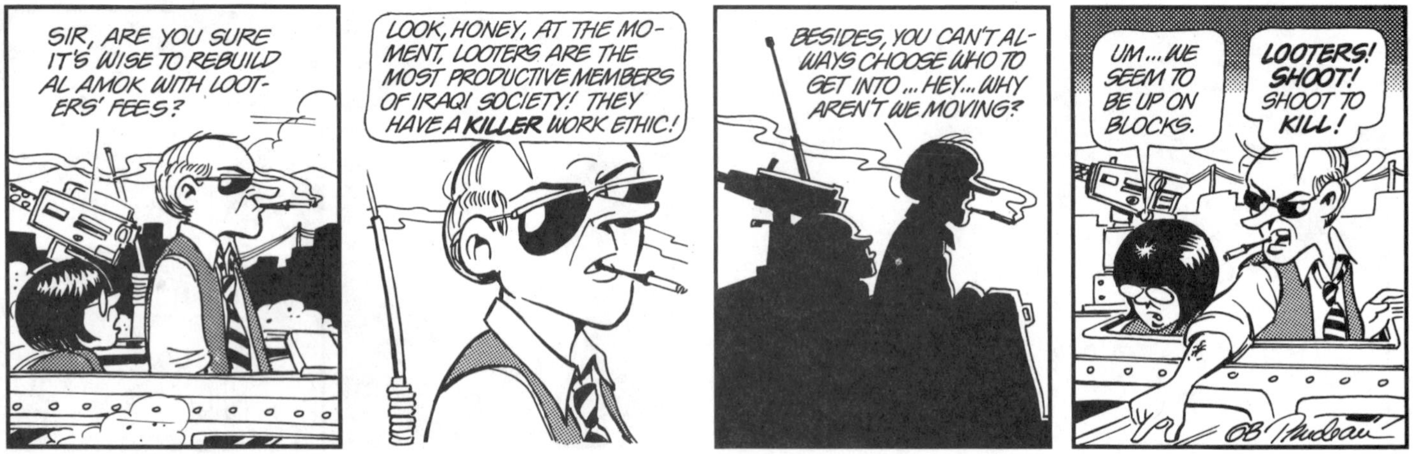
SIR, ARE YOU SURE IT'S WISE TO REBUILD AL AMOK WITH LOOT-ERS' FEES?
LOOK, HONEY, AT THE MO-MENT, LOOTERS ARE THE MOST PRODUCTIVE MEMBERS OF IRAQI SOCIETY! THEY HAVE A KILLER WORK ETHIC!
BESIDES, YOU CAN'T AL-WAYS CHOOSE WHO TO GET INTO ... HEY... WHY AREN'T WE MOVING?
UM... WE SEEM TO BE UP ON BLOCKS.
LOOTERS! SHOOT! SHOOT TO KILL!
©B Trudeau

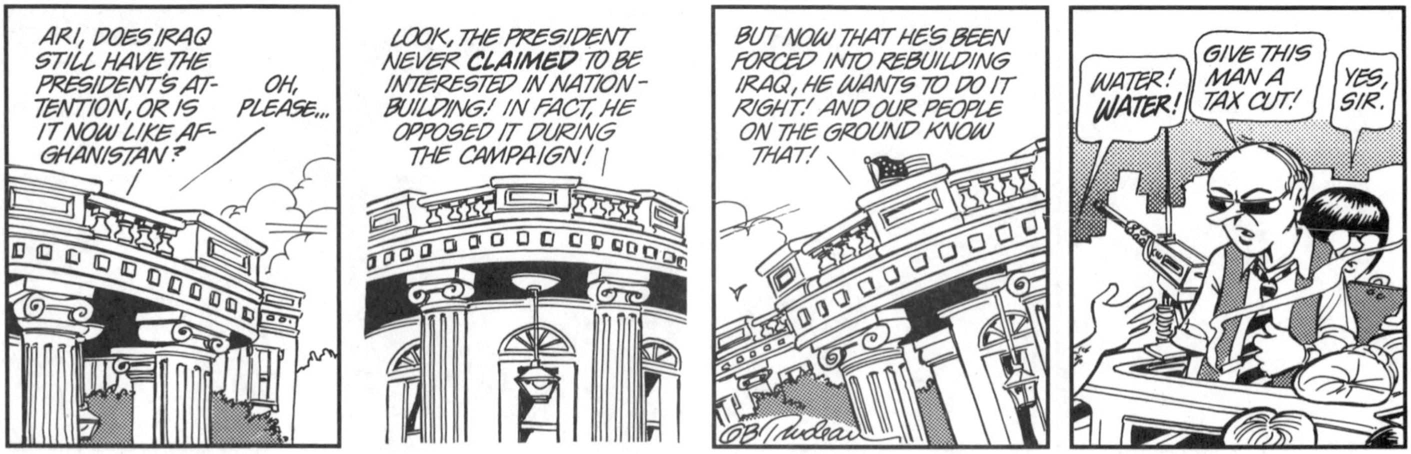
ARI, DOES IRAQ STILL HAVE THE PRESIDENT'S AT-TENTION, OR IS IT NOW LIKE AF-GHANISTAN?
OH, PLEASE...
LOOK, THE PRESIDENT NEVER CLAIMED TO BE INTERESTED IN NATION-BUILDING! IN FACT, HE OPPOSED IT DURING THE CAMPAIGN!
BUT NOW THAT HE'S BEEN FORCED INTO REBUILDING IRAQ, HE WANTS TO DO IT RIGHT! AND OUR PEOPLE ON THE GROUND KNOW THAT!
©B Trudeau
WATER! WATER!
GIVE THIS MAN A TAX CUT!
YES, SIR.

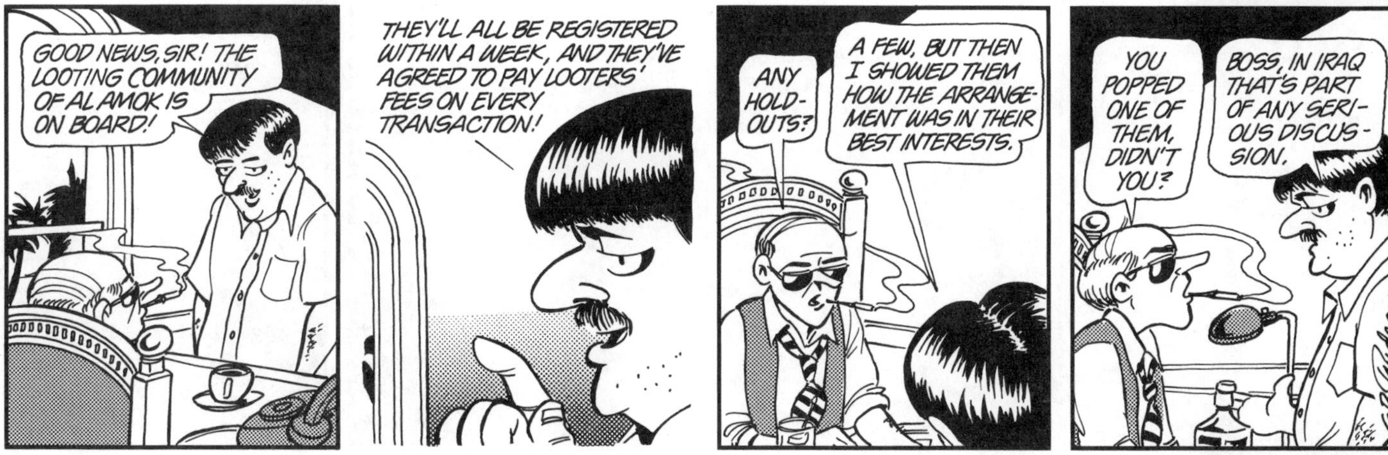
GOOD NEWS, SIR! THE LOOTING COMMUNITY OF AL AMOK IS ON BOARD!
THEY'LL ALL BE REGISTERED WITHIN A WEEK, AND THEY'VE AGREED TO PAY LOOTERS' FEES ON EVERY TRANSACTION!
ANY HOLD-OUTS?
A FEW, BUT THEN I SHOWED THEM HOW THE ARRANGE-MENT WAS IN THEIR BEST INTERESTS.
YOU POPPED ONE OF THEM, DIDN'T YOU?
BOSS, IN IRAQ THAT'S PART OF ANY SERI-OUS DISCUS-SION.

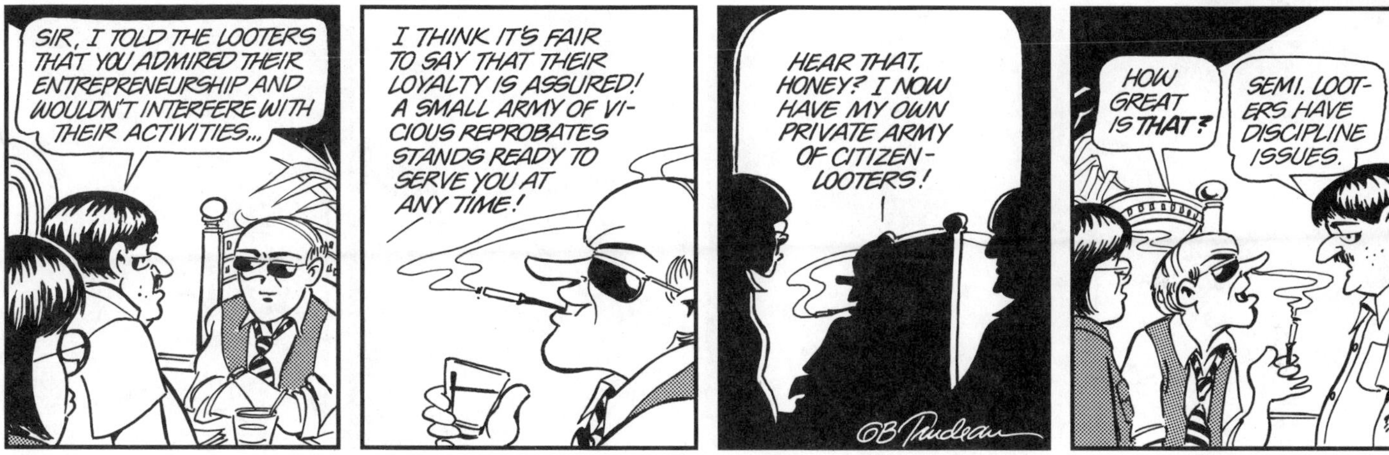
SIR, I TOLD THE LOOTERS THAT YOU ADMIRED THEIR ENTREPRENEURSHIP AND WOULDN'T INTERFERE WITH THEIR ACTIVITIES...
I THINK IT'S FAIR TO SAY THAT THEIR LOYALTY IS ASSURED! A SMALL ARMY OF VI-CIOUS REPROBATES STANDS READY TO SERVE YOU AT ANY TIME!
HEAR THAT, HONEY? I NOW HAVE MY OWN PRIVATE ARMY OF CITIZEN-LOOTERS!
HOW GREAT IS THAT?
SEMI. LOOT-ERS HAVE DISCIPLINE ISSUES.

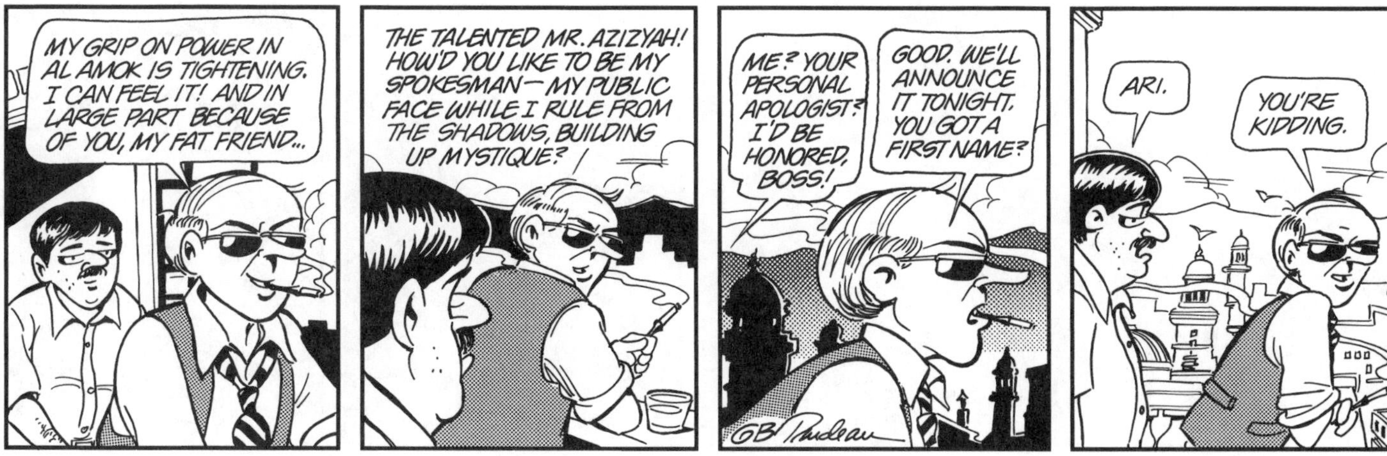
MY GRIP ON POWER IN AL AMOK IS TIGHTENING. I CAN FEEL IT! AND IN LARGE PART BECAUSE OF YOU, MY FAT FRIEND...
THE TALENTED MR. AZIZYAH! HOW'D YOU LIKE TO BE MY SPOKESMAN— MY PUBLIC FACE WHILE I RULE FROM THE SHADOWS, BUILDING UP MYSTIQUE?
ME? YOUR PERSONAL APOLOGIST? I'D BE HONORED, BOSS!
GOOD. WE'LL ANNOUNCE IT TONIGHT. YOU GOT A FIRST NAME?
ARI.
YOU'RE KIDDING.

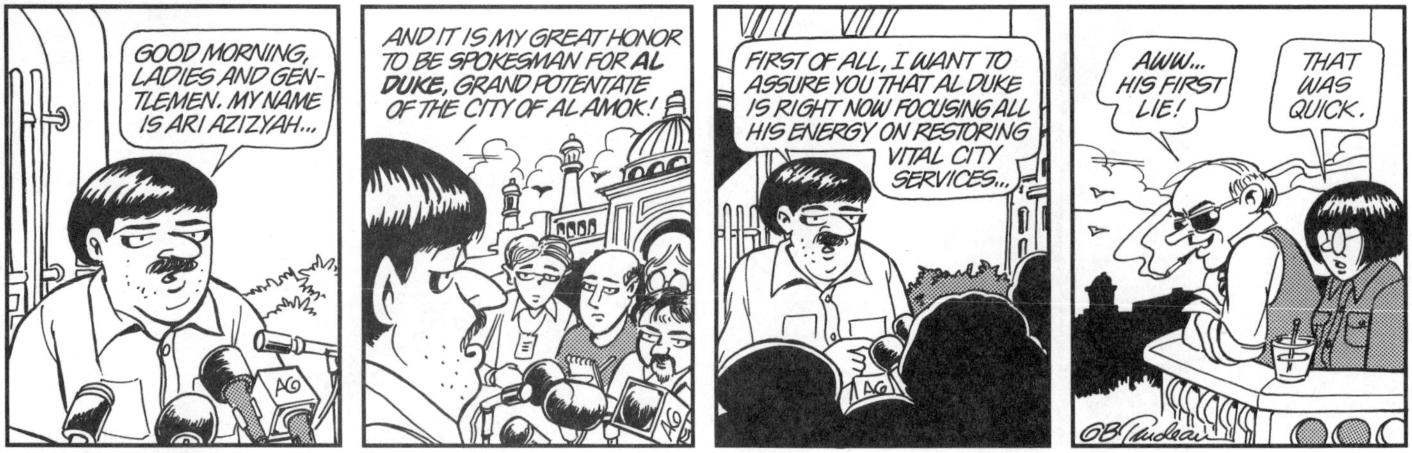
GOOD MORNING, LADIES AND GENTLEMEN. MY NAME IS ARI AZIZYAH...
AND IT IS MY GREAT HONOR TO BE SPOKESMAN FOR AL DUKE, GRAND POTENTATE OF THE CITY OF AL AMOK!
FIRST OF ALL, I WANT TO ASSURE YOU THAT AL DUKE IS RIGHT NOW FOCUSING ALL HIS ENERGY ON RESTORING VITAL CITY SERVICES...
AWW... HIS FIRST LIE!
THAT WAS QUICK.
GB Trudeau

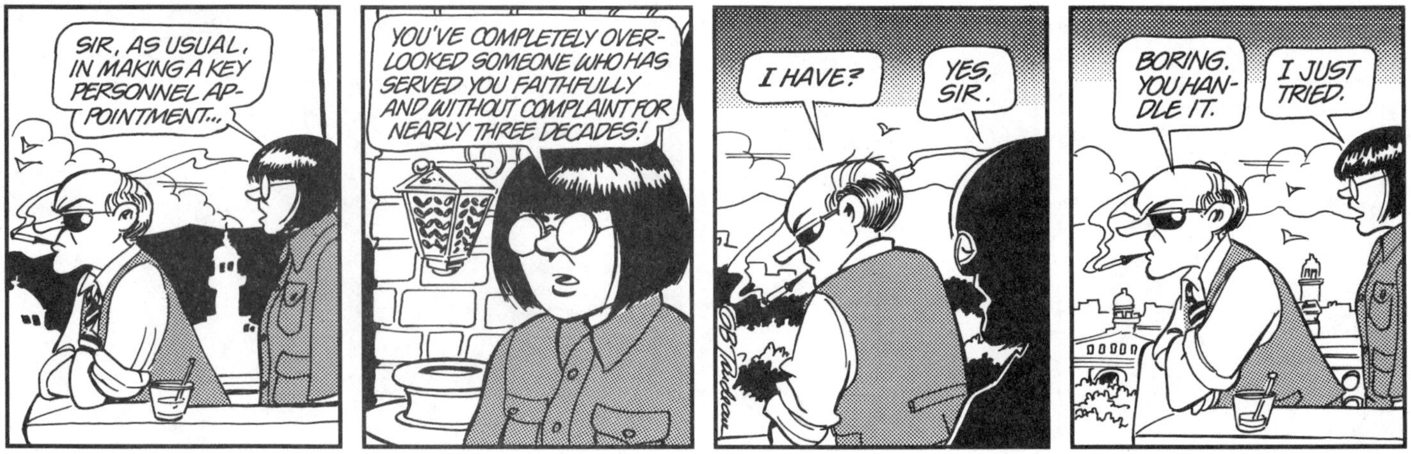
SIR, AS USUAL, IN MAKING A KEY PERSONNEL APPOINTMENT...
YOU'VE COMPLETELY OVERLOOKED SOMEONE WHO HAS SERVED YOU FAITHFULLY AND WITHOUT COMPLAINT FOR NEARLY THREE DECADES!
I HAVE?
YES, SIR.
GB Trudeau
BORING. YOU HANDLE IT.
I JUST TRIED.

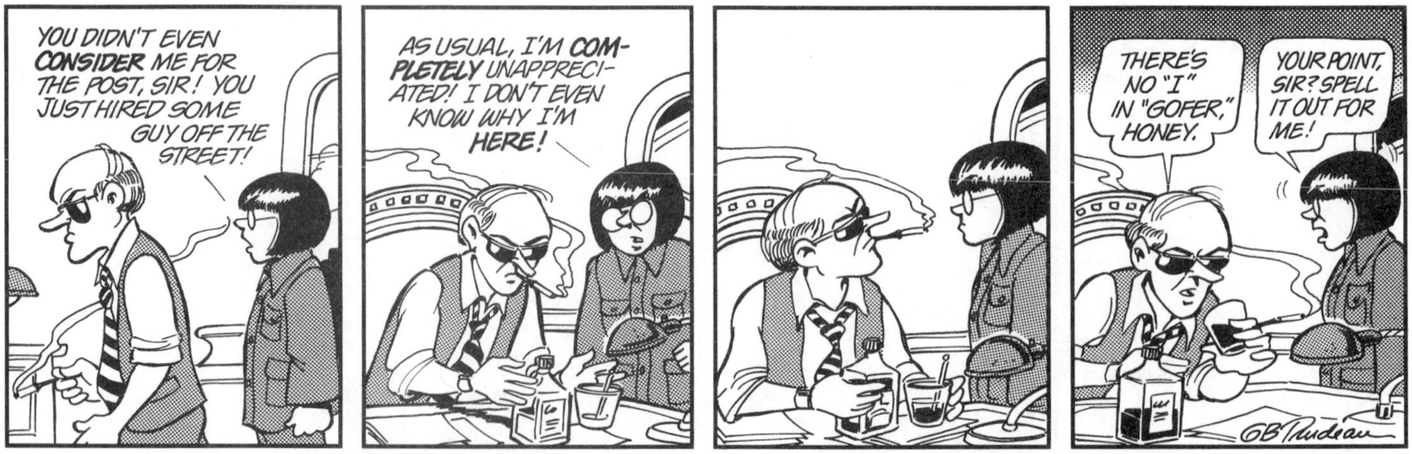
YOU DIDN'T EVEN CONSIDER ME FOR THE POST, SIR! YOU JUST HIRED SOME GUY OFF THE STREET!
AS USUAL, I'M COMPLETELY UNAPPRECIATED! I DON'T EVEN KNOW WHY I'M HERE!
THERE'S NO "I" IN "GOFER," HONEY.
YOUR POINT, SIR? SPELL IT OUT FOR ME!
GB Trudeau

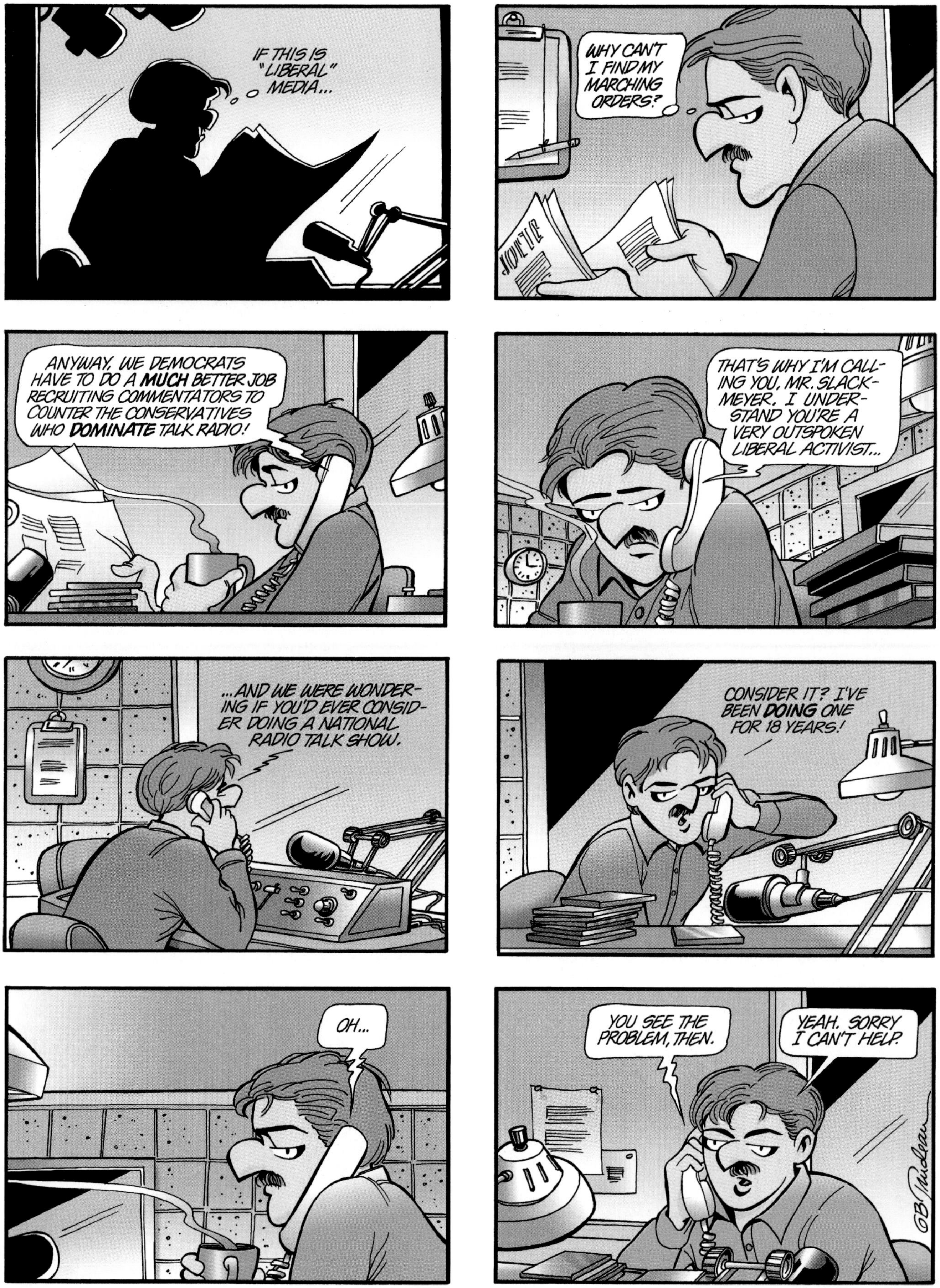
IF THIS IS "LIBERAL" MEDIA...
WHY CAN'T I FIND MY MARCHING ORDERS?
ANYWAY, WE DEMOCRATS HAVE TO DO A **MUCH** BETTER JOB RECRUITING COMMENTATORS TO COUNTER THE CONSERVATIVES WHO **DOMINATE** TALK RADIO!
THAT'S WHY I'M CALLING YOU, MR. SLACKMEYER. I UNDERSTAND YOU'RE A VERY OUTSPOKEN LIBERAL ACTIVIST...
...AND WE WERE WONDERING IF YOU'D EVER CONSIDER DOING A NATIONAL RADIO TALK SHOW.
CONSIDER IT? I'VE BEEN **DOING** ONE FOR 18 YEARS!
OH...
YOU SEE THE PROBLEM, THEN.
YEAH. SORRY I CAN'T HELP.
©B. Trudeau

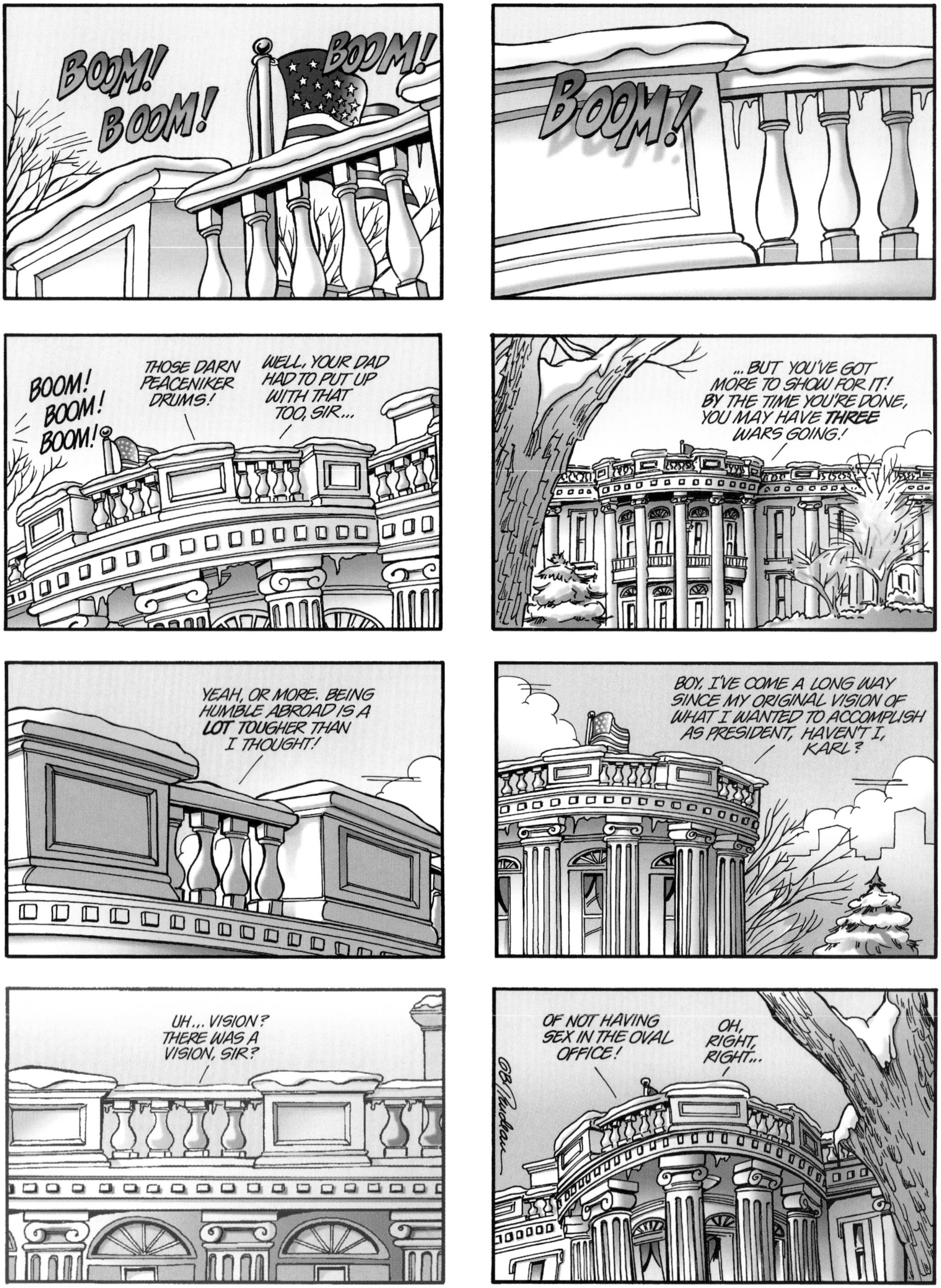
BOOM!
BOOM!
BOOM!
BOOM!
BOOM! BOOM! BOOM!
THOSE DARN PEACENIKER DRUMS!
WELL, YOUR DAD HAD TO PUT UP WITH THAT TOO, SIR...
... BUT YOU'VE GOT MORE TO SHOW FOR IT! BY THE TIME YOU'RE DONE, YOU MAY HAVE **THREE** WARS GOING!
YEAH, OR MORE. BEING HUMBLE ABROAD IS A **LOT** TOUGHER THAN I THOUGHT!
BOY, I'VE COME A LONG WAY SINCE MY ORIGINAL VISION OF WHAT I WANTED TO ACCOMPLISH AS PRESIDENT, HAVEN'T I, KARL?
UH... VISION? THERE WAS A VISION, SIR?
OF NOT HAVING SEX IN THE OVAL OFFICE!
OH, RIGHT, RIGHT...

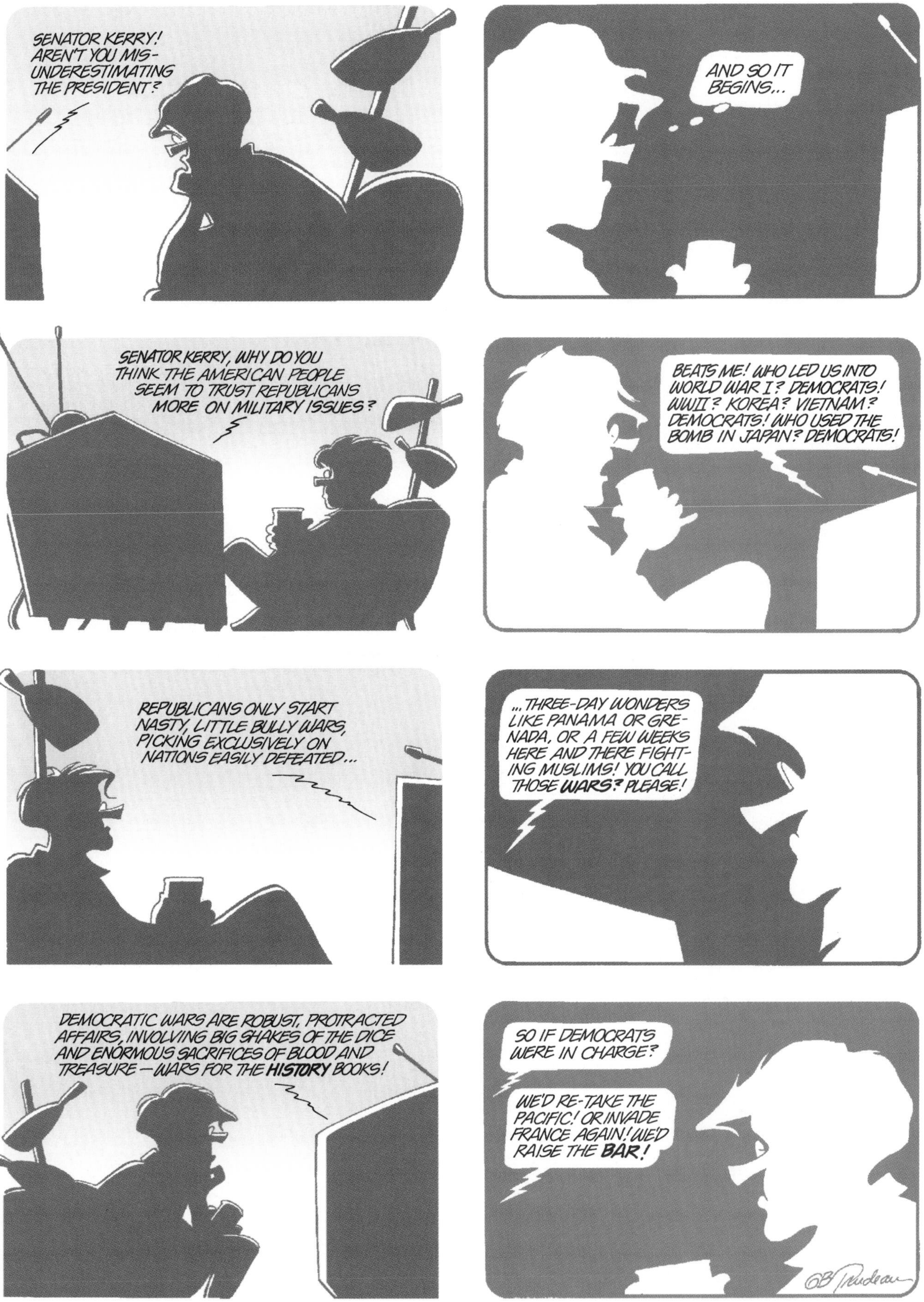
SENATOR KERRY! AREN'T YOU MIS-UNDERESTIMATING THE PRESIDENT?
AND SO IT BEGINS...
SENATOR KERRY, WHY DO YOU THINK THE AMERICAN PEOPLE SEEM TO TRUST REPUBLICANS MORE ON MILITARY ISSUES?
BEATS ME! WHO LED US INTO WORLD WAR I? DEMOCRATS! WWII? KOREA? VIETNAM? DEMOCRATS! WHO USED THE BOMB IN JAPAN? DEMOCRATS!
REPUBLICANS ONLY START NASTY, LITTLE BULLY WARS, PICKING EXCLUSIVELY ON NATIONS EASILY DEFEATED...
...THREE-DAY WONDERS LIKE PANAMA OR GRE-NADA, OR A FEW WEEKS HERE AND THERE FIGHT-ING MUSLIMS! YOU CALL THOSE WARS? PLEASE!
DEMOCRATIC WARS ARE ROBUST, PROTRACTED AFFAIRS, INVOLVING BIG SHAKES OF THE DICE AND ENORMOUS SACRIFICES OF BLOOD AND TREASURE—WARS FOR THE HISTORY BOOKS!
SO IF DEMOCRATS WERE IN CHARGE?
WE'D RE-TAKE THE PACIFIC! OR INVADE FRANCE AGAIN! WE'D RAISE THE BAR!

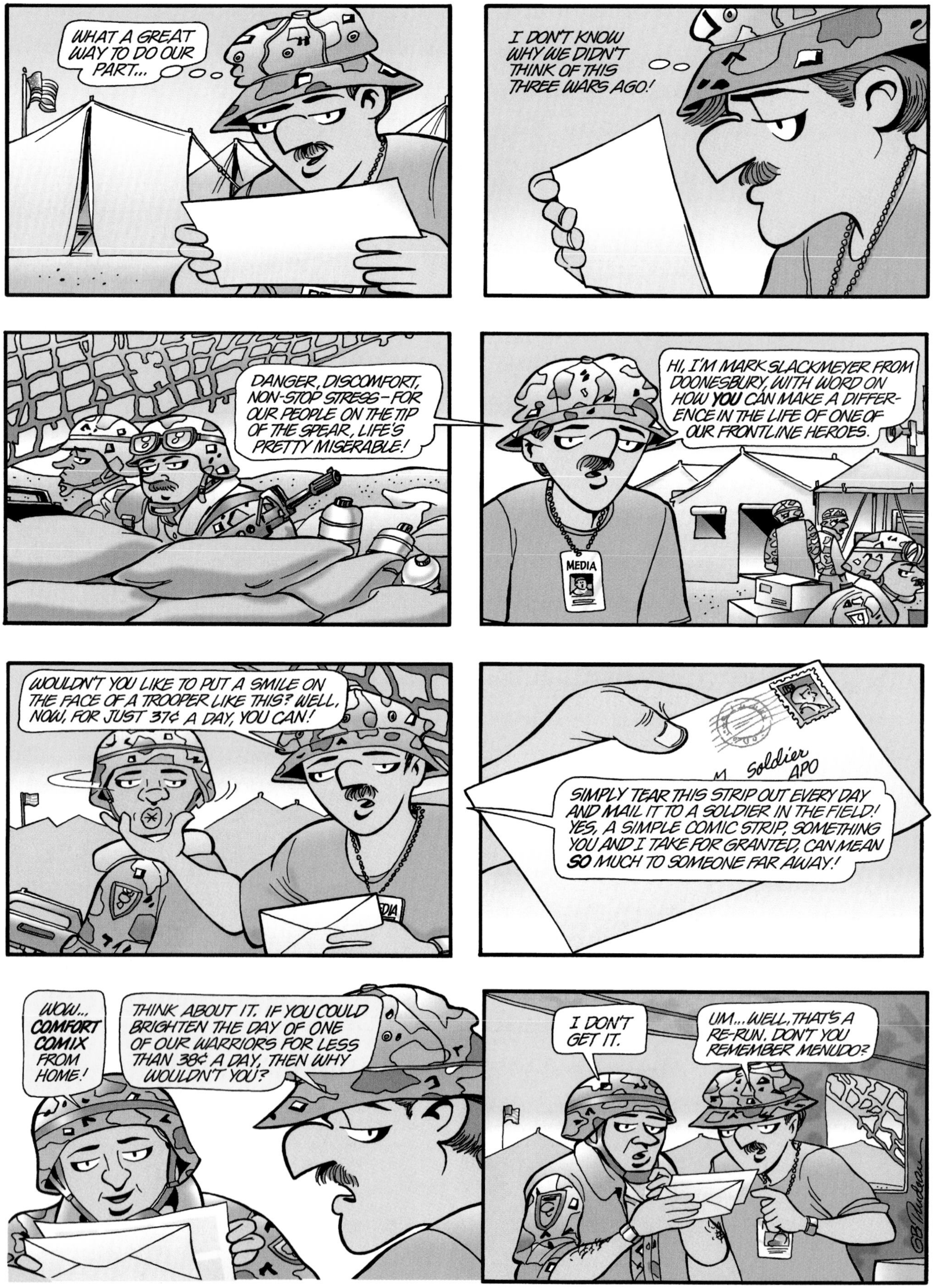
WHAT A GREAT WAY TO DO OUR PART...
I DON'T KNOW WHY WE DIDN'T THINK OF THIS THREE WARS AGO!
DANGER, DISCOMFORT, NON-STOP STRESS—FOR OUR PEOPLE ON THE TIP OF THE SPEAR, LIFE'S PRETTY MISERABLE!
HI, I'M MARK SLACKMEYER FROM DOONESBURY, WITH WORD ON HOW **YOU** CAN MAKE A DIFFERENCE IN THE LIFE OF ONE OF OUR FRONTLINE HEROES.
MEDIA
WOULDN'T YOU LIKE TO PUT A SMILE ON THE FACE OF A TROOPER LIKE THIS? WELL, NOW, FOR JUST 37¢ A DAY, YOU CAN!
Soldier
APO
SIMPLY TEAR THIS STRIP OUT EVERY DAY AND MAIL IT TO A SOLDIER IN THE FIELD! YES, A SIMPLE COMIC STRIP, SOMETHING YOU AND I TAKE FOR GRANTED, CAN MEAN **SO** MUCH TO SOMEONE FAR AWAY!
WOW... **COMFORT COMIX** FROM HOME!
THINK ABOUT IT. IF YOU COULD BRIGHTEN THE DAY OF ONE OF OUR WARRIORS FOR LESS THAN 38¢ A DAY, THEN WHY WOULDN'T YOU?
I DON'T GET IT.
UM... WELL, THAT'S A RE-RUN. DON'T YOU REMEMBER MENUDO?
©B Trudeau

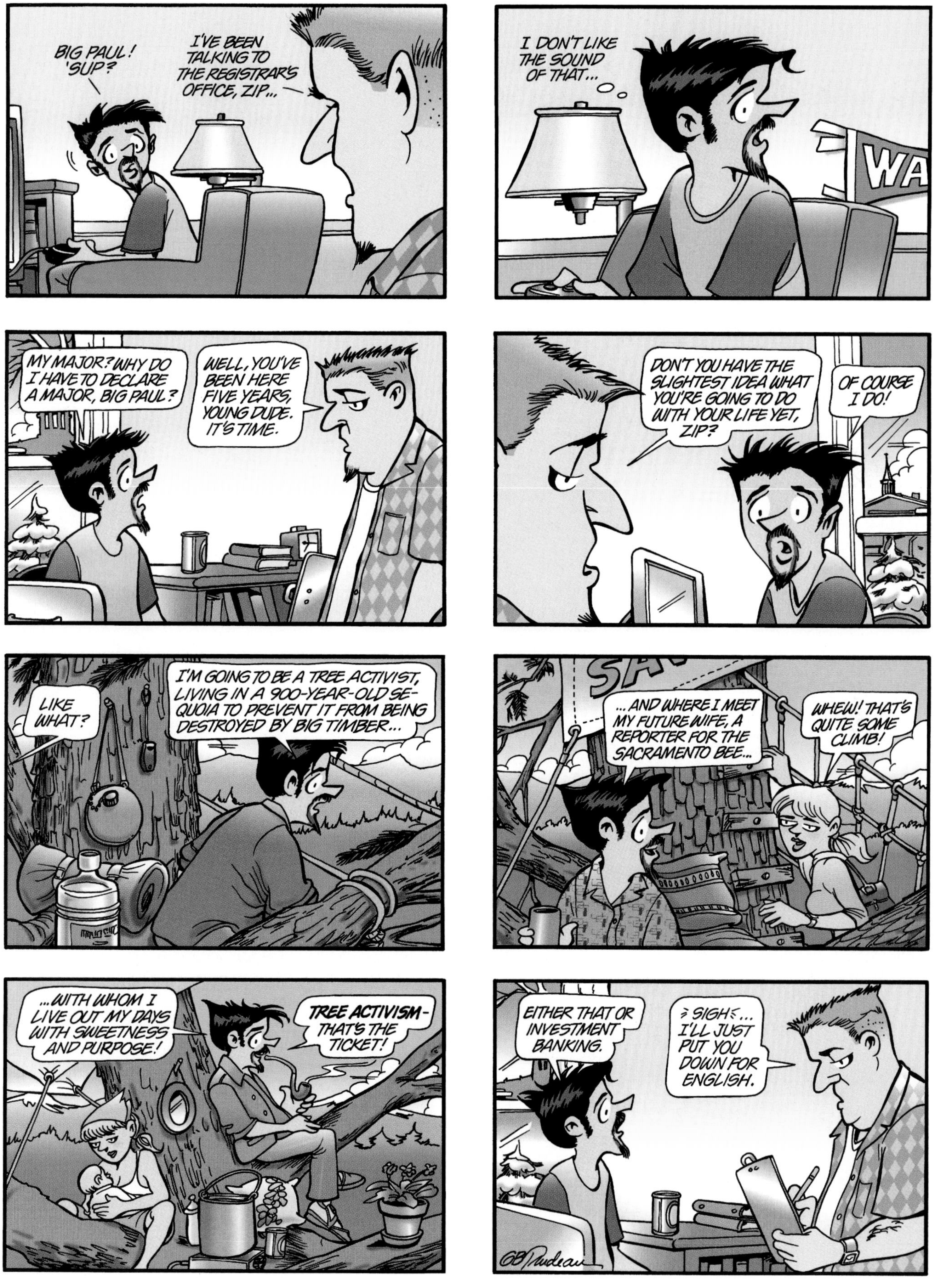
BIG PAUL! 'SUP?
I'VE BEEN TALKING TO THE REGISTRAR'S OFFICE, ZIP...
I DON'T LIKE THE SOUND OF THAT...
MY MAJOR? WHY DO I HAVE TO DECLARE A MAJOR, BIG PAUL?
WELL, YOU'VE BEEN HERE FIVE YEARS, YOUNG DUDE. IT'S TIME.
DON'T YOU HAVE THE SLIGHTEST IDEA WHAT YOU'RE GOING TO DO WITH YOUR LIFE YET, ZIP?
OF COURSE I DO!
LIKE WHAT?
I'M GOING TO BE A TREE ACTIVIST, LIVING IN A 900-YEAR-OLD SEQUOIA TO PREVENT IT FROM BEING DESTROYED BY BIG TIMBER...
...AND WHERE I MEET MY FUTURE WIFE, A REPORTER FOR THE SACRAMENTO BEE...
WHEW! THAT'S QUITE SOME CLIMB!
...WITH WHOM I LIVE OUT MY DAYS WITH SWEETNESS AND PURPOSE!
TREE ACTIVISM - THAT'S THE TICKET!
EITHER THAT OR INVESTMENT BANKING.
SIGH... I'LL JUST PUT YOU DOWN FOR ENGLISH.

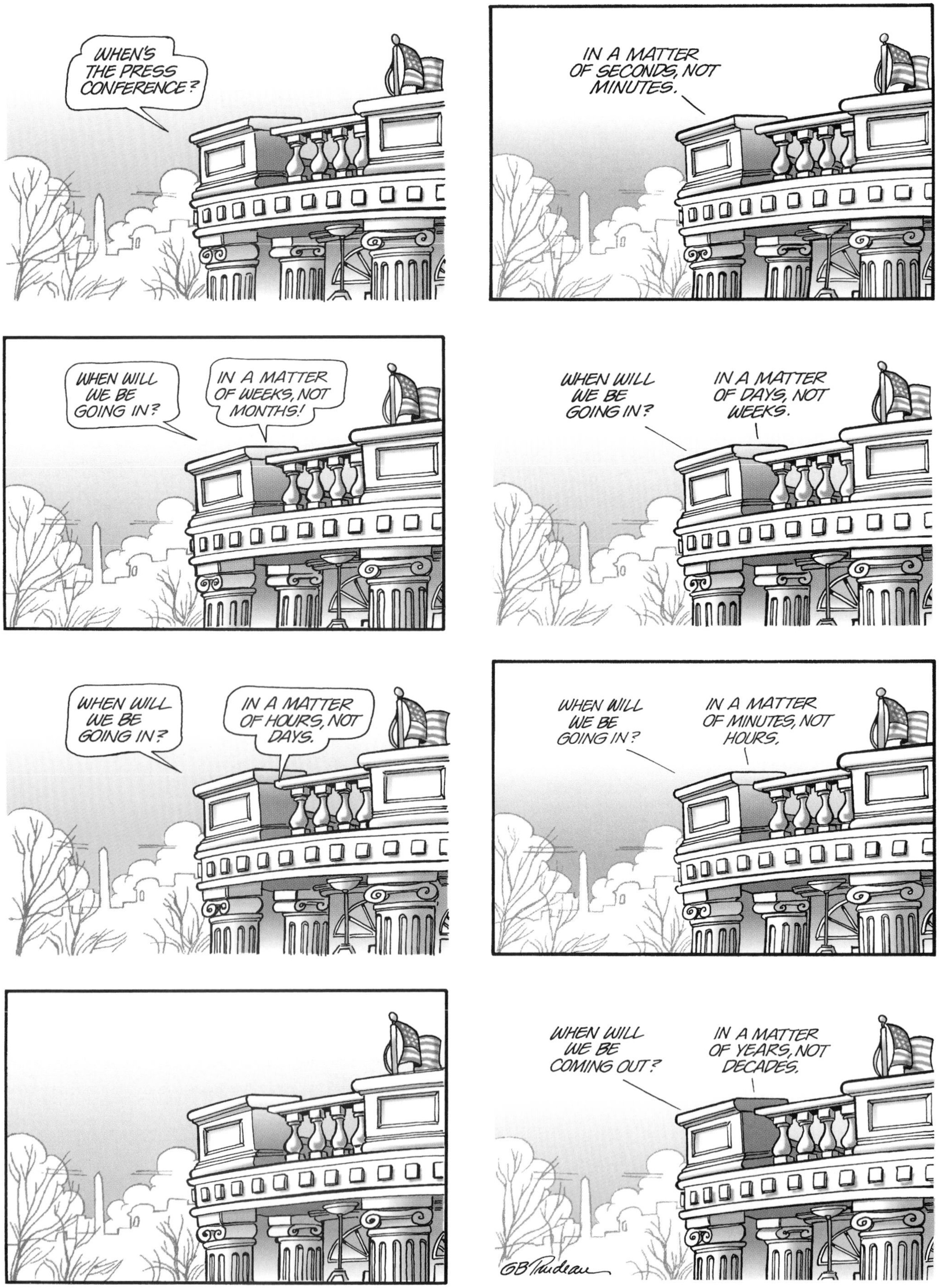
WHEN'S THE PRESS CONFERENCE?
IN A MATTER OF SECONDS, NOT MINUTES.
WHEN WILL WE BE GOING IN?
IN A MATTER OF WEEKS, NOT MONTHS!
WHEN WILL WE BE GOING IN?
IN A MATTER OF DAYS, NOT WEEKS.
WHEN WILL WE BE GOING IN?
IN A MATTER OF HOURS, NOT DAYS.
WHEN WILL WE BE GOING IN?
IN A MATTER OF MINUTES, NOT HOURS.
WHEN WILL WE BE COMING OUT?
IN A MATTER OF YEARS, NOT DECADES.
GB Trudeau

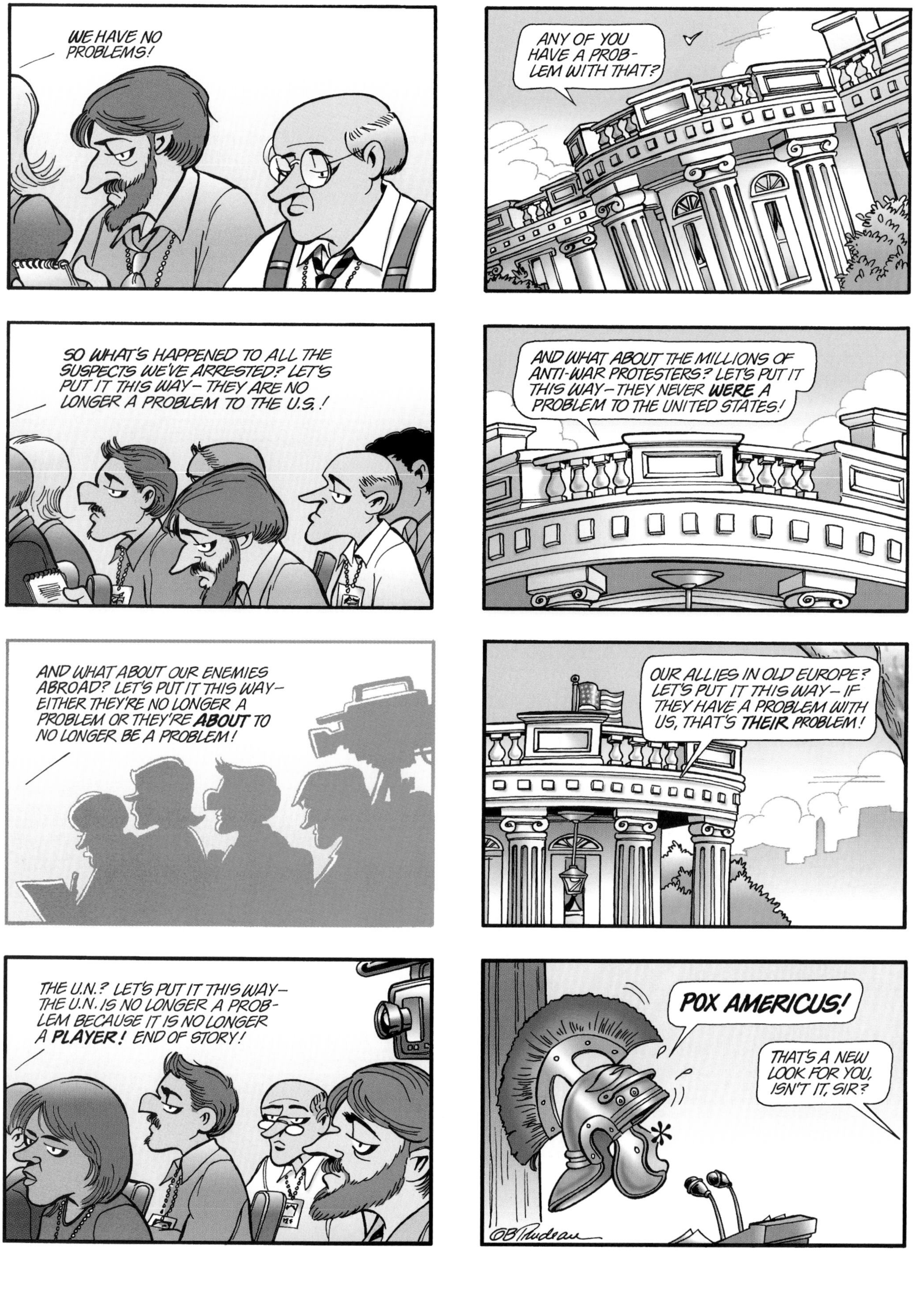
WE HAVE NO PROBLEMS!
ANY OF YOU HAVE A PROB-LEM WITH THAT?
SO WHAT'S HAPPENED TO ALL THE SUSPECTS WE'VE ARRESTED? LET'S PUT IT THIS WAY—THEY ARE NO LONGER A PROBLEM TO THE U.S.!
AND WHAT ABOUT THE MILLIONS OF ANTI-WAR PROTESTERS? LET'S PUT IT THIS WAY—THEY NEVER **WERE** A PROBLEM TO THE UNITED STATES!
AND WHAT ABOUT OUR ENEMIES ABROAD? LET'S PUT IT THIS WAY—EITHER THEY'RE NO LONGER A PROBLEM OR THEY'RE **ABOUT** TO NO LONGER BE A PROBLEM!
OUR ALLIES IN OLD EUROPE? LET'S PUT IT THIS WAY—IF THEY HAVE A PROBLEM WITH US, THAT'S **THEIR** PROBLEM!
THE U.N.? LET'S PUT IT THIS WAY—THE U.N. IS NO LONGER A PROB-LEM BECAUSE IT IS NO LONGER A **PLAYER!** END OF STORY!
POX AMERICUS!
THAT'S A NEW LOOK FOR YOU, ISN'T IT, SIR?
©BTrudeau

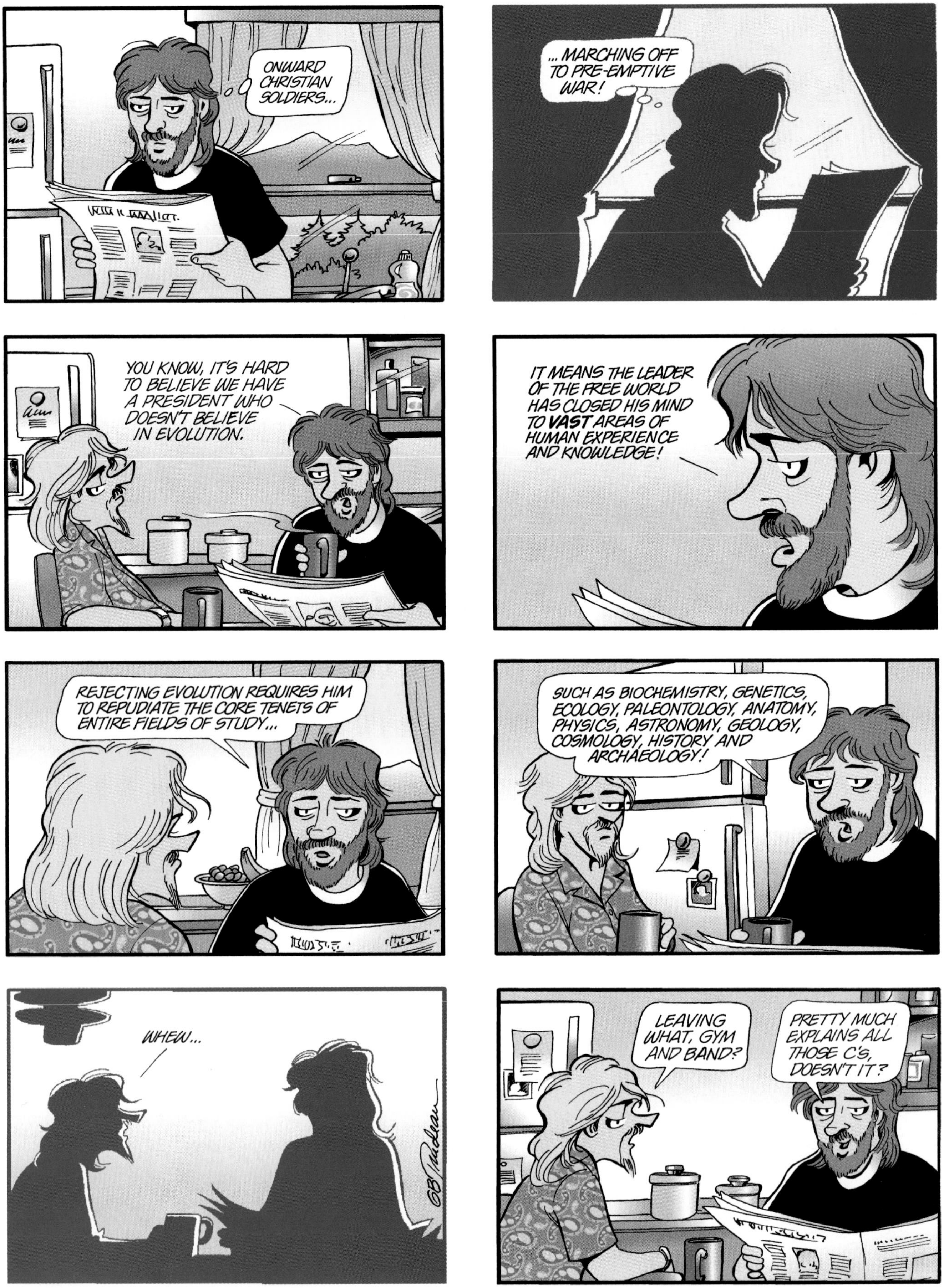

ONWARD CHRISTIAN SOLDIERS...
...MARCHING OFF TO PRE-EMPTIVE WAR!
YOU KNOW, IT'S HARD TO BELIEVE WE HAVE A PRESIDENT WHO DOESN'T BELIEVE IN EVOLUTION.
IT MEANS THE LEADER OF THE FREE WORLD HAS CLOSED HIS MIND TO VAST AREAS OF HUMAN EXPERIENCE AND KNOWLEDGE!
REJECTING EVOLUTION REQUIRES HIM TO REPUDIATE THE CORE TENETS OF ENTIRE FIELDS OF STUDY...
SUCH AS BIOCHEMISTRY, GENETICS, ECOLOGY, PALEONTOLOGY, ANATOMY, PHYSICS, ASTRONOMY, GEOLOGY, COSMOLOGY, HISTORY AND ARCHAEOLOGY!
WHEW...
GB Trudeau
LEAVING WHAT, GYM AND BAND?
PRETTY MUCH EXPLAINS ALL THOSE C'S, DOESN'T IT?

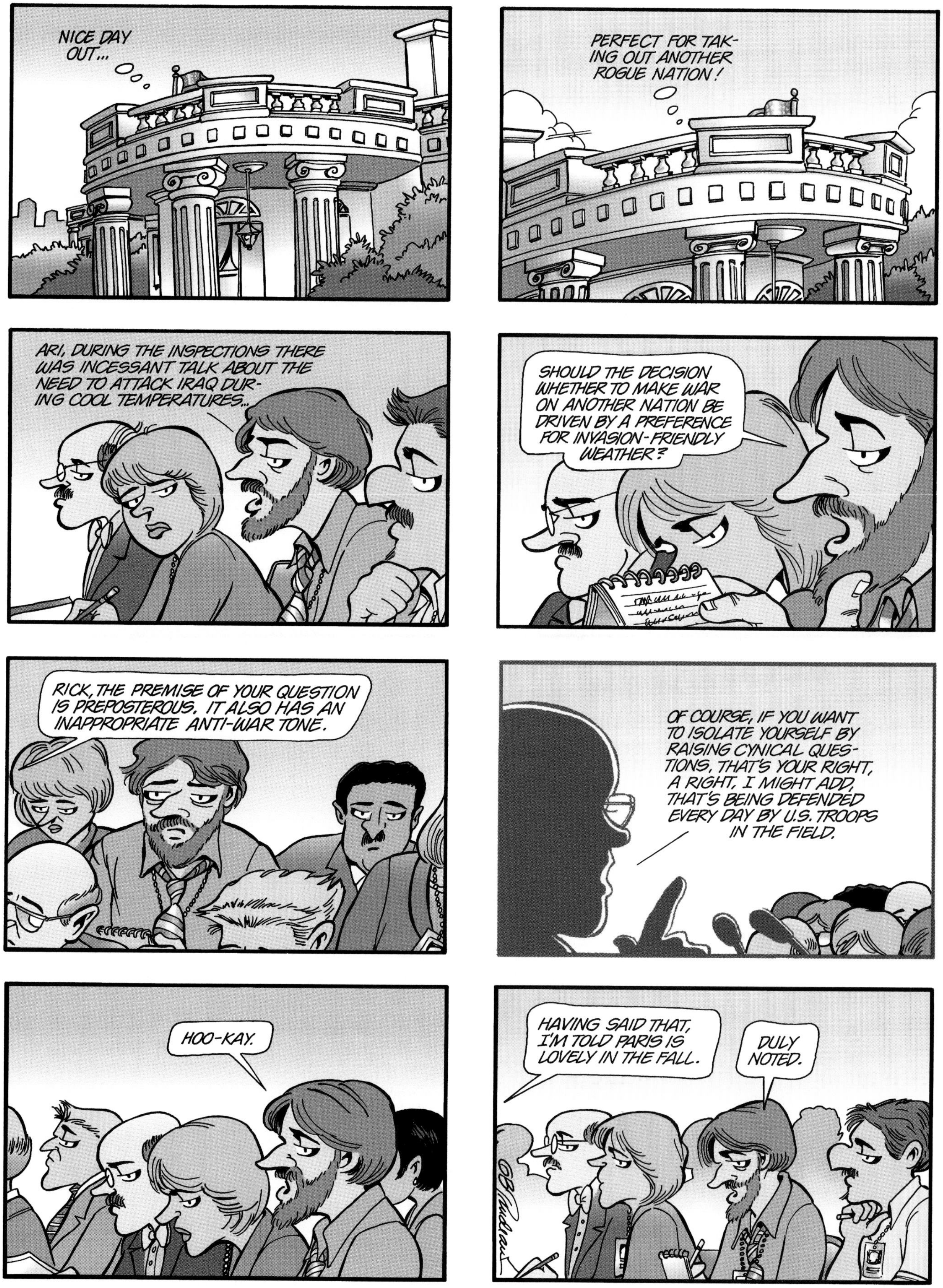
NICE DAY OUT...
PERFECT FOR TAKING OUT ANOTHER ROGUE NATION!
ARI, DURING THE INSPECTIONS THERE WAS INCESSANT TALK ABOUT THE NEED TO ATTACK IRAQ DURING COOL TEMPERATURES...
SHOULD THE DECISION WHETHER TO MAKE WAR ON ANOTHER NATION BE DRIVEN BY A PREFERENCE FOR INVASION-FRIENDLY WEATHER?
RICK, THE PREMISE OF YOUR QUESTION IS PREPOSTEROUS. IT ALSO HAS AN INAPPROPRIATE ANTI-WAR TONE.
OF COURSE, IF YOU WANT TO ISOLATE YOURSELF BY RAISING CYNICAL QUESTIONS, THAT'S YOUR RIGHT, A RIGHT, I MIGHT ADD, THAT'S BEING DEFENDED EVERY DAY BY U.S. TROOPS IN THE FIELD.
HOO-KAY.
HAVING SAID THAT, I'M TOLD PARIS IS LOVELY IN THE FALL.
DULY NOTED.

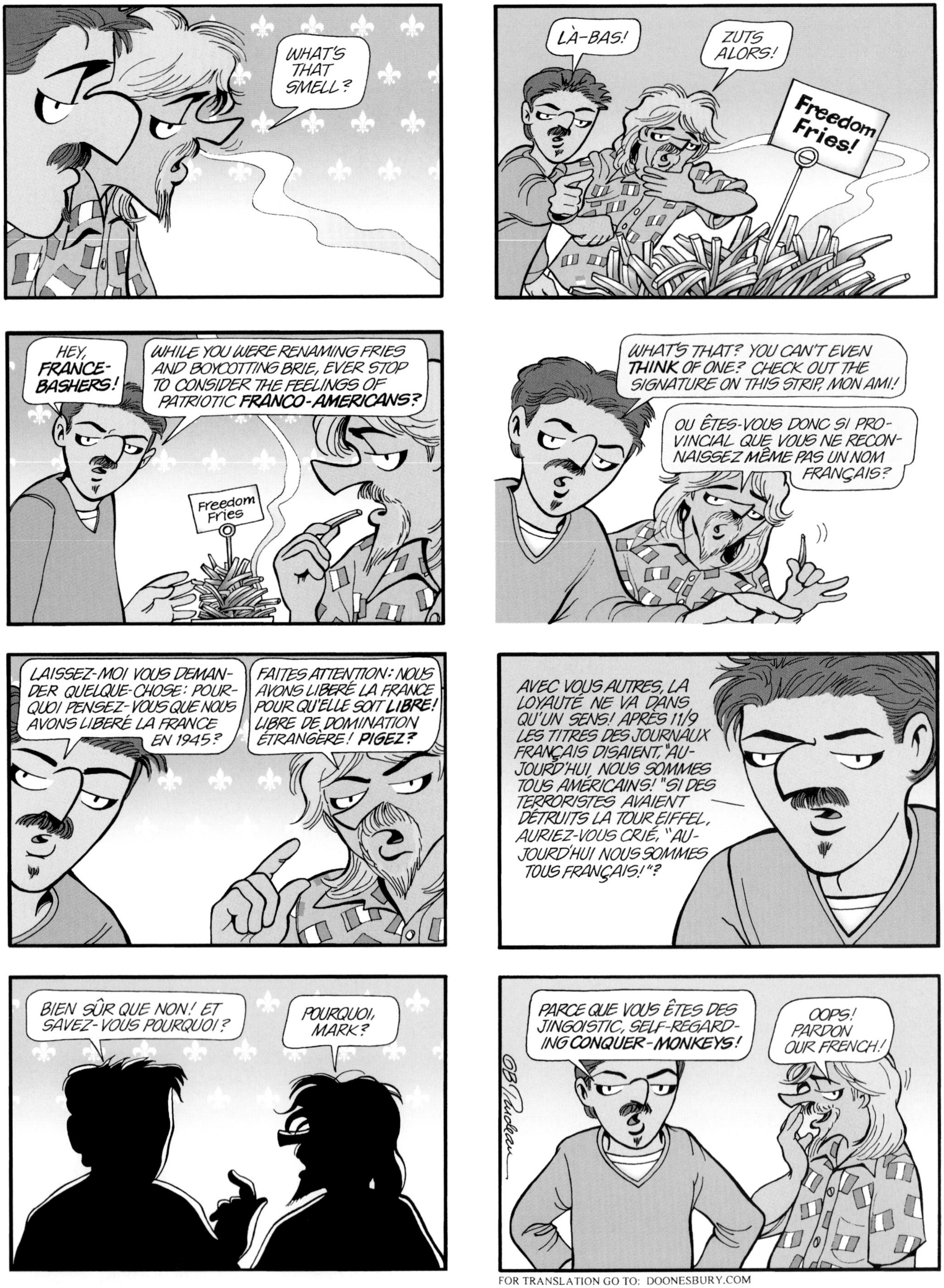
WHAT'S THAT SMELL?
LÀ-BAS!
ZUTS ALORS!
Freedom Fries!
HEY, FRANCE-BASHERS!
WHILE YOU WERE RENAMING FRIES AND BOYCOTTING BRIE, EVER STOP TO CONSIDER THE FEELINGS OF PATRIOTIC FRANCO-AMERICANS?
Freedom Fries
WHAT'S THAT? YOU CAN'T EVEN THINK OF ONE? CHECK OUT THE SIGNATURE ON THIS STRIP, MON AMI!
OU ÊTES-VOUS DONC SI PROVINCIAL QUE VOUS NE RECONNAISSEZ MÊME PAS UN NOM FRANÇAIS?
LAISSEZ-MOI VOUS DEMANDER QUELQUE-CHOSE: POURQUOI PENSEZ-VOUS QUE NOUS AVONS LIBÉRÉ LA FRANCE EN 1945?
FAITES ATTENTION: NOUS AVONS LIBÉRÉ LA FRANCE POUR QU'ELLE SOIT LIBRE! LIBRE DE DOMINATION ÉTRANGÈRE! PIGEZ?
AVEC VOUS AUTRES, LA LOYAUTÉ NE VA DANS QU'UN SENS! APRÈS 11/9 LES TITRES DES JOURNAUX FRANÇAIS DISAIENT, "AUJOURD'HUI, NOUS SOMMES TOUS AMÉRICAINS!" SI DES TERRORISTES AVAIENT DÉTRUITS LA TOUR EIFFEL, AURIEZ-VOUS CRIÉ, "AUJOURD'HUI NOUS SOMMES TOUS FRANÇAIS!"?
BIEN SÛR QUE NON! ET SAVEZ-VOUS POURQUOI?
POURQUOI, MARK?
PARCE QUE VOUS ÊTES DES JINGOISTIC, SELF-REGARDING CONQUER-MONKEYS!
OOPS! PARDON OUR FRENCH!

FOR TRANSLATION GO TO: DOONESBURY.COM

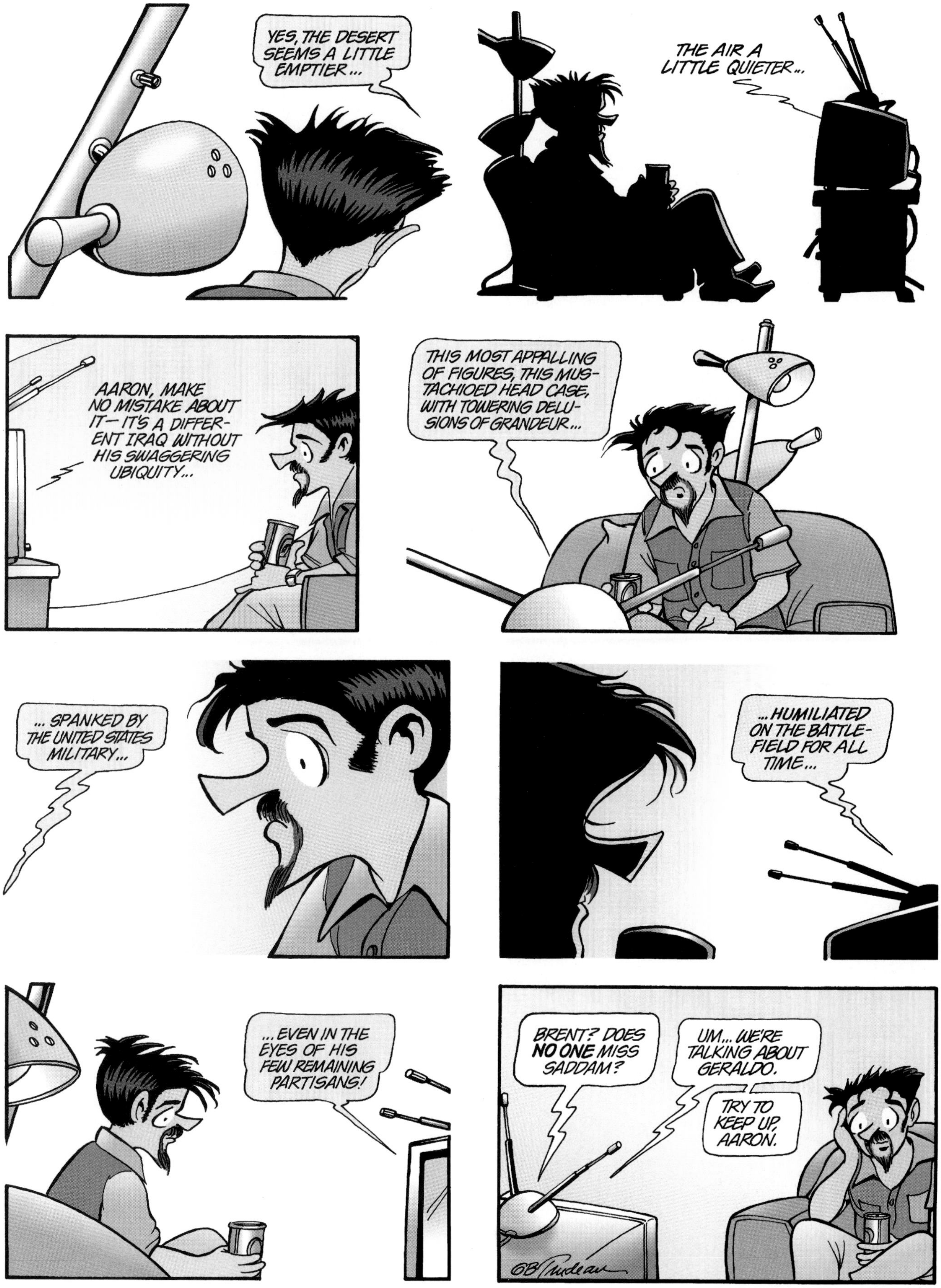
YES, THE DESERT SEEMS A LITTLE EMPTIER...
THE AIR A LITTLE QUIETER...
AARON, MAKE NO MISTAKE ABOUT IT— IT'S A DIFFERENT IRAQ WITHOUT HIS SWAGGERING UBIQUITY...
THIS MOST APPALLING OF FIGURES, THIS MUSTACHIOED HEAD CASE, WITH TOWERING DELUSIONS OF GRANDEUR...
... SPANKED BY THE UNITED STATES MILITARY...
... HUMILIATED ON THE BATTLEFIELD FOR ALL TIME...
... EVEN IN THE EYES OF HIS FEW REMAINING PARTISANS!
BRENT? DOES NO ONE MISS SADDAM?
UM... WE'RE TALKING ABOUT GERALDO.
TRY TO KEEP UP, AARON.

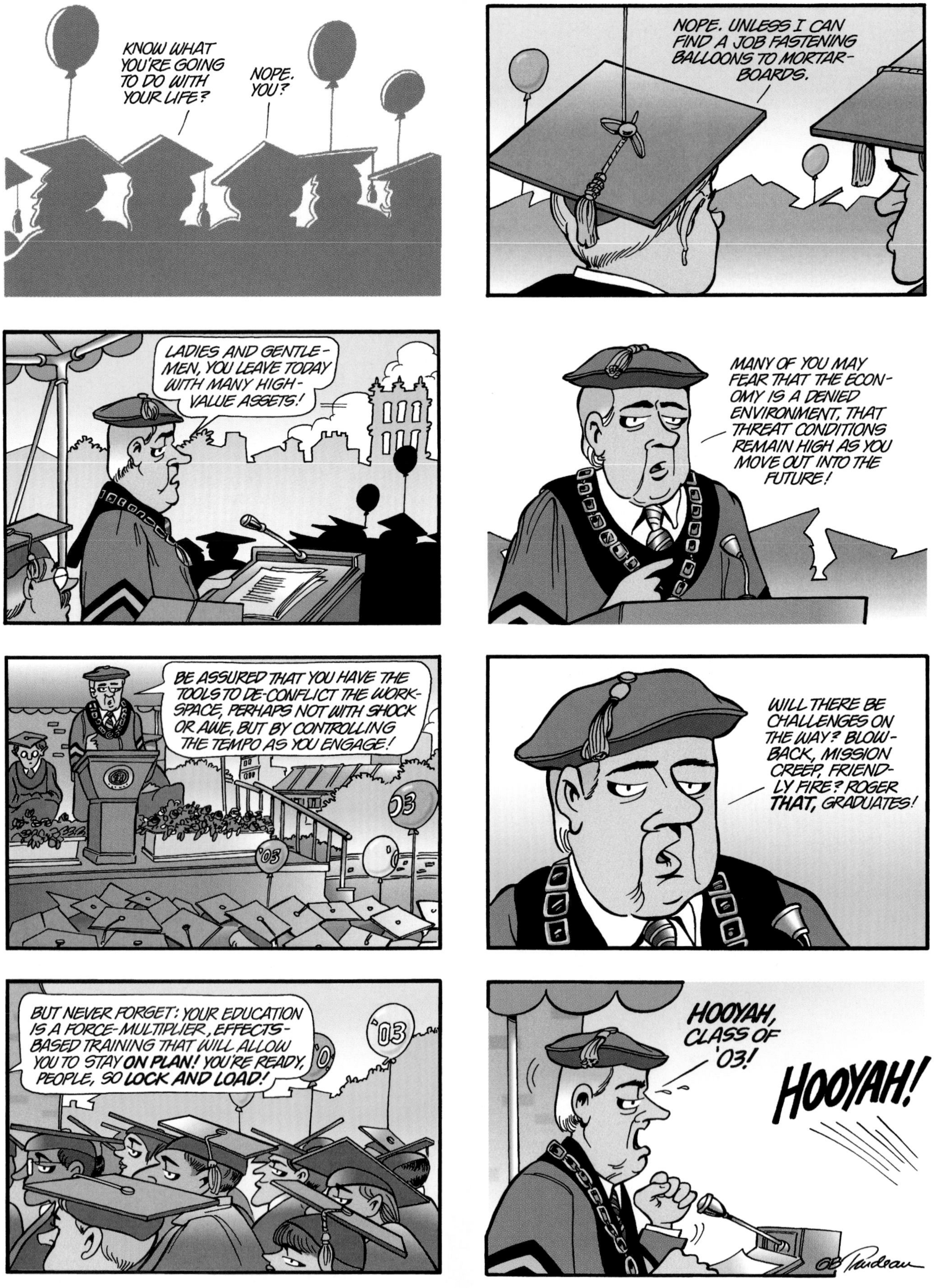
KNOW WHAT YOU'RE GOING TO DO WITH YOUR LIFE?
NOPE. YOU?
NOPE. UNLESS I CAN FIND A JOB FASTENING BALLOONS TO MORTAR-BOARDS.
LADIES AND GENTLE-MEN, YOU LEAVE TODAY WITH MANY HIGH-VALUE ASSETS!
MANY OF YOU MAY FEAR THAT THE ECON-OMY IS A DENIED ENVIRONMENT, THAT THREAT CONDITIONS REMAIN HIGH AS YOU MOVE OUT INTO THE FUTURE!
BE ASSURED THAT YOU HAVE THE TOOLS TO DE-CONFLICT THE WORK-SPACE, PERHAPS NOT WITH SHOCK OR AWE, BUT BY CONTROLLING THE TEMPO AS YOU ENGAGE!
'03
'03
WILL THERE BE CHALLENGES ON THE WAY? BLOW-BACK, MISSION CREEP, FRIEND-LY FIRE? ROGER THAT, GRADUATES!
BUT NEVER FORGET: YOUR EDUCATION IS A FORCE-MULTIPLIER, EFFECTS-BASED TRAINING THAT WILL ALLOW YOU TO STAY ON PLAN! YOU'RE READY, PEOPLE, SO LOCK AND LOAD!
'03
HOOYAH, CLASS OF '03!
HOOYAH!
GB Trudeau

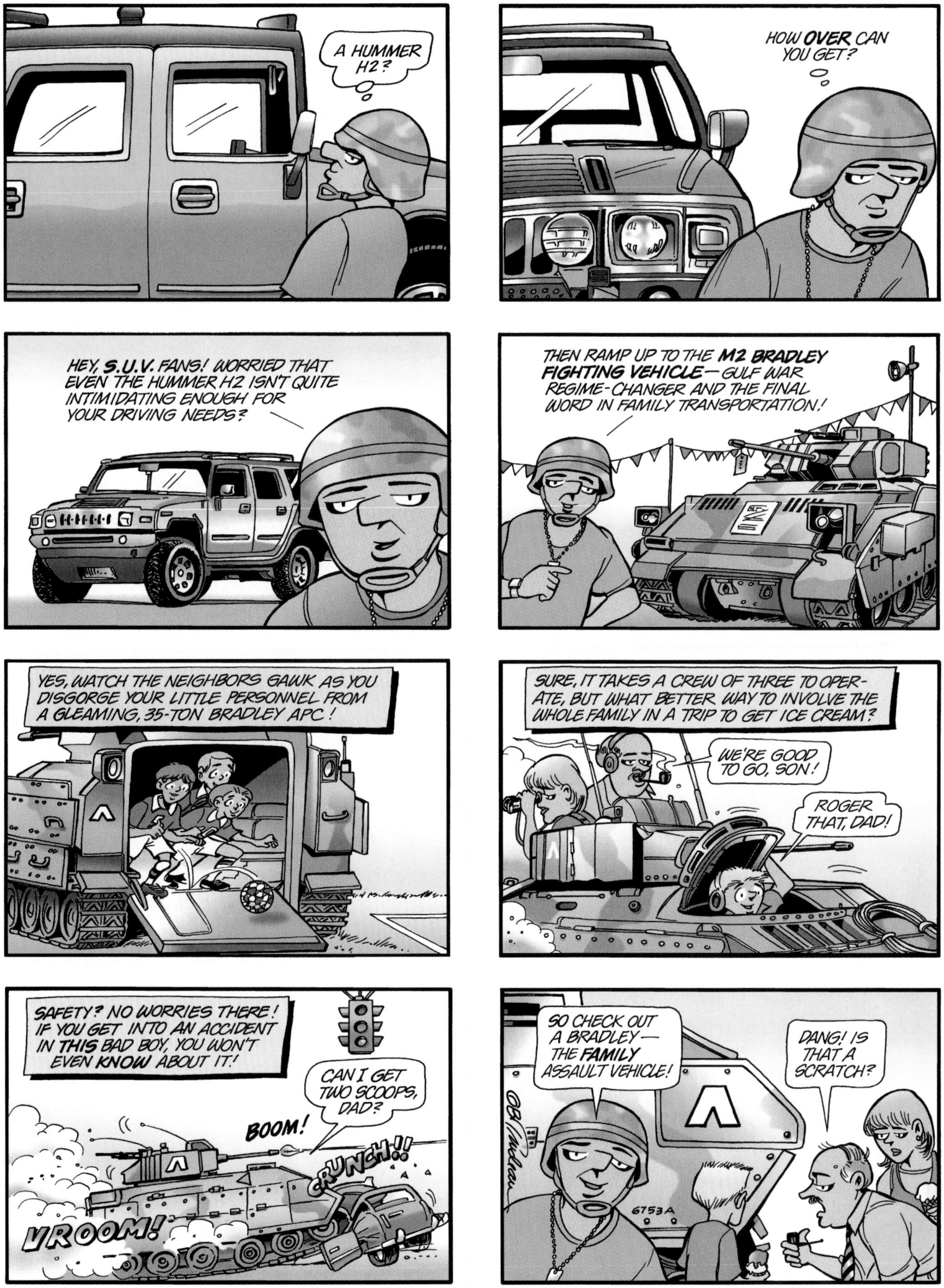
A HUMMER H2?
HOW OVER CAN YOU GET?
HEY, S.U.V. FANS! WORRIED THAT EVEN THE HUMMER H2 ISN'T QUITE INTIMIDATING ENOUGH FOR YOUR DRIVING NEEDS?
THEN RAMP UP TO THE M2 BRADLEY FIGHTING VEHICLE — GULF WAR REGIME-CHANGER AND THE FINAL WORD IN FAMILY TRANSPORTATION!
YES, WATCH THE NEIGHBORS GAWK AS YOU DISGORGE YOUR LITTLE PERSONNEL FROM A GLEAMING, 35-TON BRADLEY APC!
SURE, IT TAKES A CREW OF THREE TO OPERATE, BUT WHAT BETTER WAY TO INVOLVE THE WHOLE FAMILY IN A TRIP TO GET ICE CREAM?
WE'RE GOOD TO GO, SON!
ROGER THAT, DAD!
SAFETY? NO WORRIES THERE! IF YOU GET INTO AN ACCIDENT IN THIS BAD BOY, YOU WON'T EVEN KNOW ABOUT IT!
CAN I GET TWO SCOOPS, DAD?
BOOM!
CRUNCH!!
VROOM!
SO CHECK OUT A BRADLEY — THE FAMILY ASSAULT VEHICLE!
DANG! IS THAT A SCRATCH?

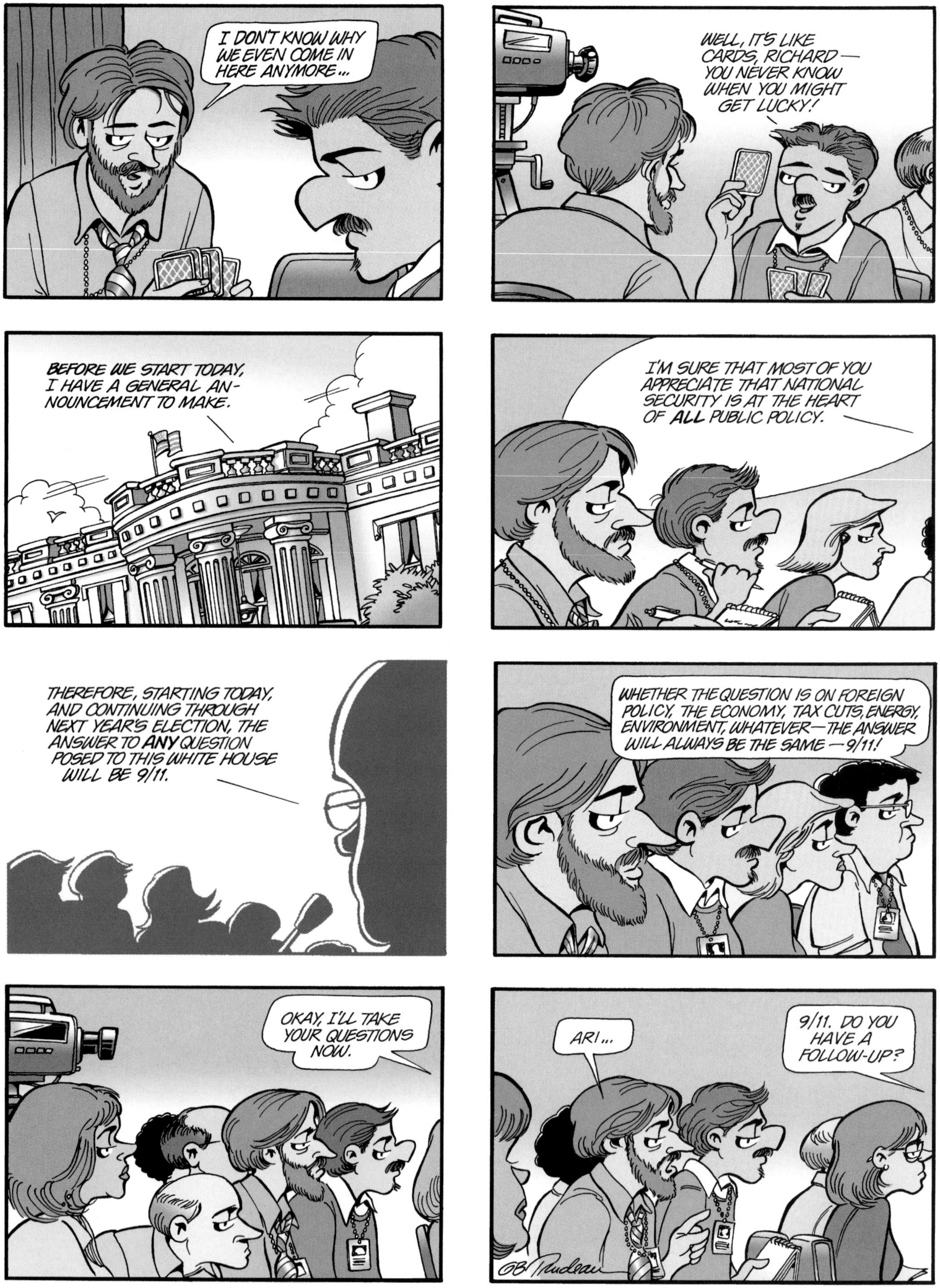
I DON'T KNOW WHY WE EVEN COME IN HERE ANYMORE...
BEFORE WE START TODAY, I HAVE A GENERAL ANNOUNCEMENT TO MAKE.
THEREFORE, STARTING TODAY, AND CONTINUING THROUGH NEXT YEAR'S ELECTION, THE ANSWER TO **ANY** QUESTION POSED TO THIS WHITE HOUSE WILL BE 9/11.
OKAY, I'LL TAKE YOUR QUESTIONS NOW.
WELL, IT'S LIKE CARDS, RICHARD— YOU NEVER KNOW WHEN YOU MIGHT GET LUCKY!
I'M SURE THAT MOST OF YOU APPRECIATE THAT NATIONAL SECURITY IS AT THE HEART OF **ALL** PUBLIC POLICY.
WHETHER THE QUESTION IS ON FOREIGN POLICY, THE ECONOMY, TAX CUTS, ENERGY, ENVIRONMENT, WHATEVER—THE ANSWER WILL ALWAYS BE THE SAME —9/11!
ARI...
9/11. DO YOU HAVE A FOLLOW-UP?
GBTrudeau

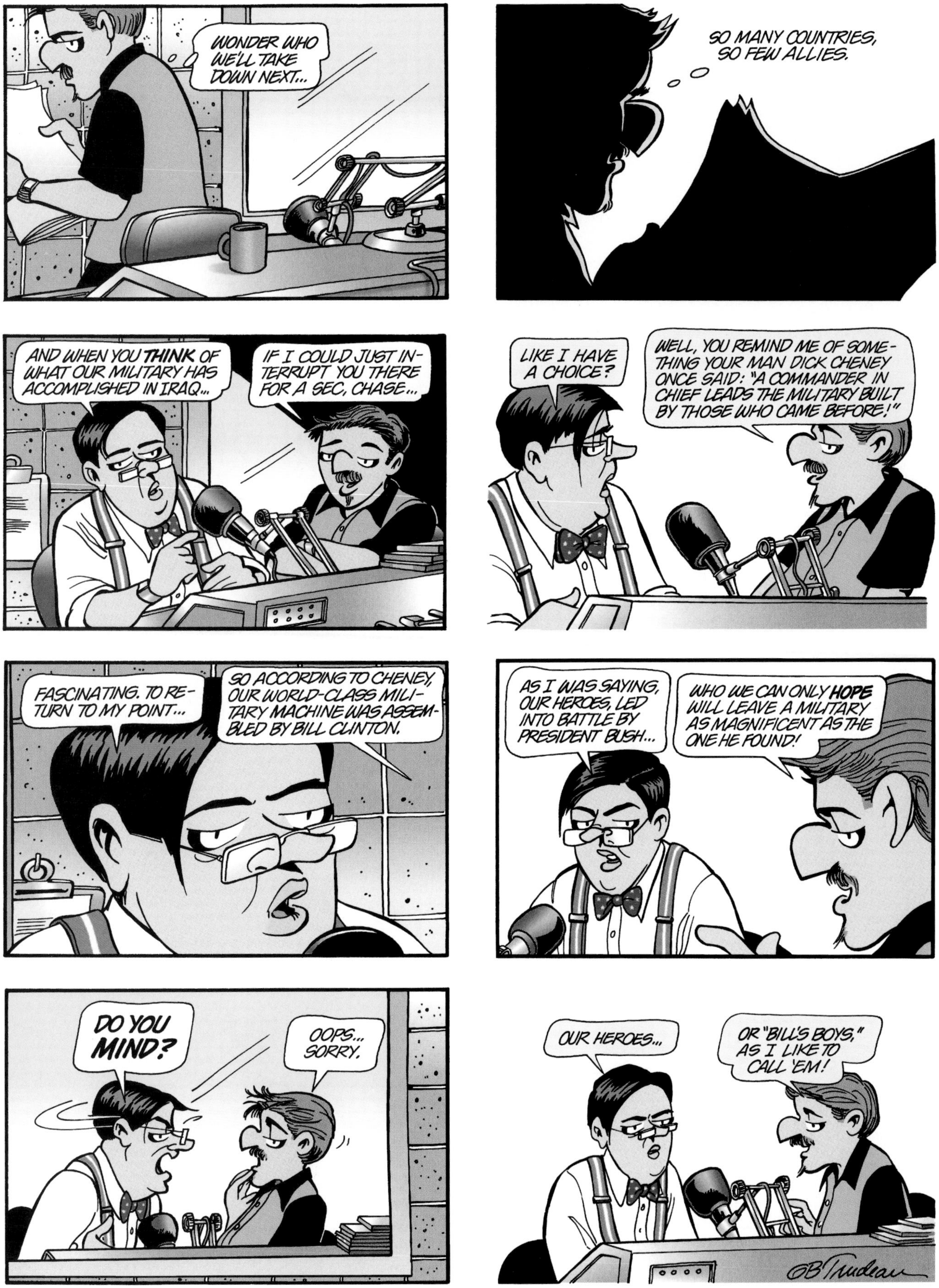
WONDER WHO WE'LL TAKE DOWN NEXT...
SO MANY COUNTRIES, SO FEW ALLIES.
AND WHEN YOU **THINK** OF WHAT OUR MILITARY HAS ACCOMPLISHED IN IRAQ...
IF I COULD JUST INTERRUPT YOU THERE FOR A SEC, CHASE...
LIKE I HAVE A CHOICE?
WELL, YOU REMIND ME OF SOMETHING YOUR MAN DICK CHENEY ONCE SAID: "A COMMANDER IN CHIEF LEADS THE MILITARY BUILT BY THOSE WHO CAME BEFORE!"
FASCINATING. TO RETURN TO MY POINT...
SO ACCORDING TO CHENEY, OUR WORLD-CLASS MILITARY MACHINE WAS ASSEMBLED BY BILL CLINTON.
AS I WAS SAYING, OUR HEROES, LED INTO BATTLE BY PRESIDENT BUSH...
WHO WE CAN ONLY **HOPE** WILL LEAVE A MILITARY AS MAGNIFICENT AS THE ONE HE FOUND!
DO YOU MIND?
OOPS... SORRY.
OUR HEROES...
OR "BILL'S BOYS," AS I LIKE TO CALL 'EM!
GBTrudeau

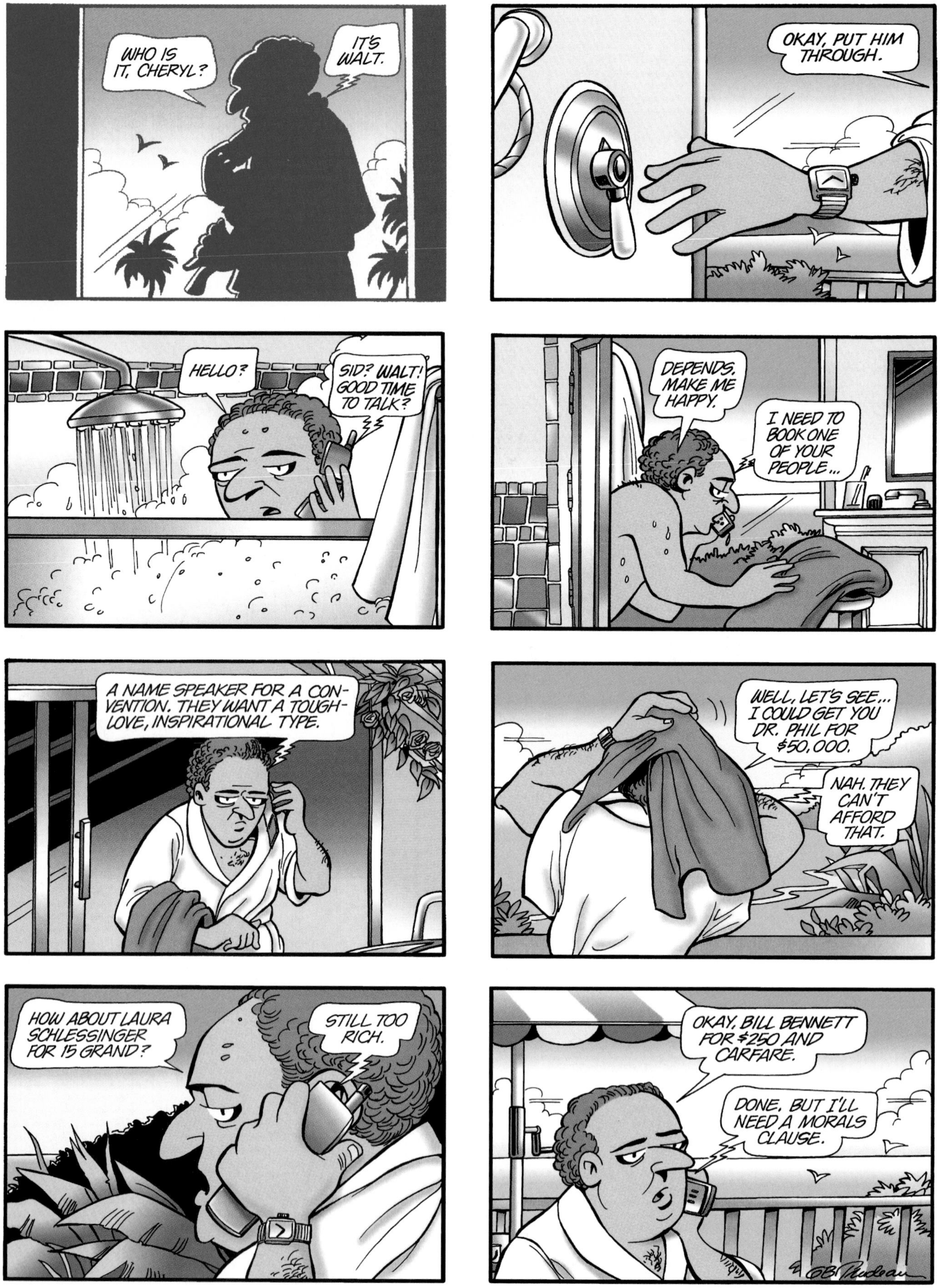
WHO IS IT, CHERYL?
IT'S WALT.
OKAY, PUT HIM THROUGH.
HELLO?
SID? WALT! GOOD TIME TO TALK?
DEPENDS. MAKE ME HAPPY.
I NEED TO BOOK ONE OF YOUR PEOPLE...
A NAME SPEAKER FOR A CONVENTION. THEY WANT A TOUGH-LOVE, INSPIRATIONAL TYPE.
WELL, LET'S SEE... I COULD GET YOU DR. PHIL FOR $50,000.
NAH. THEY CAN'T AFFORD THAT.
HOW ABOUT LAURA SCHLESSINGER FOR 15 GRAND?
STILL TOO RICH.
OKAY. BILL BENNETT FOR $250 AND CARFARE.
DONE. BUT I'LL NEED A MORALS CLAUSE.

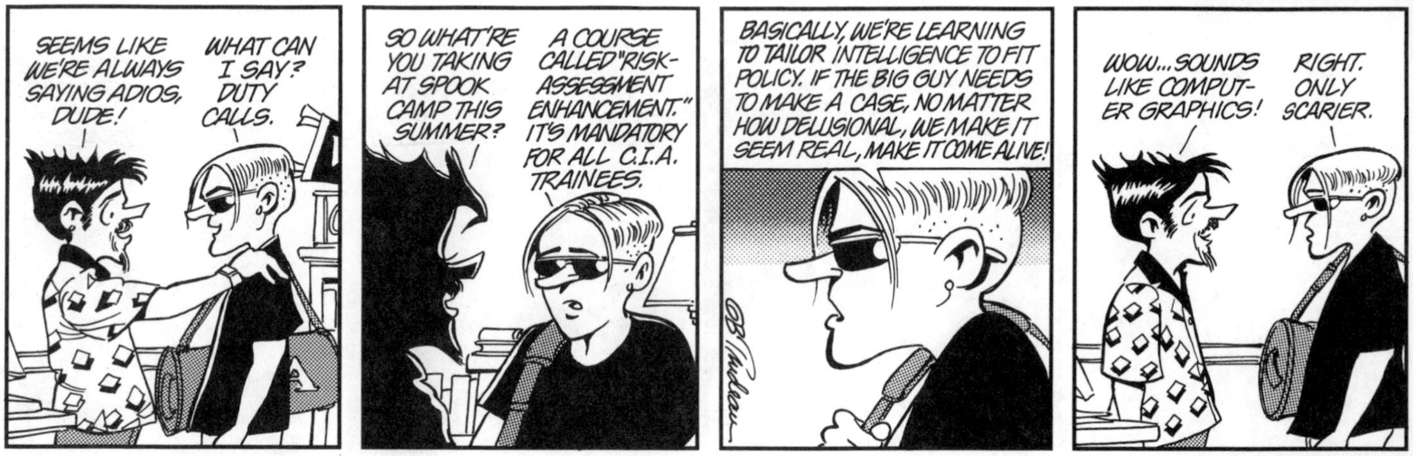
SEEMS LIKE WE'RE ALWAYS SAYING ADIOS, DUDE!
WHAT CAN I SAY? DUTY CALLS.
SO WHAT'RE YOU TAKING AT SPOOK CAMP THIS SUMMER?
A COURSE CALLED "RISK-ASSESSMENT ENHANCEMENT." IT'S MANDATORY FOR ALL C.I.A. TRAINEES.
BASICALLY, WE'RE LEARNING TO TAILOR INTELLIGENCE TO FIT POLICY. IF THE BIG GUY NEEDS TO MAKE A CASE, NO MATTER HOW DELUSIONAL, WE MAKE IT SEEM REAL, MAKE IT COME ALIVE!
WOW... SOUNDS LIKE COMPUTER GRAPHICS!
RIGHT. ONLY SCARIER.

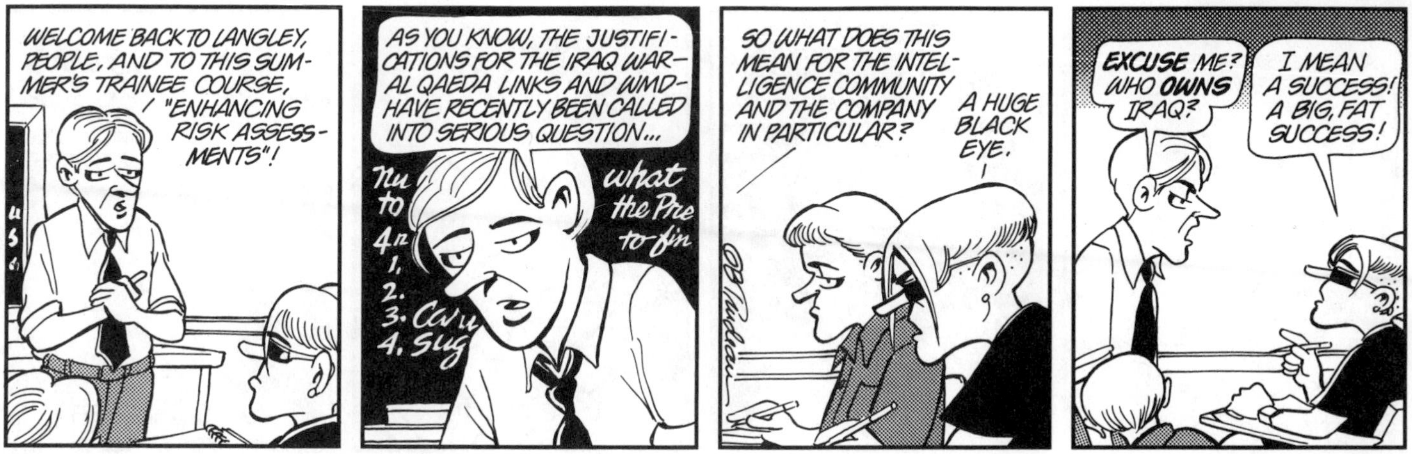
WELCOME BACK TO LANGLEY, PEOPLE, AND TO THIS SUMMER'S TRAINEE COURSE, "ENHANCING RISK ASSESSMENTS"!
AS YOU KNOW, THE JUSTIFICATIONS FOR THE IRAQ WAR—AL QAEDA LINKS AND WMD—HAVE RECENTLY BEEN CALLED INTO SERIOUS QUESTION...
SO WHAT DOES THIS MEAN FOR THE INTELLIGENCE COMMUNITY AND THE COMPANY IN PARTICULAR?
A HUGE BLACK EYE.
EXCUSE ME? WHO OWNS IRAQ?
I MEAN A SUCCESS! A BIG, FAT SUCCESS!

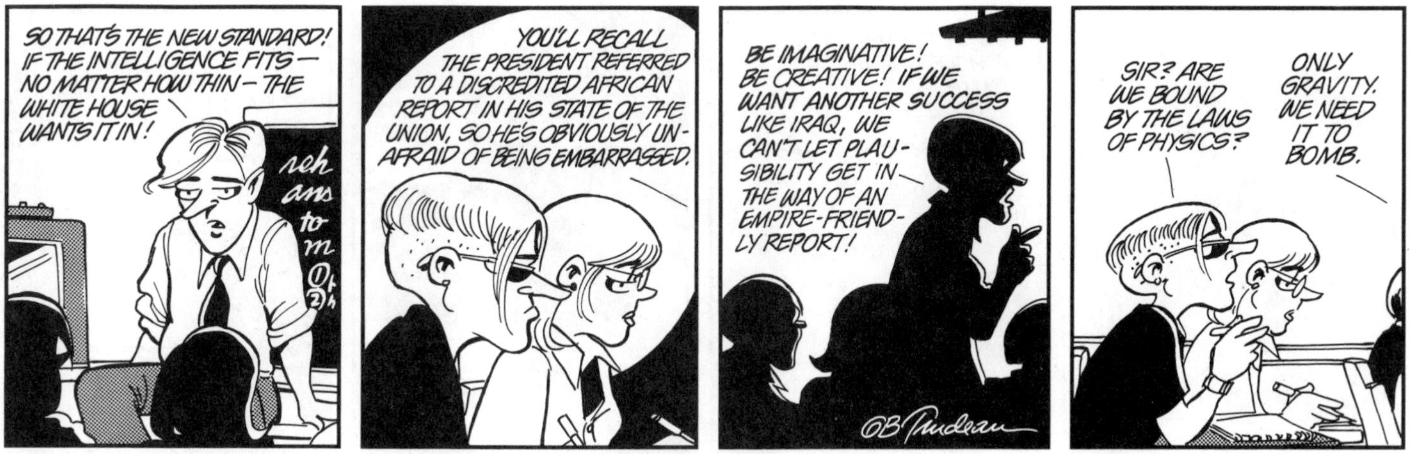
SO THAT'S THE NEW STANDARD! IF THE INTELLIGENCE FITS—NO MATTER HOW THIN—THE WHITE HOUSE WANTS IT IN!
YOU'LL RECALL THE PRESIDENT REFERRED TO A DISCREDITED AFRICAN REPORT IN HIS STATE OF THE UNION, SO HE'S OBVIOUSLY UNAFRAID OF BEING EMBARRASSED.
BE IMAGINATIVE! BE CREATIVE! IF WE WANT ANOTHER SUCCESS LIKE IRAQ, WE CAN'T LET PLAUSIBILITY GET IN THE WAY OF AN EMPIRE-FRIENDLY REPORT!
SIR? ARE WE BOUND BY THE LAWS OF PHYSICS?
ONLY GRAVITY. WE NEED IT TO BOMB.

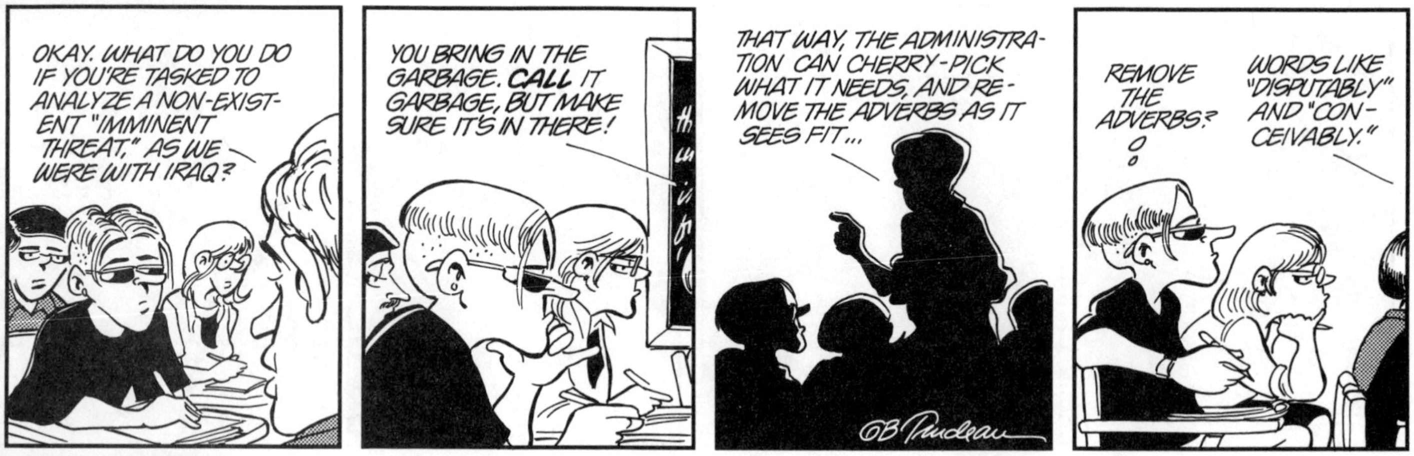
OKAY. WHAT DO YOU DO IF YOU'RE TASKED TO ANALYZE A NON-EXISTENT "IMMINENT THREAT," AS WE WERE WITH IRAQ?
YOU BRING IN THE GARBAGE. **CALL** IT GARBAGE, BUT MAKE SURE IT'S IN THERE!
THAT WAY, THE ADMINISTRATION CAN CHERRY-PICK WHAT IT NEEDS, AND REMOVE THE ADVERBS AS IT SEES FIT...
REMOVE THE ADVERBS?
WORDS LIKE "DISPUTABLY" AND "CONCEIVABLY."

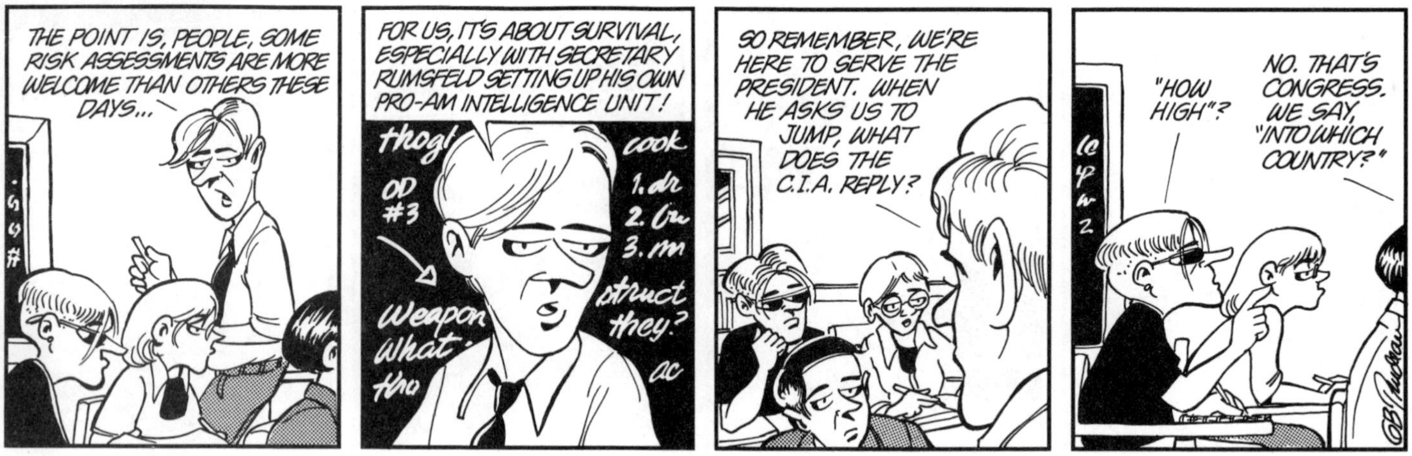
THE POINT IS, PEOPLE, SOME RISK ASSESSMENTS ARE MORE WELCOME THAN OTHERS THESE DAYS...
FOR US, IT'S ABOUT SURVIVAL, ESPECIALLY WITH SECRETARY RUMSFELD SETTING UP HIS OWN PRO-AM INTELLIGENCE UNIT!
SO REMEMBER, WE'RE HERE TO SERVE THE PRESIDENT. WHEN HE ASKS US TO JUMP, WHAT DOES THE C.I.A. REPLY?
"HOW HIGH"?
NO. THAT'S CONGRESS. WE SAY, "INTO WHICH COUNTRY?"

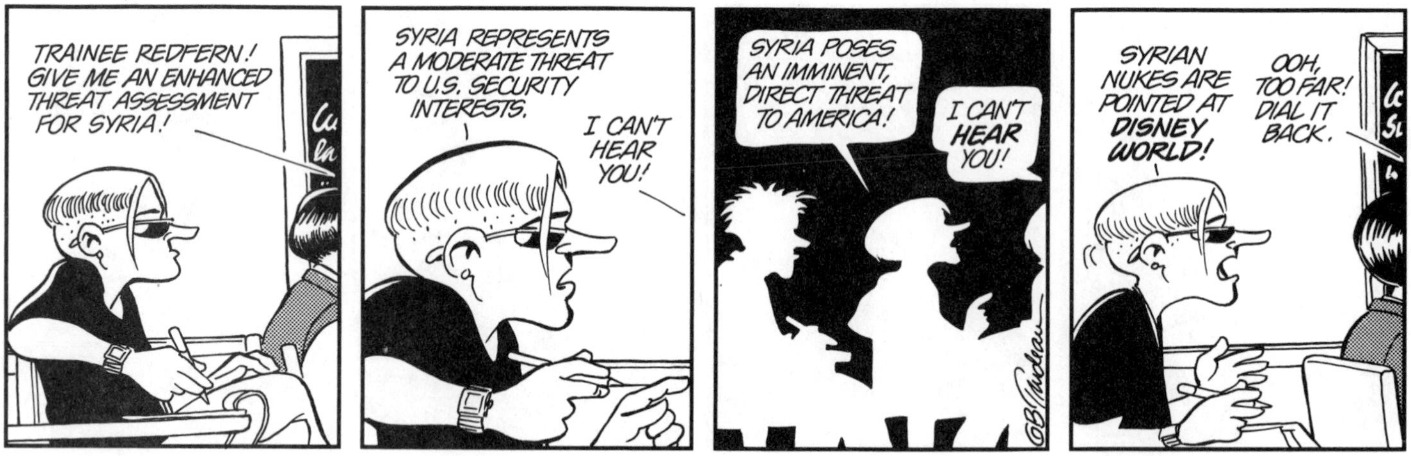
TRAINEE REDFERN! GIVE ME AN ENHANCED THREAT ASSESSMENT FOR SYRIA!
SYRIA REPRESENTS A MODERATE THREAT TO U.S. SECURITY INTERESTS.
I CAN'T HEAR YOU!
SYRIA POSES AN IMMINENT, DIRECT THREAT TO AMERICA!
I CAN'T **HEAR** YOU!
SYRIAN NUKES ARE POINTED AT **DISNEY WORLD!**
OOH, TOO FAR! DIAL IT BACK.

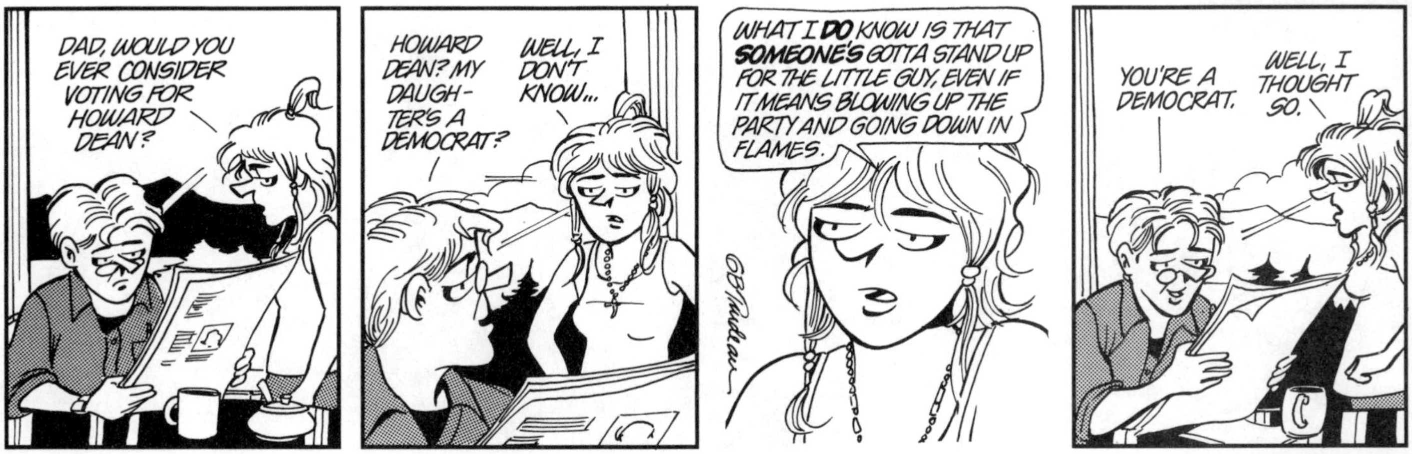
DAD, WOULD YOU EVER CONSIDER VOTING FOR HOWARD DEAN?
HOWARD DEAN? MY DAUGHTER'S A DEMOCRAT?
WELL, I DON'T KNOW...
WHAT I **DO** KNOW IS THAT **SOMEONE'S** GOTTA STAND UP FOR THE LITTLE GUY, EVEN IF IT MEANS BLOWING UP THE PARTY AND GOING DOWN IN FLAMES.
©B Trudeau
YOU'RE A DEMOCRAT.
WELL, I THOUGHT SO.

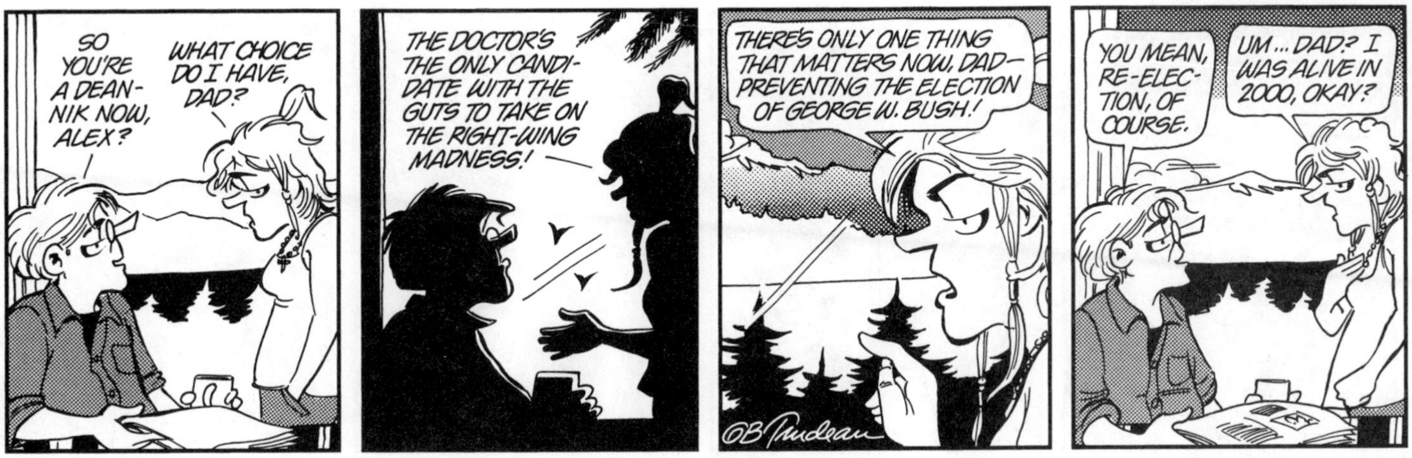
SO YOU'RE A DEANNIK NOW, ALEX?
WHAT CHOICE DO I HAVE, DAD?
THE DOCTOR'S THE ONLY CANDIDATE WITH THE GUTS TO TAKE ON THE RIGHT-WING MADNESS!
THERE'S ONLY ONE THING THAT MATTERS NOW, DAD—PREVENTING THE ELECTION OF GEORGE W. BUSH!
©B Trudeau
YOU MEAN, RE-ELECTION, OF COURSE.
UM... DAD? I WAS ALIVE IN 2000, OKAY?

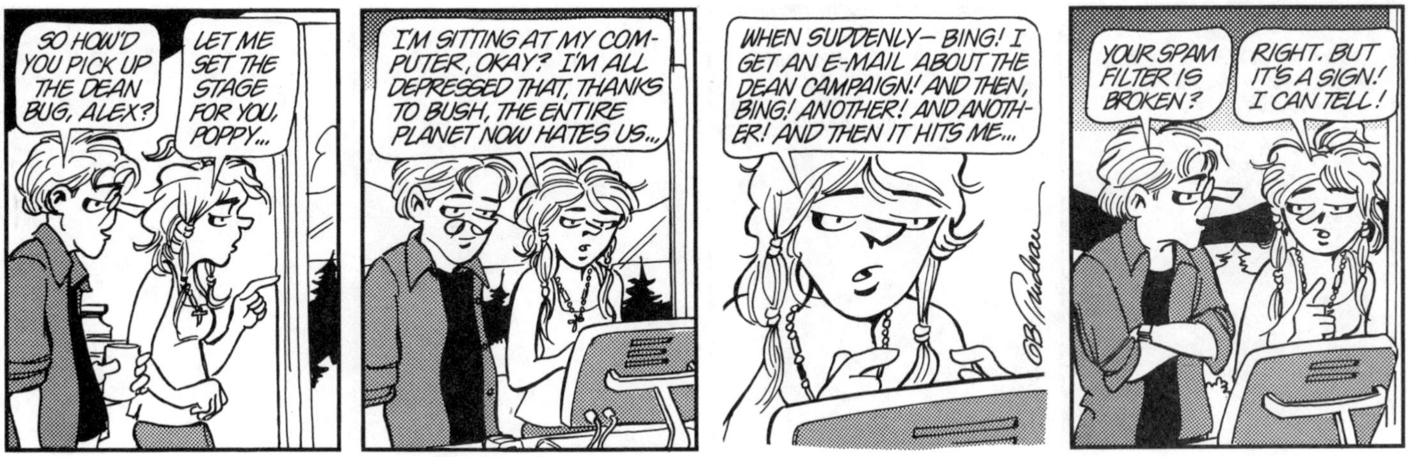
SO HOW'D YOU PICK UP THE DEAN BUG, ALEX?
LET ME SET THE STAGE FOR YOU, POPPY...
I'M SITTING AT MY COMPUTER, OKAY? I'M ALL DEPRESSED THAT, THANKS TO BUSH, THE ENTIRE PLANET NOW HATES US...
WHEN SUDDENLY— BING! I GET AN E-MAIL ABOUT THE DEAN CAMPAIGN! AND THEN, BING! ANOTHER! AND ANOTHER! AND THEN IT HITS ME...
©B Trudeau
YOUR SPAM FILTER IS BROKEN?
RIGHT. BUT IT'S A SIGN! I CAN TELL!

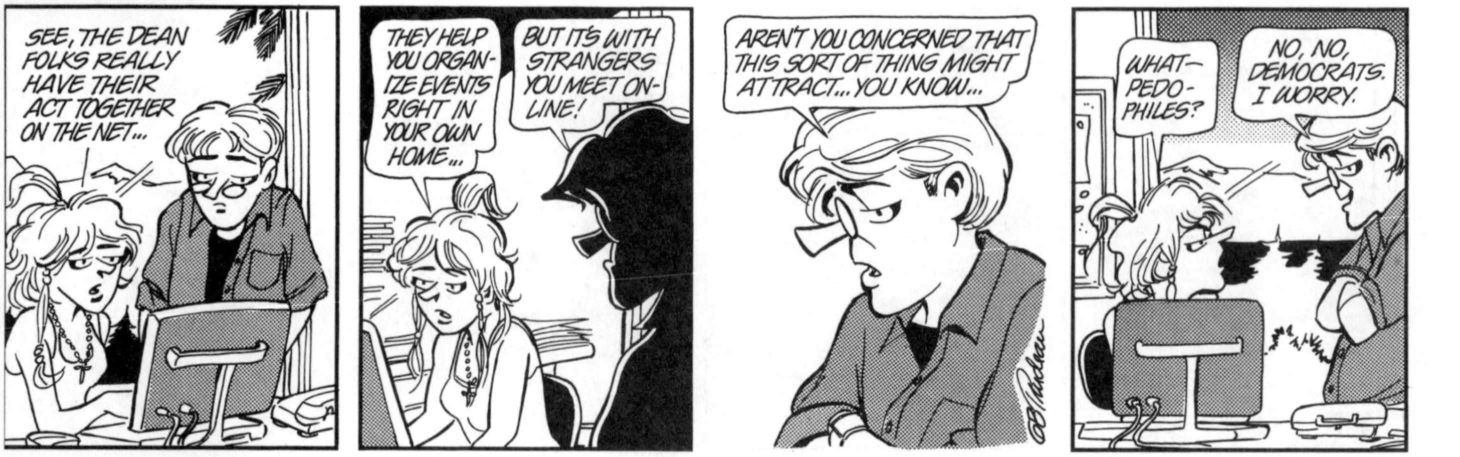
SEE, THE DEAN FOLKS REALLY HAVE THEIR ACT TOGETHER ON THE NET...
THEY HELP YOU ORGANIZE EVENTS RIGHT IN YOUR OWN HOME...
BUT IT'S WITH STRANGERS YOU MEET ON-LINE!
AREN'T YOU CONCERNED THAT THIS SORT OF THING MIGHT ATTRACT... YOU KNOW...
WHAT-PEDOPHILES?
NO, NO, DEMOCRATS. I WORRY.

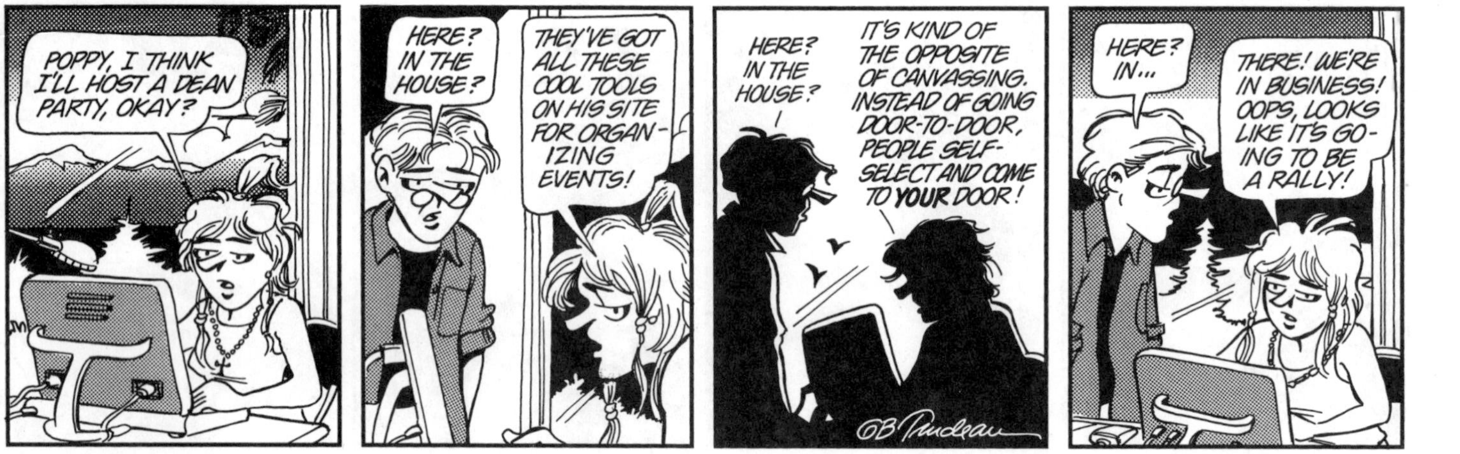
POPPY, I THINK I'LL HOST A DEAN PARTY, OKAY?
HERE? IN THE HOUSE?
THEY'VE GOT ALL THESE COOL TOOLS ON HIS SITE FOR ORGANIZING EVENTS!
HERE? IN THE HOUSE?
IT'S KIND OF THE OPPOSITE OF CANVASSING. INSTEAD OF GOING DOOR-TO-DOOR, PEOPLE SELF-SELECT AND COME TO YOUR DOOR!
HERE? IN...
THERE! WE'RE IN BUSINESS! OOPS, LOOKS LIKE IT'S GOING TO BE A RALLY!

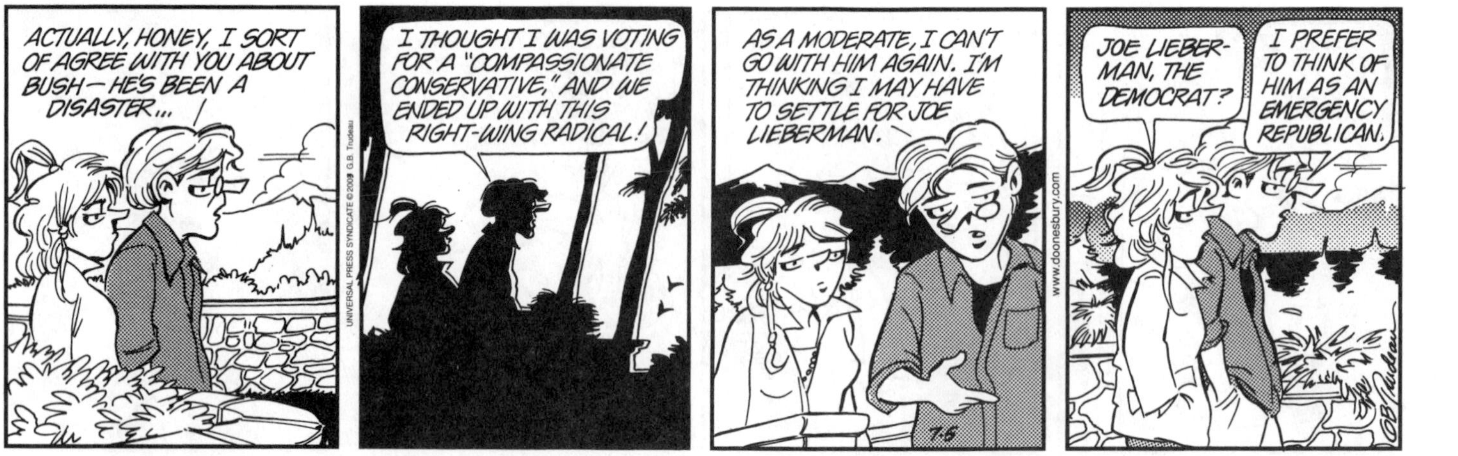
ACTUALLY, HONEY, I SORT OF AGREE WITH YOU ABOUT BUSH— HE'S BEEN A DISASTER...
UNIVERSAL PRESS SYNDICATE © 2003 G.B. Trudeau
I THOUGHT I WAS VOTING FOR A "COMPASSIONATE CONSERVATIVE," AND WE ENDED UP WITH THIS RIGHT-WING RADICAL!
AS A MODERATE, I CAN'T GO WITH HIM AGAIN. I'M THINKING I MAY HAVE TO SETTLE FOR JOE LIEBERMAN.
www.doonesbury.com
JOE LIEBERMAN, THE DEMOCRAT?
I PREFER TO THINK OF HIM AS AN EMERGENCY REPUBLICAN.

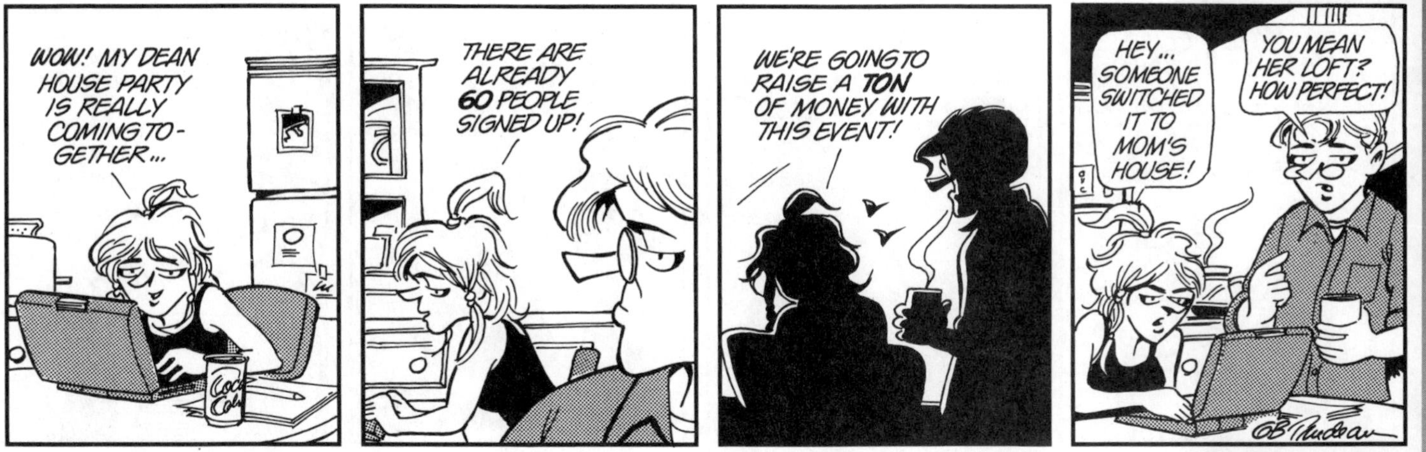
WOW! MY DEAN HOUSE PARTY IS REALLY COMING TOGETHER...
THERE ARE ALREADY 60 PEOPLE SIGNED UP!
WE'RE GOING TO RAISE A TON OF MONEY WITH THIS EVENT!
HEY... SOMEONE SWITCHED IT TO MOM'S HOUSE!
YOU MEAN HER LOFT? HOW PERFECT!

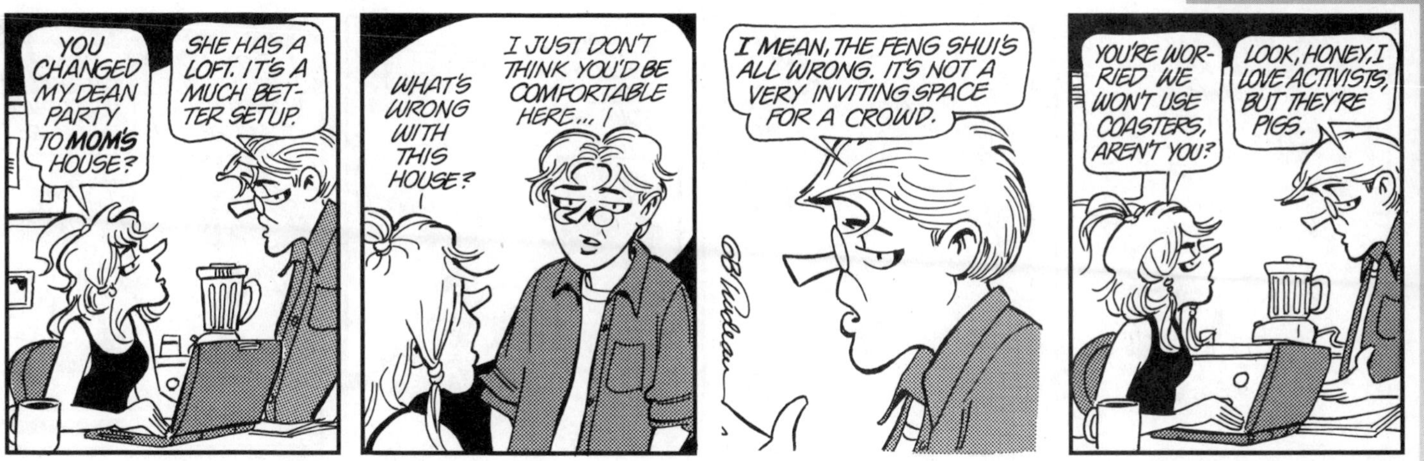
YOU CHANGED MY DEAN PARTY TO MOM'S HOUSE?
SHE HAS A LOFT. IT'S A MUCH BETTER SETUP.
WHAT'S WRONG WITH THIS HOUSE?
I JUST DON'T THINK YOU'D BE COMFORTABLE HERE...
I MEAN, THE FENG SHUI'S ALL WRONG. IT'S NOT A VERY INVITING SPACE FOR A CROWD.
YOU'RE WORRIED WE WON'T USE COASTERS, AREN'T YOU?
LOOK, HONEY, I LOVE ACTIVISTS, BUT THEY'RE PIGS.

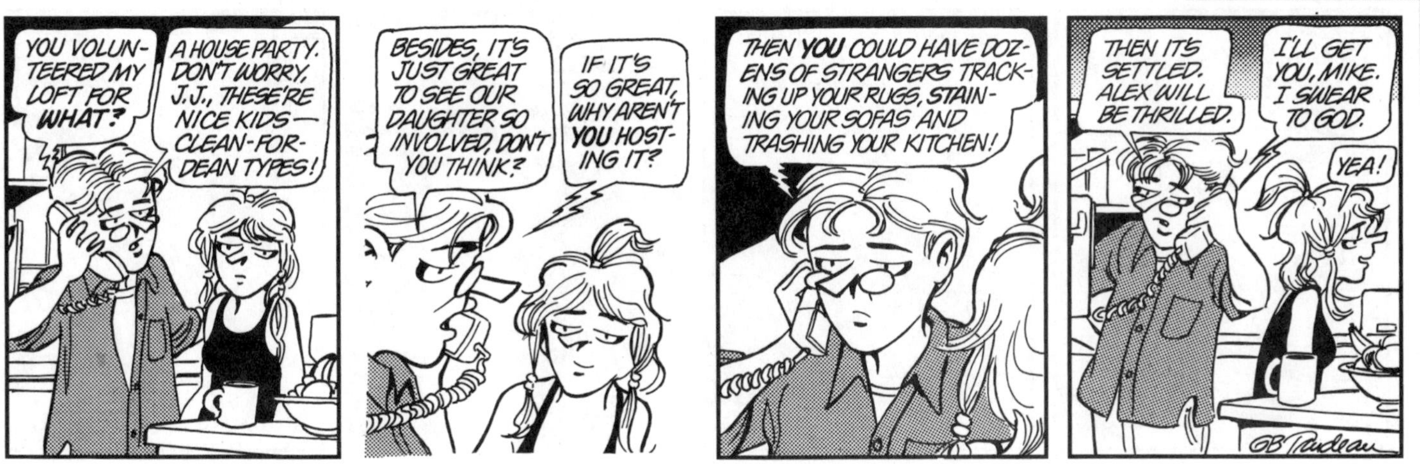
YOU VOLUNTEERED MY LOFT FOR WHAT?
A HOUSE PARTY. DON'T WORRY, J.J., THESE'RE NICE KIDS—CLEAN-FOR-DEAN TYPES!
BESIDES, IT'S JUST GREAT TO SEE OUR DAUGHTER SO INVOLVED, DON'T YOU THINK?
IF IT'S SO GREAT, WHY AREN'T YOU HOSTING IT?
THEN YOU COULD HAVE DOZENS OF STRANGERS TRACKING UP YOUR RUGS, STAINING YOUR SOFAS AND TRASHING YOUR KITCHEN!
THEN IT'S SETTLED. ALEX WILL BE THRILLED.
I'LL GET YOU, MIKE. I SWEAR TO GOD.
YEA!

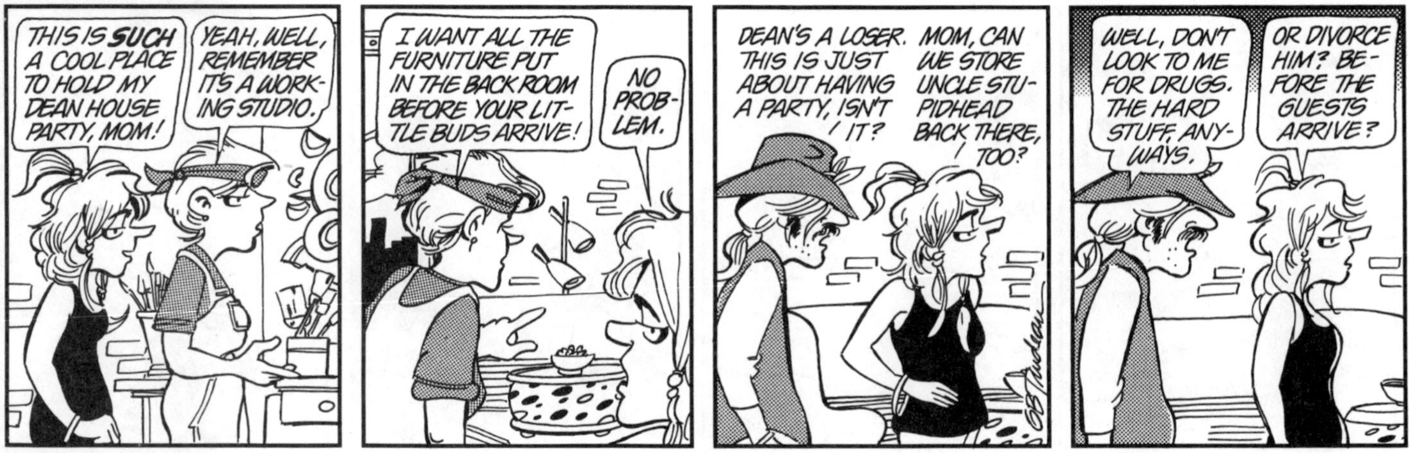
THIS IS SUCH A COOL PLACE TO HOLD MY DEAN HOUSE PARTY, MOM!
YEAH, WELL, REMEMBER IT'S A WORKING STUDIO.
I WANT ALL THE FURNITURE PUT IN THE BACK ROOM BEFORE YOUR LITTLE BUDS ARRIVE!
NO PROBLEM.
DEAN'S A LOSER. THIS IS JUST ABOUT HAVING A PARTY, ISN'T IT?
MOM, CAN WE STORE UNCLE STUPIDHEAD BACK THERE, TOO?
WELL, DON'T LOOK TO ME FOR DRUGS. THE HARD STUFF, ANYWAYS.
OR DIVORCE HIM? BEFORE THE GUESTS ARRIVE?

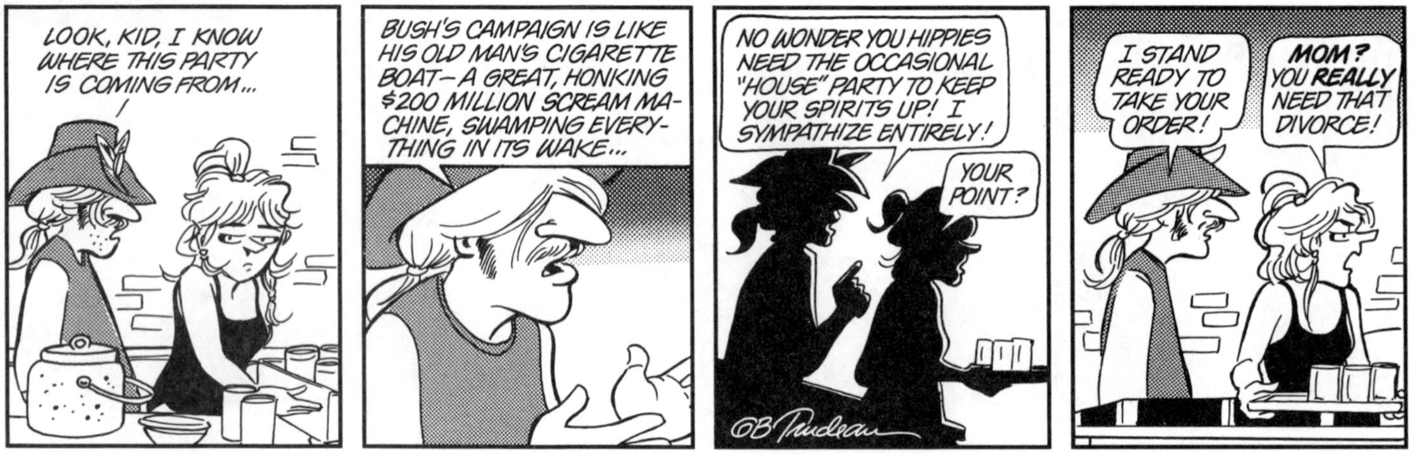
LOOK, KID, I KNOW WHERE THIS PARTY IS COMING FROM...
BUSH'S CAMPAIGN IS LIKE HIS OLD MAN'S CIGARETTE BOAT—A GREAT, HONKING $200 MILLION SCREAM MACHINE, SWAMPING EVERYTHING IN ITS WAKE...
NO WONDER YOU HIPPIES NEED THE OCCASIONAL "HOUSE" PARTY TO KEEP YOUR SPIRITS UP! I SYMPATHIZE ENTIRELY!
YOUR POINT?
I STAND READY TO TAKE YOUR ORDER!
MOM? YOU REALLY NEED THAT DIVORCE!

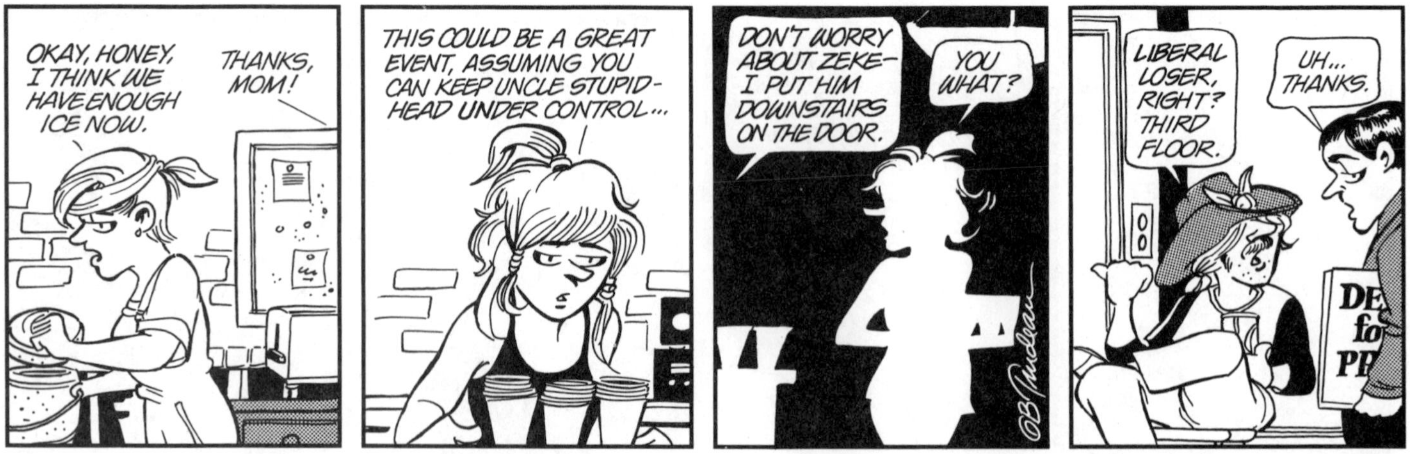
OKAY, HONEY, I THINK WE HAVE ENOUGH ICE NOW.
THANKS, MOM!
THIS COULD BE A GREAT EVENT, ASSUMING YOU CAN KEEP UNCLE STUPIDHEAD UNDER CONTROL...
DON'T WORRY ABOUT ZEKE—I PUT HIM DOWNSTAIRS ON THE DOOR.
YOU WHAT?
LIBERAL LOSER, RIGHT? THIRD FLOOR.
UH... THANKS.

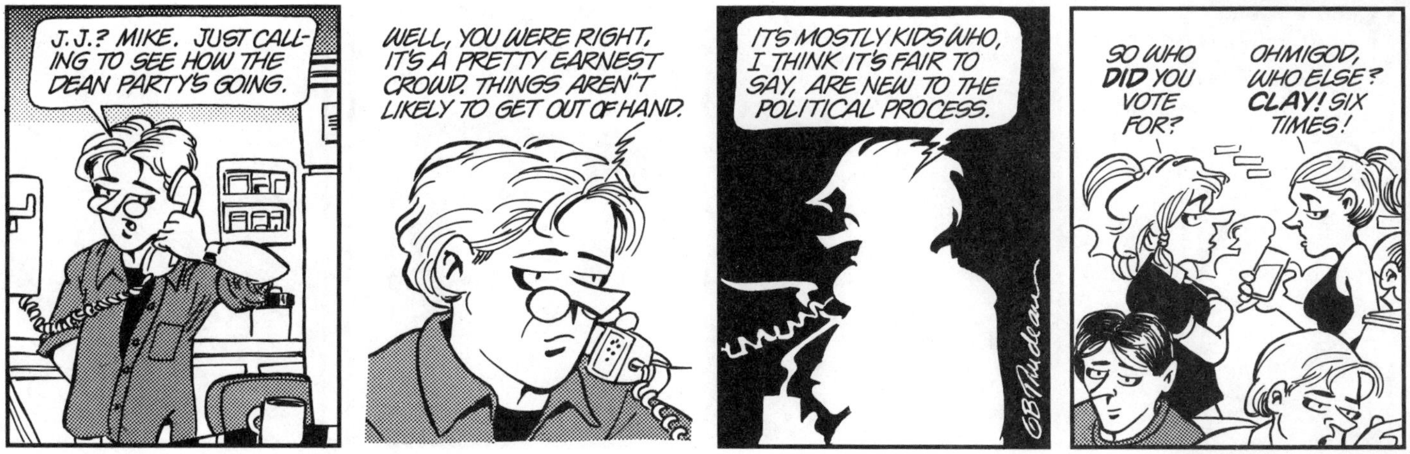
J.J.? MIKE. JUST CALLING TO SEE HOW THE DEAN PARTY'S GOING.
WELL, YOU WERE RIGHT. IT'S A PRETTY EARNEST CROWD. THINGS AREN'T LIKELY TO GET OUT OF HAND.
IT'S MOSTLY KIDS WHO, I THINK IT'S FAIR TO SAY, ARE NEW TO THE POLITICAL PROCESS.
SO WHO DID YOU VOTE FOR?
OHMIGOD, WHO ELSE? CLAY! SIX TIMES!

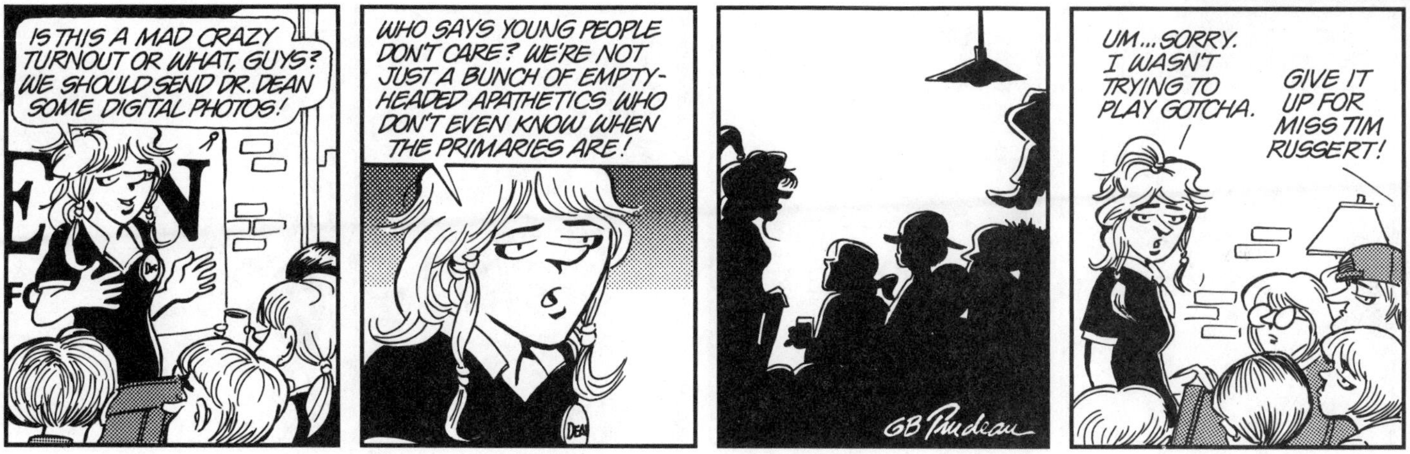
IS THIS A MAD CRAZY TURNOUT OR WHAT, GUYS? WE SHOULD SEND DR. DEAN SOME DIGITAL PHOTOS!
WHO SAYS YOUNG PEOPLE DON'T CARE? WE'RE NOT JUST A BUNCH OF EMPTY-HEADED APATHETICS WHO DON'T EVEN KNOW WHEN THE PRIMARIES ARE!
UM... SORRY. I WASN'T TRYING TO PLAY GOTCHA.
GIVE IT UP FOR MISS TIM RUSSERT!

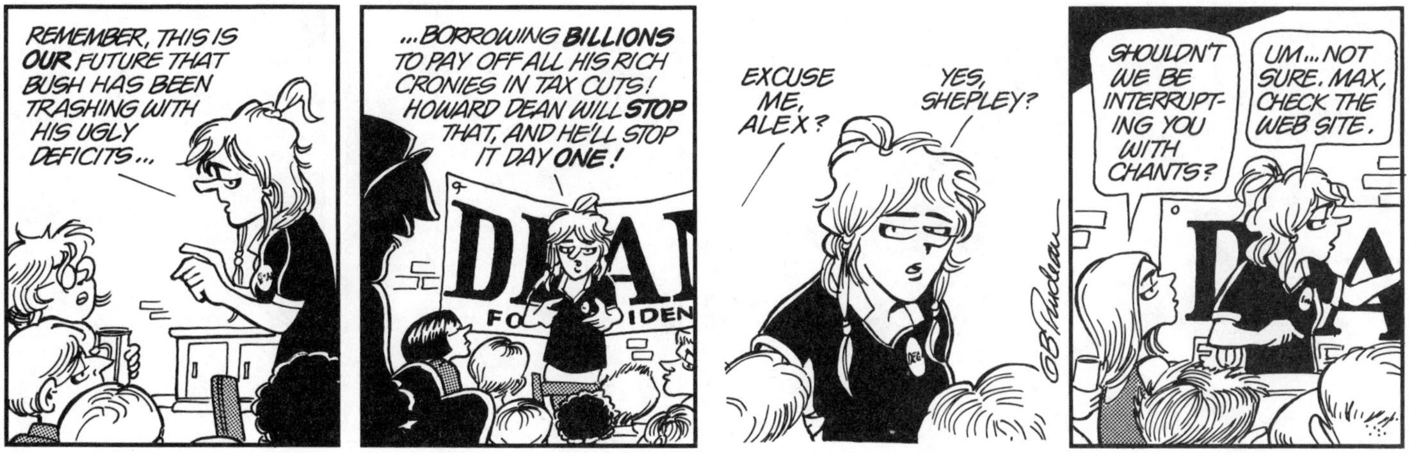
REMEMBER, THIS IS OUR FUTURE THAT BUSH HAS BEEN TRASHING WITH HIS UGLY DEFICITS...
...BORROWING BILLIONS TO PAY OFF ALL HIS RICH CRONIES IN TAX CUTS! HOWARD DEAN WILL STOP THAT, AND HE'LL STOP IT DAY ONE!
EXCUSE ME, ALEX?
YES, SHEPLEY?
SHOULDN'T WE BE INTERRUPTING YOU WITH CHANTS?
UM... NOT SURE. MAX, CHECK THE WEB SITE.

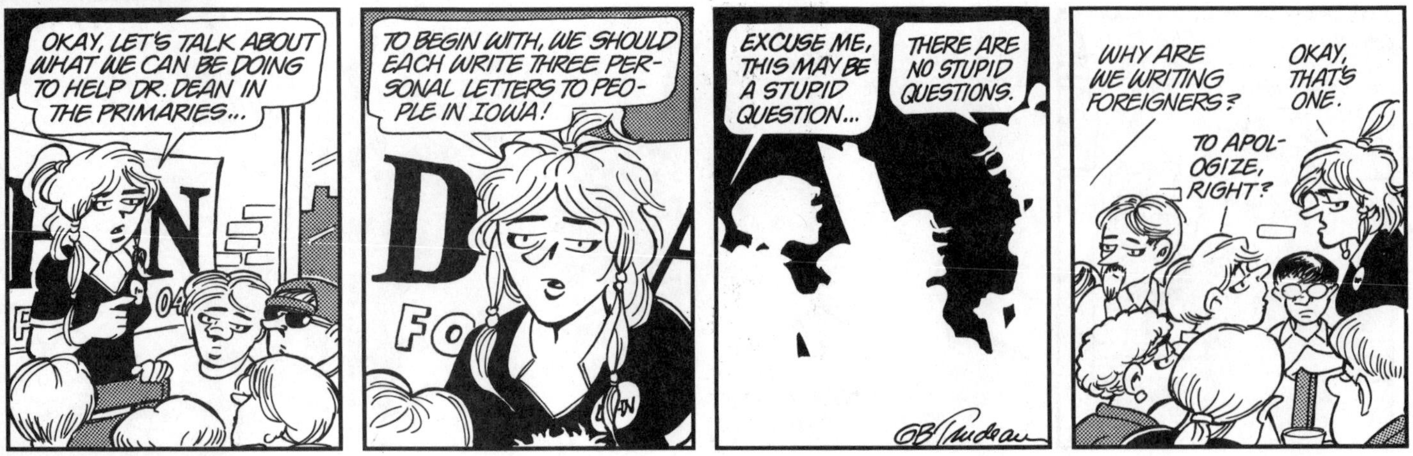
OKAY, LET'S TALK ABOUT WHAT WE CAN BE DOING TO HELP DR. DEAN IN THE PRIMARIES...
TO BEGIN WITH, WE SHOULD EACH WRITE THREE PERSONAL LETTERS TO PEOPLE IN IOWA!
EXCUSE ME, THIS MAY BE A STUPID QUESTION...
THERE ARE NO STUPID QUESTIONS.
WHY ARE WE WRITING FOREIGNERS?
OKAY, THAT'S ONE.
TO APOLOGIZE, RIGHT?

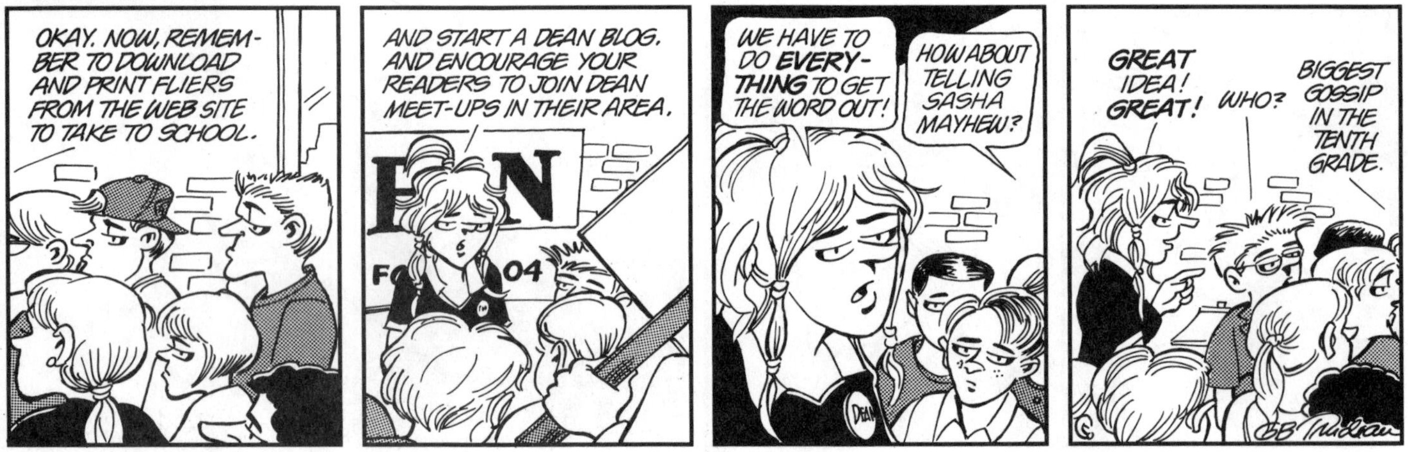
OKAY. NOW, REMEMBER TO DOWNLOAD AND PRINT FLIERS FROM THE WEB SITE TO TAKE TO SCHOOL.
AND START A DEAN BLOG, AND ENCOURAGE YOUR READERS TO JOIN DEAN MEET-UPS IN THEIR AREA.
WE HAVE TO DO EVERYTHING TO GET THE WORD OUT!
HOW ABOUT TELLING SASHA MAYHEW?
GREAT IDEA! GREAT!
WHO?
BIGGEST GOSSIP IN THE TENTH GRADE.

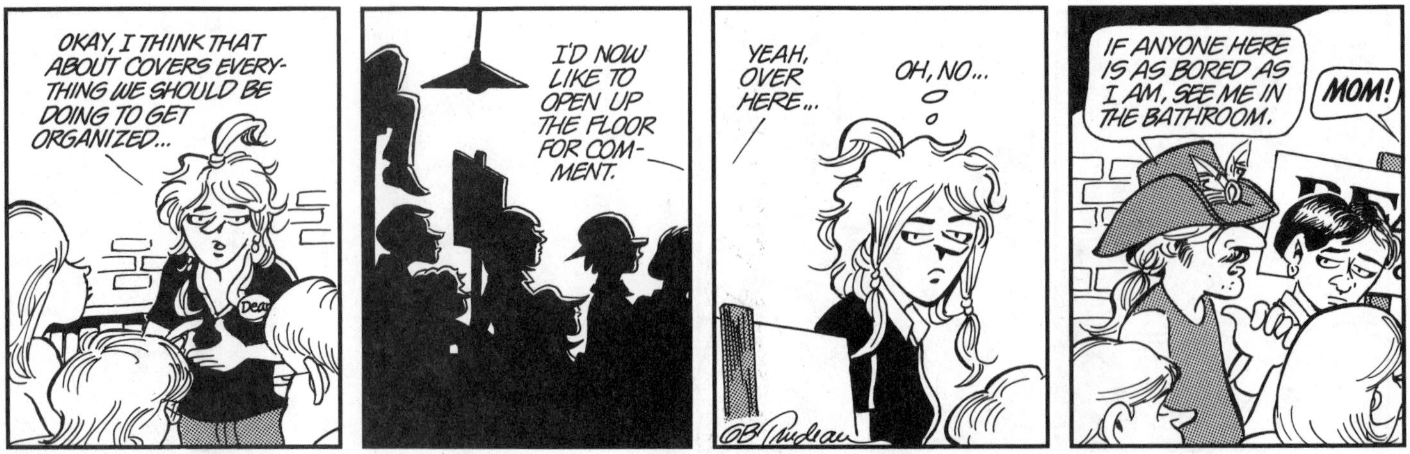
OKAY, I THINK THAT ABOUT COVERS EVERYTHING WE SHOULD BE DOING TO GET ORGANIZED...
I'D NOW LIKE TO OPEN UP THE FLOOR FOR COMMENT.
YEAH, OVER HERE...
OH, NO...
IF ANYONE HERE IS AS BORED AS I AM, SEE ME IN THE BATHROOM.
MOM!